LEARNING

LEARNING

Fourth Edition

A. Charles Catania

University of Maryland Baltimore County

Prentice Hall, Upper Saddle River, New Jersey 07458

Library of Congress Cataloging-in-Publication Data

Catania, A. Charles
  Learning / A. Charles Catania. — 4th ed.
    p.   cm.
  Includes bibliographical references and index.
  ISBN 0-13-235250-8
    1. Learning, Psychology of.   2. Conditioned response.
  3. Psychology, Comparative.   I. Title.
  BF318.C37   1998
  153.1'5—dc21   97-9015
                                                        CIP

Editor-in-Chief: Nancy Roberts
Executive Editor: Bill Webber
Editorial Assistant: Tamsen Adams
Managing Editor: Mary Rottino
Production Liaison: Fran Russello
Project Manager: Karen Trost
Prepress and Manufacturing Buyer: Tricia Kenny
Cover Director: Jayne Conte
Marketing Manager: Mike Alread

This book was set in 10/12 Palatino by ComCom
and printed and bound by R.R. Donnelley & Sons Company.
The cover was printed by Phoenix Color Corp.

Acknowledgments appear on pages 418–419,
which constitute a continuation of the copyright page.

 © 1998, 1992, 1984, 1979 by Prentice-Hall, Inc.
Simon & Schuster/A Viacom Company
Upper Saddle River, NJ 07458

10   9   8   7   6   5   4   3

ISBN 0-13-235250-8

Prentice-Hall International (UK) Limited, *London*
Prentice-Hall of Australia Pty. Limited, *Sydney*
Prentice-Hall Canada Inc., *Toronto*
Prentice-Hall Hispanoamericana, S.A., *Mexico*
Prentice-Hall of India Private Limited, *New Delhi*
Prentice-Hall of Japan, Inc., *Tokyo*
Simon & Schuster Asian Pte. Ltd., *Singapore*
Editora Prentice-Hall do Brasil, Ltda., *Rio de Janeiro*

To Connie, to Bill, and to Ken

Brief Contents

Contents

Chapter 15 Verbal Behavior and Nonverbal Behavior 261

Chapter 16 Psycholinguistics: Language Structure 279

Chapter 17 Verbal Learning and Transfer 297

Preface

A little learning is a dang'rous thing;
Drink deep, or taste not . . .
                    —*Alexander Pope*

Learning is central to the problems of psychology. To ask what an organism can learn is to ask how much of its behavior depends on its evolutionary history and how much depends on what it has experienced during its own lifetime. Studies of learning have ranged from relatively simple animal procedures to the complexities of human language and problem solving. Research in these areas is so different and the literatures are so extensive that the temptation is great to restrict attention solely to issues of animal behavior and learning or solely to issues of human learning and memory. Many texts in learning yield to this temptation. In turn, the study of learning has become more and more divided, with each approach developing its own languages and research methodologies.

In this book, part of my purpose has been to bring these literatures together and to explore some continuities between human learning and the learning of other organisms. Humans are undoubtedly unique, but they share an evolutionary heritage with other species. The properties of nonhuman learning are therefore likely to be relevant to learning in humans. If we only show that some types of human learning aren't reducible to types of learning known to occur with other organisms, we've at least begun to define what is peculiarly human.

This book surveys the major areas in the psychology of learning from a consistent behavioral point of view. I won't attempt to outline the nature of a behavioral orientation here. That view has evolved considerably from its parochial origins and is better treated in the context of specific psychological issues (some are taken up in the text). I'll only note that a behavioral position needn't exclude aspects of human behaving such as thinking and feeling and imagining. For those who like to think in terms of scientific paradigms and paradigm shifts, this text illustrates a behavioral paradigm that has emerged among behavior analysts over recent years; with selection at its core, it encompasses all of the phenomena of behavior. Thus, topics often regarded as the province of contemporary cognitive psychology will be treated here along with those more traditionally regarded as behavioral.

In its overall structure, this book has three major parts (II through IV) framed by an introduction (I) and a conclusion (V). Part II deals with behavior without learning, and does so in an evolutionary context. Part III (Chapters 5 through 13) covers learning without words; in so doing, it surveys basic topics in nonhuman behavior and learning. Part IV (Chapters 14 through 20) covers learning with words; in so doing, it examines human learning and memory. These parts are in some places fairly independent, but more often the concepts developed earlier are prerequisites for the treatment of more complex issues later. The new chapter organization may allow someone teaching a 14-week course to use Chapters 1 through 13 plus the concluding Chapter 21 conveniently in a course devoted just to the basic topics of animal learning.

I've made a special effort to include examples of human behavior in discussing the relevance of nonhuman studies of learning, and to refer to appropriate concepts from nonhuman behavior in discussing human learning and memory. One major difference between this and the last edition is that many examples of important human applications of basic processes have been added throughout. They often show how behavior analysis may contribute to education in significant ways. It would be surprising if the topic of learning did not yield such implications. The choices of particular examples were dictated by both the logic of the subject matter and the availability of appropriate cases in the relevant research literature.

Students often miss the use of human behavior to illustrate the relevance of findings from nonhuman research. For example, one multiple-choice exam question I used for several semesters asked how many instances of human behavior were mentioned in the text through the chapters corresponding to the present Chapter 6. The four choices were: a) none; b) fewer than 10; c) about 20; d) more than 40. By actual count, there were more than 50 human examples throughout those chapters in the first and second editions (there are even more now), but the modal answer was typically a or b; students who challenged d as the correct answer sometimes found it instructive to check the number of human examples for themselves.

Further information on students' responses to questions based on the text is available in a *Test-Item File* that includes a variety of tested objective and essay items keyed to chapters; adopters can obtain copies of the *Test-Item File* from the publisher. Another supplement to the text is a set of computer programs, *Behavior on a Disk* (ISBN 0-922077-23-1), that includes simulations of shaping and other behavioral processes, experiments in memory and verbal learning, and vocabulary review exercises (the programs are available in 3.5-inch MS-DOS format for IBM and compatible computers, from CMS Software, P.O. Box 5777, Santa Fe, NM 87502-5777).

Like the previous editions, this fourth edition of *Learning* includes some etymological notes at the beginning of each chapter. These capsule word histories are important reminders of how easily our language changes. Consistencies in vocabulary are essential to technical treatments, but the language must also grow and adapt to new findings and new perspectives. We must use our language of behavior with care, but perhaps we'll be less likely to become rigid about it if we know something of its origins.

This edition, like the last, also includes a glossary that summarizes the major terminology of the field and may provide a convenient organizer for study and review. The preparation of a glossary forces an author to attend to potential contradictions and ambiguities in basic concepts, and may serve that function for the reader as well. The glossary includes an introduction with some comments on its scope and its special features. In the reference section, entries are keyed to the pages on which they're cited in the text; they've been chosen as useful starting points for exploring the literature of learning as well as for documenting specific points.

To study learning, one should know what it is. Chapter 1 begins with the problem of defining learning (but doesn't solve it). Chapter 2 is primarily organizational, providing an outline of topics treated in detail in Chapters 4 through 12 in the context of some of the history of the field. Chapter 3 deals with selection as a core concept for what follows and provides some background on evolution. Chapter 4 examines the reflex and other relations generated when stimuli are presented to an organism. Other texts typically introduce conditioning at this point, but within the present organization that topic is more effectively deferred until later.

Chapters 5 and 6, on reinforcement and on aversive control, show how the consequences of responding can affect behavior. These topics raise the issue of classes of responses and classes of stimuli as behavioral units. They therefore lead to the concept of the operant in Chapter 7, and the concept of the discriminated operant in Chapters 8 and 9. Chapter 9 also considers the implications of higher-order units of behavior. These concepts are further illustrated in Chapters 10 and 11, which examine how complex behavior can be synthesized within the context of reinforcement schedules. Chapter 12 then takes up conditioning and shows how it's related to processes discussed in earlier chapters. Chapter 13 on social learning provides a transition to verbal behavior, that eminently social outgrowth of human behavior.

In their treatment of language, Chapters 14 and 15 deal with the complexities of human verbal behavior. Some features of behavioral and cognitive approaches are explicitly compared in Chapter 16, on psycholinguistics. These three chapters set the stage for an examination of verbal learning and transfer in Chapter 17, and of memory in Chapters 18 and 19. Cognition and problem solving, the focus of Chapter 20, present an opportunity for synthesis, because they bring together topics considered separately at various points throughout the text. The final chapter is an overview and integration of some major issues in the psychology of learning.

Many topics have been given expanded or revised coverage. Some of these are: naming as a verbal class; higher-order classes of behavior; language development and the argument from the poverty of the stimulus; equivalence classes; discrimination of one's own behavior; autoclitic processes; verbally governed behavior and instructional control; the distinction between artificial and natural selection; the shaping of verbal behavior; animal language; distorted and repressed memory; and metaphor and other phenomena of language. Continuity between the nonhuman learning and conditioning chapters and the human learning and memory chapters has also been enhanced.

Throughout its history, the psychology of learning has been concerned with theories. Particular learning theories were developed, elaborated, and then displaced by others. Many remain with us, typically more restricted in their scope than when they were first introduced. Whatever their current status, the data that gave rise to these theories are still to be dealt with. For that reason, this text emphasizes research findings rather than learning theories. It's theoretical mainly in that it adheres to a consistent behavioral language and attempts a systematic organization that accommodates the various procedures and processes of learning. Although theory isn't emphasized, I've tried to include enough information about experimental procedures, terminology, and data to provide an effective starting point for the student, instructor, or general reader who wishes to pursue particular theories. The emphasis of the book isn't so much on the interpretation of particular findings as on the relations among the varied phenomena included within the psychology of learning. My intent has been to make this book useful not only to those who are already behaviorally inclined, but also to those who are decidedly not of the behavioral persuasion.

The content of this book grew over successive offerings of an introductory lecture course in the Psychology of Learning, first at the University College of Arts and Science of New York University and then at the University of Maryland Baltimore County. I am indebted to my students and colleagues at both campuses, and especially to Eliot H. Shimoff. As my teachers and my colleagues, numerous others contributed by their comments, discussions and encouragement. As in the earlier editions, I name only a few, mainly because I can still identify particular contributions of each: Abraham Amsel, Kenneth C. Catania, William J. Catania, Joseph Cautelli, Daniel Cerutti, Leonard Cook, Willard F. Day, Israel Goldiamond, Lewis R. Gollub, Ernest S. Graham, Stevan Harnad, Eliot Hearst, Ralph F. Hefferline, Philip N. Hineline, Per Holth, Koji Hori, Pauline Horne, Herbert M. Jenkins, Victor G. Laties, Kennon A. Lattal, Richard A. Littman, C. Fergus Lowe, Ernst L. Moerk, J. A. Nevin, Koichi Ono, Michael J. Owren, Robert R. Provine, Robert Remington, George S. Reynolds, Marc Richelle, Terje Sagvolden, B. F. Skinner, Deisy de Souza, William C. Stebbins, S. S. Stevens, Mark Sundberg and Vicci Tucci. In such a listing, omissions are inevitable; fortunately, the contributions of many others are acknowledged by their inclusion among the references. I wish also to express my appreciation for the invaluable help of Madelon Kellough, Terri Harold and Mary Johnston, for Jack Burton's encouragement, and for Ilene Kalish's and Karen Trost's guidance of the book through its successive stages to publication.

I would also like to thank the following reviewers of the manuscript for this fourth edition: Rebecca M. Chesire, University of Hawaii; Robert H. I. Dale, Butler University; Lewis R. Gollub, University of Maryland at College Park; and David K. Hogberg, Albion College.

Above all, and as in past editions, one further acknowledgment remains. This time, sadly, they're no longer with us to receive it. I owe more than I can say to Nat and Fred: W. N. Schoenfeld and Fred S. Keller. Their courses and their *Principles of Psychology* introduced me to the analysis of behavior and irrevocably committed me to the exploration of its wonders. I hope that this book is true enough to their teaching that readers who knew them and learned from them will recognize something of them in these pages.

A. Charles Catania
Columbia, Maryland

PART I   INTRODUCTION

Chapter 1
Learning and Behavior

A. The Language of Learning and Behavior
Behavioral and Cognitive Languages
The World and the Laboratory

B. Antecedents, Behavior, Consequences
Stimuli and Responses
Behavior Hierarchies

The English word learning *probably comes from an Indo-European root, leis-, which meant a track or furrow. Before reaching its present form, it went through many changes: læstan, leornian, lernen. At various times in the evolution of our language it might have been understood as following a track, continuing, coming to know, or perhaps even getting into a rut. The verb* last, *to endure, came from the same root.*

The word behavior, *like* habit, inhibit *and* ability, *is related to the Latin* habere, *to hold or have. The prefix* be- *became attached in such words as the Old English* behabban. *As a word for how one held oneself, it was closer to the sense of comportment or demeanor than to the more contemporary sense of activity, just as* habit *was once more commonly what was worn than what was habitually done.*

Suppose you were unfamiliar with the word *phenomenon* and then noticed it in a few sentences. You might decide from its context that it means something like a thing that happens or an event worth noticing. At that point you could look it up in a dictionary, which might define it as an event that can be observed; a secondary entry might define it as a remarkable or unusual person or thing. The dictionary would show that the word is a singular noun and its plural is *phenomena*. Even after reading the definition, you might hardly ever use the word yourself. Still, you'd have learned something about it that could be useful the next time you come across it.

But what about the definition of the subject matter of this book? What is this phenomenon called *learning*? The word doesn't give us trouble in everyday conversation, but a dictionary definition that tells us it means getting to know something or gaining knowledge and skill isn't very helpful. The word *learning* is a lot more familiar than *phenomenon* and yet it is a lot harder to define. We can usually say whether we've learned something and we can usually agree on what counts as learning. Even so, we run into problems when we try to frame a definition.

For example, a textbook might define learning as a relatively permanent change in behavior resulting from experience (cf. Kimble, 1961, pp. 1–13). But what is meant by *behavior* or by *experience*, and how permanent is *relatively permanent*? Staring at an eclipse of the sun is an experience and if it damages your eyes it will certainly change your behavior. Yet if someone claimed that this damage was an example of learning, we'd probably disagree.

Section A   The Language of Learning and Behavior

This book is about learning, but from the start we have to face the fact that we won't be able to define it. There are no satisfactory definitions of learning. Still, we can study it. We do so whenever we look at how organisms come to behave in new ways. In our study of learning, we'll ask two types of questions: (1) what is the nature of these events we call learning? and (2) what is the best way to talk about them?

Consider words like *learning* or *knowledge*. They seem obviously important. But when they function in different ways in different contexts we often don't notice, and that can cause confusion. For example, sometimes we speak of learning *about* something; at other times we speak of learning *how to do* something. Someone who's learned how an automobile works may not know how to drive one; conversely, someone who's learned to drive a car may not be able to say how it works.

Some kinds of learning involve deeds and others involve words. Should we treat these two kinds together or separately? Philosophers are concerned with this type of distinction when they debate the difference between "knowing how" and "knowing that" (e.g., Ryle, 1949). Psychologists sometimes make the distinction by contrasting *procedural* knowledge or memory with *declarative* knowledge or memory. The distinction is so fundamental that, as the table of contents shows, this book is divided into two major parts. One is concerned with learning that doesn't involve words, and the other is concerned with learning that does.

If *learning* could be defined in a sentence or two, we'd have no problem. We'd define the word and then discuss the conditions under which learning takes place, the kinds of things that are learned, ways in which different instances of learning can be combined, the limitations of learning, and so on. But learning means different things at different times to different people.

Consider some examples. A pigeon discovers food in its travels and returns to the same place later when hungry. A child becomes able to read a story or to spell simple words. A dog is taught to sit or lie down on command. A patient who once had a bad experience in a dentist's office feels uneasy in the waiting room. A young cat, after its early hunting expeditions, comes to avoid skunks and porcupines. A shopper sees an announcement for a sale that's not yet begun, and several days later returns to the store to take advantage of bargain prices. An author who encounters an unfamiliar word later uses it in a short story. A student, after reading a chapter in a mathematics book, finds a way to solve a problem that once was baffling.

What do these examples have in common? They involve dogs and cats, children and adults, and we'd probably agree that they're all instances of learning. But is it reasonable to group a pigeon who learns a route to food with a student who discovers a solution to a mathematical problem?

Someone might suggest that we could resolve our problem of definition by adding that learning had to come about through some change in the brain. But do we ever look at an organism's brain to decide whether it's learned something? We've all learned to say when we or others have learned something, but how many of us have ever seen a brain do anything? Even if we could watch a brain do something, how would we know that what it was doing was learning?

This isn't to say that learning has no physiological basis. Of course it does, and it would be fascinating to know what neurological changes accompany learning. Yet we'd have trouble figuring out what to look for in the nervous system if we didn't know much about learning. In fact, we can't have an adequate neuroscience of learning unless we understand its behavioral properties. Those properties determine what sorts of things neuroscientists interested in learning must look for in the nervous system. That's why our main concern will be with the behavioral properties of learning rather than with its physiological basis.

We've hardly worried about the facts of learning so far; we've mainly worried about how we talk about it. Languages are changeable; their vocabularies reflect what is currently important to their speakers. One trouble is that the language that has evolved in our everyday interactions with others isn't necessarily well suited for a language of learning (and that's one reason for the etymologies, or word histories, included at the beginning of each chapter).

We're usually more interested in what other people know and in what they're likely to do than in how they came to be that way. For example, a parent might be concerned about a child who consistently fought with other children and never played cooperatively. But if the child began to play cooperatively, the parent might not care whether this happened because of the natural rewards of cooperative play or because cooperative play was explicitly taught or because the fighting and other alternatives to play were punished.

Our language for describing what people do is useful. It's important to know what to expect of others, and that's probably why we describe people in terms of how they're likely to behave. We speak of each other as outgoing or reserved, easygoing or compulsive, trustworthy or unreliable. Describing people with words like *artistic*, *athletic*, *social*, *intellectual* or *musical* specifies their preferred activities. Yet this kind of vocabulary isn't suitable for discussing how particular interests or traits develop in an individual.

Consider another example. There's an important difference between lying and telling the truth. But if one child learned to keep out of trouble by telling lies and another by telling the truth, we wouldn't be surprised if the first child grew up to be less truthful than the second. Yet the behavior of each child was shaped by its consequences; each child behaved so as to keep out of trouble. This shaping of behavior should concern us, but our everyday vocabulary doesn't equip us well for discussing it.

Similar problems exist in fields other than psychology. When physicists look at events in the world, they don't find the everyday vocabulary adequate. They coin new terms or take over existing ones. The latter course can create difficulties. Words like *work, force* and *energy*, for example, mean different things to physicists in their technical talk than they do to most other people in casual conversation. Fortunately for physicists, much of what they now study is far enough removed from our daily experience that we don't confuse their technical language with our ordinary discourse.

This isn't so in psychology. We're all inescapably involved with behavior. We speak of how people grow and change, we speculate about the reasons people have for doing things, and we ourselves learn new facts and acquire new skills. If we want to create new ways of talking about these events, we must take care that we don't confuse our new language with the old one. We've all spent most of our lives talking in certain ways about what we do, and these familiar ways may interfere with any new ways we try to establish. Some parts of this book will introduce a language of behavior, and that language won't just be a paraphrase of everyday usages; it will instead require some new ways of dealing with familiar phenomena or events.

BEHAVIORAL AND COGNITIVE LANGUAGES

Sometimes we talk about what people do and sometimes we talk about what they know. On the one hand, what someone does is the only thing accessible to us. There's nothing else for us to study but behavior. For example, a person in a learning experiment may describe thoughts or feelings, but these descriptions are still only behavior (verbal behavior may be special, but it's behavior nonetheless). No matter what phenomena we study in psychology, our terminology and theories must ultimately be derived from behavior, from what organisms do.

On the other hand, there's more to an organism than shows in its behavior. Two students may sit silently through a lecture, and yet it may be clear to the instructor that one can answer certain questions and solve certain problems while the other can't. Although the students might be distinguished on the basis of past performances, it remains that they aren't currently behaving differently. The difference is in what each potentially can do; we might say simply that one student knows more than the other. When we study this knowledge, it's tempting to say that we study the mind.

The debate between psychologists who call themselves behaviorists and those who call themselves cognitivists or mentalists has been long-standing. To some extent, it's been about appropriate ways of talking about psychological events. The behaviorist argues that, because behavior is all that is available to measure, the language of mental events can be misleading, especially when a mentalistic account is accepted as explanatory and therefore discourages further inquiry.

For example, we sometimes casually say that an idea, a feeling or a hunch led someone to do something. The behaviorist doesn't dispute the existence of ideas, feelings and hunches, but rather criticizes their invoca-tion as causes of behavior. It's too easy to be satisfied with an explanation in these terms; for a behaviorist, it isn't enough to say that someone did something because of an idea, a feeling or a hunch. Ideas, feelings and hunches are about the world and therefore must have their origins in our experiences with the world. We must look further, to these past experiences or, in other words, to past behavior, to account for what we do. If we're successful, we may also have something useful to say about the origins of our ideas, feelings and hunches.

The cognitivist maintains that such a view is unnecessarily narrow. Processes must occur in our dealings with the world that aren't observable in our behavior. When we try to recall a word that is "on the tip of our tongue" or try to solve a problem by "sleeping on it," things are happening that don't show directly in our behavior, and we may not even be able to report them. If we can find out something about such processes, it's bound to be relevant to our study of learning.

But the dispute between behaviorists and cognitivists may stem as much from different ways of talking about behavior as from differences in research findings. Some difficulties arise because the two kinds of psychologists are often interested in different types of questions. Behaviorists tend to deal with questions of function and cognitivists with questions of structure.

Suppose we'd like to teach a child to read. On the one hand, we could become concerned with what we have to do to involve the child in reading. We'd worry about what would keep the child alert, what would help the child pay attention to the words presented, and what would help the child remember what the various words are. Will we be more successful if we reward the child for being correct or penalize the child for being wrong? When we arrange different consequences for different answers the child may give, we determine the functions of these various answers or, more precisely, the functional relations between behavior and its consequences.

On the other hand, no amount of concern with the effects of reward and punishment on the child's mastery of reading will tell us the most efficient way to present reading materials to the child. How is reading structured? What's the best way to order the materials? Should we teach the child to read by starting with single letters, with syllables or with whole words? When we present the materials to be learned in different orders, we're concerned with the effective structural relations within the subject matter. Are words best taught as unitary structures or as complex structures built up from simpler units such as letters or syllables? Problems of structure are concerned with how behavior and the environment are organized.

Both problems are important. Any attempt to improve how children learn to read that ignores either will be deficient. Consider another example. Suppose we discovered that children who read from text accompanied by pictures are more likely to attend to the pictures than the words. One of our problems would be functional and might lead us to ask whether we could improve the teaching of reading by putting words on one page and a relevant picture on the next. That might also help the teacher, who must judge whether a child has really read a word or has only guessed the word from the picture. We might even try to create a system of computer instruction in which the child gets to see the picture only as a consequence of correctly reading the words.

But another of our problems will be structural, because it will still be important to know which pictures should accompany which words and the order in which different reading materials should be presented. However good the computer-assisted instruction is in handling relations among words and pictures and the child's responses, its effectiveness could be undermined if we tried to teach difficult words before easy ones or irregular spellings before regular ones. A reading program to teach an alphabetic language such as English would probably be quite different from one to teach an ideographic language such as Chinese. Each program would have to take into account the structure of the spoken and written language being taught.

Historically, some controversies in psychology arose because those interested in functional problems tended to speak a behavioral language whereas those interested in structural problems tended to speak a cognitive or mental language. Even though behaviorists could have studied structural problems, just as cognitivists could have studied functional ones, the problems in which behaviorists and cognitivists were interested tended to be correlated with the words they used.

It's easy to see how this correlation can come about. If you're concerned with function, you study the consequences of particular relations between specified environmental events and specified actions; you can conveniently express these in the behavioral language of stimuli and responses. If you're concerned with structure, you study the properties of particular capacities or abilities; you can conveniently express these in the cognitive language of knowledge and mind. (A parallel distinction between structure and function, the separation of anatomy and physiology, occurred in the history of biology; see Chapter 21.)

We needn't be sidetracked by this controversy. We'll consider both function and structure in learning and we'll therefore examine both types of research. In either case, it will often be useful to describe situations in terms of *antecedents*, or the circumstances that set the occasion for behavior, the *behavior* that occurs in those circumstances, and the *consequences* of the behavior (these three terms are conveniently abbreviated as ABC). We can consider either *function*, the relations among the terms (e.g., given certain antecents, what consequences are produced by behavior) or *structure*, the properties of particular terms (e.g., what are the critical properties of those antecedents).

The orientation from which this book is written deals with both function and structure, and therefore encompasses both behavioral and cognitive concepts. These two psychological positions differ in their languages and in the research problems they emphasize, but they have in common the reliance on experimental method, the anchoring of concepts to experimental observations, and the assumption that our subject matter, however complex, is orderly and not capricious. Our concern is with what determines behavior. And if we're worried about how our knowledge of behavior might be misused, we must recognize that we can't eliminate a determinant of human behavior simply by choosing not to study it; in fact, we can best defend against the misuse of techniques for controlling human behavior if we understand how they work.

THE WORLD AND THE LABORATORY

How then do we find out about behavior? The problems of language are made even more difficult because we live in a complex world. The events that influence our behavior don't occur in isolation. Thus, to understand a situation we must strip away its unessential details and analyze it. To analyze something is simply to break it down into its component parts. For this purpose, we turn to the laboratory. We begin with the study of organisms simpler than ourselves, in simple environments. Of course, we must face the objection that a laboratory experi-

ment is artificial and therefore may not be appropriate for establishing generalizations about learning outside of the laboratory. But starting with simple events will help us to develop techniques and vocabularies that can be applied to complex ones.

The laboratory environment enables us to look at one thing at a time. We arrange circumstances so that we know what goes into an experimental situation; if we're careful, we can exclude some of the distractions that might otherwise obscure what we wish to study. The simplicity of our laboratory environment may also help us to see the varied features of learning more easily. We have to be able to identify events before we can study their properties. One place to start is to look at behavior that doesn't involve language, because it will probably be simpler than behavior that does involve language. The easiest way to do that is to look at the behavior of nonhuman organisms. What they tell us about behavior without words may later help us to appreciate what's special about behavior with words.

Even after we've studied behavior in the laboratory, we can't expect to be able to interpret every instance of behavior outside the laboratory. There are limits to what we can know. It is tempting to ask a psychologist to explain why someone behaved in a certain way, what led up to a certain incident, or how someone came to have certain interests, fears or attachments. But the psychologist often has so little information available that only a plausible interpretation is possible.

This situation differs only in degree from that in other sciences. Just as the principles of aerodynamics aren't invalidated if we can't account for every twist and turn in the path of a particular falling leaf, the principles of behavior aren't invalidated if we can't account for every detail of an organism's performance on a particular occasion. In our study of learning, it's important to recognize what remains out of our reach. In what follows, we'll find that the most profitable course is one that stays close to the data; we'll worry less about psychological theory than about properly describing our findings. For example, it will often be more useful to *describe* what an organism has learned or remembered than to attempt to *explain* its learning or its memory.

Section B Antecedents, Behavior, Consequences

Now let's turn to behavior as subject matter. The study of learning is about how behavior can be modified, so we must first consider what behavior is, how it can be investigated, and what vocabulary might best describe it. Behavior is no easier to define than learning. We may say glibly that behavior is anything an organism does, but this definition is too global. Should we count respiration or metabolism along with muscular movements and glandular secretions? We describe behavior with verbs: people walk, talk, think, do things. But we also distinguish between active and passive actions. Although we may say that someone breathes, we aren't likely to say that someone "heartbeats." People bleed when cut but maybe we won't want to speak of such bleeding as behavior.

Let's not try to resolve this problem. Our aim is to examine some properties of behavior. Although they sometimes share common names, the phenomena of behavior are varied, so we'll probably do better by considering examples than by attempting definitions. We can deal with specific examples without much risk of misunderstanding. When we observe an organism, we see properties of its environment and properties of its behavior. We call these properties *stimuli* and *responses*, but neither a stimulus nor a response is of interest by itself. An experimental analysis determines what kinds of relations exist between stimuli and responses, and how these relations can come about. It must also consider broader contexts, the situations within which these relations between stimuli and responses are embedded.

Imagine a pigeon in an experimental chamber. On one wall is an opening to a feeder that can be used to dispense food. Above the feeder opening is a recessed translucent disk that can be lit from the other side of the chamber wall. The pigeon has been trained to earn food by pecking the key whenever it's lit. Now suppose that the key is lit, the pigeon hasn't eaten for a while, and its peck on the key immediately produces a small amount of food. It's one thing if the alternative, not pecking, is never followed by food; it's another if not pecking is followed by a delayed but much larger amount of food. In each case a response, the key peck, is followed by a stimulus, food. But the contexts are very different. We would expect the pigeon to peck the key in the first case, but what about the second? If the pigeon doesn't peck, we might be tempted to say that it shows self-control, forgoing the small amount of immediate food for the larger amount it receives later. We'll discuss this type of situation in more detail in Chapter 11. For now, the point is that we must consider not only the moment-to-moment details of events but also their contexts over extended periods of time.

Let's examine the relation between environment and behavior further by observing a human infant. We might like to start by asking what the infant feels, but there'd be many complications if we did so. The infant isn't yet verbal and so can't tell us. Even if this were an older child who could tell us, we'd have to wonder how the child learned the appropriate words and whether they'd mean the same thing to us as to those who taught them to the child. When we get to language, in Chapter 14, we'll examine the role it plays in molding our knowledge of ourselves and others, but it won't help us here.

We know the infant is active, learning from the environment and interacting with it. But how do we find out what's going on? We can begin simply by observing. We watch for a while, and we notice movements of the hands or arms or legs. Perhaps at some point the infant begins to cry. If the crying stops without our intervention, the infant might sleep or might lie quietly with open eyes. If we look closely, we might see the infant's eyes moving, although it's difficult to judge just what, if anything, the infant is looking at. We could begin to catalogue the various things the infant does, and we might discover that particular movements usually occur in particular sequences. But if we only watch, we can say little more than certain movements occur more or less often and more or less in certain orders.

STIMULI AND RESPONSES

We needn't be restricted to watching. We might touch or rock the infant, move objects in or out of view, make sounds or offer a nipple. We'd expect the infant to respond to each event in a characteristic way. If we touched the infant's palm, for example, the infant would probably clench that fist, grasping the object that touched it. The vocabulary for these events is already familiar: we call the touch to the palm a *stimulus*, and the grasping a *response*.

In this case, we aren't interested in the stimulus alone or in the response alone; we're interested in their relation to each other. We call this relation, the reliable production of some response by some stimulus,

a *reflex*. We'll consider reflexes in Chapter 4. The important point here is that the term *reflex* is simply a name for a behavioral relation: an observed correlation between a particular stimulus and a particular response (Skinner, 1931). It's neither a theory nor an explanation, and it's only one of many possible relations between behavior and environment.

Besides the production of grasping by a touch to the palm, we might catalogue other examples of reflex relations: crying caused by a loud noise; sucking produced by a nipple in the mouth; blinking triggered by a flash of light. These aren't the only types of relations possible, however. The environment acts on the infant when stimuli produce responses, but the infant can also act on the environment. Crying, for example, often brings attention from mother. Crying, then, is a response that can produce a consequence: mother's presence. This relation involves stimuli and responses, but we can't call it a reflex. For one thing, here the responses come first, not the stimuli; for another, here behavior has consequences.

The relations can get even more complicated. If the infant's eyes move while the lights are on, those eye movements change what the infant sees. Eye movements can't have this effect with the lights off. Thus, the infant may come to look around in the light but not in the dark. In the presence of one stimulus, the light, moving the eyes has consequences; it produces other stimuli, some new things seen. Eye movements can't have this consequence in the dark. The relation involves three terms: an antecedent stimulus, the light; a response, eye movement, in the presence of this stimulus; and a consequence, what's newly seen given this response in the presence of this stimulus. This three-term relation, stimulus-response-consequence, is sometimes called a *three-term contingency*, and it is important because an organism's behavior depends on both antecedents and consequences.

An *antecedent* is simply something that comes before, and a *consequence* is simply what's caused by or what happens as a result of some event. Thus, everyday usage corresponds reasonably well to the senses of these terms when we use them technically. It's important to note that consequences should not be identified with stimuli. Responses can have many types of consequences. They sometimes produce stimuli that would otherwise have been absent, but they can also prevent things from happening or change the consequences of other responses. For example, food produced by a response is both a stimulus and a consequence, but food presented independently of behavior is a stimulus only; shock prevented by a response is a stimulus, but the consequence of the response is the absence of shock, which isn't a stimulus.

For *stimulus* and *response*, the relation between technical and everyday usages is not so simple. Stimuli are events in the world and responses are instances of behavior. The term *stimulus* is often restricted to specific physical events such as lights or sounds or touches. But organisms respond to varied features of the environment, including relations (e.g., to the left of, on top of), complex behavior (e.g., facial expressions, tones of voice), functional properties (e.g., edible, comfortable), and so on (cf. Gibson, 1979). We'll often speak of such environmental features as stimuli, even though we might not be able to specify physical dimensions that characterize them.

The line between stimuli and responses is rarely ambiguous. Even so, special cases sometimes complicate our definitions. For example, what about stimuli that originate within the organism? Consider the differ-

ence between a loud noise and the pain of a toothache. Both are events in the world and each might function as an antecedent of behavior (the toothache might set the occasion for going to a dentist). They differ in that the noise is public and the toothache is private; in other words, the noise may be heard by more than one person whereas the toothache can be felt only by the person with the bad tooth. That would be a problem if we insisted that all stimuli had to be outside of the organism, but if appropriate receptors exist we have no reason to exclude as stimuli the important parts of the world that are within the organism's skin.

As for the term *response*, everyday usage often implies that a response is *to* something (typically a stimulus). The term won't function that way here, however, because an account of what causes responses typically includes other factors (e.g., their past consequences, characteristics of the organism) along with the stimuli in the presence of which they occur. With these reservations noted, we now consider some other properties of stimuli and responses.

A stimulus is an environmental event, but such events vary in complexity. In the example in which the infant's crying produced mother's attention, we regarded the infant's mother as a stimulus. The infant's environment is certainly different when mother is present than when she is absent. Yet what sort of stimulus is she? We don't know which aspects of her looks, her voice or her touch are important to the infant early in life. We might guess that the infant would not react to her as usual if she approached wearing a surgical mask, but we couldn't be sure unless we did the experiment. Despite our ignorance with respect to these questions, we don't doubt that the mother is an important part of the infant's environment, and we may still find it useful to speak of the effects she has as she comes and goes in the infant's world.

This example again illustrates the different problems of structure and function. When we try to analyze which of mother's visual, auditory and tactile features are important to the infant, we deal with the structure of this complex stimulus, mother. We might ask how the infant learns to respond to a particular individual as mother despite changes in her dress or hair style, her facial expression or posture. But if we concentrate instead on how mother interacts with the infant's responses, we're concerned with the functional significance of mother in the infant's environment. For example, if an infant was crying, we might not care whether the infant recognized mother by her face, her hair or her voice as long as her presence made a difference; it would be enough to see that when she went to the infant the crying stopped.

Later, we'll often be interested in simpler stimuli: lights, sounds, food in the mouth. But even with simpler stimuli we'll have to distinguish between structural problems, as in analyzing stimulus properties, and functional problems, as in analyzing the interactions between stimuli and responses.

And what about responses? How should we deal with them? In describing responses, we encounter at least two difficulties. The first is that behavior isn't repeated exactly from one instance to the next. If the infant grasps an object on two different occasions, the grasping won't be the same each time. The difference may be small, in the force of the grasp, for example, or in the exact placement of the fingers. But if there's any difference at all, we must worry whether the two grasps should be regarded as two instances of the same response or as two different responses. We must speak not of individual responses but of classes of responses having common properties.

The second difficulty is that responses are sometimes adequately described in terms of movements, but at other times the description must include the environment in which the responses occur. For example, suppose we want to compare the infant's grasping of an object with clenching a fist. If we look just at muscles, grasping an object with the right hand and clenching that fist have more in common than grasping an object with the right hand and grasping an object with the left hand. Yet sometimes it's more important to speak of the act of grasping an object, no matter which hand is used, than to speak of the movement of closing a particular hand.

An account of behavior must distinguish between *movements*, responses defined by their form or the musculature used, and *actions*, responses defined by their relations to the environment. We'll find that actions are more important for our purposes. Consider how often we speak of doing things, going places or manipulating objects, without regard to the details of how these actions are performed.

Even in the absence of movement, we sometimes conclude that behavior has occurred. For example, an infant will typically grasp an adult's fingers so tightly that the infant can be lifted into the air. Once lifted, the infant may not move while holding on and yet the very fact that the infant doesn't fall leads us to conclude that the grasping response continues. Similarly, if we see an adult standing still, our judgment that the adult is behaving stems partly from our knowing that the adult would fall down if unconscious or dead. We could argue that the standing adult is in fact moving in small, unnoticed ways, but even if minor postural adjustments occur in standing still, we don't have to observe them to conclude that the adult is behaving. The critical feature of the infant's grasping and the adult's standing is simply that these responses have an effect; neither the child nor the adult falls.

Thus, not all movements need be instances of behavior, and not all instances of behavior need be movements. We do many things that don't involve any obvious movement. For example, while listening to music we may shift our attention from one instrument to another. That shift of attention is behavior even though we don't measure it as movement. Many aspects of thinking and imagining involve no movement, but as things we do they are varieties of behavior.

Whether behavior involves movement or not, it typically has consequences, and one of the most significant consequences of behavior is that it provides opportunities for other behavior. For instance, if a child is given a cookie, the cookie gives the child an opportunity to eat. The significance of the cookie is based on the child's eating, its behavior with respect to that stimulus. As we'll see again and again, we can't characterize stimuli independently of an organism's behavior, nor can we characterize responses independently of an organism's environment.

BEHAVIOR HIERARCHIES

One way to classify an organism's behavior is to rank responses according to the relative frequencies with which the organism engages in them. For example, if we gave a child an opportunity to eat, to play with toys or to take a bath, we might find that the child plays a lot, eats occasionally and hardly ever volunteers for a bath. Playing, as the most likely or most probable behavior, comes first in this ranking, followed by eating and then by taking a bath. Such a ranking has been called a *behavior hierarchy*

(cf. the habit family hierarchy of Hull, 1943). An equivalent way of describing the ranking is in the language of preference: We could also say that the child prefers playing to eating and prefers either of these to taking a bath.

Behavior hierarchies are changeable. For example, if we waited until the child's usual mealtime and provided a choice between eating and playing, we might find that eating had become more probable than playing or, in other words, that eating had moved up in the hierarchy relative to playing. While eating, the child is neither playing nor taking a bath, but we could find out about the relative rankings of those responses by giving the child a choice between the toys and the bathtub. We might discover that this child almost always prefers the toys. We therefore conclude that right now playing with toys ranks above taking a bath in this child's behavior hierarchy.

We might even find that this child always leaves the bathtub area even when there isn't much else to do elsewhere. Maybe the child recently had a bad experience there. For any kind of behavior, we must consider when it stops as well as when it starts.

It's often convenient to speak of stimuli rather than of opportunities for responding. Thus, for this child we might describe food as an *appetitive* stimulus or event and taking a bath as an *aversive* one, with events that are neither appetitive nor aversive categorized as *neutral*. Unfortunately, even though we may be able to use such terms in specific situations, stimuli in general can't be grouped so neatly. Context makes too much of a difference. We can't just divide the environment into three simple classes of events called appetitive, neutral and aversive. Instead, we must evaluate each stimulus relative to the others available.

With changes in the behavior hierarchy

come changes in the significance of stimuli. For example, consider how food may change from appetitive to aversive over the course of an unusually large holiday dinner. In the bathtub example, if the parents handle things carefully the child may begin to tolerate baths and eventually even come to prefer toys in the tub to toys in other places. In any case, as the child's behavior changes we might want to say that the child is learning something about toys and tubs.

So now we've surveyed some general properties of stimuli and responses as they enter into the relations among antecedents, behavior and consequences. With these preliminaries behind us, we are ready to move on to some classic experiments and findings in the psychology of learning.

Chapter 2
A Behavior Taxonomy

A taxonomy *is a system of classification. The word is derived from the Greek* tassein, *to arrange, plus the Greek* nomia, *method. It shares its first root with the grammatical term* syntax, *with* tactic, *and with* taxis, *a kind of movement; it shares its second root with systematic disciplines such as as-tronomy* and economics, *with* metronome *and* autonomy, *and probably even with* number.

Responses, depending on their relations to elic-iting stimuli, consequences, establishing operations and discriminative stimuli, are variously said to be elicited, emitted, evoked *or* occasioned. *All four terms have Latin roots. The first three share a pre-fix abbreviated from* ex-, *out:* elicit, *derived from* laqueus, *noose or snare, is related to* delight *and* latch; emit, *derived from* mittere, *to send or let go, is related to* omit *and* intermittent; evoke, *de-rived from* vocare, *to call, is related to* vocal *and* invoke. Occasion, *derived from the prefix* ob-, *against, and* cadere, *to fall, is related to* case, ac-cident, chance *and* coincidence.

This chapter offers the outlines of a behav-ioral taxonomy or, in other words, a vocab-ulary in terms of which the various procedures and phenomena of behavior can be organized. Instead of attempting to ex-plain instances of behavior in terms of formal laws, we'll seek a systematic classification of behavior in terms of its origins. The taxon-omy won't be exhaustive, because we can't anticipate everything we'll run into as we study behavior. The science of behavior is sometimes complex, so it is and will likely remain work in progress. But we can at least aim for a descriptive system that organizes the phenomena we know something about while not excluding those we've yet to in-vestigate.

Procedures for studying behavior are sometimes called experimental *operations*, and the changes in behavior they produce are sometimes called behavioral *processes*. We study the relation between environmen-tal events and the organism's behavior by manipulating the environment and observ-ing how this affects what the organism does. We operate on the organism's environment or, in other words, we perform experimental operations. In the analysis of behavior, operations are *what the experimenter does or arranges*, and processes are *the changes in behavior that result*. (A convenient analogy comes from medicine, where the surgical operation is what the physician does to the patient and the processes that follow are the effects of the operation, such as changes in circulation, respiration and so on.) Learning procedures can be described in terms of these operations, taken either alone or in some combination.

The simplest operation, of course, is merely (1) to *observe behavior*. The behavior we observe tells us what an organism is capable of doing. But we have no control over events when we only observe, so we may not be able to draw conclusions about the causes of behavior. We therefore must intervene, and the simplest intervention is (2) to *present stimuli*. Another more complicated intervention is (3) to arrange the environment so that the organism's behavior has *consequences*. Once responses have consequences, the responses may occur more or less often, and therefore consequential operations lead to the processes sometimes called *reinforcement* and *punishment*.

We haven't exhausted the possibilities: We can arrange things so that (4) stimuli *signal* the presentation of other stimuli or so that (5) the stimuli *signal* the opportunity to produce consequences. We then speak of *signaling* or *stimulus-control* operations; these operations can only occur in combination with one of the simpler operations, either presenting stimuli or arranging consequences. Behavior may then depend on whether the signaling stimulus is present or absent. We must also consider operations that (6) can change the effects of the consequences of behavior, as when food becomes a more potent reinforcer after a period of food deprivation. Such operations are called *establishing operations*, in that they establish the conditions under which consequences may become effective as either reinforcers or punishers.

Thus, the basic operations that we'll consider are (1) observing behavior, (2) presenting stimuli, (3) arranging consequences for responses, (4) signaling stimuli, (5) signaling consequences and (6) establishing the effectiveness of consequences. We now survey several classic experiments to illustrate these operations and to introduce some major researchers from the history of the psychology of learning.

Section A The Observation of Behavior

What must we do to observe behavior? In the last section, we argued that interesting behavior depends on interesting environments. What would happen if we tried to move in the other direction, avoiding the contamination of behavior by the environment? For example, imagine taking a rat and fitting it with goggles to exclude visual stimuli and with ear plugs to exclude sounds. We then remove odors with a ventilating system. Realizing that the rat can still touch things, including its own body, we arrange a suit of hollow tubes that holds the rat's legs, reducing tactile contact at least for its paws. This still may not satisfy us, because the rat's weight produces pressure where the suit meets part of its body and so allows it to orient spatially. The next step is to send the suited rat up to an orbiting space station, where gravity is eliminated. Yet after we'd accomplished this much, what could we say about the rat's behavior? What might we observe the rat doing?

The rat example is hypothetical, but experiments on sensory deprivation place humans in environments approximating the minimal stimulation we imagined for the rat.

The problem is that in such environments, for both human and rodent, there isn't much to do; there's no place to go and no one to speak to. Although humans in such environments report a range of activities during their waking time, from thinking to hallucinating, it's no surprise that they spend much of their time asleep.

We were right in the first place. To observe interesting behavior, we have to observe the organism in an interesting environment. Let's consider some examples. Early in the study of the psychology of learning, speculations about the nature of learning were often based upon anecdotal evidence derived from simple observation, as in the following:

> The way in which my dog learnt to lift the latch of the garden gate, and thus let himself out, affords a good example of intelligent behaviour. The iron gate outside my house is held to by a latch, but swings open by its own weight if the latch be lifted. Whenever he wanted to go out the fox terrier raised the latch with the back of his head, and thus released the gate, which swung open. . . . How did he learn the trick? In this particular case the question can be answered, because he was carefully watched. When he was put outside the door, he naturally wanted to get out into the road, where there was much to tempt him—the chance of a run, other dogs to sniff at, possibly cats to be worried. He gazed eagerly out through the railings . . . and in due time chanced to gaze out under the latch, lifting it with his head. He withdrew his head and looked out elsewhere; but the gate had swung open. . . . After some ten or twelve experiences, in each of which the exit was more rapidly effected with less gazing out at wrong places, the fox terrier had learnt to go straight and without hesitation to the right spot. In this case the lifting of the latch was unquestionably hit upon by accident, and the trick was only rendered habitual by repeated association in the same situation of the chance act and the happy escape. Once firmly established, however, the behaviour remained constant throughout the remainder of the dog's life, some five or six years. (Morgan, 1920, p. 144)

Observing this behavior was perhaps a lucky accident, like the dog's lifting of the latch. More can be learned about learning by arranging the environments within which behavior is observed. One researcher who did so was Wolfgang Köhler, one of the founders of gestalt psychology. Köhler studied the behavior of chimpanzees maintained from 1913 to 1917 at the Anthropoid Station on Tenerife, an island northwest of Africa (Köhler, 1927; chimpanzees aren't native to Tenerife and the station was probably a front for German espionage activity involving World War I naval operations: Ley, 1990). In some of Köhler's experiments, bananas or oranges were placed in visible but inaccessible locations and the chimpanzees used materials within the area as tools to obtain the fruit. The following describes the behavior of the male chimpanzee, Sultan:

> The six young animals of the station colony were enclosed in a room with perfectly smooth walls, whose roof—about two metres in height—they could not reach. A wooden box . . . , open on one side, was standing about in the middle of the room, the one open side vertical, and in plain sight. The objective was nailed to the roof in a corner, about two and a half metres distant from the box. All six apes vainly endeavored to reach the fruit by leaping up from the ground. Sultan soon relinquished this attempt, paced restlessly up and down, suddenly stood still in front of the box, seized it, tipped it hastily straight towards the objective, but began to climb upon it at a (horizontal) distance of half a metre, and springing upwards with all his force, tore down the banana. About five minutes had elapsed since the fastening of the fruit; from the momentary pause before the box to the first bite into the banana, only a few seconds had elapsed, a perfectly continuous action after the first hesitation. (Köhler, 1927, pp. 39–40)

In many instances, of course, chimpanzees made fruitless attempts to solve such problems.

Köhler discussed these and related observations in terms of the chimpanzees' intelligence and insight. More important perhaps, he demonstrated how much they were capable of doing. Chimpanzees were much less familiar in those days than now, and the readers of his time were impressed by Köhler's descriptions of chimpanzee behavior. The problem was that it wasn't possible to say from observation alone where the behavior came from. Was Sultan able to solve a problem because of some inherited cognitive disposition? Because the problem had features in common with some situation he'd already encountered? Because he'd seen other chimpanzees whose behavior he could imitate? Because of some combination of these and other factors?

The term *insight* seemed appropriate to Köhler because of the suddenness with which a solution to a problem typically emerged. Problem solving that seemed insightful led to further questions: whether learning took place abruptly or gradually, and whether this type of problem solving could be explicitly taught. Debates about how much nonhuman primates can learn continue to the present. But observation alone rarely identifies the sources of behavior and therefore rarely resolves such issues.

Strictly, Köhler did more than simply observe behavior. He arranged environments within which to make his observations. Observation without intervention is difficult to achieve. To observe organisms successfully in the wild, one must know the possible effects of a human presence on their behavior. Even bringing an organism into captivity is itself an intervention. To study such effects, one must present appropriate stimuli. In any study of behavior, therefore, presenting stimuli is virtually inevitable.

Section B   The Presentation of Stimuli

Köhler did in fact present stimuli, by arranging environments for his chimpanzees. So let's now turn to a set of examples in which the role of stimuli is examined more directly. The following, by the ethologist Niko Tinbergen, describes the first feeding of newly hatched herring gull chicks:

Sometimes the parent stands up and looks down into the nest, and then we may see the first begging behavior of the young. They do not lose time in contemplating or studying the parent, whose head they see for the first time, but begin to peck at its bill-tip right away, with repeated, quick, and relatively well-aimed darts of their tiny bills. They usually spread their wings and utter a faint squeaking sound. The old bird cannot resist this, and if only the chicks persist it will feed them. First the parent stretches its neck, and soon a swelling appears at its base. It travels upward, causing the most appalling deformations and the most peculiar turnings and twistings of the neck. All at once the parent bends its head down and regurgitates an enormous lump of half-digested food. This is dropped, and a small piece is now picked up again and presented to the chicks. These redouble their efforts, and soon get hold of the food, whereupon the parent presents them with a new morsel. Now and then the chicks peck at the food on the ground, but more often they aim at the parent's bill, and although this aiming is not always correct, it rarely takes them more than three or four attempts until they score a hit. (Tinbergen, 1960, p. 178)

So far we have here only some observations of chick behavior. But they involve the effects of stimuli and therefore prompt some questions. What exactly are the critical features of these special stimuli presented by the parent gull? Are some more important than others? Are they the most effective ones possible?

Tinbergen set out to answer these questions by preparing stimuli that resembled the parent gull in various ways. He then measured the pecking generated when these stimuli were presented to recently hatched herring gull chicks. The herring gull parent has a white head and a yellow beak with a red patch near its tip. A beak with a black or blue or white patch produced less pecking than one with a red patch, but a beak with a patch of any color produced more pecking than one without any patch at all. Compared to the red patch, the color of the beak or the head was relatively unimportant in generating pecking. In fact, as long as the model had a beak with a red patch on it even the presence or absence of a head made little difference.

Tinbergen also varied the shape of the beak, as illustrated in Figure 2-1. Next to each stimulus, pecking is shown as a percentage of pecks generated by the normal beak shape at the top. With the red patch and other color differences eliminated, changes in pecking depended solely on changes in shape. Most models produced less pecking than the one with the normal shape. The model with an elongated beak (Figure 2-1, bottom) produced considerably more pecking than any of the others, including the one with the normal shape. Because of its effectiveness relative to the normal shape, Tinbergen called this model a *supernormal* stimulus, but he speculated that its shape might be more like what the chick first sees of its parent's beak, as it looks up from beneath the parent's head, than the profile view used for most of the other models.

Tinbergen varied other properties of the beak such as movement, slant and height above the ground. His analysis enabled him

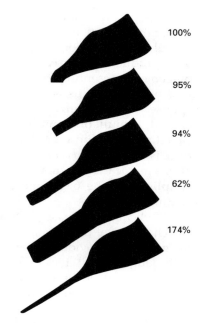

100%

95%

94%

62%

174%

FIGURE 2-1   A series of models used to analyze which properties of the parent gull's beak produced begging pecks in the hatchling herring gull. Pecks to each other model are expressed as a percentage of the reference level (100%) given by pecks to the top model. (Adapted from Tinbergen & Perdeck, 1950, Figure 15.)

to construct a truly supernormal stimulus, a red pencil-shaped rod with three narrow white bands that generated more pecking than an accurate three-dimensional model of a herring gull head. More important, he could specify which features of the parent's head were important in generating pecks and could distinguish them from unimportant features. In other words, by presenting stimuli and observing their effects, Tinbergen was able to identify the critical *structure* of the stimuli that generated pecking in the hatchling herring gulls.

Stimulus presentations are a common feature of research conducted by ethologists, whose concern is the evolution of species-specific behavior patterns in an organism's natural habitats. One effect of stimulus presentations, as we've just seen, is to produce responses. This process, an outcome of presenting stimuli, is called *elicitation*; the stimulus is said to elicit a response. In the language of ethology, the critical stimuli or stimulus features are called *releasers*, and the behavior they produce is called a *fixed action pattern*. But variations in vocabulary shouldn't obscure the simplicity of the basic operation of presenting stimuli.

The eliciting or releasing effects of stimuli can change over time. Data from the laughing gull chick provide an example. Feeding in the laughing gull chick differs in some details from that of the herring gull but includes the begging peck at the parent's beak followed by the parent's regurgitation of partly digested food that the chick then eats. The accuracy of the begging peck was tested by presenting beak models to chicks of various ages. Only about one-third of the pecks of newly hatched chicks struck the model, as opposed to more than three-quarters of those of two-day-old chicks (Hailman, 1969). Did the improved accuracy depend on changes in coordination or visual experience or other factors? Some kinds of behavior might be built in ("prewired") whereas others might have to be learned. How do we tell which is which?

The consequences of accurately aimed pecks differ from those of poorly aimed pecks. In the laughing gull's natural habitat, a more accurately aimed peck is more likely to hit the parent's beak and therefore to be followed by the parent's regurgitation of food than a poorly aimed one. Accurately aimed pecks might increase relative to poorly aimed pecks because of their different consequences. Hailman's observations are consistent with that idea:

> If an inexperienced chick is too close to the target at first, its pecking thrust against the bill or model is so strong that the chick is thrown backward as much as an inch. If the chick starts out too far from the target, the pecking thrust misses and the chick falls forward as much as two inches. Older chicks rarely make such gross errors, suggesting that the experience of overshots and undershots has helped the chick learn to adjust its distance. (Hailman, 1969, p. 100)

To study such cases, it isn't enough simply to present stimuli. A more complex operation must be arranged: Stimuli must be presented as consequences of the organism's behavior.

Section C   Consequential Operations

Again we move to a new set of examples, this time from research on animal intelligence by the American psychologist, Edward L. Thorndike. The critical difference between Thorndike's research and Köhler's was that Thorndike systematically observed changes in behavior over many repetitions of behavior in a given setting rather than looking only at single instances of a problem solution. Thorndike typically noted gradual changes in behavior over repetitions rather than the abrupt changes typically reported by Köhler, perhaps in part because the problems he studied didn't lend themselves to sudden or insightful solutions. More important, Thorndike's experiments showed how responding often depends on its past consequences.

Near the end of the 19th century, Thorndike described his procedures in this way:

> I chose for my general method one which, simple as it is, possesses several other marked ad-

vantages besides those which accompany experiment of any sort. It was merely to put animals when hungry in enclosures from which they could escape by some simple act, such as pulling at a loop of cord, pressing a lever, or stepping on a platform. . . . The animal was put in the enclosure, food was left outside in sight, and his actions observed. Besides recording his general behavior, special notice was taken of how he succeeded in doing the necessary act (in case he did succeed), and a record was kept of the time that he was in the box before performing the successful pull, or clawing, or bite. . . . If, on the other hand, after a certain time the animal did not succeed, he was taken out, but *not fed*. (Thorndike, 1898, pp. 5–6)

One of Thorndike's problem boxes is illustrated in Figure 2-2. In such devices, Thorndike studied cats, dogs and chicks. He gave the following description as typical of the behavior of most cats:

When put into the box the cat would show evident signs of discomfort and of an impulse to escape from confinement. It tries to squeeze through any opening; it claws and bites at the

FIGURE 2-2 In most boxes that Thorndike (1898) used, the animal had only a single way to free the door. In the one shown, three different methods are illustrated: a treadle inside the box (A); a wire or string that can be reached from inside (B); and two outside latches that can be reached from inside (C). The door (D) was usually counterweighted so that it opened by itself once the animal made the appropriate response.

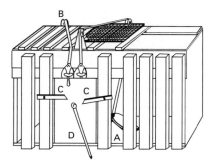

bars or wire; it thrusts its paws out through any opening and claws at everything it reaches; it continues its efforts when it strikes anything loose and shaky; it may claw at things within the box. . . . The cat that is clawing all over the box in her impulsive struggle will probably claw the string or loop or button so as to open the door. And gradually all the other non-successful impulses will be stamped out and the particular impulse leading to the successful act will be stamped in by the resulting pleasure, until, after many trials, the cat will, when put in the box, immediately claw the button or loop in a definite way. (Thorndike, 1898, p. 13)

As a consequence of its behavior, the cat escaped from confinement and also gained access to food. We can assume that both escaping and eating helped make the successful response gradually dominate over other, unsuccessful ones. In either case, the procedure can't be reduced simply to the presentation of stimuli. A new part of the environment wasn't just presented to the cat; it became available as a consequence of what the cat did. As a result of this consequential operation, the cat's behavior changed. Contemporary experiments often examine simpler responses in simpler situations, but they are similarly concerned with relations between responses and their consequences.

We arrange consequences for responses by constructing environments. If we place food in the goalbox of a maze, for example, we create an environment in which a consequence of a rat's movement from the startbox to the goalbox is finding food. After the rat has reached the food once, we can find out how this consequence affects its behavior by seeing what it does the next time we put it in the startbox.

The consequences we arrange can vary from events of obvious biological significance such as presenting food or water to relatively minor changes in things seen or heard or touched. But not all consequences involve producing stimuli: responses can alter stimuli, as when turning a dimmer switch changes the brightness of a lamp; they can remove stimuli, as when operating a switch turns off a light; they can prevent stimuli, as when unplugging a lamp before repairing it eliminates the possibility of an electric shock; they can change the consequences of other responses, as when replacing a burned-out lightbulb makes the previously ineffective response of operating the light switch effective again. Any environmental change can be a change that is produced by a response.

Two classes of consequences are often distinguished on the basis of their effects on behavior. *Reinforcing* consequences are those that increase or maintain responding; *punishing* ones are those that decrease or suppress it. (It's also useful to have a term that doesn't prejudge whether the consequences will reinforce or punish. *Consequation* has been introduced for that purpose. For example, if we don't know whether gold stars will reinforce the classroom behavior of a kindergarten child, it would still be appropriate to speak of *consequating* the behavior with gold stars; e.g., Powers & Osborne, 1976.)

Section D   Signaling or Stimulus-Control Operations

When stimuli become effective as signals, we speak of them as *discriminative* stimuli, and operations that involve signals are called *signaling* or *stimulus-control* operations. The presentation of stimuli and the arrangement of consequences seldom occur in isolation; they're often signaled by other events. A flash of lightning typically precedes a clap of thunder. A traffic light typi-

cally alerts drivers to possible consequences of proceeding or stopping at an intersection. These two examples illustrate that the signaling or discriminative effects of stimuli may be combined either with stimulus presentations or with consequential operations. We'll come back to them later. Both demonstrate the signalling functions of stimuli even though, as we shall see, the two types of signaling can have very different properties.

SIGNALING STIMULUS PRESENTATIONS

Stimuli that signaled the presentation of other stimuli were the basis for experiments on conditional or conditioned reflexes by the Russian physiologist, Ivan P. Pavlov. Pavlov (1927) studied how stimuli acquired signaling properties by showing that responses to stimuli such as food were sometimes produced by other stimuli that had reliably preceded the food. Pavlov spoke of the effects of food in a dog's mouth in terms of the alimentary reflex (for Pavlov, its components included both the glandular response of salivating and motor responses such as chewing and swallowing). He concentrated on salivation because the technology available to him made salivating easier to measure than motor responses. Through surgery, he brought the duct of one of the dog's salivary glands to the outside of the dog's cheek, where he connected it to a fluid system that allowed drops of saliva to be counted.

For one dog, the sound of a metronome consistently preceded food presentations. Pavlov gave the following account of the conditions necessary to make a stimulus function as a signal:

> On several occasions this animal had been stimulated by the sound of the metronome

and immediately presented with food—i.e., a stimulus which was neutral of itself had been superimposed upon the action of the inborn alimentary reflex. We observed that, after several repetitions of the combined stimulation, the sounds from the metronome had acquired the property of stimulating salivary secretion and of evoking the motor reactions characteristic of the alimentary reflex. . . . Hence a first and most essential requisite for the formation of a new conditioned reflex lies in a coincidence in time of the action of any previously neutral stimulus with some definite unconditioned stimulus. Further, it is not enough that there should be overlapping between the two stimuli; it is also and equally necessary that the conditioned stimulus should begin to operate before the unconditioned stimulus comes into action. If this order is reversed, the unconditioned stimulus being applied first and the neutral stimulus second, the conditioned reflex cannot be established at all. (Pavlov, 1927, pp. 26–27)

Pavlov's conditioning experiments demonstrated how a signaling operation can be superimposed on the simpler operation of stimulus presentation.

SIGNALING CONSEQUENCES

Instead of signaling the presentation of stimuli, a stimulus may signal when responses will have consequences. The signaling of consequences played an important role in the history of the psychology of learning long before it began to be studied experimentally. For example, it was involved in the analysis of the case of Clever Hans, a horse that seemed to have been taught to solve arithmetic problems (Pfungst, 1911). The horse apparently took not only addition and multiplication but also square roots in its stride.

The visitor might walk about freely and if he wished, might closely approach the horse and its master, a man between sixty and seventy years of age. His white head was covered with a black slouch hat. To his left the stately animal, a Russian trotting horse, stood like a docile pupil, managed not by means of the whip, but by gentle encouragement and frequent reward of bread or carrots. . . . Our intelligent horse was unable to speak, to be sure. His chief mode of expression was tapping with his right forefoot. (Pfungst, 1911, pp. 18–19)

Clever Hans gave its answers by the number of times it tapped. Its performance was investigated by Oskar Pfungst, who discovered that the horse performed accurately only in the presence of its master. Furthermore, Clever Hans knew the answers only if its master knew them too. Pfungst therefore turned his attention from the horse to the master, and determined that the horse was responding to subtle cues provided by the master's behavior.

. . . we sought to discover by what movements the horse could be made to cease tapping. We discovered that upward movements served as signals for stopping. The raising of the head was most effective, though the raising of the eyebrows, or the dilation of the nostrils—as in a sneer—seemed also to be efficacious. . . . On the other hand, head movements to the right and to the left or forward and back . . . remained ineffective. We also found that all hand movements, including the "wonderfully effective thrust of the hand into the pocket filled with carrots," brought no response. (Pfungst, 1911, p. 63)

The master had cooperated in the investigation and there was no evidence that he'd been aware of the signals he'd provided. Pfungst noted that

Hans's accomplishments are founded . . . upon a one-sided development of the power of perceiving the slightest movements of the questioner . . . . we are justified in concluding from the behavior of the horse, that the desire for food is the only effective spring to action. . . . The gradual formation of the associations mentioned above, between the perception of movement and the movements of the horse himself, is in all probability not to be regarded as a result of a training-process, but as an unintentional by-product of an unsuccessful attempt at real education. (Pfungst, 1911, pp. 240–241)

In this case, the master's movements provided the stimuli in the presence of which the horse's taps were followed by food. The case of Clever Hans demonstrates that even very subtle properties of stimuli can signal the consequences of responding, and it is often cited when critics wonder whether sophisticated behavior depends on cues that have unwittingly been provided by participants.

Facilitated communication, for example, was an attempt to provide therapy for nonverbal autistic children. The children's hands were guided on a typewriter keyboard by facilitators, individuals who were supposed to provide emotional support and motor help. Even though the children did not speak, some soon seemed able to produce complex typed messages. When it was discovered that the children could answer questions correctly only when the facilitators knew the questions, however, it became clear that facilitated communication was a sort of modern Clever Hans phenomenon (Montee, Miltenberger, & Wittrock, 1995). The facilitators had been actively guiding the typing, though in many cases, like the master of Clever Hans, they were unaware that they were doing so.

Signaling effects such as those displayed by Clever Hans were eventually examined more systematically. They came to be called the *discriminative functions of stimuli*, and differed in many ways from the kinds of signaling functions that had been studied by

Pavlov. The research that most decisively established the distinction was conducted by the American psychologist, B. F. Skinner, who arranged an environment in which a rat's lever presses produced food when a light was on but not when it was off, as illustrated in the following passage:

[The apparatus] consists of a dark, well-ventilated, sound-proofed box . . . containing . . . a horizontal bar, made of heavy wire, which may be pressed downward approximately 1.5 cm. against a tension of 10 grams. As the lever moves downward, a mercury switch directly behind the wall is closed. We are concerned with the response of the rat in pressing this lever, which we may define as any movement by the rat which results in the closing of the switch. The switch operates a food-magazine, which discharges a pellet of food of standard size into the tray, where it is accessible to the rat. The connection between the lever and the magazine may be broken at will by the experimenter. . . . The only additional requirement for the investigation of a discrimination is an extra source of stimulating energy . . . a small (3 c.p.) electric bulb. . . . The experimenter controls the current to the light and the connection between the lever and the magazine in such a way that the response to the lever-plus-light is always followed by the discharge of a pellet of food into the tray, while the response to the lever alone is never so reinforced. The animal eventually learns to respond to the lever when the light is on but not to respond when the light is off. (Skinner, 1933, pp. 304–305)

In this example, the light signals the consequences of pressing the lever, in that the lever press is reinforced in the presence but not the absence of the light. The light is a *discriminative stimulus*, and the rat comes to press the lever more often when it's on than when it's off. As the rat begins to respond differently in the presence than the absence of the light, its behavior is said to come *under the control* of the light as a discriminative stimulus; the light can also be said to *occasion* the behavior. The development of this differential responding has been called *discrimination learning*.

The relations between a discriminative stimulus and the consequences of responding are elaborated in the following passage by Skinner (the term *operant* refers to a class of responses having certain consequences, and the term *reinforcement* refers to these consequences):

> . . . the operant must *operate* upon nature to produce its reinforcement. Although the response is free to come out in a very large number of stimulating situations, it will be effective in producing a reinforcement only in a small part of them. The favorable situation is usually marked in some way, and the organism . . . comes to respond whenever a stimulus is present which has been present upon the occasion of a previous reinforcement and not to respond otherwise. The prior stimulus does not elicit the response; it merely sets the *occasion* upon which the response will be reinforced. . . . Three terms must therefore be considered: a prior discriminative stimulus (S^D), the response (R^0), and the reinforcing stimulus (S^1). Their relation may be stated as follows: only in the presence of S^D is R^0 followed by S^1. (Skinner, 1938, p. 178)

Skinner explored this three-term relation experimentally with lights as discriminative stimuli, the lever presses of rats as responses, and food pellets as reinforcing consequences, but his next example, reaching for and touching objects in the seen environment, illustrates the broad range of situations to which the concept applies.

> A convenient example is the elementary behavior of making contact with specific parts of the stimulating environment. A certain movement of my arm (R^0) is reinforced by tactual stimulation from a pencil lying on my desk (S^1). The movement is not always reinforced because the pencil is not always there. By virtue of the visual stimulation from the pencil (S^D) I make the required movement only when it will be reinforced. The part played by

the visual stimulus is shown by considering the same case in a dark room. At one time I reach and touch a pencil, at another time I reach and do not. . . . In neither the light nor the dark does the pencil *elicit* my response (as a shock elicits flexion), but in the light it sets the occasion upon which a response will be reinforced. (Skinner, 1938, p. 178)

The three-term relation, discriminative-stimulus—response—consequence, will be a recurrent theme. Each term is critical. Their combination distinguishes them from other, simpler behavioral relations. In the Pavlovian situation, for example, in which a stimulus is signaled, the organism's behavior has no effect on the sequence of events; no consequences are arranged for responses.

Consider again the examples of lightning flashes and traffic lights. Our blinking or startling at the lightning flash won't prevent the subsequent clap of thunder. But if a traffic light is red as we approach an intersection, our stepping on the brakes is occasioned by this stimulus only because we have learned the potential consequences of doing or not doing so. The second of these two examples is the only one that involves all of the terms of Skinner's three-term contingency. An important difference in vocabulary accompanies these distinctions: (i) *when a stimulus is the primary cause of a response, we say that the stimulus elicits the response or that the response is elicited*; but (ii) *when a response occurs in the presence of a stimulus because the stimulus signals some consequence of responding, we say that the stimulus occasions the response and that the response is emitted.*

Early animal experiments often were concerned not so much with the nature of discrimination learning as with the sensory capacities of organisms. For example, rodent vision was studied by arranging two paths, only one of which led to food (Yerkes & Watson, 1911). Where a rat had to choose the left or the right path, two stimuli were presented (e.g., a black card and a white card). The path to food varied from left to right but was always indicated by the same card (e.g., black). Once the rat learned to take the path indicated by the card correlated with food, the limits of its vision could be studied by substituting other cards (e.g., light-gray and dark-gray) for the original pair. Such experiments were laborious; to demonstrate discrimination learning might take hundreds of trials if the rat learned at all. Several problems existed in this type of study, not the least of which was ensuring that the rat looked at the cards when it reached the choice point.

Apparatus improved over time. Figure 2-3, for example, shows the jumping stand developed by Karl S. Lashley (1930). Lashley described its advantages:

> . . . it requires the animal to jump against the stimulus patterns from a distance, instead of to run past them. . . . I have usually trained the animals by placing the stand against the screen and allowing the animals to step through the open holes to the platform, then gradually withdrawing the stand until, in ten or fifteen trials, the distance of 25 cm. is reached. Cards are then placed in position and training in discrimination begun. (Lashley, 1930, pp. 454–457)

In Lashley's apparatus, rats typically learned to discriminate black from white with perfect accuracy within 4 or 5 trials, and even more difficult discriminations, such as vertical versus horizontal, could usually be mastered within less than 50 trials.

These cases in which discriminative stimuli signal consequences are more complex than the example in which a rat's lever presses produced food in the presence but not the absence of light. There our concern was only with how often presses occurred when the light was on and when it was off. Consider the jumping stand, however. It seems to involve just two responses and their consequences: jumping toward verti-

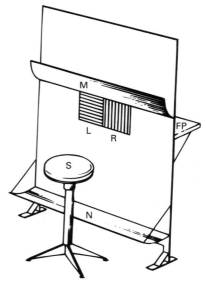

FIGURE 2-3 The Lashley jumping stand (Lashley, 1930, Figure 1). A rat was trained to jump from the stand (S) to one of two doors (L and R). If it jumped to the correct door, the door gave way and the rat reached the food platform (FP). If it jumped to the incorrect door, the door remained fixed and the rat fell into the net below (N). The projecting metal sheet (M) prevented the rat from jumping too high. In the illustration, the right door (R) would be correct for a rat being trained to jump toward vertical lines.

cal and finding food and jumping toward horizontal and landing in the net. But left and right are not irrelevant to the rat. The situation involves at least four responses, each with its own consequence: jumping to vertical on the left, to vertical on the right, to horizontal on the left and to horizontal on the right. Rats may be more likely to respond on the basis of position, left or right, than on the basis of stimulus cards. For example, if the first three trials of vertical-horizontal training were set up with vertical on the right, as in Figure 2-3, it would be no surprise if on trial 4, with vertical on the left for the first time, the rat jumped right, toward horizontal. Until trial 4, jumping to the right led to food just as reliably as jumping toward vertical.

The kind of discrimination in which a single stimulus is present or absent, as in the lever-pressing example, is called a *successive* or *go–no go* discrimination. That in which two or more stimuli are present at the same time and in which each is correlated with a different response, as in the jumping-stand example, is called a *simultaneous* discrimination. Both illustrate signaling operations superimposed on consequences of responding. The comparison between successive and simultaneous discriminations shows that such operations come in varying degrees of complexity.

Section E   **Establishing the Effectiveness of Consequences**

Some consequences of behavior are more important than others, and their effectiveness can vary over time. For example, water is likely to be an effective reinforcer if someone has been deprived of water for some time, but is less likely to be so after a lot of water has been consumed. The things that can be done to change its effectiveness are called *establishing operations*. *Deprivation* and *satiation* are two examples but aren't the only possibilities. For example, heavy exertion in a hot and dry climate or a mouthful of very salty food can have the same effect as a period of water deprivation. Establishing operations change the effectiveness of consequences by changing the likelihood of behavior, as illustrated in the following passage from B. F. Skinner:

> . . . the probability of drinking becomes very high under severe water deprivation and very low under excessive satiation. . . . The biological significance of the change in probability is obvious. Water is constantly being lost through excretion and evaporation, and an equal amount must be taken in to compensate for this loss. Under ordinary circumstances an organism drinks intermittently and maintains a fairly steady and presumably optimal state. When this interchange is disturbed—when the organism is deprived of the opportunity to drink—it is obviously important that drinking should be more likely to occur at the first opportunity. In the evolutionary sense this "explains" why water deprivation strengthens all conditioned and unconditioned behavior concerned with the intake of water. (Skinner, 1953, pp. 141–142)

Skinner spoke of such phenomena in terms of drives:

> The term is simply a convenient way of referring to the effects of deprivation and satiation and of other operations which alter the probability of behavior in more or less the same way. It is convenient because it enables us to deal with many cases at once. There are many ways of changing the probability that an organism will eat; at the same time, a single kind of deprivation strengthens many kinds of behavior. (Skinner, 1953, p. 144)

Behavior that occurs because of establishing operations is sometimes said to be *evoked*. Skinner pointed out, however, that the effects of establishing operations mustn't be equated with those of stimuli:

> A common belief is that deprivation affects the organism by creating a stimulus. The classic example is hunger pangs. When an organism has been without food for a sufficient time, the contractions of the stomach stimulate it in a characteristic way. This stimulation is often identified with the hunger drive. But such stimulation is not closely correlated with the probability of eating. Hunger pangs are characteristic of only a small part of the range through which that probability varies continuously. We usually eat our meals without reaching the condition of deprivation in which pangs are felt, and we continue to eat long after the first few mouthfuls have stopped any pangs which may have occurred. (Skinner, 1953, pp. 144–145)

As Skinner's example indicates, effects of discriminative stimuli must be distinguished from those of establishing operations. Consider another example (cf. Michael, 1982). You'd like a snack, and on locating a vending machine you look in your change purse or pocket for a coin. The vending machine is a discriminative stimulus, because it sets the occasion on which you can get your snack. But with respect to the coin you check for, it is an establishing event: It makes the coin important. It isn't a discriminative stimulus with respect to looking into your purse or pocket and finding a coin, because you'd have found the coin by looking there whether or not you'd seen the vending machine. In other words, the vending machine isn't a stimulus in the presence of which you're more likely to find coins on your person; instead, it makes the coin significant as a reinforcing consequence of checking your purse or pocket.

In contrast with the language of stimulus control, in which changes in discriminative stimuli are said to occasion responses, the responding said to be evoked by establishing operations may occur in a relatively constant environment. For example, if you're more likely to check the refrigerator a long time after a meal than right after a meal, it's your behavior and not the refrigerator that changes from one time to another. In this case, checking the refrigerator is said to be evoked by the establishing operation, food deprivation. But it is still also occasioned by the refrigerator, because the checking can occur in the presence but not in the absence of the refrigerator. And when we want to talk about such behavior without mentioning either the establishing operations or the discriminative stimuli, it remains okay to say that the behavior was emitted. In other words, establishing operations *evoke*, discriminative stimuli *occasion*, and the responses they evoke and/or occasion *are emitted*.

Our treatment of establishing operations

has been brief, because in themselves they don't provide examples of learning. As we shall see, however, they provide the contexts within which learning typically occurs, and it is therefore difficult to study learning without them.

Section F   Summary

As we have seen, the study of behavior is concerned with relations between environmental events, *stimuli*, and the organism's actions, *responses*. We can examine these relations by analyzing how changes in the environment produce changes in responding. A critical first step is *observation* of behavior, but it's typically not enough simply to watch. To understand behavior we must intervene by changing the environment. We can describe environmental changes in terms of classes of experimental operations: *stimulus-presentations*, *consequential* operations, *signaling* or *stimulus-control* operations, and *establishing* operations. We will return to these operations often throughout this book, and they will especially help us to organize the topic of *learning without words* in Part III. They are summarized in Table 2-1.

Aside from observation, presenting stimuli is the simplest operation. When we present stimuli, we can observe the responses produced. For example, a touch to the cheek might make a newborn infant turn and begin to suckle. Stimulus presentations are relevant to learning because the responses produced by stimuli can vary depending upon the conditions under which stimuli are presented.

Sometimes the organism changes its environment: Behavior can have consequences. Arranging the environment so that it is modified by the organism's responses is called a consequential operation. Consequences can include the presentation, removal or pre-

TABLE 2-1 Basic Behavioral Operations

OPERATION	DESCRIPTION	EXAMPLES	USAGE
1. Observation	No intervention.	We watch an animal behaving.	—
2. Stimulus-presentation operation	Stimulus A is presented.	*Loud noise* (A) startles child. Physician shines *light* (A) in patient's eye.	Stimulus *elicits* response; response *is elicited by* stimulus.
3. Consequential operation	Response B has consequence C (e.g., a stimulus is produced or terminated).	*Putting coin in vending machine* (B) produces *soft drink* (C). *Touching hot stove* (B) produces *burn* (C). *Light goes out* (C) when *switch is thrown* (B).	Response is *emitted*.
4. Signaling or stimulus-control operation: Superimposed on stimulus presentation	Stimulus D signals presentation of stimulus E.	*Lightning* (D) precedes *thunder* (E).	Stimulus *elicits* response; response *is elicited by* stimulus.
5. Signaling or stimulus-control operation: Superimposed on consequences	Stimulus F signals that response G will have consequence H.	*Red traffic light* (F) signals that *driving through intersection* (G) may lead to *traffic ticket* (H). *Ringing telephone* (F) signals that *answering* (G) may provide *opportunity for conversation* (H).	Stimulus *occasions* response; response *is emitted* in presence of stimulus.
6. Establishing operation	Effectiveness of consequence I as a reinforcer or punisher is established.	*Food* (I) becomes an effective reinforcer after food deprivation. The presentation of shock makes *shock removal* (I) a reinforcer. When it is important to unlock a door, *the key to the door* (I) becomes a reinforcer.	An event is *established* as a reinforcer or punisher. Behavior is *evoked* by the establishing operation.

vention of stimuli, or more complex events such as changes in the consequences of other responses. For example, a child may learn to ask for a cup of milk, or the child may discover that what is in a parent's coffee cup is usually hot and bitter tasting, or the child may find that taking an offered cup of fruit juice is allowed only after saying *please*. Some responses that have consequences may occur more often and others less often. If an organism responds more often because its behavior changed its environment, we say that the behavior was rewarded or *reinforced*; if an organism responds less often for the same reason, we say that the behavior was suppressed or *punished*.

We can signal either stimulus presentations or consequential operations by arranging them only when some stimulus is present. Organisms don't behave indiscriminately. They do some things in some circumstances and other things in other circumstances.

One stimulus can signal the imminent occurrence of another. For example, the child may learn that the sound of a key in the door reliably precedes the return home of a working parent, or that a lightning flash is often followed by the sound of thunder. In these cases, signaling is superimposed upon stimulus presentations: The sound of the key signals the parent's appearance, and the lightning warns of thunder. On the other hand, a stimulus might signal the conditions under which a response has some consequence. For example, a child may learn that requests are more likely to be granted in the presence of either parent alone than in the presence of both parents together, or that misbehavior is more likely to be followed by a scolding in the presence of one parent than in the presence of the other. In these cases, signaling is superimposed upon a consequential operation: The presence of the parents signals various consequences of requests or of misbehavior.

The changes in behavior produced by stimulus-presentation operations or consequential operations may begin to occur only in the presence of the signaling stimuli. When a stimulus signals that some event is about to occur or that an organism's behavior might have certain consequences, the organism may come to respond differently when the stimulus is present than when it is absent. This process is called *discrimination*, and the organism's behavior is said to be *occasioned by* the discriminative stimulus.

Finally, the significance of events as consequences of behavior can be altered by establishing operations, such as *deprivation* and *satiation*. For example, whether a child asks for a drink of water may depend in large part on how long it's been since the last one. These operations can evoke behavior, and they work by changing the effectiveness of events as reinforcers or punishers.

Behavior can be complicated. Different stimuli can have different effects on different responses, and different responses can have different consequences. Nevertheless, as we shall see, a variety of learning procedures can be treated as combinations of these basic types of experimental interventions: *stimulus presentations*; *consequential* operations, such as reinforcement and punishment, in which responses act on the environment; *signaling* or *stimulus-control* operations, in which these other operations are signaled by discriminative stimuli; and *establishing* operations, which alter the significance of the consequences of behavior. As our behavioral taxonomy, these categories will take us a long way, but later, especially when we consider the transition from learning without words to learning with words, we'll find that they don't exhaust the possibilities.

PART II BEHAVIOR WITHOUT LEARNING

Chapter 3
Evolution and Behavior

A. The Nature of Evolution
Recipes and Blueprints
Variation and Selection
Kinds of Selection
Summary

B. Phylogeny, Ontogeny and Behavior

Evolution *and* revolution *are descendants of the Latin* volvere, *to roll; they differ in that* evolution *implies an unrolling or rolling out whereas* revolution *implies a rolling over or turning around. Se-* lection *can be traced to the Latin* legere, *originally to gather or to choose (cf. the etymology of* logos, *Chapter 14). The prefix,* se-, *adds the implication of a weeding out from a large number, as contrasted with the bringing together implied by* con-, *the root prefix for* collection.
    Phylogeny, *evolutionary history, and* ontogeny, *the life history of the individual organism, share the Greek root* gen-, *in the sense of kind or sort (cf. the etymology of* generalization, *Chapter 8).* Phylo- *has a Greek root implying a tribe or clan or racial stock and* onto- *has one implying being or reality. In their combination with* gen-, *each implies origin: the origin of a biological phylum or population or the origin of a living entity.*

Our planet is roughly 4.6 billion years old. That's a very long time. If you tried to count to a billion, you'd take more than 30 years to finish even if you kept up an uninterrupted pace of a count per second. If you took time out to sleep, of course, you'd take much longer. (The one-per-second estimate is very generous; it's easy to count quickly when numbers are small, but bigger numbers like 374,516,982 would surely slow you down, especially if you worried about losing count.)

Life existed on earth for most of those years (see Gould, 1989, for a detailed account). Chemical and fossil evidence indicates that it began within the first billion years or so, and over most of the next 3 billion years, it consisted of single-celled organisms. Multicellular organisms only appeared roughly 600 million years ago, in the geological period called the Cambrian. An explosion in the diversity of multicellular life that occurred during that period was followed by a weeding out; the survivors provided the major groupings from which contemporary species evolved. One such grouping was the vertebrates. The evolution from amphibians to reptiles included many significant events, such as the colonization of land. The dinosaurs were a spectacular part of the story, but by 65 million years ago they were gone. Their passing made room for the evolution of mammals, and by perhaps 4 million years ago primates that walked upright had evolved. We humans eventually emerged from that line only a little more than 100,000 years ago. All of us are cousins, and all are descendants of a very long line of survivors.

Evolution continues today, and it is rapid enough that it can be observed within individual human lifetimes (Weiner, 1994). It occurs in natural habitats, such as the Galápagos Islands, where different species of finches continue to evolve with changes in the local habitats on each island, but it also happens as a result of human interventions, as when disease organisms become resistant to antibiotics or insect pests become resistant to insecticides.

These are merely a few of many facts about evolution. The fossil record is incomplete and there's much detail we don't know, but the evidence from biology and geology and other disciplines shows that evolution has happened and continues to happen. In other words, evolution is not a theory; it is a name for certain kinds of changes that happen to the biological populations we call *species*. Theories of evolution aren't about whether contemporary species are descended from the very different ancestors we find in the geologic record. All theories of evolution take that for granted. They differ in what they say about how evolution came about. The theory that has been most successful in accommodating the facts of evolution is Charles Darwin's account of evolution in terms of natural selection.

Section A   The Nature of Evolution

Natural selection refers to Darwin's account of evolution in terms of the differential survival and reproduction of the members of a population; the environment selects the individuals who pass their characteristics on from one generation to the next and thereby shapes the characteristics of those in later populations (for discussions of the details of natural selection, see Dawkins, 1976, 1986). Evolution by natural selection requires variations within populations; these variations are the stuff upon which selection works.

Selection was well-known even before Darwin but was the sort used by humans in horticulture and animal husbandry. People knew how to breed plants or livestock selectively for hardiness or yield or other characteristics. This selective breeding was called *artificial selection*, and it created new varieties of vegetables and flowers and so on. Workhorses were selected for strength and racehorses were selected for speed. One part of Darwin's insight was that a similar kind of selection occurred in nature, without human intervention; that was *natural selection*.

Darwin's main arguments were first published in his book, *On the Origin of Species* (Darwin, 1859). The arguments were warmly received in some quarters, but in others they were strongly resisted. The resistance grew, and by the end of the nineteenth century the belief was widespread that Darwinism was dead. It didn't recover until well into the 20th century. The half century or so that preceded that recovery has been called the eclipse of Darwinism (Bowler, 1983; cf. Catania, 1987).

The reason for the eclipse wasn't that evolution itself had been discredited but rather that other theories than Darwin's became dominant. The main alternatives to Darwin's (1) *natural selection* were (2) *Lamarckism*, (3) *orthogenesis*, and (4) the combination of *Mendelian genetics* with *mutation theory*. Lamarckism was based on the work of an 18th-century French scientist who in his time had done much to make a case for the fact of evolution. Lamarck's theory was that characteristics acquired during an organism's lifetime could be passed on to its offspring, through changes in its own genetic material or germ plasm. One problem with this theory was that it could not show why advantageous acquired characteristics should be any more likely to be passed on than disadvantageous ones such as injuries.

According to the theory of orthogenesis, evolution was directed by forces within organisms, without reference to the demands of the environment; it could be likened to a developmental unfolding. One manifestation of this unfolding was supposed to be the recapitulation of phylogeny by ontogeny. *Ontogeny* is the development of the individual organism and *phylogeny* is its evolutionary history. During ontogeny the embryo was thought to pass through stages corresponding to its phylogeny. This idea of recapitulation, however, has severe limitations and is no longer central to evolutionary theory (Gould, 1977).

The problem with Mendelian genetics was that by itself it provided no mechanism for variation. In strict Mendelian descent, dominant and recessive genes in one generation determined their proportions in the next. Without variation, natural selection had nothing to work on. To provide for the appearance of new forms, Mendelian accounts added mutation theory, which held that evolution proceeded through spontaneous and usually large genetic changes. At the time, however, too little was known about mutation for it to be the basis of a convincing account.

RECIPES AND BLUEPRINTS

In the 19th century, genes were theoretical entities. The techniques of cell biology hadn't yet reached the point at which genes had been located in actual cells. Nevertheless, all of these evolutionary theories assumed that hereditary material of some sort was passed on from one generation to the next and that evolution was determined by the properties of this material. A major flaw in some theories was the assumption that

genetic material constituted a representation or copy of the organism. In the earliest versions of orthogenesis, called *preformationist*, the embryo was literally a homunculus, a tiny individual complete in all its parts; in later variations of the theory, the embryo was seen as taking on ancestral forms, as ontogeny was said to recapitulate phylogeny. As for Lamarckism, the transmission of acquired characteristics required that they be preserved in the germ plasm in some way, so the germ plasm had to contain some kind of plan of those parts of the organism that were to be altered in subsequent generations. In either case, the germ plasm could be regarded as a representation or copy of the organism.

A *recipe* is a sequence of procedures or instructions. It describes how to create a product, but it doesn't necessarily incorporate a description of the product (a recipe for a cake doesn't look like a cake). A recipe can be informative but it isn't likely to contain information about its origins, such as the number of tries it took to make it work. A *blueprint*, on the other hand, doesn't ordinarily say how to construct the structure that it shows. Like a recipe, it can be informative, but it too is likely to omit information about its origins, such as the order in which different parts were designed. A blueprint is a representation or copy but a recipe isn't. Lamarckism and the preformationist orthogenetic accounts treated genetic materials as blueprints rather than recipes.

A major achievement in contemporary biology was to reinterpret genetic material not as a blueprint for the organism's structure but rather as a recipe for its development (see Dawkins, 1986, Chapter 11, on the metaphors of blueprint and recipe). The modern formulation demanded rethinking of the sense in which genetic material can be said to contain information, whether about evolutionary history or about the structure of the organism (cf. Dawkins, 1982, Chapter 9). Genetic materials provide limited information about the past environments in which they've been selected, in part because they don't include the genetic materials of all those other organisms that didn't survive. And they provide limited information about the eventual structure of an organism because they're recipes for the production of proteins rather than blueprints for body parts. One implication is that Lamarckism and at least some varieties of orthogenesis are untenable alternatives to Darwinian selection because their implicit copy theories are inconsistent with what we've learned about how the genetic material works.

It's ironic that, along with Lamarckism and orthogenesis, Mendelian genetics had also been seen as a serious challenge to Darwinian selection. The integration of Mendelian genetics with Darwinian selection in the 1920s and 1930s, known as the *modern synthesis*, became the core of contemporary biology. The problem with Mendelian genetics had been that it provided no mechanism for variations. Then genetic experiments with fruit flies not only elaborated on genetic mechanisms but also brought mutations into the laboratory. With fruit flies, many generations could be studied within a relatively short time. The research gave evidence on natural rates of mutation and on the magnitude of mutation effects, which were relatively small compared to the changes assumed in prior mutation theories. The combination of Mendelian genetics with the facts of mutation provided the variability needed for the workings of natural selection.

The Darwinian view had to face and overcome other hurdles besides the competing theories (cf. Mayr, 1982). Earlier we mentioned the incompleteness of the fossil record. Our understanding of prehistoric life depends on finding occasional members of earlier species preserved in that record, but the accidents of both their preservation and their discovery leave inevitable gaps. Furthermore, hard parts such as bones or shells are much more likely to be preserved than soft parts. And even if we find all of the parts intact, our information about how those creatures behaved is limited. We must often resort to indirect evidence (e.g., analogies with living species; fossil records of behavior such as fossil footprints).

The age of the earth was another problem. In the 19th century the estimate was too short to make evolution through natural selection plausible, but that age has been revised vastly upward during this century. Another misunderstanding was the likelihood of improbable events when these events have many opportunities to occur over extended time periods. For example, suppose that some organic molecule is a crucial prerequisite for life, that it occurs in nature with odds of a million to one only when lightning creates it by passing through some mixture of gases that were present in the early atmosphere of the earth. The creation of that organic molecule might seem a very long shot. But the many lightning storms over many millions of years during the early history of our planet would have repeated those conditions many millions of times, making it a virtual certainty that the molecule would be created not just once but many times, even though the particular moment of its creation wouldn't have been predictable (cf. Dawkins, 1986; Gleick, 1987).

VARIATION AND SELECTION

Now let's consider an example of natural selection. We start with a population of prey animals (e.g., antelopes) the members of which vary in the speed with which they can evade predators; the reasons might include differences in anatomy (e.g., bone length, muscle size), sensory differences that allow some to get off to a quicker start than others, metabolic differences that affect endurance, and so on. If these animals are preyed upon by predators, the ones most likely to be caught are the slowest ones, everything else being equal.

The proviso that everything else must be equal is important. To speak only of speed is an oversimplification. For example, an individual who is fast at the expense of requiring much more to eat might forage longer and thus run a higher risk of being seen by predators during foraging. That higher risk might counterbalance its speed advantage, because this animal will presumably tire more quickly than the others if it is chased more often than them. Or, as another example, one individual might run faster than another, but the other might be harder to catch because it can change direction more quickly or unpredictably. As long as the members of the population vary, our argument can be recast in terms of the effects of such factors on the probability of being caught. We'll speak of speed because that's convenient for our purposes, but we must note that the effective dimensions of escape from predators are probably much more complex than that.

At any time during its history, our prey population has some mean or average speed, with some members above that mean and others below it. The ones below are those most likely to be caught and so are less likely to pass their genes on to the next generation. The next generation will then include more descendants of those above the mean than of those below or, in other words, fewer of the previous slow and more of the previous fast runners. The mean speed in this generation will therefore be higher than in the last one. But the same kind of selection still operates: Again, slower ones are more likely to be caught than faster ones. Over many genera-

tions, therefore, the mean speed becomes faster and faster. (A similar kind of selection will also operate on the predators, because their effectiveness in catching prey will vary across individuals too.)

The evolution of the horse provides striking evidence for this kind of selection (Simpson, 1951; Gould, 1996). Over the 50 million years or so since *eohippus*, the so-called dawn horse (technically, its proper name is *Hyracotherium*), the individuals in the populations from which modern horses are descended gradually increased in size. These size changes were accompanied by other changes (e.g., toes becoming hooves), presumably including changes in behavior. Eohippus was the ancestor of modern horses, but it is unlikely that an eohippus population could survive in the habitats of contemporary horses. The fact that eohippus is extinct is relevant to our story. Many descendants of eohippus must have been the most evasive of their kind in their time, but they're no longer around. When selection operates on some relative property, such as speed relative to the mean for a population, the mean for the population changes. For example, after capture by predators has repeatedly selected faster escape in a population, few descendants of the originally slow runners will be left even if that slower running speed had provided a selective advantage at a time when it was a very fast speed relative to the population mean. In other words, as eohippus demonstrates, we mustn't expect to find examples of ancestral forms within current populations.

According to these arguments the source of selection is in the environment (the environments of predators include their prey and the environments of prey include their predators). Selection creates the features of organisms, but selection is necessary to maintain them as well as to create them. For example, the ancestors of whales were once land mammals. After they moved back into the sea, the environmental contingencies that made legs advantageous no longer maintained the selection of well-formed legs. Instead, selection began to favor limbs that were effective for movement through water. The legs of the ancestors of whales gradually disappeared; in a sense it's appropriate to say that the legs had extinguished or become extinct (Skinner, 1988, p. 73; cf. Provine, 1984). Selection operates on species, but does so by acting on particular organs and systems and body parts.

Consider another example. Environments that include tall trees with edible leaves are environments in which long necks may be advantageous, especially if shorter trees are scarce or if their leaves are often depleted by competitors. Giraffes arose through the natural selection of relatively long necks; such selection couldn't occur in environments that lacked tall trees (the tall trees set the occasion for the selection of long necks). But the selection also depended on what there was to start with. In one species variations among individuals might allow selection of those with longer necks, but in another they might allow selection of those who climb trees more efficiently. The environment selects from populations of organisms, but that selection can only operate on the available range of variations within those populations. Structural factors must be included among the constraints on possible variations. In the human species, for example, our four-limbed mammalian ancestry precludes the evolution of a pair of wings emerging from our shoulder blades.

The kind of phylogenic selection we've discussed so far involves gradual changes taking place over long periods of time (we'll see later that it has much in common with a kind of selection that occurs within the lifetime of the individual; see Chapter 7 on shaping). Some controversies about evolu-

tion have been about whether evolution takes place gradually, as in the example of the horse, or in fits and starts (punctuated evolution or saltation). For example, the fossil record includes evidence of major changes in species over periods of time that are relatively short by evolutionary standards (e.g., the explosion of multicellular life in the Cambrian period; or, at the end of the Cretaceous period, the extinction of the dinosaurs, perhaps as a result of the impact of a comet or some other planetary catastrophe, and the later proliferation of large mammals). Given the strong evidence for both kinds of evolutionary change, perhaps it's most reasonable to conclude that evolution can take place either way, with some features selected gradually and continuously relative to some population mean and others selected following punctuated events that produced massive environmental changes (perhaps including large-scale extinctions).

As indicated in our treatment of running speed, evolution by natural selection involves more than changes along single dimensions. It results in organized complexity, such as the intricate structure of the human eye. Is it reasonable to believe that natural selection could have produced such organized complexity? Using an analogy from aeronautical design, Dawkins (1982) posed the problem this way:

> The designers of the first jet engine started with a clean drawing board. Imagine what they would have produced if they had been constrained to "evolve" the first jet engine from an existing propeller engine, changing one component at a time, nut by nut, screw by screw, rivet by rivet. A jet engine so assembled would be a weird contraption indeed. It is hard to imagine that an aeroplane designed in that evolutionary way would ever get off the ground. Yet in order to complete the biological analogy we have to add yet another constraint. Not only must the end product get off the ground; so must every intermediate along

the way, and each intermediate must be superior to its predecessor. (Dawkins, 1982, p. 38)

If the eye is a product of natural selection, it couldn't have emerged full blown. But what good is part of an eye? What selective advantage could it confer? The answer is that even 1% of an eye is a substantial advantage if all of one's contemporaries have even less. Any sensitivity to light is better than none, 2% is better than 1%, 3% is better than 2%, and so on. Dawkins here describes the advantages of a lensless eye over no eye at all:

> You can tell if you are about to walk into a wall or another person. If you were a wild creature, you could certainly use your lensless eye to detect the looming shape of a predator, and the direction from which it was approaching. In a primitive world where some creatures had no eyes at all and others had lensless eyes, the ones with lensless eyes would have all sorts of advantages. . . . each tiny improvement in sharpness of image, from swimming blur to perfect human vision, plausibly increases the organism's chances of surviving. (Dawkins, 1986, p. 81)

Once a complex system such as an eye evolves in a given species, it becomes exceedingly unlikely that another system with the same function will ever displace it. For example, the 1% of seeing that might be an evolutionary precursor of a complete human eye provides considerably less of an advantage if a complete eye already exists than if the alternative is not seeing at all. Selection doesn't replace existing mechanisms with others that do the same job, so we shouldn't expect a third eye ever to evolve in the middle of human foreheads.

What about other cases, such as animal mimicry? A stick insect may look so much like a stick that a bird that otherwise would have eaten it will pass it by. But how much good would it do to have merely a 5% resemblance to a stick? In response to this question, Dawkins (1986, pp. 83–84) points out that a 5% resemblance may be just enough to make a difference in twilight or in fog or if the bird is far away. Once individuals in the population vary in their resemblance to sticks, natural selection based even on small differences may drive the population to more and more convincing mimicry.

Resemblance to sticks is an unusual property and is of course only one of many possible directions of selection. We've already noted that selection can operate on different features in different populations, and not every feature that seems adaptive is necessarily a product of natural selection. Darwin regarded natural selection as the most important mechanism of evolution, but he took pains to point out that natural selection wasn't the only possible one: "I am convinced that Natural Selection has been the main *but not exclusive* means of modification" (Darwin, 1859, p. 6; italics added). Selectionist accounts of the features of a population demand more than just a plausible story about how those features might be advantageous.

Some features might come about as incidental byproducts of selection. Gould and Lewontin (1979) use the spandrels of San Marco as an analogy. San Marco is a cathedral in Venice with a dome supported by arches. Any two adjacent arches come together at the top of a common pillar, and in the construction of San Marco the tapering triangular space above the pillar and between the two arches was filled in and its surface was used for a mosaic. The space is called a *spandrel*:

> Each spandrel contains a design admirably fitted into its tapering space. An evangelist sits in the upper part flanked by the heavenly cities. Below, a man representing one of the four Biblical rivers (Tigris, Euphrates, Indus and Nile) pours water from a pitcher into the

narrowing space between his feet. The design is so elaborate, harmonious and purposeful that we are tempted to view it as the starting place of any analysis. (Gould & Lewontin, 1979, pp. 581–582)

The point is that the cathedral of San Marco wasn't built in order to create the spandrels. The spandrels were an inevitable but incidental architectural byproduct of constructing a dome on top of rounded arches. Analogously, some features of contemporary populations may not be direct products of natural selection; instead, they may be incidental byproducts of other unrelated features that have arisen through selection. When the source of an inherited feature is uncertain, the question is sometimes put in terms of the San Marco analogy: is it a product of natural selection or is it a spandrel?

We've so far concentrated on properties of selection, but what can we now say about the evolution of behavior (cf. Skinner, 1984)? We've already noted that behavior has left only indirect evidence in the fossil record. It's safe to assume, however, that response systems evolved before sensory systems. For an organism that can't do anything about what it sees, there's no advantage to seeing. Some organisms remained immobile but others began to twitch and squirm. Some organisms were passively moved by ocean currents and others anchored themselves to particular places. The organisms from which we are descended developed ways to get from one place to another.

As motor systems developed, the advantages of responding differentially to environmental events were presumably the basis for the selection of sensory systems. Withdrawal upon being touched might be enough to avoid a predator and would certainly be more advantageous than withdrawing at random. Ingesting things on the basis of their chemical properties would certainly be more advantageous than ingesting

things randomly. These properties of behavior are so important that it's hard to imagine a world in which all creatures lacked them. But then we can recall that we shouldn't expect to find examples of ancestral forms within current populations.

The most primitive patterns of movement were probably driven primarily by eliciting stimuli. For example, suppose bright light elicits random movement. An insect larva in the light starts moving and continues to do so until, by chance, it moves into darkness; once there it stops. We won't find many of these larvae in the light, but we may find large numbers in dark places (e.g., under the rotting bark of a fallen tree limb). Once we expose them to light, they all begin to move. But their behavior isn't directed toward dark places; they get there by chance, some sooner than others, and they end up congregated there only because that's where they stop.

Orientation that occurs on such a basis is called a *kinesis* (plural *kineses*); it's distinguished from orientation directed toward or away from some stimulus, which is called a *taxis* (plural *taxes*; Fraenkel & Gunn, 1961). Examples of taxes include movements toward light (positive phototaxis) and upward movement, away from gravity, as in climbing a tree (negative geotaxis). The details of these and other types of orientation vary (for example, in an organism with two eyes a phototaxis may come about because the organism consistently moves so as to equalize the amount of light received by each eye).

These examples, like reflex relations, share the property that each involves a fixed pattern of responding to environmental events. First there was movement; then the movement came under the control of stimuli. Such patterns were particularly advantageous in stable environments. For example, given a sharp stimulus to its paw, a dog flexes its leg, drawing its paw up toward its body. For an animal that walks on the ground, that response is advantageous: If the dog steps on a thorn, its flexion pulls its paw away from the thorn. The sloth, however, lives in a very different environment. It hangs from trees and its comparable reflex involves an extension rather than a flexion of its limb. If the sharp stimulus is a thorn, the hanging sloth that pulls its limb toward its body instead of extending it will only drive the thorn in deeper (cf. Hart, 1973, p. 176).

But not all environments are stable. It must have been a major evolutionary step when such patterns of behavior became modifiable or, in other words, when some organisms became able to learn. Learning may at first have been selected within restricted domains. For example, upon leaving its nest the digger wasp flies in ever-widening circles; its later return to the nest is based on landmarks, such as the rocks or plants it flew over before its departure (Tinbergen, 1972). Its capacity to learn landmarks is part of its phylogenic heritage and is probably very specific to finding its nest.

The capacity to learn must itself have been selected. The selection of this capacity presumably occurred in many different ways in different species at different times. Things about environments that ordinarily remain constant over a lifetime need to be learned only once, whereas things about changeable environments need to be learned and then discarded and then learned again (in our own lives, the names of people we know don't change very often, whereas the items on our shopping lists usually change from one shopping trip to the next). We should therefore expect some kinds of learning to be difficult to reverse while others remain transient and easily modified. For example, the survival of a newborn calf may depend on how well and quickly it learns about the features that distinguish its mother

from others; in a stable environment, such learning (sometimes called imprinting) may be effectively permanent. Under such conditions, the time of life during which learning occurs may also be limited. But as the calf grows and becomes more independent, it will also learn about many things that change from day to day, such as the passage of predators or the places where food or water are found.

Those who look for mechanisms of learning in the nervous system must expect that evolutionary contingencies have selected different kinds, with some producing fairly permanent changes in behavior and others producing changes that are easily reversed, with some restricted to relatively narrow situations and others broadly general, and with some operating at different times in an organism's life than others. In other words, the selection of different kinds of nervous systems depends upon the different kinds of behavior they produce. We'll return to this topic in Chapter 12, when we consider some biological constraints on learning.

KINDS OF SELECTION

The selection we've considered so far, the selection of populations of organisms over evolutionary time, can be called *phylogenic selection*. But it isn't the only kind of selection that should interest us. Of the various kinds of learning we'll explore in the chapters that follow, one is the case in which responses are affected by their consequences. For example, if an organism is food-deprived and some response produces food, that response is likely to occur more often. We've already discussed such cases as instances of reinforcement. Reinforcement can also occur in particular environments or settings, when we say that a situation sets the occasion on which responses are reinforced. These cases involve a kind of selection that operates within the lifetime of the individual rather than over successive generations.

This kind of selection can be called *ontogenic selection*; it involves *selection by consequences* (cf. Skinner, 1981). For the food-deprived organism, for example, responses that produce food continue to occur; other responses don't. Food is the consequence that selects some responses and not others. This is a way of saying that the responding is selected by its environment (it is important to notice how very different this is from saying that the organism itself selected some way to respond). We could say that the responses that produce food survive and the others extinguish. Parallels between these two varieties of selection, phylogenic selection or Darwinian natural selection and ontogenic selection or the selection of behavior by its consequences, have been explored in considerable detail (e.g., Catania, 1978; Skinner, 1981; T. L. Smith, 1986); we'll note some of the parallels as we explore the phenomena of learning.

Behavior acquired through learning during one individual's lifetime will disappear unless it's somehow passed on to others. A third variety of selection occurs when behavior can be passed on from one organism to another, as in imitation or, more important, in language. For example, what someone has said or written can survive the person's death if it's passed on to and repeated by others. The verbal behavior that survives within and is shared among the members of a group is part of the culture of that group. We'll give special attention to this third kind of selection, which has been called *cultural selection*, in the chapters on social learning and on verbal behavior (Chapters 13 through 15).

We've been considering three kinds of selection: (1) phylogenic selection, the evolution over biological time of populations of organisms and their characteristic features, such as behavior; (2) ontogenic selection, the shaping of behavior by its consequences during the lifetime of an individual organism; and (3) cultural selection, the survival of patterns of behavior as they're passed on from some individuals to others. These kinds of selection depend on behavior that changes during ontogeny as well as during phylogeny.

SUMMARY

We began this section with a brief survey of the evolution of life on earth. Darwin's account of that evolution, natural selection, faced challenges from other approaches, such as orthogenesis and Lamarckism. It overcame those challenges when it was integrated with Mendelian genetics and mutation theory, and when it began to be recognized that the genetic material was more like a recipe than a blueprint for an organism. The cumulative changes produced over time by natural or phylogenic selection created organized complexity, but also often meant that ancestral forms didn't survive in current populations. Some biological systems were shaped directly by selection and others were incidental byproducts (spandrels). The advent of learning was one important event in the evolution of behavior; it allowed for a second kind of selection, ontogenic selection or the selection of classes of behavior within an organism's lifetime, as when responding persists because it has certain consequences. A third kind of selection became possible when behavior could be passed on from one individual to another, in cultural selection. The analysis of behavior must consider behavior as a product of phylogenic, ontogenic and cultural selection; we must understand each kind of selection to understand where behavior comes from. We now turn briefly to the relation between the phylogeny of behavior and its ontogeny.

Section B Phylogeny, Ontogeny and Behavior

Behavior is a joint function of *phylogenic contingencies*, those that operated in ancestral environments during the evolution of a species, and *ontogenic contingencies*, those that operated during interactions between an organism and its environment within its own lifetime (cf. Skinner, 1966). Ontogeny doesn't recapitulate phylogeny, so we can't expect to trace the evolution of behavior by following the development of behavior in an individual (or vice versa). Whether in spite of these limitations or because of them, a recurrent issue has been the relative contributions of phylogeny and ontogeny to behavior: To what extent does behavior depend on evolutionary history and to what extent on learning? Heated controversy often results when such questions are addressed to socially significant issues such as the inheritance of intellΔigence, especially when the alternatives are presented as oppositions (e.g., nature versus nurture, heredity versus environment).

The research of Spalding, a 19th-century British naturalist, provides an eloquent case for the role of phylogeny in behavior.

> . . . we have only to look at the young of the lower animals to see that as a matter of fact they do not require to go through the process of learning the meaning of their sensations in relation to external things; that chickens, for example, run about, pick up crumbs, and follow the call of their mother *immediately* on leaving the shell. . . . I have observed and experimented on more than fifty chickens, taking them from under the hen while yet in the eggs. But of these, not one emerging from the shell was in a condition to manifest an ac-

quaintance with the qualities of the outer world. On leaving the shell they are wet and helpless. . . . (Spalding, 1873/1954, pp. 2–3)

Spalding noted that the chicks advanced rapidly. Within four or five hours of hatching they were pecking at objects and preening their wings. But he also recognized that a lot could be learned in four or five hours.

> To obviate this objection with respect to the eye, I had recourse to the following expedient. Taking eggs just when the little prisoners had begun to break their way out, I removed a piece of the shell, and before they had opened their eyes drew over their heads little hoods, which, being furnished with an elastic thread at the lower end, fitted close round their necks. (Spalding, 1873/1954, p. 3)

Spalding kept the chicks blind for one to three days and then removed their hoods.

> Almost invariably, they seemed a little stunned by the light, remained motionless for several minutes, and continued for some time less active than before they were unhooded. Their behaviour, however, was in every case conclusive against the theory that the perceptions of distance and direction by the eye are the result of experience, of associations formed in the history of each individual life. Often at the end of two minutes they followed with their eyes the movements of crawling insects, turning their heads with all the precision of an old fowl. (Spalding, 1873/1954, p. 3)

Our primary interest in this text is in behavior that is learned, but we must always entertain the possibility that the behavior we study has phylogenic sources. We can try to create arbitrary environments to minimize the role of phylogeny. For example, a standard pigeon chamber is an arbitrary environment, because natural environments don't include keys on which a pigeon's pecks produce food only when the key is lit. But arbitrary environments aren't always arbitrary enough; they won't necessarily make the behavior that occurs in them arbitrary. Consider a pigeon's key pecks:

> Such responses are not wholly arbitrary. They are chosen because they can be easily executed, and because they can be repeated quickly and over long periods of time without fatigue. In such a bird as the pigeon, pecking has a certain genetic unity; it is a characteristic bit of behavior which appears with a well-defined topography. (Ferster & Skinner, 1957, p. 7)

Behavior may start very early in an organism's life, but that in itself is not evidence that its sources are phylogenic rather than ontogenic. Recall that Spalding had misgivings about how much a chick could learn within just a few hours after hatching. Creatures may be prepared by phylogeny to do the same sorts of things that their ancestors have done, but they also may be prepared to start learning right away. Behavior begins in the embryo (e.g., Hall & Oppenheim, 1987). Both prenatally and postnatally some of that behavior is independent of sensory input and of consequences. Other behavior, perhaps even prenatally, is modifiable: Behavior changes even with the organism's earliest interactions with its environment (e.g., Jo-

hanson & Hall, 1979; Rudy, Vogt, & Hyson, 1984). By this point it should be evident that the answer to the question of whether behavior is a product of phylogeny or of ontogeny is that it is a product of both (to questions about the relative magnitudes of their contributions, of course, the answer is usually "It depends").

Before we turn to behavior that is learned, we must note the variety of behavior that is available before learning. Behavior that isn't learned comes in many varieties (Gallistel, 1980; von Holst, 1973). Some types have characteristics of oscillators (e.g., the beating of the heart). Others have characteristics of servomechanisms (e.g., the maintenance of balance, during which small displacements produce compensating adjustments). Still others are produced in various ways by stimuli (e.g., as in reflex relations or as in kineses and taxes or as in the continuous change in pupil size with changes in light intensity). The various sources of behavior provide our taxonomy, our system for classifying behavior. In the chapters to come, we'll examine respondents, operants, discriminated operants, meanings and rememberings as some of the classes that emerge from this taxonomy.

Chapter 4
Elicited and Emitted Behavior

Reflex is derived from the Latin re-, *back, plus* flectere, *to bend. A reflexive response was thought of, in effect, as a reflection of the stimulus. It is debatable whether* flectere *and the Latin* plicare, *to fold, share a common Indo-European root. If they do,* reflex *is closely related to* reply, complex *and* multiple. *The origins of* stimulus *and* response *are better established.*

Stimulus can be traced to an Indo-European root steig-, *to stick. The same root also generated* distinguish, instinct, *and, via* stylus, *a writing instrument,* style *(but it is probably not closely related to* extinction*). Through the Old French* estiquet, *to impale and later to label, it also produced*

a modern French word now related to behavior, etiquette.

The Indo-European root spend-, *to pour a libation or to make a treaty, led to the Greek* sponde, *a drink offering, and the Latin* spondere, *to promise. Through these words,* response, *originally an undertaking in return, is linked to* spouse, sponsor, *and perhaps even* spontaneous. *The latter relation is interesting because* response *now refers to a unit of behavior that needn't be produced by a stimulus; responses may be elicited by stimuli but they may also occur spontaneously, when they are said to be emitted.*

In the psychology of learning, the concept of the reflex has played an important historical role. The first section of this chapter presents the vocabulary of reflexes and deals with some effects of presenting stimuli. It starts with some relatively simple situations in which a stimulus produces or elicits a response, and it shows that we can't judge the effect of the stimulus if we don't also know about the responding that occurs in its absence. The concepts of probability and conditional probability provide a way to cope with this problem; these concepts are involved in the treatment of several different phenomena throughout this book.

After we examine simple reflex relations in terms of conditional probabilities, we deal with some circumstances under which elicited behavior changes over successive stimulus presentations. These cases set the stage for the second section of the chapter, which explores how behavior can emerge when it hasn't been produced by an eliciting stimulus; such behavior is said to be emitted. The chapter closes with a discussion of how the behavioral significance of a stimulus may change over time; imprinting is an example used to relate such effects to the concept of drive or motivation.

Section A   **The Reflex: Elicitation**

A simple way to change behavior is to present a stimulus. For someone standing and talking, for example, a sudden loud noise will probably stop the talking and produce the change in posture called the *startle reaction*. This reliable relation between a stimulus and the change in behavior it produces has been called a *reflex*. The application of the vocabulary of the reflex to behavior has a history that begins with René Descartes, a seventeenth-century French philosopher (Fearing, 1930). Descartes was familiar with hydraulic devices constructed to amuse visitors in the royal gardens of France. Stepping on a concealed trigger released a flow of water that made statues move. Descartes saw a similarity between such devices and behavior. According to Descartes, stimuli were comparable to the garden visitors who,

> entering into one of the grottoes containing many fountains, themselves cause, without knowing it, the movements which they witness. For in entering they necessarily tread on certain tiles or plates, which are so disposed that if they approach a bathing Diana, they cause her to hide in the rosebushes, and if they try to follow her, they cause a Neptune to come forward to meet them threatening them with his trident. (Descartes, translated in Fearing, 1930, pp. 20–21)

Just as a step on the concealed plate triggers the movement of a statue, a stimulus triggers a response. For Descartes, the role of pipes and water in these statuary systems was played by nerves and animal spirits in living organisms.

For our purposes, the most important part of the concept of the reflex as formulated by Descartes was that it captured the fact that behavior is sometimes caused by environmental events, as when you quickly withdraw your hand upon touching a flame. Eventually physiologists turned their attention to the mechanism of such behavioral relations and began to explore the components of the reflex arc, the path from the original sensory impact of the stimulus through the central nervous system and then back to the muscular or glandular system within which the response occurred. Analyses of the reflex became more and more sophisticated (e.g., Sherrington, 1906), and the conditioned-reflex concepts of Pavlov (1927) and the related behaviorism of Watson (1919) treated the reflex as the basic unit of behavior.

We noted two illustrations of reflexes above, in the startle reaction and in the withdrawal of a hand from a flame. Many others are familiar: the knee jerk produced by a tap on the patellar tendon; salivation caused by food in the mouth; the postural adjustments triggered by an abrupt loss of support. These examples have the common feature that some stimulus reliably produces some response. This is what defines a reflex. In these circumstances, we say that the stimulus *elicits* the response, or that the response is *elicited* by the stimulus; the stimulus is an *eliciting* stimulus, and the response is an *elicited* response (we never use *elicited* the other way around, to refer to the effect of a response on the occurrence of a stimulus).

The reflex is neither stimulus nor response; it's the relation between them (Skinner, 1931). For example, we wouldn't speak of a reflex if we set off a firecracker but observed no startle response; the noise alone is insufficient to justify using the term. Neither would we speak of a reflex if we observed a response without an identifiable stimulus; by itself, the startle reaction isn't a reflex. And we shouldn't confuse startle reactions produced by loud noises with those produced in other ways. Many reflexes have been named after their characteristic responses. The startle and patellar reflexes are examples. But it's useful to remember that these are *not* names for responses; the reflex terminology would be inappropriate if it was applied to knee jerks that occurred in the absence of eliciting stimuli.

Consider another example. The production of pupillary constriction by bright light to the eye has usually been called the pupillary reflex, but this relation involves a response that adjusts continuously to stimulus levels: As brightness increases, the pupil constricts; as it decreases, the pupil dilates. In very bright light, the human pupil may become roughly one-twentieth of its area when the eye is relaxed in total darkness. Here the language of the reflex diverts attention from the inverse functional relation between pupil size and brightness by focusing on only a particular change in pupil size taken from a continuous range of possibilities.

For still other cases that superficially seem to involve reflex relations, the language of the reflex may be misleading. In everyday talk, for example, we sometimes speak of people having quick or slow reflexes, often with regard to the skilled behavior of athletes in competitive sports. But such usages are usually technically inaccurate. For example, a fast reaction to the starting gun of a race is operant behavior, or behavior that depends on both its antecedents and its consequences, even though it occurs very rapidly.

These qualifications make it clear that reflexes are just one subset of the many kinds of relations that can exist in behavior. Furthermore, we will restrict our attention here to reflex relations that involve external stimuli. We won't be concerned with reflex coordinations among responses, as when, in limb flexion or extension, the contraction of a muscle is accompanied by the relaxation of an opposing one, or with other more complex coordinations (e.g., rhythmic coordinations in locomotion; Gallistel, 1980). Some examples will be treated in Chapter 7.

PROPERTIES OF ELICITED BEHAVIOR

Once we identify a reflex relation between some stimulus and some response, we can examine its properties (cf. Skinner, 1938, on the Laws of the Reflex). Consider an eliciting stimulus such as an acid- or sour-tasting solution on the tongue (e.g., vinegar) and an elicited response such as salivation. Above some *threshold* value, acid on the tongue reliably elicits salivation, but a very low concentration or small quantity may not do so. When the magnitude of a stimulus is too small to elicit a response, the stimulus is said to be *below threshold*.

The threshold isn't a fixed quantity; it's a statistical summary of our measurements. As we concentrate the solution or increase its quantity, we're more likely to produce salivation. At a given concentration, we can find out how many drops on the tongue will reliably elicit salivation; conversely, for a given number of drops, we can find out what concentration is required. Some concentrations and quantities will have only marginal effects, sometimes eliciting salivation and sometimes not.

Note that a stimulus doesn't itself have a threshold. Rather, threshold values are determined for particular features of stimuli, with other features held constant. For example, the threshold number of drops for eliciting salivation would typically be smaller given a strong than a weak acid solution; it therefore wouldn't be meaningful to specify the threshold number of drops without also specifying acid concentration, or vice versa.

Some time always elapses between stimulus and response; this time period is called the response *latency*. In addition, the response must exist in some *magnitude* and have some *duration*. Because these properties often vary together, they're sometimes given a common name, *reflex strength*. Thus, responding with long latency, small magnitude and short duration corresponds to weak reflex strength, whereas responding with short latency, large magnitude and long duration corresponds to strong reflex strength. (The rate at which the elicited response occurs isn't relevant to reflex strength, because it's determined by the rate at which the eliciting stimulus is presented.)

Sechenov (1863), a Russian physiologist, noted that the organism's energy expenditure in many responses (e.g., sneezes and coughs) far exceeds the energy provided by the eliciting stimulus. The eliciting effect of a stimulus doesn't depend on a direct transfer of energy from the environment to the organism; rather, observed Sechenov, the stimulus should be regarded as a trigger, releasing energy that the organism already has available in muscles or glands or other structures. This view was, of course, consistent with the way in which Descartes conceived of the reflex.

Even though the eliciting stimulus is most accurately regarded as a trigger that releases energy that is already available, the magnitude of the eliciting stimulus may affect the elicited response. Response latency typically varies *inversely* with stimulus magnitude; in other words, response latency decreases as stimulus magnitude increases. And response magnitude and response duration typically vary *directly* with stimulus magnitude; in other words, these measures increase as stimulus magnitude increases. Saying that reflex strength increases with stimulus magnitude just summarizes these relations.

With talk of reflex relations in terms of strength instead of in terms of specific measures, it became easier to regard the reflex relation as a fundamental unit of behavior, and reflexes began to be treated as basic building blocks from which more complex behavior was constructed. The concept of the reflex had a tempting simplicity. As it came to be more widely accepted as a behavioral unit, it seemed reasonable to conclude that reflex relations might be a basis for understanding a variety of behavioral processes. Some stimuli had been identified as causes of some responses, and the faulty assumption was made that for *every* response there must exist a corresponding eliciting stimulus.

Pavlov's conditioned-reflex system and Watson's behaviorism of the 1920s and 1930s grew out of such an assumption. With reflexes serving as units of behavior, complex behavior was treated as nothing more than the combination of such units. When a response occurred with no observed eliciting stimulus, stimuli with appropriate properties were hypothesized. In addition, the responses of one reflex were assumed to have stimulus properties that enabled them to elicit other responses in turn. Thus, behavior extending over long periods of time could be interpreted as a sequence or chain of reflexes, with each response functioning simultaneously as the elicited response of one reflex and the eliciting stimulus of the next. These reflex systems were elaborated in various and sometimes ingenious ways, but they no longer command major attention in the psychology of learning. The concept of the reflex has its place, but its scope is limited and it can't stand alone.

ELICITING STIMULI
AND RESPONSE PROBABILITIES

Of the possible relations between stimuli and responses, the reflex is only one relation among many. In a reflex, some stimulus reliably produces some response. But the stimulus of that reflex may affect other responses differently, and the response of that reflex may be affected differently by other stimuli. Any stimulus may raise the likelihood of some responses, lower the likelihood of others, and have no effect on still others. Similarly, the likelihood of any response may be raised by some stimuli, lowered by others and unaffected by still others.

Furthermore, simply noting that a response reliably follows a stimulus isn't enough to justify talking about reflexes. We must also know how likely the response is without the stimulus. For example, if a rat in a running wheel spent much of its time running and ran when a noise was on as well as when it was off, we couldn't say that noise had elicited running just because we saw the rat run after we presented noise; it might have run anyway, without the noise. To speak of reflex relations, we must know how likely the response is in the absence of the stimulus as well as in its presence.

Consider a dog scratching. If a cat approaches, the scratching stops as the dog growls and assumes an aggressive posture. If the cat leaves and then the dog's master

enters, the dog barks and jumps and wags its tail. But if the master now scolds, the dog whines and drops its tail between its legs. We can't even say whether the dog's responses to its master are strictly elicited or depend to some extent on the consequences of past responses in the master's presence.

The cat, the master and the master's scolding each make some responses more likely and others less likely. Some of these responses might be observed from time to time even without these stimuli, and none necessarily occurs every time a particular stimulus is presented. In a reflex relation, a response that is infrequent in the absence of some stimulus occurs reliably when that stimulus is presented, but this is only one among many possibilities. Barking, for example, is affected by several different stimuli, and we may be interested in stimuli that make it less likely as well as those that make it more likely.

Probabilities or Relative Frequencies

These relations among stimuli and responses can best be described quantitatively in terms of probabilities or relative frequencies. We can define the effects of stimuli by comparing the probability of a response when a stimulus is present with its probability when the stimulus is absent. A probability or relative frequency is a proportion or ratio: the number of times an event occurs compared with the number of times it could have occurred.

For example, in the Babinski reflex, a splaying or spreading of the toes is elicited by a light stroke across the bottom of an infant's foot. We calculate response probability by counting how many times a response is produced over some number of stimulations. In the newborn, the splaying of the toes may be produced by each of 20 touches to the foot; the proportion of responses is therefore 20 out of 20, or a probability of 1.0. The Babinski reflex ordinarily diminishes with age, so if we test again at a later date, only 6 out of 20 touches may produce a response; the probability is now 0.3. Eventually the reflex completely disappears: None of the 20 touches produces a response, and the probability becomes 0.0.

In the mathematical notation for probabilities, these examples may be written respectively as

$$p(R_1) = 1.0; \ p(R_2) = 0.3; \ \text{and,} \ p(R_3) = 0.0.$$

Here, p stands for probability and the parentheses contain abbreviations for the events whose probabilities are specified (in this instance, R for responses, with subscripts 1, 2 and 3 corresponding to the three successive tests). These examples also show that probabilities must fall in the range from 0.0, when the event never occurs, to 1.0, when the event always occurs.

Conditional Probabilities

The Babinski reflex is uncomplicated for our purposes, because the toe splaying doesn't occur often without its eliciting stimulus. But what about blinking elicited by a puff of air to the eye? If we study this reflex with an infant who already blinks every second or so, how can we tell elicited blinks from those that would have occurred even without an airpuff (Spence & Ross, 1959)? In fact, we may not be able to say whether any given blink is elicited. We can assess the overall effect of the stimulus, however, by comparing the probability of a blink after an airpuff with the probability after no airpuff.

Our procedure is illustrated in Figure 4-1. We watch the eyelid and record blinks within some time period after each stimulus, and we compare responding in those time periods with responding in equivalent time periods that don't follow a stimulus.

FIGURE 4-1 Estimating eyeblink probability with and without eliciting puffs of air. Each solid vertical line represents a blink. In Line A, no airpuffs were presented. Dashed lines mark off five 1-s periods during which blinks were recorded (s=seconds); blinks occurred within three of these, so blink probability without a stimulus is 0.6. In Line B, arrows represent airpuffs to the eye. A blink occurred in each 1-s period that followed these stimuli, so blink probability given an airpuff is 1.0. Only the first of the two blinks following stimulus X counted toward this probability; we score a time period as either containing no blinks or containing at least one blink, and then calculate probability by dividing time periods with at least one blink by total time periods. The airpuff raised blink probability from 0.6 to 1.0. (An actual experiment would use a much larger sample of observations to calculate probabilities.)

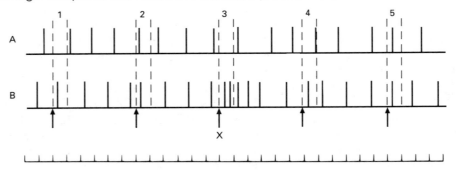

Time (Seconds) ⟶

The probabilities in this example are expressed as:

$$p(R/S) = 1.0; \ p(R/no \ S) = 0.6.$$

In this notation, R is a response and S is a stimulus. The first equation says that the probability of a response given a stimulus (blink given airpuff) equals 1.0. The second says that the probability of the response given no stimulus (blink given no airpuff) equals 0.6. This kind of probability, in which the probability of one event is given in terms of the presence or absence of another event, is a *conditional probability* (the terminology shouldn't be confused with that of Pavlov's conditioned or conditional reflexes, even though both have the feature that one event is a condition for some other event). In other words, $p(A/B)$ can be read as: probability of A given B, or probability of A on the condition that B is present. Similarly, $p(X/no \ Y)$ can be read as: probability of X given no Y, or probability of X on the condition that Y is absent.

Our later analyses will favor the language of probabilities over other ways of describing behavior. Saying that a stimulus caused a response is pretty much the same as saying that the stimulus elicited the response. Either usage can be applied to single instances of a reflex relation (as when this particular stimulus, M, is followed by this particular response, N). Similarly, saying that a stimulus increased response likelihood is pretty much the same as saying that it raised response probability. Either usage can be applied to average effects over many instances (as when stimulus O usually produces response P).

TYPES OF STIMULUS–RESPONSE RELATIONS

We've discussed cases involving one stimulus class and one response class. But behavior is usually more complicated: Environments include various stimuli and organisms produce various responses. For example, we might notice two kinds of chirps produced by a recently hatched duckling. We'll refer to those produced when the mother duck is present as contentment calls and those when a strange bird appears as distress calls (e.g., Hoffman, 1996). We could lower the likelihood of contentment calls and raise the likelihood of distress calls either by removing the mother duck or by presenting the strange bird. Our language must allow us to describe the effects of either stimulus on either response. We don't deal with stimuli alone or responses alone; we deal with stimulus–response relations.

Now we can summarize these relations using the coordinate system in Figure 4-2. The y-axis represents response probability given that a stimulus has been presented;

FIGURE 4-2 Stimulus–response relations represented as conditional response probabilities given the presence of a stimulus, $p(R/S)$, and its absence, $p(R/no \ S)$. Examples are shown in which a stimulus raises response probability (A), has no effect on response probability (B), or lowers response probability (C); the increase in response probability called a reflex, in which the stimulus reliably produces or causes the response, is illustrated at D.

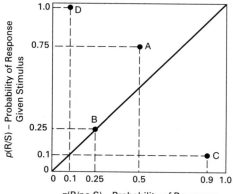

the x-axis represents response probability given that the stimulus hasn't been presented (cf. *coordinate* in the glossary). In other words, any point on this graph represents two conditional probabilities: response probability given a stimulus, $p(R/S)$, and response probability given no stimulus, $p(R/\text{no }S)$. For example, point A represents a stimulus–response relation in which response probability is 0.75 when the stimulus is presented and only 0.50 when it isn't; in this instance, the stimulus raises the probability of the response.

The diagonal in Figure 4-2 is of special interest. A response that occurs without being elicited by a stimulus is said to be *emitted*. The diagonal represents stimulus–response relations in which response probability is unaffected by or is independent of the stimulus. Thus, at point B response probability is 0.25 whether or not the stimulus is presented. For example, the duckling's contentment calls and distress calls might be unaffected by the presence or absence of some of its siblings. To say a response has been elicited we must know more than that it followed a stimulus. A response can just happen to follow a stimulus; we can't say it was elicited unless we know that it was actually caused by the stimulus.

A third class of stimulus–response relations is illustrated by point C, for which a probability of 0.90 without the stimulus is reduced to 0.10 by the stimulus; in this instance, the stimulus reduces response probability. Such reductions of response probability by a stimulus are sometimes called *reflex inhibition*. For example, if the duckling's contentment calls stopped when the strange bird appeared, we could say that the strange bird inhibited the contentment calls.

Point D represents a case in which a stimulus raises response probability from about 0.1 to about 1.0. This is the sort of stimulus–response relation we've called a reflex. While it inhibits contentment calls, the strange bird might have this effect on the duckling's distress calls.

The graph shows that this is only one among a range of possibilities. Somewhere between the upper edge of the graph, where $p(R/S)$ is near 1.0, and the diagonal, where S has no effect on R, we must decide that the eliciting effect of the stimulus is no longer reliable enough to justify calling the relation a reflex. But where should that boundary be? Probably we'd include cases in which $p(R/S)$ is just a little less than 1.0 (e.g., 0.95; maybe even 0.90). But probably we'd also exclude small effects of stimuli. For example, if a stimulus raised response probability from 0.26 to 0.32, would this relation qualify as a reflex? Almost certainly not.

All points above and to the left of the diagonal in the figure represent *excitation*, cases in which stimuli raise response probability; those below and to the right of the diagonal represent *inhibition*, cases in which stimuli lower it. Within those areas, any boundary marking off reflex relations would be arbitrary. This conclusion is important. We noted that some earlier behavioral systems, such as those of Watson and Pavlov, were based on reflexes as fundamental units of behavior. Highly reliable reflex relations were surely easier to work with than other less reliable stimulus-response relations. But if Figure 4-2 is appropriate for describing stimulus–response relations and if the reflex is just one special case among them, then any system of behavior built solely on the reflex as a behavioral unit was bound to be incomplete.

One property of behavior left out of early accounts was the emission of responses, the occurrence of responses without eliciting stimuli. Emitted responses were given such names as *instrumental* or *operant*, because they were studied in terms of how they were instrumental in changing the environment or how they operated on the environment. They derived their importance not from their relation to eliciting stimuli but from their consequences. By contrast, elicited responses were called *reflex* or *respondent*.

Once that distinction had been made, qualifications were added. In particular, some argued that instrumental or operant behavior consisted of skeletal responses, such as movements of the limbs, whereas reflex or respondent behavior consisted of autonomic responses, such as glandular secretions. This was also seen as paralleling the traditional distinction between voluntary and involuntary action. Such distinctions have since been seriously questioned.

For example, the crouching posture elicited by a sudden loud noise in the startle reflex is a motor response best described as involuntary. But swallowing seems voluntary and yet also involves a reflex relation. It's elicited by stimulation of the back of the throat, which is why you can't swallow if your mouth is dry and you have nothing in it to pass back so it will stimulate that area. On the other hand, driving certainly seems both voluntary and operant. Yet an experienced driver sitting in the passenger seat of a car may involuntarily press hard on the floor even though there's no brake pedal there when something suddenly looms up ahead on the road. We have here all of the possibilities: whether behavior is operant or respondent, we can identify examples that seem either voluntary or involuntary. In other words, the everyday distinction between voluntary and involuntary actions has nothing to do with our distinction between operant and respondent behavior. (As we'll note when we get to verbal behavior in Chapter 14, the most important determinant of whether we call behavior voluntary or involuntary may be whether the person acting can identify the source of those actions.)

Skeletal responses can be elicited and au-tonomic responses can be emitted. It's important to maintain the distinction between elicited and emitted responding. But the same response may be sometimes elicited and sometimes emitted; we can't classify responding effectively into these two categories on the basis of physiological criteria such as the difference between skeletal and autonomic responses.

Figure 4-2 supports an earlier point. When we defined the reflex, we argued that the reflex is neither stimulus nor response but rather the relation between them. The graph represents stimulus–response relations; it cannot represent stimuli by themselves or responses by themselves. Thus, the strange bird as a stimulus doesn't have a location in the graph; its location depends on which response we're measuring. Similarly, the duckling's distress call as a response doesn't have a location in the graph; its location depends on which stimulus we're presenting.

EFFECTS OF SUCCESSIVE ELICITATIONS

We've described some effects of stimulus presentations on behavior. A complication is that two different presentations of the same stimulus may have different effects. For example, you may startle much more to the first lightning flash in a thunderstorm than to later flashes. Furthermore, the effects of stimuli may depend on how quickly they follow each other. If you're peeling onions, for example, the tears elicited by the present onion may depend on whether you began working on it right after finishing the last one or just after taking a break. And in another effect, called *summation*, a stimulus that is below threshold in eliciting a response if presented once may become an effective elicitor if presented repeatedly at a high enough rate. In other words, elicited responding often depends on the number of stimulations and on their spacing in time.

Habituation

The startle reaction is produced by an unexpected event such as a lightning flash or a sudden loud noise. Even without other events to signal it, a repeated loud noise usually produces successively smaller startle reactions, until eventually there's no startle at all. Many stimuli elicit responses called orienting or observing responses; for example, a dog pricks up its ears in response to a novel sound or begins sniffing in response to an unusual odor. As these stimuli recur, the dog's responding decreases; it occurs with smaller magnitude and longer latency, perhaps even vanishing completely (we'll see later, however, that orienting or observing responses may depend not only on eliciting stimuli but also on their consequences).

We'll call this reduction in responding with repeated stimuli *habituation*. (Another possible term, *adaptation*, sometimes refers instead to changes in behavior in the continued presence of some stimulus or situation, as when an organism is said to adapt to a laboratory setting; some features of the vocabularies of habituation and related terms depend on whether changes in responding can be attributed to specific kind of changes in the nervous system; cf. Groves & Thompson, 1970.)

Habituation is a characteristic of the elicited responding produced by a variety of stimuli. It occurs with such diverse responses as changes in skin resistance produced by electric shock (the galvanic skin response or GSR), distress calls of birds to a silhouette of a predator passing overhead, and contractions in earthworms exposed to light, not to mention the startle reactions and orienting responses already mentioned (e.g., Ratner, 1970). It may also be an important component of the dynamics of emotion (Solomon & Corbit, 1974).

Potentiation

But stimuli sometimes have opposite effects. For example, electric shocks elicit squealing in rats; if several shocks are delivered, later ones produce more responding than earlier ones (Badia, Suter, & Lewis, 1966). This effect has been called *potentiation* (another term sometimes used is *facilitation*; e.g., Wilson, 1959). Potentiation is more likely with stimuli regarded as aversive or punishing than with stimuli regarded as neutral or as appetitive or reinforcing.

Potentiation mustn't be confused with another phenomenon called *sensitization* (cf. Ison & Hoffman, 1983). In sensitization, the eliciting effects of one stimulus are enhanced as a result of presentations of some *other* stimulus; one stimulus amplifies the eliciting effect of another stimulus. For example, an electric shock may make it more likely that a later loud noise will produce a startle reaction; the shock is said to *sensitize* the organism to the noise.

The method of stimulus presentation can determine whether habituation or potentiation occurs. For example, in the wiping reflex of the frog a bristle touched to a frog's back elicits a movement over the back by the hind foot (Kimble & Ray, 1965). In one group, successive touches were made to a region of the frog's back but within this region the exact location varied from one touch to the next; in a second group, touches were made to precisely the same location on the frog's back each time. In both groups, 100 touches were delivered at 10-s intervals each day for 12 days. The groups began with roughly equal probabilities of elicited wiping movements, but this probability increased over days for the first group and decreased for the second. In other words, potentiation occurred when location varied slightly from touch to touch, whereas habituation occurred when location was constant.

Effects of Time Since the Last Eliciting Stimulus

If the stimulus is absent for a while after habituation or potentiation, the probability that responding will be elicited returns to earlier values. For example, the startle reaction to loud noise may diminish or even disappear after several noises in succession, but after hours of silence it's likely to appear again in full strength to the next noise. If elicited responding decreases over successive stimuli, it usually recovers to its earlier higher levels after the stimuli are discontinued. Conversely, if elicited responding increases over successive stimuli, it usually returns to its earlier lower levels after the stimuli are discontinued. Habituation and potentiation aren't permanent, and the return to earlier levels takes place as time passes.

Figure 4-3 (p. 52) summarizes these relations. Each line shows hypothetical effects of 10 successive stimuli on response probability or reflex strength. The upper part of Figure 4-3 (A, B, C) illustrates habituation; the lower part (D, E, F) illustrates potentiation. In both cases, the three examples differ only in the time separating the first 5 stimuli from the second 5 stimuli. As this time lengthens (A to C and D to F), the responding produced by the second 5 stimuli becomes more like the responding produced by the first 5. In other words, responding returns to its earlier levels with the passage of time. For example, in A responding is elicited by the later stimulus *x* with a lower probability than by the first stimulus *w*. But when *x* is presented after successively longer periods without stimuli, as in B and C, the probability with which *x* elicits responding approaches that with which *w* elicited responding. Analogous relations exist for stimuli *y* and *z* in D, E and F.

If habituation was irreversible, it could either occur only once in an organism's lifetime or else successive habituations would drive responding to lower and lower levels until it disappeared altogether. Irreversible potentiation would similarly lead either to a single case of potentiation in the organism's lifetime or to continuing and unlimited increases in elicited responding. Such things may sometimes happen. For example, reactions of the immune system, which may be regarded as instances of elicited behavior, sometimes seem to show irreversible potentiation (e.g., for someone who has developed an allergic reaction to bee stings after having been stung several times, the reaction may diminish little if at all as time passes).

Section B From Elicited to Emitted Behavior

We've seen that the reflex is just one of the many possible relations among stimuli and responses. Now we examine how stimulus presentations affect the way in which responding is distributed over time. When stimuli occur repeatedly, they can produce temporal patterns of behavior. The topics in this section involve the order and temporal patterning of responses that occur when two or more different responses are generated by a stimulus. Adjunctive behavior, in which one response reliably follows some other response, is one example. Other effects of repeated stimulus presentations are explored in a treatment of the law of exercise. Taken together, these topics identify possible sources of responding when it is emitted rather than elicited. The chapter closes with a discussion of ways in which the behavioral significance of stimuli may change over time; imprinting as an example relates such effects to estab-

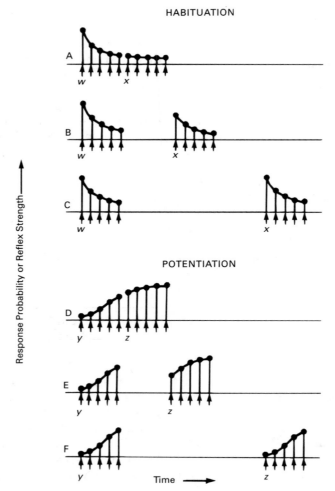

FIGURE 4-3   Habituation and potentiation. Arrows indicate stimuli; vertical lines represent the probabilities with which the stimuli elicit responses. *Habituation* is illustrated in A, B and C; probability decreases with successive stimuli. *Potentiation* is illustrated in D, E and F; probability increases with successive stimuli. In both cases, response probabilities return to earlier levels as the time since the last stimulus increases.

lishing operations and the concept of drive or motivation.

THE TEMPORAL PATTERNING OF BEHAVIOR

Presenting a stimulus may determine the sequence of responses over an extended time.

If we give a rat food, for example, it will eat. Once it's finished eating, it will then typically drink if water is available. This relation between eating and subsequent drinking is so strong that by repeatedly delivering food in small amounts we can make the rat drink several times its ordinary daily ration of water (Falk, 1977; Wetherington, 1982). This increase in drinking is called *polydipsia,* and responding that depends in this way on other responding is called *adjunctive* behavior. Adjunctive behavior is behavior in which one response reliably accompanies some other response.

As one type of adjunctive behavior, polydipsia follows at least partly from the rat's normal feeding and drinking pattern. With food and water freely available, the rat ordinarily takes a few large meals daily and drinks after each meal. If we force the rat to take many small meals by delivering food in many small portions every few minutes, the rat still drinks after each meal but doesn't reduce the size of each drink enough to compensate for its more frequent drinking. Thus, a rat going from 5 large to 50 small meals per day now drinks 10 times as often. But if the rat drinks only half as much after each of the 50 small meals instead of a tenth as much, it will drink 5 times as much as before. Such increases in the rat's water intake are so reliable that polydipsia can be used to get rats to consume substances that they ordinarily reject (e.g., alcohol: Meisch & Thompson, 1971).

Adjunctive behavior can include other responses besides eating and drinking. For example, with a running wheel instead of water available to the rat, running follows eating much as drinking follows eating in the polydipsia procedure (Levitsky & Collier, 1968).

The presentation of a stimulus may impose temporal structure on behavior in other ways. One experiment examined patterns of behavior generated in pigeons by repeated food presentations (Staddon & Simmelhag, 1971). Each pigeon was placed in a chamber on one wall of which was an opening to a feeder, a tray of grain ordinarily out of the pigeon's reach; food was presented by lighting the tray and lifting it to a position where the pigeon could eat from it. The pigeon was ob-

served through a window and its responding was scored in various categories, such as pecks directed toward the feeder wall or toward the floor and postures such as orientation toward the feeder wall.

Early in each interfood period, one bird usually made quarter-turns, and then, but less frequently, put its head into the feeder opening or pecked toward the floor. Other pigeons showed patterns that included different responses, such as preening or pacing. These responses became less likely and as the time of the next feeder operation approached, pecking became the dominant or most likely response.

The repeated stimulus presentations imposed temporal structure on behavior. Responding early in interfood intervals varied from one pigeon to another, whereas later responding was fairly constant across pigeons and usually included some form of pecking. Pecking is also the behavior occasioned by food presentations; the bird takes food into its mouth by pecking. At least in this case, the later behavior seems to have something in common with the responses produced by stimulus presentations (cf. temporal conditioning in Chapter 12). Repeated stimuli seem not only to elicit responses but also to produce behavior at other times that is closely related to the elicited responding. The problem is that it's hard to show that sequences of behavior generated by successive stimuli are unaffected by other variables, such as their consequences or the discriminative effects of stimuli (e.g., Reid & Staddon, 1982).

THE ROLE OF EXERCISE

"Practice makes perfect" is a familiar saying about the role of repetition in behavior. Before the effects of the consequences of responding were appreciated, it was believed that the mere repetition of responding, without regard to its consequences, was sufficient to maintain behavior. Consider the following from Sechenov:

> . . . an infant is able to cough, sneeze and swallow immediately upon birth. The act of sucking also belongs to this category of complex movements. . . . Indeed, everybody knows that a newborn child is able to suck. . . . Moreover, it is a well-known fact that the activity of this complex mechanism in the infant is called forth by irritation of the lips; put, for example, your finger, or a candle, or a wooden stick between the child's lips, and it will begin to suck. Try to do the same with a child three months after it has been weaned, and it will no longer do so; however, the ability to produce sucking movements at will is retained by man for life. These are highly remarkable facts: on the one hand, they show that the conduction of sensation from the lips to the central nervous mechanisms which produce the sucking movements apparently ceases in the child after weaning; on the other hand, they indicate that the integrity of this conduction is maintained by the frequent repetition of the reflex. (Sechenov, 1863, pp. 28–29)

Sechenov here emphasizes the complexity of the sucking response, but more important is his observation on the role of repetition. Not only does repetition maintain the response, according to Sechenov, but the response also becomes independent of the effects of eliciting stimuli. In the infant, sucking is elicited by stimuli ("irritation of the lips"); later, these stimuli no longer elicit the response, but the organism through adulthood remains able to produce the response even in the absence of these stimuli (cf. Schoenfeld, 1966; see also Hall & Oppenheim, 1987, p. 113: "For most altricial species, the ability to suckle from the mother is reduced if suckling is not practiced. . . . virtually all of the organized maternally oriented behavior of most infant animals can be shown to be heavily influenced by experienced events").

Based on such phenomena, we might conclude that the repeated elicitation of a response increases the likelihood that the response will be emitted. Early accounts of learning (e.g., Thorndike, 1921; Verhave, 1967) treated effects of response repetition as basic components of learning, described in terms of laws of *exercise* or laws of *practice*. These laws were usually ambiguous on questions such as whether it mattered if the repeated response were elicited or emitted. In any case, they soon were overshadowed by other concerns. As the psychology of learning turned to such phenomena as reinforcement and the signaling functions of stimuli, the possible role of exercise or practice became neglected. The evidence is too scanty to allow firm conclusions about whether exercise or practice might be a basic component of learning, but some tantalizing data exist.

One example is provided by research on the escape responses of a tropical fish, the zebra danio, from a stimulus designed to resemble the rapid approach of a larger predatory fish (Dill, 1974). As the stimulus loomed, the danio began to swim away from it (despite the aquatic medium, this swimming response of the fleeing fish can aptly be called a flight reaction). The latency with which swimming began decreased with repeated exposures; in other words, the stimulus more and more strongly elicited the escape response. After 10 days without further elicitations, the response hadn't returned to its earlier levels. The change produced by the stimulus wasn't reversible (cf. the section on potentiation above; see also Chapter 6 on species-specific defense reactions).

But not all responses begin with elicitation. Some of the earliest responses in an organism's lifetime occur spontaneously, in the absence of identifiable eliciting stimuli. For example, inside its egg the embryo chick makes uncoordinated movements of its limbs and body. These movements may prevent the developing bones from becoming fixed in their sockets, or may modify the form of growing bones and connective tissue. Later in the embryo's development, eliciting effects of stimuli appear, perhaps simply as the embryo's sensory apparatus matures. This progression from spontaneous responding to elicited responding may be summarized by saying of chick embryos that "they 'act' before they 'react' " (Provine, 1976, p. 210). Stimuli become more important later, as when the chick's rotating movements in pecking its way out of its shell during hatching are affected by whether the chick continues to encounter intact portions of the shell.

Pecking in the young chick depends not only on the conditions that elicited pecks and the consequences of earlier pecks but also on how much the chick has already pecked (Hogan, 1971). Once responding occurs, whatever its origin, it may have consequences, and the chick's survival may depend on whether those consequences in turn affect its behavior. Among gulls, for example, pecking at but missing the parent's beak has different consequences from striking the beak; only in the latter case is the parent gull likely to feed the chick. These differential consequences affect the accuracy of the chick's later pecking only as the response becomes independent of its eliciting stimulus. That development corresponds to one possible formulation of a law of exercise: Once a response has been elicited by a stimulus, the response may become more likely even in the absence of the stimulus.

In experiments on salivation, dogs at first salivate only when food is presented, but after several food presentations they begin to salivate even when food is absent (Zener & McCurdy, 1939). Such responding, *spontaneous* salivation, had been attributed to conditioning of the salivary response to features of the setting (e.g., the eliciting stimulus might have been a spot on the wall that the dog just happened to see when food deliveries began). No other eliciting stimuli were identifiable, so including all salivary responses in a reflex relation could be justified only by assuming that salivation could be elicited by such arbitrary features. Yet the problem of identifying stimuli simply vanishes once we admit the possibility of responses that occur without eliciting stimuli; in fact, we can't otherwise conceive of emitted responding at all. The concept of emitted responding will be essential to our treatment of consequential operations such as reinforcement and punishment.

Early behavior theories held that simple repetition was important in its own right to the development and maintenance of behavior. Consider the following from Sechenov: "If a child which has just learned to walk becomes ill and remains in bed for a long time, it forgets the previously acquired art of walking. . . . This fact testifies once again to the great import for nervous activity of frequent repetition" (Sechenov, 1863, p. 29).

We can't be sure of the evidence upon which Sechenov based his conclusion (e.g., did he observe one child or many children?), but we can consider a more recent example, in Zelazo, Zelazo, & Kolb (1972). The walking reflex appears in newborns and disappears at about eight weeks (McGraw, 1945). The response of the walking reflex has much in common with what the child does later when learning to walk. Coordinated walking movements resembling those of an adult can be elicited by holding the infant under its arms with its feet touching a level surface. When parents exercised their infants' walking reflexes by holding them so as to elicit the walking response, the walking reflex was less likely to drop out and these infants learned to walk earlier on the average than others whose walking wasn't exercised. Thus, exercising this reflex during the first eight weeks of life not only increased elicited responding that ordinarily decreases during this time; it seemed to shorten the time to its later appearance as a component of emitted behavior, walking.

But the researchers recognized that walking movements produce changes in the infant's world (visual, kinesthetic or tactile) that might reinforce such responses. Even during the eight weeks of exercise, walking was sometimes emitted rather than elicited, and more was going on than simple elicitation: "Walking . . . seemed to progress from a reflexive to an instrumental response. There is little doubt that learning occurred. . . . Not only were there more responses . . . but they were better executed" (Zelazo, Zelazo, & Kolb, 1972, p. 315). The situation is further complicated as an example of elicitation by changes in the infants' weights and in the supporting capacities of their limbs over the time course of such studies (Thelen et al., 1982).

We've speculated that after a response is produced by a stimulus it may become more likely even in the absence of the stimulus. In other words, eliciting a response may raise its probability of emission. This formulation differs from the classical laws of exercise or practice to which we've related it. It depends only on the simple experimental operation of presenting stimuli. But we needn't try to establish such laws. Some emitted responses may originate because they're first elicited whereas others may be emitted from the start. The issue isn't the universality of laws of exercise or such alternatives as spontaneous emission; rather, it's the source of responding in particular cases. We'll treat other problems in behavior analysis in this way in later chapters. Instead of trying to explain instances of behavior in terms of ex-

haustive formal laws, we'll seek to improve our taxonomy of behavior by classifying behavior in terms of its origins.

STIMULUS PRESENTATIONS IN IMPRINTING

So far, we've concentrated on how stimuli affect responding. Virtually all of the phenomena we've considered in this chapter can be described in terms of response probabilities. For example, in a reflex relation a stimulus raises the probability of a response to near 1.0, in habituation response probability decreases over successive stimulus presentations, and in adjunctive behavior the elicitation of one response changes the probability of some other response. We now examine an outcome of stimulus presentations, *imprinting* (Lorenz, 1937), that must be discussed in terms other than effects on response probability. Imprinting provides a bridge to the treatment of response consequences in the next chapter.

When a duckling hatches, the first moving thing it ordinarily sees is its mother, and even on this first day of life outside the egg the duckling will probably stay close to her. But if the mother is gone and the duckling first sees something else in motion, such as a human, the duckling will behave toward this stimulus as it otherwise would have toward its mother. Such stimuli are said to be *imprinted*, or, in a figurative sense, stamped into the duckling.

Imprinting has been demonstrated in both laboratory and field with a variety of stimuli, ranging from real and model birds to electric trains (some stimuli, of course, work better than others). The development of imprinting is sometimes said to have a *critical period* of one or a few days, so that it may not occur at all if it doesn't occur during this critical period. Actually, things are more complicated than that (Hoffman, 1996). For example, fear of novel stimuli develops toward the end of the critical period; as the birds get older, they move away from novel stimuli, making distress calls. Thus, older birds don't ordinarily stay near such stimuli long enough for imprinting to occur, but it can occur if this effect of novel stimuli is prevented or reversed.

In any case, the duckling begins behaving in significant ways to a stimulus, whether mother duck, human or some arbitrary moving object, if the stimulus is introduced under appropriate conditions and at appropriate times in the duckling's life. One response is following the imprinted stimulus as it moves; it's sometimes said that the duckling's following is elicited by the imprinted stimulus, but speaking of elicitation is misleading.

If the imprinted stimulus is the mother duck, the duckling follows her about and emits distress calls in her absence. But how does the imprinted stimulus produce following? When the duckling walks toward the mother, it finds itself closer to her; when it walks from her, it finds itself farther away. In other words, the natural consequence of walking in different directions is to change its distance from its mother. If closeness to the mother is important to the duckling, it's no surprise that it walks toward her rather than away from her. It follows that if we change the duckling's world so that the mother' closeness requires some response other than walking, the walking should be replaced by that other response.

In such an experiment (Peterson, 1960), a dark compartment on one side of a window contained a moving imprinted stimulus, and on the other side a duckling was given a response that could light up the dark side. The duckling did so even when the response was one incompatible with following, such as

pecking at a disk on the wall or standing still on a platform near the window. In other words, the critical property of the imprinted stimulus wasn't that it could elicit responses such as following or pecking or standing still, but rather that it had become important to the duckling and therefore could reinforce such responses as following or pecking or standing still. In natural environments, the duckling's following ordinarily keeps it close to the imprinted stimulus (usually its mother), but a laboratory environment shows that ducklings can learn other responses if they instead of following have the important consequence of keeping the imprinted stimulus close.

In imprinting, the initial presentations of the to-be-imprinted stimulus don't change response probabilities. Rather, they are establishing operations. They change the significance of the stimulus. The imprinted stimulus acquires its significance simply by being presented under appropriate circumstances. It begins as a stimulus toward which the duckling is relatively indifferent but ends as a stimulus that functions as a reinforcer and therefore shapes the duckling's behavior.

ESTABLISHING OPERATIONS AND THE SIGNIFICANCE OF STIMULI

The significance of stimuli can be changed in other ways. Some were treated in Chapter 2 as cases of establishing operations. For example, if a rat is more likely to eat than to run in a running wheel, we'd expect the rat to press a lever more often if its presses produce food than if its presses produce only access to the wheel. But suppose we continue to give the rat free access to food while we lock the wheel, thereby preventing the rat from running. After we deprive the rat of wheel running in this way, it will be more likely to run than to eat when we give it the opportunity to run again, and more likely to press the lever if presses produce access to the wheel than if presses produce food. In other words, we changed the relative significance of eating and running; through the deprivation of one or the other, we made eating more likely than running or running more likely than eating.

Changes in the significance of stimuli that occur with establishing operations are sometimes discussed in terms of *drive* or *motivation* (e.g., Bolles, 1975). Stimuli become more or less reinforcing or more or less aversive, depending upon factors such as the time since their last presentation. Food, for example, becomes more reinforcing as time passes without eating, but it may become aversive right after the eating of an unusually large amount.

The significance of stimuli can be changed through means other than deprivation; for example, as we shall see in later chapters, conditioned reinforcers and conditioned aversive stimuli are stimuli that have acquired their reinforcing or aversive properties through their relation to other stimuli (for a discussion of interactions between motivation and habituation, see Solomon & Corbit, 1974).

Physiological studies of motivation are typically concerned with relations between organic factors and the significance of stimuli (e.g., effects of blood levels of glucose on behavior with respect to food, effects of

hormonal levels on sexual behavior, etc.). Motivation or drive, therefore, isn't a special force to be located somewhere inside an organism; rather, it's a term applied to the many environmental and organic variables that make stimuli significant to the organism.

This chapter has concentrated on how stimuli affect responding. Many phenomena we've considered here can be described in terms of response probabilities: In a reflex relation, a stimulus raises response probability to near 1.0; in reflex inhibition, a stimulus reduces response probability; over successive stimulus presentations, the probability of elicited responding may decrease (habituation) or increase (potentiation); in adjunctive behavior, the elicitation of one response changes the probability of some other response; repeated presentations of stimuli can produce temporal patterns of behavior; successive elicitations may raise response probability in the absence of stimuli, as in the phenomenon of exercise. The example of imprinting involved additional effects of stimulus presentations and set the stage for a discussion of establishing operations.

We're now ready to move on to the consequential operations of reinforcement and punishment. When responding has consequences, the consequences also have their effects as stimuli. We'll therefore find our understanding of stimulus presentation operations useful in dealing with the effects of consequences.

PART III   LEARNING WITHOUT WORDS

Chapter 5
Consequences of Responding: Reinforcement

The Indo-European root, sekw-, *to follow, links* consequence *to* signal *and* designate *(from the Latin* signum, *something that one follows) and to* social *and* association *(from the Latin* socius, *a companion or follower). It shares its prefix,* con-, *with* conditioning, contingency *and* contiguity. Conditioning, *through the Indo-European root* deik-, *to show or pronounce, has many relatives:* dictation, *from the Latin* dicere, *to say;* teach, *from the Old English* taecan, *to show or instruct;* judgment, *from the Latin* judex, *he who pronounces the law; and* paradigm, *from the Greek* para, *beside, plus* deiknunai, *to show.* Contingency, *from the Latin* contingere, *to touch on all sides or to happen, has varied meanings: a possibility; a condition of depending on chance; some-*

thing incidental to something else. Like contact, *it combines the roots* com-, *together, and* tangere, *to touch.* Contiguity, *the condition of touching or being in contact, has the same origins. Curiously,* contingency *and* contiguity *are usually contrasted in learning theories:* contingency, *in its technical use, stresses how the likelihood of one event is affected or caused by other events, whereas* contiguity *implies the juxtaposition of events in space or time without regard to causation.*

Behavior has consequences, and an important property of behavior is that it can be affected by its consequences. We can study this phenomenon by arranging consequences for behavior, but to do so involves more than just presenting stimuli. The stimuli must occur in some relation to behavior. We have to arrange the environment so that responses make something happen.

Consequences for behavior already exist in natural environments. Even before we intervene, organisms change their environments by doing things or by going from one place to another. But we can better study how consequences affect behavior by arranging consequential operations in the laboratory. For example, we can build a maze in which a water-deprived rat will find water after making an appropriate sequence of turns, or we can build a chamber in which a food-deprived pigeon can produce food by pecking a key on the wall. Then we can see how water affects the turns the rat takes as it runs through the maze or how food affects the rate at which the pigeon pecks the key.

We'll begin this chapter by exploring the historical development of experiments on the consequences of behavior. We'll then treat some properties of the contemporary concept of reinforcement, such as the significance of discontinuing reinforcement (extinction), the relativity of reinforcement, the kinds of consequences that can be reinforcing, and the range of responses that can be reinforced. We'll conclude by showing how reinforcement is relevant not only to behavior maintained by physiologically significant consequences such as food and water but also to sensory–motor interactions, as when eye movements affect what is seen.

Section A   Reinforcement and Extinction

Chapter 2 introduced Thorndike's experiments, in which animals learned to escape from problem boxes by operating a device that released the door. Typically, a food-deprived animal was placed inside the box with food available outside. In its varied activity, the animal sooner or later operated the device and was free to leave the box. At first this was a low probability response, but because it opened the door its probability went up over repeated trials.

Thorndike described how the consequences of responding affected later responding with a principle he called the *Law of Effect*. The law went through many revisions, but its essence was that response probability could be raised by some consequences and lowered by others. In language closer to Thorndike's, responses with satisfying effects were stamped in whereas those

with annoying effects were stamped out. (The earliest version of Thorndike's law was called the *strong* Law of Effect. Later, he repudiated the second half of the law, keeping the probability increase or stamping in but discarding the probability decrease or stamping out. What remained was then called the *weak* Law of Effect. This historical point will be relevant in Chapter 6, when we deal with punishment.)

Figure 5-1 shows data from one of Thorndike's cats. To escape from its box, this cat had to pull a string that ran from a wire loop at the front of the box to a bolt holding the door. The first time in the box the cat took 160 s to escape. Its time decreased gradually and irregularly over successive trials until, during the last few trials, the cat reliably escaped in less than 10 s. This gradual decrease in the time taken to complete a task came to be called *trial-and-error learning* (Köhler later contrasted this gradual change with the sudden or insightful solutions he observed with chimpanzees).

MAZES AND LEARNING CURVES

In later years, trial-and-error learning was studied with many different organisms in many types of situations. Experimenters believed that the intelligence of different species could be compared by seeing how rapidly learning went in problem boxes, mazes, runways and other apparatuses (e.g., Hilgard, 1951). Apparatus design began to be dictated by theoretical questions: whether learning took place in discrete steps, on an all-or-none basis, or instead occurred gradually and continuously; whether organisms learned movements (response learning) or properties of the environment (stimulus learning); whether the

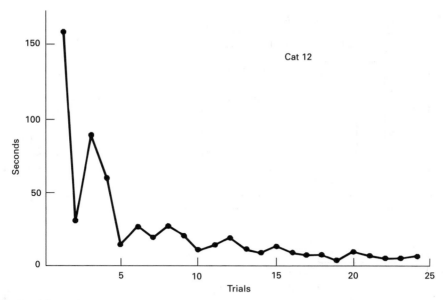

FIGURE 5-1   A learning curve. A cat's time to escape from a problem box as a function of trials. (From Thorndike, 1898, Figure 1)

consequences of responding led directly to learning or only made the organism perform so as to demonstrate what it had learned in other ways.

A common feature of these experiments was that responding became more probable when it had certain consequences. The change in probability was measured differently depending on the apparatus and the experimental aims. Graphs showing how behavior changed during an experiment were called *learning curves*: time to complete a response as a function of number of trials (e.g., Figure 5-1); percentage of correct responses; proportion of animals reaching some criterion of successful performance. Sometimes these measures were transformed to ease comparisons among them. When rats ran through a maze, for example, the time to run from startbox to goal-box ordinarily decreased, whereas the percentage of correct turns and the proportion of rats making errorless runs increased. Converting the time to run through the maze to speed (the reciprocal of running time) made all three measures increase with learning. But the shapes of learning curves depended so much on the apparatuses used and measures taken that the progress of learning couldn't be described in any unitary way.

The problem was that these experiments produced complicated performances. For example, measuring the time course over which a rat stopped entering blind alleys as it learned its way through a maze didn't show how learning proceeded at a single choicepoint. This consideration led to the gradual simplification of mazes, as illustrated in Figure 5-2.

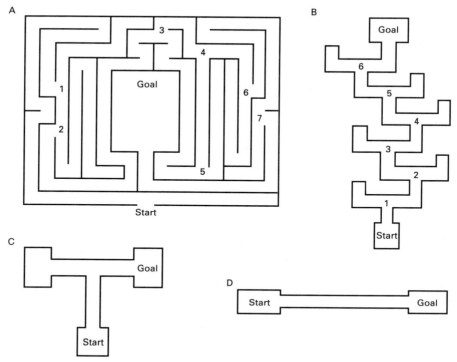

FIGURE 5-2 Stages in the evolution of mazes in studies of animal learning: A, the Hampton Court maze, as adapted by Small (1899–1900); B, a U-maze with six choicepoints; C, the single choicepoint T-maze; and D, the runway or straight alley.

Diagram A shows the plan of the earliest maze used to study animal learning (Small, 1899–1900), a 6-by-8-foot modification of the hedge maze at Hampton Court in England. (Curiously, such mazes may also have provided the setting for the hydraulically operated statues that inspired Descartes in his formulation of the concept of the reflex; cf. Chapter 4.) When a cage door at the start was lifted, rats could enter the maze; food was in the goal area at the center. With more experience in this maze they reached the goal area more rapidly and with fewer wrong turns along the way. But it was difficult to examine learning at any given choicepoint. Choicepoint 1 in diagram A might be learned more quickly than 7 either because

1 was earlier in the maze than 7 or because their floor plans differed; 4 might be learned more quickly than 5 either because of the different ways in which 4 could be approached (from 3 or from 5) or because of the fewer occasions on which 5 would be encountered if the rat often went from 3 to 4 directly rather than by way of 5.

Gradually, mazes evolved into more systematic forms, as in diagram B. In this maze, sometimes called a *U-maze* after the form of the successive units, choicepoints were essentially the same as the rat approached each one; they differed only in where they were in the sequence and in whether left or right turns were correct. This kind of systematic arrangement made it easy to specify the correct sequence (in B, right-left-right-left-left-right) and to keep track of errors. Even here, however, position and sequence interactions complicated the analysis. For example, is the rat's choice of left at 4 affected by the preceding right turn at 3 or the following left turn at 5; would it matter if the rat approached 4 after coming back from the blind alley at 3, having made an error there, instead of after a correct right turn at 3; does it matter that 4 is in the middle rather than near the beginning or end?

It was perhaps inevitable that the maze would be reduced to a single choicepoint, as in the *T-maze* shown with a goalbox on the right in diagram C in Figure 5-2. Here, when leaving the startbox the rat had only to make a single choice of right or left. But complications were still possible. For example, suppose one rat in its first trial in this maze turned right while a second rat turned left. Should the second one be allowed to retrace its steps after reaching the empty box at the end of the left arm? If it is returned to the startbox instead, should it be forced to the goalbox (e.g., by blocking the left arm) to make sure it has time in the goalbox equal to the first rat's? The next logical step was to eliminate choicepoints completely, leaving nothing but a simple runway, as in diagram D. Now no errors were possible, and measures of behavior were reduced simply to the speed with which the rat moved from startbox to goalbox.

There were other problems. Average measures of the performance of a group didn't necessarily represent performances of the individuals in the group. Suppose that single rats running in a T-maze usually change abruptly from making frequent errors to making consistently correct choices, but that this change occurs on different trials for different rats. In a large group of rats, 65% might make correct turns by trial 5, 72% by

trial 6, 79% by trial 7, 83% by trial 8, and so on, until performance becomes stable at 98% to 100% by trial 20. This group performance, giving the appearance of a gradual increase in correct choices, would completely obscure the abrupt change in performance by individual rats (Sidman, 1952).

Even the simple runway wasn't an ultimate solution, because the speed of a rat's running down a straight alley can be affected by many trivial factors. If trials began with the opening of a startbox door, it depended on which way the rat was facing when the door opened. Other factors included the experimenter's handling of the rat when moving it between trials from goalbox to startbox, odor trails left by other rats, and even whether the goalbox had enough room to allow a running rat to slow down before banging its head against the goalbox back wall (Killeen & Amsel, 1987).

With mazes or runways, the experimenter had to return the rat from goalbox to startbox to begin a new trial. Thus, the experimenter rather than the organism determined when behavior occurred. Furthermore, measuring how long the rat took didn't specify what it was actually doing during that time. Two experimental innovations helped to solve these problems. The first was an apparatus designed so that the organism could repeatedly emit an easily specified response without the experimenter's intervention; the second was a recording method based directly on the rate or frequency of responding rather than on indirect measures derived from response sequences or groups of organisms. These innovations, inspired partly by an interest in reducing the handling of the organism and thereby simplifying the experimenter's work, were important features of a direction of research initiated by B. F. Skinner (1930, 1938, 1950; see especially Skinner, 1956, for a history of these developments).

EXPERIMENTAL CHAMBERS
AND CUMULATIVE RECORDS

Figure 5-3 illustrates two representative apparatuses: on the left a standard rat chamber with a single lever, and on the right a three-key pigeon chamber. They share response devices, mechanisms for delivering reinforcers such as food or water, and stimulus sources.

In a typical arrangement, a rat that has been food deprived is placed in the chamber. A lever protrudes from one wall. Near the lever is a food cup into which food pellets can be dispensed from a delivery system on the other side of the wall; a distinctive sound accompanies each pellet delivery. The house-light provides general illumination, and noise can be broadcast from the speaker to mask sounds from outside the chamber.

The first step is feeder training. Pellets are delivered into the food cup. Sooner or later, the rat finds and eats them. Once this happens, pellet deliveries continue until the rat comes quickly to the food cup from any location upon each delivery; 10 or so pellets are usually enough. Once feeder training is done, the apparatus is changed so that pellet deliveries depend on lever presses. Eventually the rat presses the lever, the press produces a pellet, and the pellet occasions eating. The rat will then probably go back to the lever and press it again. (Alternatives to waiting for the lever press are considered in Chapter 7.) The outcome of interest is the rate at which the rat presses the lever. If it increases, we call the food pellet a *reinforcer*. In the type of chamber shown in Figure 5-3, other kinds of reinforcers can be substituted. For example, the pellet dispenser could be replaced by a dipper that delivers small amounts of water or milk.

A pigeon chamber differs from one for rats in that keys substitute for levers and the feeder works by bringing a tray of pigeon food (mixed grain or commercially available pellets) within the pigeon's reach for a few seconds. The feeder opening is centered

FIGURE 5-3 A rat chamber (left) and a three-key pigeon chamber (right). The rat chamber includes a lever (A), a food cup and pellet delivery tube (B), a speaker (C), and a lamp or houselight (D); some rat chambers include a grid floor through which shock can be delivered (E). The pigeon chamber includes three keys (F, G, H) and the opening to a food hopper (I); lamps or projectors behind each key allow colors or patterns to be displayed on them.

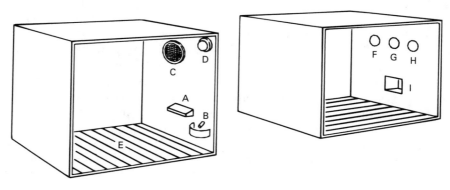

below the keys. It's common practice to light the feeder and turn off all other lights whenever the feeder is operated. The chamber typically includes other features, such as a houselight for dim general illumination, masking noise or other auditory stimuli, and so on.

A pigeon key is a piece of plastic mounted behind a hole in the chamber wall. It's attached to a switch that records the pigeon's pecks if they're forceful enough (keys are routinely sensitive to forces of less than 0.1 N, which is about 10 g or one-third of an ounce). The plastic is usually translucent or transparent, so that lamps or miniature projectors or a computer monitor behind the key can present patterns or colors on it. The chamber in Figure 5-3 contains three keys, arranged horizontally about 23 cm (9 in.) above the chamber floor. A given experiment might use only one key, some combination of two, or all three. Keys are typically lit when they're in use. As with the rat, if a food-deprived pigeon's key pecks produce food, the rate at which the pigeon pecks the key will ordinarily increase.

The rat and the pigeon are common laboratory organisms. They each have idiosyncratic species-specific behavior patterns that must be taken into account, and we mustn't assume that anything we observe with rats or pigeons can be generalized to other organisms. Nevertheless, the diet, housing, susceptibility to disease, and other characteristics of these animals are reasonably well understood, and their size, relatively long lifespan and economy make them particularly convenient. Thus, we'll find that they've often served in research on the consequences of responding.

Responding in apparatuses like those in Figure 5-3 has sometimes been called *free-operant* responding: *free* because the organism is free to emit the response at any time rather than waiting for the experimenter (like the rat in a goalbox, which can't run through the maze again until it's placed back in the startbox and the experimenter opens the startbox door); and *operant* because the response operates on the environment.

Free-operant responding lends itself to a recording method, the cumulative record, that gives a convenient, detailed picture of how responding changes over time. Most contemporary cumulative records are produced by computer, but in the original cumulative recorder, illustrated in Figure 5-4, a roll of paper was threaded around a roller. A motor drove the roller at a constant speed, feeding out the paper. A pen or other writing device rested on the paper as it passed over the roller, and each response (e.g., a pigeon's key peck) moved the pen a small distance at right angles to the movement of the paper. Thus, at any time during a session this record shows the total responses accumulated.

Figure 5-5 shows examples of cumulative records. Because the record advances at a constant speed, its slope is steeper the higher the rate of responding, as illustrated in records A and B. In the scale for Figure 5-5, rates are roughly 30 and 12 responses/min in records A and B respectively. Record C includes only a few responses; the horizontal portions indicate periods of time without responses (note that a cumulative record can't have a negative slope, because the pen can record responses only by moving in one direction across the page).

In record D, a magnified section of record C that includes a few responses accompanies an event record on the same time scale. For each response in the event record, a small step occurs in the cumulative record; this property of cumulative records isn't al-

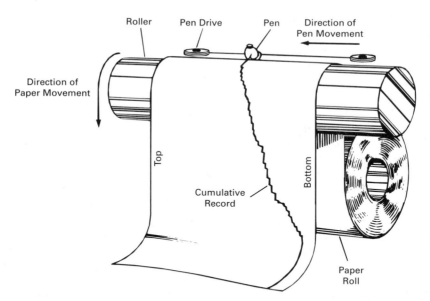

FIGURE 5-4 Main components of a cumulative recorder. A roller drives the paper at a constant speed and each response moves the pen a fixed distance across the paper. Paper speed and step-size per response vary with the behavior under study. A common scale is about 1 cm/min (about 2.5 min/in.) and 1100 responses across the width of the paper (about 200 responses/in.). At this scale, a slope of 45° represents a rate of about 40 responses/min. When the pen moves near the top of the paper, it resets automatically to its starting position near the bottom.

ways obvious because typical response and time scales are often too small for such fine resolution of detail.

Even so, different patterns of responding are easily distinguished in cumulative records. For example, response rates in E and F are roughly the same, but E is steplike whereas F is relatively smooth. This means that E was produced by short high-rate bursts of responding (steep segments) separated by pauses (flat segments), whereas F was produced by more uniform responding. This property is sometimes called *grain*; of the two records, E has a rougher grain than F.

Records G and H illustrate other proper-ties of behavior made visible in cumulative records. In G, the rate begins at roughly 25 responses/min but gradually decreases as time passes; in H, it changes in the opposite direction, increasing from a relatively low rate to roughly 30 responses/min (records in which slopes decrease over time are called *negatively accelerated*; those in which they increase are called *positively accelerated*).

Figure 5-6 shows other features sometimes incorporated into cumulative records. Records A and B show how pen displacements can indicate other events besides responses. Here only some responses produced food, irregularly in A (as at *a, b* and *c*) and regularly in B (as at *d* and *e*). The

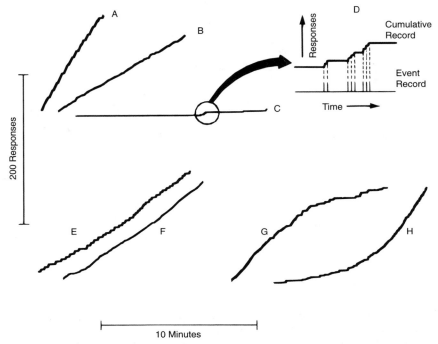

FIGURE 5-5 Sample cumulative records. A 45° slope represents about 20 responses/min. Records A and B differ mainly in response rate, higher in A than in B. Rate is zero through most of C; a magnified segment of C with a few responses is shown in D in relation to an event record. Records E and F are about equal in rate but show different patterns of responding: E is steplike, indicating periods of responding alternating with pauses; the smoother-grained F indicates relatively steady responding. Records G and H show rates that change over time, decreasing in G (negative acceleration) and increasing in H (positive acceleration).

repeated concave pattern in B, as between *d* and *e*, is sometimes called *scalloping*. In C, responding that began at *f* produced food at *g*, as indicated by the pen displacement. The pen then reset to *h* and the sequence repeated at *h* to *i* and so on. This type of record makes successive segments easy to compare (e.g., the segment ending at *g* contains more responses than the one ending at *i*). Record D shows how sustained pen displacements can distinguish different conditions. Here responding occasionally produced food

only in the presence of a tone; the pen stayed in its normal position during the tone, in segments *j*, *l* and *n*, but was displaced downward in its absence, in segments *k*, *m* and *o*.

With this treatment of free-operant behavior and cumulative records, we've explored part of the technology of the science of behavior. Before we can effectively consider the findings made available through such analyses, we must turn our attention to some aspects of the language of behavior.

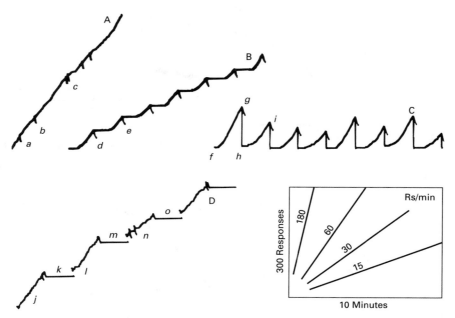

FIGURE 5-6   Additional features of cumulative records. In A and B, pen displacements superimpose a record of other events, such as food deliveries, on cumulative responses (as at *a* through *e*). In C, pen resets make it easy to compare successive segments of the record (*f* to *g*; *h* to *i*). In D, sustained pen displacements distinguish responding during a stimulus (at *j*, *l*, *n*) and nonresponding in its absence (at *k*, *m*, *o*). A slope of 45° represents about 40 responses/min (the scale differs from that in Figure 5-5).

REINFORCEMENT

Lever pressing becomes more probable when a water-deprived rat's lever presses produce water than when they don't. Key pecking becomes more probable when a food-deprived pigeon's key pecks produce food than when they don't. And perhaps a child's cries become more probable when they produce a parent's attention than when they don't. These cases illustrate the principle of reinforcement: Responding increases when it produces reinforcers. The principle is simple, but as it evolved from Thorndike's initial versions of the Law of Effect to its con-

temporary status, it carried problems of language and logic with it. Table 5-1 summarizes some properties of the contemporary vocabulary of reinforcement.

The vocabulary of reinforcement includes the term *reinforcer* as stimulus and the terms *reinforce* and *reinforcement* as either operation or process. For example, when a rat's lever presses produce food pellets and lever pressing increases, we say that the pellets are reinforcers and that the lever presses are reinforced with pellets. The response that increases must be the one that produces the consequences. For example, if a rat's lever press produces shock and only the rat's

TABLE 5-1   The Vocabulary of Reinforcement. This vocabulary[a] is appropriate if and only if three conditions exist: (1) a response produces consequences; (2) the response occurs more often than when it doesn't produce those consequences; and (3) the increased responding occurs *because* the response has those consequences.

TERM	RESTRICTIONS	EXAMPLES
reinforcer (noun)	A stimulus	Food pellets were used as reinforcers for the rat's lever presses.
reinforcing (adjective)	A property of a stimulus	The reinforcing stimulus was produced more often than the other, nonreinforcing stimuli.
reinforcement (noun)	As an operation, the delivery of consequences when a response occurs	The fixed-ratio schedule of reinforcement delivered food after every tenth key peck.
	As a process, the increase in responding that results from the reinforcement	The experiment with monkeys demonstrated reinforcement produced by social consequences.
to reinforce (verb)	As an operation, to deliver consequences when a response occurs; responses are reinforced and not organisms	When a period of free play was used to reinforce the child's completion of school work, the child's grades improved.
	As a process, to increase responding through the reinforcement operation	The experiment was designed to find out whether gold stars would reinforce cooperative play among first-graders.

[a]A parallel vocabulary is appropriate to punishment (including *punisher* as a stimulus and *punish* as a verb; cf. Chapter 6), with the difference that a punishing consequence makes responding occur less rather than more often.

jumping increases, it would be inappropriate to speak of either pressing or jumping as reinforced.

A reinforcer is a type of stimulus, but reinforcement is neither stimulus nor response. As an operation, reinforcement is presenting a reinforcer when a response occurs; it is carried out on responses, and so we speak of reinforcing responses rather than organisms. We say that food reinforced a rat's lever press or that a pigeon's key peck was reinforced with water, but not that food reinforced the rat or that the pigeon was reinforced for pecking or that a child was reinforced. The main reason for this restriction is illustrated in the last examples: When we speak of reinforcing organisms, it's too easy to omit the response or the reinforcer or both. The restriction forces us to be explicit about what's reinforced by what. Nor must we omit the organism; we can always say whose response it was (e.g., the child's crying).

The term *reinforcement* has also often served as a name for a process, the increase in responding that follows from reinforcing consequences. This dual usage as both operation and process complicates things, but it's been around a long time and is unlikely to change. For example, the statement that a response was reinforced can be interpreted in two ways: Either the response produced a reinforcer (operation) or responding increased because it produced a reinforcer (process). We'll favor the usage of reinforcement as an operation. The process can be described so easily in terms of changes in responding (i.e., responding increased) that substituting other terms for a direct description of what happens to responding seems hard to justify. But the process usage has so much precedent that it can't be avoided. In addition, the overlap between operation and process vocabularies extends to many other terms (e.g., extinction, punishment; Ferster & Skinner, 1957).

The vocabulary of reinforcement leads to some logical difficulties even when restricted to operations. When a response becomes more likely because it's produced a stimulus, we say the response has been reinforced and we call the stimulus a reinforcer. If asked how we know the stimulus was a reinforcer, we point to the increase in responding. If we're then asked why the increase occurred, we might say it did so because the response was reinforced. Soon we begin to repeat ourselves. Once we define a reinforcer by its effect on behavior, we create a problem of circular definition if we simultaneously define the effect by the reinforcing stimulus (Meehl, 1950).

One solution is to recognize that the term *reinforcement* is descriptive, not explanatory. It names a relation between behavior and environment; it doesn't explain the relation. The relation includes at least three components. First, responses must have consequences. Second, their probability must increase (i.e., they must become more probable than when not having these consequences). Third, the increase must occur *because* they have these consequences and not for some other reason. For example, if we knew only that responding increased, it wouldn't be appropriate to say that the response must have been reinforced (maybe it was elicited). It wouldn't even be enough to know that the response was now producing some stimulus it hadn't been producing before. We'd still have to know whether responding increased *because* the stimulus was its consequence.

Suppose a parent attends to an infant whenever the infant makes cooing sounds, but suppose also that the infant is more likely to make them with the parent present than with the parent absent. The infant coos and the parent comes, and now the cooing increases. How do we decide whether the infant is now cooing because cooing has been reinforced or because the parent is now present and makes cooing more likely? It's even more complicated, because the infant's cooing may also reinforce the parent's attention. In working out these interactions, it's important to distinguish reinforcing effects of consequences from other effects (cf. Poulson, 1984).

Consider another and less pleasant example. Assume an abusive parent gets annoyed whenever an infant cries and tries to suppress the cries with slaps. The infant cries and then gets slapped and this produces even more crying. In this case, the consequence of crying is getting slapped and getting slapped produces more crying, but we wouldn't want to say the slapping reinforces the crying. Two criteria for reinforcement are satisfied but the third isn't. Crying doesn't increase because slapping is a consequence; the slapping brings on crying even if the infant isn't crying at the time of the first slap. Stimuli may have eliciting or other effects along with or instead of their effects as consequences of responding. (Under these unhappy circumstances, by the way, the infant may learn eventually to suppress the crying; as we'll see in Chapter 6, it would then be appropriate to say that the slapping punishes the crying.)

The vocabulary of reinforcement requires that responding has consequences, that responding increases, and that this increase occurs because responding has its consequences and not for other reasons. Once these conditions are met, we say the response was reinforced and the stimulus was a reinforcer.

We might also assume the stimulus will continue to be an effective reinforcer in the future and will reinforce other responses in other situations. But either assumption may be incorrect. The effectiveness of reinforcers changes over time, and any consequence may reinforce some responses but not others. For example, money is more likely than a smile to reinforce the services of a plumber or an electrician, but the opposite is likely to be the case if the behavior to be reinforced is a lover's embrace. Despite these reservations, the reinforcers used in many standard experimental situations (e.g., food with food-deprived organisms) are likely to reinforce a variety of responses; the experimenter who chooses a stimulus that will reinforce some responses but not others will sooner or later have to cope with the difference. More about the relativity of reinforcement will come up later in this chapter.

EXTINCTION

The consequences of many responses remain reasonably constant throughout life. For example, we usually touch the objects we reach for and we usually get from one floor to another when we climb a flight of stairs. But for other responses, consequences change. Responses reinforced during childhood may no longer be reinforced in adulthood. Educational systems may arrange consequences such as praise or grades for solving arithmetic problems or answering factual questions, but sooner or later these artificial consequences are discontinued (with the hope that more natural consequences will maintain the responses when the student moves on to other settings). When a response is reinforced, its probability increases. But the increase isn't permanent: responding decreases to its earlier levels when reinforcement is discontinued.

The operation of discontinuing reinforcement is called *extinction*; when responding decreases to its earlier level as a result it's said to be *extinguished*. This return of responding to its prereinforcement level mainly demonstrates that the effects of reinforcement are temporary. Responding is maintained only while reinforcement continues and not after it stops. Thus, the decrease in responding during extinction isn't a special process requiring a separate treatment; it's one of the properties of reinforcement.

At one time, responding during extinction was a primary measure of reinforcement. *Resistance to extinction* was expressed as the time elapsed until responding dropped to some specified level. Two hypothetical records of extinction of a rat's lever presses are shown in Figure 5-7. Response rate decreases over time in both (negative acceleration), but depending on the extinction criterion either might represent more resistance to extinction. If the criterion is the time until 2 min go by without a response, then A shows more resistance to extinction than B; A doesn't include 2 min without a response but such a period begins halfway through B. If instead the criterion is total responses, then resistance to extinction is greater for B than for A. Resistance to extinction diminished in significance because its definition permitted such ambiguities.

But resistance to change, of which resistance to extinction is a special case, remains an important property of behavior (Nevin, 1992). For example, arithmetic facts, spelling

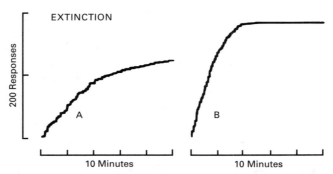

FIGURE 5-7 Hypothetical cumulative records of extinction of a rat's lever presses after food reinforcement. Either A or B might be said to demonstrate greater resistance to extinction, depending on whether it is measured by the time taken until 2 min go by without a response or by total responses during the session.

and other academic skills are said to be *fluent* when they have been practiced and reinforced to the point where they occur with high accuracy and short latency (Johnson & Layng, 1992). Once such skills become fluent, they also become less likely to be disrupted by changes in settings or other distractions.

Extinction Versus Inhibition

If extinction didn't occur, the effects of reinforcement would be permanent. Any responding engendered by reinforcement would last through a lifetime. Clearly that isn't generally so. For example, if you wear a watch you probably often turn your wrist to look at it; the consequence of looking is finding out the time. But if you stop wearing the watch for some reason, you'll eventually stop looking; seeing a bare wrist isn't an effective reinforcer.

The history of the concept of extinction, however, wasn't so simple. It was long assumed that extinction actively suppressed responding. Extinction was said to have *inhibitory* effects, in contrast to assumed *exci-*

tatory effects of reinforcement. This treatment went back to a language that had been applied to data from Pavlov's conditioning experiments (cf. Chapter 12; see also Skinner, 1938, pp. 96–102). Once that language was carried over to the language of consequences, it was kept because it seemed consistent with other effects that often accompanied extinction. Thus, texts on learning tended to devote separate chapters to reinforcement and extinction rather than treating them as two aspects of one phenomenon.

Consider *spontaneous recovery*. In a typical extinction session, responding decreases as the session continues. But the rate at the beginning of the next extinction session is usually higher than it was at the end of the last one. Some hypothetical cumulative records illustrating spontaneous recovery are shown in Figure 5-8. Responding at the start of a session was said to have recovered spontaneously from inhibition built up by the end of the last session; it was assumed that this inhibition increased within sessions, actively suppressing responding, and dissipated between sessions.

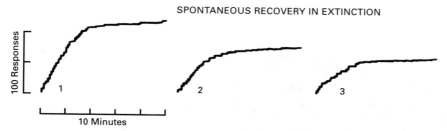

FIGURE 5-8 Spontaneous recovery shown in hypothetical cumulative records of a rat's lever presses in sessions of extinction after food reinforcement. The response rate at the start of session 2 is higher than it was at the end of session 1; similarly, the rate at the start of session 3 is higher than it was at the end of session 2.

Phenomena such as spontaneous recovery were taken to mean that responding that had been reduced by extinction was somehow "there all the time but inhibited" (Reid, 1958). Various accounts of extinction were formulated in terms of inferred processes such as inhibition, frustration, interference or fatigue (Kimble, 1961). They differed mainly in how they characterized the events that generated the inhibition. But these accounts explained extinction in terms of fictional events or processes. When a response was said to be inhibited in extinction, the inhibited response could be measured but not anything that was doing the inhibiting.

It wasn't necessary to assume suppressive processes in extinction. For example, the effects of presession conditions such as handling may make the start of a session different from later times. If so, effects of extinction late in one session might not transfer to the start of the next session. On these grounds, Kendall (1965) reasoned that the usual pattern of response rates in extinction sessions could be reversed under the right conditions. The key pecks of three pigeons were first reinforced in 1-hr sessions. Repeated 1-min sessions of extinction followed. The first long extinction session came only

after responding had reliably decreased to zero in the brief sessions. Within a few minutes, each pigeon began to respond. Until this session, responding had never extinguished at times later than 1 min into a session; responding occurred at these later times when the opportunity was finally available. In a sense, Kendall had demonstrated spontaneous recovery within a session rather than at its start.

Another example of recovery of extinguished responding has been called *regression* or *resurgence* (Epstein & Skinner, 1980; Keller & Schoenfeld, 1950, pp. 81–82). Suppose a rat's chain pulls are extinguished and then lever presses are reinforced. If the lever presses are later extinguished the previously extinguished chain pulls are likely to reappear. By analogy to clinical terminology, the phenomenon suggests regression from current behavior (lever presses) to older behavior that was once effective (chain pulls).

Response-Reinforcer Contingencies and Reinforcer Deliveries

Controversy over the nature of extinction may have occurred because discontinuing reinforcement has not one but two effects:

(1) the contingency between responses and reinforcers ends, so (2) reinforcers are no longer delivered. In this context, the term *contingency* simply describes the consequences of responding; here it's *the effect of a response on stimulus probability*. For example, in a contingency in which a rat receives food if and only if it presses a lever, a lever press raises the probability of food from zero to 1.0, but in a contingency in which lever presses do nothing, the probability of food is independent of lever presses. (Strictly, a response-stimulus contingency is virtually always part of a three-term contingency, but we needn't address that issue here; cf. Chapter 8.)

Contingencies expressed in terms of probability relations between responses and their consequences can be summarized in graphic form much like those between stimuli and the responses they elicit (Figure 4-2). The coordinate system is illustrated in Figure 5-9. The y-axis shows the probability of a stimulus given a response, $p(S/R)$; the x-axis shows its probability given no response, $p(S/no\ R)$. Relative to Figure 4-2, the S and R terms have been reversed. The earlier figure showed effects of stimuli on responses; this one shows effects of responses on stimuli.

At A, the probability of the stimulus is high given a response but is otherwise low, as when a rat's lever presses produce food. At B, stimulus probability is independent of responses, as when food is delivered without regard to lever presses. At C, stimulus probability is zero whether or not a response has occurred, as when food is discontinued in extinction. We'll later consider other kinds of contingencies in other contexts. For example, cases in which responses reduce stimulus probability, as at D, illustrate avoidance (Chapter 6), and those in which responses produce a stimulus with a probability of less

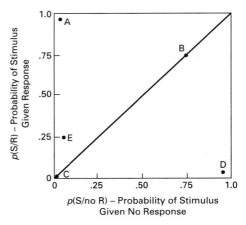

FIGURE 5-9   Response–stimulus contingencies represented in terms of stimulus probability given a response, $p(S/R)$, and stimulus probability given no response, $p(S/no\ R)$. The graph includes reliable production of stimuli by responses (A), response-independent stimuli (B), extinction (C), prevention of stimuli by responses, as in avoidance (D: see Chapter 6), and intermittent production of stimuli by responses, as in reinforcement schedules (E: see Chapter 10). Cf. Figure 4-2.

than 1.0, as at E, illustrate reinforcement schedules (Chapter 10).

Let's now compare procedures in terms of changes in contingencies and changes in stimuli. Consider first the food-deprived rat whose lever presses are reinforced with food. Once every 10 or 15 seconds the rat presses the lever and eats the food delivered. If lever pressing is then extinguished, lever presses no longer produce food and the rat no longer eats. This rat is now different in two ways: (1) its lever presses no longer have their earlier consequences, and (2) it's no longer eating.

Here's a different arrangement. The rat stays food-deprived, but when we stop reinforcing lever presses we begin to deliver food automatically every 10 or 15 seconds. In this case, as in the last example, lever presses that once produced food no longer have an effect. But even though food is no longer a consequence of lever presses, this rat continues to get food every 10 or 15 seconds. Both rats will press less often, but only one will still be eating.

The standard extinction procedure terminates both a contingency and reinforcer deliveries. The last example shows, however, that the contingency can be terminated while reinforcers continue. In both cases, responding that had been reinforced decreases. But terminating reinforcers, which occurs only in the first procedure, affects more than just the reinforced response. If food is suddenly taken away from a food-deprived rat that's been eating, for example, the rat becomes more active and perhaps urinates or defecates. If food was produced by lever presses, the rat might bite the lever (Mowrer & Jones, 1943). If other organisms are in the chamber, the rat might attack them (Azrin, Hutchinson, & Hake, 1966). And the opportunity to engage in such aggressive responses may reinforce other responses (e.g., the organism might pull a chain if chain pulls let it get at something it can sink its teeth into: Azrin, Hutchinson, & McLaughlin, 1965). These effects, though observed in extinction, aren't results of terminating the reinforcement contingency. They occur when response-independent food deliveries stop as well as during extinction. In both cases, a rat that's been eating stops receiving food. In extinction, these side effects get superimposed on decreases in the previously reinforced responding because the termination of reinforcers is necessarily a part of extinction.

These observations have considerable practical significance. For example, experi-ments with children sometimes use response-independent reinforcers rather than extinction to avoid the side effects of terminating reinforcer deliveries (e.g., see Hart, et al., 1968, on the social reinforcement of a child's cooperative play). Behavioral operations often have more than one effect. A stimulus that reinforces one response may elicit some other response and serve as a discriminative stimulus for still another. The phenomena thought to show that extinction was more than the temporary effect of reinforcement were probably only side effects. Many, such as the aggressive responding generated by terminating reinforcer deliveries, could have been observed in situations that didn't involve the consequences of responding.

Extinction and Superstition

As we've just seen, the effects of terminating contingencies in extinction are superimposed on the more general effects of terminating reinforcer deliveries. Why then has extinction remained the primary way to study the effects of terminating contingencies for so long? Disconnecting the lever from the feeder is more convenient than disconnecting the lever and at the same time substituting a clock that operates the feeder periodically, but it's unlikely that the answer lies in a mere change in apparatus. It more likely lies with some other properties of behavior.

In a phenomenon called *superstition* (Skinner, 1948), food is repeatedly presented to a food-deprived pigeon at short intervals (e.g., every 10 or 15 seconds). Responses that occur just before food deliveries are likely to be repeated and therefore to be followed closely by still more food deliveries. The effect of the accidental succession of responses and reinforcers

> is usually obvious. The bird happens to be executing some response as the hopper appears; as a result it tends to repeat this response. If the interval before the next presentation is not so great that extinction takes place, . . . [this] strengthens the response still further. . . . The bird behaves as if there were a causal relation between its behavior and the presentation of food, although such a relation is lacking. (Skinner, 1948, pp. 168–171)

Skinner noted that the topography or form of each pigeon's responding usually changed gradually as the procedure continued, as accidental relations developed between responding and food deliveries. Skinner referred to these changes as *topographical drift*. A pigeon responded temporarily as if its responses were producing food as a consequence, but no particular response consistently remained as superstitious behavior. Over long periods of time with this procedure, Staddon and Simmelhag (1971) observed that pecking often dominates as the response just preceding food deliveries (cf. Chapter 4 on the contributions of elicitation).

Superstitious responding generated by accidental successions of responses and reinforcers is a recurrent problem in behavior analysis, because such accidental sequences can occur whether reinforcers are independent of responses or are their consequences. If one response is followed by a different response that's reinforced, the reinforcer may affect both even though its delivery depends only on the second one (Catania, 1971; Kazdin, 1977). Even when responses have consequences, properties unrelated to reinforcement may become stereotyped if they typically accompany reinforced responses. For example, a bowler's gestures after releasing the ball may persist because they are so often closely related to earlier responses and the impact of the ball (Herrnstein, 1966). Furthermore, if reinforcement contingencies change so that features of responding that once were relevant become irrelevant and if these old features aren't incompatible with the newly relevant ones, the old ones may persist simply because they continue to be followed by reinforcers (Stokes & Balsam, 1991). Another difficulty is that superstition is too easily invoked to explain behavior not accounted for in other ways (Guthrie & Horton, 1946; Moore & Stuttard, 1979).

We can now reconsider what happens when a reinforcement contingency is terminated while reinforcer deliveries continue. First, a rat's lever presses are reinforced with food; then, when presses no longer produce food, food deliveries continue independently of behavior. Lever pressing continues for some time, with presses still followed closely by food. Lever pressing declines slowly because the frequent incidental succession of responses and reinforcers counteracts the effects of terminating the reinforcement contingency. Eventually lever pressing is replaced by other responses, but it would be difficult to argue that this decrease in pressing is simple. For this reason, arranging a transition from a reinforcement contingency to response-independent reinforcer deliveries may be a poor way to examine the effects of terminating reinforcement contingencies (Boakes, 1973; Catania & Keller, 1981).

Once again, there are practical implications. Suppose an institutionalized developmentally disabled boy often engages in self-injurious behavior such as head-banging or eye-poking. Suppose further that we discover that his behavior is in large part maintained by staff attention as a reinforcer. Extinction is not well-advised because of the harm he might do to himself if we ignore the self-injurious behavior. Giving him attention independently of the self-injurious behavior is one possibility, but as we've seen that might reduce the behavior only slowly. A better procedure is to use attention to reinforce an alternative response, and especially one that is incompatible with the self-injurious behavior (Repp & Deitz, 1974). The self-injurious behavior will inevitably decrease as the alternative response increases. Such procedures, sometimes called *differential reinforcement of other behavior*, have been widely applied to problem behavior (e.g., see Skiba, Pettigrew, & Alden, 1971, on thumbsucking). One way to reduce a child's bad behavior is to reinforce good behavior. That's one reason why "Catch 'em being good" is such an effective slogan for either parents or teachers.

Section B   **Reinforcers as Opportunities for Behavior**

Reinforcers are inevitably oversimplified by treating them merely as stimuli. The presentation of any reinforcer involves a transition from one situation to another (cf. Baum, 1973). So far, we've identified reinforcers only in terms of their effects. Without making a stimulus a consequence of responding we can't say if it will serve as a reinforcer. Even demonstrable reinforcers such as food vary in effectiveness depending on deprivation. Food as a consequence of lever presses might not do much to the rat's rate of pressing if the rat already has food continuously available. We'll see that an important property of a reinforcing situation is the responding for which it sets an occasion.

Chapter 2 introduced establishing operations, the procedures that make events more or less effective as reinforcers. Chapter 4 discussed some effects of establishing operations as examples of *motivation* or *drive*. We can now define these terms more precisely. When we study motivation or drive we're concerned with what makes consequences more or less effective as reinforcers or as punishers. In the taxonomy of establishing operations, deprivation and satiation are important ways, but not the only ways, to change the effectiveness of stimuli as reinforcers or punishers. In this context, we can now survey the variety of events that may serve as reinforcers.

Reinforcers are sometimes distinguished on the basis of the types of operations that established them. For example, a *conditioned reinforcer* is one that's become effective by virtue of its relation to some other reinforcer (e.g., the light that comes on when a pigeon feeder is operated will eventually become a conditioned reinforcer because of its relation to food delivery). The establishing operation here is that of arranging the relation between the stimuli (i.e., setting up the feeder so that food deliveries are accompanied by the light). In human behavior, money often works as a conditioned reinforcer, and because of its relation to so many other possible reinforcers (all of the things we've bought with it), it's sometimes called a *generalized* conditioned reinforcer. A reinforcer that doesn't depend on a relation to other reinforcers is called an *unconditioned reinforcer*.

Many events that are regarded as unconditioned reinforcers have obvious biological significance (e.g., food, water, sexual contact; cf. Richter, 1927). But reinforcers are not limited to events of obvious biological significance. For example, sensory stimuli such as flashing lights can be powerful reinforcers for the behavior of autistic children (Ferrari & Harris, 1981). And when developmentally disabled children were briefly deprived of music or social praise, these events became more effective reinforcers of other behavior such as operating a switch; conversely, when the children were satiated with music or social praise, the effectiveness of these events as reinforcers decreased (Vollmer & Iwata, 1991).

Reinforcers have also been distinguished on the basis of their relation to responses. An *intrinsic* reinforcer (sometimes also called an *automatic* reinforcer) is one that has a natural relation to the responses that produce it (as when a musician plays because of the music that the playing produces), whereas an *extrinsic* reinforcer (sometimes also called a *contrived* reinforcer) has an arbitrary relation to those responses (as when the musician plays for money). The term *extrinsic* has also been applied to stimuli presumed to function as reinforcers because their function has been instructed (as when a child is told that it's important to earn good grades); despite their label, such stimuli are often ineffective reinforcers.

We've discussed eliciting, discriminative and reinforcing functions of stimuli. The presentation of stimuli can also have establishing functions (cf. Michael, 1982). Consider two examples: Tasting unsalted soup doesn't make it more likely that salt will be passed when you ask for it, and arriving in front of a locked door doesn't make it more likely that you'll find the key in your pocket. But you will be more likely to ask for the salt or to reach into your pocket. In each case something that had been neutral (the salt or the key) has become reinforcing. (Such effects have sometimes been called *incentive* functions; the term *incentive*, however, has been applied to both the establishing and the discriminative functions of stimuli; e.g., Bolles, 1975; Logan, 1960.)

THE RELATIVITY OF REINFORCEMENT

Reinforcers exist in great variety. Some are consumed. Others aren't. Some appear effective on the organism's first experience with them. Others acquire their reinforcing properties during the organism's lifetime. No common physical properties allow us to identify reinforcers independently of their effects on behavior. For example, it's difficult for us to say what it is about teacher attention that reinforces student behavior, but we do know that when a teacher moves to a first-grader's desk with perhaps a pat on the shoulder or an encouraging comment contingent on the student's reading, the student's study behavior increases and other nonstudy behavior such as dawdling decreases (Hall, Lund, & Jackson, 1968). We also know that changes in student behavior can reinforce the behavior of the teacher (Sherman & Cormier, 1974).

It's tempting to equate reinforcers with events that colloquially are called rewards, but that would be a mistake. Reinforcers don't work because they make the organism "feel good" or because the organism "likes" them. Our everyday language doesn't capture what's important about reinforcers. For example, in a study of the reinforcers that might be effective in managing the behavior of people with profound handicaps, predictions based on staff opinion of what would work for each individual were inconsistent with the reinforcers identified by systematically assessing each individual's preferences among those events (Green et al., 1988; cf. Fisher et al., 1992).

Some events that superficially seem "rewarding" may not function as reinforcers; others that seem the opposite may have powerful reinforcing effects. For example, falling from high places or being violently twisted and shaken hardly seem like potential reinforcers. Yet they surely contribute to the reinforcing effects of roller coasters and other amusement-park rides. Restraint also seems an unlikely reinforcer, but an analysis of the self-injurious behavior of three children with severe developmental disabilities showed that restraints that prevented the children from poking or biting themselves could reinforce arbitrary responses such as putting marbles in a box (Favell, McGimsey, & Jones, 1978). Once such a reinforcer is identified, it can be used to reinforce behavior that is incompatible with self-injury.

Laughter seems like a reinforcing consequence for the telling of jokes. Suppose an instructor tells some jokes, the class laughs, and as a result the instructor tells jokes more often. We can say that the laughing reinforced the telling of jokes, but on just this evidence we can't say that laughter in general is a reinforcer. Suppose now the instructor puns, the class laughs, and as a result the instructor puns less often. The laughing didn't reinforce the punning (in fact, we should say it punished the punning: Chapter 6). Whether laughter reinforced or punished depended on whether it was contingent on telling jokes or on punning. Actually, punning is more likely to be reinforced by groaning than by laughing. Suppose the instructor puns, the class groans, and as a result the instructor puns more often. Now we can say that the groaning reinforced the punning. Depending on whether the consequences are laughter or groans, punning is either reinforced or punished. (In fact, laughing at puns can be bad enough to make a groan man cry.) The effectiveness of a reinforcer depends on its relation to the responses that produce it.

When a rat's lever press produces food, the food gives the rat an opportunity to eat. If we make lever and food simultaneously available to the rat, the rat is more likely to eat than to press. Now consider the hypothesis that the probability of a response will go up if it provides an opportunity to engage in another response more probable than itself (Premack, 1959, 1971). Another way of stating it is that if response A is more probable than response B, an opportunity to engage in A can be used to reinforce B. If this is so, food is an effective reinforcer for a food-deprived rat's lever presses simply because eating is usually more probable than pressing.

Consider an experiment that reversed the reinforcing effects of two stimuli by varying the probabilities of the responses occasioned by each (Premack, 1962). A rat's running in a wheel was controlled by engaging or releasing a brake on the wheel. The rat's drinking was controlled by moving a drinking tube into or out of an opening in a stationary wall on one side of the wheel; licking was recorded with an electrical device called a drinkometer. As tested during brief periods when both responses were available, running became more probable than drinking after the wheel was locked with water freely available, but drinking became more probable than running after the drinking tube was removed with the wheel freely available. In each case, the opportunity to engage in the more probable response reinforced the less probable response. When running was more probable than drinking (after the wheel was locked), licking became more likely if it released the brake and allowed the rat to run than if it didn't allow an opportunity to run. Conversely, when drinking was more probable than running (after the drinking tube was removed), running became more likely if it produced the drinking tube and allowed the rat to drink than if it didn't allow an opportunity to drink.

This demonstrates that reinforcers can't be defined independently of the responses that they reinforce. In Premack's experiment, drinking reinforced running when drinking was more probable than running, but running reinforced drinking when the probabilities were reversed. According to this account, reinforcers are relative and their important properties are based on the responses for which they provide an opportunity.

This relativity had long been unrecognized. Most learning experiments had been restricted to responses of relatively low probability (e.g., a rat's lever press) and to reinforcers that occasioned highly probable responses (e.g., food and eating). These were common and convenient but nonetheless special cases. Few thought to ask whether situations might be arranged in which opportunities to press a lever or peck a key could be used to reinforce eating (e.g., Sawisch & Denny, 1973). The question isn't so far-fetched. The opportunity to eat a good meal can be an effective reinforcer, but consider how often children are persuaded to finish their dinners by making other activities depend on that eating. Eating can reinforce, as when a child's dessert depends on whether the child has completed homework, or it can be reinforced, as when the opportunity to watch television depends on whether the child has finished dinner.

The relativity of reinforcement can be illustrated further by expanding the previous experiment to three responses. Let's add a feeder to the running wheel and the drinking tube. By restricting access appropriately, we can make eating more probable than running and running in turn more probable than drinking. We then find that running can be reinforced by the opportunity to eat but the opportunity to run can reinforce drinking; running can simultaneously reinforce and be reinforced. These relations are shown on the left in Figure 5-10. If by water deprivation we now make drinking the most probable response, the reinforcement relations change, as shown on the right in Figure 5-10. In other words, by changing the relative probabilities of the three responses, we can make an opportunity to engage in any one an effective reinforcer with respect to either or both of the others. The relative likelihoods with which different children prefer coloring in books, building with blocks or playing in the playground can be useful information to someone who has to manage the behavior of children in daycare centers or the early grades of elementary school (e.g., Wasik, 1970).

FIGURE 5-10 Reinforcement relations given different response probabilities in a behavior hierarchy. When eating is most probable and drinking is least probable (left), an opportunity to eat reinforces running or drinking but an opportunity to run reinforces only drinking. At another time (right), when drinking is most probable and running is least probable (e.g., after water deprivation), eating still reinforces running but both eating and running can now be reinforced by an opportunity to drink.

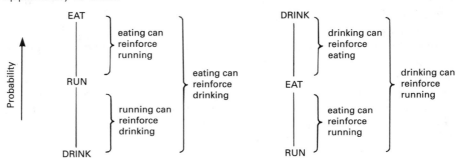

Deprivation makes reinforcers effective because the probability of a response ordinarily goes up when we restrict the organism's opportunities to engage in it (e.g., Timberlake, 1980). But the detailed operation of Premack's principle has engendered controversy, mainly because its operation depends on how probabilities are calculated. Choice among simultaneously available responses may be more satisfactory than the proportion of time occupied by each (e.g., Dunham, 1977; Eisenberger, Karpman, & Trattner, 1967). A further complication is that some responses are more likely than others to substitute for each other (Bernstein & Ebbesen, 1978; Rachlin & Burkhard, 1978). For example, deprivation of the opportunity to eat one food may not make its eating effective as a reinforcer if another food is available, but it might do so if water was available instead of the second food. Here eating one food and eating the other are substitutable responses (either will replace the other as a reinforcer) but eating and drinking aren't.

We introduced reinforcers as types of stimuli, but now we're treating them in terms of responding. The treatment shifted because we found that an important prop-

erty of a reinforcer is the responding that it occasions. Like the reflex, reinforcement is a relation and not a theory or hypothesis. This relation includes responses, their consequences and the changes in behavior that follow from them.

THE ACQUISITION OF BEHAVIOR

Let's return now to learning, by examining how an organism may acquire responses through reinforcement. Record A of Figure 5-11 shows a hypothetical cumulative record of a rat's very first session of reinforced lever pressing. The first few responses are separated by long pauses. Within 5 min or so, the long pauses disappear and responding increases for the rest of the session. The acquisition of lever pressing seems gradual. To repeat these observations, we extinguish lever presses until responding decreases to previous levels and then conduct another reinforcement session. Record B of Figure 5-11 shows what it might look like. Because of the prior extinction, there's no responding at first. When responding finally occurs and is reinforced, it immediately rises to a rate

FIGURE 5-11 Hypothetical cumulative records of a rat's initial acquisition of lever pressing during the first session with each response reinforced with food (A) and reacquisition of lever pressing with reinforcement introduced again after a period of extinction (B).

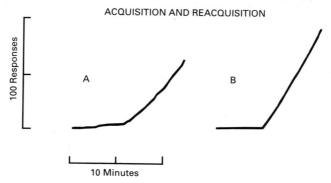

ACQUISITION AND REACQUISITION

100 Responses

A

B

10 Minutes

roughly equal to that at the end of the first reinforcement session. This time, acquisition of lever pressing was abrupt rather than gradual. How do we reconcile these two very different performances?

Sidman (1960) has presented an alternative to the view that the initial learning produced an irreversible change.

> The animal learned not only those responses that succeeded in depressing the lever but also learned to go to the tray, to pick up the small pellet, to bring it to its mouth, etc. And these responses were learned in their correct sequence, because their reinforcement was correlated with the appropriate stimuli both from the environment and from the preceding behavior. The tray approach, for example, could be reinforced only after the sound from the food magazine; reaching for the pellet could be reinforced only after the pellet had dropped into the tray, etc. . . . What did we extinguish when we disconnected the feeding mechanism? . . . There is no magazine sound, no pellet sound, no visual pellet, no tactual pellet, etc. Tray-approach is still possible, but only in the absence of some of its controlling stimuli. The responses involved in picking up and ingesting the pellet can no longer occur in their originally learned context. While our extinction procedure may have returned the lever-pressing response to its preconditioning level, other components of the total learned sequence could not have undergone complete extinction. (Sidman, 1960, pp. 101–103)

From this analysis, Sidman summarized the reasons for the difference in acquisition in the two sessions: "When reinforcement was again introduced . . . , the animal did not have to relearn the whole sequence, because the whole sequence had not been extinguished" (Sidman, 1960, p. 103).

Reinforcement, then, doesn't produce learning; it produces behavior. In looking to see whether a rat presses a lever when a reinforcement contingency operates and not otherwise, we're concerned with the extent to which the rat has learned the consequences of its lever pressing. The consequences of responding are critical to learning not because learning follows from them but because *they are what is learned*. Contingencies involve the ways in which the environment is affected by behavior and are therefore important features of the environment for organisms to learn.

Latent Learning

These issues were implicit in a controversy based upon a phenomenon called *latent learning* (Thistlethwaite, 1951). Consider the experiment illustrated in Figure 5-12 (Tolman & Honzik, 1930; Tolman, 1948). Food-deprived rats in each of three groups negotiated a maze. In one group, the rats found food in the goalbox, and over successive daily trials their entries into blind alleys gradually decreased. In a second group, the rats found no food in the goalbox. Their entries into blind alleys decreased but remained substantially higher than those for the first group. In a third group, food was introduced in the goalbox only after 10 sessions. This group, which had been like the second group (no food), quickly became like the first group (food); the rats that previously negotiated the maze without food in the goalbox now began to run with as few entries into blind alleys as did the rats that had always found food there. Until food was introduced, the learning of the third group had been latent; what had been learned was demonstrated by introducing food.

The argument at first was that rats learned the maze equally well whether or not food was in the goalbox, so that learning could not to be attributed to food reinforcers. It was then extended to reinforcers in general, and latent-learning experiments were said to have shown that learning could occur without reinforcement. But soon came the

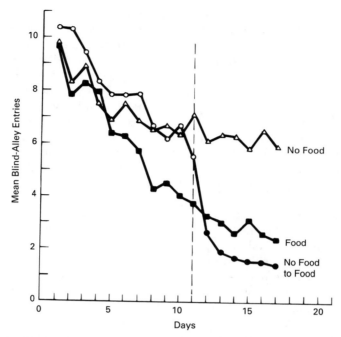

FIGURE 5-12   A latent-learning experiment. Rats were allowed one trial per day in a 14-choice-point maze. One group (filled squares) always found food in the goalbox and a second (un-filled triangles) never did. A third group found no food in the goalbox through day 10 (unfilled circles) but thereafter found food there (filled circles). This group, which had been perform-ing like the second one, quickly became like the first one. They'd been learning the maze all along, so food in the goalbox was necessary only to get them to demonstrate what they'd already learned. (From Tolman & Honzik, 1930)

counterargument that food in the goalbox isn't the only possible reinforcer of a rat's maze-running. Its removal from the maze at the end of the run, its escape from the con-strained spaces of blind alleys, or its return to its home cage where it's fed might all function as effective reinforcers. Experi-ments then varied the rat's handling at the end of the run, the width of the alleys it ran and its home cage feeding. Each time one experiment showed that some reinforcer could generate maze learning, some other one showed latent learning in such a way that that reinforcer couldn't have been ef-fective. And so it went.

Even in principle the argument couldn't have been resolved, and latent learning gradually faded away as a critical theoreti-cal issue. The reason was that a rat's negoti-ation of a maze inevitably involves the consequences of responding. At any choice-point, one turn is followed by entry into a blind alley and the other by an opportunity to move farther through the maze; at the final choicepoint, only one turn is followed by entry into the goalbox, whether or not food is there. The rat's sniffing, touching, looking and moving through the maze are consequential responses, even if they aren't as easily accessible to us as correct turns or entries into blind alleys. These consequences are what the rat learns. Whether to call them reinforcers is mostly a matter of preference, but the language of latent learning seems to have led to a blind alley.

Sensory-Motor Learning

The consequences in these rat experiments have mainly included stimuli with biological significance for the organism's survival (e.g., food or water). But, as implied by latent learning, many presumably lesser consequences are important in day-to-day interactions with the environment. Response-reinforcer contingencies are all around us, but are easily overlooked (see Parsons, 1974, for a human example). We open a book to read it. We listen to hear what someone says. We reach toward a pencil to pick it up. Each consequence sets the occasion for new responses. When we finish reading one page, we turn it and read the next; when we've heard what's been said, we ask a question or make a comment; when we pick up the pencil, we write something with it. To the extent that each case involves behavior maintained by its consequences, each may be discussed in the vocabulary of reinforcement. Seeing reinforces looking; hearing reinforces listening; contacting the pencil reinforces reaching for it.

The interaction of sensory processes with behavior has been a longstanding source of controversy in the psychology of learning. Theorists took sides in debates over whether learning was sensory or motor. Did organisms learn responses or did they learn relations among stimuli? Did they learn response-stimulus or stimulus-stimulus associations?

One issue is whether sensory processes should be treated as behavior. Doing so is consistent with the view that behavior must be dealt with in terms of relations among stimuli and responses rather than in terms of stimuli alone or responses alone. We can't measure seeing and hearing as unambiguously as we can measure a rat's lever presses or a pigeon's key pecks, but they're still behavior. They depend not only on whether visual or auditory stimuli are present but also on what the organism does. Looking makes seeing more likely, and listening makes hearing more likely. The organism isn't passive in its contact with its environment.

Sounds and lights and other basic events have sometimes been described as neutral relative to potentially strong reinforcers or punishers (e.g., food and shock). But the label *neutral*, though convenient, is a misnomer. Events that are consequences of behavior are unlikely to be truly neutral; it's unlikely they'll have absolutely no effect on behavior. Nevertheless, reports of the reinforcing effects of stimuli such as lights and sounds were received with skepticism before the relativity of reinforcers was appreciated. Repeated demonstrations, however, led to the acceptance of *sensory reinforcement* (Kish, 1966). For example, if a rat's lever pressing in darkness briefly turned on a light, its pressing transiently increased. In other words, the light served temporarily as a weak reinforcer. Phenomena like these were discussed in terms of *exploratory behavior* and *curiosity*, and experiments were extended to varied sensory consequences. For a monkey alone in an enclosure, for example, the opportunity to look at other monkeys outside will reinforce the operation of a switch (Butler, 1957).

In this research, responses chosen for ease of measurement were used to assess the effects of sensory consequences. But in any environment behavior inevitably has such consequences. The organism changes its environment simply by moving from one place to another; the things it sees and touches change as it moves, and spatial relations among the components of its environment are a fundamental part of what it learns (Gallistel, 1990).

An experiment by Held and Hein (1963) illustrates these relations between behavior and sensory consequences. Pairs of kittens were raised in darkness; their first visual experience was in the apparatus shown in Figure 5-13. Both kittens received the same kind of visual stimulation: Each wore a shield that prevented it from seeing its own feet and body; each was prevented from seeing the other by the wide central post; and each saw the same pattern of black and white vertical stripes uniformly covering the walls of the circular enclosure. A sort of miniature carousel linked them, but one kitten (A) moved actively whereas the other (P) was

moved passively. The active kitten stood on the floor; the passive kitten stood inside a carrier suspended above the floor. As the active kitten walked around the post, the passive one in its carrier moved a corresponding distance on the other side. If the active kitten turned around in place to walk in the other direction, the pulley system turned the passive one's carrier so that it too turned to face the new direction.

The kittens were exposed to similar visual stimuli, but those for the active kitten were consequences of its own behavior whereas those for the passive kitten were not; they depended on the active kitten's movements rather than its own. The kittens were then both given standard tests of visual-motor coordination, such as visual paw placement (normal kittens held in the

FIGURE 5-13   An apparatus for studying the relation between behavior and visual stimuli. Both the active kitten (A) and the passive one (P) are harnessed to a pulley system with its fulcrum at the central column. Kitten A stands on the floor and Kitten P rides in a carrier. As Kitten A moves about, the pulley system duplicates its changes in position for Kitten P (see arrows). (From Held & Hein, 1963, Figure 1)

air a short distance away from a table edge or other horizontal surface extend their paws toward it). Even though their exposure to visual stimuli was equivalent, only the active kitten responded appropriately in these tests; the passive kitten became able to respond appropriately only later, after it was allowed to walk about freely in a lighted room.

This experiment has much in common with a classic one by Stratton (1897), who for eight days wore prisms that inverted and reversed his visual fields. At first his world looked upside-down and backwards, and his movements weren't coordinated with his surroundings. For example, in walking he looked down to see where he was going, but with the inverting prisms he was looking at the ceiling instead of the floor. Similarly, he had difficulty in pointing at or reaching for objects, because things once seen below eye level were now seen above and things on the right were now seen on the left, and vice versa. As time passed, however, his coordination improved and Stratton reported that the world no longer even looked so upside-down.

The consequences of behavior are again crucial. Looking and moving in the visual field have different consequences with and without inverting prisms, and adjustment to the prisms requires that the new consequences be learned. For example, seeing the floor as one walks is important, but when one begins wearing inverting prisms, seeing the floor, once a consequence of looking down, becomes a consequence of looking up (in these situations, of course, up and down can be defined either relative to the visual field or relative to the body; cf. Harris, 1965). Thus, if seeing the floor is a reinforcer while one is walking and one walks while wearing inverting prisms, seeing the floor will reinforce the response of looking up instead of the response of looking down.

In discussing Stratton's inverted vision, we moved from the locomotion to responses of smaller magnitude, such as eye movements. Even such small-scale responses can have profound consequences. If you notice something out of the corner of your eye, you're more likely to see it clearly if you look toward it than if you look away from it (except in dim light, when you see an object best by looking a little bit away from it). Suppose that in a uniform visual field a contour such as the edge of an object can reinforce eye movement. We'd expect eye movements to become coordinated with events in the visual field. Data from the eye movements of newborns are consistent with this view. For example, when shown a simple figure such as a triangle in a uniform visual field, with continued visual experience infants tend to fixate more and more accurately on the edges and vertices of the triangle (e.g., Salapatek & Kessen, 1966).

We've much to learn about how arbitrary such relations between responses and consequences can be (cf. Hein, et al., 1979). For example, suppose we set up an optical system that projects visual stimuli in an infant's field of view and alters the natural consequences of eye movement. It presents stimuli only when the infant looks straight ahead. A stimulus appears in the right visual field. If the infant looks right, the stimulus disappears. But if the infant looks left, the stimulus moves left, to where the infant is now looking (and vice versa for stimuli appearing in the left visual field). In other words, this optical system creates a world in which the infant can fixate on an object only by looking away from it (cf. Schroeder & Holland, 1968).

The infant would probably learn how to look at things in this experiment, but we'd want to think twice about doing it. Visual areas of the brain develop dramatically in infancy in humans as well as in cats (e.g.,

Blakemore & Cooper, 1970; Freeman, Mitchell, & Millidot, 1972). Some early changes may later be modifiable, but others may be relatively permanent. For example, a child with early problems of binocular vision may never acquire proper depth perception if the problems remain uncorrected until adulthood. Some things are more easily learned, whether in general or at some times rather than others, and some things learned are more easily changed than others. On the one hand, we may be reluctant to invoke reinforcement in accounts of behavior that is learned early and relatively permanently; on the other, we must take care not to rule it out when the permanence of the behavior might depend on the constancy throughout life of the contingencies that originally created it. Contingencies and consequences are part of the description of what we learn even with respect to our simplest interactions with events in the world.

We began this chapter with a brief history of the Law of Effect: puzzle boxes, mazes, runways and operant chambers. Out of these apparatuses and methods, the principle of reinforcement emerged as a descriptive term appropriate when responding increased because of its consequences. Extinction demonstrates that reinforcement has temporary effects, but other events accompany extinction and can be superimposed on the decrease in responding it produces. Extinction is complicated because it involves both terminating a contingency and terminating stimulus presentations. The contributions of contingencies and stimulus presentations can be disentangled by comparing behavior during reinforcement, extinction and superstition procedures. The reinforcement relation is relative. A stimulus providing an opportunity to engage in one response can reinforce another less probable response, and reinforcement relations can be reversed by changing response probabilities through establishing operations such as deprivation. Phenomena such as latent learning and sensory-motor learning demonstrate that reinforcement isn't an explanation of learning; rather, it's part of the description of what is learned. Organisms learn the consequences of their own behavior.

Chapter 6
Consequences of Responding: Aversive Control

A. Punishment

B. Negative Reinforcement: Escape and Avoidance

Punishment *and* reinforcement *have fairly straightforward histories.* Punishment *stems from the Latin* poena, *pain or penalty, and* reinforcement *from the Latin* fortis, *strong, which is related to such structural words as* fort *and* burg.

Escape, *as* ex-, *out of, plus* cappa, *cape, seems to be derived from the Old North French* escaper, *to take off one's cloak or, by extension, to free oneself from restraint.* Avoidance *shares its sense of getting out of, as in making empty, with several of its relatives:* vacant, evacuate, vanish, waste.

Aversive *is derived from the Latin* a, *away, plus* vertere, *to turn.* Vertere *has a Germanic relative, the suffix* -ward *or* -wards, *which has had senses of warding off, guarding or regarding; the suffix appears in* reward, *a word often inaccurately treated as a substitute for* reinforcement.

So far we've emphasized a relation, *reinforcement*, in which the consequences of responding make responding more likely. There's another relation, *punishment*, in which the consequences of responding make responding less likely. Furthermore, a stimulus that reinforces responding when the responding produces it may serve the opposite function when responding removes it: Its removal may punish the responding. Inversely, a stimulus that punishes responding when the responding produces it may reinforce responding when that responding removes it. For example, money may reinforce, as when a child is paid for completing a chore, but its removal may punish, as when the child's allowance is canceled because of a misdeed. Similarly, a painful burn may punish, as when you learn not to touch a pan just taken from a hot oven, but its removal or prevention may reinforce, as when you learn to treat a burn with appropriate medication or to put on a kitchen glove while handling things around a stove.

Except for positive reinforcement (reinforcement by presenting a stimulus: cf. Chapter 5), these relations are often grouped together as instances of *aversive control*. In other words, aversive control includes both *punishment* and *negative reinforcement* (reinforcement by removal or prevention of aversive stimuli). This chapter first treats punishment and then turns to negative reinforcement, in escape and avoidance procedures.

Section A   Punishment

As an operation, *punishment* is arranging a consequence of responding that makes responding less likely. The stimulus arranged as a consequence is called a *punisher*. For example, if a rat's lever presses produce electric shock, the lever press is said to be punished and the shock is said to be a punisher, because this operation reduces lever pressing. In these respects, the vocabulary of punishment parallels the vocabulary of reinforcement (cf. Table 4-1).

Like *reinforcement*, the term *punishment* has been applied to both operations and processes. Thus, saying that a response was punished may mean either that the response produced a punisher or that responding decreased because it produced a punisher. As with reinforcement, preferred usage will be to restrict the term *punishment* to the vocabulary of operations and to describe the process directly in terms of changes in responding. As with reinforcement, however, the process usage has so much precedent that it can't be avoided.

The vocabulary of punishment also parallels that of reinforcement in its object: Responses, not organisms, are said to be punished. If a rat's lever pressing produces shock and lever pressing decreases, it's appropriate to say that the rat was shocked and that the lever press was punished; it goes

against colloquial usage, but it's *not* appropriate to say that the rat was punished. As with reinforcement, this grammatical distinction encourages us to be precise when we observe and describe behavior. One reason it differs so dramatically from everyday usage is that the everyday concern is too often with retribution rather than with changing behavior.

Consider a child misbehaving. A parent calls the child and administers a spanking when the child comes. To say simply that the parent punished the child may be convenient, but this usage makes it too easy to omit the responses that might be affected. The immediate consequence of the child's misbehaving was that the parent called; the spanking occurred after the child obeyed the call. Although the child might misbehave less in the future because of the spanking, the spanking may also reduce the likelihood that the child will approach next time the parent calls. (But this doesn't mean that the parent intent on spanking should go to the child rather than having the child come; too many better alternatives, such as reinforcing responses incompatible with the misbehavior, don't require spanking at all.)

The point isn't just grammatical. We're more likely to see what's happening if we state the punished response explicitly (spanking punished the child's approach) than if we settle for a less precise description (spanking punished the child). In endorsing the grammar of reinforcing responses and punishing responses, we needn't prejudge how these operations affect behavior; we'll assume that they'll often affect other responses besides those for which they're arranged (e.g., a spanking may also elicit crying). A vocabulary that states the consequences of behavior unambiguously helps us to describe such effects.

COMPARING REINFORCEMENT AND PUNISHMENT

The effect of punishment is simply the opposite of that of reinforcement. The relation between the two is illustrated in Figure 6-1, which presents hypothetical reinforcement and punishment data. The top graph shows changes in a rat's lever pressing during food reinforcement and then during extinction. During *baseline*, when lever pressing has no consequences, responding occurs infrequently. When *reinforcement* begins, responding increases over the first sessions, after which it remains at a fairly stable level. *Extinction* then gradually reduces responding to the former baseline level.

The bottom graph of Figure 6-1 shows changes in the rat's lever pressing during and after punishment of lever presses with electric shock. Because punishment reduces responding, some responding must exist to

FIGURE 6-1   Effects of reinforcement and punishment on the hypothetical lever pressing of a food-deprived rat. The top graph shows unreinforced pressing (baseline), the increase when it produces food (reinforcement), and the return to earlier lower levels when reinforcement ends (extinction). The bottom graph shows pressing maintained by reinforcement (baseline), its decrease when response-produced shock is added (punishment), and the return to earlier higher levels when punishment ends (recovery). Pressing maintained by reinforcement is the baseline against which the effects of punishment are illustrated in the bottom graph because a decrease in responding can't be seen as easily when responding is already infrequent.

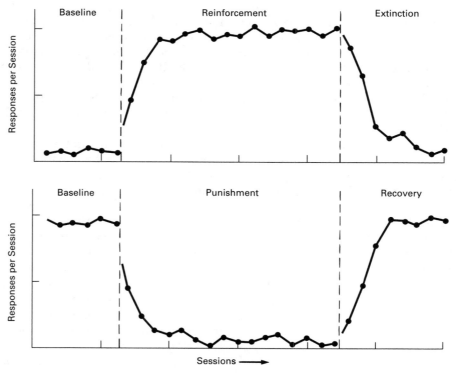

begin with or we couldn't observe a decrease. In this example, responding is already maintained by food reinforcement, which continues throughout all sessions; the effects of punishment are then assessed by superimposing it on this baseline. The *baseline* shows the responding maintained before lever pressing is punished. When *punishment* begins, lever pressing decreases to a maintained low level. In *recovery*, punishment is discontinued and responding gradually returns to the former baseline level.

Reinforcement and punishment are symmetrical: The former increases responding whereas the latter decreases it, but their effects continue as long as the procedures are maintained and disappear after they end (responding returns to earlier levels). Actual rather than hypothetical effects of punishment are shown in Figure 6-2 (Estes, 1944).

FIGURE 6-2   Cumulative record of the effect of punishment superimposed upon a baseline of food reinforcement that continued throughout the session. The response was a rat's lever press and the punisher was shock. The rate of pressing decreased during punishment and recovered after punishment was discontinued. (From Estes, 1944, Figure 10.)

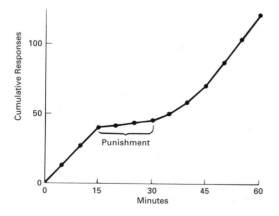

The effects in Figure 6-2 are clear. Nevertheless, the effectiveness of punishment has long been controversial. Punishment was incorporated into Thorndike's early versions of his Law of Effect (cf. Chapter 5). Thorndike argued then that behavior could be stamped out by annoyers as well as stamped in by satisfiers. Statements of Thorndike's law that included the punishment component were called the *strong* Law of Effect. Later, Thorndike withdrew the punishment component and the version that remained, which included only the stamping in of behavior, was called the *weak* Law of Effect. Thorndike based his conclusion on experiments on human verbal learning in which saying "right" to the learner enhanced responding whereas saying "wrong" had less effect than saying nothing. Thorndike accepted the finding as general evidence against the effectiveness of punishment.

Thorndike's conclusion had so much impact that even the data in Figure 6-2 were interpreted to mean that punishment was an ineffective procedure. The argument, based on the recovery of responding after punishment, was that punishment wasn't to be taken seriously as a way of changing behavior because it suppressed responding only temporarily. Yet on the basis of this criterion, reinforcement should also be judged ineffective. For some reason, the effectiveness of punishment was judged by different criteria than the effectiveness of reinforcement. Even though responding was reduced during punishment, investigators looked not at that reduction but rather at the recovered responding after punishment was discontinued. What follows provides reasons for concluding that techniques other than punishment should be used when possible. But if this conclusion is correct, that's because Thorndike and his successors were right for the wrong reasons.

In more recent times, investigators turned again to punishment and studied conditions that can modify its effectiveness in suppressing behavior (e.g., Azrin & Holz, 1966; Church, 1963). For example, experiments with electric shock as the punisher of a pigeon's food-reinforced key pecking showed that the more intense and immediate the punisher, the more effective it is. A punisher introduced at its maximum intensity suppresses responding more effectively than a punisher introduced at low intensity and gradually increased to maximum intensity. Also, the effectiveness of the punisher may change over extended periods of punishment, as when a punisher of low intensity gradually becomes ineffective after many presentations (cf. Azrin & Holz, 1966, pp. 426–427). And, as with extinction, it's easier to reduce the likelihood of a response when some other response that produces the same reinforcer is available than when there are no other alternative responses that produce the same reinforcer.

Experiments on the properties of punishment not only changed the criteria for the effectiveness of punishment; they also raised questions about whether punishment had been judged adequately according to the old criteria. On occasion a single punisher or a few punishers, if intense enough and the consequence of a weakly maintained response, might make a response disappear for most or all of a lifetime. Such exceptional effects might as well be regarded as permanent, but why should we be surprised that recovery can sometimes be so slow that it exceeds an individual life span? Consider the analogous argument for reinforcement. Would we be surprised if winners of million-dollar lottery prizes continued to buy occasional lottery tickets throughout their lives even if that behavior was never again reinforced by a win? We wouldn't reject the existence of extinction on those grounds, so we shouldn't reject the existence of recovery after punishment because punishment occasionally has very durable effects.

Some incidental features of punishment probably contributed to its unusual treatment. A reduction in responding can be studied only if some responding already exists. A response that's never emitted can't be punished. That's why experiments on punishment usually superimpose punishment on reinforced responding. But the effects of punishment then depend on what maintains responding. For example, punishment by shock will probably reduce food-reinforced lever pressing less if a rat is severely food-deprived than if it's only mildly food-deprived.

Another difficulty is that punishing stimuli are likely to have other effects that occur whether or not they're produced by responses. As in reinforcement, the punishment effect must depend on the *relation between responses and punishers* (contingency) and not simply on the *delivery of punishers*. For example, shocks may reduce the rate at which a pigeon pecks a key even when they're delivered independently of key pecks, so before we speak of them as punishers we should be sure that they reduce responding more when they're produced by pecking than when they occur independently of pecking (cf. Azrin, 1956).

Prejudices against recognizing punishment were at times so strong that effective procedures were even given a different name, *passive avoidance*. For example, consider a rat on a platform above an electrified grid that's shocked when it steps down to the grid, so that it's less likely to step down again later. It's appropriate to say that stepping down is punished by shock, but some would say instead that this rat is passively avoiding the punisher, by holding back from stepping down. This usage allowed effective punishment procedures to be discussed in the vocabulary of passive avoidance while other procedures that didn't reduce responding were used to defend the claim that punishment was ineffective.

Punishment is a name for a relation between responding and consequences. The issue is mainly when it's appropriate to apply this name. Early analyses of punishment emphasized the impermanence of its effects. For this reason, punishment long went unacknowledged as a fundamental behavioral operation. But the existence of consequences that reduce responding is no longer questioned. Except that the effects differ in sign, punishment parallels reinforcement: Reinforcement increases reinforced responding and punishment decreases punished responding. Both operations have temporary effects; when they're discontinued, responding returns to earlier levels. Because punishment can modify human behavior, questions inevitably arise about the ethics of its application. But we can't hope to resolve such questions without an adequate analysis of its properties.

THE RELATIVITY OF PUNISHMENT

In experiments on punishment, punishers are usually chosen for their reliable effect on a variety of responses, because such stimuli reveal the effects of punishment most clearly. One such punisher is electric shock, which can be measured accurately and can be presented at levels that are effective and yet don't damage tissue. Such stimuli, however, are only extreme instances of punishers. For example, as we've already seen, some developmentally disabled children chronically engage in head banging, hand biting and other self-injurious behavior. A brief squirt in the face with water mist from the sort of spray bottle that's used to moisten indoor plants is at worst a minor annoyance. When

applied contingent on such behavior, however, it's an effective punisher (Dorsey et al., 1980). As such it's relatively innocuous, especially when compared with the serious damage these children can do to themselves (unfortunately, some who oppose any use of punishment find even this application unacceptable).

Punishment is inevitable because it is arranged by many natural contingencies. The child who teases a barking dog may get bitten and the child who plays with fire may get burned. Furthermore, even stimuli that ordinarily serve as reinforcers can become punishers under appropriate conditions. For example, food that is reinforcing at the beginning of a holiday feast may become aversive by the time the meal has ended. On the other hand, events that superficially seem aversive, such as falling from a height, may be reinforcing under certain circumstances (consider sky diving and ski jumping). Like reinforcers, punishers can't be defined in absolute terms nor in terms of common physical properties. Rather, they must be assessed in terms of the relation between punished responses and the responses occasioned by the punisher.

The Premack principle of reinforcement (Chapter 5) stated that an opportunity to engage in more probable responses will reinforce less probable responses. That analysis has also been extended to punishment (Premack, 1971). Let's return to the apparatus that can control a rat's opportunities to run in a running wheel or drink from a drinking tube. It's been modified by a motor that can either lock the running wheel in position, thereby preventing the rat from running, or rotate it at a fixed speed, thereby forcing the rat to run.

In this apparatus, depriving the rat of opportunities to run while giving it free access to water makes running more probable than drinking; depriving it of water while giving it opportunities to run makes drinking more probable than running (cf. the probabilities of running and drinking in the two parts of Figure 5-10). Rotation of the wheel can now be made a consequence of drinking: Each time the rat drinks, the wheel begins to turn and the rat is forced to run. When running is more probable than drinking, this operation increases drinking, and it's appropriate to say that drinking is reinforced by running. But when running is less probable than drinking, this operation has an opposite effect: Now drinking decreases when running is its consequence, and it's appropriate to say that drinking is punished by running. If their relative probabilities can be reversed, as illustrated in this example, any given response can be either reinforced or punished by any other response.

The stimuli and responses in typical experiments on reinforcement and punishment had been chosen to make those procedures work (e.g., with food-deprived rats, eating is far more probable than lever pressing). They thereby obscured the potential reversibility of consequences as reinforcers and punishers. Responding can be raised or lowered by changing its consequences, and these effects are determined by the behavioral and not the physical properties of the consequences.

SIDE EFFECTS OF PUNISHMENT

As with reinforcers, punishers can have effects independent of their contingent relation to responses. If an organism is shocked or burned or pinched, some of its responses may have little to do with whether these events were brought on by the organism's own behavior. Difficulties arise in analyzing punishment because such effects must be distinguished from those that depend on the relation between responses and their consequences. Some effects of shock may be primarily physiological, as when successive shocks systematically reduce a rat's skin resistance. Depending on the nature of the shock source, the effectiveness of later shocks may then vary with the rat's resistance. Other effects are primarily behavioral, as when the apparatus fails to prevent responses by which the organism can reduce its contact with the shock source (e.g., fur is an insulator, and rats have sometimes minimized effects of shock as a punisher by pressing the lever while lying on their furry backs; Azrin & Holz, 1966). In either case such side effects must be taken into account.

Eliciting Effects of Punishers

Figure 6-3 is from an experiment (Camp, Raymond, & Church, 1967) that compared effects of response-produced and response-independent shock. Lever pressing was maintained by food reinforcement in three groups of rats. Measured against a no-shock control group, shock reduced responding in both groups, but response-produced shock suppressed responding much more than response-independent shock (see also Church, 1969). This difference makes it appropriate to call the response-produced shock a punisher. Events affect behavior most when behavior affects those events in turn (Rachlin, 1967, p. 87). Just as we must distinguish between effects of reinforcer deliveries and effects of the contingent relation between responses and reinforcers, so also we must distinguish between effects of punisher deliveries and effects of the contingent relation between responses and punishers.

The punishment of two classes of species-specific behavior in the Mongolian gerbil (Walters & Glazer, 1971; see also Shet-

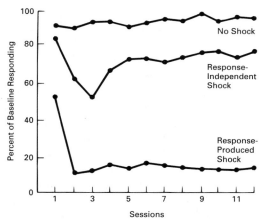

FIGURE 6-3 Effects of response-independent and response-produced shock on rats' lever pressing maintained by food reinforcement. Shock rate in the group given response-independent shock was matched to that in the group given response-produced shock, but response-produced shock reduced responding more than response-independent shock. (From Camp, Raymond, & Church, 1967, Figure 5.)

tleworth, 1978) provides another example. Sand digging, part of the gerbil's nesting behavior, consists of scooping sand and kicking it backwards; alert posturing, a defense reaction occasioned by sudden or aversive stimuli, consists of standing erect on the hindpaws with ears cocked. Delivering shock was difficult in the sandbox where the experiment was conducted, so a tone was established as an aversive stimulus by repeatedly pairing it with shock in a different setting. When contingent upon digging, the tone was an effective punisher. Digging decreased on producing it and recovered after the contingency was discontinued; while digging decreased, alert posturing increased. But contingent on alert posturing, the tone wasn't effective. Alert

posturing increased and didn't return to earlier levels for several sessions after the contingency was discontinued; there was no appreciable change in digging. The eliciting effect of the tone on alert posturing was more powerful than its punishing effect. In punishment as in reinforcement, it's important to acknowledge the separate effects of response-stimulus contingencies and stimulus deliveries.

As another example, consider a monkey in a restraining chair with shock electrodes on its tail (e.g., Morse & Kelleher, 1977, pp. 193–198). At 5-min intervals, the monkey's lever press delivers shock to its own tail. A little while after being placed in the chair, it begins to press. Eventually 5 min pass and its next press delivers a shock (this arrangement is called a 5-min fixed-interval schedule; see Chapter 10). The monkey briefly jumps and for a while stops pressing. But soon it starts again, pressing more and more rapidly until shocking itself once more at the end of the next 5-min interval. It repeats this performance throughout daily sessions. When shock is discontinued, lever pressing virtually ceases; when shock is reinstated, it returns. If shock level is raised, lever pressing increases; if shock level is lowered, it decreases. Shocks depend completely on the monkey's behavior; it would receive no shocks if it didn't press the lever. Why doesn't it just stop pressing?

The paradox is that the same shock that maintains lever pressing when produced by pressing according to a 5-min fixed-interval schedule suppresses lever pressing when produced instead by every press; the same shock can also be used to initiate and maintain escape and avoidance behavior (e.g., Barrett & Stanley, 1980). So how do we decide whether the language of punishment is appropriate? If every lever press produces shock, we call the shock a punisher because it reduces responding. But when a lever presses produces shock only at 5-min intervals, should we call the shock a reinforcer because it generates responding? (It wouldn't help to yield to the temptation to call the monkey a masochist. Masochism is just a name we use when a stimulus that we think should be a punisher serves as a reinforcer; it doesn't explain anything.)

Other experiments showed that even though a schedule in which lever presses produce shock every 2 min usually maintains higher rates of pressing than one in which they produce shock every 6 min, monkeys switch to the one with the longer time between shocks when allowed to choose between them (Pitts & Malagodi, 1991). In other words, the monkeys preferred shocking themselves less often to shocking themselves more often. We might be reminded of the effectiveness of restraints as reinforcers with some children who engage in self-injurious behavior (Chapter 5); they preferred the situation with restraints, in which they couldn't injure themselves, to situations without restraints in which they could (and did).

As long as human behavior includes such problems as self-injury, our concern with such phenomena is justified. We've seen that it's sometimes more appropriate to compare response-produced shock with response-independent shock rather than with no shock at all. Electric shock elicits manual responses such as lever pressing in monkeys. These eliciting effects of shock can be strong enough to override the punishing effects, so that lever pressing occurs in spite of and not because of the punishment contingency. If so, the case is analogous to that of the parent who tries to stop a child from crying by punishing the crying and has trouble because the punisher elicits the very response that the parent is trying to suppress.

Discriminative Effects of Punishers

Another side effect of punishment comes about because punishers can acquire discriminative properties, as when a response is reinforced only when it's also punished. An experiment designed to make response-produced shock signal the availability of food arranged two alternating conditions (Holz & Azrin, 1961). In one, a pigeon's key pecks had no consequences; in the other, every peck produced shock and some pecks produced food reinforcers. A low rate of pecking was maintained when pecks produced no shock, because then they never produced food either; but pecking increased once pecks began to produce shock, because only then did they occasionally produce food. Sample records with food reinforcement completely discontinued are shown for two pigeons in Figure 6-4. With no shock, the rate of pecking was low. When responses began to produce shock, the rate increased. When shock was discontinued, a brief increase in rate (arrows) was followed by a decrease to the earlier low levels.

Again we can ask whether the shocks should be called punishers. In fact, we should conclude from Figure 6-4 that shock was a reinforcer. The main difference between the shock and other more familiar reinforcers is that the shock acquires its power to reinforce through its relation to food; it loses its power if that relation is discontinued. Perhaps these procedures are relevant to human behavior. For example, a battered child might provoke a parent to the point of a beating because the beatings are often followed by more attention from the then-remorseful parent than ever follows less traumatic parent-child interactions. In this example, the beating is analogous to the shock in Figure 6-4 and the parent's attention is analogous to the food. A parent's attention

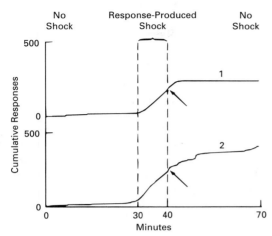

FIGURE 6-4 Discriminative effects of shock. First, two conditions alternated: Pigeons' pecks produced neither food nor shock, or the pecks always produced shock and occasionally produced food. In the sessions shown here, no food was presented. For both pigeons, initially low rates of pecking increased when pecks began to produce shock and decreased to earlier levels when shock was discontinued. (From Holz & Azrin, 1961, Figure 3.)

make the reduction in responding easily visible; for that reason, experiments on punishment often superimpose it on a baseline of reinforced responding. The effectiveness of punishers, like that of reinforcers, is determined by the relative probabilities of the punished response and the responses occasioned by the punisher; punishment occurs when a more probable response forces the organism to engage in a less probable response. Punishment can be complicated by eliciting or discriminative effects of punishers. The task of an experimental analysis is to separate such side effects from the primary effects of the punisher. These effects occur because punishment necessarily includes both stimulus presentations and a contingency between responses and stimuli; the effects of the stimulus presentations must be distinguished from those of the contingency. We now leave punishment and return to reinforcement. We'll see that there are different kinds of complications when responding, instead of being punished by presentation of an aversive stimulus, is reinforced by removal or prevention of that stimulus.

can be a potent reinforcer and may sometimes override the effects of consequences that would otherwise serve as punishers. Thus, a behavioral analysis may be relevant to human problems such as child abuse.

We've seen that punishment is the inverse of reinforcement; it's defined by decreases in consequential responding whereas reinforcement is defined by increases. Its vocabulary parallels that of reinforcement: punishers are stimuli and punishment is an operant or a process. Its effects are ordinarily temporary; responding usually recovers to earlier levels after punishment is discontinued. In studying punishment, baseline levels of responding must be high enough to

Section B   Negative Reinforcement: Escape and Avoidance

Organisms get rid of as well as produce stimuli. For example, a rat doesn't ordinarily expose itself to shock, and if shock does occur the rat escapes from it, given the opportunity. If presenting an aversive stimulus punishes a response, removing or preventing that stimulus may reinforce the response. When a response terminates or prevents an aversive stimulus and becomes more probable for that reason, the stimulus is called a *negative reinforcer* and the operation is called *negative reinforcement*. Positive and negative reinforcement are distinguished by whether a response produces or removes a stimulus.

Later we'll encounter some problems in the vocabulary of positive and negative reinforcement. But the vocabulary has substantial precedent. It's standard usage that *positive* and *negative*, as modifiers of the term *reinforcement*, refer to the consequence produced by responding (whether the response adds something to the environment or takes something away), and that *negative reinforcer* refers to the stimulus itself and not to its removal (if removal of shock reinforces a rat's lever press, shock, not the shock-free period that follows the response, is the negative reinforcer). This vocabulary was established gradually (at one time, negative reinforcement was defined as above in some textbooks but as equivalent to punishment in others; such misunderstandings still appear occasionally: e.g., Kimble, 1993). As indicated by the etymologies introducing each chapter of this text, language evolves. Thus, the evolving language of reinforcement may eventually make the distinction between positive and negative reinforcement of marginal value (cf. Michael, 1975). Nevertheless, when we do invoke the vocabulary of positive and negative reinforcement and punishment, we'll adhere to standard usage, summarized as follows:

1. *Reinforcement* makes the reinforced response *increase*.
2. *Punishment* makes the punished response *decrease*.
3. The modifier *positive* means that the consequence of responding is the *addition* of a stimulus to the organism's environment.
4. The modifier *negative* means that the consequence of responding is the *subtraction* of a stimulus from the organism's environment.

5. *Reinforcers* and *punishers* are stimuli and not the absence of stimuli (given that it's possible to make an unambiguous distinction).

The last item above is parenthetically qualified because the distinction is sometimes difficult. For example, is it more appropriate to think of a traffic ticket in terms of the piece of paper presented to you or your loss of money when you pay the fine? Similarly, is it more appropriate to think of an exam in terms of getting a high grade or avoiding a poor one?

[handwritten marginalia: bad examples]

ESCAPE

Escape procedures are the simplest examples of negative reinforcement: An organism's response *terminates* an aversive stimulus. They differ from avoidance procedures, in which the response prevents or delays an aversive stimulus. This vocabulary is consistent with everyday usage: We *escape* from aversive circumstances that already exist, but we *avoid* potential aversive circumstances that haven't yet happened. For example, you might leave a party to escape from the company already there or to avoid someone expected to arrive later.

In institutional settings for developmentally disabled children, the children sometimes behave aggressively because in that way they escape from simple demands placed upon them, such as working on tasks designed to teach them how to fasten and unfasten clothing buttons. For two such children, aggression dropped to near-zero levels when they could escape from demand situations by engaging in other behavior that was incompatible with aggression (Carr, Newsom, & Binkoff, 1980). But such cases of escape might of course imply that typical demand situations in such settings don't provide enough reinforcers.

Conditions for escape can be arranged for a rat by constructing a compartment with an electrified grid floor. Movement from one place to another as the escape response is illustrated in Figure 6-5, from a shock-escape experiment with rats in a runway (Fowler & Trapold, 1962). Running speed was fastest when the shock was turned off as soon as the rat reached the end of the runway. The longer the delay between reaching the end of the runway and the shock turning off, the slower the rat ran. This is one of many examples of quantitative effects of reinforcement. For example, with both positive and negative reinforcement, immediate reinforcement is more effective than delayed reinforcement (*delay* parameter) and large reinforcers are more effective than small ones (*magnitude* or *intensity* parameter; see parameter in the glossary).

FIGURE 6-5 Relative running speed as a function of delay of shock termination in the escape responding of rats in a runway. The longer the delay between reaching the end of the runway and shock termination, the slower the rats ran. Each point is based on the last 4 of 28 escape trials. (From Fowler & Trapold, 1962, Figure 1)

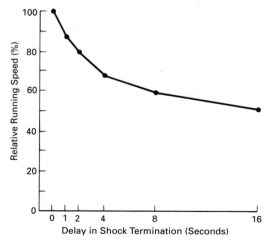

Movement from one place to another makes an effective escape response, but discrete responses such as lever presses are easier to record. A rat's lever press in the presence of shock can turn off the shock, or in the presence of bright light it can turn off the light (e.g., Keller, 1941). If in either case responding increases because of its consequences, we say that the response has been reinforced. Let's therefore compare positive and negative reinforcement: In the absence of food, responding that produces food increases; in the presence of shock, responding that removes shock increases. The parallel is straightforward. Yet escape procedures receive less attention than more complex procedures. Research on negative reinforcement is dominated by avoidance, in which aversive stimuli are prevented or delayed by responses that occur in their absence.

Elicited Responding and Escape

The reason for the relative neglect of research on escape is that it's usually easy to raise the probability of a rat's lever presses or a pigeon's key pecks using positive reinforcement, but it's sometimes difficult to do so using negative reinforcement in escape procedures (e.g., Hoffman & Fleshler, 1959). This is at least in part because the temporal relation between reinforced responses and responses produced by the reinforcer in positive reinforcement differs from that in negative reinforcement. The two conditions are diagrammed in Figure 6-6.

In positive reinforcement, the reinforcer is absent when the reinforced response is emitted. After the response, the reinforcer is presented and occasions other responses. For example, if a rat's lever press is the reinforced response and food is the reinforcer, food is absent while the rat presses; eating doesn't occur until after the press, when food is presented. Lever pressing and eating occur

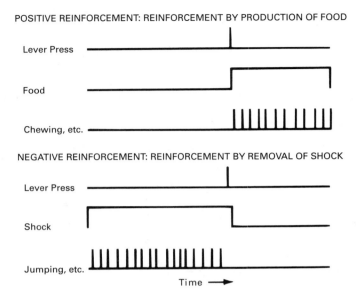

FIGURE 6-6   Different temporal relations between reinforced responses and other responses produced by the reinforcer, in positive reinforcement (top) and in negative reinforcement (bottom). In food reinforcement, the reinforced lever press has already occurred when food delivery produces behavior (e.g., handling the food), so those responses don't compete much with pressing. In shock escape, responses produced by shock (e.g., jumping) occur at the same time that reinforced lever pressing must occur, so those responses do compete with pressing.

at different times and so don't compete directly with each other.

In negative reinforcement, however, the negative reinforcer is present before the reinforced response is emitted; only after the response is it removed. For example, if a rat's lever press is the reinforced response and shock is the negative reinforcer, shock is present before lever presses occur. The shock generates responses such as elicited jumping or behavior that reduces contact with the shock source. As long as shock is present and produces these responses, some of them will compete with lever pressing. Once a lever press turns off the shock, they decrease and

no longer compete. But once shock is absent, further presses can't have the consequence of terminating shock.

Similarly, if the negative reinforcer is bright light from which the rat can escape by pressing a lever, the rat may reduce the effects of the light by closing its eyes and hiding its head in a corner. Any movement from that position is punished by greater exposure to the light, so the rat isn't likely to come out of the corner and press the lever. Getting a rat to escape from light by lever pressing requires procedures that reduce the likelihood of such competing responses (Keller, 1941).

The Ambiguity of Distinguishing Between Positive and Negative Reinforcement

Whether stimuli are presented or removed may be a less important criterion for distinguishing between positive and negative reinforcement than whether responses generated by the reinforcer occur at times when they can compete with the reinforced response. An experiment on escape from cold illustrates the point (Weiss & Laties, 1961). A rat was placed in a cold chamber in which its lever presses were reinforced by the operation of a heat lamp. On the one hand, this procedure could be called positive reinforcement: It involves adding energy in the form of heat to the environment when a lever press occurs. On the other hand, cold may function as a stimulus through its effects on temperature receptors in the rat's skin. Cold is the absence of heat, but it's also a significant and potentially aversive environmental event. By this interpretation the procedure should be called negative reinforcement, because turning on the heat lamp after a response terminates the effects of cold.

In escape from cold, a case can as easily be made that reinforcement involves presenting a stimulus as that it involves removing a stimulus. It's easy to find ambiguities in other instances of reinforcement. For example, we can argue that water reinforcers terminate aversive stimuli generated by a dry mouth, or that food reinforcers terminate aversive stimuli generated by the depletion of nutrients in the bloodstream (cf. Hull, 1943). Why then did the distinction between positive and negative reinforcement take on behavioral significance?

Let's reconsider the rat in the cold. Before the reinforced lever press occurred, the rat huddled in a corner and shivered. Those responses reduced the likelihood that the rat would press the lever. Once a lever press occurred, the heat lamp turned on and those competing responses became less likely, but a rat that's no longer cold can't escape from cold. Responses that competed with the reinforced response occurred before rather than after reinforcement, so this example is more like escape from shock than like production of food or water (cf. Figure 6-6). Thus, it's probably more appropriate to call this negative instead of positive reinforcement.

We haven't completely eliminated the ambiguity. Reinforcement always involves a change in an organism's situation, so it inevitably leads to differences in responding before and after the change. At best, we can regard such changes as producing a continuum of effects, ranging from those in which other responses are highly likely to precede and compete with the reinforced response to those in which they don't do so or perhaps even raise the likelihood of the reinforced response.

AVOIDANCE

In avoidance, the aversive stimulus isn't present when the reinforced response occurs. The two major varieties of avoidance procedure are called *deletion* and *postponement*. Deletion procedures are analogous to swatting a mosquito before it gets to you: Once you've swatted it, you've permanently prevented that particular mosquito from biting you. Postponement procedures are analogous to putting coins in a parking meter: You postpone the violation flag as long as you put in coins and reset the meter, but once you stop putting in coins, the meter eventually runs out.

As an example of a deletion procedure, imagine a rat placed in a chamber with a lever and a floor grid through which brief shocks may be delivered. Shocks are scheduled to be delivered once a minute, but if the rat presses the lever before the next one is due, that shock is omitted. In this procedure, the rat can avoid shock completely by pressing at least once a minute. Deletion procedures are sometimes conducted in discrete trials. For example, a light comes on for 30 s. If the rat presses the lever during the 30 s, no shock is delivered at the end of the trial; it's delivered only if the rat fails to press.

Let's now consider an example of a postponement procedure (Sidman, 1953). Two clocks control shock deliveries. Which clock runs depends on whether the last event was a shock or a lever press. The first clock times the *shock-shock* or *SS interval*, the time between shocks if the rat doesn't press the lever. Whenever a shock is delivered, this clock resets to zero and starts timing a new SS interval. Whenever the rat does press the lever, control shifts to the second clock. This clock times the *response-shock* or *RS interval*, the time by which each lever press postpones the next possible shock. While this clock runs, each press resets it to zero and starts a new RS interval. In these circumstances, the rat can postpone the shock indefinitely by always pressing the lever before the current RS interval ends. If no response occurs and a shock is delivered at the end of an RS interval, the SS-interval clock takes over again. With this procedure, called *Sidman avoidance* or *continuous avoidance*, avoidance responding can be studied independently of escape responding; shock can be prevented by avoidance responses, but once delivered the shock is so brief that there's little if any opportunity to escape from it.

Data for one rat's lever pressing are shown in Figure 6-7, which presents rate of responding as a function of RS interval with SS interval as a parameter. Across functions, the RS interval that produced the highest rate depended on the SS interval. First consider an avoidance schedule with a 6-s RS in-

FIGURE 6-7 Rate of Rat 46's lever pressing as a function of RS interval, with SS interval as a parameter. The SS interval is the time between shocks if no responding occurs between shocks. The RS interval is the time by which each press postpones the next possible shock. (From Sidman, 1953, Figure 1A)

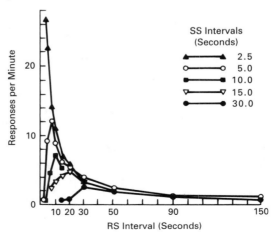

terval and a 2-s SS interval. Any responding at all reduces shock, and a rate of one response every 4 s or so avoids shock completely. When the RS interval is shorter than the SS interval, however, some patterns of pressing increase rather than decrease shock. For example, consider a schedule with a 2-s RS interval and a 6-s SS interval. A rat that never presses receives a shock every 5 s, or 12/min. But if the rat presses every 3 s, a shock is delivered 2 s after each press and the rat receives 20 shocks/min (strictly speaking, if this increase in shock rate reduces responding, it's appropriate to say that responding is punished). The rat can avoid shock completely by responding so fast that 2 s never go by without a press, but the increase in shock produced by lower rates may prevent the rat from ever attaining such a performance.

Avoidance behavior may be persistent after a long history of avoidance; as we'll see below, it can be slow to extinguish. But the consequence of an effective avoidance response is that nothing happens: The aversive event is successfully avoided. So despite the persistence of avoidance behavior once it's adequately in place, it's often hard to get it started. This may explain why safety measures and other preventive procedures are not often shaped by natural contingencies. Someone who's never been in a serious automobile accident may be less likely to fasten a seat belt than someone who has, and someone who's never had a bad experience with fire may be less likely to install a smoke detector than someone who has. One significant problem in medicine is the compliance of patients with regimens such as taking prescribed medications. Many patients stop taking their medications once their symptoms have disappeared even though further doses may have continued benefits. And with vitamin or mineral supplements that can prevent dietary deficiencies, taking a dose is

followed by nothing happening right from the start. This problem exists over a wide range of preventive measures, from immunizations to birth control and from purifying drinking water to using sterile surgical equipment. We shouldn't be surprised that such measures are sometimes difficult to shape up and maintain.

Species-Specific Defense Reactions

An advantage of avoidance over escape procedures is that the reinforced response occurs in the absence of the aversive stimulus. Thus, other responses generated by the aversive stimulus don't compete continuously with the avoidance response. But just as it's easier to turn some responses than others into escape responses, it may be easier to turn some responses than others into avoidance responses. For example, pigeons avoid shock more readily if they can do so by moving from one side of a chamber to another than if they can do so only by pecking (e.g., Macphail, 1968). In avoidance procedures, it's more difficult to make the case that such differences depend on competition between reinforced responses and other responses generated by the aversive stimulus. It's been argued instead that the differences arise because organisms are variously equipped with defense responses that are species-specific. If so, success with avoidance procedures will depend upon whether the experimenter chooses a response that the organism is already prepared to emit in aversive situations (Bolles, 1970; Seligman, 1970).

Bolles summarizes the argument as follows:

> What keeps animals alive in the wild is that they have very effective *innate* defensive reactions which occur when they encounter any kind of new or sudden stimulus. . . . These defensive reactions are elicited by the appearance of the predator and by the sudden appearance of innocuous objects. These re-

sponses are always near threshold so that the animal will take flight, freeze, or threaten whenever any novel stimulus event occurs. It is not necessary that the stimulus event be paired with shock, or pain, or some other unconditioned stimulus. The mouse does not scamper away from the owl because it has learned to escape the painful claws of the enemy; it scampers away from anything happening in its environment, and it does so merely because it is a mouse. The gazelle does not flee from an approaching lion because it has been bitten by lions; it runs away from any large object that approaches it, and it does so because this is one of its species-specific defense reactions. Neither the mouse nor the gazelle can afford to *learn* to avoid; survival is too urgent, the opportunity to learn is too limited, and the parameters of the situation make the necessary learning impossible. (Bolles, 1970, p. 33)

Avoidance, as the Bolles passage implies, has sometimes been a focus of controversy. Bolles' point concerns the extent to which avoidance behavior is learned. Without doubt, current behavior can be significantly determined by evolutionary variables (even the capacity for responding to be reinforced must have evolved in some way). It's generally accepted that species-specific behavior often limits what can be learned.

Consider, for example, the transition from elicited to emitted responding in a rat's acquisition of signaled avoidance (a deletion procedure). In this procedure, a warning stimulus such as a buzzer precedes shock. If the rat responds during the buzzer and before shock, the shock is omitted; if it responds after the shock starts, the shock is removed. In other words, the rat avoids shock by responding during the warning stimulus; if it fails to avoid and shock starts, it then escapes from shock by responding.

In such experiments, a frequent choice of response is some form of locomotion, such as jumping a hurdle or running from one side of the chamber to the other. Furthermore, the avoidance response is typically the same as the escape response. With rats, such locomotor responses are likely to be elicited by aversive stimuli even in the absence of a response-shock contingency. Once they've been produced by shock, they may continue when shock is absent. Thus, the rat's first few avoidance responses may occur mainly because of their earlier elicitation by shock (cf. Chapter 4 and Azrin, Hutchinson, & Hake, 1967). After avoidance responding begins, it's an experimental question whether it continues because it prevents shock or because it's an instance of species-specific behavior that's easily generated by aversive situations.

Some differences may also depend on species-specific determinants of what is aversive. For example, demonstrations of escape from or avoidance of the sound of running water by beavers raise the intriguing possibility that the aversiveness of such sounds contributes to the building and maintenance of their dams and lodges (cf. Hartman, 1975).

The Nature of the Reinforcer in Avoidance

Another issue is specifying what reinforces avoidance responding. When a successful avoidance response occurs, its important consequence is that nothing happens to the organism. How can the absence of an event affect behavior? According to one view, avoidance responding is maintained because the organism is escaping from some properties of the situation that accompanied past aversive stimuli. This view evolved from earlier procedures in which a warning stimulus preceded shock and the organism prevented shock by responding in the presence of the warning stimulus. Avoidance was most easily acquired when the avoidance response terminated the warning stimulus as well as prevented shock. It was assumed that the aversiveness of the warning stimulus was established through its consistent relation to shock, and therefore that this immediate consequence, escape from the warning stimulus, was the effective reinforcer. In fact, one purpose of Sidman's avoidance schedule was to demonstrate avoidance without a warning stimulus.

This view, that the warning stimulus acquired its own aversive properties through its consistent relation to the aversive stimulus and that the termination of the warning stimulus therefore reinforced the avoidance response, was called a *two-process theory of avoidance* (e.g., Kamin, 1956). The main issue was the nature of the reinforcer. Some theorists were willing to accept the fact of avoidance without appealing to some reinforcing event occurring at the moment of the avoidance response. Others felt that it was necessary to specify such an event. When, as in Sidman avoidance, the event couldn't be located in some environmental warning stimulus that terminated with a response, these theorists instead located it inside the organism. It was argued, for example, that the organism's state just after a response, when shock wasn't imminent, was reinforcing relative to its state long after a response, when shock might occur at any moment. The latter state acquired aversive properties through its relation to shock and, like a warning stimulus, was terminated by a response. This change of state presumably occurred immediately with each avoidance response, so it was assumed that an account based on other temporally remote events was unnecessary.

Debates on the status of such avoidance theories have a complex history (e.g., Anger, 1963; Herrnstein & Hineline, 1966; Hineline, 1977), with some even changing sides (e.g., Schoenfeld, 1950, 1969). Gradually the issues shifted to experimental questions about the conditions under which avoidance responding can be maintained: Must the organism be able to reduce the total number of shocks in a session or is it sufficient for the organism to be able to postpone individual shocks even though the same number of shocks is eventually delivered? It turns out that either condition can maintain avoidance responding, so these questions were soon replaced by ones about the establishing operations that make negative reinforcers effective (Hineline, 1970, 1981).

An establishing operation that makes positive reinforcers more effective is *deprivation*. The analogous operation for negative reinforcers is *presentation* (it would be called *satiation* were the stimulus food instead of shock); it's the presentation of aversive stimuli that makes their removal reinforcing. Even more so than with positive reinforcement, these establishing effects must be distinguished from discriminative, eliciting and other effects of stimuli. Furthermore, the relativity of reinforcement holds for negative as well as positive reinforcement. An avoidance procedure involves response-contingent transitions from one situation to another, and its effectiveness is determined by the situation that follows the avoidance response as well as the one that precedes it.

An example is provided by a case in which not every shock is avoidable. Can avoidance responding be maintained when responding reduces the likelihood of shock but, unlike Sidman avoidance, doesn't reliably postpone each one? Herrnstein and Hineline (1966) arranged an avoidance schedule in which a rat was shocked with some probability at the end of every 2 s. Shock occurred with one probability if no lever press occurred and with a different probability if a press did occur. For example, in one condition a starting shock probability of 0.3 was reduced to 0.2 by a press: If the rat pressed at least once every 2 s, it reduced the shock rate from 9 to 6 shocks/min. Lever pressing was maintained by this procedure.

Now consider a case in which each lever press raises the shock probability from 0.1 to 0.2: now, by pressing at least once every 2 s the rat increases the shock rate from 3 to 6 shocks/min. Even though the consequence of pressing is still a shock probability of 0.2, the rat stops pressing. Relative to a starting shock probability of 0.3, the transition to a shock probability of 0.2 reinforces responding; relative to one of 0.1, it punishes responding.

Shocks were delivered probabilistically in this procedure, so even with shock probabilities that maintained avoidance responding (e.g., 0.3 reduced to 0.1 by lever pressing) some presses were immediately followed by shock and some periods without presses passed without shock. Thus, no consistent temporal relation existed between individual responses and individual shocks. Nevertheless, the likelihood of shock increased more rapidly on the average over time after no pressing than over time after a press. Thus, those who sought an immediate consequence of responding could argue that the reduction in average aversiveness produced by a lever press was sufficient to reinforce avoidance responding. And so the debate went.

These positions illustrate the difference between *molecular* and *molar* orientations toward the analysis of behavior. The first deals with behavior in terms of moment-to-moment sequences of events in a given setting; the second deals with properties that can be measured only over extended time periods. For example, a molecular approach to avoidance examines the individual time intervals separating individual responses and individual shocks, whereas a molar view examines the more general relation between rate of responding and rate of shock over a large sample of responses and shocks (note that rate can be determined only by sampling events over an extended period of time).

The issues haven't been and perhaps can't be resolved. The relative importance of molecular or molar properties of behavior can be different in different settings. It's also reasonable to assume that evolution has equipped organisms with the capacity to respond differentially to many properties of the situations in which they find themselves. Situations can be created in which a rat postpones shocks within trials even though it doesn't reduce the overall shock rate, and in which it reduces the overall shock rate even though responding shortens the time to the next shock (Hineline, 1981). Thus, there seems no reason to assume that an organism whose responding is determined by the molecular properties of one situation (e.g., the consistent temporal relations between responding and shocks created by the RS and SS intervals of Sidman avoidance) would be incapable of responding according to the molar properties of another (e.g., the consistent overall relations between response rate and shock rate created by a probabilistic avoidance schedule). If this is so, it's not a matter of choosing one or the other approach but rather of deciding which is more appropriate to the analysis of a given situation.

EXTINCTION

As with positive reinforcement and punishment, the effects of negative reinforcement are temporary. And as with these other operations, the effects of terminating contingencies between responses and aversive stimuli must be distinguished from the effects of simply terminating the aversive stimuli. In shock escape, turning off the shock eliminates responding simply because there's no occasion for escape in the absence of the aversive stimulus. But in avoidance, turning off the shock source is sometimes considered an extinction operation. If avoidance responding is maintained at such a rate that shocks are rare, the absence of shocks will make little difference and responding will continue for a long time. In fact, one widely acknowledged property of avoidance responding is its persistence after aversive stimuli are discontinued. For that reason, some have seen avoidance as relevant to some cases of persistence of human behavior, as in compulsions.

Consider the alternatives. With food reinforcement, we can arrange extinction either by turning off the feeder or by breaking the connection between responses and the feeder. Both have the same effect: Food is no longer delivered. That isn't so with shock escape or avoidance. Shock continues if responses can no longer remove or prevent it. In Sidman avoidance, for example, all shocks would be determined by the SS clock; responses would no longer operate the RS clock. This procedure would discontinue the response-shock contingency, but it would also increase the number of shocks if responding had been keeping shock rate low. Thus, by itself this procedure could not separate the effects of changing shock rate from those of changing the contingency.

Discontinuing the aversive stimulus has been the more common extinction procedure in avoidance, but presenting the aversive stimulus while discontinuing the consequences of responding more closely parallels extinction after positive reinforcement. The time course of extinction depends on which operation is used and on the way in which the operation changes the rate at which aversive stimuli occur (cf. Hineline, 1977, pp. 377–381). In any case, paralleling our accounts of extinction after positive reinforcement and of recovery from punishment, extinction after negative reinforcement shows that the effects of negative reinforcement are temporary.

POSITIVE AND NEGATIVE PUNISHMENT

The distinction between positive and negative reinforcement is easily extended to positive and negative punishment (though here, too, ambiguous cases are possible). Responses can be punished by some events, such as shock or forced running in a running wheel. Responses also can be punished by the termination of events. For example, removing food contingent on a food-deprived rat's lever presses is likely to reduce the rate of pressing. The problem is that if this is negative punishment it might be hard to demonstrate. If the rat is food deprived and food is available, it will probably eat rather than press, so we won't have many opportunities to punish lever pressing by removing the food (consider Figure 6-6 with food and shock reversed). For this reason, studies of negative punishment haven't usually removed the positive reinforcer itself; paralleling the emphasis on avoidance rather than escape in studies of negative reinforcement, they've instead removed a stimulus in the presence of which responses are reinforced.

For example, suppose two levers are available to a monkey and that presses on one lever produce food whenever a light is on. We can expect some presses on the other lever, but we can punish them by making each one produce a time period during which the light turns off and presses on the first lever won't produce food. Such periods are called *timeout*. (These procedures are sometimes called *punishment by timeout from positive reinforcement*: e.g., Ferster, 1958. Those that signal negative punishment have been called *omission training*: Sheffield, 1965; see also Chapter 12.)

Timeout originated in experiments with pigeons and rats and monkeys, but it's now probably best known in its human applications (e.g., Wolf, Risley, & Mees, 1964). For example, a period of time in an isolation room has sometimes been used to punish the problem behavior of institutionalized children. But as we've seen in other examples, judgments about whether particular events will be reinforcers or punishers are sometimes difficult. When timeout in isolation was used in an attempt to punish the tantrums of a 6-year-old autistic girl, her tantrums increased substantially instead of decreasing. This child often engaged in self-stimulation (e.g., creating visual flicker by waving her fingers closely in front of her eyes), but this behavior was often interrupted by the staff. For her, time in the isolation room was a reinforcer because there she could engage in the self-stimulation without interruption (Solnick, Rincover, & Peterson, 1977).

As with any form of punishment, the main function of timeout is to reduce behavior, but it's too often applied without attention to alternative behavior that could be reinforced (Winett & Winkler, 1972). Some who use timeout without understanding its behavioral basis apply it counterproductively. For example, contemporary daycare centers for preschoolers are likely to use a designated area rather than an isolation room for timeout. A child who disturbs other children in a playgroup might be sent to sit for 5 min on a piece of carpet near the play area, in view of the other children. Suppose that the child sits quietly for 4 min and then begins to cry or act up. The staff person who rigidly requires 5 min of timeout might then let the child return to the playgroup at the very time when the child is again acting disruptively; it would have been better to "catch the child being good" and to have allowed the return at the end of 3 or 4 min (after all, 4 min of sitting quietly is already a very long time for a preschooler).

THE LANGUAGE OF AVERSIVE CONTROL

The presentation or removal of stimuli can reinforce or punish behavior. Reinforcement is most effective if the reinforced response is compatible with the responding occasioned by the reinforcer. Inversely, punishment is most effective if the punished response is incompatible with or at least independent of the responding occasioned by the punisher. Thus, it may be easy to reinforce jumping with shock removal (escape) but hard to punish it with shock presentation.

Stimuli that can reinforce by their presentation can also punish by their removal, and vice versa. We therefore spoke of *punishers*, *negative reinforcers* and *aversive stimuli*. We introduced each one in a different context, but this was fitting because context determines the behavioral functions of any stimulus. Thus, we introduced aversive stimuli in connection with elicitation, punishers in the discussion of consequences that reduced responding, and negative reinforcers in the treatment of consequences that increased responding. It would be convenient if we could assume that each term identified different aspects of a single category of events. We might then speak of shock interchangeably as an aversive stimulus, a punisher or a negative reinforcer, depending on the situation.

For many stimuli much of the time, this assumption is probably correct. If we know a stimulus is effective as a punisher, we can reasonably expect it to be effective as a negative reinforcer; this consistency is part of our justification for calling it aversive. Consistencies are to be expected because these categories have their origins in relations among the probabilities of different response classes. But these very probabilities should remind us of the relativity of reinforcers and punishers. We must beware of taking the assumption too much for granted. The fact that we may easily reinforce jumping with shock removal whereas we may not so effectively punish it with shock presentation shows that the symmetry of reinforcement and punishment has limits.

Failures of symmetry between reinforcement and punishment have perhaps encouraged attempts to reduce either one to a special case of the other. Some instances of punishment have been described in the language of *passive avoidance*: By not responding, the organism was passively avoiding the stimulus arranged as a punisher for responding. But then we might as well say that not responding (e.g., not stepping down from a platform onto an electrified grid) is a response that can be reinforced. If the language works in this case, why not in any case of punishment?

The question of what counts as behavior is implicit in such arguments. Whenever responding is punished, we could say that not-responding is reinforced; whenever responding is reinforced, we could say that not-responding is punished. Once we extend our vocabulary that way, the difference between reinforcement and punishment seems to vanish. Yet we usually can tell the difference between cases of reinforcement and cases of punishment. In fact, the differences are often of serious concern. For example, we can't be indifferent to whether a parent reinforces a child's cooperative behavior

with praise or punishes the failure to cooperate with beatings.

It's easier to speak in terms of discrete responses than in terms of their absence. When we can, therefore, we'll choose direct descriptions in terms of recordable responses such as lever presses or key pecks over indirect ones in terms of what's not happening. An organism exhibits more or less behavior at different times, and we don't have to assume that all failures to act are in themselves actions. Just as we don't have to achieve absolute zero to acknowledge that temperature is a dimension that varies in quantity, we don't have to produce a totally nonbehaving organism to acknowledge that an organism's behavior is a dimension that can change in quantity. The behavior called not-responding (or other behavior) is a class that allows the totality of behavior to be constant, so that when summed the probabilities always add up to one, but that gives us one degree of freedom too many. If we punish a response, we should know what happens to it before we go looking for an account in terms of other behavior, and we should know what else the organism is doing before we start speaking of not-responding as behavior.

The Ethics of Aversive Control

The behavioral properties of aversive control have implications that are consistent with ethical arguments against aversive control. For example, a parent who arranges aversive consequences for a child's behavior may acquire aversive properties. To the extent that the child then learns to escape from or avoid the parent's company, contingencies other than those available to the parent are likely to begin to influence the child's behavior. But if punishment seems the only effective technique for reducing the self-mutilating behavior of an autistic child, punishment might be a lesser evil than the permanent damage the child might self-inflict. Ethical precepts are concerned with the acceptable and unacceptable outcomes of our actions, which implies that the consequences of behavior mustn't be ignored.

In a discussion of the status of our culture and its progress in finding alternatives to aversive control, B. F. Skinner came to the following conclusion:

> Even in politics and government the power to punish has been supplemented by a more positive support of the behavior which conforms to the interests of the governing agency. But we are still a long way from exploiting the alternatives, and we are not likely to make any real advance so long as our information about punishment and the alternatives to punishment remains at the level of casual observation. (Skinner, 1953, pp. 192–193)

Skinner included techniques of reinforcement among his "alternatives to punishment." Unfortunately, if we look at the behavior of those who deliver reinforcers or punishers, we see that effects of reinforcement often show up long after the reinforcer is delivered (the effect of reinforcing a child's diligent schoolwork each day might not be obvious until several days have gone by), whereas the effects of punishment often show up right away (one effect of slapping or scolding a child who is teasing a sibling is that the teasing stops immediately). Thus, delivering a punisher is much more likely to produce immediate consequences than delivering a reinforcer. That means that people probably find it easier to learn techniques of aversive control than to learn techniques of reinforcement. But it doesn't mean that the aversive techniques are better.

Some argue against any kind of modification of behavior, whether involving aversive stimuli or positive reinforcers. But those who make such arguments should recognize that our behavior is being modified all the time, both by natural contingencies and by the artificial ones created by those around us. Denying it won't make those contingencies go away, and a counterargument is that our best defense against the misuse of behavioral techniques is to learn as much as we can about how they work.

Chapter 7
Operants: The Selection of Behavior

A. Shaping: Differential Reinforcement of Successive Approximations
Natural and Artificial Selection in Shaping

B. Differentiation and Induction
Response Classes
Some Examples of Differential Reinforcement
Operant Classes: Function Versus Topography

C. Operant Structure
Differential Reinforcement of Temporal Organization
Complex Behavior: Maze Learning
Response Sequences: Chaining Versus Temporally Extended Units
Operant Classes and Novel Behavior

Operant, *a class of responses, can be traced to the Latin* opus, *work, which is also a source of* operation *and* copy. Class *can be traced to the Latin* classus, *a division of Roman citizens eligible for military draft and perhaps thereby a summons or call. In* classify, *it is linked to the suffix,* -fy, *a form of the Latin* facere, *to do.*

Forms of facere *appear in* fact, modify, difficult *and* effect. *In* specify, *it is linked to* species, *a name for another type of class that is selected. By way of Latin, these come from the Indo-European* spek-, *to see or observe, and are closely related to* expect, introspect, skeptic, telescope *and* spy. *In* office, *from* opi- *plus* -ficere, *and thus the doing of work, it is also linked to* operant. Work *itself has Greek origins, and is related to* organism *through the Greek* organon (tool).

We've seen how we can change behavior by presenting stimuli and by arranging consequences for responding. One way to discuss the effects of these operations is in terms of the relative positions of responses in a behavior hierarchy: The organism's behavior consists of a repertory of responses, each with a different probability. But if we restrict our attention only to these responses, we miss some of the most interesting features of those changes in behavior we call learning; we miss the circumstances in which an organism comes to respond in new ways. We must therefore examine how we can add new responses to an organism's repertory. In this chapter we begin by considering *shaping*, a procedure for generating new responses. This will lead us to consider how classes of responses are defined as units of behavior, in the concept of the *operant*. This concept provides a basis for discussing the structure of behavior.

The rat's lever press and the pigeon's key peck have often served as our examples of responses. But if we simply place a rat in front of a lever or a pigeon in front of a key, we might not observe presses or pecks. We might be fortunate with some organisms, when responses occur right away. But others might remain so long without responding that they exceed our patience. Reinforcement can't have any effect if the response to be reinforced is never emitted. Fortunately, there's an alternative. Instead of waiting for the response, we can generate it by successively reinforcing others that more and more closely approximate it.

Section A   **Shaping: Differential Reinforcement of Successive Approximations**

Consider the pigeon's key peck. Once the pigeon begins to eat whenever the feeder is operated, you operate the feeder only when the pigeon turns toward the key. After you reinforce two or three movements toward the key, you then reinforce not just any movement toward the key but only those that include forward motion of the beak. By this time, the pigeon is spending most of its time in front of the key, so you can shift your attention from its turning toward the key to its forward beak movements. These more closely approximate key pecking than turns toward the key, and once you've guaranteed that they'll continue to occur by reinforcing them, it's no longer necessary for you to reinforce turning toward the key. By this time, the pigeon's beak movements are full-fledged pecks and soon one strikes the key. At this point, you can withdraw, because you've arranged the apparatus so that further pecks operate the feeder automatically.

An experienced experimenter can shape a pigeon's key peck with just 10 or 15 reinforcer deliveries. Some aspects of skill in shaping can be stated explicitly. For example, reinforcing movements is more likely to shape responding efficiently than reinforcing postures. Other aspects can't be formulated so readily. For example, shaping usually compromises between extremes of frequent and infrequent delivery of reinforcers. Frequent delivery leads to quicker satiation and may overly strengthen some early responses that later won't be part of the

response to be shaped. On the other hand, infrequent delivery may reduce responding in general, and once the organism becomes inactive the progress in shaping up to that point may be lost. The experimenter must work within the limits imposed by these extremes, but no explicit rules exist for judging just where these limits lie (cf. Platt, 1973; Eckerman et al., 1980).

Furthermore, some features of shaping are fairly specific to the particular response and organism being studied, whereas others are relevant to shaping a variety of responses in a variety of organisms. For example, an experimenter who has worked often with pigeons knows that reinforcing a small beak movement aimed directly at the key will more effectively produce key pecking than reinforcing a large sidewise beak movement that finishes in front of the key. On the other hand, whatever the response and the organism, an opportunity to reinforce a response shouldn't be missed if it more closely approximates the response to be shaped than any other response that's been reinforced before.

NATURAL AND ARTIFICIAL SELECTION IN SHAPING

Shaping is a variety of selection that provides an ontogenic parallel to the phylogenic selection that occurs in biological evolution (Donahoe, Burgos, & Palmer, 1993). It's most obvious when used by a human trainer, as in the teaching of skills to a seeing-eye dog (cf. Pryor, 1985; Squier, 1993). In such cases, it's an example of *artificial* selection, just as the breeding of cattle is artificial selection in the phylogenic case. But shaping can also occur as a result of *natural* contingencies.

For example, male cowbirds in different parts of the United States sing different dialects of birdsong (as is usually the case among songbirds, the female cowbird doesn't sing). A female is most likely to respond with mating-pattern postures to songs that sound most like the ones she heard in her youth, which were in the dialect of local males. When a foreign male is introduced, he begins singing in his own dialect. But he sings with variations, and the more time he spends in her presence, the more his song takes the form of the local dialect. His acquired dialect is a product of natural ontogenic selection: her differential reactions were reinforcers, and they shaped his song (e.g., King & West, 1985).

Shaping typically involves quantitative changes along one or more dimensions of an organism's behavior, but sometimes it appears to produce qualitative changes. Consider the following example involving the shaping of a rat's high-force lever presses (Catania & Harnad, 1988, p. 476). The rat produces food by pressing on a counterweighted lever that protrudes into the chamber at a height requiring the rat to stand on its hind legs to reach it. We begin with the counterweight set at a modest level. At this setting the rat presses easily by resting one or both forepaws on the lever. Over successive reinforcers, we gradually raise the counterweight until the required force is near the rat's own weight. Once the force exceeds the rat's weight, pressing will be effective only if a new topography emerges. Pushing down on the lever with both hind legs on the floor doesn't work any more. Instead, the rat's paws come up off the floor. While hanging on the lever the rat must now lift its hind legs to the chamber wall, where a wire mesh allows it a firm grip. Even with the counterweight exceeding its own weight, the rat can now depress the lever by pulling between its forelegs and hind legs. Whether the rat makes the change to the new topography depends jointly on its behavior, its anatomy and the apparatus. For example, it will be less likely to produce the new topography

involving both forelegs and hind legs if it got up to high-force pressing by jumping on the lever instead of by pressing it.

This example illustrates two kinds of ontogenic selection, one gradual and the other relatively abrupt. The first occurred with the counterweight below the rat's own weight, and the second occurred when that weight was exceeded. (There are analogies in phylogenic selection, as when the gradual quantitative changes produced by selection relative to a population mean are contrasted with the more abrupt changes produced by catastrophic environmental events. In phylogenic evolution, the latter changes are sometimes called *saltations*. Cf. Chapter 3.)

As illustrated by this example, the different properties of different responses that might be shaped make shaping an art. This art may be applicable to many varied skills, such as gymnastics, lovemaking, playing a musical instrument, seduction, penmanship and setting someone up as a victim of a con game. As these examples suggest, shaping can be put to either good use or bad, and many use it without even knowing that they're doing so (those too might be called cases of ontogenic natural selection). As with reinforcement and punishment, when shaping is put to good use, it might as well be done effectively; when it's put to bad use, the best defense against it is knowing how it works.

Shaping is based upon *differential reinforcement*: At successive stages, some responses are reinforced and others aren't. In addition, the criteria for differential reinforcement change as responding changes, in *successive approximations* to the response to be shaped. The property of behavior that makes shaping effective is that behavior is variable. No two responses are the same, and reinforcement of one response produces a spectrum of responses, each differing from the reinforced response along such dimensions as topography (form), force, magnitude and direction. Of these responses, some are closer to the response to be shaped than others and may be selected to be reinforced next. Reinforcing these responses produces still others, some of which may come even closer to the response to be shaped. Thus, reinforcement can be used to change the spectrum of responses until the one to be shaped occurs.

This aspect of shaping is sometimes supplemented by other effects of reinforcers. Some reinforcers increase activity. For example, food delivery makes a food-deprived pigeon active (it's therefore difficult to use food to reinforce its holding of a posture; cf. Blough, 1958). Thus, a response more closely approximating the one to be shaped occasionally occurs simply because the delivery of some reinforcers makes an organism more active.

There's a paradox to shaping. Reinforcement is said to raise the probability of the reinforced response. But no response is ever repeated exactly. How then can we appeal to reinforcement as the basis for the shaped response when reinforcers are delivered after responses that only approximate that response? In fact, if individual responses are never repeated, how can we speak of reinforcement at all? We acknowledged this problem in Chapter 1 but didn't resolve it. In what follows, we'll see that we can't deal with just single responses; we must deal with *classes* of responses.

Section B **Differentiation and Induction**

If we watched a rat's lever presses we might see the rat press the lever with either paw or both paws or by sitting on it or perhaps even by biting it. Each is a different response; even if two presses were made with the same paw they wouldn't be identical. Nevertheless, we call all of them lever presses. On the other hand, if the rat made similar movements at the other end of its chamber, distant from the

lever, we wouldn't call those responses lever presses no matter how closely they resembled the earlier ones that did operate the lever.

We can't discuss behavior just in terms of individual responses. Responses are instances of behavior, so each can occur only once; responses can have common properties but they can't be identical in all respects. Later responses will resemble the earlier reinforced response more or less closely, but they can't match it exactly. On the other hand, we can't group all responses together without distinction, because we'd be left with nothing to speak about but behavior in general. We have to settle for an intermediate level of analysis, at which we speak of neither individual responses nor behavior in general, but of *classes of responses* defined by common properties (Skinner, 1935a).

RESPONSE CLASSES

In experiments on the rat's lever press, the lever is attached to a switch that closes whenever the rat moves the lever with enough force through a sufficient distance. The common property of all lever presses is this consequence: Each response that closes the switch qualifies. Defining response classes in terms of common environmental effects is the basis for both recording responses and arranging their consequences. For example, an experimenter could record presses by counting closures of the switch and arrange to reinforce all such responses with food.

But this class produced by the experimenter has behavioral significance only if it's affected by the operations imposed on it. We must ask a fundamental question: Do consequences modify the likelihood of responses in this class? If so, it can be called an *operant* class; an operant class is a class of responses affected by the way in which it operates on or works on the environment.

Lever presses and key pecks are convenient examples, but operant classes include more extensive and complex cases.

Early in the psychology of learning, when operant behavior was called *instrumental*, it was assumed that only responses of the skeletal musculature could enter into classes modifiable by their consequences. Other classes of responses called *autonomic*, those of glands and smooth muscles, hadn't been shown to be modifiable in this way. Such responses were typically elicited, and Pavlov's conditioning procedures (see Chapters 2 and 12) had shown how new stimuli could come to elicit them. At that time, evidence that these responses could be modified through reinforcement or punishment was negligible. Furthermore, it was always possible to argue that such changes in autonomic responses were mediated by other kinds of behavior (as when exercise raises heart rate).

Despite controversy (e.g., Dworkin & Miller, 1986), some autonomic responses seem modifiable by their consequences. Consider the salivary response. Salivation occurs spontaneously as well as when elicited by a stimulus such as food in the mouth (Zener & McCurdy, 1939; cf. Chapter 4). Consequences can be arranged for spontaneous or emitted salivation, measured in drops of saliva. The consequences of emitted salivation mustn't be food, though, because the effect of food as a reinforcer would be hard to distinguish from its effect as an elicitor of salivation. Thus water, which doesn't elicit salivation, was used to reinforce salivation in water-deprived dogs (Miller & Carmona, 1967). Salivation increased when it produced water (reinforcement) and decreased when it prevented the delivery of water (punishment). These autonomic salivary responses were modified by their consequences; in other words, emitted salivation could appropriately be called an operant class, and these salivary responses were members of that

class (cf. Harris & Turkkan, 1981, on shaping of blood pressure elevation).

An operant is a response class that can be modified by the consequences of the responses in it. This definition of a response class depends on behavioral properties of responding and not on physiological properties such as the somatic–autonomic distinction. The behavioral properties of operant classes are based on the operation called *differential reinforcement*, the reinforcement only of responses that fall within a specified class. This operation makes subsequent responding conform more and more closely to the defining properties of the class. The essential feature of an operant is the correspondence between a class of responses defined by its consequences and the spectrum of responses generated by these consequences.

SOME EXAMPLES OF DIFFERENTIAL REINFORCEMENT

Let's place a food-deprived rat in a chamber with a horizontal slot 30 cm long on one wall (30 cm is about 12 in.). Photocells record where the rat pokes its nose through the slot. We'll label successive 2-cm segments along the slot as positions 1 through 15, reading from left to right. Food can be delivered into a cup in the wall opposite the slot. Food deliveries are accompanied by a distinctive noise, and the rat quickly comes to the cup and eats whenever food is delivered (cf. Antonitis, 1951).

At the start, the rat spends little time near the slot. Occasionally it sniffs at it and puts its nose in it as it moves about, but these responses are relatively infrequent and aren't systematically related to the positions along the slot. A frequency distribution of the rat's responses as a function of position is shown in A of Figure 7-1.

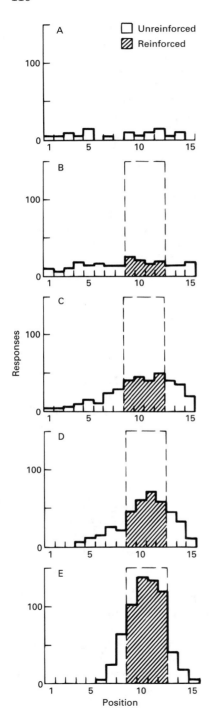

Now let's reinforce the poking of the rat's nose through the slot, but only if the pokes occur at positions 9 through 12. The initial effect of reinforcement, in B, isn't restricted just to positions correlated with reinforcement; it increases responding at all positions. This phenomenon, the spread of the effect of reinforcement to other responses not included in the reinforced class, is called *induction* (an occasional synonym is *response generalization*). In the example, reinforcing responses at positions 9 through 12 affected responding not only there but also at other positions across the entire slot.

As we continue differential reinforcement, reinforcing responses at positions 9 through 12 but not elsewhere, responding gradually increases at positions correlated with reinforcement and decreases at other positions, as shown in C, D and E. Eventually, most responses are within the boundaries that determine whether a response is to be reinforced, as in E, and a point may be reached at which, even though some unreinforced responses still occur, the distribution of responses across positions doesn't

FIGURE 7-1 Hypothetical differential reinforcement of response location. A rat pokes its nose into a horizontal slot in the chamber wall; photocells register this response at any of 15 positions reading from left to right. A shows the distribution of response positions when no responses are reinforced. In B through E, responses at positions 9 through 12 (bounded by dashed vertical lines) are reinforced with food; filled areas show reinforced responding. In B, the effects of reinforcement spread across the length of the slot; this spread is called *induction*. In C through E, responding becomes restricted to positions correlated with reinforcement; this concentration of the effects of reinforcement is called *differentiation*. With continued differential reinforcement, the distribution becomes stable and, as in E, corresponds fairly closely to the class of responses correlated with reinforcement.

change any further with continued differential reinforcement.

In the example, the distribution of emitted responses came to conform closely to the boundaries of the class of reinforced responses. This process is called *differentiation*, and responding produced in this way is said to be *differentiated*. Differential reinforcement created a response class defined by response position. Yet if the distribution of responses in E represents the maximum differentiation possible, what can be said about the responses that continue at positions 6, 7 and 8, or 13, 14 and 15? They're outside the boundaries of the class of responses correlated with reinforcement and, according to a strict interpretation of the defining properties of operants, can't be counted as members of the operant class. They can at least be talked about in terms of induction: These responses are so close to the class of reinforced responses that the effects of reinforcement have spread to them from the reinforced class. This view simply attributes responding within the boundaries of the reinforced class to differentiation, and responding outside these boundaries to induction. The same operation generates responding outside as well as inside these boundaries, and this responding can be represented as one continuous distribution.

The difficulty can be resolved by recognizing that the example actually involves two different classes. The first (1) is the basis for reinforcement and is represented by dashed vertical lines in Figure 7-1; these lines show how consequences (food) depend upon response position. The lines show the conditional probabilities of food given a response as a function of position; probability is 1.0 given responses in positions 9 through 12, and zero elsewhere. This distribution defines a class of responses in terms of the consequences of responses within that class. The second class of responses (2) is given by the actual performance produced by reinforcement. At any time this class is represented by the current response distribution (e.g., early during differential reinforcement, as at C, or late, as at E). The two classes needn't correspond exactly. In fact, a fundamental dimension of any class of reinforced responses is the degree of correspondence between (1) the behavior that is reinforced and (2) the behavior generated by reinforcement. The behavior that is reinforced is sometimes called (1) the *descriptive* or *nominal* class; the behavior generated by reinforcement is sometimes called (2) the *functional* class.

Let's now consider another hypothetical example, illustrated in Figure 7-2. Again we use photocells to record the positions at which the rat pokes its nose through a slot, but this time the slot is vertical rather than horizontal. The 15 positions are numbered consecutively, reading from the bottom to the top. At the start, the rat occasionally pokes its nose in the slot as it sniffs about the chamber, but these responses mostly occur at the lower positions, as in A of Figure 7-2. Perhaps a response will eventually occur at 15, the top position, if we're patient enough. But maybe not. Shaping is a better option.

First we arrange reinforcement for responses at position 7 or higher, as in B. Responding increases but most of it remains at the lower positions. Later we raise the criterion for differential reinforcement to 9, as in C. By this time, responding at the lower positions has decreased, the distribution has shifted toward higher positions, and responding has occurred for the first time at 13. Responding becomes more concentrated in the region correlated with reinforcement in D, when we raise the shaping criterion to 11. Finally, in E, we raise the criterion to 13. Had we imposed this criterion on the starting performance, in A, no reinforceable responses might ever have occurred. With differential reinforcement of successive approximations,

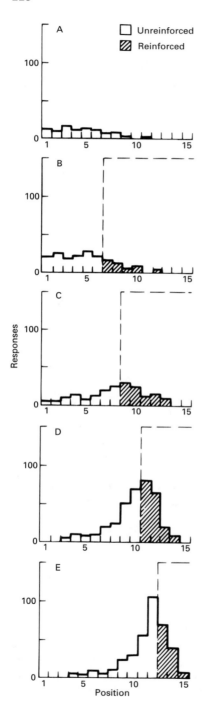

however, the distribution has shifted to higher levels, with maximum responding at 12. Nevertheless, this maximum remains below the boundary separating reinforced from unreinforced responses, and more responses are unreinforced than reinforced. The basis for this outcome is simple: The rat can reach some positions more easily than others. But what are the implications of such an outcome for defining response classes in terms of their consequences?

In this instance, the class of responses defined by consequences (responses at positions 13 and higher, which were reinforced) differed from the class generated by those consequences (responding up to 15, but with the maximum at 12). Responding was obviously modified by its consequences, but some of it was outside the boundaries of the reinforcement criterion. We can't speak of either class alone; operants must be defined in terms of the relation between (1) the environment (the consequences it arranges for responses) and (2) behavior (the responding produced by these consequences). For con-

FIGURE 7-2 Hypothetical example of shaping (differential reinforcement of successive approximations to a response). The situation is like that in Figure 7-1, except that the slot is vertical with the 15 positions numbered from the bottom to the top. Again, unfilled areas represent unreinforced responding and filled areas represent reinforced responding. Before reinforcement, in A, more responding occurs at lower than at higher positions. In B, responses at position 7 or higher are reinforced; the dashed vertical line shows the lower boundary for reinforced responses. After this differential reinforcement has some effect, the criterion is moved up to position 9, in C. Later it's moved to 11, in D, and finally to 13, in E, when shaping produces some responses at 15, the top of the slot, that weren't seen before reinforcement. At this point, the response distribution has its maximum at 12, just below the minimum required for reinforcement.

venience, we'll sometimes speak of operants solely in terms of classes defined by consequences or solely in terms of the distributions generated by these consequences, but it's important to remember that they're more strictly defined in terms of the correspondences between the two classes

Reinforcement inevitably involves differentiation. Responses such as lever presses and key pecks must occur at particular locations and be of sufficient force or they won't produce the consequences arranged for them. We could repeat the examples of Figures 7-1 and 7-2 by substituting such dimensions as force of a press or a peck. These examples illustrate the selection of behavior by its consequences. Within the lifetime of the individual organism, the selection of populations of responses is analogous to the selection of populations of organisms over evolutionary time. Both types of selection involve classes created by contingencies (cf. Chapters 3 and 21).

OPERANT CLASSES: FUNCTION VERSUS TOPOGRAPHY

We've seen how classes of behavior can be created through differential reinforcement. It might seem at first that these classes are defined by their topographical properties (what they look like). But that's not so. Consider even a superficially simple response like the rat's lever press. The rat might press the lever with its left paw or with its right paw or with both paws. It might also do so by pushing the lever down with its chin or by jumping on it or by sitting on it. These responses look very different, but they all count as lever presses; they're all members of the same operant class. Despite their differences, they're members of that class because they share a common function: They all produce the same consequences.

In other words, operants are defined by their functions and not by their forms. The problem of self-injurious behavior in children with developmental disabilities illustrates the importance of this distinction (e.g., Iwata et al., 1990, 1994; Lovaas & Simmons, 1969; Wahler, 1975). Such behavior can include head banging, biting one's own flesh until drawing blood, poking a finger into the space between the eyeball and the eye socket, and many other topographies. It is dangerous behavior, and the children who engage in it can do permanent damage to themselves.

Consider three male children who indulge in self-injurious behavior. They're housed in a treatment center, and each one spends time in head banging and in biting himself, so we can't distinguish among the children on the basis of the topographies of their behavior. Yet we find that the first child increases this behavior mostly when people are around but not paying attention to him; the second does so mostly when others ask him to complete some task (e.g., reading or simple arithmetic); and the third engages in this behavior independently of its social context. For these three, their self-injurious behavior is very similar in topography but its functions are quite different. For the first child, the self-injurious behavior gets attention; for the second it avoids compliance with demands; and for the third the behavior doesn't seem to depend on any environmental contingencies.

This analysis recommends very different treatment programs for each child. The first one must be taught other and more effective ways of engaging the attention of others and must be brought into situations where he'll be less deprived of attention. Tasks must be selected for the second child that are appropriate to his competence, and his success at those tasks must be reinforced (his behavior suggests that it's been too often punished in the past). The source of the third child's self-injurious behavior is unknown, and we must consider the possibility that it has some organic source (perhaps the child was born to a drug-addicted mother and suffered prenatal damage to the developing brain).

The point is that it's more important to define behavior classes by their consequences than by their topographies. Even though the self-injurious behavior looks alike across the three children, the attention produced by that of the first child distinguishes it from the avoidance achieved by that of the second child; some aspect of self-stimulation may be involved in the behavior of the third child but, unfortunately, we don't know enough about such cases.

Let's now concentrate on the first child. Suppose we try to extinguish the self-injurious behavior by ignoring it. First of all we might have trouble doing so because we can't tolerate the damage the child may do to himself. We persevere nevertheless and discover that the self-injurious behavior doesn't decrease. One possibility is that we haven't adequately identified the relevant class of behavior. Topography has again misled us. If the function of this behavior is to produce attention, it's probably part of a much larger class of behavior that includes shouting and acting up, hitting or otherwise abusing the caregivers in the treatment center, and any number of other responses that might function to get attention. This tells us how important attention is to this child. It also reminds us that we can't define response classes by what they look like. In this case, we must define a treatment program that uses attention to reinforce more effective and appropriate behavior. Both the child and his caregivers will benefit if the program is successful.

The self-injurious behavior was one class of behavior embedded in the larger class of attention-getting behavior (cf. Lalli et al., 1995). The larger class was held together by

the common consequences of its members, just as the various topographies of lever pressing (left or right paw, both paws, sitting on it) were held together by the common consequence of producing food. Common consequences are the glue that holds classes of behavior together (cf. Malone, 1990, p. 296). Furthermore, when a class of responses seems insensitive to its consequences, as when the first child's self-injurious behavior seemed not to extinguish, we must entertain the possibility that we've improperly defined the class, and that it's part of a larger class the other members of which continue to have the consequences it once shared with them (e.g., the attention-getting of the current example; cf. Chapter 9 on higher-order classes of behavior).

Section C   **Operant Structure**

We've seen that responding can vary not only in location or force but also in topography or form, direction, and so on. Differential reinforcement can be based on any response dimension, so any dimension or combination of dimensions might provide the defining properties of an operant class. We'll now explore the differentiation of operant classes along dimensions that have entered into significant theoretical issues in the history of the psychology of learning. Our examples include the temporal organization of behavior, its sequential patterning, and its novelty and variability.

DIFFERENTIAL REINFORCEMENT OF TEMPORAL ORGANIZATION

Temporal properties of responding include latency, duration and rhythm, any of which may provide the basis for differential reinforcement. For example, a procedure that differentially reinforces long latencies might reinforce a pigeon's peck on a lit key only if some minimum time has elapsed since the key light turned on. With criterion latencies shorter than 10 s, the pigeon's mean latency usually exceeds criterion, and more pecks are reinforced than unreinforced, but with a longer criterion fewer latencies are long enough to qualify for reinforcement and so fewer pecks are reinforced (the tendency for responding to exceed a short latency criterion and to fall below a long one is a common feature of the differential reinforcement of temporal properties of behavior in human as well as nonhuman performances: Catania, 1970).

Differentiation of temporal properties of behavior is relevant to reinforcement schedules, treated in detail in Chapter 10. We'll see that substantial quantities of behavior can be maintained even when only occasional responses produce a reinforcer. In reinforcement schedules, responses can be made eligible for reinforcement on the basis of the number of responses emitted, the time elapsed since some event or some combination of these conditions. A property of special interest is the separation of responses in time.

For example, you'll successfully start a car with a flooded engine only if you wait long enough after your last attempt to start it; conversely, you'll successfully inflate a bicycle tire using a pump with a leaky connection to the valve only if you pump rapidly enough. Analogously, reinforcement might be arranged for a pigeon's key peck only if that peck is preceded by 10 s of no pecking, or only if pecking has been so rapid that at least 20 pecks were emitted during the last 5 s. In the first case, pecking decreases; in the second, it increases.

If we concentrate just on the pecks, we might be tempted to say that the first case isn't an instance of reinforcement. But the unit of responding reinforced in the first case isn't a peck. Instead, it's a sequence consist-ing of a pause plus a peck. To the extent that this combination becomes more likely (thereby demonstrating the effect of the reinforcers on the response class that produced them), the rate of pecking necessarily decreases.

The procedure in the first example, in which a response is reinforced only if preceded by a minimum time without a response, is called a *differential reinforcement of low rate* or *DRL* schedule (Ferster & Skinner, 1957); it's sometimes also called a schedule of *interresponse time* or *IRT* reinforcement (Malott & Cumming, 1964), because reinforcement is based on the spacing in time of individual responses rather than on the average rate generated by many responses over an extended time. In general, the longer the interresponse time required for reinforcement, the lower the rate of responding. In DRL performance, the rate of responding decreases because the likelihood of responses preceded by long pauses (long IRTs) increases. Thus, DRL contingencies differentially reinforce a complex operant consisting of an IRT plus a response, in that order.

In the second example, in which reinforcement depends on 20 or more pecks within no more than 5 s, responding might increase, but only because the high rate of responding itself is differentially reinforced. Such a schedule is called a *differential reinforcement of high rate* or *DRH* schedule. The DRH schedule has received less attention than the DRL schedule, mostly because it's harder to work with DRH than with DRL schedules. Consider the pigeon whose pecking has been raised to a rate of more than 4 pecks/s by a DRH schedule requiring 20 pecks/5 s. (In fact, a skillful experimenter can routinely produce rates in excess of 10 pecks/s in pigeons by gradually raising the criteria.) As long as the pigeon maintains this rate, pecks produce reinforcers frequently. But if for any reason the pigeon slows down, pecking meets the rate criterion less often and thus produces fewer reinforcers. This in turn reduces the pigeon's rate of pecking further, which leads to a further decrease in reinforcers. This vicious circle will probably end in a rate of pecking so low that the reinforcement criterion is never met, so the pigeon's pecking ceases completely. To reinstate responding, the experimenter has to produce the high-rate performance again through shaping.

In the DRL schedule, however, an initial effect of reinforcers following pecks is that pecks occur more often. This higher rate of pecking means that pecks occur closer in time, so fewer IRTs are long enough to meet the reinforcement criterion. Thus, reinforcers decrease and the rate of pecking decreases in turn. But this decrease in rate just makes it more likely that IRTs will again be long enough to meet the criterion. Thus, pecking oscillates between increased rates accompanied by decreased reinforcement and decreased rates accompanied by increased reinforcement. Pecking can be maintained over long periods of time by such contingencies.

The significance of these examples is that we must be cautious about taking response rate as a fundamental measure of the effects of reinforcement. Response rate was once regarded as a measure of response strength (cf. reflex strength in Chapter 4; Nevin, 1992), but once it was recognized that rate was a property of behavior that could be differentiated like other properties such as force and topography, this view became less tenable. Although DRL responding occurs at a low rate, it's easily produced and maintained; and although DRH responding occurs at a high rate, it's hard to produce and fragile once it has been produced.

Other classes of differential-reinforcement schedules exist, such as the *differential reinforcement of paced responding*, which sets both upper and lower limits on the IRTs that can precede reinforced responses and which tends to maintain a fairly constant response rate. The *differential reinforcement of other behavior* (usually abbreviated *DRO*, and occasionally also called *differential reinforcement of zero behavior*) delivers a reinforcer if a specified time elapses without a response. This is in fact the technical name for a procedure often used to arrange reinforcement of alternative responding during extinction in applied settings (cf. the example of self-injurious behavior at the end of Section A, Chapter 5).

Consider a DRO schedule of 10 s arranged for a pigeon's pecks. This schedule reinforces the class of responses defined by 10 s without pecking. But if a reinforcer is delivered after every 10 s without pecking, then each peck must delay the reinforcer by at least 10 s. If pecks occur less often because they delay reinforcers, it would be appropriate to say they're negatively punished. In this case, as in distinguishing positive reinforcement of not-responding and negative punishment of responding, speaking in terms of specified responses may seem preferable to speaking in terms of their absence. But the DRO vocabulary is well established, and though potentially troublesome it defines a procedure rather than attributing functional properties to such events as not-responding.

COMPLEX BEHAVIOR: MAZE LEARNING

Most of our examples so far have involved relatively discrete response units, such as the rat's lever press or the pigeon's key peck. But complex sequences of responses can also be treated as operant classes. For example, a rat's negotiation of a maze could be regarded as a single complex response. Consider the simplest maze, the T-maze (C in Figure 5-2).

If the left goalbox is empty and the right goalbox contains food, a response sequence that includes running from startbox to choicepoint, turning right and then running to the right goalbox will be reinforced. Sequences that include turning left won't be reinforced or (if we allow the rat to retrace its way from left to right goalbox) at least won't lead to the reinforcer as quickly. As the rat comes more and more frequently to choose the right path we may say that this T-maze performance has become differentiated.

But maze learning can involve more complex sequences. Consider the sequence of responses in the *double-alternation problem* (e.g., Hunter, 1928). At one end of a central runway, a choicepoint offers a left turn (L) and a right turn (R), but both paths lead back to the other end of the runway. Without being removed from the apparatus the organism comes back up the central runway and again chooses left or right at the choicepoint. If it makes a series of left and right turns in the appropriate order, food is presented to it as it returns to the central runway.

In such apparatuses, the question was whether organisms could learn a double-alternation sequence, either LLRR or RRLL. The sequence was learned with varying degrees of success by different species and different organisms of the same species, but the more general issue was whether the organism's behavior at one time could determine its behavior later. An organism couldn't complete a double-alternation sequence successfully unless its behavior at the choicepoint somehow took into account the turns it made the preceding times around (in Chapter 14 we'll find that discrimination of features of one's own behavior is critical to some aspects of language).

A difference between this and our earlier examples of differentiation is in how the response class is specified. Linear position or force or duration are single dimensions along which responses can be located, but sequences of responses in double-alternation learning can't be ordered unambiguously along any one dimension. For example, the sequence LLLR contains only a single transition from L to R and the sequence LRLR contains as many Ls as Rs, but then which is more closely related to the reinforced sequence, LLRR? Another question is whether we should treat a sequence of turns as a single unit of behavior or subdivide it into smaller components. For example, in learning the LLRR sequence only R is followed immediately by a reinforcer, but if more Rs occur than Ls, should individual turns or entire sequences be treated as units?

As an organism learns response sequences in these and related tasks, differential reinforcement acts upon the behavior that the organism brings to the experiment. This behavior is often systematic. For example, a rat learning a maze at first might always take left turns, then later always right, then still later alternations between left and right, and so on until mastering the components of the maze. In a Lashley jumping stand with light and dark stimuli in which choices of the dark stimulus lead to food and in which light and dark irregularly change sides, a rat at first might mostly choose the light stimulus, then mostly the left one, then mostly the right one, until finally the rat begins consistently choosing only the dark one. Such systematic patterns were noted by Krechevsky (1932), who called them hypotheses and discussed their implications as follows:

Almost every description of animal learning includes such phrases as "*random* exploratory movements"; "chance entrances"; "chance errors." It is either implicitly assumed or explicitly stated in most descriptions of learning that in the beginning of the process the animal is a "chance" animal. His responses are without purpose, without form, and without meaning. Helter-skelter trial and error seems to be the rule at first, and then, after such behavior has eventually led the animal to experience the "correct" pattern, the various laws of learning step in to stamp in the correct responses and stamp out the incorrect. (Krechevsky, 1932, p. 157)

Based upon his data, Krechevsky contrasted this view with a different one, according to which the animal

brings to each new situation a whole history of experiences. These experiences the animal is ready to apply. *From the very beginning*, perhaps, the animal goes about solving his problem in a straightforward, comprehensive manner wherein each response is . . . a meaningful part of his total behavior. The animal, in executing a series of movements which we call "perfect," "errorless," "learned," "integrated," is not doing something which has arisen from a series of "imperfect," "unintegrated," "chance" responses. He is now merely running through a different set of integrated responses, which series of integrated responses were *preceded by other just as integrated responses*. Such responses, "false solutions," "early systematic attempts," etc., we have dubbed with the dubious name of "hypotheses". . . . When the human individual *behaves* in the very same such and such way we must also say that he has an "hypothesis." However, we are primarily interested not in defending our terminology but in describing certain behavior. The term "hypothesis" has merely been chosen as a convenient tag for such behavior. (Krechevsky, 1932, pp. 528–529)

RESPONSE SEQUENCES: CHAINING VERSUS TEMPORALLY EXTENDED UNITS

Once we break down a behavior sequence into components, we can treat the sequence as a succession of different operants, each defined by the reinforcing consequence of producing an opportunity to engage in the next one until the sequence is terminated by a reinforcer. Such a sequence is called a response *chain*. An example was provided in Chapter 5 by Sidman's detailed analysis of a rat's lever pressing reinforced by food. Rising up to the lever produced contact with the lever, which set the occasion for pressing the lever, which produced a seen food pellet, which set the occasion for moving to the food cup, and so on. Any segment of the sequence serves the dual function of reinforcing the last response and producing the conditions that occasion the next one. A discriminative stimulus that serves such a reinforcing function is sometimes called a *conditioned reinforcer* (some experiments on conditioned reinforcement are treated in Chapter 11).

Some behavior sequences can be reduced to smaller units in this way, and the analysis into such components can be confirmed experimentally by checking how independent the components are from one another (Skinner, 1934). For example, if lever pressing no longer produces food, lever pressing may decrease, but by delivering food independently of lever pressing we may find that food continues to occasion movement to the food cup. This procedure demonstrates that the integrity of one component isn't affected by altering the reinforcement contingencies for another.

Some sequences present different problems, however. In one experiment (Straub et al., 1979), for example, four keys in a pigeon chamber were lit green, white, red and blue, with the location of each color varying from trial to trial. If the pigeon pecked the green, white, red and blue keys in that order, the final peck on blue produced food; the trial was cancelled if it pecked them out of order. The pigeon learned to peck white after green and red after white and blue after red even though the color locations changed from trial to trial and even though successive pecks in the sequence didn't produce stimulus changes. Furthermore, the pigeon's pecks were likely to conform to the reinforced sequence even with one of the colors absent (e.g., after pecking white, pecking blue rather than green if red was missing). As in the maze-learning task of double alternation, the current response in the sequence must depend on the organism's past behavior. The same issue arises whenever an organism learns an arbitrary sequence in which responses are not accompanied by stimulus changes (e.g., Boren & Devine, 1968); can the organism's own behavior provide the discriminative stimuli that will occasion future behavior?

The critical question, however, isn't so much whether some behavior sequences are held together like this; rather, it's whether this is the only way in which behavior sequences can develop. In the history of the psychology of learning, the positions taken on this issue were often symptomatic of serious divisions among researchers of different orientations, some holding that sequential behavior could always be interpreted in terms of the concatenation of components (variously called associations, chains, stimulus–response bonds or conditioned reflexes), and others holding that sequential behavior couldn't be interpreted adequately in such terms. We'll conclude that sequential behavior of both sorts is possible; the significant question in any particular case is determining the nature of the sequential ordering.

Perhaps the most telling argument was made by Lashley (1951), who summarized earlier conceptions as follows:

> . . . the only strictly physiological theory that has been explicitly formulated to account for temporal integration is that which postulates chains of reflexes, in which the performance of each element of the series provides excitation

of the next. This conception underlay the "motor theories" of thinking which . . . sought to identify thought with inaudible movements of the vocal organs, linked together in associative chains. The . . . kinesthetic impulses from each movement serve as a unique stimulus for the next in the series. (Lashley, 1951, p. 114)

Lashley then described cases, including illustrations from language and music, that made such accounts implausible. For example, in answer to the argument that each movement serves as a unique stimulus for the next, Lashley considered the complex sequence of movements required to pronounce the sounds of the word "right" in proper order. The order isn't given by the sounds themselves, because the sounds can occur in a variety of orders and combinations (e.g., in the opposite order, as in "tire"). Thus, the sound sequence can't be based solely on direct connections, but must depend on some larger organization. Lashley extended the case from sequences of sounds within words to sequences of words within sentences:

> The word "right," for example, is a noun, adjective, adverb, and verb, and has four spellings and at least ten meanings. In such a sentence as "The millwright on my right thinks it right that some conventional rite should symbolize the right of every man to write as he pleases," word arrangement is obviously not due to any direct associations of the word "right" itself with other words, but to meanings which are determined by some broader relations. (Lashley, 1951, pp. 115–116)

Lashley used music to point out that the sheer rapidity of some sequences constrains how the sequences might be generated:

> The finger strokes of a musician may reach sixteen per second in passages which call for a definite and changing order of successive finger movements. The succession of movements is too quick even for visual reaction time. In

rapid sight reading it is impossible to read the individual notes of an arpeggio. The notes must be seen in groups. . . . Sensory control of movement seems to be ruled out in such acts. (Lashley, 1951, p. 123)

Lashley's argument, then, was that some sequential patterns of responding can't be reduced to a succession of stimulus–response or S–R units. When a skilled typist rapidly types the letters *the*, these letters can't be discriminative stimuli for the next stroke, first because the typist will be executing that next stroke even before the typed letters on the page can have any stimulus effects, and second because these letters can't be unique discriminative stimuli if they can be followed by hitting the space bar or various other keys depending on what the typist is typing (e.g., the words *the* or *these* or *then* or *thermometer*).

The historical problem was probably that, in the face of such arguments, researchers felt a choice had been forced between assuming that sequential behavior depended upon stimulus–response sequences and assuming that it depended on temporally extended units of behavior not reducible to such sequences. The issue may instead be regarded as an experimental one. Some sequences clearly can be put together in such a way that each response produces stimulus conditions that set the occasion for the next one, whereas others must be integrated so that responses appear in the proper order without each depending on the consequences of the last. For any given sequence, the issue is deciding which type it is.

OPERANT CLASSES AND NOVEL BEHAVIOR

The close correspondence between the class of responses with consequences and the class of responses generated by these consequences is the criterion for speaking of an operant class. As we've seen, these classes may be defined along single dimensions such as force or location or may have more complex properties. Our examples included differential-reinforcement schedules, mazes and integrated response sequences.

In each case, our major interest is with the dimensions along which responding conforms to the class of responses that is reinforced. The structure of behavior is such that we can't always define such dimensions independently of reinforcement contingencies. For example, consider the reinforcement of novel responses in porpoises (Pryor, Haag, & O'Reilly, 1969). The novel performances were shaped by reinforcing, in each session, some class of responses not reinforced in any previous session. For example, if the porpoise's backflips were reinforced in one session, slapping the water with its tail might be reinforced in the next and beaching itself at the side of the pool in the one after. After several sessions, the porpoise began to emit responses in each new session, such as leaping up from the water with a corkscrew spin, that the experimenters had never seen before. Response novelty had been differentiated, but how else is this operant class to be specified except by describing the criteria for reinforcement? The fact that we have difficulty measuring them doesn't rule out novelty or other complex dimensions of behavior as properties that can define operant classes. Novel behavior must be emitted before it can be incorporated into other behavior.

Even the variability of responding can be a basis for differential reinforcement (Neuringer, 1986; Page & Neuringer, 1985). But differential reinforcement with respect to novelty or variability raises questions. Reinforcers are produced by individual responses, and yet properties such as novelty and variability can't be properties of individual responses. They can only be properties of responses in the context of other responses that occurred earlier. A given response might be variable in the context of one sequence of past responses and stereotyped in the context of another. Thus, the fact that novelty and variability can be differentially reinforced means that organisms are sensitive to populations of responses and consequences over extended periods of time, and not merely to individual response–stimulus sequences (cf. Chapter 6 on molar and molecular analyses).

We'll return to the issue of behavioral classes later, especially in connection with verbal behavior, when we'll treat the finding that some grammatical structures are more easily learned than others as similar in kind to the finding that rats learn single-alternation sequences (LRLR) more easily than double-alternation sequences (LLRR). In each case, the problem is to identify the dimensions along which responding may come to conform to the class of responses that has consequences. Perhaps these dimensions can sometimes be specified only by verbal description (e.g., the class of all responses not reinforced on earlier occasions, as in reinforcing the porpoise's novel responses).

Chapter 8
Discriminated Operants: Stimulus Control

A. The Nature of Discriminated Operants

The Latin habere, *to have,* and capere, *to take or seize, are traceable to closely related Indo-European roots.* Habere *is an ancestor of* behavior, habit *and* inhibit. Capere *led to* concept *and* perception, *words relevant to stimulus classes; thus, these words and* behavior *are distant relatives.*

There are no obvious ties among differentiation *and* induction, *applied to response classes, and* discrimination *and* generalization, *applied to stimulus classes.* Differentiation, *from the Latin* dis-, *apart, plus* ferre, *to carry, is related through the Indo-European* bher-, *to carry or bear, to* birth, transfer, preference *and* metaphor *(but not to* interfere).* Induction, *from the Latin* in-, *in, plus* ducere, *to lead, is related through the Indo-European* deuk, *to drag or to lead, to* duke, adduction, edu-

cate *and* conduct. Discrimination, *from the Latin* dis-, *apart, plus* crimen, *judgment, is related by way of the Indo-European* skeri-, *to cut or separate, to* crime, describe *and* criterion. *And* generalization, *from the Latin* genere, *to produce or cause, is related through the Indo-European* gen-, *to give birth or beget, to* ingenious, kind *and* nature.

We've dealt with reinforcement based on response dimensions, but differential reinforcement can also be based on the stimuli in the presence of which responses occur. For example, a rat's lever presses in light are different from its presses in darkness, and reinforcement can be arranged for presses in the presence but not the absence of light. Similarly, a pigeon's key pecks during green light are different from its pecks during red. When responding is reinforced only in the presence of some stimulus, we say that reinforcement is *correlated with* that stimulus. A response class created by such differential reinforcement with respect to stimulus properties is called a *discriminated operant.*

Discriminated operants are pervasive. When driving, you proceed through an intersection if the traffic light is green but not if it's red. When speaking to someone, what you say is affected by what the other person said, the other's posture and facial expression, the setting of the conversation, and so on. Many earlier examples of reinforcement included discriminative control of responding. In discussing the rat's learning of a maze, we emphasized the increase in the choice of correct turns, but the rat that failed to discriminate the appropriate place at which to turn right or left would repeatedly bump the walls as it moved through the maze and could hardly master the maze as a whole.

In fact, there's probably no such thing as an operant class without discriminative stimuli. A pigeon's key peck can't be emitted in the absence of a key and a rat's lever press can't be emitted in the absence of a lever. The features that remain relatively constant throughout an experiment, such as the chamber itself along with the devices in it, are sometimes referred to as *contextual* stimuli. We'll usually be most interested in the stimuli that change within experimental sessions, but we must remember that the environment within which a pigeon or rat responds exists in a broader context that includes its living quarters, the scales on which it is weighed and other features of the laboratory outside the experimental chamber (cf. Donahoe & Palmer, 1994).

Discriminative stimuli correspond to those colloquially called signals or cues. They don't elicit responses. Rather, they *set the occasion* on which responses have consequences and are said to *occasion* responses (cf. affordance: Gibson, 1979). An example of the development of stimulus control, control of responding by a discriminative stimulus, is shown in Figure 8-1 (Herrick, Myers, & Korotkin, 1959). Rats pressed a lever in the alternating presence and absence of light. When the light was on, lever presses were occasionally reinforced with food. When it was off, presses weren't reinforced. The notation for the stimulus correlated with reinforcement is S^D for *discriminative stimulus* or S+ for *positive stimulus*; that for the one correlated with nonreinforcement or extinction is S^Δ, also for discriminative stimulus (Δ is delta, the Greek letter *d*), or S- for negative stimulus (strictly, S^0 is more appropriate to

denote the absence of a stimulus, but S- is a much more common usage).

In the procedure of Figure 8-1, light and dark alternated irregularly; when lit, the lamp remained on for periods ranging from 5 to 30 s. Lever presses were reinforced according to a *variable-interval* or *VI* schedule: On the average, only one lever press per 30 s was reinforced while the light was on. The important features of this schedule are that (1) it maintains a moderate and relatively constant response rate and (2) the varying times between successive reinforcers make time since the last reinforcer an unreliable predictor of when the next response will be reinforced. With this arrangement, stimulus changes and reinforcer deliveries vary unsystematically over time, so if the rat presses more in the light than in the dark we can be confident that the functional discriminative stimulus is the light and not the temporal regularities of those other events.

Over sessions, lever pressing increased during light and decreased in its absence. Such increases often accompany such discriminations (behavioral contrast: see Chapter 10). Figure 8-1 also shows changes in a discrimination index, responding in light as a percentage of total responding. The index increased over sessions. Equivalent ways of describing this outcome are saying that lever pressing in the presence of light was a discriminated operant, or that the light functioned as a discriminative stimulus for lever pressing, or that lever pressing was under the stimulus control of the light.

Section A   The Nature of Discriminated Operants

We can illustrate some properties of discriminated operants with a hypothetical example comparable to that of Figure 7-1 in the previous chapter. Again, a rat is in a

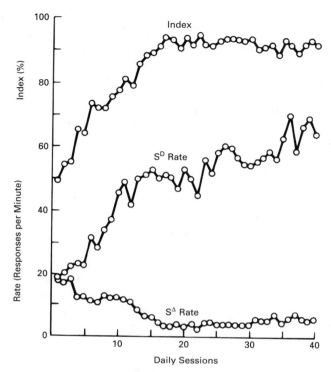

FIGURE 8-1   Rats' lever pressing in the presence and absence of light. The light (S^D) was correlated with variable-interval reinforcement and its absence (S^Δ) with extinction. The discrimination index is the percentage of the total presses emitted during light (100 times S^D rate divided by S^D plus S^Δ rates). Data are medians from eight rats. (From Herrick, Myers, & Korotkin, 1959, Figure 2)

chamber with a slot in one wall, but this time it can't poke its nose into the slot. Instead, the slot is covered by a translucent plastic strip that can be lit by a row of 15 lamps behind it. In other words, the lamps provide a stimulus dimension analogous to the response dimension of Figure 7-1. A lever is centered just below the slot and just above a feeder. Now we light the lamps behind the strip one at a time and in irregular order and we record the lever pressing that occurs in the presence of each. If we don't reinforce presses, pressing is infrequent and bears no systematic relation to the part of

the strip that we light. In fact, the data might look like those in A of Figure 7-1, with the main difference that the x-axis now represents stimulus position instead of response position.

At this point, we reinforce lever presses only with the slit lit at positions 9, 10, 11 or 12; when any other lights are lit, we don't reinforce presses. The initial effect of reinforcement is much like that in B of Figure 7-1: Responding increases across all positions. In other words, the effect isn't restricted just to the stimuli at positions correlated with reinforcement; instead, it spreads to other positions. The spread of the effect of reinforcement from one stimulus correlated with reinforcement to other stimuli is called *generalization*. In this example, reinforcing responding when lights 9 through 12 are lit affects responding in the presence of lights at all other positions. This example differs from the original one mainly in the dimension correlated with reinforcement: In Chapter 7 we dealt with a response dimension, but now we're dealing with a stimulus dimension.

Suppose we continue differential reinforcement with respect to stimulus location, reinforcing responses only when we light positions 9 through 12. Responding gradually increases when these positions are lit and decreases when others are lit. The effects are like those of Figure 7-1 in C, D and E. Eventually most responses occur when we light positions correlated with reinforcement, as in E, and even though some responses still occur when we light other positions, we reach a point at which the distribution of responses doesn't change much with continued differential reinforcement.

In this example, the stimuli that occasioned responding came to conform closely to the class of stimuli correlated with reinforcement. This process is called *discrimination* and responding controlled in this way by stimuli is said to be *discriminated*. Differential reinforcement created a response class defined by the stimuli in the presence of which responses occurred. But what about responses in the presence of stimuli outside the boundaries correlated with reinforcement (e.g., positions 6, 7 and 8, or 13, 14 and 15)? According to a strict interpretation, we shouldn't count these as members of the discriminated operant; we should speak of them in terms of generalization. But differential reinforcement generated the responding both inside and outside those

boundaries, so it's part of a continuous distribution.

We can resolve this problem in the same way as in Chapter 7. We have to recognize two classes of stimuli: One is the class correlated with a reinforcement contingency; the other is the class in the presence of which responding occurs. We're interested not in either class alone but rather in the correspondence between them. This closely parallels our discussion of differentiation and induction in Chapter 7. This is appropriate, because we can think of a stimulus in the presence of which a response occurs as another property of that response, like its force or duration or topography. Why then do we speak of differential reinforcement with respect to response properties in terms of differentiation and induction, whereas we speak of differential reinforcement with respect to stimulus properties in terms of discrimination and generalization?

One methodological factor is probably crucial to the distinction. When we study differential reinforcement with respect to response properties, we record responses in different classes, but aside from arranging contingencies there isn't much else we can do about them. If we see a rat about to poke its nose into position 7 along the slot, we can't stop the rat from emitting that response at this instant even if it's responded there a lot more often than elsewhere. But suppose instead that we're working with stimulus properties. We could choose among many possible orders and relative frequencies of presenting the lights. For example, instead of presenting lights equally often at each position we could present lights at some positions but not others, so that the rat never gets a chance to press the lever in the presence of some stimuli. This is why we say that stimuli in discrimination procedures set the occasion for responses: When a class of responses is defined by the presence of a stimulus, responses in that class can't occur when the stimulus is absent.

Even this methodological distinction has exceptions. For example, consider the differential reinforcement of long interresponse times (the DRL schedule: Chapter 7). If a pigeon's pecks are reinforced only after at least 5 s of no pecking, it may come to space its pecks about 5 s apart. We discussed this behavior in terms of the differentiation of a complex operant consisting of a pause plus a peck. We could as easily treat the duration of the pause as a stimulus property and argue that the behavior should be dealt with as a discrimination based on time elapsed since the last peck. In this instance, in fact, the vocabularies are interchangeable. Whether we speak of differentiation and induction or discrimination and generalization, the underlying operation is differential reinforcement. Both differentiation and discrimination involve correspondences between the dimensions upon which differential reinforcement is based and the dimensions of the resulting behavior. But we'll adhere to the established distinction between the vocabularies of response properties and of stimulus properties, because they have an extensive and widely accepted historical foundation.

ATTENDING TO PROPERTIES OF STIMULI

In discussing the correspondence between the stimuli with which reinforcement contingencies are correlated and those to which the organism responds, we spoke in terms of the stimulus dimension selected by the experimenter. But stimuli have varied properties, and there are no guarantees that the organism will respond to just those properties we select. In differentiation, a rat's lever presses might have fairly constant form even

though only force is the basis for differential reinforcement. For example, the rat might reliably press with its left paw even though this property isn't critical to whether the press is reinforced. Similarly, in discrimination a rat might respond on the basis of the intensity of a visual stimulus even though differential reinforcement is based only on its shape; we might then say that the rat is attending to intensity. (Stimulus properties to which an organism is likely to respond are sometimes called *salient*, but salience isn't a property of a stimulus; it's a property of the organism's behavior with respect to that stimulus.)

The concept of *attention* is essential to an account of discriminated operants because organisms typically respond to some stimulus properties and not others. To the extent that attending to one stimulus property or another is something organisms do, we can treat attending as a kind of behavior (see Chapter 20). The important reason for treating it in this way is that attending can have consequences. For example, if a reinforcement contingency is correlated with the brightness of a visual stimulus but not with its size, it will make a difference whether the organism attends to brightness or to size (and if attending to brightness occurs more often because of its consequences, it's appropriate to talk about that attending as an operant).

Consider a pigeon whose key pecks are occasionally reinforced with food. One of two stimulus combinations is presented on the key: a triangle on a red background or a circle on a green background. After 3 min of triangle-on-red, the next peck in the presence of this stimulus is reinforced; after 3 min of circle-on-green, the stimulus turns off without reinforcement. The arrangement during triangle-on-red is called a *fixed-interval* or *FI* schedule of reinforcement; the arrangement during circle-on-green is extinction. We'll examine the fixed-interval schedule in Chapter 10. For the present, it's enough to note that this schedule usually maintains responding that increases in rate as time passes in the interval rather than the relatively constant rate ordinarily maintained by a variable-interval schedule. If every peck during triangle-on-red produced a reinforcer, then the reinforcer deliveries themselves could acquire discriminative functions, but we don't have to worry about such effects with FI rein-

forcement because no peck is reinforced until the interval ends.

Figure 8-2 (Reynolds, 1961a) shows data for two pigeons. The left graphs show rates of pecking during each stimulus combination after 18 hours of training. Both pigeons emitted more than 40 pecks/min during triangle-on-red but pecked at relatively low rates during circle-on-green. In a test without reinforcement, the elements of each combination were presented separately. Almost all of Pigeon 105's pecking occurred during the triangle; red, the color correlated with

FIGURE 8-2 Key pecking of two pigeons during reinforcement correlated with triangle-on-red and extinction correlated with circle-on-green (left: training), and during extinction tests with forms and colors presented separately (right: attention tests). Pigeon 105 was responding to form but not color; Pigeon 107 was responding to color but not form. (From Reynolds, 1961a, Figure 1)

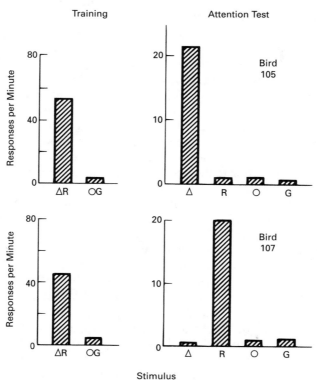

reinforcement, occasioned little more responding than either the circle or green, the elements previously correlated with extinction. On the other hand, almost all of Pigeon 107's pecking occurred during red; even though the triangle had been correlated with reinforcement during training, by itself it occasioned even less pecking than the circle or green. Pigeon 105 was attending to form and not color, and Pigeon 107 was attending to color and not form. Form and color had been similarly correlated with reinforcement during training. Only by separately examining the effects of the elements were we able to see what their discriminative functions were.

The pigeons' responding here isn't just an instance of generalization. The responding of Pigeon 105 generalized from triangle-on-red to triangle without red but not to red without triangle. We usually speak of attention not as a response to a particular stimulus but rather as attention to some stimulus dimension (paying careful attention means listening to everything that's said and not just to some parts). We say that Pigeon 105 attended to form and not color because discriminated responding occurred with changes in form but not with changes in color. When stimuli are discriminated along one stimulus dimension but not another, we say that the organism is attending to the first dimension but not the second.

Once an organism has attended to some stimulus properties in one situation, it's likely to attend to those properties in new situations (Lawrence, 1949). We can also change the likelihood that an organism will attend to stimulus properties simply by changing the way in which reinforcement is correlated with them (Johnson & Cumming, 1968). In the training phase of Figure 8-2, form and color were correlated equally well with reinforcement. For this reason, the experiment was particularly suitable for demonstrating some properties of attention.

But if our major interest was form discrimination in the pigeon, we'd make color irrelevant and correlate changes in reinforcement only with changes in form.

Place Learning Versus Response Learning

The preceding issues are indirectly related to a long-standing controversy in psychology, on place learning versus response learning (Restle, 1957). The response of moving from one place to another has had a privileged place in behavioral analyses (e.g., Olton, 1979). Going to food isn't the same as producing food while remaining in place. One important difference between the two cases is that the environment changes more drastically when we move to a new location than when we introduce a new stimulus into our present one. Humans in particular have found ways to substitute other responses for ordinary locomotion: To go places, we step on gas pedals, turn steering wheels, press elevator buttons and stand on escalators or moving walkways. Furthermore, movement produces continuous changes in the environment, whereas sequences of other responses may produce no change until the sequence is completed. Beyond these differences, then, does it matter whether an organism moves to a new place or produces new stimuli where it is?

Such questions were implicit in the controversy over place learning versus response learning. We can differentiate the right turns of a rat at the choicepoint of a T-maze by reinforcing right but not left turns. We can then ask whether the rat's responding is based on response dimensions (movements to the right as opposed to movements to the left) or on stimulus dimensions (movements toward a particular place, without regard to the direction from which the rat approaches). For example, suppose the right arm of the T-maze points toward the brighter windowed east wall of a laboratory. The rat might learn right turns or it might learn to run toward the window. We could test these alternatives by turning the T-maze around so that the right arm points west and the rat now approaches the choicepoint from the north. If the rat turns right and therefore away from the window, it shows *response learning*. If it turns left toward the window, it shows *place learning*: It moves toward the same place, even though it does so by turning in a different direction. The question is whether the rat learns right versus left turns or east versus west turns.

The rat's performance depends on the stimuli available both inside and outside the maze. The typical maze used to be topped by wire mesh or some other cover that allowed the experimenter to watch what the rat was doing. If an experimenter can look in, a rat can look out. Although it's nearsighted, the typical rat can discriminate the general direction of lights and other gross features of a room. As long as stimuli are available outside the maze, they may become the basis for the rat's turn in a particular direction. But if those stimuli are eliminated by placing an opaque cover over the maze, the direction that the maze faces in the room becomes irrelevant and the rat can't show anything but response learning. Place learning or response learning therefore depend on how the experimenter prepares the problem for the rat. By judiciously choosing conditions, an experimenter can make things come out either way.

In natural environments, food at a given location isn't necessarily replenished as it is in the goalbox of a laboratory maze. In foraging, an animal is more likely to move to a new location than to return to one where it has already consumed the available food. Again, the properties of the environment to which the organism attends may vary with constraints imposed by the experimenter (cf.

Collier & Rovee-Collier, 1981; Lea, 1979). For example, when a rat is given daily sessions in an apparatus in which food is located at the ends of each of several alleys and the food isn't replenished during the session, the rat learns not to repeat visits to alleys where it's already eaten (Olton & Samuelson, 1976). Spatial properties of environments are particularly important, but in appropriate circumstances a rat may learn their other properties.

STIMULUS-CONTROL GRADIENTS

Discrimination procedures place a heavy burden on the experimenter. In differentiation procedures the organism determines the order of responses, but in discrimination procedures the experimenter must determine the order of stimuli. An experimenter who is interested in some stimulus continuum (i.e., some dimension along which stimuli can vary, such as intensity or position of a light) must worry about how many stimuli to present, how long and in what order to present them and how they should be correlated with reinforcement and nonreinforcement, to mention some of the most important possibilities. Research on gradients of stimulus control bears on the effects of some of these variables. Such procedures usually involve a training phase during which some correlation between stimuli and reinforced responding is arranged, and then a test phase during which reinforcement is discontinued while various old and new stimuli are presented.

Generalization Gradients

If responding is reinforced during some stimulus and a property of that stimulus is then varied, responding may depend on how much the stimulus has changed. For example, if a pigeon's key pecks are reinforced when the key is lit yellow during a training phase, the pigeon will ordinarily peck at lower rates as the light is changed to orange and red and violet in a test phase. This demonstrates generalization: the effects of reinforcement during yellow spread to the other colors.

Figure 8-3 presents data on generalization of pigeons' key pecks to tones of different frequency after pecks were reinforced only during a tone of 1000 cycles/s (Jenk-

ins & Harrison, 1960). In one procedure (no discrimination training), the tone was always present and pecks were reinforced according to a variable-interval or VI schedule. In a second procedure (presence versus absence training), the tone was sometimes present and sometimes absent and pecks were reinforced according to the VI schedule only during the tone. After training, reinforcement was discontinued and tones of other frequencies were presented for the

FIGURE 8-3 Generalization gradients as a function of frequency of a tone after reinforcement of key pecks during a 1000-cycle/s tone (top: 3 pigeons) or after reinforcement during the tone and extinction during its absence (bottom: 5 pigeons). Without discrimination training, gradients were relatively flat; after presence versus absence training, they peaked at the reinforcement stimulus (S^D). (From Jenkins & Harrison, 1960, Figures 1 and 2)

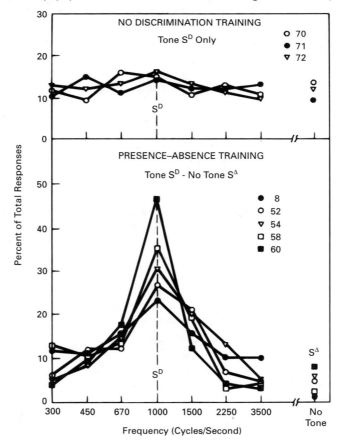

first time, along with no tone and the original training tone; the stimuli were presented eight times each in mixed order during this test phase.

For the three pigeons without discrimination training (Figure 8-3, top), neither the frequency of the tone nor its presence or absence had much effect on pecking. The generalization gradient was relatively flat or, in other words, the effect of reinforcement during the original tone spread uniformly to all the other stimuli. We can say that these pigeons weren't attending to the tone because changes in its frequency made no difference to them.

For the five pigeons given discrimination training (Figure 8-3, bottom), the original frequency produced higher rates of pecking than any other during the test phase; in general, the closer to the original frequency, the higher the rate of pecking. It isn't surprising

that low rates of pecking occurred when the tone was absent; absence of tone was correlated with extinction. But for these pigeons response rate varied with frequency even though discriminated responding depended only on the presence or absence of the tone and not on its frequency. We therefore can say that these pigeons were attending to the tone. (The form of generalization gradients is also affected by other variables, such as level of deprivation or the reinforcement schedule during training: e.g., Hearst, Koresko, & Poppen, 1964.)

Postdiscrimination Gradients

Stimulus-control gradients can also be obtained after discrimination between two or more stimuli along a dimension. Figure 8-4 compares such a postdiscrimination gradient with a generalization gradient (Hanson,

FIGURE 8-4   Gradients of stimulus control. The generalization gradient shows pigeons' key pecking after reinforcement at a wavelength of 550 millimicrons (S^D); the gradient peaks at the S^D. The postdiscrimination gradient shows key pecking after reinforcement at 550 millimicrons (S^D) and extinction at 570 (S^Δ); it shows a peak shift, in that maximum responding has shifted from the S^D in a direction away from the S^Δ. The spectrum goes from violet and blue at short wavelengths to red at long wavelengths, so the S^D and S^Δ were in the green-yellow region. (From Hanson, 1959, Figure 1)

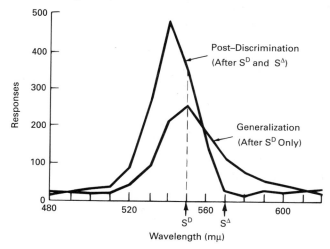

1959). For one group of pigeons (generalization), key pecks during a single wavelength on the key were reinforced according to a VI schedule, and then rates of pecking during this and other wavelengths were obtained during nonreinforcement. The gradient peaked at the reinforcement stimulus; in other words, rate decreased as distance from this stimulus increased.

For a second group (postdiscrimination), key pecks were reinforced according to a VI schedule during the same wavelength as the first group, but this wavelength alternated with another during which pecks weren't reinforced (extinction); as for the first group, rates of pecking during this and other wavelengths were obtained during nonreinforcement. In this case, the peak of the gradient was displaced from the reinforcement stimulus in a direction away from the extinction stimulus; this displacement is called a *peak shift*. (Similar effects occur when the discrimination is based on a higher frequency of reinforcement during one stimulus than another: Guttman, 1959.)

One account of the form of the postdiscrimination gradient (Spence, 1937) assumed that reinforcement during one stimulus creates a gradient of increased responding centered on that stimulus (excitatory gradient), that extinction during another stimulus produces a gradient of decreased responding centered on that second stimulus (inhibitory gradient), and that after discrimination training the responding produced by other stimuli could be predicted by subtracting the inhibitory from the excitatory gradient. Spence's theoretical gradient showed a peak shift: Its maximum was displaced from the reinforcement stimulus in a direction away from the extinction stimulus. But the new gradient, produced by subtraction, was everywhere lower than the original excitatory gradient; thus, it was consistent with the form but not with the absolute values of postdis-

crimination gradients (cf. Hearst, Besley, & Farthing, 1970).

Effects of discrimination training on the shape of gradients raised questions about the origins of peaked generalization gradients. One suggestion was that gradients should be steeper or shallower depending on whether stimuli in that region of the gradient were easier or harder to discriminate. But when the steepnesses of generalization gradients around stimuli in different regions of the spectrum were compared with the thresholds for the detection of a change in wavelength in those regions, no simple relations between generalization and discriminability were found (Guttman & Kalish, 1956).

Another suggestion was that the peaked gradients depend on discrimination learning that occurs before the organism is brought into the experimental situation. For example, a pigeon presumably learns to discriminate among the grains it eats long before it sees yellow projected on a pigeon key; its discriminations of color might be sharpest in the yellow region of the spectrum simply because yellow predominates as a color in its food. It's hard to control the color discriminations acquired in natural environments, but we can create environments in which color discriminations aren't possible. In an environment lit only by monochromatic light, a very narrow band of wavelengths such as the yellow emitted by a sodium vapor lamp, objects have no color; to a human in such an environment, everything appears in shades of gray. An organism reared in such an environment has no opportunity to learn color discriminations.

A suitable organism for monochromatic rearing is the duckling, which is capable of walking and pecking soon after it hatches; thus, reinforcement procedures can start early. Generalization gradients across wavelengths from ducklings reared monochromatically have been sometimes flat (Peterson, 1962; cf. Figure 8-3, top) and sometimes peaked (e.g, Rudolph, Honig, & Gerry, 1969; cf. Figure 8-3, bottom), suggesting that ducklings sometimes attend to color even without color experience. When ducklings reared monochromatically were trained to discriminate between only two wavelengths, however, their postdiscrimination gradients were similar to those of normally reared duckings and included peak shifts, even though the stimuli consisted mostly of wavelengths they'd never seen before (Terrace, 1975).

Inhibitory Gradients

Once Spence's account was offered to handle the form of postdiscrimination gradients, interest arose in finding a way to record inhibitory gradients directly. The difficulties were both methodological and theoretical. To determine whether a stimulus reduced responding, there had to be some responding to start with. A procedure was needed that would separate the dimension along which the extinction gradient was determined from the one correlated with reinforcement. Such a procedure is illustrated in Figure 8-5 (Honig et al., 1963). With one group of pigeons, the reinforcement stimulus was a vertical line on the key and the extinction stimulus was a lit key without a line; with a second group, these stimuli were reversed. For both groups, VI schedules were used during training and gradients along the dimension of line orientation were

FIGURE 8-5 Excitatory and inhibitory stimulus-control gradients after variable-interval reinforcement of pigeons' key pecks during one stimulus (S^D) and extinction during another (S^Δ). For one group, a vertical line was correlated with reinforcement and its absence with extinction (filled circles); for another, the stimuli were reversed (unfilled circles). Data obtained during nonreinforcement show responding during various line orientations and absence of the line. (From Honig, Boneau, Burstein, & Pennypacker, 1963, Figure 1)

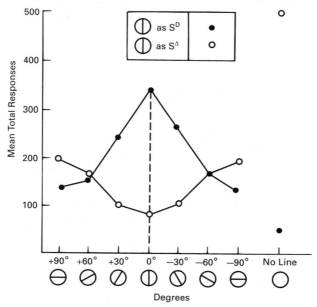

obtained during nonreinforcement in the test phase.

In the group with the vertical line correlated with reinforcement and its absence correlated with extinction (filled circles), pecking decreased with greater deviations from vertical; this is a reinforcement gradient like that of Figure 8-3 (bottom). But in the group with the vertical line correlated with extinction and its absence correlated with reinforcement (unfilled circles), pecking increased with greater deviations from vertical. In this group, changing the orientation of the line affected its distance from the vertical extinction stimulus but not its distance from the reinforcement stimulus, the absence of a line. This is an inhibitory gradient.

Inhibitory gradients are often shallower than the corresponding excitatory gradients, probably because organisms are more likely to attend to stimulus properties correlated with reinforcement than to those correlated with extinction (cf. Dinsmoor, 1995). A condition like that of the first group, in which the line was a feature present only during reinforcement, is called a *feature-positive* discrimination; a condition like that of the second group, in which the line was a feature present only during extinction, is called a *feature-negative* discrimination (Jenkins & Sainsbury, 1970). Because it's easier to get organisms to attend to stimuli correlated with reinforcement than to those correlated with extinction, training a feature-positive discrimination is easier than training a feature-negative one. We'll consider some implications of these phenomena in more detail when we discuss observing responses in Chapter 11.

We've now considered the four main types of stimulus-control gradients: (1) the relatively flat generalization gradient, without attention to the relevant stimulus dimension; (2) the peaked generalization gradient, with attention to the dimension; (3) the postdiscrimination gradient, typically with a peak shift, after reinforcement correlated with one stimulus along the dimension and extinction correlated with another; and (4) the inhibitory gradient, after reinforcement in the presence of a stimulus not on the dimension and extinction in the presence of a stimulus on the dimension.

Whatever the gradient, we can always raise questions about the actual stimulus dimensions to which an organism attends. For example, suppose the pigeon looks only at the upper edge of a key with a line projected on it. If we change the line orientation from vertical, the top of the line moves away from the upper edge of the key, so the edge looks more like it did when there was no line there. In this case, the line is the nominal stimulus, but the functional stimulus is what appears at the upper edge of the key. We can only evaluate such a possibility experimentally (e.g., by removing portions of the line and seeing whether this produces the same sorts of changes in the pigeon's behavior as rotating the line: cf. Touchette, 1969). The point may seem trivial with regard to a pigeon's pecks, but it can be exceedingly important in application, as when a teacher tries to find out whether a child is attending to the words in a storybook or is faking reading by attending mainly to the pictures.

FADING: STIMULUS CONTROL BY SUCCESSIVE APPROXIMATIONS

Just as the response properties that define an operant can be changed gradually by shaping procedures, the stimulus properties that define a discriminated operant can be changed gradually by analogous procedures called *fading*. Training doesn't have to start with stimuli that are difficult to discriminate.

Instead, it can start with stimuli that are easy to discriminate and then move gradually to more difficult ones. For example, it's usually harder to teach a pigeon to discriminate between vertical and horizontal lines than between red and green. Once a discrimination between red and green exists, however, one between vertical and horizontal can be successively approximated by superimposing vertical on red and horizontal on green and then gradually fading out the colors (Terrace, 1963b). (Some rough fading has been arranged in this chapter, by dropping out *variable-interval* in favor of its abbreviation, *VI*, after both appeared together more than once.)

Creating stimulus control through fading is often effective (e.g., Sidman & Stoddard, 1967), but as with shaping no rules exist to determine how rapidly stimuli should be faded in or out in different situations. For example, if we superimpose vertical on red and horizontal on green and then partially fade out the colors, we might remove the colors completely and find that the pigeon has learned to discriminate between vertical and horizontal. On the other hand, fading might be unsuccessful; if the pigeon attends only to the colors even when they became very faint, we might find that discriminated responding disappears every time we dim the colors below certain minimum levels.

Just as shaping requires that some behavior is available to be shaped, fading requires that some discriminative responding is available to be shifted to a new stimulus dimension. For example, consider *errorless discrimination learning* (Terrace, 1963a). Soon after a pigeon's pecks on a red key had been shaped with food reinforcement, reinforcement during 3-min periods of red was continued according to a VI schedule. The periods of red alternated with another stimulus, during which pecks weren't reinforced.

At first, this other stimulus was a dark key lasting 5 s. Over three sessions, its duration was gradually lengthened and it was changed from dark to dim and then to brighter and brighter green, until, to the human eye, its brightness matched that of the red key. By the end of these conditions, 3 min of red correlated with reinforcement alternated with 3 min of green correlated with extinction. Each pigeon treated in this way pecked the extinction key fewer than 10 times in the entire course of training; pecking occurred almost without exception on the red key rather than on the green key. Pigeons introduced to this procedure later after initial training or introduced abruptly to green at full duration and intensity pecked the green extinction key hundreds and even thousands of times during equivalent periods of training.

The gradual fading in of green was effective in part because turning the red key dark early in training stopped the pigeon's pecking for a few seconds (any abrupt stimulus change might have had such an effect). Pecking wasn't likely to start again before the 5-s extinction stimulus ended. Thus, a difference in responding to the two stimuli occurred at the outset, and the gradual changes in the duration and intensity of the extinction stimulus built upon that difference. After such a history, we might change the extinction stimulus to a reinforcement stimulus and the pigeon might never respond during that stimulus and discover that we had done so. The sense in which such a performance is errorless isn't obvious. We must be cautious about the language of errors; the term *error* implies a judgment about the value of responding and may be inappropriate to a behavioral analysis. The fading procedure isn't solely of theoretical interest; its possible applications to education give it practical significance (e.g., see Chapter 17).

THE VOCABULARY
OF DIFFERENTIAL REINFORCEMENT

Both differentiation and discrimination involve differential reinforcement. The major difference is whether differential reinforcement is imposed on properties of responding or on properties of the stimuli during which responding occurs. The main implication of the difference is procedural: In studies of differentiation the experimenter must wait for the organism's responses, whereas in studies of discrimination the experimenter controls the order and duration of stimulus presentations. The vocabulary of differentiation and discrimination is summarized in Table 8-1.

Differential reinforcement can be based on simple dimensions of stimuli, such as intensity or location. The experimental question is whether responding conforms to the differential consequences, in that more responding occurs in the presence of the stimuli correlated with reinforcement than in the presence of those correlated with nonreinforcement. The implications are profound. What we've learned from training simple discriminations in pigeons or rats has been used to develop methods for training primates to discriminate among different drugs that have been administered to them (e.g., Schuster & Balster, 1977), for teaching young parents to identify their children's illnesses (e.g., Delgado & Lutzger, 1988) and for instructing women in breast self-examination (e.g., Pennypacker & Iwata, 1990), to mention just a few of a vast number of successful applications.

As illustrated by these applications, differential reinforcement can be arranged for complex properties of stimuli that aren't easily quantified. For example, children learning to read must be able to name the letters of the alphabet. But the properties important for distinguishing among some letters are different from those important in distinguishing among others (e.g., straight line versus curve is important in distinguishing *U* and *V* but not *V* and *N*), and different distinctions are important for lowercase than for uppercase letters (e.g., no pair of uppercase letters has the up-down or left-right reversals that must be mastered to read *b*, *p*, *d* and *q*). The way in which a child learns to distinguish among letters of the alphabet depends on relations among such stimulus properties as symmetry, curvature and closure. Those properties essential to discriminating among different letters are called *critical features* (e.g., Gibson, 1965).

It isn't enough, however, to enumerate critical features. For some letters, the upper-case and lowercase forms differ more from each other than they differ from other letters

TABLE 8-1   The Vocabulary of Differential Reinforcement

DIFFERENTIAL REINFORCEMENT (OPERATION)	CONCENTRATION OF EFFECTS OF REINFORCEMENT (PROCESS)	SPREAD OF EFFECTS OF REINFORCEMENT (PROCESS)	DIFFERENTIAL REINFORCEMENT BY APPROXIMATIONS (OPERATION)
With respect to response properties	Differentiation	Induction	Shaping
With respect to stimulus properties	Discrimination	Generalization	Fading

(e.g., *e*, *E* and *F*, or *h*, *n* and *N*). Given the multitude of forms, what then defines the class of stimuli that occasions our saying *A* or *B* or *C*? This question is about the stimulus structure of the letters of the alphabet. The problem becomes even more complicated when different contexts are considered. For example, *O* could be either a letter or zero, and *I* could be either a letter or a roman numeral. The concept of an *X* or a *Y* or a *Z* is defined by the class of stimuli to which we respond with the corresponding letter name, but we'll see that such classes are based on behavior, not on common physical properties (cf. Chapter 14).

Discriminated operants are behavior classes defined by the stimuli that occasion responding. We often identify such classes in our everyday vocabulary, as when we speak of stopping at a red traffic light or answering a telephone. The red light can vary in brightness and size and the telephone ring can vary in loudness and timbre, but our behavior is reasonably independent of variations along such dimensions, so we speak in terms of these classes rather than in terms of specific instances.

We often treat stimuli as if they were restricted to concrete objects or environmental events. But though we can learn to respond in consistent ways to objects or events, we also discriminate among features, sometimes called *abstract* or *relational*, that are independent of particular objects or events. The term *stimulus* often functions in this more general way, in the sense of some property of environmental events. For example, we might say that a chair had been placed to the right of a table. Although the chair and the table are concrete objects, being-to-the-right-of isn't, and yet we discriminate this relation from being-to-the-left-of. In some discrimination experiments, therefore, relations among stimuli have been dimensions of special interest.

Section B Animal Cognition

The field of animal cognition is concerned with what animals know. It addresses this problem by identifying the events and relations that can be discriminated by different species. Studies of animal cognition have examined a variety of discriminative performances and are of special interest when they involve discriminations of complex relational properties of the environment. Examples include judgments of visual symmetry (e.g., Delius & Nowak, 1982); discriminations of numerousness (e.g., Davis & Pérusse, 1988); visual search (e.g., Blough, 1989); discriminative control by reinforcement contingencies or stimuli correlated with those contingencies (e.g., Washburn, Hopkins, & Rumbaugh, 1991); the organization of behavior within a sequentially discriminated sequence (Terrace & Chen, 1991); and responding under the stimulus control of the organism's own behavior (e.g., Shimp, Sabulsky, & Childers, 1989), to mention just a few. Many examples of research on animal cognition are presented elsewhere in this book, so this section presents only a highly selective sample.

Consider a pigeon who watches a clock hand as it is projected on the center key of three pigeon keys (Neiworth & Rilling, 1987). The hand starts at vertical and rotates at a constant rate from vertical through 90°; then it disappears. A little later it reappears farther along, at 135° or 180°. The timing of its reappearance is either consistent or inconsistent with a constant rate of rotation while it was invisible. After a trial consistent with a constant rotation rate, left-key pecks are reinforced; after an inconsistent one, right-key pecks are reinforced. Pigeons learned to discriminate trials consistent with a constant rotation rate from those in which the constant rate was violated even though the rotating stimulus was absent some of the time; the discrimination also transferred to new locations of reappearance of the clock hand. This performance wasn't based on trial durations or specific locations of the clock hand. It therefore demonstrates visual tracking in the absence of the visual stimulus; such tracking is sometimes called imagery (cf. Chapter 20). Colloquially, we might say that the pigeon knew where the stimulus was even while it was invisible (a useful skill, as when an edible insect passes behind an obstruction and a bird awaits its emergence from the other side).

Studies of animal cognition are concerned with what organisms know, and accounts are often framed in terms of the structure of relevant stimuli (cf. Chapter 1 on structural and functional languages). For example, if an organism discriminates among stimuli on the basis of some critical feature, an animal cognitivist might say that the organism represents the stimuli to itself in terms of that feature (e.g., in the clock hand example, that the pigeon represents or imagines its constant motion, or in the case of search for prey, that a predator compares potential targets with a search image). We discussed the role of representations in biological theories in the context of natural selection in Chapter 3. We'll take the issue up again in the context of remembering in Chapters 18 and 19, where we'll discuss remembering as the reconstructing and thus the "re-presenting" (in the literal sense of presenting again) of features of earlier events, and in the context of cognitive and behavioral theories in Chapter 20, where we'll argue that imagery is best treated as a kind of behavior.

COGNITIVE MAPS

Whenever local environments have different properties it's advantageous for an organism to be able to find its way from one to another. An environment with a rich and stable supply of food is preferable to one with a poor and variable supply; an environment in which the food is easily accessible is preferable to one in which the same food exists but is less accessible; an environment with safe areas for breeding and for the rearing of offspring is preferable to one that's more dangerous; and so on. (The argument holds for most animal groups. It would take us too far afield to consider the phylogenic contingencies that operated in the evolution of plants, but it's appropriate to note that many plants disperse their seeds; animals are often involved in that dispersal, as when bees pollinate flowers.)

Once some kind of orientation has emerged, natural selection is likely to sharpen it over phylogenic time (cf. Chapter 3). It's therefore not surprising that many animal species readily find their way around in the world. Some of their navigation is learned and some is unlearned. Gallistel (1990) provides a detailed treatment that ranges from foraging in ants to echolocation by bats and choice of routes by chimpanzees, and ranging from orientations based on simple stimulus dimensions such as gradients of odor or light to varieties that are functionally equivalent to celestial navigation. Organisms that leave their nesting areas must be able to return to them; the more accurately they can do so, the more widely they can forage. Organisms that store food over the winter must be able to locate the food later; the more variable their sites and the more sites they can keep track of, the less likely they'll be to lose what they've stored to their competitors (e.g., Balda, Kamil, & Grim, 1986). Organisms that evade predators must be able to locate escape routes; those that allow themselves to be pursued into blind alleys don't survive.

We considered some issues relevant to

spatial orientation in discussing place learning versus response learning. The two kinds of behavior were distinguished mainly by whether stimuli outside the maze were available to the rat. If they were, the rat oriented itself within the larger stimulus complex, the room within which the maze was located; it learned places. If not, it mastered only specific turns within the maze; it learned responses. Additional complexities were introduced in other maze experiments (cf. Olton, 1979). For example, it was demonstrated that a rat sometimes chooses the shortest available route through a maze when another route preferred earlier is blocked, or that it sometimes takes appropriate shortcuts that have just been added to a maze even though it never traveled those shortcuts before. These outcomes provide the justification for speaking of *cognitive maps* (Tolman, 1948); the finding that organisms can locate an area even when approaching it from a new direction demonstrates that they learn spatial relations in addition to or perhaps instead of specific paths.

The problems of determining the environmental features to which organisms attend as they move from one place to another emerge on a grander scale in animal homing and migration. Wasps return to their nests, bees to their hives, salmon to their rivers of origin and birds to seasonal nesting grounds. Among the environmental features that may be important are landmarks, the location and movement of the sun and stars, polarized light, chemical gradients and magnetic fields (e.g., Tinbergen, 1972; Walcott, Gould, & Kirshvink, 1979). In some cases organisms navigate in isolation to regions they've never visited before; in others, they do so in the company of other members of their species. Both cases must involve substantial phylogenic components, either with respect to important properties of environments or with

respect to the contingencies that lead to group migration (or both). With respect to long-distance migrations, the phylogenic contingencies may have involved the selection of those able to maintain orientation over gradually longer journeys as continents very slowly drifted apart over geologic time (Skinner, 1975). A more detailed account of these phenomena is beyond the scope of this text, but they illustrate that an analysis of the stimulus properties that determine behavior is relevant to both phylogeny and ontogeny.

NATURAL CONCEPTS
AND PROBABILISTIC STIMULUS CLASSES

We can speak of concepts as generalization within a class of stimuli and discrimination between classes of stimuli (Keller & Schoenfeld, 1950). Thus, our concept of red must involve generalization among all stimuli we call red and discrimination between these and the others we don't call red. Thus, concepts are to classes of stimuli what operants are to classes of responses. (Responding on the basis of some single property of stimuli is sometimes called *abstraction*, and the language of concepts is sometimes restricted to responding that is based on some combination of properties. But these are ambiguous distinctions. For example, being-to-the-left-of can be treated either as a single relational property or as a combination of properties necessarily including both a reference point and a stimulus to the left of that reference point.)

We've already noted that it's often difficult to define discriminative stimuli by physical dimensions. For example, the properties that define the letter *A* vary according to whether it's uppercase or lowercase and whether it appears as type or as script. The capacity to discriminate among such stimuli exists in animals as well as humans (e.g., discriminations between various forms of the letter *A* and the digit *2* have been demonstrated in pigeons: Morgan et al., 1976). But the difficulty of defining stimuli in terms of measurable physical properties isn't limited to arbitrary classes created by humans, such as letters and numbers. They exist also with everyday objects and events. What distinguishes dogs from other animals? On what basis do we generalize between huskies and chihuahuas by calling both dogs, while we discriminate between huskies and wolves even though they look more alike than huskies and chihuahuas?

Pigeons have been taught to discriminate between pictures that contain a human form and those that don't (e.g., Herrnstein & Loveland, 1975). Such discriminations have been called *natural concepts*. In one study (Herrnstein, Loveland, & Cable, 1976), slides were presented on a screen next to a pigeon's key and its pecks were reinforced in the presence of some slides but not others. Some pigeons learned discriminations between pictures with and without trees; others learned discriminations between pictures with and without water; still others learned discriminations between pictures with and without a person. After training with one set of slides (e.g., slides with and without trees), the pigeons discriminated among slides of the same classes of stimuli that hadn't been presented before. The new slides were sometimes more accurately discriminated than those used in training. The implications were that

we cannot begin to draw up a list of common elements. To recognize a tree, the pigeons did not require that it be green, leafy, vertical, woody, branching, and so on (overlooking the problem of common elements nested within terms like leafy, vertical, woody, and so on). Moreover, to be recognizable as a nontree, a picture did not have to omit greenness, wood-

iness, branchiness, verticality, and so on. Neither could we identify common elements in the other two experiments. If not common elements, what? No other theory is so easily characterized, though in crude terms an alternative suggests itself. Pigeons respond to clusters of features more or less isomorphic with the clusters we respond to ourselves. The green should be on the leaves, if either green or leaves are present. However, neither is necessary or sufficient. The vertical or branching parts should be the woody parts, although neither of these features is necessary or sufficient either. What we see as trees comprises a complex list of probabilistic conjunctions and disjunctions, the discovery of which would require far more effort than seems justified by any possible benefit. (Herrnstein, Loveland, & Cable, 1976, pp. 298–299)

Natural concepts are examples of *probabilistic stimulus classes*, classes in which each member contains some subset of features but none is common to all members. The number of features in the subset may vary from one class member to another. Such classes, sometimes called *fuzzy sets*, don't have well-defined boundaries, though class members may have family resemblances (Rosch, 1973).

Some probabilistic stimulus classes are defined by reference to a *prototype*. A prototype is a typical member of a probabilistic class; it's derived from a weighted average of all of the features of all members of the class. For example, birds are a probabilistic stimulus class; most fly, but ostriches and penguins don't. In the production of a prototypical bird, feathers must be weighted more heavily than webbed feet because more birds have feathers than have webbed feet. Thus, a robin is more prototypical than a duck because it shares more features with other birds than does a duck.

Other types of stimulus classes include polymorphous stimulus classes (Lea & Harrison, 1978: see Glossary) and equivalence classes (about which more in the next chapter). In fact, the class of stimulus classes is itself a probabilistic stimulus class, in the sense that its definition changes as we expand the boundaries of relevant research.

DEFINING STIMULUS CLASSES

The problem of defining stimulus classes is a general one. It isn't resolved by appealing to the procedures of physical measurement, because the reading of meters or other instruments is also discriminative behavior. As we'll see in the next chapter, behavior classes depend on the common contingencies that created them and not on their physical properties. Even the behavior of the scientist depends on discriminations learned in the laboratory. As we've already seen, distinctions among reinforcement, punishment, elicitation and other behavioral processes are based upon such discriminations. They are where our taxonomy of behavior comes from. Stimulus control is as fundamental with respect to our own scientific behavior as it is with respect to the behavior of the organisms that we study. Thus, any effective philosophy of science must take it into account.

We began this chapter by exploring parallels between differentiation and induction on the one hand and discrimination and generalization on the other. Both are outcomes of differential reinforcement; they differ mainly in whether we arrange the operation for stimulus properties or response properties. We treated functional aspects of stimulus control in the context of experiments on attention, stimulus-control gradients and fading procedures. In dealing with discriminable properties of the environment in the context of animal cognition, we then considered how complex relational features of the environment could define stimulus classes. Cognitive maps and natural concepts provided relevant examples. In the next chapter, we'll explore complex stimulus classes further and we'll find them relevant to important human judgments.

Chapter 9
Conditional Discrimination and Higher-Order Classes

A. Relational Stimulus Dimensions
Matching-to-Sample and Oddity
Symbolic Behavior: Equivalence Classes

B. Higher-Order Classes of Behavior
Learning Set
Properties of Higher-Order Classes
Origins of Structure

C. Sources of Novel Behavior

Matching comes by way of Old English from the Indo-European mag- *or* mak-, *to knead or fashion; it is related to* make, among *and* mass. Sample *can be traced to the Indo-European root,* em-, *to take or distribute. Like* example, *it combines the Latin* ex-, *out, and* emere, *to buy or obtain; it is related to* exempt, prompt *and* consume. Comparison *is derived from the Latin* com-, *with, plus* par, *equal; it is related to* part, pair *and perhaps also* repertory. Oddity *fittingly has a more singular etymology; it is derived from the Old Norse* oddi, *a point or a triangle.*

The concept of classes is implicit in the etymology of symbolic, *which by combining the Greek* sym-, *together, and* ballein, *to throw, suggests the creation of a unit from separate parts. Combined with* dia-, *across,* ballein *provides via* diabolic *the root for* devil, *and combined with* pro-, *before, it provides the root for* problem.

Like contingencies, discriminations may be effective under some conditions but not others. For example, your response to a green traffic light will depend on whether you're facing it or looking at it from the cross traffic. Such discriminations, in which the role of one stimulus depends on others that provide its context, are called *conditional discriminations*. Consider the case of attention in the pigeon, discussed in Chapter 8 (Figure 8-2). The available stimuli are triangles or circles on red or green backgrounds. Suppose we add a lamp above the key and reinforce pecks in the presence of triangles when it's lit and pecks in the presence of red when it isn't. Under these circumstances, when the lamp is on the pigeon comes to peck triangles but not circles without regard to color; when it's off, it comes to peck red keys but not green without regard to form. In other words, whether the pigeon discriminates form or color is conditional on whether the lamp is lit.

In this chapter, we'll consider several experimental procedures in which discriminative contingencies depend upon the context within which they're arranged. We'll see that these procedures generate higher-order classes of behavior, in the sense that the classes are defined not by particular stimuli or responses but rather by relations that include those stimuli and responses as special cases (cf. Chapter 7). Among the procedures we'll review are matching-to-sample, oddity, arbitrary matching and learning set. They provide a context in which we'll explore the conditions under which one stimulus can become the functional equivalent of another (as when, in varied settings, uppercase *A* and lowercase *a* function as the same letter).

Section A   Relational Stimulus Dimensions

Many conditional discriminations involve arbitrary relations between a conditional discriminative stimulus and the discriminations for which it sets the occasion. Some cases in which those relations aren't arbitrary are of special interest. For example, whether one stimulus in a set of stimuli matches one or more of the others or is an odd stimulus depends on, or is conditional on, the context of other stimuli within which it's presented. For example, if stimuli A and B are blue and stimulus C is yellow, then in relation to A, B is a matching stimulus and C is an odd stimulus. We'll now consider some properties of such conditional discriminations.

MATCHING-TO-SAMPLE AND ODDITY

Matching-to-sample is illustrated as we might arrange it in a three-key pigeon chamber in Figure 9-1 (cf. Skinner, 1950; Ferster, 1960). During an intertrial interval, all keys are dark. A trial begins when the center key

FIGURE 9-1   Diagram of a matching-to-sample trial in a three-key pigeon chamber. After an intertrial interval of *t* s, a sample stimulus (green: G) appears on the center key. A center-key peck turns on the two side keys. One comparison stimulus matches the sample; the other (red: R) doesn't. A peck on the matching comparison stimulus produces food, after which the next intertrial interval starts; a peck on the nonmatching comparison starts the next intertrial interval without food. The sample stimulus and the left-right locations of the matching comparison vary from trial to trial.

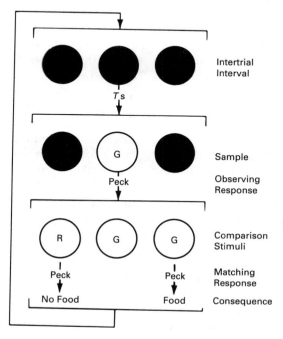

is lit, presenting the *sample* stimulus. Typically a peck is then required on the center key. This peck, sometimes called an *observing response*, turns on new stimuli and also makes it likely that the pigeon has looked at the sample (cf. the discussion of observing responses in Chapters 8 and 11). The two stimuli produced by the center-key peck are called *comparison* stimuli; one matches the sample and the other doesn't. A peck on the matching key then produces a reinforcer followed by a new intertrial interval, but one on the nonmatching key is followed directly by the intertrial interval without a reinforcer (sometimes nonmatching pecks also produce an extended intertrial interval, which perhaps functions as a mild punisher; cf. Holt & Shafer, 1973).

Both the sample stimulus and the position of the matching comparison usually change over trials. A common feature of matching-to-sample is a correction procedure, which repeats the same sample and comparison stimuli on the next trial if a trial ends with a peck on a nonmatching key. This procedure prevents the development of responding that's restricted to only one key or color (but as we'll see in Chapter 10, it also guarantees that errors are often closely followed by reinforcers produced by correct responses).

Suppose a pigeon pecks only the comparison stimulus on the left. If the matching key alternates irregularly between left and right, these pecks will be reinforced on half the trials (those with the matching stimulus on the left). Reinforcement on half the trials will probably be enough to maintain pecking on the left key indefinitely. With a correction procedure, however, the pigeon has to switch to the right key sooner or later, because a trial with a matching stimulus on the right will repeat itself until a right-key peck occurs and is reinforced. Similarly, if the pigeon always pecks red comparisons, these pecks will be reinforced on half the trials unless a correction procedure forces the pigeon to switch occasionally to green.

Another procedural refinement is to enhance the pigeon's attention to the sample by modifying the contingencies arranged for pecks on the sample key. For example, if production of the comparison stimuli depends on different patterns of responding for each sample (e.g., different response rates), the response patterns the pigeon produces can tell us how well it's discriminating between the samples. Such procedures sometimes produce faster acquisition of matching, but unfortunately the enhanced attention to the sample sometimes also reduces attention to the comparisons (e.g., Urcuioli, 1985).

In any case, suppose now that a pigeon is responding accurately given red (R) and green (G) in a matching-to-sample procedure. How should we describe its performance? Has it just learned to peck left given the configurations RRG and GGR and right given GRR and RGG? Or has it learned matching in general, the identity relation? If we now present blue or yellow and the pigeon matches the new sample colors we'll feel more confident about speaking of generalized matching (in fact, matching in pigeons doesn't transfer easily to new colors, though the likelihood of such transfer depends on the details of training). Even if we saw matching with new colors, what if we failed to get matching with geometric figures? We might just say the pigeon has learned color but not form matching, noting that the human concept of matching seems not so limited by specific dimensions of the stimuli. Matching-to-sample has sometimes been called *identity matching*, but we reserve that term for cases in which matching generalizes to novel sample and comparison stimuli, such as matching of forms after training with colors. With a limited stimulus set, what looks like matching on the basis of identity too often turns out to be matching based on specific stimulus configurations.

There are many variations on matching-to-sample. If reinforcement is arranged for pecks on the nonmatching rather than the matching comparison, the procedure becomes an instance of *oddity* responding, because this key is necessarily the odd one of the three keys. This version of oddity requires a minimum of two pecks per trial, one on the sample and the other on the nonmatching comparison. In other versions of oddity procedures, no sample is used; with pigeons in a three-key chamber, for example, each trial consists of lighting all three keys, with the odd key any one of them. This procedure requires just one peck per trial.

The relations among stimuli can also involve *arbitrary matching*. For example, we could train the pigeon to peck green given a square as a sample and red given a circle as a sample. We might then ask whether the pigeon might peck a square given a green sample and a circle given a red sample. We often expect such reversibility when we deal with words and objects, as when a child who's learned to point to a picture of a car on seeing the word *car* can also point to the word on seeing the picture. This reversibility, a property of *symbolic behavior*, isn't to be taken for granted. For example, a child may show such reversibility without explicit training but a pigeon won't. Arbitrary matching can also be extended to cases in which the same matching response is trained with more than one comparison (e.g., pecking a green comparison given either a circle or an ellipse as a sample, and pecking a red one given either a square or a triangle; cf. Zentall & Urcuioli, 1993, on many-to-one and one-to-many matching).

The various tasks we've just considered all involve relations among different stimulus classes. Some are arbitrary, as when we designate pecks on green as correct given

square as a sample and pecks on red as correct given circle as a sample; but others such as matching and oddity seem to involve more fundamental dimensions. How then should we deal with relations such as same and different and opposite, and what can we say about the contingencies that created them (cf. Hayes, 1994, on relational frames)? Questions about stimulus structure seem to be inevitably interwoven with questions about contingencies and the structure of behavior (e.g., Fujita, 1983; Lamb & Riley, 1981; Wasserman, Kiedinger, & Bhatt, 1988).

SYMBOLIC BEHAVIOR: EQUIVALENCE CLASSES

If a pigeon's pecks are reinforced in the presence of green but not red, we wouldn't be likely to consider the possibility of the pigeon's greening in the presence of pecks. Such a reversal makes no behavioral sense. This isn't so in matching, though. Both the sample stimulus and the comparison response are defined by the stimuli presented on the keys. We could therefore ask about a red response to a red stimulus, or about the reversibility of a vertical response to a diagonal stimulus, or about whether round responses to dim stimuli can be created by training round responses to large stimuli and then large responses to dim stimuli.

These cases illustrate properties of relations called *reflexivity*, *symmetry* and *transitivity*. Reflexive properties are those that hold between a term and itself (e.g., A = A); symmetrical properties are those in which the order of terms is reversible (e.g., if A = B then B = A); and transitive properties are those in which the common terms in two ordered pairs determine a third ordered pair (e.g., if A = B and B = C then A = C). Equivalence relations are those that have all three properties, and the terms that enter into them (here, A, B and C) are said to be members of an *equivalence class* (Sidman, 1994).

For other relations, only some of these properties hold. For example, the relation of *oppositeness* is symmetrical (if D is the opposite of E, E is the opposite of D), but it's neither reflexive (D is not the opposite of itself) nor transitive (if D is the opposite of E and E is the opposite of F, D isn't the opposite of F; instead, D is the same as F). And a magnitude relation such as *greater than* is transitive (if G is greater than H and H is greater than

I, then G is greater than I), but it's neither reflexive nor symmetrical.

Figure 9-2 illustrates how standard and arbitrary matching procedures can be used to demonstrate reflexivity, symmetry and transitivity. Each procedure includes two sample stimuli, shown as A in the three-key array on the left and as B in that on the right. For convenience, the matching comparison stimulus is always shown on the left in the three-key array, even though in practice the side positions of the comparisons vary from

FIGURE 9-2 Matching procedures for studying three properties of equivalence relations: reflexivity (identity matching), symmetry (reversal of arbitrary matching), and transitivity (transfer across ordered pairs of arbitrary matches). Each three-key array is shown in only one of its two possible arrangements, with the matching comparison on the left. Stimuli include red (R) and green (G), triangles and circles, and light and dark.

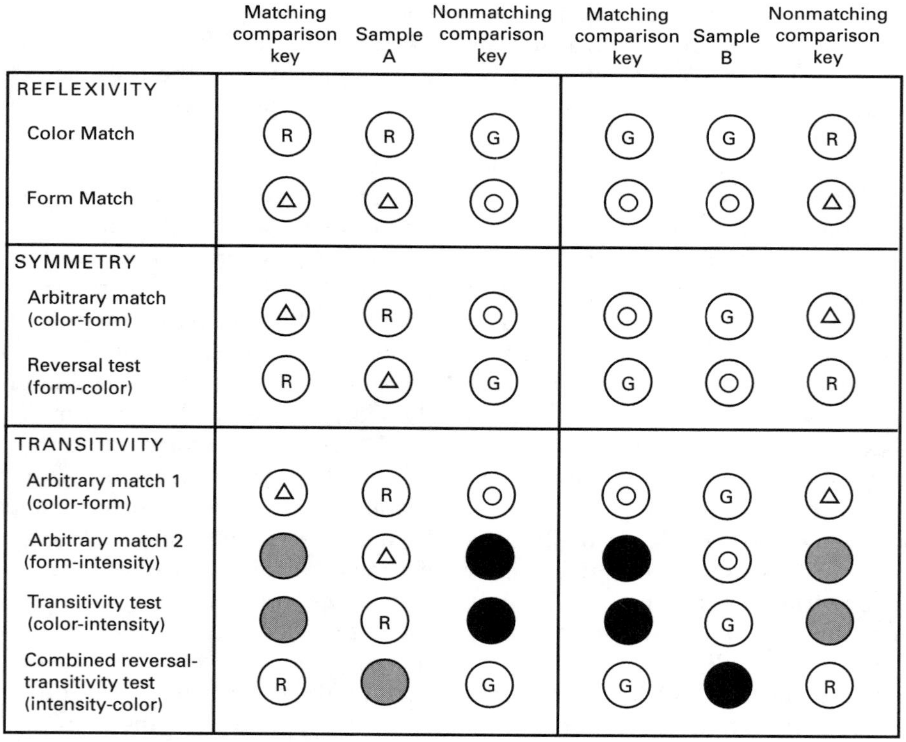

trial to trial. As in Figure 9-1, a peck on the sample produces the comparisons, and a peck on the matching comparison produces food whereas one on the nonmatching comparison doesn't.

The top two rows of Figure 9-2 (reflexivity) illustrate standard matching procedures with color and with form. The next two rows (symmetry) illustrate symbolic matching with color samples and form comparisons and then a reversal test with form samples and color comparisons. The bottom rows (transitivity) show how the common stimuli in two symbolic matching procedures (color to form and form to intensity) can be combined in a test of transitivity (color to intensity). An alternative test, illustrated in the last row, combines the reversal and transitivity tests (intensity to color); it's sometimes called an equivalence test, and the relation between the stimuli of the equivalence test is sometimes called an equivalence relation. The relations of the reversal and equivalence tests were never explicitly taught. If appropriate matching occurs in these tests, the new relations demonstrated by that behavior are called *emergent* relations, in the sense that they've emerged without explicit training; they are examples of novel behavior produced by the arbitrary matching contingencies.

When we say that a pigeon that pecks in the presence of green can't green in the presence of pecks, we're saying that the relations between antecedent stimuli and the responses they occasion in a three-term contingency aren't symmetrical. This means that we can't reduce equivalence classes to classes of discriminative stimuli. Equivalence relations are symmetrical, but the relations among the terms of a three-term contingency aren't.

We've already questioned whether the pigeon's standard matching performance depends on the identity relation in general or only on relations among specific stimuli. We might assume that the identity relation between sample and comparison stimuli would make standard matching easier than arbitrary matching. For pigeons, however, acquisition of matching depends more on the stimulus dimensions chosen for samples and comparisons than it does on whether the procedure is standard or arbitrary matching. For example, both standard and arbitrary matching develop more rapidly with red and green samples than either does with vertical and horizontal samples (e.g., Carter & Werner, 1978). Symmetry and transitivity have been demonstrated in a limited way with pigeons, but the effects have not ordinarily been robust (e.g., D'Amato et al., 1985; Richards, 1988). Furthermore, there are technical as well as logical pitfalls to be avoided in the analysis of equivalence relations via transfer tests, such as whether the relevant conditional discriminations have been learned as picking out the matching comparison rather than as *exclusion*, or rejecting the nonmatching one (e.g., Carrigan & Sidman, 1992). Thus, the case for equivalence relations in the pigeon's matching behavior is at best not compelling (probably all of the component relations could be explicitly taught, of course, but that outcome would be mainly of procedural interest).

Equivalence relations are easily generated in humans. For example, retarded youths who'd already shown reflexivity (identity matching) were taught matches involving (A) spoken words, (B) pictures corresponding to those words and (C) the corresponding printed words (e.g., car, dog, boy: Sidman, Cresson, & Willson-Morris, 1974). First, given any one of 20 spoken picture words they learned to pick out the corresponding pictures from a comparison set (AB). Then, given the same 20 spoken words they learned to pick out the corresponding printed words from a set (AC). For all 20 words, these two kinds of matches (spoken words to pictures and spoken words to printed words) also generated four other relations without additional training: two new relations through symmetry (BA, given a picture saying its name; and CA, given a printed word saying it) and two through transitivity (BC, given a picture picking out the corresponding printed word; and CB, given a printed word picking out the corresponding picture). Forty relations had been taught (20 each in AB and AC) and another 80 emerged indirectly (in BA, CA, BC and CB). The reinforcement of arbitrary matching had created the beginnings of a reading repertory in these youths. The emergent relations justify calling their performances *symbolic matching* rather than arbitrary matching.

Each of the 20 equivalence classes consisted of a picture and the corresponding printed and spoken words. New classes could have been added with new pictures and corresponding words, and the number of equivalences could have been expanded by adding new relations (e.g., printed words and words written in longhand, or pictures and actual objects). There aren't any obvious limits to the number of classes that can be created or the number of stimuli that can be included within each class. The status of such classes in the behavior of nonhumans remains a matter of controversy (e.g., Dube et al., 1993; Horne & Lowe, 1996; Schusterman & Kastak, 1993; Zentall & Urcuioli, 1993). But equivalence classes define symbolic behavior, so maybe they're an exclusive property of human behavior, or maybe we share this property only with our close primate relatives. In fact, much of the interest in equivalence classes arises because of their possible relevance to the phenomena of language, which we'll consider in Chapters 14 through 16.

The members of an equivalence class are equivalent in the sense that we can exchange one for another in the context of arbitrary matching procedures. But this doesn't necessarily mean that they're functionally equivalent, in the sense that one will substitute for another in other contexts. In other words, *functional equivalence* isn't the same as membership in an equivalence class, and it mustn't be assumed that the logical properties of these classes are fully consistent with their behavioral ones (Saunders & Green, 1992). The functional equivalence of the members of an equivalence class must be tested experimentally. The question is whether a function acquired by one member of an equivalence class, such as a discriminative function, will transfer to other members of that class (cf. Sidman et al., 1989).

Consider an example. A child has learned to obey a parent's words, *go* and *stop*, when crossing with the parent at a traffic intersection. In a separate setting, the child is taught that *go* and green traffic lights are equivalent and that *stop* and red traffic lights are equivalent (in other words, *go* and green become members of one equivalence class and *stop* and red become members of another). If the discriminative functions of the words *go* and *stop* transfer to the respective traffic lights, the child will obey the traffic lights without any additional instruction. An analogous type of transfer has been demonstrated experimentally with children: High and low rates of responding occasioned by one set of stimuli transferred to another set when the stimuli in the sets were made members of equivalence classes (Catania, Horne, & Lowe, 1989; cf. de Rose et al., 1988).

Section B   Higher-Order Classes of Behavior

In our examples of matching-to-sample and related procedures, we've typically described performances at more than one level of analysis. We described pecks to red comparisons given a red sample as conditional discriminations, but we also asked whether we could characterize this performance as identity matching. Our decision depended on whether we had created an operant class defined by particular stimuli in a particular context, or one that generalized across relations over a range of different stimuli. It makes a difference whether a pigeon that matches green to green and red to red also matches with other colors, or whether a pigeon that matches to sample across a range of colors also does so when we present problems that instead involve shapes or textures or other dimensions. Similarly, it makes a difference whether a pigeon's arbitrary matching is an operant class restricted to a particular set of samples and comparisons or instead includes all of the reflexive, symmetrical and transitive relations that define equivalence classes.

These examples involve classes embedded within other classes. If we demonstrate identity matching, each specific match defines a class, but identity matching is then a higher-order class that includes all of the specific matches as its components. In matching-to-sample, the matching of green to green or red to red may exist as separate operants. They can be treated as instances of identity matching only if they can be shown to be components of a single higher-order operant defined by the identity relation between sample and comparison. One test for this higher-order operant is whether novel

relations can be demonstrated, such as the matching of new colors (e.g., blue to blue or yellow to yellow); another is whether all of the matching subclasses hang together as a class if we change contingencies only for some subset of them. In what follows, we'll examine some higher-order classes, we'll review some of their properties, and we'll consider some implications that can be drawn from them.

LEARNING SET

The learning of a new discrimination can depend on what the organism has already learned (we sometimes call what it has learned in the laboratory its *experimental history*). As illustrated by the phenomenon called *learning set* (Harlow, 1949), responding may depend on relations among stimulus properties independent of specific stimuli. Two different objects were presented to a food-deprived monkey in successive trials. Their positions varied from trial to trial. Food was under only one of them, and therefore picking that one up was differentially reinforced. After a number of trials, the monkey mastered the discrimination. Then, in a new problem, another pair of objects was presented, with differential reinforcement again arranged for picking up only one of the two objects. Again a discrimination emerged. A new problem with another new pair was then presented, and later still another, and so on.

Data averaged across eight monkeys are shown in Figure 9-3. Each set of points shows percent correct responses over the first 6 trials across blocks of successive problems. Over the first 8 problems (1–8), correct responses increased gradually over trials; by the sixth trial, they hadn't even reached 80%.

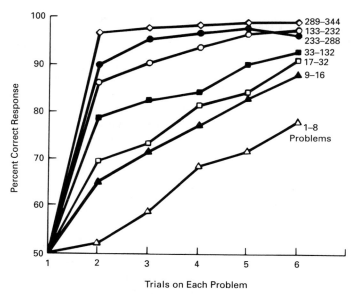

FIGURE 9-3   Learning set or learning-to-learn. Eight monkeys learned a variety of two-choice discrimination problems. Each set of points shows percent correct responses over the first 6 trials of each problem for blocks of successive problems (the y-axis starts at 50%, chance level). The rate of learning increased over successive problems. By the last block of problems (problems 289–344), responding was almost 100% accurate by trial 2 of each new problem. (Adapted from Harlow, 1949, Figure 2)

In the next block of 8 problems (9–16), correct responses increased more rapidly over trials. Over successive blocks, correct responding rose more and more rapidly over trials until, by the last block (trials 289–344), responding reached nearly 100% accuracy on the second trial of each new problem. In other words, the more problems the monkey had mastered, the more rapidly it mastered each new one.

In this procedure, we can't describe the discriminated operant just in terms of a stimulus pair. When a monkey acquires successive discriminations so rapidly that it consistently picks the stimulus correlated with reinforcement after a single trial with a new pair, its performance depends on relations between stimuli and their correlated consequences over successive problems and not on the particular stimulus pairs that appear within single problems. Within each early problem, the monkey had to learn many other features of the procedure besides which stimulus was correlated with food. It had to learn that food was correlated with just one of the two stimuli rather than with position or other dimensions of the setting, that this correlation didn't change within a problem, that reaching simultaneously for both stimuli wasn't reinforced, and so on. During early problems, learning took place slowly because the monkey was learning many things such as these; eventually, when the monkey had learned these other things, all it had to learn in any new problem was which stimulus was correlated with food.

At this point, we can define the discriminated operant as follows: If picking up one of the objects is reinforced on the first trial of a new problem, pick that one on all subsequent trials; if it isn't reinforced, switch to the other object on all subsequent trials. In learning set, this is the behavior that is reinforced, and this is what the organism's behavior becomes. Thus, the correspondence between the reinforcement contingencies and the behavior generated by these contingencies remains an appropriate criterion for this operant class. Learning set qualifies as a higher-order class because it's defined by these relations and not by the stimuli and responses of any particular problem.

A phenomenon that can be viewed as a variation on learning set is *learned helplessness* (Maier, Seligman, & Solomon, 1969). For example, rats that receive inescapable and unavoidable electric shock in one situation are sometimes less likely to learn avoidance when that becomes possible in a new situation than rats never exposed to inescapable and unavoidable shock (cf. Maier, Albin, & Testa, 1973). Here again it's difficult to define the response class, except to note that the rats given inescapable and unavoidable shock apparently learned that their responses didn't have important consequences; the behavior generated by these contingencies transferred to situations in which responding could have consequences. Maybe learned helplessness as a higher-order class could be brought under the control of discriminative stimuli through differential contingencies.

Learning set illustrates the range and complexity of what organisms can learn; it also shows that we can't treat what happens when we introduce an experimentally naive organism into a laboratory setting as a simple case (cf. Chapter 5 on acquisition). To study learning, some investigators have therefore turned to the repeated acquisition of simple discriminations or simple response sequences. Paradoxically, they've come to study learning, defined by changes in performance, in the context of steady-state procedures, defined by stability in performance. For example, with four groups of three levers each in a monkey's chamber, only one particular sequence of presses was reinforced within any session (e.g., left lever of group 1; right lever of group 2; middle lever of group 3; right lever of group 4), but the sequence changed from session to session (Boren & Devine, 1968). Once the monkey's rate of mastering a new problem each day became stable, these repeated acquisitions provided a baseline for studying a variety of phenomena: effects of different fading procedures; effects of drugs on learning; effects of different types of consequences for responses at various positions in the sequence; effects of creating the response sequence as a whole as opposed to building it up either from the beginning or from the end; and so on.

PROPERTIES OF HIGHER-ORDER CLASSES

A significant property of higher-order classes was implicit in our treatment of self-injurious behavior in Chapter 7. In that example, self-injurious behavior maintained by attention was not easily reduced by extinction as long as it remained part of a larger class (attention-getting), most other members of which continued to be effective. Whenever the contingencies maintaining a higher-order class differ from those maintaining one or more of its subclasses, we must ask which contingencies will prevail. For example, imagine a higher-order class consisting of a child's imitations of the actions modeled by a puppet. When the puppet claps, the child claps; when the puppet laughs, the child laughs; when the puppet jumps, the child jumps; and so on. Let's identify a dozen different imitations by letter, A through L. Once we've reinforced those, one way we can tell whether we've created a higher-order class is to see whether the child also imitates new actions that the puppet has never modeled before.

Now suppose we stop reinforcing G while we continue reinforcing all of the other imitations, A through F and H through L. Whether imitations of G will decrease or whether they'll persist long after they've been excluded from the reinforcement contingencies that continue for the others is an experimental question. If they decrease, we've demonstrated that we can pull G apart from the other members of the higher-order class. But if they don't, we'll have to assume that G is still functioning as a member of the higher-order class called imitation, which is defined by the correspondences between what the puppet does and what the child does. As long as a higher-order class maintains its integrity, its subclasses are maintained along with the other members even if they're not consistently involved in the contingencies that maintain the others. When that happens, the lower-order subclasses will seem insensitive to the changed contingencies that have been arranged for them.

When we arrange new contingencies for subclasses of higher-order classes, we ordinarily expect those subclasses eventually to be differentiated from the others. But if the subclasses overlap in various ways with other classes that share in other contingencies, this may not happen. For example, imitating what someone has said shares class membership with other imitations but it may also participate in social contingencies that don't involve imitation. This may be enough to maintain it as a subclass when contingencies change for it but not for other kinds of imitations. These complexities are implicit in the following account of ontogenic selection, where the "rules, principles, strategies and the like" correspond to what we've been calling higher-order classes:

In more mature human beings, much instrumental behavior and, more especially, a great part of verbal behavior is organized into higher-order routines and is, in many instances, better understood in terms of the operation of rules, principles, strategies and the like than in terms of successions of responses to particular stimuli. . . . In these situations it is the selection of strategies rather than the selection of particular reactions to stimuli which is modified by past experience with rewarding or punishing consequences.

If one who is attempting to describe and predict the behavior of an adult human learner fails to take account of these behavioral organizations, and attempts to construct an account in terms only of individual stimulus–response units, the principles of operation of rewards and punishments may appear to be quite different from those revealed in simpler experiments with animals or immature human learners. Actually, it may be that the principles of operation of these factors are the same in all cases and that the difference lies in the nature of the behavioral units whose probabilities are being modified as a result of the experience with various types of outcomes. (Estes, 1971, p. 23)

We've considered potential higher-order classes in matching-to-sample, learning set and imitation. In these and other cases, training with many specific instances may sometimes be a sufficient prerequisite for higher-order or generalized classes (e.g., training with many symmetry problems may produce generalized symmetry, training with many transitivity problems may produce generalized transitivity, and so on; such generalized classes have also been called *relational frames*: Hayes, 1994). We'll encounter various other examples of higher-order classes in other contexts, as when we deal with social learning and verbal behavior. For example, we'll return to generalized imitation in Chapter 13, and we'll consider classes of verbal responding such as naming in Chapter 14 and the following of instructions in Chapter 15.

ORIGINS OF STRUCTURE

Most of the classes we've considered so far have been structured classes. The properties that defined them weren't arbitrary, but instead were derived from systematic relational properties of environmental events (e.g., matching, oddity, symmetry). Let's now examine some arbitrary classes, as created in an experiment by Vaughan (1988). A group of photographic slides was arbitrarily divided into two sets of 20 slides each. The slides were presented one at a time, and pigeons' pecks were reinforced given a slide from one set but not the other. After blocks of sessions with fairly consistent performance, the correlation between slide sets and reinforcement was occasionally reversed. After several reversals, the pigeons began to switch their responding from one slide set to the other after only some of the slides had been shown. In other words, the common contingencies arranged for the 20 slides in a set made them functionally equivalent, in the sense that once contingencies changed for just a few of the slides in the set, behavior changed appropriately for all of them. This functional equivalence emerged because the same consequences were arranged for responses in the presence of all of the stimuli within a set.

This procedure created two arbitrary discriminated operants, pecks to one slide set and pecks to the other, by arranging common contingencies for the members within each set. The correlation with reinforced pecks was the only thing that distinguished one class from the other. We probably think of classes differently when their constituents are arbitrary, as in Vaughan's study, than when the constituents have some natural coherence (e.g., when they're selected from a narrow band of spectral stimuli or are all instances of some natural category: cf. Chapter 8). But the point is that common contin-

gencies select the members of operant classes. A rat's left paw presses and right paw presses and both paw presses are arbitary too, until they share in the common contingencies of depressing the lever. We can view Vaughan's experiment as just another example of using common contingencies to create a discriminated operant; it differs from others mainly in the particular classes that it created. Whatever structure then existed in the two slide sets was imposed by the two sets of common contingencies (reinforcement for one and extinction for the other).

One expression of the problem of how structure emerges from undifferentiated beginnings is familiar to psychologists in the form of William James' metaphorical description of a newborn's response to the world as "one great blooming, buzzing confusion" (James, 1890, p. 488). James appealed to the child's earliest discriminations as the basis for the child's organization of what started out as disorganized. We know a lot more about discrimination than was available to James. He didn't have the benefit of Thorndike's research on the consequences of behavior or Pavlov's on the signalling functions of stimuli or Skinner's on operant classes and three-term contingencies.

To tackle James' problem, we can start by considering how discriminated operants are created by contingencies. Operants, defined in terms of their response properties and the stimuli in the presence of which they occur, are selected by their consequences. But we must distinguish between common contingencies and common consequences. Common consequences aren't sufficient for creating differentiated classes because a single reinforcer can maintain two or more different response classes. For example, when a pigeon's left-key pecks produce food according to one interval schedule while its right-key pecks produce the same food according to a different interval schedule, left-key pecks and right-key pecks are different operants even though they produce the same consequence, food.

In other words, each operant is created not just by common consequences but rather by common consequences that depend on common contingencies. Operant contingencies make all members of an operant functionally equivalent, and the Vaughan experiment demonstrated a totally arbitrary discriminated operant based only on common contingencies. But accounts of complex discrimination too often appeal to the relative contributions of the stimulus and the organism without including the contingencies (e.g., Fetterman, 1996). We considered some of these issues in Chapter 8, in the context of natural concepts. When the class members have no common physical features, then any approach that looks to stimulus properties to define how such a class was formed must fail (cf. Lakoff, 1987). It's necessary to look instead to the behavioral processes that created these classes, and the only consistently common feature of their members is the common contingencies they enter into.

We've just argued that common contingencies can create the sometimes arbitrary functional classes called operants. But when class members do share physical properties, nonarbitrary functional classes may arise not because of direct effects of those shared properties but rather because, by virtue of those shared properties, all class members are necessarily involved in common contingencies. For example, running one's hand over a sphere differs from running it over a cube; only in the latter case does one encounter an edge. These natural contingencies may therefore be the basis for discriminating between spheres and cubes. In other words, what seem to be nonarbitrary natural categories may well be created in just

the same way as arbitrary ones, over a lifetime of experience with the common contingencies they engender (cf. the discussion of sensory consequences in Chapter 5). Doesn't anything that's significant involve contingencies of some sort, and aren't there plenty of opportunities for these contingencies to bring order, in the form of discriminated operants, out of the "great blooming, buzzing confusion"?

Undoubtedly some aspects of operant selection must be constrained by properties of the sensory and motor systems and neural organizations that have been selected phylogenically (we'll explore some of these constraints in Chapter 12). Skinner spoke of such constraints as the "natural lines of fracture along which behavior and environment actually break" (Skinner, 1935a, p. 40); "We divide behavior into hard and fast classes and are then surprised to find that the organism disregards the boundaries we have set" (Skinner, 1953, p. 94). But ontogenic contingencies are so pervasive that we must never discount them when we're trying to identify the origins of behavior. Behavior structure is determined by contingencies, but contingencies are determined in turn by environmental structure.

Section C   Sources of Novel Behavior

One theme in the discussions of many of the examples we've considered is where novel behavior comes from. Ontogenic selection must have variations on which to do its work, and it's therefore of special interest to identify the sources of novelty and variation.

We identified one method for producing new behavior when we examined shaping in Chapter 7, and another when we examined fading in Chapter 8. We also saw that novelty and variability were themselves properties of behavior that could be reinforced (e.g., Neuringer, 1986; Page & Neuringer, 1985; Pryor, Haag, & O'Reilly, 1969). But these aren't the only possibilities, as we discovered when we explored equivalences and higher-order classes. Tests for equivalence sometimes demonstrated emergent relations, relations that emerged without explicit training. For example, after arbitrary AB and BC matches, children typically performed accurately with matches involving other relations they'd never seen before, such as BA or AC or CA. And one of our criteria for calling a class a higher-order operant was the emergence of novel instances. For example, one way to tell whether a matching-to-sample performance qualifies as identity matching is to see whether the matching generalizes to novel stimuli, as in the matching of forms after training with colors. Similarly, one way to tell whether a child's imitations of modeled behavior qualify as a higher-order class is to see whether the child imitates actions that have never been modeled before.

Many examples of novel behavior implicitly involve the novel combination of existing classes. Our example of the transfer of function across members of equivalence classes involved the combination of discriminated operants (going at the spoken word *go*, and stopping at the spoken word *stop*) with classes engendered by equivalence relations (*go* and green traffic lights, and *stop* and red traffic lights). The novel coming together of separate operants has been called *adduction* (Andronis, 1983; Johnson & Layng, 1992).

Consider the following example (cf. Esper, 1973, and see Chapter 15). Suppose we set up a three-by-three array of keys next to a window on which we can project stimuli of different colors, shapes and sizes to a pigeon. We first restrict the pigeon's pecking to the middle row of keys in the array, and we make food contingent on a left peck if the stimulus in the window is red, a middle peck if it's blue, and a right peck if it's green. After the pigeon's performance has become accurate with respect to color, we restrict the pigeon's pecking to the middle column of keys, and now we make food contingent on a top peck if the stimulus is a blue circle, a middle peck if it's a blue square, and a bottom peck if it's a blue triangle. And after the pigeon's performance has become accurate with respect to shape, we restrict the pigeon's pecking just to the middle key of the array, and we reinforce fast pecking if the stimulus is a large blue square, moderate pecking if it's a medium blue square, and slow pecking if it's a small blue square.

We've created three classes of discriminated operants based respectively on color, shape and size. Now the question is what happens when we make all of the keys of the array available and present combinations of color, shape and size that the pigeon has never seen before. If we present a small blue circle, will the pigeon peck slowly on the middle key of the top row? If we present a large green square, will the pigeon peck fast on the middle key of the right column? And if we present a medium red triangle, will the pigeon peck at a moderate rate on the left key of the bottom row?

The example is hypothetical, and whether adduction occurs with any particular novel combination of stimulus dimensions would probably depend on details of training, the sequencing of various stages of the procedure, the accuracy of the pigeon's performance at the time the tests are conducted, and other details. For example, it would probably help, after the test of each new stimulus combination, to add it to the set of stimuli used in training for awhile before going on to a new test. The above conditions involve 27 possible stimulus combinations, and the training conditions involved only 7 of them; transfer to a novel combination would probably be much more likely after the pigeon had mastered 20 or more of them than after just the original 7. It's also possible that transfer to novel combinations will become more likely as levels of accuracy become higher in training (cf. Johnson & Layng, 1992, on fluency).

In any case, such training along these three stimulus and response dimensions is certainly feasible (cf. Catania & Cerutti, 1986). But even if we were unable to demonstrate adduction with pigeons in such procedures, we'd be able to find it in other contexts. For example, a child who's learned to identify colors and who can tell horses from other animals will surely be able to identify a horse of a different color upon seeing one for the first time. In fact, we'll find in Chapters 14 and 15 that the coming together of different response dimensions given novel combinations of discriminative stimuli is an important property of human verbal behavior. Besides, what we've considered here might not be the only sources of novel behavior. In fact, our several examples suggest that the taxonomy of processes that can generate novel behavior has yet to be exhausted.

Chapter 10
Reinforcement Schedules

Schedule *is derived from the Middle English* sedule, *a slip of parchment or paper, which is in turn derived from the Latin* scheda, *papyrus leaf, and the Greek* skhizein, *to split. The Indo-European root,* skei-, *to cut or split, links* schedule *to* schizo-, *as in* schizophrenia, *and to* science *and* conscious, *from the Latin* scire, *to know, in the sense of being able to separate one thing from another.*

Not all classes of responses have consistent consequences. The reinforcement of some responses but not others, sometimes called *intermittent* or *partial* reinforcement, is a general feature of behavior. You don't always find what you're looking for when you shop and you don't always get a satisfactory reply when you ask a question. Consider phoning someone. Sometimes you get to talk to that person, but other times you get no answer or the line's busy or you get an answering machine. *Continuous* or *regular* reinforcement, the reinforcement of every response within an operant class, is the exception rather than the rule. For this reason, we must examine the effects of *schedules of reinforcement*, arrangements that specify which responses within an operant class will be reinforced.

The three most basic types of schedules are (1) those that allow a response to be reinforced after some number of responses (ratio schedules), (2) those that allow a response to be reinforced after some time has elapsed since some event (interval schedules), and (3) those that allow a response to be reinforced depending on the rate or timing of prior responses (schedules that differentially reinforce rate or interresponse times). Such number, time and rate requirements can also be combined in diverse ways to produce more complex schedules. We considered interval schedules in Chapter 8 and differential-reinforcement schedules in Chapter 7. In this chapter we'll concentrate on ratio schedules and some properties of interval schedules that were beyond the scope of Chapter 8. We'll be concerned with the effects of reinforcement schedules not only as valuable experimental tools but also as ubiquitous properties of behavior in their own right (cf. Ferster & Skinner, 1957; Schoenfeld & Cole, 1972).

Let's return to the telephone example. Suppose you call a friend who has no answering machine and you get no answer. Your chance of getting an answer later will depend on when and not on how many times you call. Your friend will answer only if you call when your friend is there; if your friend isn't there, it doesn't make any difference how many times you try calling. Similarly, suppose you call and get a busy signal. Calling again won't affect how long the busy signal lasts. Some variable time will pass that depends only on how long it is until your friend hangs up. You have to call at the right time to get an answer. These cases are everyday approximations to *variable-interval* or *VI* reinforcement schedules. The schedules reinforce a single response that occurs after a specified time has elapsed, and this time varies from one instance to the next; earlier responses do nothing. A VI schedule is designated by the average time to the availability of a reinforcer.

Now consider a different situation. You'd like to get something from a vending machine, but the machine won't accept the change that you have. You can start asking those who pass by for change and you may get what you need. In this case, whether you get change doesn't depend on when you ask. Instead, only a few of those you ask are likely to be able and willing to make change for you. You have to keep asking until you find such a person. You might succeed after asking just one or two people or you might have to ask many. In other words, getting change depends on the number of times you ask, and this number will vary from one occasion to another. Such schedules are called *variable-ratio* or *VR* schedules. They're designated by the average number of responses required per reinforcer or, in other words, the average ratio of responses to reinforcers.

In the following survey we'll concentrate on simple responses such as pigeons' key pecks and simple reinforcers such as food deliveries. It's important to remember, however, that accurately applying the language of reinforcement schedules to settings outside the laboratory demands that we carefully specify the responses and reinforcers that enter into these contingencies. For example, consider phoning to get people to pledge to a fund drive for a charity or a political campaign. Whether any particular call is answered will depend on when you make the call, but the number of pledges you get will depend on the number of calls you make. At the level of whether your call is answered, the contingencies are those of interval schedules, but at the level of whether you get a pledge, the contingencies are those ratio schedules. Furthermore, when you're trying to call it makes a difference whether your last call resulted in no answer or a busy signal; calling someone who keeps an irregular schedule differs from calling a business that opens promptly at a given time; and calling after a busy signal to someone who usually leaves the line free after calls differs from calling an active number at which the line doesn't remain open very long.

Section A   Variable-Ratio and Variable-Interval Schedules

In a variable-ratio or VR schedule, the delivery of a reinforcer depends on a variable number of responses without regard to the passage of time. In a variable-interval or VI schedule, the delivery of a reinforcer depends on the passage of a variable time and then a single response; responses that occur earlier do nothing. Some properties of the contingencies arranged by VR and VI schedules are illustrated by hypothetical cumulative records in Figure 10-1. Three records that

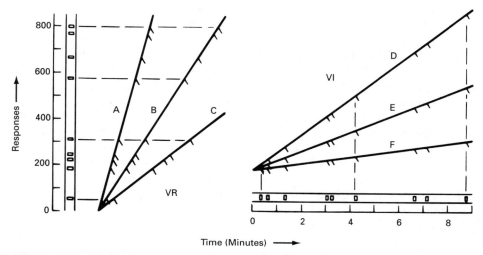

FIGURE 10-1   Hypothetical segments of cumulative records of responding maintained by a 100-response variable-ratio schedule (VR 100) and a 1-min variable-interval schedule (VI 1-min). The vertical strip to the left of the VR records and the horizontal strip below the VI records represent portions of punched tapes used to select responses for reinforcement (but contemporary laboratories would use computers to arrange these schedules). The three left records (ABC) show that VR response rate affects reinforcement rate but not responses per reinforcer; the three right records (DEF) show that VI response rate affects responses per reinforcer but not reinforcement rate.

might be generated by a 100-response VR schedule (VR 100) are shown on the left (A, B and C); three that might be generated by a 1-min VI schedule (VI 1-min) are shown on the right (D, E and F).

A VR schedule is usually arranged by a computer that randomly selects responses for reinforcement; a VR schedule that randomly selects some fraction of responses for reinforcement is sometimes called a *random-ratio* or *RR* schedule. Before computers were available, VR schedules were arranged by a loop of tape that was driven across a switch by responses. Each response moved the tape a small constant distance. The tape had holes punched in it, and whenever the switch sensed a hole the next response was reinforced. For illustrative purposes, a portion of

a tape for a VR 100 schedule is shown vertically just to the right of the response scale that accompanies the VR records in Figure 10-1. In a VR 100 schedule, one response is reinforced per 100 responses on the average, but the number varies from one reinforcer to the next. The figure shows correspondences between the holes on the tape and reinforced responses, indicated by pips on the records.

In the examples in Figure 10-1, the highest response rate, A, produces reinforcers most rapidly; the lowest, C, produces them least rapidly. In VR schedules, in other words, higher response rates produce higher reinforcement rates. With a pigeon's key pecks, an actual VR 100 schedule would probably produce a performance that looked most like record A. With moderate ratios of responses to reinforcers, VR schedules ordinarily generate high and roughly constant response rates between reinforcers. When the ratio becomes very large (e.g., hundreds or thousands of responses per reinforcer), response rate decreases; this is not so much because responding slows down overall, but rather because continued high rate responding is often interrupted by pauses.

Like VR schedules before computers were available, VI schedules also were typically arranged by a loop of tape driven across a switch. For these schedules, the tape was driven by a motor at constant speed instead of by responses. Whenever the switch sensed a hole the next response was reinforced. This arrangement allowed a response to be reinforced after some time had passed instead of after some number of responses. A portion of such a tape is shown just above the time scale on the right in Figure 10-1. Again, the figure shows correspondences between the holes on the tape and reinforced responses, indicated by pips on the records.

Once the switch operated in a VI schedule, the tape usually stopped until the reinforcer was delivered; at this point, the reinforcer was said to be *set up*, in the sense that the next response was eligible to produce a reinforcer. An alternative method now commonly used when VI schedules are arranged by computer is generating pulses at a fixed rate and randomly selecting some proportion of them to set up a reinforcer for the next response; for example, if pulses at a rate of 1/s are selected with a probability of .1, a setup would be created about once every 10 s on the average, thereby arranging a VI 10-s schedule. Schedules arranged in this way are sometimes called *random-interval* or *RI* schedules.

Records D through F of Figure 10-1 illustrate an important property of VI schedules: Even though response rates differ considerably across the three records, they all include the same number of reinforcers. The VI schedule provides a relatively constant reinforcement rate over a substantial range of possible response rates. But reinforcers aren't delivered unless responses occur, so reinforcers are produced less often than specified by the VI schedule if the time between responses becomes long relative to the time between scheduled reinforcers.

In practice, with response classes such as a pigeon's key pecks, the difference between scheduled and actual or obtained reinforcement rates is usually small. This relative independence of reinforcement rate from response rate, coupled with the relatively constant response rate that it generates, makes VI reinforcement a preferred baseline schedule, a schedule that can be used to study the effects of other variables such as drugs or chemical pollutants (cf. Chapter 8 on stimulus-control gradients). With a pigeon's key pecks, an actual VI 1-min schedule would probably produce a moderate-rate performance that looked most like record D. Notice that the moderate rate of record D is not very different from the rate in VR record C. A DRL 10-s schedule, as discussed in Chapter 7, would probably produce a low-rate record like VI record F. The point is that the several records in this figure show what different response rates do to reinforcement rates given VR or VI schedules; they don't represent typical performances produced by each schedule.

Response rates maintained by VR and VI schedules are presented in Figures 10-2 and 10-3. Both figures show data obtained with pigeons' key pecks reinforced with food. In Figure 10-2, rate of pecking is plotted as a function of the ratio, responses per reinforcer, arranged by a VR schedule. At VR 1 (leftmost point), every response is reinforced. Even with reinforcement duration

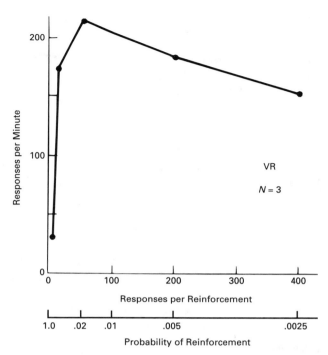

FIGURE 10-2   Rate of key pecking as a function of VR schedule for three pigeons. The two bottom scales show correspondences between responses per reinforcement and probability of reinforcement. (Adapted from Brandauer, 1958, Table 2)

excluded, responding only slightly exceeds 25 responses/min. Response rate is substantially higher at VR 10 (second point), and reaches its maximum, more than 200 responses/min, at VR 50. Response rate then decreases gradually with increasing VR size.

In Figure 10-3, rate of pecking is plotted as a function of the reinforcement rate provided by a VI schedule (e.g., VI 1-min provides a maximum of 60 reinforcers/hr). Rate of pecking increased as a function of reinforcement rate, but the function was negatively accelerated; the change in response rate produced by a given change in reinforcement rate became smaller as reinforcement rate increased.

The two figures show that VR and VI schedules differ considerably. For example, the different y-axis scales indicate that VR response rates are higher than VI response rates over most of the range of values for each schedule; with pigeons, VR rates often exceed 200 responses/min, whereas VI rates rarely exceed 100 responses/min. Even so, the detailed effects of each schedule can vary with other conditions. For example, the shapes of the functions can be affected by whether the organism receives all of its food within experimental sessions or receives some outside the sessions (these two situations have been called *closed* and *open* economies: Hursh, 1980).

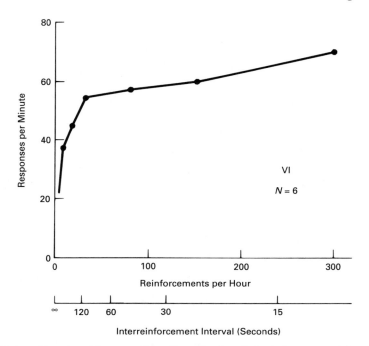

FIGURE 10-3 Rate of key pecking as a function of rate of VI reinforcement for six pigeons. The two bottom scales show correspondences between rate of reinforcement and average interreinforcement interval in VI schedules. (Adapted from Catania & Reynolds, 1968, Figure 1)

Ratio and interval schedules also differ in the way responding changes when reinforcement is reduced or discontinued. The idealized cumulative records of Figure 10-4 illustrate responding maintained by VR and VI reinforcement and responding during extinction after VR or after VI reinforcement. With VR reinforcement, responding decreases with larger ratios (cf. VR 50 and VR 1000). The decrease with larger ratios comes about mostly because responding begins to be interrupted by long pauses (the appearance of long pauses in ratio performance is sometimes called *ratio strain*). Extinction after VR reinforcement also usually produces abrupt transitions from high response rates to periods of no responding (a *break-and-run* pattern of responding). With VI schedules, on the other

hand, a high rate of VI reinforcement produces more responding than a low rate of VI reinforcement (cf. VI 1-min and VI 15-min), but in both cases responding is distributed fairly uniformly in time. In addition, in contrast to the break-and-run pattern of extinction after VR, extinction after VI produces gradual decreases in the rate of responding.

What makes VR and VI schedules generate such different performances? It seems reasonable that VR schedules should produce higher response rates than VI schedules. After all, when VR responding increases reinforcers are delivered more often, but this doesn't happen when VI responding increases. Yet the separation between successive reinforcers is variable in both schedules, so how can the different ratio and interval re-

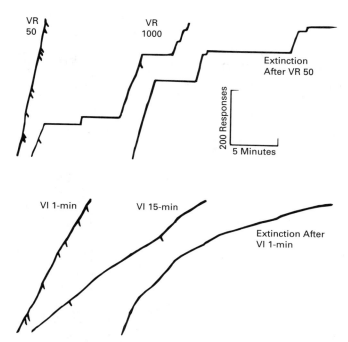

FIGURE 10-4   Patterns of responding during VR and VI reinforcement and during extinction after VR or VI reinforcement. These somewhat idealized cumulative records contrast effects of the two types of schedules: with VR, a higher maintained response rate, and abrupt transitions between high rates and long pauses with large response requirements or during extinction; with VI, a relatively constant response rate that decreases gradually during extinction. Both schedules generate substantial amounts of responding in extinction.

lations between responding and reinforcers act on behavior?

YOKED SCHEDULES

The *yoked-chamber* procedure (Ferster & Skinner, 1957) lets us study some variables that operate within schedules. In yoked chambers, an organism's performance in one chamber determines the events that occur in another organism's chamber. The procedure can be used to equate reinforcement rates in VR and VI schedules: Each reinforcer produced by a VR schedule for one pigeon's key pecks schedules a VI reinforcer for the next peck of a second pigeon. In other words, the second pigeon's pecks are maintained by a VI schedule in which successive interreinforcer intervals match those produced by the first pigeon's VR performance. In these circumstances, the two schedules differ in responses per reinforcer but not in time between successive reinforcers.

Conversely, yoked schedules can equate responses per reinforcer for the two schedules by arranging things so that the responses emitted per VI reinforcer by one pigeon determine the ratios of a second pigeon's VR schedule. In this case, the second pigeon's pecks are maintained by a VR schedule in which successive ratios match those produced by the first pigeon's VI performance.

Cumulative records from both types of yoking are illustrated in Figure 10-5 (Catania et al., 1977). For one group of pigeons, pairs were assigned to yoked schedules in which one pigeon's pecks per reinforcer in a VI 30-s schedule generated a second pigeon's VR schedule, as illustrated by Pigeons 402 and 410. For another group, pairs were assigned to yoked schedules in which one pigeon's interreinforcer intervals in a VR 25 schedule generated a second pigeon's VI schedule, as illustrated by Pigeons 414 and 406. Independent of whether VR is yoked to VI or VI is yoked to VR, VR schedules generate higher response rates than VI schedules.

These differences emerge quickly: The records are from the last of just three sessions of 50 reinforcers each. The phenomenon is so reliable that the records in Figure 10-5 were obtained from a routine laboratory exercise in an undergraduate course in experimental psychology.

The yoking experiment shows that the rate difference between VR and VI schedules can't be attributed to responses per reinforcer or time per reinforcer, because the rate difference remains even when these are the same in both schedules. One other possibility is that, even with yoking, reinforcement rate on the average changes with response rate in VR but not VI schedules. It might be argued that the organism simply

FIGURE 10-5 Cumulative records from the third session of yoking for two pairs of pigeons. Responses per reinforcer from Pigeon 402's VI performance generated a yoked VR schedule for Pigeon 410's pecks. Interreinforcer times from Pigeon 414's VR performance generated a yoked VI schedule for Pigeon 406's pecks. Horizontal arrows connecting the left records show correspondences of responses per reinforcer for that schedule pair; vertical arrows connecting the right records show correspondences of interreinforcer intervals. In both cases, VR response rate was higher than VI response rate. (From Catania, Matthews, Silverman, & Yohalem, 1977, Figure 1)

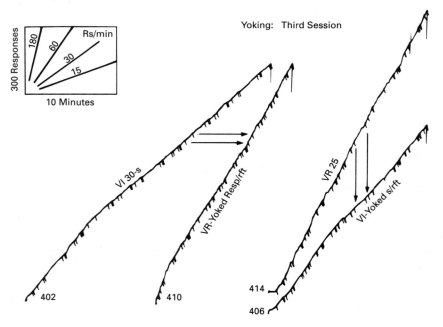

learns that in VR but not VI schedules faster responding produces reinforcers more often.

Another possibility derives from a relation between interresponse times (IRTs) and reinforcement probability (Anger, 1956). An IRT is just the time between two successive responses (cf. DRL schedules, Chapter 7). In VR schedules, the probability that a response will be reinforced depends only on the ratio; it doesn't vary with time since the last response. In VI schedules, on the other hand, the longer it's been since the last response, the more the chance that an interval has ended and therefore that the next response will be reinforced. In other words, a larger share of long than of short IRTs is followed by reinforcers in VI than in VR schedules; thus, relative to VR schedules, VI schedules differentially reinforce long IRTs. When long IRTs occur more often, response rate is necessarily lower. But differential reinforcement of IRTs can't be the whole story, even if it makes some contribution to schedule performances. For example, temporally spaced responding develops relatively slowly when DRL schedules explicitly arrange the differential reinforcement of long IRTs, and that's not consistent with the rapid separation of yoked VR and VI response rates.

Limited Hold

One temporal contingency sometimes added to schedules is called the *limited hold* or *LH*. With a limited hold, a setup or scheduled reinforcer remains available only for a limited time; if no response occurs within that time, the reinforcer is lost. For example, if you get busy signals when phoning into an overloaded switchboard, getting an answer may not become more likely as time passes since your last try, because the lines never remain open very long. If those lines are busy again within only a few seconds after someone hangs up, the schedule is a VI schedule with a limited hold. You're most likely to get

through such a switchboard by hanging up after the busy signal and immediately dialing again. In this phone example, the limited hold will vary in duration; in the laboratory, it's usually constant. A limited hold typically produces increased response rates, but a very short limited hold may allow so few responses to be reinforced that the schedule fails to maintain responding (Hearst, 1958).

REINFORCEMENT SCHEDULES AND CAUSATION

The effects of reinforcers depend on the responses they follow, but reinforcers can follow responses either when produced by responses or when delivered independently of responses. Does responding change in the same way when it produces a reinforcer as when it happens by accident to be followed by a reinforcer? We considered this question briefly in examining the phenomenon called superstition (Chapter 5). The following suggests that causal relations between responses and reinforcers may affect behavior differently than coincidental temporal contiguities:

> Is it possible that the accidental correlations in time among responses, stimuli, and reinforcers do not exert control over behavior? . . . One of the characteristics of accidental correlations between behavior and environmental events is *variability*. Every aspect of behavior may vary and yet be contiguous with a reinforcer that is independent of the behavior. In contrast, behavior that is instrumental must have at least one aspect that has a more or less fixed correlation with the reinforcer. Were animals sensitive to this difference, they could detect those events over which their behavior has no real control. (Herrnstein, 1966, pp. 42–43)

In one experiment (Lattal, 1974), pigeons' key pecks were reinforced according to a VI schedule. Once VI performance was stable, the schedule was changed: At the end of some intervals, the reinforcer was delivered immediately, without regard to responding. With decreasing percentages of response-produced reinforcers, response rate decreased. When the percentage of response-produced reinforcers was zero, so that food was completely independent of behavior, response rates approached zero. This decrease in response rate has interesting implications. For example, when a third of the reinforcers were response-produced, response rates were roughly half those when all reinforcers were response-produced, but even the pigeon with the lowest response rate responded at about 30 responses/min, or a response every 2 s. A third of the reinforcers (the response-produced ones) followed responses immediately, and all the rest were likely to follow within a second or two of the last response if responses were occurring every 2 s or so. Why then didn't these accidental temporal contiguities between responses and reinforcers maintain responding at a rate close to that when all reinforcers were response-produced?

When reinforcers are delivered independently of responses, the time between the most recent response and the reinforcer is likely to vary from one reinforcer to the next. Lattal's data suggest that this variability counteracts superstitious responding. But what about cases in which the time between the most recent response and the reinforcer varies even though the reinforcer is response-produced? This occurs, for example, when delay of reinforcement is added to a schedule (Dews, 1960).

A case is illustrated in the event records of Figure 10-6 (left). Vertical lines represent responses; arrows represent reinforcers. The top record shows a segment from a standard VI schedule: The interval ends at the dashed line and the next response, a, is followed immediately by a reinforcer. A segment from a VI schedule to which a 3-s delay of reinforcement has been added is shown in the middle record: The interval ends at the dashed line and response b produces a reinforcer 3 s later. Because other responses occur during this time, the time from the last response to the reinforcer (c) is shorter than the scheduled delay (d); it varies depending on the spacing of responses during the delay. The bottom record shows a segment from a schedule that delivers reinforcers independently of responses (technically, this is a *variable-time* or *VT* schedule):

FIGURE 10-6 Hypothetical segments of event records from VI, VI with delay and VT schedules (left), and three pigeons' rates of key pecking maintained by these schedules (right). The highest response rates were maintained by VI reinforcement and the lowest by VT. (Adapted from Sizemore & Lattal, 1977, Table 1)

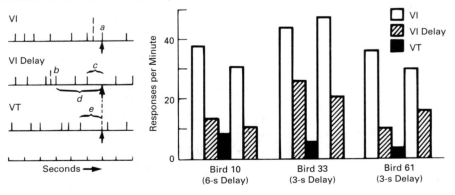

At the dashed line, the reinforcer is delivered. It is independent of responses, so the time between the last response and the reinforcer (e) varies.

The bar graph in Figure 10-6 shows data obtained with these schedules (Sizemore & Lattal, 1977). The rates of pecking maintained by VI with delay were between the moderate rates maintained by the VI schedule and the low rates maintained by the response-independent reinforcers of the VT schedule. We just concluded that the difference between VI and VT must depend in some way on the variable times between the last response and the reinforcer (c and e). What then makes the rates with delayed VI reinforcement higher than those with VT reinforcement?

These issues remain open to experimental analysis. The different effects of response-dependent and response-independent reinforcers depend in a complex way on how correlations among events are integrated over time. The complexity is perhaps best illustrated by a human analogy (cf. Catania & Keller, 1981). If a lobby elevator has no floor indicator, the only consequence of your pressing the elevator button will probably be the arrival of the elevator after a variable delay. But the elevator might also arrive because someone pressed the button earlier and then took the stairs instead, or because someone already in the elevator pressed the button for the lobby floor, or because this elevator always returns to the lobby after calls to other floors. One day the elevator door might open just as you reached out to press the button; on another it might arrive and leave and arrive again, even though you didn't press the button in the meantime. When the elevator arrives, you can never be sure your button press brought it to your floor. Nevertheless, you'll probably continue to press elevator buttons. Your judgments about causation depend not on constant conjunctions of events but rather on a sampling

of contingencies that are sometimes very complex.

Research on the effects of contingencies shows that organisms are sensitive to the consequences of their own behavior. This sensitivity may depend sometimes on detailed or molecular relations between responses and reinforcers, and sometimes on overall or molar properties of response and reinforcer rates, and sometimes even on both in combination (cf. Chapter 6). The distinction between events caused by behavior and events accidentally correlated with behavior is central to our concepts of causation. For this reason, the study of reinforcement schedules is fundamental. Demonstrating that humans may be similarly sensitive to the consequences of their own behavior may be of practical as well as theoretical significance. For example, in vigilance tasks such as monitoring a radar screen, the detection and report of a signal can be used to reinforce the behavior of looking at the screen. If an observer has a button that lights up a radar screen and button presses produce detectable signals according to a VR schedule, a high rate of observing is maintained; this observer will more accurately detect real targets not scheduled by the experimenter than will an observer sitting in front of a continuously lit radar screen without such a schedule in operation (Holland, 1958; but see also Chapter 15).

Section B   Fixed-Ratio and Fixed-Interval Schedules

If the probability that a response will be reinforced is greater at some times than at others, rate of responding is likely to be higher at those times than at others (Catania & Reynolds, 1968). For example, suppose most intervals in a VI schedule are 10 s long and the rest are between 50 and 100 s. Response rate will probably be high at about 10 s after reinforcement, and if a response isn't reinforced then it might decrease over the next 20 or 30 s before increasing again later on. We've mostly considered VR and VI schedules designed to hold the probability of reinforcement roughly constant over number of responses (in VR) or over time (in VI). But schedules can be arranged in which the number of responses per reinforcer or time to the availability of a reinforcer is constant from one reinforcer to the next; such schedules are respectively called *fixed-ratio* or *FR* schedules and *fixed-interval* or *FI* schedules (in addition, schedules in which the time between response-independent reinforcers is constant are called *fixed-time* or *FT* schedules). One important property of fixed schedules is that they introduce discriminable periods during which no reinforcers can occur.

Let's turn first to fixed-ratio or FR schedules. In an FR schedule, the last of a fixed number of responses is reinforced. For example, if a vending machine takes only quarters and the snack you want costs a dollar, inserting the fourth quarter completes a fixed ratio of exactly four responses (let's assume the vending machine is in good working order). Each fixed ratio ends with a reinforcer; the count doesn't start over if the FR responding is interrupted. The first response of the ratio is never reinforced, so FR responding typically consists of a pause followed by a high response rate. As FR size increases, the average duration of the pause increases (Felton & Lyon, 1966). The pause is called a *postreinforcement pause* or *PRP*, but it may be more appropriate to think of it as a preresponding pause; for example, pauses in FR occur as consistently when a ratio starts after a stimulus onset as when it starts after the reinforcer produced at the end of the last ratio.

Once responding begins after the pause, it typically occurs at a high rate and without interruption until the next reinforcer (FR pauses and high rates are another example of break-and-run responding; cf. VR schedules). The cohesiveness with which FR responding is maintained once it begins suggests that we should regard the FR sequence not simply as a succession of responses but rather as a behavioral unit in its own right.

The treatment of schedule performances as response units in their own right led to the development of higher-order schedules of reinforcement. For example, if reinforcement depends on completing a variable number of fixed ratios, the arrangement is a second-order schedule in which successive FRs are reinforced according to a VR schedule (e.g., Findley, 1962). An analysis of the component performances in such schedules is concerned with the structure of behavior and is analogous to examining the properties that define an operant class (cf. Chapters 7 and 11).

Ordinarily, FR responding develops so rapidly that we can't easily see the details. Figure 10-7, however, shows FR responding developing gradually. In a two-key pigeon chamber, the pigeon's pecks on one key were reinforced according to an FR 100 schedule while a VI schedule operated concurrently on the other key. The VI schedule on the other key retarded the development of the typical FR performance and in effect made it possible to examine it in slow motion; the change in temporal patterning that usually emerges in two or three sessions took place over 150 sessions. In early sessions, responding was fairly uniformly spaced between reinforcers. With continued exposure, lower response rates and eventually pauses began to follow reinforcers. The portion of the ratio consisting of uninterrupted high-rate responding gradually became longer, so that in later sessions responding continued with few if any interruptions after each pause. With successive

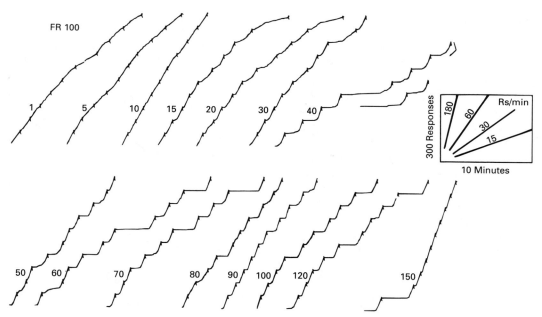

FIGURE 10-7 Development of a pigeon's performance under an FR 100 schedule of food reinforcement. The typically rapid development of FR responding was slowed down by the concurrent operation of a VI schedule (not shown) that operated for pecks on a second key. The cumulative record segments are from early portions of the numbered sessions of FR reinforcement.

sessions, the FR run was built up backwards from the reinforcer.

Now let's turn to the fixed-interval or FI schedule: A response is reinforced only after some constant interval has passed since some environmental event, such as the last delivery of a reinforcer or a stimulus onset; responses before this interval ends have no effect. An example is looking at your watch as time passes during a lecture. Here we're assuming that the reinforcer is seeing that the time has come at which you can leave the classroom. Looking at your watch before then doesn't make it run any faster. Responding maintained by FI schedules usually occurs at zero or low rates early in the interval and increases as the end of the interval approaches, so we'd expect you to

look at your watch rarely at the start of the lecture but more often as it nears its end. (We'd obviously have different things to say about the reinforcers involved if a lecture kept you so interested that you never glanced at your watch until it was over.)

Two sample cumulative records of FI performance in Chapter 5 (see B and C of Figure 5-6) show sequences of fixed intervals. The concave-upward pattern of such records is sometimes called FI *scalloping*. Depending on the sessions of exposure to FI schedules and other variables, FI scallops may show relatively abrupt transitions from no responding to a roughly constant rate of responding, as in B, or gradually increasing rates after responding starts, as in C. The pattern of FI responding tends to be consistent over relative rather than absolute time in the interval. For example, if responding reaches half its final or terminal rate 40 s into a 100-s fixed interval, it's likely to do so 20 s rather than 40 s into a 50-s fixed interval.

Treatments of FI performance must consider the finding that the FI scallop survives repeated interruptions. The phenomenon is illustrated in Figure 10-8 (Dews, 1962). Key pecks of four pigeons were reinforced with food according to FI 500-s schedules. The left graph shows average rates of pecking in successive 50-s portions of the interval. In another procedure, the houselight was turned on and off in successive 50-s portions of the interval; after the last 50 s of the interval, it remained on until the peck at the end of the interval was reinforced. Pecking while the houselight was off decreased (dark bars in Figure 10-8). Nevertheless, when the houselight was on, the FI responding increased throughout the interval (shaded bars) just as it had when it was uninterrupted during the interval.

Findings such as these have raised questions about the relative contributions to the FI scallop of a gradient of temporal discrim-

ination (in that the organism's different rates at different times in the interval imply discrimination of the elapsed time) and a gradient of delayed reinforcement (in that responses at various locations in the interval are consistently followed by the reinforcer at the end of the interval). The two gradients must exist together, because responding at any time in an interval depends on what happened after that time in previous intervals; it can't depend on the reinforcer at the end of the current interval, because that reinforcer hasn't been delivered yet.

DELAY OF REINFORCEMENT

The suggestion that the FI scallop involves some kind of gradient of delayed reinforcement carries the implication that the reinforcer produced by the last of a sequence of responses has effects that depend on its relation to all of the preceding responses and not just the one that produced it. In the early days of reinforcement schedules, schedule effects were discussed as *partial reinforcement*, and it was seen as a paradox that more be-

FIGURE 10-8 Rate of pecking in 50-s periods during a standard FI 500-s schedule of reinforcement (FI, left), and during an FI 500-s schedule in which a light and its absence alternated every 50 s (FI and added stimuli, right), for 4 pigeons. With the added stimuli, periods when the light was off produced low response rates and therefore interrupted FI responding, but rate when the light was on increased in much the same way as in the standard FI. (Adapted from Dews, 1962, Figure 2)

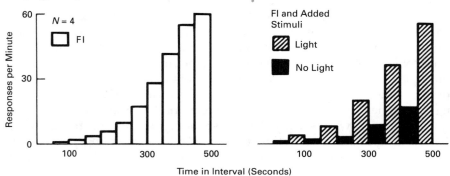

havior could be generated by reinforcing some fraction of the total responses than by reinforcing every response. But looking at schedules in terms of the delayed reinforcement of all the responses that precede the reinforced response suggests that intermittent or partial reinforcement works as it does because it allows each reinforcer to reinforce many responses instead of just one.

The earlier responses in a sequence that ends with a reinforcer contribute less to future responding than the later ones, because of the longer delays that separate them from the reinforcer (Dews, 1962). This means that in interpreting effects of schedules, we need to know the form of the delay gradient. The delay gradient has entered successfully into some mathematical models of operant behavior (e.g., Killeen, 1994), but technical problems complicate its experimental determination. For example, if we arrange delayed reinforcers only some fixed time after a response, we must either allow additional responses to occur in the interim, in which case the actual time from the last response to the reinforcer will often be shorter than the one we scheduled, or we can reset the delay with each subsequent response, in which case the resetting of the timer will differentially reinforce pauses at least as long as the delay interval, and that differentiation will be confounded with the delayed effects of the reinforcer (e.g., Catania & Keller, 1981). And we can't avoid these problems by presenting a stimulus during which the delay operates, because then we've just substituted an immediate conditioned reinforcer for the delayed one.

Furthermore, under most circumstances we can't attribute particular later responses unambiguously to the relation between particular responses and the reinforcer. Imagine that the second of a pigeon's two key pecks produces a reinforcer and then several additional pecks follow. The later pecks occurred because pecking was reinforced, but how many occurred because the second peck produced the reinforcer and how many because the first peck, after a delay, was followed by the reinforcer?

Some practical implications may be more important than these technical problems. We know that the effects of delayed reinforcement on responses that precede the one that produces a reinforcer aren't restricted to responses in a single operant class. For example, a pigeon's pecks on one key may be maintained because they're followed later by reinforced pecks on another key (Catania, 1971). Now let's consider a task that involves correct responses and errors over successive trials (e.g., an experiment on natural concepts: cf. Chapter 8). We'll use a procedure in which we reinforce every correct response and repeat any trial with an error until the pigeon gets it right. But now we've guaranteed that any string of errors will be followed, after some delay, by a reinforced correct response. Correct responses will probably dominate eventually, because they're most closely followed by the reinforcer, but errors may diminish only slowly and may even continue at a modest level even though they never actually produce the reinforcer, because they're reliably followed after a delay by a reinforced correct response. (Errorless learning procedures may be effective because errors that never occur are never closely followed by later reinforcers produced by correct responses: cf. Chapter 8.)

The moral of this story is that teachers must be alert for sequences in which a student's errors are followed by corrections, so that they don't strengthen incorrect responses along with the correct ones that they reinforce. A reinforcer that follows a sequence of correct responses will probably do a lot more good than a reinforcer that follows a single correct response after several errors. The best teacher will be the one who can judge whether correct responses are so

TABLE 10-1 Basic Schedules

NAME AND ABBREVIATION		CONTINGENCY*	COMMENT
Variable interval (Random interval)	VI (RI)	*t* s, then 1 response	*t* varies; with random intervals, response rate is roughly constant
Fixed interval	FI	*t* s, then 1 response	*t* constant; generates FI scallops
Variable ratio (Random ratio)	VR (RR)	*n* responses	*n* varies; high constant rates, but large *n* may produce ratio strain
Fixed ratio	FR	*n* responses	*n* constant; generates postreinforcement pauses and high-rate runs
Variable time	VT	*t* s	*t* varies; reinforcers are response independent
Fixed time	FT	*t* s	*t* constant; reinforcers are response independent
Continuous reinforcement	(FR 1)	1 response	All responses reinforced; also abbreviated CRF
Extinction	EXT		As procedure, often used even if response has never been reinforced
Limited hold	LH	Reinforcer cancelled if no reinforced response within *t* s	*t* constant if not otherwise specified; LH, added to other schedules, cannot stand alone
Differential reinforcement of low rate (or long IRT)	DRL	*t* s without response, then 1 response	Maintains responding easily; decreased responding increases reinforcement and thus prevents extinction
Differential reinforcement of high rate	DRH	1 response within *t* s or less of last response	Alternatively, at least n responses within *t* s; sometimes difficult to maintain, because decreased responding reduces reinforcement
Differential reinforcement of paced responding	DRP	1 response between *t* and *t'* s of last response	Sets both upper and lower limits on reinforceable response rates
Differential reinforcement of other behavior	DRO	*t* s without response	A negative-punishment or omission procedure; ordinarily decreases rate of designated response

**t s = time in seconds; *n* = number of responses

infrequent that they should be reinforced even though preceded by errors or frequent enough that the reinforcer can wait until the student has made several correct responses in a row. Examples like these should remind us that shaping is often more art than science (but see Galbicka, Kautz, & Jagers, 1993).

Section C **The Vocabulary of Reinforcement Schedules**

We've considered a variety of reinforcement schedules. Some parts of the vocabulary of schedules are logical, but others are admittedly idiosyncratic. For example, the names for FI and VI versus FT and VT schedules are arbitrary (either pair could instead have been fixed-duration and variable-duration, presumably abbreviated FD and VD). Still, the different names are correlated with very different contingencies. Even though FI, DRL and FT schedules all require the passage of a constant time, what responses can do is different in each. An FI schedule imposes no conditions on responding during the interval but one response must occur at its end. Some time passes during which responses do nothing, and then the next response is reinforced. A DRL schedule, however, requires a specified time without responses, and then the next response is reinforced. Responses that occur too soon do something: They start the time over. And in an FT schedule, the reinforcer is delivered at the end of the specified time without regard to responding. In this schedule, responses never do anything. These schedule names emerged incidentally as research evolved,

and are now so well established they'd be hard to change.

Of several noteworthy attempts to classify reinforcement schedules more systematically (e.g., Schoenfeld & Cole, 1972; Snapper, Kadden, & Inglis, 1982), none has attained general usage. Table 10-1 summarizes some major schedules. The definitions apply whether reinforcers are arranged successively and without interruption, or occur within separate trials (e.g., an FI is usually timed from the last reinforcer, but if other events are arranged between successive intervals, timing can begin with the onset of some stimulus, such as a color presented on a pigeon key). The glossary provides additional details about schedules.

The first two columns of Table 10-1 provide schedule names and their standard abbreviations. In practice, designations of time or number usually accompany the abbreviations (e.g., VI 30-s, LH 5-s, DRL 10-s, FR 50). The third column describes schedule contingencies, the conditions under which responses are eligible to produce reinforcers (cf. FI versus FT and DRL versus DRO). The last column briefly comments on each schedule. The vocabulary of this table, presented in terms of reinforcement schedules, can also be extended to punishment schedules (e.g., Azrin, 1956). The symmetry of reinforcement and punishment, illustrated in Chapter 6 (Figure 6-1), applies also to scheduling effects. For example, superimposing an FI schedule of punishment on maintained responding produces an inverted scallop, a gradually decreasing response rate as the end of the interval approaches, instead of the increasing rate that an FI schedule of reinforcement ordinarily produces.

Chapter 11
Schedule Combinations: Behavior Synthesis

A. Multiple and Mixed Schedules
Observing Responses
Schedule Interactions: Behavioral Contrast

B. Chained, Tandem and Second-Order Schedules
Conditioned Reinforcement
Brief Stimuli in Second-Order Schedules

C. Concurrent Schedules
Matching, Maximizing and Choice
Concurrent-Chain Schedules
Natural Foraging and Behavior Synthesis
Free-Choice Preference
Self-Control

D. Schedule Combinations and Behavior Synthesis

The vocabulary of schedule combinations offers a mixed etymological bag. Multiple, *from the Indo-European* mel-, *strong or great, plus* pel-, *fold, is related to* meliorate, imply *and* complicate. Mixed, *from the Indo-European* meik-, *to mix or mingle, is related to* promiscuous *and* miscellaneous. Chain *comes from a Latin word of obscure origin,* catena, *and may be related to* enchant. Tandem, *applied to bicycles after the Latin* tandem, *lengthwise, is related to* tantamount *and* though. Concurrent *and* conjoint *share the Latin prefix* con-, *with. From the Latin* currere, *to run,* concurrent *is related to* carry, intercourse *and* curriculum; *from the Latin* iungere, *to join,* conjoint *is related to* juxtapose, conjugate, yoga *and* yoke.

Schedules don't operate in isolation. They can alternate with one another, either with correlated stimuli (*multiple* schedules) or without them (*mixed* schedules). The consequence of completing one schedule can be the onset of another schedule, either with correlated stimuli (*chained* schedules) or without them (*tandem* schedules); in such contexts, one schedule can be the unit of behavior upon which another schedule operates (*higher-order* schedules). Schedules can operate at the same time, either for different responses (*concurrent* schedules) or for the same response (*conjoint* schedules), and schedules operating concurrently can each produce other schedules (*concurrent-chain* schedules). But these schedule combinations aren't of interest just for their own sakes. Instead, we'll find that they bear on problems of historical significance, such as discrimination learning (multiple schedules), conditioned reinforcement (chained and second-order schedules) and choice (concurrent and concurrent-chain schedules).

An experimental analysis involves taking complex behavior apart to find out what it's made of. The taxonomy of behavior that we've been developing in this book provides the behavioral units for our analysis. Once we've finished an analysis by teasing the pieces apart, we can validate it by seeing if we can put them back together again. The reversal of an analysis is a synthesis (as when, in chemistry, a compound is synthesized after an analysis has determined its elements and its structure). We'll be using various schedule combinations to synthesize complex behavior. The success of our syntheses will tell us something about the adequacy of our analyses. Among issues we'll address as we review specific research areas involving schedule combinations are the nature of informative stimuli, free choice and self-control.

Section A   **Multiple and Mixed Schedules**

We encountered multiple schedules as examples of stimulus control (e.g., multiple VI EXT in Figure 7-1; see Table 10-1 for abbreviations). Two schedules alternate, each correlated with a different stimulus; we speak of stimulus control when the performance appropriate to each schedule occurs during the corresponding stimulus. For example, if an FI schedule operates for a pigeon's pecks in green and a VI schedule for its pecks in red, FI scallops in green may alternate with roughly constant VI response rates in red (reinforcement can alternate with extinction in multiple schedules, but in this example a different reinforcement schedule is correlated with each stimulus).

Multiple schedules often serve as baselines in studies of variables that affect behavior. With multiple FI FR schedules, for example, drug effects on both FI and FR responding can be obtained with a single set of doses; drug effects often vary with the schedule that maintains responding. In *behavioral pharmacology* and *behavioral toxicol-*

ogy, such baselines sometimes reveal large behavioral effects of substances such as pollutants at concentrations with only small physiological effects. Substances that act on behavior can be classified on the basis of such effects (e.g., Dews, 1970; Weiss & Laties, 1969).

OBSERVING RESPONSES

Discriminative stimuli are effective only if the organism observes them. We can get a pigeon to observe stimuli by requiring it to peck a key to produce them. Let's start with the irregular alternation of extinction and VR reinforcement of a pigeon's key pecks. In this mixed schedule (mix EXT VR), we'll keep the same white keylight on during both EXT and VR, so the pigeon usually pecks throughout both. But now we add an observing key, a second key on which pecks produce stimuli correlated with the component schedules. During EXT, pecks on this key turn the first key red for a while; during VR they turn it green. In effect, pecks on the observing key change the mixed schedule to a multiple schedule (mult EXT VR); with the multiple-schedule stimuli present, the pigeon comes to peck at near-zero rates during red, the EXT stimulus, and at high rates during green, the VR stimulus. (These contingencies differ from those for observing responses in matching-to-sample, which produce stimuli by turning on the comparisons, because the contingencies here correlated with our multiple-schedule stimuli operate when those stimuli are absent as well as when they're present: cf. Chapter 9.)

Pecks on the observing key are maintained by the observing-response procedures we've just described (Kelleher, Riddle, & Cook, 1962). But what keeps them going? One possibility is that the reinforcing effectiveness of the discriminative stimuli de-

pends on their relation to the food reinforcers arranged by their schedules; another
is that they're observed because they allow
the pigeon to behave more efficiently with
respect to the component schedules (the pigeon doesn't stop pecking during EXT when
that key is always white, but it does stop
when it turns red). The question can be
posed as one of whether observing is maintained because discriminative stimuli are
conditioned reinforcers or because they're
informative.

If information is involved, then the two
discriminative stimuli should be equally
informative, even though one is correlated
with extinction and the other with reinforcement. Suppose observing responses just
turn on red during EXT and do nothing during VR. If observing responses occur because
they allow the pigeon to behave more efficiently with respect to the component schedules, turning on red in this new procedure is
just as useful as turning on both red and
green. But it turns out that observing behavior is well maintained when it produces
just the VR stimulus but not when it produces just the stimulus correlated with extinction (Dinsmoor, 1983). Similarly, stimuli
correlated with differential punishment (reinforcement in one component and reinforcement plus punishment in the other)
don't maintain observing responses very
well; if there are any informative effects,
they're overridden by the aversiveness of the
stimulus correlated with reinforcement plus
punishment, even though that stimulus
would allow the pigeon to respond more efficiently by slowing down only when it appeared (Dinsmoor, 1983).

In other words, the reinforcing effectiveness of a discriminative stimulus depends
not on informativeness but rather on the
particular consequences with which it's
correlated. Thus, a central problem in dis-

crimination learning may simply be that of
getting the organism to observe the relevant
stimuli. For example, organisms are more
likely to attend to features of stimuli correlated with a reinforcement schedule than to
those correlated with extinction. Suppose the
stimuli of a reinforcement–extinction discrimination consist of an array of circles or
the same array with a triangle substituted
for one of the circles. The triangle is the
distinctive feature of these stimuli, and a pigeon will probably acquire this discrimination more quickly if the triangle is correlated
with reinforcement (feature positive) than if
the triangle is correlated with extinction (feature negative), because looking at a stimulus
is an observing response. The pigeon is
much more likely to look at the triangle in
the former case than in the latter (cf. Jenkins
& Sainsbury, 1970, and Chapter 8 on feature-
positive discrimination).

We humans aren't immune to such contingencies. For example, suppose you're
shown cards with letters on one side and
numbers on the other, and you're told that
every card with a vowel on one side has an
odd number on the other. Four cards are
now dealt out with A, 8, X and 7 facing up
and you're asked to turn over the minimum
number of cards to verify the rule *if vowel
then odd number* (cf. Wason & Johnson-Laird,
1970). How many do you turn over and
which should they be? Most people will turn
over the A, to see whether an odd number is
on the other side. Those that do turn over a
second card usually try the 7, to check for a
vowel on the other side. But it won't disconfirm the rule if they find a consonant, because the rule doesn't say that consonants
can't have odd numbers too. You need to
turn over two cards, but the other one to try
is the 8, which will disconfirm the rule if
there's a vowel on the other side. Only a
small proportion of people choose this card.

Why? The point is that people are more likely to seek confirmation than disconfirmation of their hypotheses. Turning over a card is an observing response, and we all have long histories of checking out our guesses about things. Presumably we check on things that are important to us, so in the past it's been nicer to have our guesses confirmed than disconfirmed. Over time we've probably learned that some kinds of guesses can only be confirmed and others can only be disconfirmed, and we guess accordingly. If that's true, it unfortunately means that sometimes we think we've confirmed something when we haven't; perhaps then the truth was something we didn't want to know.

The effectiveness of a message depends more on whether its content is reinforcing or aversive than on whether it's correct or complete. For example, it's consistent with this finding that people often hesitate to have medical symptoms diagnosed. The phenomenon has long been recognized in folklore, as in accounts of the unhappy treatment of messengers who brought bad news. That organisms work for information correlated with reinforcers rather than information per se is just one more fact about behavior that's been derived from behavior analysis, and sometimes it's a fact that is resisted. When that happens, it's a fact that illustrates itself.

pecking during the first stimulus is often accompanied by increased pecking during the second, even though the schedule that operates during the second is unchanged. The phenomenon, called *behavioral contrast*, is illustrated in Figure 11-1 (Reynolds, 1961b). A multiple VI 3-min VI 3-min schedule operated for a pigeon's key pecks in green and red. The schedule in green was changed from VI to EXT and then back to VI while VI reinforcement was maintained in red. Response rate in red increased during EXT in green even though the red VI schedule hadn't changed; both rates returned toward their earlier values when the green VI schedule was reinstated.

Contrast effects vary with responses, reinforcers and organisms (e.g., Hemmes, 1973) and range from sustained increases to increases lasting only a while after a schedule change (e.g., Catania & Gill, 1964). They have been interpreted as the summation of two types of pecking: operant pecking maintained by food reinforcers and respondent pecking produced by the correlation of discriminative stimuli with reinforcers (e.g., the delivery of reinforcers during the VI but not the EXT stimulus of multiple VI EXT; cf. the topic of autoshaping in Chapter 13). The two classes have different durations and topographies (Keller, 1974; Schwartz, Hamilton, & Silberberg, 1975).

SCHEDULE INTERACTIONS: BEHAVIORAL CONTRAST

In multiple schedules, behavior in one component is often affected by what happens in the other. For example, if the schedule that maintains a pigeon's pecks during one stimulus changes from VI reinforcement to extinction while VI reinforcement continues during a second stimulus, decreased key

Section B   Chained, Tandem and Second-Order Schedules

Chained schedules have been used extensively to study *conditioned reinforcers*, reinforcers that acquire their capacity to reinforce through their relation to other stimuli already effective as reinforcers (Kelleher & Gollub, 1962). For example, the feeder light becomes a reinforcer only through its

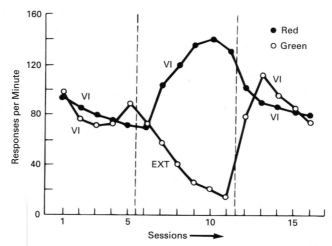

FIGURE 11-1 Effects of extinction in one component of a multiple schedule during maintained VI reinforcement in the other. Red and green alternated every 3 min. Over sessions, the schedule in green changed from VI 3-min to EXT and back to VI 3-min; a VI 3-min schedule was maintained throughout in red. Behavioral contrast refers to the increased responding in the unchanged component (red) during decreased reinforcement in the other (green). (After Reynolds, 1961b, as adapted by Terrace, 1966, Figure 10)

relation to food in the feeder. Because the opportunity to engage in highly probable responses reinforces less probable responses only if the opportunity is signalled, the conditioned reinforcing functions of stimuli have something in common with their discriminative functions.

CONDITIONED REINFORCEMENT

Assume that we've gradually increased the size of an FR schedule arranged for a pigeon's pecks on a white key to a value of FR 200. In this situation, with only the food produced by pecking, the pigeon easily maintains an adequate daily ration. In fact, since a pigeon can eat its daily diet in as little as 4 or 5 min and each food delivery lasts only 4 or 5 s (including time to get from key to food

hopper), the pigeon may be done for the day after just 60 reinforcers. At FR 200, the pigeon must peck 12,000 times per day to earn this much food. We can expect typical FR performance: postreinforcement pauses followed by rapid and uninterrupted pecking. Our pigeon will earn enough food daily to keep itself alive and healthy for an indefinite time (its life expectancy may be as high as 20 years).

But pigeons can't count very well, and we might wonder whether the pigeon is at a disadvantage each time it goes through its 200 pecks. Suppose we try to help it estimate how many pecks are left in the ratio by changing the color on the key after every 50 pecks. Each ratio starts with the key blue for the first 50 pecks; it turns green for the next 50, yellow for the next 50 and red for the final 50 pecks, the last of which produces the reinforcer. The pecks per reinforcer remain the same; only the key colors have changed.

With no distinctive stimuli, the pigeon worked well enough, earning an adequate daily ration. Have we helped by providing the colors? The stimuli have the surprising effect of slowing the pigeon down. The pause at the start of the ratio, when the key is blue, lengthens. When the pigeon finally responds, the pecks that once came in rapid succession now occur sporadically. When the key turns green after 50 pecks, the pigeon may pause again before starting the next 50 pecks. When the key was always white, the pigeon didn't pause at this point. In green, another 50 pecks, and the key turns yellow. This time the pigeon is less likely to pause: 50 more pecks turn the key red, and the pigeon now quickly completes the last 50 pecks and food is delivered. But then the key is blue again and another long pause begins.

The added colors didn't help. The pigeon takes much longer to earn each food delivery than it had when the key remained white. In fact, even though this pigeon maintained an adequate diet at 200 pecks per food delivery when the key was always white, we'd now be wise to watch carefully to be sure its daily food intake doesn't decrease drastically. And we produced this change just by adding some stimuli.

When we added the colors, we broke the 200 pecks down into four distinct units of 50 pecks each. We call these *chained* FR schedules: the separate stimuli correspond to the links of the chain. But the chain breaks the 200-peck sequence up into four FR 50 components instead of holding it together more cohesively. When the key was always white, pecking at the start of the sequence wasn't so very different from pecking at the end, just before the reinforcer. Once the stimuli were added, however, pecking during the early

stimuli became less like pecking later. In blue, for example, pecks never produced food; at best they turned the key green, but pecks never produced food during green either. With pecking reduced early in the chain, the time to complete each 200 pecks increased. In chained schedules, a stimulus supports less responding the further it is from the end of the sequence. Even severe food deprivation may not counteract this effect.

Comparable effects of chained schedules occur with other organisms besides the pigeon, with different kinds of responses and different schedules, and with different kinds and orderings of stimuli (Kelleher & Gollub, 1962). Because these effects have such generality, we may wonder whether they're relevant to human behavior. The things that people do, of course, depend on consequences more complex than food deliveries. Nevertheless, so much of what we do involves sequential behavior that we might wonder whether we sometimes operate under the strain of too many links in our chains. The ability to formulate and achieve long-range objectives is supposed to be a unique characteristic of the human species. But if adding even a single link to a chain can so devastate the pigeon's behavior, perhaps we should be alert for similar effects in our own behavior.

In this example, responding was well maintained when successive components of the schedule each operated in the presence of a single stimulus (*tandem* schedules). The introduction of different stimuli in each component (*chained* schedules) substantially reduced responding in the early components of the sequence. Similar effects occur with chained interval schedules: As in our FR example, the different stimuli reduce responding relative to that maintained with a single stimulus. How can we reconcile this finding with the assumption that the successive stimuli of the chain should become conditioned reinforcers through their relation to the food at the end of the sequence?

The low rates in the early chained-schedule components combine the discriminative effects of each stimulus (responding is never reinforced with food during these stimuli) with the reinforcing effects of the onset of the next stimulus. With component durations matched, both chained and multiple schedules involve a sequence of stimuli ending with a reinforcer; they differ only in whether stimulus changes are response-produced (cf. chained FI FI FI with multiple EXT EXT FI; both end with a single reinforcer, but only the chained schedule requires responses at the end of the first two components). Everything else being equal, rates in the next-to-last component are typically somewhat higher in chained than in equivalent multiple schedules, but it's hard to detect differences in earlier components (Catania, Yohalem, & Silverman, 1980). In other words, the stimulus changes in chained schedules have some reinforcing effects, but they're mostly restricted to the late components, close to the food reinforcers.

These effects depend on a constant ordering of the chained stimuli. The long pauses decrease markedly if the stimulus order changes from one reinforcer to the next (Gollub, 1977). Analogous but inverse effects also hold for schedules of punishment; relative to tandem schedules, chained schedules of punishment reduce responding mostly in the later components of the chain (Silverman, 1971). An implication is that punishment after a deed is done probably has its greatest effect on the behavior that precedes getting caught and only minimal effects on the much earlier behavior that led up to the misdeed.

Brief Stimuli in Second-Order Schedules

The stimuli in chained schedules can become conditioned reinforcers, but they combine with discriminative effects in such a way that responding is reduced. Yet this outcome seems inconsistent with the effects of some stimuli that acquire their reinforcing properties. In human behavior, for example, money presumably becomes a reinforcer by virtue of the various commodities for which it can be exchanged (it's sometimes called a *generalized reinforcer*, because it doesn't depend on a specific primary reinforcer; cf. Ayllon & Azrin, 1968, on token economies).

Early experiments on the effects of conditioned reinforcers were conducted during extinction, after a history of consistent pairings with a primary reinforcer (e.g., making tone a conditioned reinforcer by following it with food and testing later with tone alone). Although this procedure countered the objection that responding might be maintained directly by the later primary reinforcer rather than by the conditioned reinforcer itself, it was also one in which the effectiveness of conditioned reinforcers diminished rapidly once the primary reinforcer was removed. Convincing demonstrations of conditioned reinforcers came only when reinforcement schedules were applied to their analysis: Schedules were arranged not only for the production of conditioned reinforcers by responses but also for the contingent relation between conditioned and primary reinforcers (Zimmerman, Hanford, & Brown, 1967). For example, a tone may function as a conditioned reinforcer even if it's followed by food only 1 time in 20.

In second-order schedules, the completion of one schedule is a behavioral unit that's reinforced according to another schedule, as when the second-order schedule FR 10 (DRL 5-sec) arranges a reinforcer for every tenth IRT that's longer than 5 s (this arrangement, with a brief stimulus at the completion of each first-order schedule, is one of several types of second-order schedules). Consider a schedule arranged for a pigeon's pecks in which the peck that completes each 60-s fixed interval produces a brief green light on the key and in which every tenth such interval is followed also by food; the notation for such schedules may include the brief stimulus: FR 10 (FI 60-sec: green). Such schedules typically maintain FI scalloping within intervals even though most intervals end without food.

In contrast to chained schedules, second-order schedules with brief stimuli can greatly amplify reinforced responding. For example, when a chimpanzee's pushbutton presses were reinforced with food according to an FR 4000 schedule, postreinforcement pauses ranged from many minutes to hours. But when the light accompanying food delivery came on briefly after every 400 responses, responding increased and typical postreinforcement pauses decreased to 5 min or less. The light converted the simple FR 4000 schedule to a second-order schedule, FR 10 (FR 400: light), that amplified the amount of behavior maintained by the food reinforcers (Findley & Brady, 1965). Variables such as the relation between the brief stimuli and primary reinforcers determine the effectiveness of second-order schedules (Gollub, 1977). Both chained schedules and second-order schedules with brief stimuli involve conditioned reinforcers, but their opposite effects illustrate how critically schedule effects depend on the detailed relations among stimuli, responses and consequences (Morse & Kelleher, 1977; Malone, 1990, pp. 294–296).

Second-order scheduling can also include other kinds of operants, as when correct responses in matching-to-sample (cf. Chapter 9) are reinforced according to various schedules. In such contexts, lower levels of accuracy may be correlated with those times at which responding is least likely to be reinforced. For example, errors are more likely early in FR runs or in the early portions of FI scallops than in responding that occurs later and therefore closer to reinforcer deliveries (e.g., Boren & Gollub, 1972; Thomas, 1979). Classes defined sequentially may also imply higher-order classes. For example, individual pecks are functional units, but within FR performance the entire ratio may function as a unit. The FR performance has a property that is consistent with higher-order classes: As long as the higher-order class is reinforced, the subclasses within it may also be maintained even though they are no longer reinforced (in other words, the first peck of the fixed ratio does not extinguish, even though by itself it never produces the reinforcer).

Section C   Concurrent Schedules

Any reinforced response is likely to occur in a context of other behavior maintained by other consequences. We must therefore examine the effect on one response of reinforcement schedules operating for other responses. Concurrent schedules are schedules arranged simultaneously for two or more responses. Consider an FR 25 schedule of food reinforcement for a pigeon's pecks on one key and an FR 50 schedule operating concurrently for pecks on a second key. Alone, either schedule maintains responding, but when they operate concurrently, responding is likely to be maintained exclusively on the key with the FR 25 schedule. The outcome isn't surprising. A reinforcer requires only 25 pecks on the first key but 50 on the second.

Now consider concurrent interval schedules, such as VI 30-s reinforcement of pecks on one key and VI 60-s reinforcement of pecks on the other. In this case, the pigeon produces 120 reinforcers/hr by pecking only the first key or 60/hr by pecking only the second. By pecking both, however, it produces the reinforcers of both schedules, or 180/hr. In this case, responding is likely to be maintained on both keys.

Although pigeons distribute their pecks to both keys with concurrent VI VI schedules, there's a complication. If pecks on one key are immediately followed by a reinforced peck on the other, the reinforcer may act on the sequence, so that the pecks on one key are maintained partly by reinforcers scheduled for the other (cf. Chapter 10 on delay of reinforcement). For this reason, concurrent VI procedures often incorporate a *changeover delay*, which prevents either response from being reinforced immediately after a changeover from the other (Herrnstein, 1961). With a changeover delay, the pigeon distributes its responses to concurrent VI VI schedules roughly in proportion to the distribution of reinforcers they arrange (Herrnstein, 1961); in the example, the pigeon pecks a VI 30-s key about twice as often as a VI 60-s key.

MATCHING, MAXIMIZING AND CHOICE

This phenomenon is sufficiently general that it's been proposed as a general law of behavior, called the *matching law* (Davison & McCarthy, 1988; Herrnstein, 1970). It states that relative responding matches the relative reinforcement produced by that responding. The law even holds for concurrent ratio schedules, because exclusive responding on one schedule means that all the reinforcers will be delivered according to that schedule. Herrnstein's account has also been applied

to the responding maintained by a single reinforcement schedule (e.g., Figure 10-3), on the assumption that other events besides the reinforcers arranged by the experimenter may have reinforcing effects, even though we can't identify them.

The matching law summarizes performances in a variety of schedules, but its status as a convenient description or as a fundamental property of behavior rests on whether it can be derived from simpler processes (Catania, 1981; Rachlin, 1971). For example, consider how concurrent VI VI schedules operate when arranged for a pigeon's pecks on two keys. As the pigeon pecks one key, time passes during which the VI schedule for the other key may set up a reinforcer. A time will come when the reinforcement probability for changing over to the other key exceeds that for continuing to peck the same key. If the pigeon emits the response with the higher current reinforcement probability and this shifts from one key to the other as time passes, the pigeon will distribute its responses to both keys in concurrent VI VI schedules (Hinson & Staddon, 1981; Shimp, 1966). This has been called *maximizing*; with several responses available, maximizing means emitting the response with the maximum reinforcement probability. With unequal concurrent ratio schedules, this is always the one with the smaller ratio, but with concurrent VI VI schedules the response with the maximum reinforcement probability changes from moment to moment; concurrent VI VI performance has therefore been called *momentary maximizing*. Thus, momentary maximizing at the molecular level may lead to matching at the molar level.

Matching and maximizing seem contradictory alternatives, but they're measured in different ways. We can't speak about matching without some sample of responses and reinforcers from which to estimate relative frequencies, but we can speak about maximizing with a single response, just by noting whether it was the one with the maximum reinforcement probability. To some extent, the issues involve the level of detail at which performances are analyzed (cf. the molar–molecular distinction: Chapter 6). Furthermore, matching and maximizing don't exhaust the possibilities. For example, other analyses have examined whether concurrent performances can be described as *optimization* (the organism produces the highest possible overall reinforcement rate), *satisficing* (it meets some minimal requirement, such as a given food intake) or *melioration* (it balances performance so as to produce equal reinforcement rates under different conditions); in their quantitative details, these treatments are beyond the scope of the present account (cf. Mazur, 1991).

One feature of concurrent performances is that increases in the reinforcement of one response reduce the rate of other responses (e.g., Catania, 1969; Catania, Sagvolden, & Keller, 1988; Rachlin & Baum, 1972). If the response rate generated by a given rate of VI reinforcement is independent of how these reinforcers are distributed to the two keys, it follows that increasing the reinforcement of one response will reduce the rate of the other. The relation is illustrated in Figure 11-2, in which the curved line shows an idealized version of the function relating response rate to VI reinforcement rate (cf. Figure 10-3). The bar marked A shows response rate when response A alone is reinforced. Arranging an equal VI schedule for response B doubles the overall reinforcement rate (X to $2X$). According to the matching law, total responding will be equally distributed to the two keys, as shown by the bar at $2X$ marked A and B. The rate of A is now lower, concurrent with B, than when A was reinforced alone.

Experiments that observe the effects on pigeons' pecking on one key while responding and reinforcement are independently varied on a second key demonstrate that changes in response rate observed within

FIGURE 11-2   Combining the matching principle and the VI rate function (curved line; cf. Figure 10-3) to derive the reduction in the rate of one response (A) produced by reinforcing a concurrent response (B). The bracket shows how much reinforcement of B reduces A.

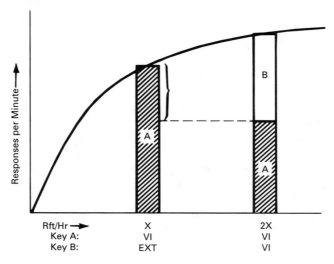

concurrent VI VI schedules depend more on the reinforcers produced by each response than on competition between responses for available time (Catania, 1963b; but cf. Henton & Iversen, 1978). In other words, decreases in one of two concurrent responses can often be attributed to increases in the reinforcement of the other response rather than to increases in how often the other response occurs. The relation between the two rates is similar to that in behavioral contrast, but even though there are superficial similarities between multiple and concurrent schedules, it's risky to generalize from one to the other (cf. Killeen, 1972, and the section on behavioral contrast in this chapter).

Variables with small effects in single-response schedules often have large effects in concurrent schedules. Concurrent schedules are therefore useful for studying effects of reinforcement variables (e.g., reinforcement duration: Catania, 1963a; response force: Chung, 1965). Furthermore, concurrent schedules make different consequences simultaneously available, so they provide appropriate baseline procedures for the study of choice or preference.

CONCURRENT-CHAIN SCHEDULES

One arrangement for studying preference is the concurrent-chain procedure illustrated in Figure 11-3 (Herrnstein, 1964b). Two equal schedules operate in *initial links*; the consequence arranged for each is another schedule, a *terminal link*. This procedure separates the reinforcing effectiveness of the terminal link from the contingencies that maintain responding in that terminal link. For example, response rates maintained by concurrent VR DRL schedules wouldn't tell us whether a pigeon prefers VR to DRL schedules; the high VR and low DRL rates maintained by these contingencies don't imply a VR preference.

Given a choice between slower DRL responding and faster VR responding, the pigeon might prefer the DRL. Concurrent chains allow this kind of choice when they arrange the VR and DRL schedules as terminal links (e.g., schedules A and B in Figure 11-3), because the initial-link pecks that produce the VR or DRL schedules don't share in either the VR or the DRL contingencies. We judge preferences among situations not by how much behavior they produce but by the relative likelihoods with which an organism enters them.

Concurrent chains have shown that reinforcement rate is a more important determinant of preference than the number of responses per reinforcer (e.g., Neuringer & Schneider, 1968) and that variable schedules are preferred to fixed schedules (e.g., Herrnstein, 1964a). Studies of preferences among various parameters of reinforcement schedules can be technically complex, because they must control for differences in time or responses per reinforcer in terminal links and for occasional biases toward particular colors or sides. One control for such bias is the occasional reversal of terminal-link conditions over sessions.

Natural Foraging and Behavior Synthesis

Beyond their use in studies of preference, concurrent chains have entered into the synthesis of complex behavior. If the interpretation of complex behavior in a natural habitat suggests that it consists of several simpler components, the interpretation can be tested by trying to assemble those components in a laboratory setting. A successful synthesis supports the interpretation; an unsuccessful one is likely to reveal inadequacies in the assumptions about what was going on in the natural setting.

In the field of *behavioral ecology*, this strategy is illustrated by studies of natural forag-

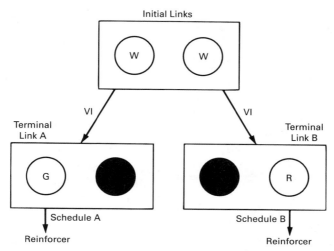

FIGURE 11-3 Schematic diagram of a concurrent-chain procedure as it might be arranged for a pigeon's key pecks. In initial links, both keys are white (W) and equal but independent schedules (usually VI) operate for both keys. According to its schedule, pecks on the left key produce terminal link A; in terminal link A, the left key is green (G), the right key is dark, and pecks on green produce reinforcers according to schedule A. Similarly, according to its schedule, pecks on the right key produce terminal link B; in terminal link B, the right key is red (R), the left key is dark, and pecks on red produce reinforcers according to schedule B. The relative rates of pecking the two initial-link keys define preferences for the respective terminal links. For example, if a pigeon pecked the right white key more often than the left white key, it would be appropriate to say that the pigeon preferred schedule B to schedule A.

ing (e.g., Fantino & Abarca, 1985; Kamil, Yoerg, & Clements, 1988). In their foraging, animals in the wild travel from one patch of food to another, staying or moving on to new ones depending on what they find. For example, a bird might fly to a bush in which the eggs of an edible insect have just hatched. As it eats, it gradually depletes its prey, and when it moves on depends on such factors as how much is left, how far it must go to find another bush and what the chances are of finding other food there (cf. Wanchisen, Tatham, & Hineline, 1988).

Some of these factors can be simulated within concurrent chains. For example, varying the schedules that operate in initial links is analogous to varying the time and effort involved in travelling from one bush

to another, and varying the schedules in terminal links is analogous to varying the availability or depletion of different food sources at different sites. Concurrent-chain schedules in the laboratory that simulate those in natural habitats have revealed some properties of foraging. For example, organisms are less selective in the food they accept if they spend more travel time (more time in initial links) between potential food sources; and if one food is preferred over another, the availability of the preferred food (the schedule that operates during the terminal link in which that food is the reinforcer) is a primary determinant of the choice of food patches (as shown by initial-link responding). In other words, natural foraging may be treated in terms of concurrent-chain schedules; properties of natural foraging, in turn, may suggest variables that are important in concurrent-chain performances.

Free-Choice Preference

Consider now another attempt to synthesize complex behavior using concurrent-chain schedules. Questions about freedom are questions about whether organisms prefer to have alternatives available. By making two keys available in one terminal link and only a single key in the other, we can ask whether pigeons prefer free choice to forced choice (Catania & Sagvolden, 1980). In free-choice terminal links, pecks on either of two keys produce a reinforcer at the end of a fixed interval; in forced-choice terminal links, the same FI schedule operates for pecks on a single key. Pigeons prefer free choice to forced choice in such schedules. These preferences don't depend on differences in the properties of terminal-link performances, such as responses per reinforcer, or on the distribution of responding to the two keys in free choice.

What, then, is the basis for the preference? Perhaps the pigeon has learned that different contingencies exist in free and forced choice. If one key fails during free choice, the other key is available as an alternative; if the single key fails during forced choice, no other key is available to fall back on. If the free-choice preference is learned in this way, we should be able to reverse it by making more reinforcers available during forced choice than during free choice. But when we do so, the effects are only temporary; the free-choice preference returns when the reinforcers in the two terminal links become equal again. We can't produce durable forced-choice preference.

Perhaps the free-choice preference has a phylogenic basis. For example, given that food supplies sometimes are lost to competitors or disappear in other ways, an or-ganism that chooses environments with two or more food sources will probably have advantages over one that chooses environments with only a single food source. If such preferences exist even in the behavior of pigeons, they can't just be products of human cultures. They may occur because evolutionary contingencies have selected organisms that prefer free choice to forced choice. If so, we may be able to mask it temporarily (e.g., by punishing responding during free choice but not forced choice), but we won't be able to eliminate it. This conclusion is based on data from pigeons, but that just makes free-choice preference more fundamental, because it suggests that our human concept of freedom has biological roots.

A behavior synthesis may exhibit properties that weren't accessible in the nonlaboratory situations from which it was derived. In this example, the free-choice preference, once demonstrated, can be used in turn to define what qualifies as free choice. For example, the pigeon prefers two FI keys to a single FI key, but not an FI and an EXT key to an FI key alone. In other words, free choice doesn't consist of just the availability of two responses; they must both be capable of producing a reinforcer.

Self-Control

Another example of behavior synthesis with concurrent-chain schedules is provided by the procedure in Figure 11-4 (Rachlin & Green, 1972). Initial links consisted of concurrent FR 25 FR 25 schedules (unlike the usual VI initial links, which equalize the pigeon's exposures to each terminal link by making them available equally often, the pigeon can enter one terminal link more often than the other with these schedules). In terminal-link A, the keys were dark for *T* s and then lit red and green respectively. A peck on red immediately produced 2 s of food; a peck on green

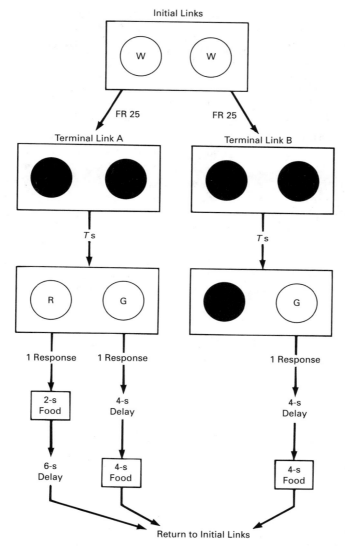

FIGURE 11-4 A concurrent-chain procedure that synthesizes some properties of impulsiveness, commitment and self-control. According to FR 25 schedules, pecks on white (W) initial-link keys are followed after *T*s by terminal links. In terminal-link A, red (R) and green (G) keys respectively make an immediate small reinforcer or a delayed large one available. In terminal-link B, the green key alone makes only the delayed large reinforcer available. (Adapted from Rachlin & Green, 1972)

produced 4 s of food after a 4-s delay. In terminal-link B, the keys also were dark for *T* s, but after that only the green key was lit. As in the other terminal link, a peck on green produced the large reinforcer after a 4-s delay.

Confronted with both red and green in terminal-link A, the pigeon almost invariably pecks red, producing the small immediate reinforcer and not the large delayed one (this has been called *impulsiveness*). Confronted with only green in terminal-link B, the pigeon necessarily produces the large delayed reinforcer. But what about the pigeon's preference for A versus B, given by its initial-link responding? The answer depends on *T*, the time until the terminal-link keys are lit. When it's short (e.g., 1 s), the pigeon usually produces terminal-link A and then pecks red. When it's longer, the pigeon is more likely to produce terminal-link B, in which only green is available. Figure 11-5 shows the relative rate of pecking the left initial-link key (left initial-link pecks divided by total initial-link pecks) as a function of *T*. As *T* increased from 0.5 s to 16 s, the proportion of pecks producing terminal-link A de-

creased; the pigeon became more and more likely to enter terminal-link B and produce the larger reinforcer.

During initial links, the time to food equals *T* for the small reinforcer but *T* plus the 4-s delay for the large one. When *T* is short, this difference is relatively large (e.g., with a *T* of 1 s, the respective delays are 1 and 5 s) and the short delay outweighs the difference in reinforcer magnitudes. When *T* is long, however, the difference becomes relatively small (e.g., with a *T* of 10 s, the respective delays are 10 and 14 s) and the difference in reinforcer magnitudes becomes effective. By producing terminal-link B when *T* is long, the pigeon commits itself to the large reinforcer even though it wouldn't do so at the onset of green if red were also present. For this reason, pecks that produce terminal-link

FIGURE 11-5   Relative initial-link pecks producing terminal-link A (left initial-link pecks divided by total initial-link pecks) as a function of *T*, the time to the onset of the terminal-link keys. (Cf. Figure 11-4; adapted from Rachlin & Green, 1972, Table 1)

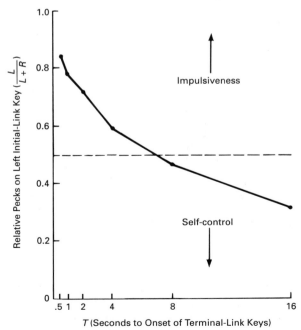

B have been called *commitment responses*: They guarantee the large delayed reinforcer by making the small immediate one unavailable. (Other syntheses can be created with other temporal arrangements: e.g., see Mazur, 1996, on procrastination by pigeons.)

Human situations discussed in terms of self-control typically involve different consequences that are pitted against each other (Skinner, 1953; Rachlin, 1974). The pigeon example involved two reinforcers. Similarly, you might get something immediately by buying now, but saving the money might make something else affordable later. Other cases can involve aversive events, as when an alcoholic refuses the immediate reinforcer of a drink and avoids the later aversive consequence of a hangover. Procedures like the one illustrated in Figure 11-4 bring such behavioral relations into the laboratory, by creating reinforcement schedules with analogous temporal properties.

With the concurrent-chain procedure we can examine impulsiveness and commitment with immediate and delayed reinforcers or with immediate and delayed aversive stimuli (e.g., Deluty, 1978). We can also examine whether commitment is modifiable and whether the components of this synthesis of self-control involve variables comparable to those that operate in human behavior (e.g., Grosch & Neuringer, 1981). Unlike the pigeon, humans sometimes do forego small and currently available reinforcers in favor of large delayed ones. Human instances of self-control presumably also involve verbal behavior (cf. Chapter 15). But if more complex processes operate in human self-control, they can only be identified by examining whether human cases are inconsistent with analyses in terms of reinforcer delays. For this reason, the behavior synthesis provides an essential reference performance for the analysis of self-control and illustrates the relevance of reinforcement schedules to human behavior.

Section D   **Schedule Combinations and Behavior Synthesis**

We've seen that reinforcement schedules are tools that can be applied to the study of a variety of behavioral phenomena relevant to human concerns. Our examples have ranged from causal relations between behavior and environment to self-control and freedom of choice. Yet even so-called simple schedules aren't simple; the complexity of schedule effects has made schedule analysis highly technical. We examined properties of ratio and interval schedules in the last chapter; in this one we've briefly sampled other topics, including multiple, chained, second-order, concurrent and concurrent-chain schedules. We've often omitted procedural details. This is perhaps inevitable. Unlike most other areas in this text, reinforcement schedules didn't even exist as a systematic subject matter until relatively recently (Skinner, 1956; Ferster & Skinner, 1957). One concern of this subject matter has been maintenance of behavior in the steady state, and yet the change in behavior that accompanies any transition from one schedule to another is an instance of learning.

We examined multiple and mixed, chained and tandem and second-order, and concurrent and concurrent-chain schedules, but we haven't exhausted the possibilities for combining the basic schedules. For example, reinforcers can be arranged for completing *either* of two schedule requirements (*alternative* schedules) or *both* of them (*conjunctive* schedules). In an alternative FI 30-s FR 50 schedule, either the first response after 30 s or the 50th response is reinforced, whichever comes first. In a conjunctive FI 100-s FR 20 schedule, a response isn't reinforced until both 100 s pass and 19 responses have already been emitted. *Adjusting* schedules vary as a function of some property of per-

TABLE 11-1 Schedule Combinations

SCHEDULE	DEFINITION*	EXAMPLE (WITH ABBREVIATION)
Multiple	A during S^A alternates with B during S^B.	(A) VI during red alternates with (B) EXT during green (mult VI EXT).
Mixed	A alternates with B (like multiple schedules but without different stimuli).	(A) DRL alternates with (B) FI, with no correlated stimuli (mix DRL FI).
Chained	During S^A, completion of A produces S^B; during S^B, completion of B produces reinforcer.	Completing (A) VR during blue produces yellow; completing (B) FR during yellow produces food (chain VR FR).
Tandem	Completion of A produces B; completion of B produces reinforcer (like chained schedules but without different stimuli).	Completing (A) VR produces (B) DRH, and completing DRH produces food, with no correlated stimuli (tand VR DRH).
Concurrent	A operates for one response; B operates for another response.	(A) One VI operates for pecks on a left key and (B) another VI operates for pecks on a right key (conc VI VI).
Conjoint	A and B operate at the same time but independently for a single response (like concurrent schedules but without different responses).	(A) VI and (B) avoidance operate simultaneously for presses on a single lever (conjt VI avoidance).
Second-order	Completion of A is reinforced according to B (reinforcing the second-order schedule according to C creates a third-order schedule, and so on).	(A) Successive FRs are treated as response units reinforced according to (B) an FI schedule (FI (FR)).
Alternative	Reinforcer depends on completion of either A or B.	Responding is reinforced on satisfying either (A) VR or (B) VI contingencies, whichever occurs first (altern VR VI).
Conjunctive	Reinforcer depends on completion of both A and B.	Responding is reinforced on satisfying both (A) FR and (B) FI contingencies, whichever occurs first (conjunc VR VI).
Interlocking	Reinforcer depends on completion of some combined function of A and B.	Responding is reinforced when (A) the sum of responses plus (B) elapsed seconds reaches some constant value (interl FR FT).
Progressive	Some schedule parameter changes systematically over successive reinforcers or blocks of reinforcers.	After every nth reinforcer, t s is added to the value of an FI (progressive FI).

*For convenience, each case is defined in terms of just two arbitrary component schedules, A and B, but combinations can include any number of components. Stimuli are designated by S with a superscript that identifies the schedule each one accompanies.

formance, as when a ratio varies in proportion to the last postreinforcement pause, or as when a shock delivery changes the RS interval of an avoidance schedule. A schedule in which time and number requirements interact is an *interlocking* schedule. For example, an interlocking FR FI schedule might shorten the interval as a function of number of responses, or lengthen the ratio as a function of time (an example is winding a grandfather clock, in which the reinforcer is the tension of the fully wound spring; until the spring is completely run down, the number of turns required to wind it increases as time passes). In a *progressive* schedule, some parameter of a schedule changes systematically over successive reinforcers or blocks of reinforcers. For example, a ratio might increase by 10 responses after every 5th reinforcer (sometimes a second response is available that resets the progression to some starting value according to some schedule).

For convenience of reference, the major schedule combinations are summarized in Table 11-1. The table provides definitions, examples and standard abbreviations. The formal designations may make some relations among the schedules more obvious. For example, multiple and mixed schedules both involve the alternation of component schedules, and chained and tandem schedules both

involve sequences in which completion of one schedule produces another. In both the multiple-mixed and the chained-tandem pairs, the only distinction is whether the component schedules each operate during different stimuli or during a single stimulus. Similarly, the only distinction between concurrent and conjoint schedules is whether the two simultaneous schedules operate for different responses or for a single response.

These schedule combinations are our tools. Once we've used schedules to explore the properties of complex behavior through a behavior analysis, we may be in a position to use these tools to put the parts back together in a behavior synthesis. For example, we can test our interpretation of complex behavior in a natural habitat by trying to assemble its components in a laboratory setting. We can't create a behavior synthesis without making explicit our assumptions about the properties of the behavior we're trying to synthesize. For that reason, when we attempt synthesis we probably profit more from our failures than from our successes. In fact, it may be a general principle of scientific research that we learn the most when our experiments produce data we didn't expect. After all, what's the point of doing the experiments if we always know exactly how they're going to turn out?

Chapter 12
Respondent Behavior: Conditioning

A. Conditional Reflexes
Types of Conditioning
Conditioning and Contiguity
Stimulus Combinations in Conditioning
  Overshadowing and Blocking
  Inhibitory Stimuli in Compounds
  Sensory Preconditioning and Second-Order
    Conditioning
Contiguity and Consequences
Autoshaping and Automaintenance

B. Operant–Respondent Interactions: Emotion
Conditioning and Emotion
Preaversive and Preappetitive Stimuli

C. Biological Constraints on Learning
Sensory Constraints
Motor Constraints
Constraints on Consequences
Preparedness

The language of emotion includes a number of etymological clusters. For example, eager, anger *and* anxiety *share the same roots, as do* choleric, melancholy, glad *and* glee, *and* wrath *and* worry, *and* sad *and* satisfy *(the last pair is also related to* satiate*). Fear, from the Indo-European* per-, *to try, to risk, to press forward or lead, has an extensive group of relatives that includes* experiment *and* apparatus, probability *and* opportunity, prepare *and* repertory, approach *and* deprivation, *and two contemporary syn-*

onyms for behavior, comportment *and* performance.

Respondent conditioning is a topic that has dominated the psychology of learning so much that it has provided the opening chapters of many learning texts. In addition to *respondent conditioning*, it's gone by such names as *classical conditioning* and *Pavlovian conditioning*, and the language of conditioned reflexes has to some extent entered the everyday vocabulary (although in popular usage it's often confused with instances of learning in operant behavior).

The term *conditioned*, from the Russian phrase for conditioned reflexes, условный рефлекс (*uslovnyi refleks*), might better have been translated as *conditional*, because the name was applied to reflexes conditional upon relations among environmental stimuli. Respondent conditioning is an instance of stimulus control applied to stimulus-presentation operations rather than to the contingencies of consequential operations. In other words, instead of signalling the consequences of responding, a stimulus simply signals the presentation of some other stimulus. Pavlov's conditioned salivary reflexes are the prototype example: When a bell repeatedly signalled food in the mouth of a hungry dog, salivation began to be elicited by the signalling stimulus as well as by the food itself.

(Ironically, Pavlov may never have used a bell in his experiments; his rare mention of bells occurs only in later work, and there probably refers to electrically operated devices. The ubiquitous references to Pavlov's bell may have originated with the common use of the dinner bell and salivation as examples in the writings of John B. Watson and others. Pavlov did own a bell, but he kept it on his desk, presumably using it to summon servants.)

In discussing operant behavior, we spoke of classes of responses rather than individual instances because individual responses are never exactly repeated. Similar problems exist for elicited behavior. For example, successive elicitations of salivation by food may differ in latency, quantity, viscosity and other properties. It's therefore appropriate to extend the language of classes to responses defined by the stimuli that produce them. These classes, called *respondents*, correspond to the behavior earlier called elicited or reflexive. Thus, salivation produced by food in the mouth is a respondent class; it must be distinguished from salivation produced by acid in the mouth, which is a different respondent class, and from spontaneous salivation, which isn't a respondent class at all because it has no eliciting stimulus (spontaneous salivation is emitted rather than elicited; if we could identify an eliciting stimulus, we wouldn't call it spontaneous).

We'll begin this chapter by discussing the behavior generated by various types of Pavlovian or respondent conditioning. Then we'll consider how such behavior may interact with operant responding. We'll find such interactions relevant to the topic of emotion. We'll end the chapter with a section on biological constraints on learning.

Section A   Conditional Reflexes

We produce respondent behavior by presenting stimuli, and we change respondent behavior by changing these stimuli. For example, different concentrations of acid in the mouth (e.g., dilutions of vinegar) elicit different quantities of saliva. This means we're limited in the extent to which we can modify respondent behavior. We can create new operants by shaping, but the properties of respondents are determined by their eliciting stimuli, so no equivalent procedure exists for respondent behavior. But we can alter the eliciting effects of stimuli. Let's examine Pavlov's (1927) procedure in more detail.

We begin with a dog in a harness with one of its salivary ducts connected to a system that records salivation. We use two stimuli: the sound of a buzzer and food in a form that can be delivered directly into the dog's mouth. First we examine the effects of each stimulus separately. When we first sound the buzzer, the dog pricks up its ears and turns its head toward it. This has been called an *orienting* response. It diminishes with successive soundings of the buzzer, perhaps even becoming undetectable; it can be reinstated by waiting awhile before sounding the buzzer again (cf. habituation, Chapter 4). When food is placed in its mouth, the dog chews and salivates. These responses may diminish a little over food presentations, but their magnitude remains substantial over the course of a session.

Suppose now that the buzzer signals food by sounding 5 s before each food delivery. After a number of trials salivation sometimes begins in the 5-s period between buzzer and food, and sometimes the buzzer is followed by salivation even on an occasional trial when the food is omitted. In neither case can we attribute the salivation to food as an eliciting stimulus: In the first the salivation began before the food was presented, and in the second the food wasn't presented at all. To the extent that the buzzer has acquired the power to elicit salivation, we say that we've created a new respondent class, salivation elicited by the sound of the buzzer. We call the relation between buzzer and salivation a conditional reflex because it's conditional on the prior relation of buzzer and food.

The sequence of events is illustrated in Figure 12-1. The buzzer at first elicits orienting responses, but these disappear with repeated presentations; at this point, the buzzer is a *neutral stimulus* (NS). In an unconditional reflex, food elicits salivation; in this relation, the food is an *unconditional stimulus* or *US* and the salivation is an *unconditional response* or *UR*. Conditioning begins when the buzzer reliably precedes food; at this point, the buzzer still has no effect on salivation and can still be regarded as a neutral stimulus. After a period of conditioning, a *conditional reflex* has been created; the buzzer elicits salivation before food is presented (a), or the buzzer elicits salivation even when food is omitted on an occasional trial (b). The buzzer is now a *conditional stimulus* or *CS* and salivation elicited by the buzzer is a *conditional response* or *CR*.

The difference between a conditional stimulus and an unconditional stimulus isn't simply which comes first. If we reversed their order, the eliciting effects of food followed by buzzer wouldn't be much different from those of food alone. In fact, we may be able to predict the relative effectiveness of stimuli as CSs and USs from the probabilities with which the stimuli elicit their respective responses (cf. Chapter 5 on the relativity of reinforcement). For example, consider salivation elicited by food in a dog's mouth and leg flexion produced by shock to its leg. A mild shock may become a conditional stimulus eliciting salivation if reliably followed by food, but a strong shock followed by food isn't likely to do so. On the other hand, food may become a conditional stimulus eliciting leg flexion if reliably followed by a strong shock, but food followed by a weak shock isn't likely to do so. The dif-

FIGURE 12-1 Relations between stimuli and responses in respondent conditioning. An initially neutral stimulus (BUZZER:NS) is followed by an unconditional stimulus (FOOD:US) that elicits salivation. If the neutral stimulus begins to elicit responding like that elicited by the unconditional stimulus, the neutral stimulus is called a conditional stimulus (CS). OR = orienting response; UR = unconditional response; CR = conditional response.

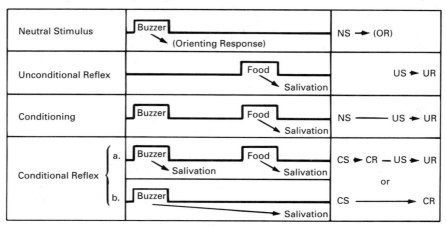

ferences are consistent with the relative probabilities with which food may elicit salivation and mild or strong electric shock may elicit leg flexion.

Differences between the CR and the UR aren't solely those of temporal order. For example, the form or topography of a conditional leg flexion typically differs from the unconditional flexion elicited by electric shock. In general, a CR isn't merely a UR now elicited by a new stimulus; in other words, respondent conditioning can't be interpreted as stimulus substitution; in Pavlov's classical case, for example, the buzzer doesn't substitute for food (the dog doesn't try to eat the buzzer). A CS can affect a broad range of responses in addition to those resembling the ones elicited by the US.

Many different conditional reflexes have been created through respondent procedures (e.g., see Hull, 1934). Pavlov's salivary conditioning is probably the most familiar, but other studies demonstrated conditioning based on such unconditional reflex relations as the knee jerk elicited by a tap of the patellar tendon (Twitmyer, 1902/1974) and limb withdrawal elicited by electric shock (Bechterev, 1933). Conditioning has worked with eyeblinks elicited by a puff of air to the eye (e.g., Gormezano, 1972), but conditioning of pupillary constriction elicited by light to the eye, once believed feasible, has been unsuccessful (Young, 1958). The Russian literature includes a variety of conditioning demonstrations (e.g., Bykov, 1957). For example, for several days a dog was placed in a waiting area at neutral temperature before being moved into a heated room, and its metabolism and oxygen consumption began to decrease in the waiting area as well as in the heated room. Inversely, after waiting area stays were followed by being moved into a cool room, the dog's metabolism and oxygen consumption began to increase in the

waiting area as well as in the cool room (Bykov, 1957, pp. 183–210).

Consider another example. The release of insulin by the pancreas is a UR produced by the US of sugar in the gut (Deutsch, 1974). This US is reliably preceded by the taste of sugar, which makes it likely that the taste will become a CS that releases insulin. Suppose now that you've just switched from consistently drinking soft drinks with sugar in them to their sugar-free diet versions. As a CS, the sweet taste of the drink elicits the release of insulin, which is ordinarily used up as you digest the sugar. But now your drink has no sugar in it, so you can expect to feel weak or heady as the insulin produces a substantial drop in your blood sugar level (hypoglycemia). This effect was especially common when sugar-free drinks were first introduced and people were familiar only with the standard varieties. The effect is less noticed nowadays, because just an occasional substitution of a sugar-free for a standard drink can weaken the effect considerably. Other conditioning effects have been demonstrated with a variety of physiological responses (e.g., reactions of the immune system: Ader & Cohen, 1985).

Respondent conditioning with some types of USs leads to CSs that elicit compensatory responses, responses that counteract the effects of the US, rather than responses similar to those elicited by the US. Such cases provide another kind of evidence that respondent conditioning isn't merely stimulus substitution. One example occurs in respondent conditioning with opiates such as morphine or heroin (Siegel, 1977). Among the effects of these drugs is analgesia, an elevated pain threshold. With continued doses, events that lead up to administration of the drug (e.g., preparing the needle) are likely to become CSs that elicit a CR. But this CR doesn't enhance the analgesia and other drug effects; instead, it counteracts them (for example, it produces hyperalgesia, a lowered pain threshold or, in other words, the opposite of analgesia). As a result, it takes larger and larger doses to produce the original drug effect (these are some of the factors involved in the development of drug tolerance). To summarize: The US is the drug in the bloodstream and one component of the UR is analgesia; the CS is any event reliably preceding the drug administration and the CR is a physiological response that counteracts the analgesia and other effects of the drug.

Heroin addicts often take their drugs in the same place in the same company, using a consistent drug ritual. Now consider the addict who for some reason takes the drug somewhere else and in different company. The dose is large but many of the CSs that usually precede it are absent, so a CR much smaller than usual is elicited. The drug effect occurs, but this time it isn't counteracted by the usual compensatory response. Under such circumstances, a drug dose that is ordinarily tolerated can instead be fatal (Siegel et al., 1982); hospital admissions and/or deaths from heroin overdose are especially likely when addicts take their drugs under unusual or unfamiliar circumstances.

TYPES OF CONDITIONING

The temporal relations between the two stimuli can be arranged in varied ways. Situations in which the onset of the CS precedes that of the US by no more than 5 s are sometimes arbitrarily grouped together as instances of *simultaneous conditioning*. This usage is perhaps based on two circumstances: The optimal interval between CS and US is roughly half a second (e.g., Kimble, 1947) and omissions of the US sometimes reduce the reliability with which conditional responding is maintained. Short

intervals like half a second provide little opportunity to observe conditional responding. The choice then was to omit the US on some trials or to lengthen the interval between stimulus onsets. Because conditioning became less reliable with stimulus omissions, lengthening the interval between stimulus onsets became favored over occasionally omitting the US, and the distinction between strict simultaneity and these relatively short delays was overlooked.

The effect of occasional omissions of the US had theoretical ramifications. In a usage that's becoming rare, presentations of the US in respondent conditioning were called reinforcement, and therefore the procedure in which this stimulus was omitted on occasional trials was called partial reinforcement. Distinctions between operant and respondent conditioning were then argued on the basis of the so-called partial reinforcement effect or *PRE*: Relative to reinforcement of every response, partial reinforcement generated substantial quantities of responding in operant behavior, as we saw in Chapter 10, whereas the analogous procedure in respondent conditioning seemed to reduce responding (but see Gibbon et al., 1980). Now that the term reinforcement has become more restricted in its scope, the comparison no longer seems relevant. In its time, however, it provided one of the most persuasive grounds for distinguishing between the two types of conditioning.

Some arrangements of CSs and USs are contrasted with simultaneous conditioning in Figure 12-2. In both *trace conditioning* and *delay conditioning* a relatively long time elapses between the onset of the CS and that of the US; they're distinguished by whether the CS turns off or remains present during that time. (The time from CS onset to US onset can vary independently of the temporal overlap of CS and US. For example, in delay conditioning the CS might end with US onset or

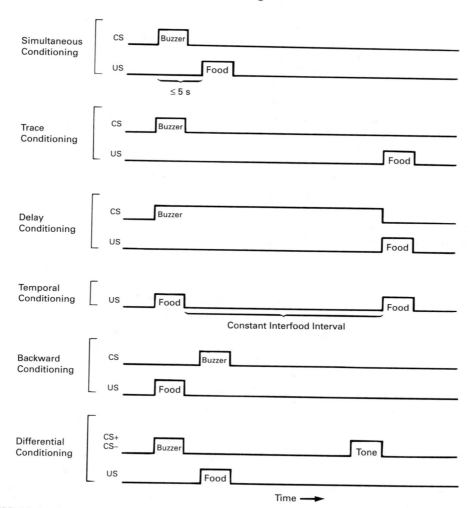

FIGURE 12-2   Schematic presentation of various respondent procedures, showing a buzzer as CS and food as US. In simultaneous conditioning, the buzzer is followed within less than 5 s by food. Different time relations are illustrated in trace, delay and temporal conditioning, and the stimulus order is reversed in backward conditioning. In differential conditioning, the buzzer is followed by food but a tone isn't. CS = conditional stimulus; US = unconditional stimulus.

end at the same time as the US; this feature of the timing of CS and US isn't relevant to the procedural distinctions in Figure 12-2.) In both trace and delay conditioning, conditional responding at first occurs shortly after the onset of the CS, but with successive trials it gradually moves closer to the time at which the US is to be delivered. Trace conditioning acquired its name from the assumption that the CS had to leave some trace in the organism's nervous system to be effective.

But successive presentations of the US itself at regular intervals (e.g., every half hour) also produce conditional responding; this procedure is called *temporal conditioning*, and responding has sometimes been spoken of as conditioned to time as a stimulus (temporal conditioning involves repeated presentation of a stimulus, and so is equivalent to some of the stimulus-presentation operations in Chapter 4).

The reversal of the order of the two stimuli is called *backward conditioning*. For theoretical reasons, it was long assumed to be ineffective in producing conditional responding. It's often less effective than other conditioning procedures, but it has occasionally been demonstrated, particularly with aversive CSs:

> . . . common sense would lead one to expect animals to have the ability to respond defensively to a novel stimulus detected after a sudden aversive event. An animal that sighted an unfamiliar predator following an abortive attack surely would not submit to another attack (i.e., a forward pairing of the predator and pain) before reacting defensively. (Spetch, Wilkie, & Pinel, 1981, p. 163; cf. species-specific defense reactions in Chapter 6)

Finally, a procedure in which one stimulus becomes a CS through its relation to the US while a second stimulus doesn't do so because it never precedes the US is called *differential conditioning*. The stimuli are sometimes called positive and negative conditional stimuli (CS+ and CS-).

In all of these cases, the CS must produce the CR because of its relation to the US, and not for other reasons. For example, if a visual stimulus and a traumatic shock occur together, a later startle to the visual stimulus might not mean it had become a CS. A startle response might be elicited by a variety of innocuous stimuli after a traumatic shock, even though these stimuli never occurred together with the shock. These are cases of

pseudoconditioning (cf. Ison & Hoffman, 1983, and sensitization, Chapter 4).

CONDITIONING AND CONTIGUITY

Some of the attention historically given to respondent conditioning may have depended on how easily it could be related to the concept of association, a principle of learning with substantial precedent in philosophy and psychology. Learning had been said to take place through the association of ideas, and conditional reflexes seemed to represent a primitive example of the formation of such associations. If ideas were associated, it was argued, then one could lead to another. In a kind of mental chemistry, ideas were supposed to become associated through such properties as having common elements or occurring together in time. It remained then to suggest that ideas could be interpreted as responses generated by environmental events, so that remembering one event in the past would call up others it had occurred with.

We needn't dwell on the details. Even those parts of the contemporary psychology of learning that can still be called associationistic have evolved considerably from earlier formulations. We've already noted that respondent conditioning can't be interpreted as simply making one stimulus a substitute for another. For the present, the point is that respondent conditioning was regarded as a process at the root of all learning, and it was assumed to take place merely through the *temporal contiguity* of events, their occurrence together in time. Theoretical debates then revolved around the primacy of respondent conditioning and other processes, and particular attention was given to finding ways of interpreting instrumental or operant behavior as an instance of behavior generated by respondent principles (for various sides of the argument, see Guthrie, 1935; Hull, 1943;

Konorski, 1948; Mowrer, 1960; Schlosberg, 1937; Skinner, 1935b; Smith, 1954).

Part of the problem was that *contiguities* among stimuli weren't adequately distinguished from stimulus–stimulus *contingencies*. Contiguity is defined by stimulus pairings, the number of times stimuli occur together. Even when the number of stimuli remains constant, however, contingency relations between CSs and USs can vary. For example, assume that buzzer (S1) and food (S2) are arranged within trials, and that we can ignore the stimuli that demarcate the trials. The rows in Figure 12-3 show samples of 10 trials from three conditioning procedures. In each, S1 is paired with S2 in trials 2, 5 and 7. In the top row, only those trials include S2, which is therefore perfectly correlated with S1: The probability of S2 is 1.0 given S1 but zero without it, and so S1 perfectly predicts S2. In the middle row, S2 occurs in every trial and so S1 is irrelevant to whether S2 occurs: The probability of S2 is 1.0 with or without S1. In the bottom row, S1 occurs in 6 trials, but in only half of these is it followed by S2, whereas S2 occurs in three-quarters of the trials in which S1 isn't presented: The probability of S2 is lower with S1 (.50) than without it (.75).

Figure 12-4 shows these three conditions

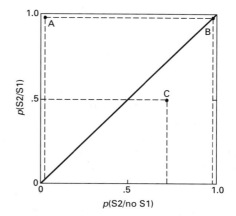

FIGURE 12-4 A stimulus–stimulus contingency space. The unit square shows conditional probabilities of stimulus S2 given stimulus S1 and given no stimulus S1. The three points, A, B and C, correspond to the three procedures of Figure 12-3. (Cf. Figures 4-2 and 5-9)

within a contingency space for stimulus–stimulus relations. Only in the first procedure is S1 likely to become an effective CS; in the last procedure, S1 might even reduce the likelihood of conditional responding elicited by the trial stimulus. The conditional relation between the two stimuli (contingency) rather than the number of pairings

FIGURE 12-3   Conditional relations between two stimuli, S1 and S2. Rows represent samples of 10 trials from three conditioning procedures. Each involves exactly three pairings of S1 and S2 (in trials 2, 5 and 7), but S1 predicts S2 only in the top procedure. In the middle one, S2 is equally likely given S1 and given no S1, and in the bottom one it's less likely given S1 than given no S1. Probabilities of S2 given S1 and given no S1 are shown at the right and are respectively plotted as A, B and C in Figure 12-4. (Cf. Rescorla, 1967)

	1	2	3	4	5	6	7	8	9	10	p(S2/S1)	p(S2/no S1)
A S1												
A S2											1.0	0
B S1												
B S2											1.0	1.0
C S1												
C S2											.50	.75

(contiguity) is the appropriate basis for classifying conditioning procedures (Rescorla, 1967, 1988).

STIMULUS COMBINATIONS IN CONDITIONING

Whether a stimulus becomes effective as a CS depends on the context of stimuli within which it appears (Kamin, 1969); an unusual stimulus or a familiar stimulus in an unusual setting is more likely to become effective than a familiar stimulus in a familiar setting. Sometimes the context itself can become effective as a CS. For example, a rat may learn that a CS is followed by a US when it's in the experimental chamber but not when it's in its home chamber. The experimental chamber is, in effect, a stimulus in the presence of which the CS–US contingency operates (as a result, the rat may not respond to a CS presented in its home chamber). In the context of respondent conditioning, such stimuli have been called *occasion-setters*, in the sense that they set the occasions on which stimulus–stimulus contingencies operate (e.g., Rescorla, 1988). Such stimuli don't elicit responding; they modify the eliciting effects of other stimuli (the occasion-setting vocabulary is sometimes also applied to individual CSs, in the sense that they set the occasion on which a US may be presented). Occasion-setting is one of many possible stimulus functions that may be produced by stimulus combinations in respondent conditioning. Let's now consider examples of a few others.

Overshadowing and Blocking

Suppose that we present loud tone and dim light together followed by some US, such as a shock that elicits leg flexion. After conditional responding develops to this stimulus pair, we could present each stimulus separately and might find tone a much more effective CS than light. (The concept of attention, as in operant discrimination, is relevant to respondent conditioning; we might say that the organism was attending more to tone than to light, or that tone was more salient than light; cf. Rescorla & Wagner, 1972.)

The tone-plus-light example assumes that the organism has no history of conditioning with either stimulus of the compound. The procedure is shown schematically as *overshadowing* in Figure 12-5. When the stimuli of a compound don't become equally effective CSs, the more effective stimulus is said to *overshadow* the less effective one. But such an effect may also occur when one of the two stimuli already has a history of conditioning. For example, suppose dim light is a CS by itself before it's presented together with tone. If simultaneous light and tone are then followed by shock until conditional flexions are observed, we might find when presenting the stimuli separately that light but not tone is an effective CS, even though tone preceded the shock as reliably as did light. When a stimulus fails to become effective as a CS because it's presented with some other already effective stimulus, we say that the stimulus with the prior history *blocked* conditioning to the new stimulus. This procedure is shown schematically as *blocking* in Figure 12-5. (Analogous phenomena can occur in operant discriminations and remind us that operant discrimination and respondent conditioning are both instances of stimulus control.)

Inhibitory Stimuli in Compounds

Stimuli can signal omissions as well as presentations of other stimuli (cf. C in Figure 12-4). When they do so, they sometimes acquire the capacity to reduce the effectiveness of other CSs, and are then described as *inhibitory*. An example is shown in Figure 12-6, which illustrates a conditioning procedure

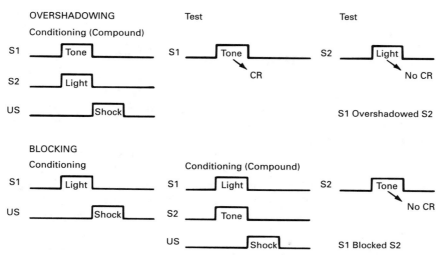

FIGURE 12-5   Schematic illustrations of overshadowing and blocking. In overshadowing, neither of two stimuli of a compound (S1 and S2) has a prior conditioning history but only one
becomes effective as a CS (or one becomes more effective than the other). In blocking, one
stimulus is made effective as a CS, and this history prevents the other from becoming effective when the two are presented together as a compound (or the first reduces the effectiveness of the second). US = unconditional stimulus; CR = conditional response.

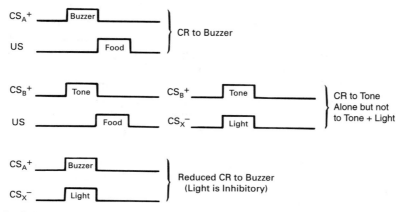

FIGURE 12-6   Schematic illustration of a procedure for demonstrating an inhibitory component of a stimulus compound. First, the succession of buzzer and food produces conditional
salivation to the buzzer. Next, tone alone is followed by food but tone accompanied by light
isn't; conditional salivation occurs to tone alone but not to tone plus light. Finally, when light
is presented with the buzzer, the buzzer elicits less salivation than if it is presented alone.

involving food-elicited salivation in a dog.
First, a buzzer is made a CS (CS_A^+). Once the
buzzer reliably elicits salivation, a tone is
presented either alone or with a light on irregularly alternating trials. When tone (CS_B^+)
is presented alone, it's followed by food.
When it's presented with the light (CS_X^-),
food is omitted. Eventually tone alone elic-

its conditional salivation but the pairing of tone and light doesn't. It might be assumed that the dog simply discriminates tone alone from the tone-plus-light combination. But the inhibitory effect of the light is demonstrated when later presentations of the buzzer with the light elicit less conditional salivation than the buzzer would have elicited if presented by itself.

In another procedure, we might follow the tone-light combination but neither of the stimuli alone by the US. In this case, we'd eventually find that the combination but not the individual stimuli elicited the CR. In other words, as this demonstration shows, organisms can respond differentially not only to individual stimuli but also to relations among them.

Sensory Preconditioning and Second-Order Conditioning

We've considered cases of respondent conditioning based on USs that serve in other situations as reinforcers (e.g., food) or punishers (e.g., shock). But does conditioning occur when relatively neutral stimuli such as lights or sounds serve as USs? The problem is that conditioning is difficult to assess in the absence of elicited responses. Two procedures concerned with effects of such stimuli, *sensory preconditioning* and *second-order*

conditioning, are illustrated for conditional leg flexions in dogs in Figure 12-7.

First, consider sensory preconditioning (Brogden, 1939). In the first phase, preconditioning, one stimulus signals a second stimulus. In the example of Figure 12-7, a buzzer is consistently followed by tone. In the second phase, a conditional reflex is created in which the second stimulus becomes a CS. In the figure, tone is followed by shock. Once the conditional reflex is created, so that the tone elicits leg flexion, the eliciting effects of the buzzer are tested. Leg flexion to the buzzer is then taken to mean that the buzzer became a CS relative to the tone during preconditioning. (For convenience, control groups used to counterbalance stimuli and to rule out sensitization and other effects have been omitted; cf. Chapter 4.)

In second-order conditioning, the order of phases is reversed (cf. Rescorla, 1980). In the example in Figure 12-7, a conditional reflex in which tone elicits leg flexion is created first, by presenting tone and then shock. Later, a buzzer is followed by the tone. In this instance, the question is whether the CS created in the first phase can function as a US for another stimulus in the second phase. The difficulty is that the tone loses its effectiveness as a CS as it's repeatedly presented without shock in the second phase, but dur-

FIGURE 12-7 A schematic diagram of the phases of sensory preconditioning and second-order conditioning procedures, using buzzer and tone as CSs and shock-elicited leg flexions in a dog as the UR.

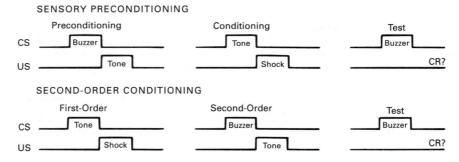

ing just this time the buzzer must acquire its conditional properties. An alternative procedure, with the buzzer followed by the tone and then shock on all trials within a single phase, would be ambiguous; we wouldn't know whether leg flexions elicited by the buzzer occurred because of the relation between buzzer and tone or the relation between buzzer and shock.

If the CS is presented alone after sensory preconditioning, thereby extinguishing the conditional reflex, the preconditioning stimulus also will no longer elicit a CR. In other words, in the example of Figure 12-7, presenting tone alone after the conditioning phase until the tone no longer elicits flexions will also make the buzzer lose its effectiveness as a CS. But the comparable procedure after second-order conditioning doesn't always extinguish the second-order conditional reflex (Rizley & Rescorla, 1972; but see also Holland & Ross, 1981). In the example of Figure 12-7, presenting tone alone until it no longer elicits flexions may not eliminate the conditional flexions to the buzzer created during the second-order phase.

This outcome is paradoxical. Consider an analogous human case history. A young man sees blood in painful circumstances and the sight of blood becomes a CS that elicits those emotional responses we call fear. At a later time (equivalent to the second-order phase), he sees blood in an elevator and thereby acquires a fear of elevators. Then he goes into hospital work and in that context gradually gets over his fear of the sight of blood. According to Rizley and Rescorla's findings, this change won't reduce his fear of elevators even though the CR to blood had been the basis for the fear. This case is hypothetical and we must generalize cautiously from experimental to real-life situations. But the analysis of such respondent contingencies is relevant to behavior therapies that are assumed to eliminate fears or phobias by extinguishing

acquired responses to conditional aversive stimuli. Examples include *flooding*, which involves exposure to intense versions of the aversive stimulus, usually for an extended time, and *systematic desensitization*, which involves the gradual fading in of the aversive stimulus (e.g., Wolpe, 1958, 1990). In any case, such findings again demonstrate that respondent conditioning isn't just the substitution of one stimulus for another.

CONTIGUITY AND CONSEQUENCES

Instances of conditioning based on aversive stimuli such as electric shock were called *defensive conditioning*, on the assumption that the responses elicited by such stimuli occurred because they had some natural defensive function (cf. Chapter 6 on species-specific defense reactions). One frequently cited example is an experiment with an infant boy named Albert (Watson & Rayner, 1920). The aversive stimulus was the sound, just behind little Albert, of striking a suspended steel bar with a hammer. This sound produced crying or withdrawal or startle responses. When the sound followed presentations of a white rat, these responses began to occur in the presence of the rat and of other stimuli having properties in common with it, such as cotton wool. Watson and Rayner called these responses *conditioned emotional reactions*. Yet the details of the experimental procedure show that the initial clangs of the steel bar weren't independent of behavior:

1. White rat suddenly taken from the basket and presented to Albert. He began to reach for the rat with left hand. Just as his hand touched the animal the bar was struck immediately behind his head. The infant jumped violently and fell forward, burying his face in the mattress. He did not cry, however.

2. Just as the right hand touched the rat the bar was again struck. Again the infant jumped

violently, fell forward and began to whimper. In order not to disturb the child too seriously no further tests were given for one week. (Watson & Rayner, 1920, p. 4)

At least at the outset, therefore, Watson and Rayner's experiment used punishment of reaching toward the rat and not merely response-independent stimulus presentations. This was presumably important in getting Albert to attend to the white rat, but it means that we can't unambiguously attribute little Albert's responses to conditioning. We can't even rule out the consequences of Albert's responses to the struck bar; after all, these responses led the experimenters to terminate the procedure for a week.

The problem, however, isn't restricted to Watson and Rayner. Once we're alert to the possibility of response consequences in supposed conditioning procedures, we often find them. For example, early demonstrations of limb withdrawal elicited by shock were indifferent to the method of attaching the electrodes. Yet if both electrodes are attached to a dog's leg, a flexion can't prevent shock delivery, whereas with either or both electrodes attached to the floor on which the dog's paws rests, a flexion prevents or terminates shock delivery by breaking the electrical circuit. In fact, the classic defensive reflex of Bechterev (1933) typically had both electrodes on a surface the organism touched, so that a response prevented or terminated the shock; Bechterev was therefore probably studying avoidance and escape behavior rather than respondent conditioning. Recognizing the different implications of the two methods of electrode placement was an important step in the evolution of the distinction between operant and respondent behavior (cf. Schlosberg, 1937; Skinner, 1935b; see also Kimmel, 1976).

Once consequences became implicated in a few cases of presumed respondent conditioning, it was tempting to seek them in all. For example, can't the flexion have conse-

quences even with both electrodes attached to a dog's leg in defensive conditioning? Suppose a buzzer reliably precedes shock. How can we tell whether the shock is as aversive passing through a flexed limb as through an unflexed one? In defensive conditioning, conditional flexions are ordinarily slower and different in magnitude than unconditional flexions. Perhaps this is because a dog whose leg is already flexed doesn't have to adjust its posture as much when shock is delivered as when it stands on all fours and must shift its weight to the remaining three legs once flexion is elicited (Wagner, Thomas, & Norton, 1967). Clearly salivation too has consequences; it affects taste and swallowing in the case of dry food and dilution in the case of acid on the tongue (e.g., Hebb, 1956).

The place of respondent conditioning in learning theory began with attempts to reduce all instances of operant learning to special cases of respondent conditioning, but the new arguments had turned the situation around. The case was made that all instances of respondent conditioning could be interpreted in terms of consequences that were earlier unnoticed. The next step was to observe that autonomic responses such as salivation and constriction or dilation of blood vessels were often accompanied by somatic responses (e.g., muscle contractions producing skeletal movement). The position could then be taken that autonomic responses in respondent conditioning were artifacts, incidental accompaniments of the behavior generated by instrumental processes (Smith, K., 1954; cf. the spandrels of Chapter 3). The status of respondent conditioning therefore came to depend on demonstrations of conditioning that couldn't be interpreted in terms of consequences of responding.

One approach was to see whether conditional responding could be modified by explicitly arranged consequences. If such consequences were ineffective, then the argument that the new reflex relation depended on other unidentified consequences would no longer be convincing. Sheffield (1965) therefore added consequences to the conditional salivation generated by the classical Pavlovian situation. Specifically, a tone CS preceded food but food was omitted if the dog salivated on that trial. (The procedure is an example of negative punishment sometimes referred to as *omission training*.) In other words, this arrangement converted the standard Pavlovian procedure to one in which the consequence of salivating was no food and the consequence of not salivating was food.

Salivation wasn't modified by its consequences in this procedure. Consider the performance of the dog Vicki. At the beginning of training, conditional salivation hadn't yet begun, so the tone was consistently followed by food. This contingency produced conditional salivation, but when Vicki salivated in a trial, food was omitted so conditional salivation decreased. Once conditional salivation decreased, the tone was again consistently followed by food so conditional salivation reappeared. Vicki repeated this cycle of conditional salivation, omitted food, decreased salivation, reinstated food, and return to conditional salivation many times over 40 days (800 trials). Although she could have received food on every trial by not salivating during the tone, she didn't learn to do so and received food on only some trials each day.

It would be premature to conclude that this settled the issue. A consequence effective as a reinforcer for one response may not be effective for another (Chapter 5). Food elicits salivation, so it isn't surprising that salivating is ineffectively reinforced by food. The reduction of salivation by the omission of a reinforcer has been demonstrated with a water reinforcer, which doesn't itself elicit

salivation (Miller & Carmona, 1967; cf. Chapter 7). Salivation, elicited in some circumstances, can be modified by its consequences in others. The issue is no longer that of reducing operant learning to respondent conditioning or vice versa, because too many lines of evidence distinguish between them. For example, operant cases require responses but respondent conditioning can occur without responses, as when stimulus–stimulus contingencies arranged during paralysis by curare affect behavior after recovery from the paralysis (cf. Solomon & Turner, 1962). Instead, the crucial issue in dealing with operant and respondent cases is to be able to tell which is which.

AUTOSHAPING AND AUTOMAINTENANCE

The cases of respondent conditioning so far have included both autonomic responses (e.g., salivation) and somatic or skeletal responses (e.g., leg flexion). Chapters 4 and 7 considered how these two classes contributed to theoretical distinctions between operant and respondent behavior. The demonstration that autonomic responses such as salivation could be modified by their consequences had substantial impact on these theories. That impact was paralleled by the demonstration that somatic or skeletal responses could be affected by respondent procedures. Both demonstrations implied that operant and respondent processes couldn't be distinguished by physiological criteria that defined kinds of responses; the critical difference was instead in the respective response–stimulus and stimulus–stimulus contingencies.

We discussed earlier the ambiguity of experiments on conditional leg flexions to shock. The problem was that procedures couldn't be designed to guarantee that leg flexions would have no consequences. Perhaps partly for this reason, the demonstration of respondent conditioning of another skeletal response, the pigeon's key peck, received special attention in a procedure called *autoshaping* (Brown & Jenkins, 1968). Because the key peck is a common response in studies of consequential responding, it was important to determine the extent to which respondent processes enter into these performances.

Autoshaping originated as a convenient alternative to shaping the key peck by successive approximations (Chapter 7). It begins with a pigeon that eats reliably from the feeder but hasn't pecked the key. At intervals the key is lit and a few seconds later the feeder is operated independently of the pigeon's behavior. Thus, the lit key becomes a stimulus that signals food. The food occasions eating, which in the pigeon includes pecking. We therefore might say that food is a US and that pecking food is a UR. After a few presentations of lit key and then feeder, the pigeon begins to face and move toward the key when it lights. Within perhaps fewer than 10 and rarely more than 100 trials, the pigeon pecks the key whenever it's lit. After pecking is generated by autoshaping, the continuation of the procedure is called *automaintenance. Autoshaping* and *automaintenance* simply distinguish the changes in behavior leading up to the first peck from the maintained behavior following this peck.

In autoshaping and automaintenance, food deliveries occur independently of behavior. It's therefore difficult to attribute autoshaped pecking to its consequences. Nevertheless, once such pecking begins it's often followed by food. An argument based solely on the observation that no consequences of pecking are obvious may not be persuasive. Autoshaped pecks were therefore studied in omission procedures analogous to Sheffield's experiment with salivation: Food was delivered after the key

light only on trials in which the pigeon didn't peck the key (Williams & Williams, 1969). As with salivation, pecks often occurred in a substantial proportion of trials even though they caused the omission of food. The pecking presumably stabilized at a level at which enough trials occurred without pecks (and therefore with food) to maintain pecking in the other trials.

When food is repeatedly presented to a hungry pigeon, pecking becomes a dominant component of its behavior between food presentations (cf. Chapter 4). The pigeon's autoshaped key pecks may therefore be interpreted as behavior generated by repeated food presentations. They occur mainly during the key light and come to be directed toward it so strongly that they strike the key. Once autoshaped pecking begins, it may be maintained indefinitely by repeated presentations of key light and food even though it has no obvious consequences (in fact, relative to keeping its head in or near the feeder, the pigeon may delay its access to food by pecking the key). The production of key pecking in autoshaping has the critical features that define respondent conditioning, so the respondent vocabulary is appropriate. The key light is a CS. It acquires its capacity to elicit a CR, key pecking, through its correlation with food. Food is the US and it elicits a UR, pecking. As in other cases, the contingent relation between key light and food, not their pairing, determines whether autoshaped pecking occurs.

A distinctive feature of autoshaping is the directed nature of the CR: Pecks generated by the key light could occur anywhere in the chamber (in the air, at the wall, around the food hopper); instead, they're directed at the key. The inverse relation also holds: Pigeons tend to move away from stimuli correlated with the absence of food (Wasserman, Franklin, & Hearst, 1974). For example, if a green key precedes food but a red key doesn't, autoshaped pecking occurs during green but the pigeon moves to the opposite side of the chamber during red. The directed nature of autoshaped pecking has been called *sign tracking* (Hearst & Jenkins, 1974). A response must be emitted before it can be reinforced, and it may sometimes be emitted because it was once elicited. Perhaps then the behavioral relations that occur in autoshaping are prototypes of the processes from which operant behavior evolves.

Chapter 11 considered behavioral contrast, the increase in response rate in an unchanged component of a multiple schedule when the reinforcement rate in the other component decreased. One account of behavioral contrast is that autoshaped pecks, generated by the differential correlation of the multiple-schedule stimuli with food, are added to operant pecks. Some experiments have distinguished two classes of key pecks on the basis of duration and topography (e.g., Keller, 1974; Schwartz & Williams, 1972). The topography of autoshaped pecks is affected more by the US than by contingencies (Jenkins & Moore, 1973). For example, the pigeon's peck at grain is briefer than and differs in form from its drinking. Autoshaped pecks produced by key light and food resemble eating pecks (when autoshaped pecks are based upon food, the pigeon looks as if it's eating the key), whereas those produced by key light and water resemble drinking (when they're based upon water, the pigeon looks as if it's drinking the key). On the other hand, autoshaping can occur even when the US elicits behavior unrelated to pecking. For example, pigeons will come to peck a lighted key if the key light is reliably followed not by food but rather by access to a social area (Peele & Ferster, 1982).

In our survey of respondent conditioning, we've covered a lot of ground. Our treatment of the basic components, CS and US and CR and UR, was followed by a brief survey of types of conditioning, including simultaneous, trace, delay, temporal and backward conditioning. We distinguished between pairings or contiguities and stimulus–stimulus contingencies defined by conditional probabilities. We also examined findings with various stimulus combinations in conditioning, including overshadowing and blocking, inhibitory stimuli in stimulus compounds, sensory preconditioning, and second-order conditioning. We concluded with an example of the conditioning of a skeletal response, the pigeon's peck, in autoshaping and automaintenance. Now we're ready to consider the ways in which respondent processes may be relevant to operant behavior.

Section B   **Operant–Respondent Interactions: Emotion**

Operant and respondent processes can interact when respondent procedures are combined with operant procedures. For example, a stimulus that reliably precedes or signals shock may not just elicit leg flexions; it may also interfere with behavior that's been maintained by its consequences, such as lever pressing maintained by food reinforcement. We sometimes describe comparable behavior in humans in terms of fear or anxiety; thus, procedures such as these are often regarded as relevant to emotion.

CONDITIONING AND EMOTION

Stimuli that signal the presentation of other stimuli can be superimposed on baselines of ongoing operant behavior. For example, suppose a rat's lever presses are maintained by food reinforcement; from time to time a tone is presented; the tone ends with the delivery of a shock. In such circumstances, the tone typically reduces lever pressing, especially as the time of shock delivery approaches. This phenomenon, originally demonstrated by Estes and Skinner (1941), has been variously called *anxiety*, *conditioned suppression* and *conditioned emotional response* or *CER*. It's illustrated in Figure 12-8, which shows development of and recovery from suppression (Geller, 1960). The rat's lever presses were maintained by a VI 2-min schedule of food reinforcement; a brief shock followed 3-min presentations of tone. After the tone came to suppress responding, shock was discontinued and pressing during the tone recovered to earlier levels.

The procedure is an instance of respondent conditioning: One stimulus, tone, signals another stimulus, shock. (The shock is presumed to be aversive, so we call the tone a *preaversive* stimulus.) This is another case in which behavior produced by the CS differs from that produced by the US. The tone suppresses reinforced lever pressing, but

pressing begins again soon after shock has been delivered.

If we looked more closely at the rat's behavior during the tone, we'd find that these contingencies affected many other classes of responses besides lever presses (e.g., heart rate, respiration; cf. Blackman, 1977; Rescorla & Solomon, 1967). We're most likely to invoke the language of emotion when an event affects a broad array of different response classes, so we may be tempted to speak of the rat's fear or anxiety. If we do so, we must recognize that such terms don't explain the rat's behavior. It wouldn't do to say later that the rat stopped pressing during the tone because it was afraid; the effect of the tone on the rat's pressing led us to speak in terms of the rat's fear in the first place.

Our language of emotions is complicated. We speak of emotions in others and in ourselves on the basis of both situations and the behavior that occurs in those situations (cf.

FIGURE 12-8   Development of and recovery from suppression during a preaversive stimulus. A rat's food-reinforced lever presses were maintained by a VI 2-min schedule (reinforcers aren't shown in the cumulative records). The left records show the effects of superimposing a 3-min tone followed by electric shock on baseline lever pressing. The downward displacements of the record between the dashed vertical lines mark off periods of tone. By trial 27, pressing was almost completely suppressed by the tone. The right records show recovery from suppression when the tone was no longer followed by shock. (Adapted from Geller, 1960, Figure 3)

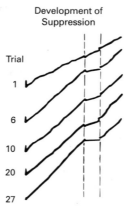

Development of
Suppression

Trial

1

6

10

20

27

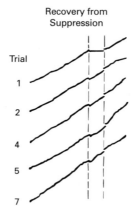

Recovery from
Suppression

Trial

1

2

4

5

7

Ortony & Turner, 1990). For example, we might speak of the behavior produced by preaversive stimuli in terms of fear or anxiety, but if we also observed aggressive behavior we'd be more likely to speak of anger. Either way, we must be clear that these names for behavioral effects don't explain them. Consider, for example, the question of why is someone acting in some way. We might answer that the person is sad or depressed. If asked how we know, we might answer that we can tell from how the person is acting. But we've said nothing more than that the person is acting that way because the person is acting that way. It would be more useful to know that the person is acting that way because of some specific event, such as the loss of a job or the breakup of a love affair.

A practical application of our understanding of preaversive stimuli is provided by the treatment of children under intensive care, as in hospital burn units (Derrickson, Neef, & Cataldo, 1993). These children are subjected to unpredictable and uncontrollable aversive events at any time of the day or night: Injections, changes of dressings, intravenous feedings and so on. A typical outcome of their long-term care is that they become lethargic and withdrawn; they don't react to the events around them (cf. Chapter 9 on learned helplessness). For these children, the hospital setting has become one massive preaversive stimulus.

We can help by giving the children at least some control over part of the environment some of the time (e.g., in social interactions with visitors or ward staff, in choices of meals whenever possible, and so on), but constraints on care delivery may limit the feasibility of this approach. Another alternative is suggested by our analysis in terms of preaversive stimuli. If we turn on a red light over a child's bed at least 10 minutes be-fore we start any aversive procedure, the red light becomes a preaversive stimulus. Its onset will become aversive too, but while it does so its absence also becomes a *safety signal*, a time when the child is safe from aversive medical procedures. The safety may be relative, in that the child may still be in pain some of the time and emergencies may sometimes not allow time for use of the red light, but relative safety is better than none at all. During the safe times, while the red light is absent, the child's physiological reactions to the conditions that signal aversive events will relax, and behavior with reinforcing events as a consequence will be more likely to be maintained; this may speed the child's recovery as well as reducing the child's lethargy and withdrawal.

PREAVERSIVE AND PREAPPETITIVE STIMULI

Although the language of emotion is important in our interactions with other people, it hasn't proved very useful in behavioral analyses of the effects of preaversive stimuli. Instead, the interactions between respondent conditioning and operant behavior, as when preaversive or preappetitive stimuli are superimposed on reinforced responding, have been analyzed more effectively in terms of experimental parameters, such as baseline reinforcement schedule, baseline response rate and so on.

The finding that positively reinforced responding can be suppressed by preaversive stimuli was later supplemented by the finding that avoidance, which is negatively reinforced responding (cf. Chapter 6), can be enhanced by such stimuli (Sidman, Herrnstein, & Conrad, 1957). In other words, a rat whose lever presses avoid shock may increase rather than decrease its pressing during a stimulus that precedes an unavoidable or inevitable shock. This enhanced responding has been called *conditional facilitation* or *conditional acceleration*. Once such enhanced responding develops during negatively reinforced responding, it may continue with positively reinforced responding. For example, rhesus monkeys' lever pressing maintained by orange juice as a reinforcer was originally suppressed during a clicking noise that preceded shock, but after they acquired a history of pressing that avoided shock and were returned to the initial procedure, their pressing during the clicking noise was enhanced rather than suppressed (Herrnstein & Sidman, 1958).

The situations were then extended to superimposing preappetitive rather than preaversive stimuli on baseline operant behavior. For example, a key light that precedes response-independent food deliveries increases pigeons' key pecking when it's superimposed on pecking maintained by DRL reinforcement (Herrnstein & Morse, 1957). By analogy to the labeling of suppression during preaversive stimuli as *anxiety*, it was tempting to speak of such enhancing effects of preappetitive stimuli in terms of *joy*. The enhancement of positively reinforced responding and suppression of negatively reinforced responding by preappetitive stimuli seemed to parallel the suppression of positively reinforced responding and enhancement of negatively reinforced responding by preaversive stimuli (e.g., Azrin & Hake, 1969; Leitenberg, 1966). But the contingencies are complicated (e.g., they sometimes allow autoshaped key pecks to combine with effects of preappetitive stimuli), and continued study of preaversive and preappetitive stimuli showed such an account to be oversimplified (Blackman, 1977).

As an example, Figure 12-9 shows that shock level and baseline response rate jointly determine whether preaversive stimuli suppress or enhance a rat's lever pressing reinforced with food (Blackman, 1968). During red light and noise, lever presses were reinforced according to a DRL 15-s schedule with a limited hold of 5 s (i.e., a press was reinforced only if emitted within 15 to 20 s of the last press); during white light and no noise, an FI 20-s schedule operated with a 5-s limited hold. In these multiple DRL FI schedules, DRL components maintained lower response rates than did FI components. Later, occasional 1-min tones that preceded brief shock were added and shock level was varied to determine the relation between shock magnitude and degree of suppression. Figure 12-9 (left) shows response rate during tone (the preaversive stimulus) as a function of shock level. In the FI component, response rate consistently decreased with increasing shock level. In the DRL component, however, response rate increased at low shock levels and decreased only at higher levels. Figure 12-9 (right) shows the same data converted to a suppression ratio, the change in response rate expressed relative to baseline response rate.

The different FI and DRL performances show how behavioral effects can vary as a function of baseline conditions. Superimposing preaversive stimuli on reinforced responding is a respondent procedure that has opposite effects depending on the baseline performance upon which it's superimposed. Similar types of interactions are critical to psychopharmacology, the analysis of the effects of drugs on behavior; there again, the effect of a drug may vary considerably depending on baseline performance.

The effects of preaversive stimuli are determined not only by properties of baseline performance but also by properties of the schedule of stimulus presentation. For example, suppression varies jointly with the duration of a preaversive stimulus and its frequency of presentation. The degree of suppression also depends in part on how

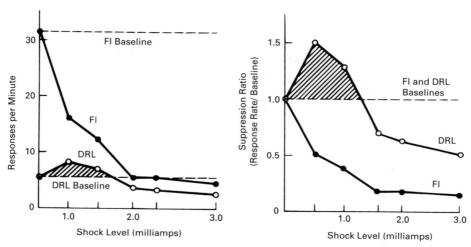

FIGURE 12-9   Response rates (left) and suppression ratios (right) during a stimulus that preceded shock. Effects of the preaversive stimulus depended jointly on shock level and the schedule that maintained responding. Data are from a rat's lever pressing maintained by multiple DRL FI schedules of food reinforcement. With FI responding, the preaversive stimulus suppressed responding at all shock levels; with DRL responding, it enhanced responding at low levels and suppressed it only at higher levels. (Adapted from Blackman, 1968, Figure 2)

much the reduced response rate affects reinforcement rate: When the reduction in responding greatly reduces the reinforcers per session, less suppression occurs than when it only slightly affects reinforcers per session (Smith, 1974).

As with other respondent cases, the effects of preaversive and preappetitive stimuli on operant behavior depend on stimulus–stimulus contingencies rather than stimulus–stimulus pairings. The point is illustrated in Figure 12-10 (cf. Figure 12-3), which shows how various combinations of shock probabilities in the presence and absence of preaversive stimuli suppress a rat's reinforced lever pressing (Rescorla, 1968). For example, if 40% of the preaversive stimuli are paired with shock (probability of shock given CS = .40), a range of effects from complete suppression to no suppression at all can be obtained depending on the probability of shock when the preaversive stimulus is absent. (We can speak of the different contingencies in terms of *predictive value*: The preaversive stimulus is said to have predictive value when shock probability in its presence differs from that in its absence; it's said to have no predictive value when those probabilities are equal; cf. Figure 12-4.)

Responding in the presence of a signalling stimulus is affected by its relation to the stimulus it signals. In the classical Pavlovian case, it seemed at first as though one stimulus substituted for the other, but with preaversive and preappetitive stimuli we've again seen that respondent phenomena can't be treated as stimulus substitution. As usual, it's appropriate to recall that stimuli have multiple functions, and it was probably inevitable that we would have to take such functions into account in dealing with situations that combined operant and respondent procedures (cf. Hoffman & Fleshler, 1962).

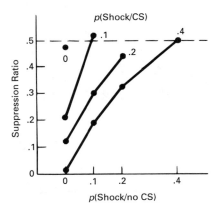
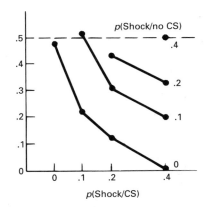

FIGURE 12-10 Suppression of a rat's lever pressing during a preaversive stimulus (CS) as a function of different shock probabilities during its presence and absence. For example, with a shock probability during the preaversive stimulus of .4, or p(SHOCK/CS) = .4, suppression depended on shock probability in its absence, or p(SHOCK/no CS). Effects ranged from complete suppression when the latter probability was zero to none when it equalled p(SHOCK/CS). The same data are plotted in both halves of the figure: on the left the parameter is p(SHOCK/CS) and on the right it's p(SHOCK/no CS). In this suppression ratio, baseline equals .5. (Adapted from Rescorla, 1968, Figure 3)

Section C   **Biological Constraints on Learning**

Chapter 3 examined the joint phylogenic and ontogenic sources of behavior and learning. Both sources may impose constraints not only on the stimuli and responses that enter into operant and respondent contingencies but also on the relations that can be established among stimuli and responses. This section considers a few examples.

SENSORY CONSTRAINTS

Some of the most obvious constraints on learning depend on the organism's sensory systems. For example, a pigeon is more likely than a bat to respond to visual stimuli, whereas a bat is more likely than a pigeon to respond to auditory stimuli. If an organism's sensory capacities aren't taken into account, learning experiments can yield misleading results. For example, the sound frequencies

at which sensitivity is maximal are much higher for rat ears than for human ears. The experimenter who uses auditory stimuli that are easily heard by rats may be unable to tell whether the stimuli are on or off, but the one who uses auditory stimuli that are easily heard by humans may be giving the rat sounds that are hard for it to hear, and may incorrectly conclude that the rat learns slowly and with difficulty.

Experimenters must be alert to the possibility that stimuli to which they're insensitive are important discriminative stimuli for the organism they're studying. For example, the results of early studies of maze learning must be interpreted with caution because rats have keen olfactory sensitivity. If a maze isn't thoroughly cleaned between subjects, a rat's performance may depend on odor trails left by other rats instead of what it learned on its own earlier runs through the maze. Similarly, if the odor of a food US reaches a dog during the presentation of the CS in a Pavlovian procedure, the salivation that follows the CS may depend on the odor instead of the CS–US contingency.

Constraints can involve stimulus configurations as well as single dimensions of stimuli. For example, in contagious yawning one person's yawn elicits yawns in others. The effectiveness of the yawn as an eliciting stimulus is determined by a complex combination of facial features that includes movements of the eyes as well as the mouth (Provine, 1989b). In humans, the properties of faces that are involved in yawns and smiles and frowns have become important over a long phylogenic history of social behavior (Provine & Fischer, 1989). If they need to be learned at all, they're more easily learned than arbitrary geometric configurations.

MOTOR CONSTRAINTS

Anatomical constraints on responding pose no problem. We don't expect flight to be the same in pigeons and bats and bees (and we don't even ask about the possibility of flight in the rat). Species differences in motor capacity are more likely to raise questions when they don't have a clear anatomical basis.

In a study of leg movements in infancy, Thelen and Fisher (1983) recorded the timing and topography with which 3-month-old infants kicked at a mobile. The visual consequences of kicking varied: Some infants saw the mobile move when they kicked at it and others didn't. These consequences affected the rate and vigor of kicking but not the temporal coordinations among the flexion and extension phases of the kick. In other words, some features of the kicks were modifiable but others weren't. Similarly, contingencies may affect the direction in which you walk but not your detailed coordinations of muscles and joints as you do so.

Locomotion has both phylogenic and ontogenic components, and the details of motor coordination don't arise from contingencies between responses and stimuli. Coordinations in walking involve relations among the muscles within a given limb and among the limbs and other parts of the body (e.g., the relaxation of one muscle as an opposing muscle contracts). Many aspects of these coordinations operate independently of the environment (cf. Gallistel, 1980; Gray, 1953); they're often called *motor programs*. The horse trainer doesn't have to shape the details of stepping or the order of leg movements as a horse speeds up from a walk to a trot to a canter to a gallop. A show horse might be taught special steps, such as the rack, but even in these cases the new topography modulates existing patterns.

Another example is flight in birds. How do the wings come to beat in synchrony? Must the bird fly to discover that it can't stay in the air by flapping with just one wing or by bringing one wing down while raising the other? Hatchling chicks were deprived of flapping and flight experience by wing restraint or other means and then their wing coordination was tested at various later stages (e.g., Provine, 1981). Flapping was synchronous from the start, showing that this aspect of flight doesn't depend on environmental contingencies. Many aspects of flight coordination are "prewired"; they're built into bird behavior. Nevertheless, the environment remains important. The evolution of flight in birds depended on the aerodynamic environments of their ancestors. And whatever the details of its flight coordination, when a bird flies and where it goes are determined by the current environment.

Species differ in many ways, and constraints on the topography of responses mustn't be confused with constraints on their functions. We can illustrate this point by contrasting a cat stalking a mouse in a natural environment with a cow that's taught to stalk:

> . . . given a prey which bears the same relation to a cow, in speed and mutual stimulation, as a mouse does to a cat, it should not be too difficult to set up contingencies under which a cow will "stalk"—that is, approach slowly when at a distance in order not to alert the prey and then move quickly to capture. The prey would have to be something like an animated bundle of corn. (Skinner, 1977, p. 1011)

Skinner then points out that this "stalking" by the cow, in speed and other characteristics, would look quite different from the stalking by a cat. Nevertheless, the functional properties of the behavior of the cow and the cat would be similar, even if they differed considerably in structural details.

CONSTRAINTS ON CONSEQUENCES

We may extend our examples to the capacities of various stimuli to reinforce or to serve as USs. Like sensory and motor capacities, these also differ across species. It hardly needs saying that the effectiveness of reinforcers has a phylogenic basis. An organism for which neither food nor water was ever effective as a reinforcer would hardly be likely to live long enough to pass its genes on to another generation. But more subtle properties of environments may also be important, such as the sensory consequences that maintain exploratory behavior or the novel consequences that may make an organism cautious in sampling an unknown food or familiar food in an unknown place (cf. *neophobia*; e.g., Mitchell, Scott, & Williams, 1973).

Before the relativity of reinforcement was recognized, findings in which standard reinforcers for a species failed to have their characteristic effects were hard to deal with.

Breland and Breland (1961) used several cases to argue against the generality of reinforcement as a behavioral process.

In one demonstration with raccoons, food was delivered when a raccoon picked up coins from the ground and deposited them in a container. After some repetitions of the procedure, the raccoon began persistently to rub the coins together instead of releasing them into the container. The Brelands and others saw this outcome as invalidating the principle of reinforcement. But a relevant aspect of raccoon behavior is that raccoons ordinarily rub and wash their food before eating it. The coins apparently provided a better opportunity for this behavior than the food that was supposed to function as a reinforcer. In other words, food wasn't effective as a reinforcer because rubbing had become sufficiently more probable than eating. It's likely that an opportunity for rubbing would have been effective as a reinforcer for other responses, perhaps including eating.

Given that reinforcement relations are based on relative probabilities of responses, the different behavioral hierarchies of different species inevitably constrain what they can learn. When an experimental procedure is applied, there's no guarantee it will be effective. A procedure that leads to learning with one response or organism may not do so with different responses or organisms, and a response or an organism affected by one procedure may be unaffected by others. An essential part of the analysis of learning is to explore such limits.

PREPAREDNESS

Constraints may also involve the relations between the stimuli and responses that enter into operant and respondent contingencies. Such relations were implicit in the examples of constraints on consequences, because we treated them in terms of the relative probabilities of the reinforced responses and the responses occasioned by the reinforcers. We considered other examples in the treatment of species-specific defense reactions in Chapter 6. For example, the ease with which avoidance responding was acquired and maintained depended on species-specific relations between various avoidance responses and aversive stimuli.

Some relations between discriminative stimuli and responses may be easier to learn than others. For example, does it help if the stimuli and responses share common properties, as in responding on the left to a stimulus on the left and on the right to one on the right, instead of responding left to green and right to red? In the first case, locations are relevant properties of both stimuli and responses; in the second stimulus qualities are correlated with response locations (e.g., Miller & Bowe, 1982). Would a shift from location to quality be easier or harder to master than a reversal of locations (recall Stratton's adaptation to inverting prisms in Chapter 5; see also the discussion of transfer in Chapter 17)? Such relations may be crucial in the design of human-machine systems and in the mastery of motor skills (e.g., Bauer & Miller, 1982; Glencross, 1977; Mazur, 1986, Chapter 12).

We've considered cases involving relations between discriminative stimuli and responses, and between responses and reinforcers. Phylogenic contingencies may have prepared organisms to learn only some of the many possible relations among stimuli and responses in operant and respondent procedures. The concept of *preparedness* grew out of the observation that discrimination learning may be a function of the context of responses and reinforcers within which it occurs (Seligman, 1970; Schwartz, 1974). Its significance was established through the analysis of a phenomenon called *bait shyness* or *taste-aversion learning*, a variety of discrimination learning based upon differential punishment (but see Rozin & Kalat, 1971).

In experiments on taste aversion, a rat stops eating a food if it later becomes sick (Revusky & Garcia, 1970). Nausea or other systemic consequences of eating can punish eating even though they follow eating only after a considerable delay. In a study of the role of discriminative stimuli (Garcia & Koelling, 1966), thirsty rats drank water sweetened by saccharin; their drinking was accompanied by clicks and flashes of light triggered electronically by their licks. In other words, the rats drank water that was bright and noisy as well as sweet. In one group, drinking was followed by X-irradiation that later produced sickness. In a second group, drinking was followed by shock. Later, the drinking of each group was measured when a sweet solution was presented and when noise and light accompanied drinking.

Figure 12-11 summarizes the results. Rats that had been X-irradiated drank less sweetened water, but their drinking was unaffected by noise and light; those that had been shocked drank less when noise and light accompanied drinking, but their drinking was unaffected by whether the water was sweetened. In other words, when the aversive stimulus was the delayed systemic consequence of X-irradiation, the rats learned only its relation to the taste of the water consumed earlier, but when the aversive stimulus was shock the rats learned only its relation to the noise and light that preceded it. The delayed effects of X-irradiation punished the drinking of sweetened water, and the immediate effects of shock punished drinking accompanied by noise and light. It's not enough to say that the rats learned

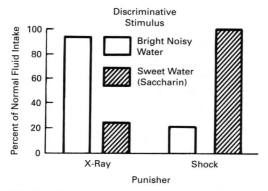

FIGURE 12-11 Percent normal fluid intake of rats whose drinking of sweetened water was accompanied by clicks and lights. In one group, drinking was followed by X-irradiation; in a second, it was followed by electric shock. Whether taste or the sound–light combination became the discriminative stimulus that was effective in reducing drinking depended on the nature of the punisher. (From Garcia & Koelling, 1966, as presented in Revusky & Garcia, 1970, Figure 9)

some stimuli or some responses more easily than others; they were predisposed to learn different relations among discriminative stimuli and contingencies in these different situations.

Revusky and Garcia (1970) discuss these findings in the context of a thought experiment in which you find $100 that's been left for you

> by an insane billionaire experimenter because, two hours ago at lunch, you ate gooseberry pie for dessert instead of your usual apple pie. The experimenter wanted to increase the future probability that you would eat gooseberry pie. It is very unlikely that this experiment will be successful. . . . Hundreds of events are bound to occur during the two hours between consumption of the gooseberry pie and the receipt of the $100. The odds are very great that you would have associated one of these intervening events with the $100. . . . The results of our thought experiment are really shocking.

We have selected an arbitrary reward of great potency and a response of which you probably were well aware . . . [and] we reached the conclusion that the nature of the environment precluded association over a two-hour delay. (Revusky & Garcia, 1970, p. 20)

These investigators then suggest an alternative thought experiment: Instead of finding money, you get sick:

> Since the gooseberry pie was new to you, you would probably conclude that the pie caused the illness. Here association over a two-hour delay agrees with our daily experience. . . . But why has a change from a consequence of $100 to a consequence of sickness changed the situation? . . . There seems to be only one reasonable answer. . . . The fact that infra-humans also can associate over long delays strongly suggests that there is an innate selective association of flavors with physiological aftereffects and, what is more important, a selective failure to associate irrelevant stimuli with toxicosis. (Revusky & Garcia, 1970, p. 21)

Such experiments are of course complicated by other differences between the two types of consequences. For example, electric shock has a more abrupt onset than do the gastric symptoms of X-irradiation. Furthermore, a case can be made that these experiments involve respondent relations rather than or in addition to operant ones. If respondent contingencies are arranged with taste as a trace CS and nausea as a US, the taste is likely to acquire its aversiveness as a result of its contingent relation to nausea even though the contingency operates over a delay.

In any case, this is another phenomenon with considerable practical significance. When radiation is used in medical procedures, such as some cancer treatments, the contingencies are analogous to those for the X-irradiation groups of Figure 12-11. Thus, the treatment setting itself may begin to elicit nausea and the patient's appetite may decrease as the palatability of foods eaten in the hours before treatment is affected. It may be appropriate to arrange treatments so that these effects are confined to a narrow range of settings and diets.

We've mainly considered phylogenic contributions to constraints. The issues can become even more complicated if we consider ontogenic as well as phylogenic contributions. For example, the adult sexual and maternal behavior of monkeys depends not only on the evolutionary contingencies that selected aspects of the rearing of young and patterns of mating. It also depends on contingencies of early development that involve contact with the mother and interaction with age mates. The deprivation of a young monkey's maternal contact during its first weeks may constrain its behavior throughout the rest of its life (e.g., Harlow & Harlow, 1966). The analysis of behavior is concerned with identifying the origins of particular instances of behavior. With both operant and respondent contingencies, our conclusions about what is learned must take both phylogeny and ontogeny into account.

Chapter 13
Social Learning

The etymologies of the personal pronouns probably extend back to the very earliest of human languages. The histories of I *and its relatives (such as* ego *and* ich*) may be separate from those of* me *and* my *and* mine*. Some forms of* I *have a verblike quality, and pronouns are incorporated into verbs in some languages (e.g., as in the Latin* sum *and* es *for* I am *and* you are*). The distinctions among these and other personal pronouns, such as* you *and* she *and* they *and* he *and* us *and* it*, may be so fundamental as to be irreducible.*

Self, which is related to sibling, separate, se-lect *and* ethnic, *carries an implication of possession (cf. the sense of its relative,* solitary, *as on one's own). Other has the etymological sense of the other one of two:* al- *(other) plus* ter *(two), as in* alter-native. Community, *like* communicate, *implies a having in common. Common is a derivative of* con-, *with, and the Indo-European* mei-, *to go or move together with; some relatives are* immune, mutate, migrate *and* mean.

One variety of selection is the sort that operates on populations of organisms over successive generations. It was considered in Chapter 3 in the context of Darwin's treatment of evolution in terms of natural selection. Another variety is the sort that operates on populations of responses within the lifetime of the individual organism. Much of our discussion of the effects of consequences in subsequent chapters was concerned with this variety of selection. Organisms persist in doing some things and they stop doing others; the procedure of shaping provided an explicit example of the selection of behavior by its consequences.

Chapter 3 also mentioned a third variety of selection. It too operated on behavior, but it involved more than one organism. Whatever behavior an organism acquires within its own lifetime is eventually lost if it isn't passed on to others. Once social learning becomes possible, behavior that's been learned can survive the death of the organism that learned it. The behavior then survives in what others do, perhaps not only in the behavior of descendants but even in the behavior of others who are genetically unrelated.

Section A   **Kinds of Social Contingencies**

Learning from others is especially important in human behavior. A very substantial part of what any of us knows is what we've learned from others, and much of it has been explicitly taught to us, either in the informal context of interactions between family members and others or in the formal context of educational institutions. But the earliest types of social learning must have been much simpler. At what point did some organisms begin to learn to do things just by watching what happened as other organisms did them?

We may think of learning by observation as commonplace because it so often enters into human behavior. But it's not clear how much of it goes on even among nonhuman warm-blooded vertebrates (mammals and birds), and there's hardly any evidence for it at all in invertebrates (e.g., insects). Among primates, one widely cited example involved the feeding of sweet potatoes to macaque monkeys on a Japanese reserve adjacent to a beach (Kawamura, 1959). The potatoes typically became sandy, but one juvenile monkey eventually discovered the practice of removing the sand from the potatoes by rinsing them in the ocean. The practice then spread to other juveniles of the colony (but it was not taken up by the adults).

Human cultures offer many examples of the social selection of behavior, the selection that occurs as behavior is passed on from one individual to another (Harris, 1977; Skinner, 1981). Certain ways of raising children, getting and preparing food, building shelters and dealing with group members and outsiders survive over successive generations. Some practices spread to other groups who aren't close genetic relatives of those who began them. In contemporary Western culture, for example, ethnic foods are prepared and eaten by many who aren't members of the ethnic groups that originated them.

Some behavior that's socially transmitted survives because of its consequences. In early human history, the person who learned from someone else how to make stone tools or fire or garments was probably also more likely to survive long enough to pass the behavior on to someone else than a person who couldn't learn in that way (in every variety of selection, we look at how selection operates at the level of the survival of individual members or units and not at the level of the survival of the group). The survival of other patterns of behavior may involve more complex contingencies.

Consider patterns of child rearing. Suppose that children reared according to most patterns are as likely as adults to rear their own children according to one pattern as according to any other. But suppose also that a very few patterns work so that when the children become adults they're likely to rear their own children in the same way as their parents reared them; we might call these self-replicating patterns of child rearing. In a large population, whenever one of the self-replicating patterns happens to be used by some parents, for whatever reasons, it will be used again in the next generation; the other patterns will come and go. Little by little, over many generations, the patterns that are self-replicating will displace the ones that aren't. Once traditional patterns of child rearing originate in this way, they're likely to survive for very long periods of time.

In earlier discussions of the first two varieties of selection, natural selection and operant selection, we noted that evolution and shaping depended upon variable populations on which selection could operate. Similar constraints exist at the level of cultural selection. For example, cultural practices that favor ethnic diversity may have advantages over ones that don't simply because they allow such variability.

LEARNING ABOUT OTHERS

In many situations, the discriminative stimuli provided by other organisms are more important than those provided by inanimate objects and events. For example, parental investment in offspring may be wasted if the parent can't discriminate between its own offspring and the offspring of others; potential mates must be distinguished from potential competitors, and among the potential mates the receptive must be distinguished from the unreceptive; and so on. In many organisms, such properties are correlated with anatomical features (e.g., colorful plumage in birds); often, behavior is the crucial dimension.

The study of animal communication is concerned with the many ways in which organisms produce stimuli that affect the behavior of other organisms. "Examples of communication are numerous: song in birds, frogs, and crickets; tail-wagging and hackle-raising in dogs; 'grinning' in chimpanzees; human gestures and language" (Dawkins, 1976, p. 67; see also Dawkins & Krebs, 1978). It's more appropriate to speak of such stimuli in terms of their behavioral effects than in terms of the information they carry. Just as it may be misleading to speak of genes as carriers of information about phylogenic contingencies (Dawkins, 1982), it may be misleading to speak of social stimuli as carriers of information (cf. Chapter 14).

Releasers and fixed action patterns provide many examples of effects of social stimuli. In some cases, sometimes called *social facilitation*, the behavior that serves as a social stimulus and the behavior produced by that stimulus are topographically similar, as when one bird's takeoff triggers the flight of the other birds in a flock, or as when a few galloping steers set off a stampede. Such cases may superficially look like imitation, but they're limited to a narrow range of response classes (e.g., contagious yawning or laughing: Provine, 1989a, 1996) and so must be distinguished from it (cf. Field et al., 1982).

Discriminating the behavior of other organisms, whether of one's own or other species, has clear selective advantages. Consider, for example, the relation between predator and prey. If one antelope in a herd is limping just a little, the lion that notices the limp may be more likely to make a capture. The antelope that can tell the difference between one lion that hasn't eaten for a while and another that's just finished eating may be more likely to move away in the safest direction. A predator that can distinguish whether it's been noticed by its prey has a distinct advantage over one that can't; an advantage also accrues to a prey that can distinguish whether it's been noticed by its predator. Such discriminations presumably have an extensive phylogenic history. Attention to the behavior of prey may be one dimension upon which natural selection operates in the evolution of predators, just as attention to the behavior of predators may be one dimension upon which natural selection operates in the evolution of prey. Following from such selection, discriminations of social behavior may become so important that they override other types of discriminations.

Discriminations of the behavior of others are at the heart of our human concept of intentionality (cf. Dennett, 1987): We say we understand someone's intentions when our discriminations of the various properties of that person's past and current behavior enable us to act appropriately with respect to what that person will do in the future. In fact, if discriminating one's own behavior is a special case of discriminating the behavior of others (e.g., Bem, 1967), it can be argued that this topic encompasses all of the phenomena considered under the rubric of intentionality. Judgments of the intentions of others are, above all, social judgments, and it takes no special assumptions about the selective contingencies that must have operated on social behavior both within and across species to see that such contingencies could shape well-prepared capacities for social discriminations.

Social discriminations within species have many functions. They may operate within dominance hierarchies or in the defense of territory or as isolating mechanisms that maintain the integrity of a group against intrusions from outsiders or in the distribution of limited resources among group members. Within species that live as social groups, such as most primates, individuals learn what sorts of behavior to expect of others with whom they have extended contact. The cooperative behavior that can emerge in such contexts (de Waal, 1989) requires social discriminations that may be the precursors of the behavior toward others that's called empathy (Hoffman, 1975).

LEARNING FROM OTHERS

It's one thing to learn about other organisms. It's another to learn something from them (Zentall & Galef, 1988). Sometimes the behavior of one organism allows another to act on the basis of stimuli available only to the first, as when a vocal call from one monkey allows another monkey to escape from a predator it hadn't seen. Warning calls are well-documented in bird behavior (e.g., Kroodsma & Miller, 1982). In monkeys, predator calls can vary with kinds of predators, and the response to the call can depend on who the caller is and who the listener is (e.g., Gouzoules, Gouzoules, & Marler, 1984; Seyfarth, Cheney, & Marler, 1980).

Observational Learning

Learning based on observing the behavior of another organism is called *observational learning* (e.g., Zentall & Levine, 1972; another occasional term is *vicarious learning*: Bandura, 1986). Sometimes what seems to be observational learning involves simpler processes. For example, food preferences in rats are learned in social contexts; it's hard to get rid of rats by poisoning because rats that don't ingest the poison may avoid it after interacting with other rats that did and became sick or died. When rats come together they sniff and lick each other, so by smell and taste one rat can become familiar with properties of the food the other has recently eaten (Galef & Stein, 1985). If the food is novel and the other rat is healthy, the first rat will later prefer that novel food over other novel foods, but if the other rat is sick, the first rat will avoid that novel food (in other words, this is a socially mediated taste aversion: cf. Chapter 12). The learning won't occur without some contact between the two rats (e.g., mouth to mouth or mouth to fur). One rat has learned about some novel foods from another, but only in the sense that the combination of food stimuli with social stimuli makes some foods more or less effective as reinforcers or as aversive stimuli, and not in the sense that one rat has learned something on the basis of observing what happens to another rat.

Observational learning has been compellingly demonstrated with rhesus monkeys (Mineka et al., 1984). Monkeys in the wild show fear of snakes by screaming and other agitated behavior and by avoidance of the snake. Even if their parents fear snakes, monkeys reared in the laboratory who have had no experience with snakes don't; for example, if food is on the other side of a container with a snake in it, they'll reach across the container for the food. But if the laboratory-reared monkeys then briefly observe one of their parents behave fearfully toward snakes, they too become fearful. Their fear is intense and persistent; if tested three months later it's undiminished. What they've learned about snakes is based only on observing the parent's behavior toward a snake. There may be a phylogenic component, however, because such observational learning is more likely to occur with snakes or snakelike objects than with some other types of stimuli.

Observational learning is sometimes treated as if it were itself a fundamental kind of learning (e.g., Bandura, 1986), but it's probably better treated as a higher-order variety of behavior. Many different skills have to come together appropriately for observational learning to work, and in the case of human observational learning it's likely that there's also a very large verbal component (Catania, 1995; cf. Chapters 14 and 15). At the least, observational learning must include subtle discriminations of another organism's actions and their outcomes and some history with respect to the effects of related actions on the part of the observer. When we see observational learning, we should try an analysis to determine its components instead of trying to use it to explain other, more complex kinds of behavior.

Imitation

The most important difference between observational learning and imitation is that in imitation the observer's behavior corresponds to that of the organism that's been observed. Imitation doesn't imply that the imitating organism has learned something about contingencies, so not all imitations are

advantageous. A coyote that sees another coyote step into a trap would do well not to imitate that behavior. A hatchling bird that hasn't yet grown its flight feathers would do well not to follow its parents when they fly from its treetop nest.

Following may sometimes be imitative. In one experiment (Neuringer & Neuringer, 1974), food-deprived pigeons learned to eat from the experimenter's hand. When the hand then approached and pecked the key, producing food, the pigeons followed the hand and began to peck the key. The procedure often worked more rapidly than shaping of the key peck. Under natural conditions, young animals may learn to behave like their parents simply by following parental sources of food. But not all following is imitative. For example, when one rat leads another to food, nearness to the leader rat may become a reinforcer of the behavior of the follower rat. Following then emerges as behavior shaped by natural contingencies (cf. the duckling's following of an imprinted stimulus; Chapter 4).

We call responding *imitative* when one organism duplicates the behavior modeled by another organism. But one kind of imitation may be limited to the duplication only of specific instances that have been explicitly taught, while another may include correspondences between the behavior of model and observer even in novel instances, when it's called *generalized imitation*; in the latter case, imitative responding is a class of responses that may be differentially reinforced or, in other words, it's a higher-order class of behavior (e.g., Poulson et al., 1991).

For example, suppose a child learns to imitate several instances of behavior modeled by a puppet, such as jumping, skipping and clapping. If we arrange consequences to maintain the child's imitation of all but the clapping, the child will ordinarily continue to imitate the clapping along with the others even though this imitation never produces those consequences (e.g., Baer, Peterson, & Sherman, 1967). To the extent that imitation of clapping doesn't extinguish, we say it's a member of the generalized class. With generalized imitation, the child will also produce novel imitations if the puppet does something it's never modeled before, such as stamping its foot (in fact, responses occasioned by novel stimuli define generalization, as when a pigeon pecks when it first sees yellow or blue after a history of pecking only in the presence of green). Because *modeling* of a new response can produce novel behavior only if a child's imitation has generalized, it's an effective supplement to shaping (e.g., in teaching skills to children with autism or other developmental disabilities: Secan, Egel, & Tilley, 1989).

We don't know the pertinent physical dimensions of imitative behavior. For example, contingencies can be arranged to create classes that include both nonimitative and imitative responses (Peterson, 1968) or that include imitations only within certain topographical boundaries (Garcia, Baer, & Firestone, 1971). These possibilities are consistent with what we understand about the contingencies that create higher-order classes (cf. Chapter 9), especially given that the behavior of model and observer may look the same to us but we can't be sure that this is also true for the observer. For example, if you touch the top of your head when that's modeled in the game of "Simon says," you see but don't feel the leader's hand and you feel but don't see your own hand. There's no simple correspondence between someone else's seen hand and your own felt hand, so how did you learn to imitate?

One way you can learn correspondences between the seen and felt parts of your body is by behaving in front of a mirror. Humans and some primates seem to learn these correspondences without explicit

training (e.g., Gallup, 1979). For example, if a chimpanzee experienced with mirrors has a spot painted on its eyebrow while it's asleep, it will touch the spot the next time it sees its face in a mirror. Such responses to one's own body have sometimes been spoken of in terms of *self-awareness*. With other organisms, such as the pigeon, the correspondences have to be taught, by training discriminations among stimuli seen in a mirror (Epstein, Lanza, & Skinner, 1981). For example, first a pigeon's pecks at blue cardboard dots pasted at various places on its body were shaped. Next, discriminations among blue dots reflected in a mirror were taught by presenting the dots behind holes in one wall only when the pigeon faced a mirror on the opposite wall; each dot was gone by the time the pigeon turned around, but only pecks at the hole where it had appeared were reinforced. When another blue dot was then attached to the pigeon's breast while it wore a short bib that allowed it to see the dot in the mirror but not by looking down, the pigeon pecked down toward the dot on its body even though it was seeing the dot only in the mirror.

The novel performance doesn't demonstrate a sense of self in pigeons, but it does illustrate a special case of discriminative control in which stimuli and responses vary together along a dimension (*continuous repertoires*: e.g., Wildemann & Holland, 1972); continuous changes in one produce corresponding changes in the other. Discriminated behavior with respect to a mirror involves correspondences between continuous movements and the seen positions of one's body. Other instances include keeping a moving object framed in a camera, mixing paints to match a sample color, tuning a musical instrument and steering a car along a winding road. In human behavior, imitation is a particularly important example of this type of stimulus-control relation; for the individual who already has an established imitative repertoire, new behavior can often be generated more quickly and effectively this way than by shaping or other means.

The Social Origins of Language

Another way to learn from another organism is through verbal behavior: you can be told about contingencies instead of observing them. But verbal behavior can't have originated in that way, because descriptions of contingencies require sentences and the earliest forms of language must have begun with single words. It's a reasonable guess that something like functional single-word utterances (protolanguage) have a history of a million years or more in our hominid ancestry; perhaps these units sometimes combined in functional ways, but their combination in the grammatical organizations we call language probably originated only as recently as forty or fifty thousand years ago. We'll have more to say about verbal behavior in the next chapter, but here we'll deal briefly with its possible origins in human social contingencies.

The simplest and most obvious function of verbal behavior is instructional: It's a way in which one organism gets another to do something. By talking, we change each other's behavior. In verbal behavior, we do things via the mediation of another organism. Sometimes what gets done involves nonverbal effects, as when we ask someone to move something or to carry something to us; sometimes it involves verbal effects, as when we change what someone else has to say about something. If the primary function of language is that it's an efficient way in which one individual can change the behavior of another, it follows that this behavior is quintessentially social and can emerge only in organisms whose behavior is already sensitive to social contingencies.

Assume that the calls of a primate leader once determined the behavior of members of its band as reliably as a releaser elicits a fixed action pattern. At first the vocabulary of releasers was limited to just a few calls, not yet qualifying as verbal behavior but with relatively simple effects corresponding to those of words such as *come* or *go* or *stop*. Over many generations, perhaps millennia, a more extensive repertory of more varied calls was differentiated. If the details of these calls were weakly determined phylogenically, this rudimentary vocal control could later be supplemented by variations produced by ontogenic contingencies. For example, a dominant speaker might learn to attack a listener who doesn't respond in the characteristic way, thereby punishing disobedience (as we'll see in Chapter 15, many contemporary contingencies continue to maintain the effectiveness of verbal control by reinforcing the following of instructions and punishing deviations from it).

Once vocal behavior had expanded to an extensive repertory including arbitrary as well as phylogenically determined calls, idiosyncratic repertories developed by particular leaders would ordinarily be lost to later generations until some way of reproducing this behavior in the leaders' successors had evolved. Thus, the next step in this evolution, perhaps long in coming, was the repetition by the follower of the leader's verbal behavior (Catania, 1994; see also Jaynes, 1976, for an alternative scenario). Once some individuals begin repeating what others say, verbal behavior becomes a kind of behavior that can survive within the behavior of the group, as a candidate for the third type of selection that we discussed earlier, that of cultural transmission. The stage is then set for human verbal memory, for instruction and educational systems, and for the rapid and wide dissemination of cultural practices.

LEARNING ABOUT ONESELF

We've discussed imitation in terms of the relation between our own behavior and the behavior of others. Implicit in that discussion was the suggestion that we learn to discriminate properties of our own behavior in the context of learning about others. The case is even more obvious with verbal behavior, because we learn the language with which we describe our own behavior from others. It follows that what we know about ourselves is a social product. We don't see ourselves as others see us; instead, we see ourselves as we see others.

Let's begin with a human example from a verbal learning experiment (Vesonder & Voss, 1985). The experiment included three kinds of participants: learners who talked aloud while learning verbal items and then predicted how well they'd remember the items on the next presentaton; listeners who heard what the learner said and made similar predictions based on what they heard; and observers who made predictions based on how well learners did on past items without hearing what the learners said. The predictions of both the learners and the listeners were substantially better than those of the observers; the crucial point, however, was that the predictions of the learners and the listeners were essentially the same. The public behavior of the learner, to which the listener also had access, was good enough for the predictions; if the learner did know private things to which the listener had no access (e.g., levels of confidence), they didn't make the learner's predictions any better. The findings are consistent with evidence suggesting that, just as we judge others on the basis of observations of their behavior, we judge ourselves on the basis of observations of our own behavior (e.g., Bem, 1967; Nisbett & Wilson, 1977).

Discriminating Properties of Our Own Behavior

The capacity to discriminate properties of our own behavior is important in many types of human behavior. For example, the student who can't tell the difference between a superficial and a thorough reading of a text may stop studying too soon. To the extent that the behavior of interest has environmental effects, it's sometimes difficult to distinguish between control of discriminated responding by the behavior itself and control by the stimuli produced by that behavior (in some other contexts, this might be called the difference between knowing and feeling that you know: e.g., Koriat, 1995). For example, some students might judge their examination performances primarily on the basis of problems they encountered in answering particular questions, whereas others might judge them primarily on the basis of the consequences of their performances (e.g., the grades later posted).

The nonhuman synthesis of such discriminations is again of potential interest. In one procedure, a pigeon's pecks on a center key were followed by the lighting of two sidekeys; pecks on the left one were reinforced if the pigeon had emitted 50 or fewer responses on the center key, and pecks on the right one were reinforced if the pigeon had emitted more than 50 (Pliskoff & Goldiamond, 1966). The pigeon's side-key pecks depended on the number of its center-key pecks, so we can regard them as responses under the discriminative control of a property of the pigeon's own behavior. Stimulus control by number of responses and other properties of behavior such as the temporal patterning of responses have been demonstrated in a variety of experiments (e.g., Reynolds, 1966; Shimp, Sabulsky, & Childers, 1989; see also Capaldi & Davidson, 1979, on discrimination of deprivation).

One technical problem in such procedures is that the organism's behavior is usually correlated with environmental stimuli. For example, the pigeon that's spent a longer time pecking has probably also spent more time in a position where it's been looking at the key. Is its discrimination then based on its behavior or on what it's been looking at?

In discriminating our own behavior, stimuli are of course available from our muscles and joints and so on. These stimuli are called *proprioceptive* or *interoceptive*. The effects of *biofeedback* may depend on the ways in which such stimuli are augmented or supplemented (e.g., Hefferline, 1958). For example, if the reading on a meter or the loudness of a tone is made proportional to the electrical activity of a muscle, an individual may learn to control levels of muscle tension and relaxation. Such feedback procedures have been extended to other systems, such as the aura that precedes some epileptic episodes or the muscle and blood vessel events correlated with some migraine headaches (e.g., Sturgis, Tollison, & Adams, 1978). It seems plausible that biofeedback control should be correlated with discriminative capacity, but it remains to be shown whether such relations between biofeedback control and discriminations of proprioceptive or interoceptive stimuli are possible (e.g., Cott, Pavlovski, & Black, 1981).

Now consider one more nonhuman example. Suppose we give a pigeon a dose of cocaine, pentobarbital or saline (an uncontrolled substance that here serves as a control). We then intermittently reinforce pecks on one of three keys depending on which drug we've administered (e.g., Lubinski & Thompson, 1987). The pigeon can learn to discriminate among these three substances in this procedure, and once the pigeon has done so we can study the properties of other dosage levels of these and other substances by administering them and observing which key the pigeon pecks. For example, we can find out how small a dose of cocaine the pigeon can discriminate from saline, or whether the pigeon can discriminate pentobarbital from other sedative drugs it's never been given before. In effect, we've taught the pigeon to report an internal condition, its own drug state. This example shows how we can use the public correlates of private events to generate reports of those events. Notice that to do this, we don't have to know what the drug state feels like; we only have to know what's circulating in the pigeon's bloodstream.

We'll return to the issue of discriminating private events in Chapter 14 (cf. Critchfield, 1993). The practical significance of being able to do so should be obvious; for example, the drinker who is a good judge of blood alcohol levels should know when to hand the car keys over to someone else. Another important feature of the drug example is that the pigeon was taught the drug discrimination by a human experimenter. In human behavior, such discriminations may sometimes be incidentally learned, but the point is that, like the pigeon, we're most likely to learn them when they're taught to us by others. In other words, discriminations of our own behavior very often originate in the context of social behavior.

We've already mentioned other circumstances in which discriminations of our own behavior are important (e.g., as in judging how well we've studied a text). Such discriminations are also critical to a phenomenon once called *self-reinforcement* but now more properly referred to as *self-regulation* (e.g., Catania, 1975, 1995; Mahoney & Bandura, 1972). For example, a student who has made a commitment to watch television only after completing a study assignment might think that this arrangement for watching television after studying will reinforce studying. But any increase in studying that follows can't be attributed to reinforcement; the student will only make the commitment to deal with studying this way if studying has already become important for other reasons. Whatever brings the student to make the commitment to "self-reinforce" studying in the first place will probably by itself make studying more likely. It's impossible to pull these variables apart.

Thus, when we speak of the standards that students set for fulfilling such commitments, we can't say that they're reinforcing their own behavior. Instead, their commitment involves setting standards for the discrimination between adequate and inadequate studying, so we can say that students who try to deal with their study habits in this way are discriminating properties of their own behavior that have become important to them. The contingencies that generate these discriminations are complex and probably involve verbal behavior. The language of self-reinforcement doesn't clarify the phenomenon. In Chapter 11 we considered related issues in the topic of self-control; we'll treat how discriminations of our own behavior are relevant to language in Chapter 14, when we deal with the class of verbal responses called autoclitics.

Section B   **Recapitulation**

In this text so far, we've considered various behavioral procedures and findings: phenomena of elicitation, reinforcement, discrimination and conditioning, among others. Before we apply these concepts to more complex types of behavior such as language, a review seems appropriate. We'll do so in the context of examples of social behavior involving parents and a child, some of which are related to topics sampled in this chapter.

Beyond mere observation, the simplest of our behavioral operations was stimulus presentation (Chapter 4): No signal precedes the stimulus and no response needs to occur before it is presented. Suppose a nursing mother starts out by feeding her newborn infant independently of his behavior (let's assume that the child is male, not for sexist reasons but rather so we can easily distinguish the mother and the infant as *she* and *he*). Her presentation of the nipple is an instance of stimulus presentation, and it may affect the infant's behavior. He's likely to turn toward her breast and begin to suckle. From the nursing mother's point of view, the suckling is also a stimulus, and it elicits the letting down of her milk. This glandular response moves the milk toward her nipples, where it becomes available to the suckling infant.

Assume now that the mother switches to demand feeding, and so feeds the infant only when he begins to cry. The feeding becomes a consequence of a response, crying. This relation is, of course, a response–stimulus contingency; we translate it as the effect of a response on the probability of a stimulus. In this instance, the infant isn't fed unless he cries; without the crying the probability of a feeding is zero. This is, of course, just one example of a contingency. Responses can raise or lower stimulus probability (Chapters 5 and 6); they can turn things off as well as turn things on (they can also change other contingencies, but our examples here don't require such levels of complexity).

The contingency between crying and feeding is likely to affect the infant's behavior. We can expect an increase in crying, but only after some time has passed since his last feeding, when milk has again become reinforcing through the establishing operation of deprivation.

Let's now add stimulus control: We superimpose a discriminative stimulus on either of the other operations. First consider the mother's behavior. When she feeds the infant, the suckling produces the letting down of milk into her breasts. Once she begins feeding the infant whenever he cries, the crying becomes a reliable antecedent of the feeding and the mother discovers that she begins to let down her milk as soon as he begins to cry. The stimulus, crying, is followed by another stimulus, the infant's suckling at her breast. This relation should be familiar as an example of Pavlov's respondent conditioning (Chapter 12). When Pavlov presented dogs with light and then food, the dogs began to salivate after light as well as after food, just as the mother lets down her milk during the crying as well as during the feeding.

But a discriminative stimulus can also be superimposed upon the consequential operations of reinforcement or punishment (Chapter 8). Now the infant has grown a bit and sleeps through the night. The mother begins the practice of feeding him when he begins to cry during the day but not when he does so at night. These times are correlated with daylight and darkness, and soon the infant begins to discriminate between them. Nighttime crying decreases relative to daytime crying, and later subtler discriminations allow the mother to begin to shape other kinds of behavior to replace the crying. Until then, during daylight the infant is fed when he cries but when it's dark he isn't; in other words, light and dark become discriminative stimuli. During the light, crying raises the likelihood of a feeding, but during the dark it doesn't.

When we examine behavioral situations, it's often a useful exercise to describe them in terms of the appropriate operations; sometimes a proper description requires a combination of operations. For example,

suppose that the mother has learned that when her infant begins to make fussy noises near bedtime, he's likely to fall asleep quickly if she picks him up and rocks him. His fussy noises set the occasion for rocking him and his subsequent falling asleep sets the occasion for tucking him into his crib. With regard to the mother's behavior, both parts of this sequence involve stimulus-control operations superimposed on consequential operations. The rocking produces a consequence, the sleeping infant, that is in turn a discriminative stimulus for the tucking in; a stimulus that's contingent on responding in one part of the situation serves as a discriminative stimulus in another (cf. chained schedules; Chapter 11).

These examples have involved interactions between the infant's behavior and the mother's. In the context of such interactions, the infant learns to give special attention to social stimuli. These later become significant in many kinds of social behavior, such as attending to what others say, taking turns in conversation and saying things that affect the behavior of others. Maybe you've noticed that many of the human examples we've used to illustrate basic processes have involved children with little or no verbal behavior, such as young infants or children with autism or other developmental disabilities. This was no accident, because the basic contingencies are most effective when they're uncontaminated by talk. As we'll see in the next chapter, verbal behavior is a very special kind of social behavior.

KINDS OF CONTINGENCIES AND CONTINGENT STIMULI

Let's call the stimuli involved in response–stimulus relations *contingent stimuli*. The preceding account used the mother's milk and the infant's suckling as examples of contingent stimuli. But stimuli are of various sorts. We could replace those of the preceding examples with others that are aversive. The infant might be less fortunate, and the shouting of an abusive parent might occur independently of the child's behavior; or it might occur only after some response, such as crying; or it might occur only in the presence of some other stimulus, as when the child learns that his father shouts only when his mother is around; or it might be that if he cries his mother always quiets his shouting father, so that her presence is an occasion when he can avoid or escape from his father's shouting by crying. Each of these examples corresponds to contingencies involving aversive stimuli that we've already discussed.

It's sometimes convenient to distinguish among different types of contingent stimuli. Organisms work to produce or remain in the presence of some, called *appetitive, rewarding* or *reinforcing*: food, entertaining company, money, among many others. They work to remove or stay away from others, sometimes called *aversive, noxious* or *punishing*: noise, dull company, extremes of heat or cold, among many others. Some of these stimuli have obvious biological significance while others acquire their significance during the organism's lifetime. It's difficult to classify any stimulus unambiguously as a reinforcer or a punisher (Chapters 5 and 6). And, having admitted appetitive and aversive stimuli as classes of contingent stimuli, we must also recognize that relatively neutral or insignificant stimuli can enter into contingencies. If the infant reaches out and touches his mother, for example, his movement is a response and contact is its consequence. Obviously, no stimulus is likely to be completely without significance; these classes represent points or regions in a continuous range of stimulus types rather than three discrete categories, and the designation of particular stimuli can change as a result of establishing operations.

A response may lower as well as raise the probability with which events occur. Suppose that the father finds the infant's cries aversive. If the infant is especially likely to start crying if his diaper hasn't been changed for some time, then the father can avoid the infant's crying by changing the diaper. The probability of crying increases as time passes without a diaper change, and decreases whenever a diaper change occurs. In other words, the diaper change is the father's avoidance response. A response–stimulus contingency is defined as the effect of a response on the probability of a stimulus, and we distinguish among contingencies in terms of whether the effect is an increase or a decrease in probability. In this last case, in which the diaper change avoided the infant's crying, the stimulus was aversive and its probability was reduced by the father's response.

Now suppose that the infant has fallen asleep and while watching television the father accidentally awakens him by turning up the sound too loud. The infant begins to cry. The contingent stimulus, the crying, is again aversive, but this time a response, turning up the sound on the television, has raised its probability. The crying may punish the turning up of the sound, in that the father may now be less likely to do so while the infant is sleeping. Changes in probability are, of course, not limited to all-or-none cases. For example, the infant might not be fed every time he cries, and he might not awaken and cry every time someone turns up the television sound (Chapter 10 on schedules).

In classifying contingent stimuli, we rec-

TABLE 13-1   Kinds of Response–Stimulus Contingencies and Contingent Stimuli

	TYPE OF RESPONSE–STIMULUS CONTINGENCY*		
Type of Contingent Stimulus	*Response Raises Probability of Stimulus*	*Response Doesn't Affect Probability of Stimulus*	*Response Lowers Probability of Stimulus*
Appetitive, rewarding or reinforcing	Positive reinforcement (operant discrimination)	Stimulus presentation (respondent conditioning)	Negative punishment (omission training)
Relatively neutral or insignificant	Sensory consequences (latent learning)	Stimulus presentation (sensory preconditioning)	Sensory consequences (latent learning)
Aversive, noxious or punishing	Positive punishment (discriminated punishment)	Stimulus presentation (defensive conditioning)	Negative reinforcement (discriminated avoidance)

*Entries are representative classes of experimental procedures; those in parentheses illustrate cases in which a discriminative stimulus is superimposed on the contingency.

ognized relatively neutral or insignificant stimuli as well as appetitive or aversive stimuli. Contingencies also range from those in which responses raise stimulus probability to those in which they lower it, and within this range is the special case in which a response has no effect on stimulus probability. This special case is equivalent to the stimulus-presentation operation. Stimulus presentations may involve the response-independent delivery of appetitive stimuli or aversive stimuli or relatively neutral or insignificant stimuli.

Kinds of contingencies and contingent stimuli are summarized in Table 13-1, in which they're shown combined with a discriminative stimulus and with some representative names in the psychology of learning applied to them. The procedures aren't exhaustive, so the list is incomplete. For any procedure in the psychology of learning, it's instructive to locate it or its various stages among the classes in Table 13-1.

Consider an example. The infant is older, and his mother now allows him to crawl around and explore some of the rooms in his home. After he's done this a few times over several days, the mother takes him to a room in the corner of which is a new toy chest. She opens the chest and gives him a favorite toy. The next day she puts him down in another room and he immediately sets out for the room with the toy chest, getting there quickly and without making any wrong turns. His exploration of the room on the previous days involved behavior that produced relatively neutral consequences. But when a more significant consequence was introduced, the new chest with some of his toys in it, the child proved that he'd learned the layout of the rooms.

The example is analogous to an experiment on latent learning.

Consider one more example. The mother has often taken the infant to the pediatrician's office for routine exams. Time in the waiting room has reliably been followed by seeing the pediatrician in the examining room. One evening the infant becomes ill and the mother takes him to a hospital urgent care unit rather than to the pediatrician's office. There the pediatrician checks the infant's symptoms and then gives him an injection. The injection makes the infant cry. A few days later the mother takes the infant to the pediatrician's office for a follow-up exam. Even though the aversive injection hadn't been given to him in the examining room, the infant begins to cry as soon as he and his mother enter the waiting room. When the pediatrician's significance was changed by the injection, the crying in the waiting room proved that the infant had learned the contingent relation between the waiting room and seeing the pediatrician. The waiting room and seeing the pediatrician are analogous to the initially neutral stimuli of a sensory preconditioning experiment. Constructing other examples that correspond to the various cells in Table 13-1 is a worthwhile exercise.

One way to judge the relative significance of events is to compare the probabilities of the responses they occasion. If we were interested in the child's playing with toys and eating, we might see which he did when both the toys and food were freely available. When the child becomes older, an opportunity to play with friends might function to reinforce eating if he's reluctant to finish a meal, but if he's just encountered some cousins he's never met before at a family get-together and is reluctant to play with them, the opportunity to eat a favorite food may function to reinforce playing. In other words,

the effect of a contingency may depend on the relation between the responses that produce and are occasioned by contingent stimuli (Chapter 5). We are again reminded that establishing operations are concerned with the conditions determining the effectiveness of contingent stimuli as reinforcers or as punishers.

These classifications don't guarantee that any stimulus or response will have just a single function; a stimulus in a contingent relation with one response may be in a discriminative relation with another, and a response elicited by one stimulus may be involved in contingencies with other stimuli. For example, the mother's presence may be a contingent stimulus when she comes at the infant's cry, and a discriminative stimulus when the infant learns that things happen when she's there that don't happen when she's not; the infant's cry is sometimes elicited by events, such as painful stimuli, while at other times it occurs because such events as the mother's presence are its consequence. We come to understand behavioral situations by separating the various stimulus and response relations that enter into them. That's the business of an experimental analysis.

On close examination, some distinctions implied by our taxonomy seem to diminish in importance. In the analysis of behavior, classifications often have fuzzy boundaries and distinctions can become arbitrary. We noted such a case with respect to presenting or removing stimuli (e.g., is water effective as a reinforcer by virtue of its presentation or because it terminates dry mouth or other events correlated with thirst?). In the final analysis, we were able to discard the distinction between presenting and removing stimuli in favor of a behavioral account that considered the relation between the responding that produced the reinforcer and the responding produced by that reinforcer. That account recognized that all consequences of responding can be characterized as environmental changes.

We might then note that every procedure takes place in some environment, so we could next get rid of discriminative stimuli, observing as we did so that we can deal with them by incorporating them into our response definitions. Thus, if a child's requests for candy are granted when his grandparents are present but not when they're absent, the response of this contingency can be defined to include only those requests he makes in the presence of his grandparents. If later analysis shows us that we can't even define response classes independently of contingencies, we might ultimately decide to dispense with that distinction too. But distinctions like these have been useful along the way. We can, so to speak, throw away the ladder after we've climbed it.

PART IV   LEARNING WITH WORDS

Chapter 14
Verbal Behavior: Language Function

A. Correspondences Between Vocal and Written Classes
Echoic Behavior
Transcription
Textual Behavior
Dictation-Taking
Relations Among the Classes

B. Intraverbal Behavior

C. The Contact of Verbal Behavior With the Environment
Abstraction
The Extension of Verbal Classes
The Language of Private Events
Verbal Classes and Naming

D. Verbal Behavior Conditional Upon Verbal Behavior
Relational Autoclitics: The Conjunction of Verbal Units
Descriptive Autoclitics: Discriminating Our Own Verbal Behavior

Our language words have diverse sources. Verbal, through Latin, and word, through Old English, are derived from a common Indo-European root, wer-, to speak. The Germanic spek- or sprek-, from which comes the German die Sprache, speech or language, leads to the English speak and speech.

The Greek legein, to speak, and logos, word, lead to lexical, legible and such relatives as logic and intelligent. Latin provides language and linguistics, through lingua, tongue, and vocal and vocabulary, through vox, voice.

Language is behavior. But when we try to talk about it, our everyday vocabulary gets in the way. For example, consider the common term *word*. When we speak of words, we seldom bother to distinguish spoken words from written ones. Yet speaking a word isn't the same as writing it, and speaking and writing usually occur in different circumstances. Even worse, we often speak of *using* words, as if words were things instead of behavior.

We also speak of language as if it were directed toward events or objects. We say that words or sentences refer to, deal with, speak of, call attention to or are about things. The language of reference implicitly includes the direction from verbal behavior to environment. Everyday language doesn't include words that emphasize the opposite direction. What if our everyday language has prejudiced us about the ways in which our verbal behavior works? We hardly ever say that we utter nouns in the presence of relevant objects or that sentences are occasioned by relevant events. Instead, we say that words refer to objects or that sentences are about events. There's good reason for these usages; as we'll see, they're appropriate to the equivalences that relate different classes of verbal behavior. But they may be misleading in an analysis of the behavior of speakers and listeners or readers and writers.

The language of meaning is another complication. Dictionaries don't contain meanings of defined words; they just contain other words. We speak metaphorically when we say that words *contain* meanings and that we *convey* these meanings to others through language (cf. Chapter 16). The metaphor of words as containers for meanings has been around for a long time, and yet the magnetic patterns corresponding to a taped voice or the patterns of pigment corresponding to a handwritten message have no meaning unless someone listens to the tape or reads the note; the meaning isn't waiting to be released from the tape or the paper. If language transmits anything, it's verbal behavior itself; in listening and reading, our own behavior re-creates some features of the behavior of the speakers and the writers who constitute our verbal community. We share our verbal behavior; it is, above all, social behavior.

A primary task of the analysis of language is classifying verbal behavior. But our taxonomy must be functional rather than structural or grammatical. A grammatical classification of words in a sentence doesn't tell us about the circumstances in which the sentence was produced or the consequences its production had for the one who produced it. Functional accounts of verbal behavior examine what verbal responses do. As with nonverbal behavior, structural and functional accounts of language complement each other. Unfortunately, verbal behavior has been controversial in the history of psychology, and structural and functional accounts have often been pitted against each

other as if they were incompatible instead of complementary (e.g., Skinner, 1957; Chomsky, 1959; Catania, 1973). We'll attempt to deal consistently with both kinds of approaches.

Verbal responses are distinguished by the occasions on which they occur and the consequences they produce. They can be occasioned by either verbal or nonverbal stimuli, and they can have either verbal or nonverbal consequences. For example, a child might say "apple" in the presence of either the written word or an actual apple; as a consequence of saying "apple," the child might get either the reply "right" or the apple.

This chapter will consider some of the functions of verbal behavior, emphasizing various classes of verbal stimuli and responses. We'll begin with relatively simple relations in which verbal behavior is reproduced in either a vocal or a written mode (as in echoing what someone has said or taking dictation). We'll also examine how verbal behavior makes contact with the environment, as when we describe objects or events; in doing so we'll discover something about the prerequisites for learning to talk about ourselves. Those topics will set the stage for explorations of more complex verbal processes, as in assertion and negation. In Chapter 15, we'll move on to some of the consequences of verbal behavior. In particular, one individual can change the behavior of another by giving instructions; this may be the primary function of language. To see how it works, we have to understand the relations between verbal behavior and nonverbal behavior or, in other words, between saying and doing. Our analyses of these functional properties of verbal behavior will prepare us to treat the structure of verbal behavior in Chapter 16.

Section A Correspondences Between Vocal and Written Classes

Our verbal communities shape correspondences between things and their names, between words and their definitions, between what we did and what we say we did, between what we promise and what we accomplish, and so on. The way in which we learn correspondences and the conditions of their maintenance may determine how they function in our verbal behavior. Our first examples consist of some formal verbal relations between vocal and written classes, because these cases are familiar and these correspondences are well defined by our verbal community (Skinner, 1957).

The term *verbal* is a general one and applies to language in any modality; we'll distinguish it from the term *vocal*, which is specific to spoken language. We could easily extend our account to other modalities (e.g., the gestural modality of sign language or the tactile modality of Braille), but we'll restrict our attention to vocal and written classes of verbal behavior.

Correspondences between verbal stimuli and verbal responses in formal verbal relations are implicit in the colloquial vocabulary: We say that words are the same whether they're heard or spoken, seen or written, or, in other words, whether they're auditory or visual stimuli or responses. One elementary verbal function is the reproduction of verbal behavior: We repeat what others say or copy what others write. Thus, our cases will include the reproduction of verbal behavior in all four possible combinations of spoken or written stimuli and spoken or written responses: vocal to vocal (echoic behavior), written to written (transcription), written to vocal (textual behavior), and vocal to written (dictation-taking).

ECHOIC BEHAVIOR

Imitation of some properties of vocal stimuli appears relatively early in human infants' acquisition of speech. We call this class of verbal relations *echoic*. When a parent says "mama" and the child repeats "mama," the child's response is echoic to the extent that (1) it's occasioned by the parent's utterance and (2) the phonemes of the child's utterance have a one-to-one correspondence to those of the parent's. Essentially, echoic behavior is generalized vocal imitation (cf. Chapter 13 and Poulson, et al., 1991).

Even though the stimulus and the response have common properties, this verbal relation isn't simple. The stimulus is a complex sound pattern. The response consists of the coordinated articulations of lungs, vocal chords, tongue, lips and so on. These produce sounds but aren't themselves sounds. How then does the child know what to do to produce the sounds heard as "mama" or "dada" by the parents (cf. Chapter 13 on imitation)?

The significant dimensions of the units of speech called phonemes are more easily defined by articulations (positions of the tongue, etc.) than by acoustic properties (Lane, 1965; Liberman, 1982). The interactions of articulation and sound are complex; for example, many English consonants (e.g., *p, b, d*) can't be produced unless accompanied by a vowel, and their acoustic properties vary as a function of context (e.g., the sounds of *l* and *k* are different in *lick* than in *kill*). Echoic behavior isn't defined by acoustic correspondence; it's defined by correspondences of phonetic units.

Voices differ in many respects: An adult voice is deeper than that of a child, a woman's voice differs from that of a man, and people speak with varying regional dialects. If a young boy from a small town in

New England repeats what a woman from Atlanta just said, their utterances differ acoustically in many ways. But differences in vocal quality and regional dialect are irrelevant to whether the boy's behavior is echoic; the criterion for echoic behavior is the vocal correspondences of verbal units such as phonemes and words. That's why the duplication of human sound patterns by parrots and other birds doesn't qualify as echoic behavior: Their duplications are acoustic rather than phonetic. For example, a parrot would reproduce the *th* sound if a child lisps an *s*, but a nonlisping adult would ordinarily use the unlisped *s* instead.

Echoic behavior depends at least in part on the shaping of articulations by their vocal consequences (cf. Risley, 1977; Skinner, 1957, p. 58). Before their own vocalizations begin to be differentiated, infants learn to discriminate among the many aspects of the speech of those around them (Eimas et al., 1971); for example, infants readily discriminate between sounds of their native language and those from an unfamiliar foreign language, but not between sounds from two unfamiliar foreign languages (Mehler, et al., 1988). This means that they can also hear the difference when they make the sounds themselves. At first their babbling includes an undifferentiated range of human speech sounds, but over time they retain native speech sounds in their spontaneous vocalizations while other kinds of speech sounds gradually disappear, and their babbling evolves to self-repetitions (echolalic speech; e.g., "ma-ma-ma-ma-ma") and then to repetitions of the speech of others (echoic speech).

Vocalizations can be reinforced (Poulson, 1984), and the vocalizations of infants are engendered and maintained by what they hear themselves saying; without these auditory consequences (as in cases of hearing im-

pairment), the behavior doesn't develop. As we know from recordings, our own voices sound different to us than they do to others, because we hear our own voices via bone conduction as well as from sound that travels through the air (rare individuals may, through accidents of anatomy, hear themselves as others hear them; those who do have the advantage, in doing vocal impressions, of knowing how well they've actually imitated the voices of others). This is one more reason why phonetic correspondence is relevant but acoustic isn't.

Perhaps native speech sounds become reinforcing relative to sounds of nonnative languages simply because they often accompany the activities of the infant's caregivers (e.g., DeCasper & Fifer, 1980). An articulation that produces something sounding more or less like what mommy says may be reinforced automatically by this correspondence between the infant's and parent's utterances. The differentiation of phonemic structure may then be attributed to the various overlapping contingencies that different speech sounds enter into (cf. Chapter 9 on the origins of structure).

But such processes may be constrained by phylogenic histories, neural development or changing ontogenic environments: Discriminations of speech sounds that are easily learned at an early age may be difficult to learn later (e.g., Werker, 1989). For example, the distinction between spoken *r* and *l* in English doesn't exist in Japanese, and it's much more easily learned by a Japanese child than by an adult Japanese speaker. Infants master simple articulations before moving on to more complex ones. If the vocal units differentiated during babbling are different from one language to another, perhaps an adult learning a new language finds it difficult to master the new phonemes mainly because the prerequisite simpler articulations were never differentiated.

This, then, is an account of the natural selection of the phonetic units of verbal behavior at an ontogenic level. The selection is based upon correspondences between the language already available in a verbal community and the vocalizations of an infant who is the language learner, so it also provides for the transmission of verbal behavior at the cultural level (in this case from one generation of speakers to the next). There are ways it can fail: for example, motor disorders may constrain articulation; or hearing may be impaired; or relevant consequences may be absent, perhaps as a result of neglect or abuse by caregivers or because neurological deficits have reduced the effectiveness of social stimuli. But once vocal articulations can be shaped and the child can hear the consequences of those articulations, the minimum conditions for the ontogenic selection of vocal units are in place. A lot may follow from that: "The human species took a crucial step forward when its vocal musculature came under operant control in the production of speech sounds. Indeed, it is possible that all the distinctive achievements of the species can be traced to that one genetic change" (Skinner, 1986, p. 117). In contrast, reinforcement of nonhuman vocalizations is typically limited to rate of vocalization; it's difficult to modify topography (e.g., Hayes & Hayes, 1951; Lane, 1960).

Echoic units can vary in size from individual speech sounds to extended phrases or sentences. A variety of verbal phenomena, such as speech errors (e.g., Fromkin, 1971), can help us to decide what these units are. The importance of the echoic production of individual sounds is demonstrated by rhyming and alliteration in poetry (Smith, 1968; Skinner, 1972). For adult speakers, the units of echoic behavior are often whole words or phrases. The echoic production of extended phrases or sentences occurs in dra-

matics, as when an actor repeats the lines whispered by a prompter, and on ritual occasions, as when a bride and groom repeat the phrases of a marriage vow spoken by a member of the clergy. Echoic units aren't defined by their size; they're defined by the correspondences into which they enter.

Echoic behavior doesn't simply accompany the acquisition of language and then vanish; it persists in the behavior of mature speakers. For example, you might repeat a telephone number just given to you or the name of someone you've just been introduced to. Nevertheless, echoic behavior doesn't imply that the speaker has understood what's been echoed; meaning doesn't enter into the definition of echoic behavior. As we'll see later, we must deal with meaning in verbal behavior in other ways.

TRANSCRIPTION

Verbal stimuli and responses can also correspond when both are written. In such cases, the behavior is called *transcription*. For example, you might copy a number from a telephone book or copy an author and title in preparing a bibliography. Just as we distinguish vocal articulations and the sounds they produce in echoic behavior, we also distinguish the movements involved in producing words from the looks of the words in transcription. And just as echoic behavior depends on correspondences of verbal rather than acoustic properties, transcription depends on correspondences of verbal rather than visual properties. A handwritten sentence may look very different from the printed text from which it was transcribed (for example, the script letters run together but the printed ones don't). Nevertheless, writing the sentence qualifies as transcription if the script sentence matches the printed one in spelling, word order and punctuation.

Just as units of echoic behavior can vary from individual phonemes to entire phrases or sentences, units of transcription can vary from individual characters to extended passages, depending on the circumstances in which the behavior occurs. A child learns to copy single letters before learning to copy whole words. In doing so, the child learns the correspondences between arbitrary visual forms, such as the printed and script *a* in upper- and lowercase. There may be no visual property common to all forms of the letter *a* (cf. Gibson, 1965).

Transcription differs from copying in the pictorial sense (cf. Shahn, 1972, pp. 49, 256). A skilled Asian calligrapher unfamiliar with the European alphabet in which a text is printed might produce an accurate copy, but such copying wouldn't be verbal. We base this distinction on the behavioral units in the two kinds of copying. The critical features of the calligrapher's copying are geometrical properties of the letters in the text and the marks produced by the calligrapher's strokes; the critical features of transcription are the verbal units (letters, words and phrases) in the original text and its copy. Visually, the calligrapher's copy might look more like the original than a handwritten copy by a speaker of the language, but only the latter counts as transcription.

Except for their respective vocal and written modes, echoic behavior and transcription are formally similar. Children ordinarily acquire echoic behavior early, even without specific instruction, but they take some time doing so. They don't ordinarily acquire transcription unless it's explicitly taught. Nevertheless, the relative ease with which one or the other is learned provides no grounds for assuming that one is simpler than the other.

Pure transcription is probably rare. It occurs only when transcription is unaccompanied by other behavior, such as responses to the meaning of the text. For example, if a skilled typist accurately transcribes a letter while not responding verbally to it in other ways (e.g., while listening to a conversation elsewhere in the office), the typist afterwards won't be able to describe what was in the letter. When we're transcribing, we're usually doing a lot more besides. As with echoic behavior, meaning doesn't enter into the definition of transcription; it must be dealt with in other ways.

TEXTUAL BEHAVIOR

When a written verbal stimulus sets the occasion for a corresponding vocal verbal response, the behavior is *textual*. Thus, you might say aloud what's on a menu or read a bedtime story to a child. In textual behavior, the arbitrary correspondence between verbal stimuli and responses is more obvious than in either echoic behavior or transcription, because the stimuli and the responses are in different modes. A written word is a visual stimulus; it has no sound. A spoken word is an auditory stimulus; it has no shape. Yet these correspondences are so familiar that we rarely notice the arbitrary nature of the relations between verbal shapes and sounds.

As with transcription, textual behavior is usually taught explicitly, and some controversies about teaching it are based on assumptions about the units appropriate to various stages of instruction (e.g., whether the teacher of reading should begin with individual letters, syllables or entire words: Gleitman & Rozin, 1973).

As with the other formal classes, we have to distinguish textual behavior from other kinds of responses to written verbal stimuli. For example, if a sign says STOP, reading the word aloud is textual but stopping isn't. In the mature reader, textual responses become less important than other kinds of responses to written verbal stimuli. Vocal responses diminish in magnitude, become subvocal and perhaps disappear completely as a child becomes a proficient reader. Reading is behavior, but textual responses are at best only one part of reading. For example, a father reading a bedtime story aloud to a child might finish a page and suddenly realize that he doesn't know what just happened in the story, even though the child he's been reading to does.

This example, without understanding, is a pure case of textual behavior. The colloquial vocabulary doesn't distinguish between reading that's simply the saying of the words on a page and the kind of behavior we call reading for understanding (e.g., Fowler et al., 1981). Most of us have occasionally found ourselves partway through a page unable to say what was in the last couple of paragraphs. Such experiences are evidence for the importance of these distinctions (see also Kolers, 1985). Reading for understanding includes other behavior along with or instead of vocal or subvocal speech, so it's more (probably a lot more) than simply textual behavior.

DICTATION-TAKING

Just as a written stimulus can set the occasion for a vocal response, a vocal stimulus can set the occasion for a written response. This class of verbal behavior is called *dictation-taking* (we're concerned with the listener who takes the dictation, not the speaker who dictates). For example, you might write down a number given to you by a telephone operator or take notes at a lecture. The units of dictation-taking are typically entire words or phrases, but individual letters may also serve (e.g., when children are taught the written alphabet or when an unusual name is spelled out for a stenographer).

As with textual behavior, dictation-taking involves stimuli and responses in different modes. Some of its special properties follow from the relatively permanent record produced in the written text. In addition, occasions for dictation-taking are limited relative to textual behavior, because, unlike our vocal apparatus, writing implements aren't parts of our anatomy. Perhaps for this reason, we aren't much tempted to pursue its covert manifestations; we're less likely to speak of submanual writing or typing than of subvocal reading (the motor theory of consciousness had argued that thought was just vocal behavior reduced in magnitude; Max, 1934). Nevertheless, textual behavior and dictation-taking are formally similar, and either can be accompanied by other kinds of verbal behavior occasioned by verbal stimuli.

RELATIONS AMONG THE CLASSES

We've limited this account of formal verbal classes to vocal and written stimuli and responses. We could have extended it to other language modes (e.g., sending and receiving Morse code). Sometimes we can ignore the distinction between verbal stimuli and verbal responses, but not always. For example, even though we speak of letters and words without regard to whether they're written or spoken, the mode matters in teaching. A teacher who has only taught a child to name letters written on a chalkboard shouldn't expect the child to be able to write the letters when they're spoken. The stimuli in the former are responses in the latter, and vice versa. Until they become equivalent, they're just one part of "knowing the alphabet."

To teach reading and writing is to teach equivalences between vocal and written modes of verbal behavior. Our everyday vocabulary obscures these distinctions, perhaps because such equivalences come easily to humans, or perhaps because language instruction is designed to eliminate them, or perhaps both. In any case, the relations are summarized in Figure 14-1.

Each mode, vocal and written, has special characteristics. For example, spoken verbal behavior varies more freely in stress, rhythm and intensity than written verbal behavior, but it's also more transient. Some properties of verbal behavior are independent of mode. For the immediate consequence of being able to dial a phone number, it hardly matters whether you call information and hear the number or read it in a phone book, or whether you repeat it aloud to yourself or write it down. Some consequences may affect how you look up a number next time (e.g., the time it took to get it or the likelihood of retrieving it later), but they're not essentially verbal. Thus, once equivalences are in place, it may be relatively unimportant in many cases to distinguish among the formal classes. But we may need the distinctions for studying certain topics, such as the language pathologies called *aphasias*, in which deficits are characterized by the verbal classes affected (e.g., Sidman, 1971).

Thus far we've emphasized classes defined in terms of verbal modes, but other formal relations may be differentiated even within a mode. For example, if a student has learned only to translate from English to German, the student may have difficulty when asked to translate in the other direction, from German to English (cf. Chapter 17 on transfer). The problems are compounded when both spoken and written languages are involved. Language instruction usually recognizes these distinctions; a course in conversational French is expected to emphasize the vocal mode, whereas one in scientific Russian is expected to emphasize the written mode. (Bilingual verbal behavior might best be characterized in terms of the extent to which equivalence classes extend across both languages; cf. Kolers, 1966; Caramazza & Brones, 1980.)

All our examples of formal classes have been variations on the theme of distinguishing verbal stimuli from verbal responses. In verbal behavior, a speaker's response is a listener's stimulus and a writer's response is a reader's stimulus, and a speaker or writer at one time becomes a listener or reader at another. The differences between three-term contingencies and equivalence relations, as set out in Chapter 9, are relevant.

___

Section B   Intraverbal Behavior

The formal classes involve verbal responses occasioned by verbal stimuli. They're each characterized by one-to-one correspondences

FIGURE 14-1 Relations among the four formal classes (S, stimulus; R, response). Similar relations can be established for any pair of verbal modes (e.g., printed text and the gestures of American Sign Language, or vocal behavior and Braille).

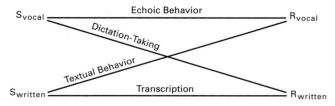

of verbal units; in transcription, for example, each word of a text has a unique equivalent in the transcribed version. But we learn many verbal relations that don't involve such formal correspondences. Such instances are called *intraverbal* (Skinner, 1957). We learn to recite the alphabet, to count, to give answers to arithmetic problems, to recite poems, to define terms and to state facts. The sequence of letters in the alphabet is no more orderly than the one on a computer keyboard: Some similar letters of the alphabet are close together and others are widely separated (e.g., *M, N* but *D, T*); some voiced consonants precede and some follow the voiceless (e.g., *B, P* but *F, V*); and so on. Despite its arbitrary character, we learn the alphabet because so much is ordered according to it: dictionaries, telephone books, indexes. We're less able to recite the order of letters on a computer keyboard because we don't have to behave with respect to keyboards the way we do with respect to alphabetized lists.

The same points apply to chronologies, geographies and much else of our everyday knowledge. No one now living ever saw Washington crossing the Delaware. You might argue that you saw the scene in a painting, but even if you'd recognized Washington, could you have known that the setting was the Delaware River without a label that told you so? We don't ordinarily learn historical details by experiencing them. Instead, given names or dates, we learn to say when or in what order events occurred.

In intraverbal behavior, one verbal stimulus sets the occasion for another verbal response. The relation between stimulus and response is arbitrary; there are no systematic correspondences between them. Free association is an example (Galton, 1879). The immediate consequences of free associations are usually minimal, and any given verbal stimulus may occasion a variety of different responses, so the procedure is assumed to tap verbal responses of relatively high probability in the speaker's verbal repertoire. In discussing intraverbal behavior, Skinner (1957) treats free association as follows:

> One verbal response supplies the stimulus for another in a long series. The net effect is revealed in the classical word-association experiment. Here the subject is simply asked to respond verbally to a verbal stimulus, or to report aloud any responses he may "think of". . . . Such an experiment, repeated on many subjects or on one subject many times, produces a fair sample of the responses under the control of a standard stimulus in a given verbal community. . . . Many different responses are brought under the control of a given stimulus word, and many different stimulus words are placed in control of a single response. For example, educational reinforcement sets up many different intraverbal operants involving the cardinal numbers. *Four* is part of the occasion for *five* in learning to count, for *six* in learning to count by twos, for *one* in learning the value of π, and so on. On the other hand, many different verbal stimuli come to control the response *four*, e.g., *one, two, three* . . . or *two times two makes*. . . . Many different connections between verbal responses and verbal stimuli are established when different passages are memorized and different "facts" acquired. The word-association experiment shows the results. (Skinner, 1957, pp. 73–74)

Word associations can be based on several words instead of single words as stimuli. Such sequences are the basis for constructing different *orders of approximation* to English. For example, suppose you're asked to complete a sentence given its first three words. The first of the three words is then dropped, and the two remaining words plus the new one are presented to someone else, who now generates a sentence that continues those three words. Again the first word is dropped, and the next three remaining words are presented to still another participant, and so on. An example of text produced this way is

> the first list was posted on the bulletin he brought home a turkey will die on my rug is deep with snow and sleet are destructive and playful students always (Miller & Selfridge, 1950)

This is called a fourth-order approximation to English, because at each point a participant sees only the last three words and must add the new fourth one. A zero-order approximation to English has words chosen randomly; a first-order approximation has words chosen randomly but in proportion to their frequencies in the language. The more closely a text approximates English, the easier it is to remember, but even with high-order approximations to English there's no guarantee that grammatical sequences will be generated.

In its simplest forms, intraverbal behavior has been the focus of much research on human verbal learning, perhaps because of the ease with which verbal materials can be manipulated as stimuli. The classic experiments of Ebbinghaus (1885) were specifically concerned with the learning of arbitrary verbal combinations. Ebbinghaus created nonsense syllables so that previous language experience wouldn't contaminate learning. Paired-associates learning (learning word pairs) and serial learning (learning ordered lists, as in learning to count) represent relatively pure cases of intraverbal behavior. Chapter 17 treats them in more detail.

Intraverbal behavior is involved only in cases in which successive parts of an utterance serve as discriminative stimuli for later parts. When extended utterances function as independent verbal units (cf. Chapter 7 on temporally extended units of behavior), it's inappropriate to say that the relations among their parts are intraverbal. Such maxims as "Haste makes waste" and "He who hesitates is lost" are best regarded as verbal units in their own right.

Intraverbal relations are an important component of standard educational practice, as when a child who's mastering the multiplication table gives 42 as the response to 6 x 7. But the response is strictly intraverbal only if it doesn't depend on other intervening arithmetic behavior (e.g., adding six sevens, counting by sixes or counting the boxes in a 6-by-7 rectangle). We'll deal with cases in which the answer is derived rather than learned intraverbally when we've considered some environmental determinants of verbal behavior and some of its consequences.

Section C　The Contact of Verbal Behavior with the Environment

Verbal behavior would never have evolved had it made contact only with other verbal behavior. At some point, it must make contact with environmental events. We speak of this contact as *tacting*; a *tact* is a verbal response occasioned by a discriminative stimulus (cf. Skinner, 1957). For example, if a child learns to say "apple" in the presence of an apple, the child is said to be tacting the apple. The tact doesn't involve any new process; it's just a name for stimulus control as it enters into verbal behavior.

Superficially they may seem alike, but tacting differs from naming in somewhat the same way that textual behavior differs from reading. For one thing, tacting is sometimes a component of naming. Unlike naming, however, it can only occur in the presence of the tacted stimulus. We can name an absent object but we can't tact it (one reason for the distinction is that, as we'll see in Chapter 18 on remembering, our responses to past events aren't determined directly by those events; instead, they're determined indirectly by our previous behavior with respect to them). We'll return to naming later in this chapter, where we'll treat it as a higher-order class of behavior and consider some of its special properties.

An unlimited number of tacts is available to the mature speaker. We tact objects (chairs and tables, pencils and books), living things (flowers and trees, birds and insects), weather conditions (rain and snow, sun and clouds), activities (walking and running, working and playing) and innumerable other features of the environment. Some tacts are general (e.g., man, woman) and others are restricted to relatively narrow circumstances (e.g., someone's name). The wealth of available tacts may be taken as a remarkable feature of human language, but we mustn't let it obscure the simple relation that defines an instance of tacting. The relation between a tact and something tacted is precisely the same as the relation between a stimulus and the response that it occasions in a three-term contingency.

It's useful to consider how tacts might be taught in a nonhuman organism; such examples force us to be explicit about their properties. Imagine a food-deprived pigeon in a chamber with a window on which we can project different colors. Next to the window are three keys. When the window's red, pecks on the left key produce food; when it's blue, pecks on the middle key do so; when it's green, pecks on the right key do so (cf. the adduction example in Chapter 9). The pigeon will eventually peck left during red, middle during blue and right during green. We can then call the pigeon's performance the tacting of red, blue and green. The stimuli are highly specific, and we wouldn't expect the pigeon to respond to red roses or flags or sunsets as it does to the red window. But the generality or specificity of the relevant stimuli isn't a criterion for the tact rela-

tion. If we doubt the generality of the pigeon's response to red, we can just call the pigeon's left peck a tact of a red window in this particular chamber.

What of the consequences of the pigeon's pecks? The pigeon would stop pecking if it weren't food-deprived or if food weren't a consequence. But even human tacting depends on its consequences. We don't go around tacting everything we see. Consequences aren't criteria for tacting. An instance of tacting may produce approval, pay, an examination grade, or the help it gives a listener; and, just as other responses aren't always reinforced, sometimes it may produce no consequences at all.

Finally, we might object that the pigeon has no audience. Its pecks are appropriately occasioned by red and blue and green, but the pigeon isn't speaking to anyone. We can easily rectify this difficulty by arranging signs, RED, BLUE and GREEN, that respectively light after the pigeon pecks the left, middle or right key. If our pigeon's performance was accurate and we couldn't look into the chamber, we could watch the signs and let the pigeon tell us which light was on.

But this arrangement isn't relevant to the issue. We don't need to check whether someone is listening to decide whether we've tacted something. Audiences are important in creating and maintaining tacts, but they aren't criteria for the tact relation. Tacting can be modified by audience variables and by consequences, but these variables don't define tacting. The pigeon's pecks in the presence of red and blue and green are relatively simple instances of discriminative responding, but any time the environment occasions what we say, stimulus control plays a role in our verbal behavior. The point warrants one more repetition: When we speak about tacting we're just speaking about stimulus control as it enters into verbal behavior.

ABSTRACTION

In many instances in which stimuli occasion responding, we're interested in specific discriminative stimuli. For example, when we're studying a pigeon's pecks on red and green keys, we're not likely to worry about the pigeon's responses to red and green stimuli in other contexts. But in verbal behavior we'll often be concerned with responding occasioned by properties of the environment rather than by particular stimuli or classes of stimuli. In the tacting of red, for example, the property of color is the critical determinant of the verbal response "red" whether it's occasioned by red fire engines, red traffic lights or red noses. We call verbal discrimination based on a single property of a stimulus *abstraction*.

The tacted property is defined by the practices of the verbal community; it doesn't depend on whether we have some independent physical measure of it. For example, stage lighting sometimes uses a color contrast effect called *Hering shadows*, in which

we see a shadowed area as some color even though there's no light of that color illuminating it. No range or distribution of wavelengths exists such that all visual stimuli within the range are called red whereas all those outside aren't, so even discriminations based on relatively simple stimulus properties (e.g., all red stimuli as opposed to specific red objects) may be to some extent arbitrary. We don't need to specify some physical dimension of the stimulus to decide whether a particular verbal relation is a tact; in defining our terms, we start from behavior and not physics (cf. Chapter 9 on structure).

A concept formation experiment illustrates how arbitrary classes can be generated (Hull, 1920; cf. Chapter 8 on concepts). Learners mastered names for the members of sets of Chinese characters (three are shown in Figure 14-2). A name was consistently related to a radical that appeared in one character in each set, but the configuration within which it appeared varied from one set to another. Each set of 12 characters

FIGURE 14-2 Radicals common to the Chinese characters in six lists. Learners had to give the radical name to the character that contained it, but no character was repeated across lists. Learners became able to name characters upon seeing them for the first time in new lists, and sometimes did so even when unable to define the common radical by sketching it. (From Hull, 1920, Figure 1)

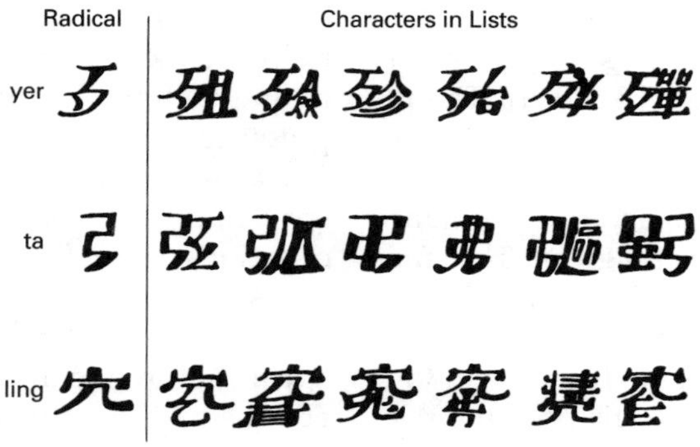

was presented until the learner gave the appropriate name for each, and then a new set of 12 was presented. By the fifth set, learners named more than half the characters upon seeing them for the first time, and sometimes they gave the name even though they couldn't sketch the radical or describe the basis for their naming.

Tacting in this experiment differs from tacting in natural languages in that we can't define the basis for many of our tacts so explicitly. For example, we can't say exactly what properties make an object a chair. The word *chair*, whether spoken or written, is an arbitrary class by virtue of the common verbal consequences arranged by verbal communities. A chair may have four legs or stand on a single pedestal, it may have a flat or a contoured seat or back, and it may be made out of a variety of materials. We can't even appeal to its function, because we call some objects chairs even though we can't sit on them (e.g., a toy chair in a set of dollhouse furniture). To make things still more complicated, they can also be embedded in other classes, as when they're pieces of furniture. This is not a traditional way of thinking. For example, this view of classes of objects and events contrasts drastically with Plato's essentialism, the idea that classes of things in the world share some common essence; the contrast also illustrates the antiquity and ubiquity of the problem.

We can tact extremely subtle properties of events. They include relations among stimuli. For example, *above* and *below*, *near* and *far*, and *larger* and *smaller* tact properties of stimuli in relation to each other or to the speaker. Relational tacting occurs when you say that two objects are alike or different, or when you note that one item in a set is an odd item. Such terms rarely stand alone, and we'll consider their joint dependence on other properties of events and on other ver-

bal responses when we consider the verbal relations called *autoclitic*. We also tact complex events extended in space or time, as when we identify a musical piece as one by Debussy or a painting as one by Monet. Identifying a musical work on the basis of just part of a melody shows how large a tacted unit can be. At another level of complexity, we might say that Debussy's music and Monet's paintings have something in common, even though it would be difficult to specify the common dimensions. Yet to call them both impressionist might be regarded as tacting common properties.

Sometimes the properties that occasion a tact can be identified more with the speaker's own behavior than with any particular stimulus feature. For example, if a painting or a musical composition or a situation occasions the word *marvelous*, this tact presumably depends on the responses generated in the speaker rather than on physical properties common to all of these stimuli. Saying that we've just done something voluntarily or involuntarily probably depends on what we know about the antecedents and consequences of our behavior, such as whether it was elicited or whether it was coerced (and it would only qualify as tacting if we said it at the time rather than an hour or a day later). An interesting verbal case is the *tip-of-the-tongue* phenomenon. When you say a word is on the tip of your tongue, you're tacting the near-threshold availability of an appropriate verbal response in your own verbal behavior. Sometimes we can even report properties of an unrecalled word, such as its length or part of its spelling (Brown & McNeill, 1966).

The vocabulary of emotion is similarly based on complex relations involving situations and behavior (cf. Chapter 12). Tacts of love, hate, joy and sorrow, whether in ourselves or others, depend on overt manifestations such as laughter or tears and on the circumstances that generated the behavior we observe. If this weren't so, a verbal community couldn't maintain any consistency in this vocabulary; the variability of the language of emotions is itself evidence of the subtlety of the relations that we tact.

Events and situations obviously have many properties that might be tacted. Whether any are tacted and which are tacted will depend on other variables acting upon the speaker. For example, we may tact the color of an apple in one circumstance and its smell in another. The situation presents no difficulties; verbal responses are determined in multiple ways.

Consider again the pigeon example. Let's alter the lighting of the window beside the three keys so that we can present bright, moderate or dim colors. During a tone, pecks on the left key produce food when the light is bright, those on the middle key do so when it's moderate and those on the right key do so when it's dim, in each case regardless of color. Without the tone, everything is as it was before. If the pigeon's pecks become appropriate to intensity when the tone is present but remain appropriate to color when it's absent, we could say that the pigeon tacts intensity during the tone and color during its absence (cf. Chapter 8 on attention and Chapter 9 on conditional discrimination).

The presence and absence of tone in the pigeon example serve the same function as questions in human verbal behavior. A question, like the tone, may be a conditional stimulus that occasions the tacting of some stimulus property (e.g., "What color is the apple?" or "What does it smell like?"). Audiences, previous verbal behavior and other factors can affect tacting. We don't tact indiscriminately. Some things we tact only in some circumstances, and we also learn that sometimes (e.g., in remarking on someone's

bad breath or dandruff) it isn't tactful to tact at all.

We tact temporal dimensions of stimuli when we say that something lasted a long or a short time. Often we respond verbally to stimuli that are no longer present, but such responding counts as tacting only if it occurs in the presence of or very soon after the events that occasioned them (responses that occur long after require special treatment because they usually include other behavior besides tacting; cf. Chapter 18).

Sentences in different tenses can sometimes be regarded as tacts occasioned by temporal properties of the environment. Consider "It's raining," "It's beginning to rain" and "It just stopped raining." Each sentence is a response to rain, but they're distinguished by different temporal properties. A past-tense response such as "It rained" is likely to be determined by other kinds of stimuli, when it isn't appropriate to call it a tact. For example, it might be uttered as an echoic or a textual response. If it's occasioned by present stimuli such as wet streets, it may be derived from other verbal behavior, such as "The streets are wet; therefore it must have rained."

THE EXTENSION OF VERBAL CLASSES

The tact is a flexible relation. In some verbal communities, the stimulus properties that occasion a tact are sharply defined. A student in a science laboratory, for example, is taught to be consistent in tacting apparatuses and materials and procedures. This precision is less common in everyday discourse. We often tact properties of the behavior of our acquaintances, but the conditions under which we say that someone is warm or reserved, energetic or lazy, interesting or dull and so on, vary considerably from one speaker to another. The etymologies or word histories introducing each chapter recognize the ways in which vocabularies have evolved over time ("Etymology is the archaeology of thought": Skinner, 1989b, p. 13).

In discriminations involving nonverbal behavior, we say a response has generalized if a response maintained during one stimulus occurs when some new stimulus is presented. For example, if our tacting pigeon pecked the left key when a novel amber light was presented, we'd say that its response to red had generalized to amber. A similar generalization of verbal responses to new stimuli occurs in the extended tact. Simile and metaphor are familiar instances. We may say that someone is as busy as a bee or as sly as a fox (simile) or that someone is a hawk or a dove (metaphor). These extended tacts presumably originated through generalization across subtle properties sometimes shared by the behavior of humans and bees and foxes and birds. Language grows and changes through metaphor (cf. Esper, 1973; Jaynes, 1976; Skinner, 1989b; see also Chapter 16).

Another type of extension of the tact occurs when new words are formed by combining existing ones (e.g., the words *dish* and *wash* predated the invention of dishwashers). Vocabularies change with environmental changes that are important to the speakers of a language. The ways in which tacts can be extended are so varied that a detailed account isn't feasible. Stewart (1975) offers interesting examples in an account of the origins of placenames, which are more likely to be based on unusual than common features of a region. A valley in a forest of fir trees wouldn't be named Fir Valley, but it might be named Oak Valley if a single oak tree stood there. Similarly, no stream where wolves are common is likely to be called Wolf Creek, but a stream where wolves are rare might get that name once a lone wolf is sighted there.

We've already noted the restriction that tacting must occur in the presence of or very soon after the event tacted. Then what about words that seem superficially to be tacts but can't occur in the presence of what they name? Do we ever see political units like states or nations, subjects like economics or politics, properties like ownership or indebtedness, processes like creation or evolution, and so on? And how about months or days of the week? Such entities must enter into our verbal behavior in other ways; they don't exist in a form that can be tacted. The point is that tacting isn't defined by parts of speech or other linguistic categories; instead, it's a type of behavior.

THE LANGUAGE OF PRIVATE EVENTS

Another important extension of the tact is to private events. Tacted stimuli are sometimes accessible only to the speaker, as when we say we have a headache. Such tacts depend on the verbal community for their origins and maintenance. The problem is how the verbal community can create and maintain these responses when it doesn't have access to the stimuli. A parent can teach a child color names because the parent can see the colors that the child sees and therefore can respond differentially to the child's correct and incorrect color naming. (So many varied consequences follow from color naming that it usually doesn't matter whether the parent teaches the color names explicitly or simply allows them to be learned through casual day-to-day interactions; we'll come back to naming in the next section.)

With private events, the vocabulary can be taught only through extension from tacts based upon events to which the verbal community has access. For example, the child may learn to report pain because the parents have access to overt manifestations such as the event that caused an injury or the child's crying or facial expression; if the child has learned the names of body parts, the two kinds of verbal responses may be extended to the tact of pain in a particular place (cf. Skinner, 1945).

A toothache is a discriminable event, but the person with the toothache has a different kind of access to it than the dentist called upon to treat it. Both respond to the unsound tooth, but one does so by feeling the tooth and the other by looking at it and probing it with instruments. Their different contact with the tooth might be compared with the different ways a seeing person and a sightless person make contact with a geometric solid if one is teaching its name to the other; the seeing person does so by sight and the sightless person by touch. One kind of contact isn't necessarily more reliable than the other. For example, in the phenomenon of referred pain, a bad tooth in the lower jaw may be reported as a toothache in the upper jaw. In this case, the dentist is a better judge than the patient of where the pain really is.

We probably think of private events such as our feelings and thoughts as ones we have privileged access to and therefore special knowledge of. But we learned the relevant words from others, and all they had access to in teaching them to us were the public correlates. If we can be mistaken even about the location of a toothache, what assurance do we have that our other reports of our private events are reliable? Skinner (1963) makes the point by describing some students who'd watched a pigeon in a classroom demonstration and then described what they saw in terms of the pigeon's expectations:

> They were describing what *they* would have expected, felt, and hoped for under similar circumstances. But they were able to do so only because a verbal community had brought relevant terms under the control of certain stimuli, and this had been done when the community

had access only to the kinds of public information available to the students in the demonstration. Whatever the students knew about themselves which permitted them to infer comparable events in the pigeon must have been learned from a verbal community which saw no more of their behavior than they had seen of the pigeon's. (Skinner, 1963, p. 955)

Some verbal responses that superficially seem to tact private events may be occasioned instead by the situation in which our behavior occurs. For example, if on sitting down to a meal you suddenly find yourself eating voraciously, you may say, "I must have been very hungry." You haven't tacted some private hunger pang; you're saying of yourself what you'd have said of someone else if you'd observed that kind of eating in another.

Once we learn to tact properties of the public behavior of others, we may come to tact the same properties of our own behavior, whether public or not. If one person works hard at something with little compensation and another does so only with substantial compensation, we'll usually assume that the task was more important to the first person than to the second. But the same observations of our own behavior may also lead us to say what's more or less important to us (Bem, 1967). Speaking of our beliefs or our understanding of the causes of our actions may follow more directly from our discriminations of our own public behavior than from anything private (e.g., Kiesler, Nisbett, & Zanna, 1969). This isn't to deny private events. It's instead a cautionary note: The language of private events can easily distract us from the public causes of behavior.

Another problem with tacts of private events is that it's hard for the verbal community to shape and maintain them, because it has inconsistent access to the events and their public correlates. For example, when someone says "I have a headache" and leaves a social gathering, it isn't clear whether the verbal response tacted some private event or just allowed the speaker to escape from unwanted company. Like the language of public events, that of private events depends on the public practices of the verbal community. The implications have been explored in detail by Skinner and by Wittgenstein (Day, 1969, discusses parallels between their treatments of private events).

For our purposes, it's enough to note that verbal behavior doesn't ordinarily require stimuli to be simultaneously available to both speaker and listener. In fact, some important consequences of verbal behavior occur when the speaker tacts an event unavailable to the listener. For example, if you're telling someone over the phone about something you're watching on television, the other person can't see what you're seeing but may be able to do something about it (e.g., by switching to the same channel that you're watching). In other words, the relation between tacting a public event and tacting a private event is pretty much the same as the relation between tacting when both speaker and listener have access to what is tacted and tacting when only the speaker has such access. Although the language of private events has its own special difficulties, we don't need new categories of verbal responding to deal with it.

By themselves, tact relations are only one part of verbal behavior, but through them verbal behavior comes into contact with the environment. Without them there'd be nothing about which we could speak. The question of truth is behavioral. Some of what we call truth depends on how verbal communities maintain correspondences between verbal behavior and environment. Those who lie do so because the consequences of lying differ from those of telling the truth, but lying can be effective only within verbal communities in which such correspondences are reasonably reliable ("Unless social interaction is to break down, the lie must always be the exception," Bolinger, 1973, p. 549; cf. Dawkins, 1976, pp. 82, 112).

VERBAL CLASSES AND NAMING

We've already made the point that we have to keep tacting distinct from naming. Naming may include tacting as one of its components, but the everyday vocabulary extends to a sufficiently wide variety of cases that any formal definition will probably be unsatisfactory for some applications of the term. Let's again consider the pigeon whose pecks tact red and green and blue lights. It's a good bet that most readers would object to any argument that suggested the pigeon was naming those colors or that the pecks on the different keys were the pigeon's names for the colors. And they'd be right to object. But the reason might be not that we do something different when we name colors; instead, it might be that in naming we do something like what the pigeon does but we do a great deal more besides.

Naming is a higher-order class that involves arbitrary stimulus classes (things or events with particular names) and corresponding arbitrary verbal topographies (the words that serve as their names) in a bidirectional relationship. Consider what a child must do before we're satisfied that the child knows the name of something, such as *shoe* as a name for one of those things that goes on your feet. Not only do we expect the child to say "shoe" when we hold up a shoe and say "What's this?" We also expect the child to look around when we say "Where's the shoe?" and then point to the shoe if it's in sight.

Superficially, this looks like an equivalence relation, or at least a relation of symmetry, because the stimulus object and response word in the first part of the example appear to change places in the second. But that's assuming too much, because, unlike a pigeon's pecks on sample and comparison keys, a seen object can't be exchanged with a point at it and a heard word can't be exchanged with a spoken one: "the relation between a name and that which it names is fundamentally asymmetrical" (Horne & Lowe, 1996, p. 234).

Naming has still another feature. If a child already does some naming but hasn't yet learned the name *glove*, we might hold one up and say "This is a glove"; the child might immediately say "glove" and point at it. We then wouldn't be surprised a little later if the child pointed to the glove when we said "Where's the glove?" or said "glove" when we held it up and said "What's this?" even though the child had never answered these questions with respect to gloves before. The prerequisites for doing so include at least three components: (1) listener behavior, in looking for things and pointing based on what someone's said; (2) echoic behavior, in repeating names when they're spoken; and (3) tacting, in saying the names given the objects. The child's responses to the questions about the glove are instances of novel behavior, and naming as a higher-order class enables them to emerge. The various social and nonsocial consequences of naming are individually small, but collectively they can sustain lots of behavior. Soon the child may initiate naming instead of waiting for it to be initiated by others, and it's common for a child who's learned some naming to turn the questioning around: On encountering something that doesn't have a name yet, the child points and asks, "What's this?"

Naming is generated from the ordinary interactions between children and their caregivers. Once it's available as a higher-order

class within a child's repertoire, it allows for expansions of vocabulary in which the introduction of new words in particular functional relations (such as tacting) involves those words in a range of other emergent functions (including but by no means limited to intraverbal behavior, echoic behavior and orienting toward or pointing at named objects). We'll consider other aspects of language development in children in Chapter 16, where we'll see how dramatically a child's vocabulary expands once naming is in place as a higher-order class. (For a more detailed account of the several verbal functions that constitute naming, the kinds of contingencies in the natural environments of children that can shape and maintain those functions, the central role of naming in enlarging and amplifying other functions of verbal behavior, and a review of the developmental literature that supports the account, see Horne & Lowe, 1996.)

Section D   Verbal Behavior Conditional Upon Verbal Behavior

Verbal behavior, like any other event, can be tacted. No new kinds of relations are involved, but the complexities created when verbal behavior is built upon other verbal behavior need special comment. Verbal behavior that depends upon other verbal behavior and that modifies the effects of other verbal behavior is called *autoclitic*. It includes both the combination and arrangement of verbal units, as in adduction (Chapter 9), and verbal usages that modify the effect on the listener of other verbal behavior. *Relational autoclitics* involve verbal units that can't stand alone because they must be coordinated with other verbal behavior; *descriptive autoclitics* involve discriminations of our own verbal behavior. Note that intraverbals also depend on other verbal behavior, but we distinguish them from autoclitics because they're limited to sequential verbal relations and they don't require discriminations of our own behavior. For example, when one person says "Red, white and . . . " someone else can give the intraverbal response "blue."

RELATIONAL AUTOCLITICS: THE CONJUNCTION OF VERBAL UNITS

Some verbal responses specify events only through their relations to other verbal responses. For example, words such as *above*, *before* and *of* don't just tact particular events. They almost always occur in combination with other verbal responses and they depend on those other verbal responses for their effects. Tense and other grammatical variations are also conditional upon properties of events tacted, so they too are autoclitic. A sentence in passive voice and past tense combines tacts of various relational and temporal properties of a set of events. For example, "The dog ran" and "The birds fly" involve several discriminations that come together in those few words: dog versus bird, running versus flying, singular versus plural, past versus present. We'll consider grammatical structure in Chapter 16, but for now we're more concerned with how the events around us combine to occasion what we say than whether it's grammatical when we say it.

These multiple dimensions are not very different from the ones along which stimuli occasioned response properties in the adduction example of Chapter 9. When environmental properties occasion classes of verbal responses that are invariant even when they occur in combination with other response classes, we can treat such classes as

verbal units (e.g., as when the present-tense active-voice sentence structure remains invariant across a variety of different tacted events). Such units have complex structures, but we can generate novel verbal behavior under novel conditions only because we can combine verbal units in novel ways; we can tact new events only on the basis of verbal behavior available with respect to things already known. Even if you've never seen a purple cow, the separate tacts of purple and cowness will allow you to say "Look at that purple cow" when you encounter one.

The new combinations that relational autoclitic processes generate are important because our own verbal behavior often occasions later behavior (for example, you might act today on a reminder you wrote for yourself yesterday). Sometimes the later behavior is verbal: We reword sentences, draw conclusions, derive solutions. These manipulations are of special interest when, as in problem solving, they lead to behavior that was unavailable earlier. Part of the power of verbal behavior resides in how it can occasion novel responding with important consequences (cf. Chapter 20 on problem solving).

Consider an example from mathematics, a convenient illustration because mathematical notation exactly prescribes the verbal responses that particular verbal stimuli should occasion. We judge the understanding of addition or multiplication by the number of ways in which someone can respond appropriately to relevant verbal stimuli. The person should be able to define the operations, to discriminate between cases where they apply and cases where they don't, to give answers to specific problems, and to derive each from simpler counting operations. Such behavior is verbal, and is necessary and sufficient for saying that someone understands addition and multiplication.

The learning of arithmetic involves intraverbal and autoclitic processes. Its particular advantages come when it combines with tacting of the numerosity of objects or events. A child might calculate the number of objects in a rectangular array by multiplying the number of rows by the number of columns or simply by counting all the objects. Either operation is verbal and the outcome is a verbal response that has a consistent relation to the quantity of objects in the array; it's a derived tact. The structure of arithmetic corresponds to the structure of the environment in such a way that new verbal responses generated arithmetically can function effectively as tacts (*twelve* tacts the number of eggs in a full box of a dozen eggs; we don't have to count the eggs every time).

Much important verbal behavior is derived from other verbal behavior. We mentioned the problem of entities that can't be tacted (e.g., how do we tact philosophy or biology or psychology?). We can progress from individuals and what they do and where we find them to groups and more general activities and broader areas, until we speak of academic institutions, governments, business organizations, religions, political parties, industries, branches of the military and so on. But we can't point to these entities, so we still can't tact them, even though they're related to events we do contact directly. Derivations of this sort, however, are much less explicitly defined than those of logic or mathematics, so maybe correspondences between the world and what we say about it become less reliable as our verbal behavior gets further removed from its points of direct contact with the environment.

Derived verbal behavior also permits us to respond to properties of the world that we can't respond to in other ways. We can't tact noon or Saturdays or February 3rd or the 21st century. These exist only by virtue of clocks and calendars; they can't stand independently of verbal behavior (cf. Austin, 1962, on speech acts such as pronouncing a couple married or bestowing a title). The analogy between these cases and mathematical derivations explains verbal behavior only in the limited sense of showing how it works and how its properties differ from those of nonverbal behavior.

DESCRIPTIVE AUTOCLITICS: DISCRIMINATING OUR OWN VERBAL BEHAVIOR

Many verbal responses tact the conditions under which other verbal behavior is emitted and thereby modify the responses of the listener. Consider the phrases *I doubt* and *I'm sure* in "I doubt the coffee is ready" and "I'm sure the coffee is ready." Each one modifies the way in which the listener is likely to act upon the statement that the coffee is ready. For the listener, *I doubt* and *I'm sure* are analogous to the conditional stimuli of a conditional discrimination: In both cases the listener has heard *the coffee is ready*, but the listener is less likely to pour the coffee after *I doubt* than after *I'm sure*.

Now consider the speaker. What has *I doubt* or *I'm sure* tacted? It can't be just the readiness of the coffee. It must be some property of the speaker's own tendency to say "The coffee is ready," and the relation of that statement to the actual state of the coffee. You can't use *I doubt* or *I'm sure* effectively unless you can discriminate your own behavior. In a situation in which you'd like to be able to say "The coffee is ready," you must be able to tell whether it's appropriate to do so.

We don't tact everything we see, and conversely we sometimes respond as though tacting when the stimulus is absent. The qualifying autoclitic accompanying such verbal behavior is typically some form of the verbal response *no*. For example, we don't continuously say "The coffee isn't ready" under conditions of unready coffee. Instead, this verbal response occurs when circumstances set the occasion for saying "The coffee is ready" (e.g., the smell of coffee, the question "Is the coffee ready?") even though that response would be inappropriate. If you do say "The coffee is ready" when the coffee in fact isn't ready, adding "Not!" makes a big difference.

Assertion, like negation, is also autoclitic, but the verb *is* serves many functions. Sometimes it specifies that it accompanies a tact ("This is a book"); sometimes it prescribes equivalences between verbal responses ("A human is a featherless biped"); and sometimes it specifies temporal properties ("It's cold now"). The particular function of *is* often depends on other verbal responses or, in other words, on context. Not only does it function as a conditional stimulus with respect to the effect of other verbal behavior, but its function may in turn be conditional on other verbal behavior.

Autoclitics can have quantitative as well as qualitative effects. Examples are *few, some* and *many*, and the plural forms of nouns and verbs. The effect of *often* in "This text is often misunderstood" can be paraphrased as a statement that it's often appropriate to say "This text is misunderstood." As we'll see in treating language structure (Chapter 16), we have no independent nonverbal means for characterizing these relations, but paraphrase is useful because it makes explicit the conditional relations among the components of the utterance. This is most obvious when autoclitics specify the listener's verbal behavior (e.g., *vice versa* is conditional upon preceding verbal behavior, and it may be interpreted as an instruction specifying that

the listener generate a new verbal response reversing the order of components in the original verbal response).

Descriptive autoclitics depend on discriminations of our own verbal behavior, and we know only a little about how they're learned or can be taught. For example, suppose we arrange a series of discrimination trials ranging from easy to hard for a pigeon's key pecks and then try teaching the pigeon to report its certainty after each trial. We could add two new keys to the chamber, designating one as the *certain* key and the other as the *uncertain* key. If we were successful, the relation between the pigeon's report of its certainty and its response on the discrimination trial would be like that between the autoclitics, *I'm sure* or *I'm not sure*, and whatever it is we're sure or unsure about.

The trouble is that we have to know whether the pigeon is certain or uncertain in each discrimination trial before we can reinforce pecks on one or the other of the new keys appropriately. This is again the problem of teaching a tact of a private event. Perhaps we can base our reinforcers on some measure of the difficulty of the discriminative stimuli; another possibility is to base them on the latencies of the pigeon's responses in those trials (but see Blough, 1992). Our verbal community somehow taught us to tact our own certainty, so its teaching too was presumably based on public dimensions such as the properties of problems and whether we responded to them promptly or with hesitation. It would certainly be tough and maybe even impossible to teach this autoclitic to a pigeon (cf. Smith et al., 1995), but the analogy is helpful because it forces us to be explicit about the details of these complex properties of our own behavior.

Our verbal behavior would be impossible without autoclitic processes. In saying "I recall that it rained yesterday" or "I read that it rained yesterday" or "I heard that it rained yesterday," the speaker specifies the source of the verbal response, "It rained yesterday." Other descriptive autoclitics tact the speaker's reaction to other things the speaker is saying, as in "I am sorry to report that you missed the point" or "I am pleased to say that you did well on the exam."

More important, descriptive autoclitics demonstrate that the analysis of verbal behavior is an issue of behavior and not logic.

Saying "This is so" or "That's probable" or "It can't be" is verbal behavior with respect to other verbal behavior. To reduce such sentences to symbolic logic or to the mathematics of probability may be useful in solving problems of logic or mathematics, but that reduction eliminates a crucial feature of human language. Discriminations of our own behavior are prerequisites for what we call consciousness or self-awareness, and we owe those discriminations to the verbal community.

Chapter 15
Verbal Behavior and Nonverbal Behavior

A. The Consequences of Verbal Operants
Multiple Causation

B. Verbally Governed and Contingency-Shaped Behavior
Instructional Control
Insensitivity to Contingencies
Intrinsic Versus Extrinsic Consequences

C. Correspondences Between Saying and Doing
Shaping Verbal Behavior

D. The Listener's or Reader's Behavior
Meanings as Equivalences

E. Verbal Behavior and Nonhuman Language

Among the labels that have been applied to behavior guided by verbal antecedents are verbally governed *and* rule-governed, *and among those applied to behavior that depends on nonverbal contingencies are* contingency-governed *or* contingency-controlled. Govern *is related to cybernetics via the Greek* kubernan, *to steer or pilot, which is probably related in turn to the Sanskrit* kubhan-, *dancing, maybe in a sense of adjusting one's steps.* Control *combines the Latin* contra-, *against, with* rotulus, *roll, which as a diminutive of* rota *implied a roll of paper as well as a wheel. Via the Indo-European root* ret-, *to run or to roll, it is*

related to rotate *and* round, *and to* role *perhaps in the sense of taking a turn. In their etymologies,* govern *implies guidance whereas* control, *almost literally as working against movement, implies constraint.*

With the exception of the tact, the verbal classes we considered in Chapter 14 were primarily ones that related verbal responses to each other. We defined the formal classes of echoic behavior, transcription, textual behavior and dictation-taking in terms of one-to-one correspondences between arbitrary vocal and written units (phonemes, letters, words). The relations in intraverbal classes did not involve such correspondences, and those in autoclitic processes added coordinations some of which depended on discriminations of properties of our own verbal behavior. It was only in tacting that we began to connect verbal behavior to environmental events, but that connection was only to the nonverbal antecedents of verbal behavior and not to its consequences. To be functional, verbal behavior must be able to do things. The classes we've discussed so far are just the raw materials that are combined in functional verbal behavior.

By itself, verbal behavior doesn't do things. It's effective through the mediation of other people. (The mode isn't critical; you can tell someone what you want when shopping by asking for it or by pointing, and you can also do so in writing, as when you place an order by mail or by computer modem.) But mediation by others is characteristic of all social behavior, so we must add another proviso. The social contingencies that shape verbal behavior don't just create the conditions for speaking; they also create verbal repertories with a special property: In the ordinary give and take of everyday talk, as speakers become listeners and listeners become speakers, the behavior of the listener reinforces the behavior of the speaker. Some nonhuman behavior may minimally qualify, as when a horse is taught to turn in response to a touch of the reins to its neck (the turns then reinforce the trainer's behavior). But the horse and trainer differ crucially from a child and an adult teacher. For the latter only, verbal contingencies soon become reciprocal: The child learns to ask as well as answer, and to say "thank you" as well as "you're welcome." Thus, in some respects all verbal cultures are mutual reinforcement societies (cf. Skinner, 1957, pp. 224–226).

Consider a simple verbal exchange: A says, "Hi"; B replies, "Hi, how are you?"; A continues, "I'm fine, thanks. And you?"; B answers "Okay"; and so on. The first reply of B is both a consequence of A's greeting and an occasion for A's continuation, but so is A's response with respect to B's antecedent and consequent verbal behavior. If there's any doubt about whether consequences that maintain verbal behavior operate here, just imagine A's or B's verbal behavior if the verbal behavior of the other simply ceased. Verbal behavior involves both listener behavior shaped by its effects on the speaker's behavior, and speaker behavior shaped by its effects on the listener's behavior. These reciprocities define verbal behavior. Verbal behavior is shaped and maintained by the practices of a verbal community, and this chapter will consider some of the varied consequences that follow from those practices.

When we define verbal behavior in this way, by its function, we distinguish it from language (cf. Skinner, 1957, p. 461). A language is defined by structure and not by function. The definitions, spellings and pronunciations in dictionaries and the rules in a grammar book describe the standard structures of various verbal units in a language. In so doing, they summarize some structural properties of the practices of a verbal community. The verbal behavior of a speaker occurs in the context of those practices, but those maintaining practices, language, must not be confused with what they maintain, which is verbal behavior.

Section A   The Consequences of Verbal Operants

Verbal behavior has consequences. As with all operant behavior, these consequences affect subsequent verbal responding. In a speech episode such as a simple two-person conversation, each person provides an audience for the other. Audiences are varied in their properties; we speak into telephones, write messages or address large groups of people. Often the consequences for the speaker are simply what a listener says later. It doesn't require a laboratory experiment to demonstrate that a listener's response can maintain a speaker's talk. We tend to stop talking to people who don't react to what we say. To this extent, we can say that the listener's responses reinforce the speaker's verbal behavior (cf. Greenspoon, 1955; Rosenfeld & Baer, 1970, on *yes* or *uh-huh* as reinforcers of verbal classes such as plural nouns or the substantive content of conversations). One of the most general consequences of verbal behavior is that through it a speaker changes the behavior of a listener. Words are ways to get people to do things.

The consequences that serve as reinforcers of human verbal behavior are many and varied. Sometimes they're nonverbal (someone comes when called); sometimes they're verbal (someone answers a question). Sometimes they're fairly reliable ("Thank you" is often followed by "You're welcome"); sometimes they're not (not all requests are granted). Often they're very specific (answers to particular questions, taking appropriate action), but the shaping of verbal behavior, whether by natural or by artificial contingencies, is likely to involve generalized reinforcers. In addition, the tendency to speak may depend on some consequences while what's said may depend on others (one difficulty with experiments on verbal reinforcers was that they sometimes attempted to modify the substance of verbal behavior with the same consequences that were supposed to keep the speaker talking; e.g., Greenspoon, 1955; Rosenfeld & Baer, 1970). Verbal behavior is maintained by varied consequences within interacting natural contingencies that can be thought of as complex nested schedules of reinforcement (Chapter 11). It's no wonder that we talk a lot.

One obvious kind of consequence of verbal behavior is illustrated when we're given something we ask for. If a child says *milk* and receives a glass of milk, we might say that the milk reinforces the verbal response. The response needn't occur in the presence of the reinforcer. For example, a child may ask for milk even if a glass of milk isn't present. Verbal responses that specify their reinforcers have been called *mands* (Skinner, 1957); demands and commands, for example, specify what the listener must do.

An analogue from animal research may be helpful. Assume a rat in a chamber with one lever that produces food and another that produces water. If the rat presses the first lever only when food-deprived and the second only when water-deprived, we could argue that the presses are, respectively, food requests and water requests. Although it wouldn't be essential, we could make the analogy more convincing by arranging signs that lit up for the experimenter when either lever was pressed, saying "Please give me food" and "Please give me water." The rat's vocabulary is limited to two levers, but the relations between the presses and their consequences are similar to those between human verbal requests and their consequences.

Yet the account isn't satisfactory. For example, imagine a child who sees a new toy, learns it's called a woozle and then asks for a woozle even though asking for woozles could never have been reinforced before. As a category of verbal behavior, the mand can't consist of many separate response classes corresponding to each of the many consequences that could be manded; rather it must be a single class of responses in which a reinforcer is specified by the verbal responses that tact it in other circumstances; in other words, manding is a higher-order verbal operant (cf. naming in Chapter 14). No such class existed in the rat example.

Within the class of mands, some subclasses specify stimuli ("May I have an apple?") and some specify the behavior of the listener ("Please wait for me"); others called questions specify the listener's verbal behavior (e.g., "What's your name?" or "Do you have the time?"). These classes may be further subdivided according to a variety of features. For example, we speak of a *prompt* when the appropriate verbal response is already known to the speaker (as in giving a hint to a child who is unable to solve a riddle) and a *probe* when it isn't known (as in a police interrogation). In everyday discourse, we also distinguish different kinds of mands on the basis of the contingencies they signal; for example, bribes specify the consequences of compliance whereas threats specify the consequences of noncompliance.

MULTIPLE CAUSATION

One problem of verbal behavior is that particular verbal topographies (e.g., words) can share in many different functions:

> . . . we cannot tell from form alone into which class a response falls. *Fire* may be (1) a mand to a firing squad, (2) a tact to a conflagration, (3) an intraverbal response to the stimulus *Ready, aim . . .* , or (4) an echoic or (5) textual response to appropriate verbal stimuli. It is possible that formal properties of the vocal response, especially its intonation, may suggest one type of controlling variable, but an analysis cannot be achieved from such internal evidence alone. In order to classify behavior effectively, we must know the circumstances under which it is emitted. (Skinner, 1957, p. 186)

Any verbal topography potentially can take on any verbal function. Furthermore, probably no instance of verbal behavior is ever uniquely determined by just one variable. For example, when a child says "milk" in the presence of milk, this verbal response may function simultaneously as a mand and a tact (especially if the child is already naming). When two or more events act together to produce behavior, we speak of their combined effect as *multiple causation*.

Humor often depends on multiple causation. For example, if the end of this paragraph is funny, that's mainly because of how it combines two different vocabularies with which we talk about things that we value. Let's change the subject to the Olympics. Is there any truth to the rumor that there was once an Olympic team whose members were so proud of their gold medals that they had them bronzed?

Audiences provide especially good examples of multiple causation. Tacting is oc-casioned by the tacted stimulus, but we might not tact unless an audience is present, and an effective audience might or might not be a person. For example, we might say something to a pet even though the pet never answers. Pets have enough in common with human audiences (e.g., most are reasonably animate and some even make eye contact when you talk to them) that our tacting often generalizes from human audiences to them.

What we say given one audience may differ from what we say given another audience or given both together. If an absent-minded professor comes to class wearing a napkin from lunch still tucked in like a bib, a student might tact the napkin aloud given another student as an audience, but only provided that the professor is not in a position to be an effective audience for the tact too. If the student just whispers the tact, the causes of the whisper are the napkin and the other student and the professor's proximity in combination; take away any one and there'll be no whispered tact. As is appropriate in an analysis, we'll usually treat causes one at a time, but once we start looking for the multiple causation of behavior, we'll find it virtually everywhere.

Section B   **Verbally Governed and Contingency-Shaped Behavior**

Verbal behavior can have either verbal or nonverbal consequences, but in one way or another, the consequence is usually a change in the listener's behavior. For example, if you tell a friend who's about to go outdoors that it's going to rain, your friend may be more likely to take an umbrella. The verbal community maintains correspondences between verbal behavior and environmental events. The listener can act on the speaker's verbal behavior only if such correspondences are consistent. If the speaker's verbal behavior is occasioned by environmental events inaccessible to the listener, it may become a potent discriminative stimulus for the listener's behavior. For example, a listener's response to the tact *fire* may have important consequences even if only the speaker has seen the fire. Through the verbal behavior of others, we can respond indirectly to events distant in space or in time (the tale of the boy who cried wolf illustrates how control by the speaker's verbal behavior may weaken if the speaker tacts unreliably).

Sometimes what people do depends on what they're told to do; people often follow instructions. Behavior mainly determined by verbal antecedents is called *verbally governed* behavior (sometimes also *rule-governed* behavior); its properties differ from those of *contingency-governed* or *contingency-shaped* behavior, behavior that's been shaped by its consequences (Skinner, 1969). Some instructions affect nonverbal behavior ("Come here," "Sit down," "Go away"); others affect verbal behavior itself ("Tell me a story," "Say please," "Be quiet").

INSTRUCTIONAL CONTROL

The most general function of language is instruction; we tell each other what to do and what to say. Language isn't an instrument of reason or a vehicle of truth; those properties are only corollaries of its primary function, changing the listener's behavior. Orders are given, advice is offered, laws are enacted and so on; each case involves instructional control. This is easiest to overlook when the instructed behavior is itself verbal. A script is a set of instructions to an actor and a text is a set of instructions to a reader. In both cases the instruction specifies verbal behavior, i.e., what's to be said. The instructor who defines a term, for example, specifies the circumstances in which the term and its definition will be appropriate in the student's future

verbal behavior (especially in those contexts called exams).

An important characteristic of instruction is that it substitutes verbal antecedents for natural contingencies, as when a parent tells a child "Don't touch the stove or you'll get burned." This property of instruction has far-reaching implications. Instructions can change the listener's behavior in situations in which natural consequences by themselves are ineffective or are effective only slowly. If we invite friends for a visit, for example, we give them directions rather than letting them search for our place on their own.

Notice that these verbal antecedents aren't necessarily discriminative stimuli. We might act appropriately when we see a sign saying "Hot surface! Don't touch!" In that case the sign would qualify as a discriminative stimulus. But the instruction isn't present to function as a discriminative stimulus when the child avoids the hot stove today after a warning about it yesterday. Many instructions alter the functions of other stimuli instead of functioning as discriminative stimuli (Schlinger & Blakely, 1987). For example, if the warning about the stove is effective, it changes the stove to a discriminative stimulus correlated with an aversive event, getting burned, but the warning itself, no longer present, isn't a discriminative stimulus.

Contingencies operate for following instructions. To the extent that instruction-following is characterized by correspondences between the instruction and the listener's behavior and thus is more than the following of particular instructions, it's another higher-order class of behavior held together by common contingencies. The higher-order contingencies that operate on the following of orders in general, which are usually social and verbal, are different from those that operate on the following of a particular order, which may be completely nonverbal. For example, following orders in the military is a product of extensive and powerful social contingencies; they're often artificial applications of aversive control. But there's nothing artificial about the immediate consequences of obeying a command to attack a heavily armed position across an open field of fire in actual combat.

Varied social contingencies maintain instruction-following. Among the consequences that might reinforce the granting of a request might be that it pleases the requester, or avoids hurting the requester's feelings, or puts the requester in debt so that the favor will probably later be returned, or gets the requester to leave, or annoys someone else who didn't want the request granted, and so on, and so on. The possibilities are endless.

Sometimes the contingencies that maintain instruction-following depend on the relation between verbal formulations and nonverbal contingencies, as when someone successfully makes a repair by following a service manual, or as when someone avoids injury by acting on a warning. The term *pliance* has been suggested for instruction-following that depends on social contingencies and the term *tracking* for instructional contingencies that involve correspondences between verbal behavior and environmental events (Zettle & Hayes, 1982). Some instructions function as establishing operations, *augmenting* the effectiveness of reinforcers (as when an advertisement that shows pictures of food makes eating more likely, or as when a sales pitch that describes special features of a car makes buying the car more likely: cf. Hayes, Zettle, & Rosenfarb, 1989, p. 206).

Consider an example of verbally governed behavior. Without instructions someone types with the index fingers, one letter at a time, in the method called hunt-and-peck. This is faster for the novice typist than touch typing, in which each finger has its own resting position at the keyboard. The immediate consequences of the two typing methods favor the former: With the familiar hunt-and-peck method, the job will get done more quickly. But in learning touch typing, the long-term consequences of following instructions to place the fingers appropriately and to type each letter with a particular finger will eventually outweigh the short-term advantages of the hunt-and-peck system: once it's mastered, touch typing is much faster than hunt-and-peck typing. What's learned isn't just a particular method of typing. To follow instructions successfully, the learner must ignore the natural consequences, in this instance that the text is at first produced more slowly by touch typing than by hunt-and-peck typing.

The student who's a hunt-and-peck typist may find it hard to switch over to touch typing, especially when a paper is due. Under this time pressure, the slowness of novice touch typing can't compete with hunt-and-peck typing (we'd probably say that the student who sticks with touch typing under these circumstances exhibits self-control: cf. the contingencies in Chapter 11). One way to get around the problem is to make the transition a gradual one, adding just one or two letters at a time to the proper placement for touch typing while continuing hunt-and-peck for the rest (new letters should be added only when the touch typing of the earlier ones is well differentiated). With this method, it's important to return to the base finger placement, with the left index finger on the *F* and the right on the *J*, as often as possible.

Because of the practical advantages of instruction, the verbal community shapes the behavior of following instructions across a substantial range of activities throughout a substantial portion of our lives. This can happen only if the contingencies that maintain instruction-following are more potent than the natural contingencies against which they're pitted (we seldom bother to ask people to do things they'd do on their own anyway). Thus, instructions may begin to override natural contingencies: People then do things when told to do them that they'd never do if just the natural contingencies operated.

A major achievement of human verbal behavior is that it allows behavior to be controlled by descriptions of contingencies, in the verbal behavior of others, as well as by direct contact with the contingencies themselves. But the advantages of this unique property of verbal behavior are accompanied by special problems. For example, a history of following instructions may make individuals susceptible to verbal control by authority figures (e.g., Milgram, 1963). But in addition to the abuses that can arise when people just follow orders, instructions can create problems in subtler ways (cf. Chase, 1938).

INSENSITIVITY TO CONTINGENCIES

Consider the simple task of pressing a telegraph key, with presses earning money according to various schedules of reinforcement. When key pressing is established in humans by instructions instead of by shaping, instructed performances are typically insensitive to the schedule contingencies, whereas shaped performances often aren't (Matthews et al., 1977). Schedule effects observed with uninstructed responding in humans (e.g., higher rates maintained by ratio schedules than by yoked interval schedules; cf. Chapter 10) don't occur reliably when responding is instructed. Just telling a human in an experimental setting to "press the key" produces persistent responding that's insensitive to its consequences (cf. Lowe, 1980; Shimoff, Catania, & Matthews, 1981). Such insensitivities have been observed across a range of sched-

ule contingencies (e.g., Baron & Leinenweber, 1995; but cf. Svartdal, 1992).

This property of instructed performances is relevant to those aspects of skill that we sometimes say can't be taught. Skilled performances are those in which behavior is sensitive to its consequences from moment to moment, as when a woodcarver adjusts to the changing patterns of grain in a woodblock or a quarterback anticipates the movements of an opposing player or a dancer accommodates to slight deviations in the steps of a partner. If verbally governed behavior is likely to be insensitive to its consequences, then skilled behavior must be contingency-shaped instead. We must learn by doing in such cases; instructions can't substitute for the subtleties of direct contact with contingencies.

Shaping provides another example. It's a skill that might be acquired through instruction or through nonverbal contingencies. If you try shaping based on the discussion in Chapter 7, your reinforcement of some responses but not others will be verbally governed. Perhaps you'll follow a rule stating that you should wait for a response closer to the one you want to shape than any you've seen before. But if too many responses go by without one that qualifies, you'll have to modify the rule or responding may extinguish.

The momentary distribution of responses includes some closer to your shaping goal than others. If you reinforce one from the end of the distribution closer to your goal, the distribution will probably shift in that direction; if you reinforce one from the farther end, it will probably shift away from it. The distribution is always changing, so your task is to judge where in it a given response comes from. If a response comes from the farther end, you should let it go without reinforcement, but if it comes from the one near your goal, you should reinforce it.

Whether you reinforce a response from the middle should depend on how long it's been since the last reinforced response and how many reinforcers you've already delivered; if you go too much one way or the other, responding will cease, either through extinction or through satiation.

What you do while shaping has many of the characteristics of *signal detection* (Green & Swets, 1966; Nevin, 1969). Signal detection theory assumes that an observer responds or doesn't respond to a stimulus that consists of either a signal in noise or noise alone. Responding to the signal is a *hit*, but responding to the noise alone is a *false alarm*; not responding to the signal is a *miss*, but not responding to the noise alone is a correct *rejection*. Probability of hits given a signal in noise and of correct rejections given just noise can be plotted in a unit square much like those for contingency relations (e.g., Figure 5-9). These probabilities can be used to compute two statistics, one called d' (d prime), an index of the observer's sensitivity to the signal, and another called *bias*, an index of whether the observer is biased toward responding or not responding (for example, if misses are costly but false alarms don't matter much, the observer will be biased toward responding).

Signal detection theory is usually applied to research on sensory systems and related topics, but its relevance to shaping is that in its terms reinforcing a response at the end of the distribution near your shaping goal is a hit, whereas reinforcing one at the other end is a false alarm; similarly, not reinforcing one at the end near your goal is a miss, whereas not reinforcing one at the other end is a correct rejection. The shaper who is better at judging where in the distribution a response came from (higher values of d') will be more successful at shaping. The shaper who is too biased toward reinforcing responses will be more likely to lose respond-

ing to satiation, and the one who is too biased the other way will be more likely to lose it to extinction.

The point is that these judgments are part of the skills of a person who has become good at shaping, but they're not easily expressed as rules. The skills come from being sensitive to the ways in which response distributions change from moment to moment over the course of shaping; the learner who depends mainly on rules may be less likely to master such judgments than one who is less dependent on rules. We often make assumptions about new situations, and our assumptions often take the form of rules that we've generated for ourselves (cf. Rosenfarb et al., 1992). But sometimes our assumptions get in the way and make our behavior insensitive to some of the contingencies that would otherwise shape and maintain it. That's probably why teachers are sometimes torn between telling students how to do something and letting the students discover it for themselves.

We usually don't want others to do what we say simply because we say it. A parent or teacher who gives instructions to a child might prefer but can't be confident that the natural contingencies will eventually control the relevant behavior and make instructions unnecessary. For example, a reason for telling a child to put overshoes on before going out to play in the snow is that the instruction may keep the child from coming home with cold wet feet. If the child always obeys the instruction, the natural contingencies will never act on the child's behavior; if the child disobeys the instructions, the aversive consequences that follow from snow and unprotected feet may enhance the control by instructions on future occasions. Thus, if we try to teach by telling others what to do, we may reduce the likelihood that they'll learn from the consequences of their own behavior.

There's no easy solution to this dilemma. We must always choose between the immediacy and convenience of verbal instructions and their longer-term effects on the learner's sensitivity to the consequences of behavior.

Cases of insensitivity to contingencies produced by verbal behavior can be found across a wide range of settings. For example, people learn the rules of an artificial language more effectively by working only with sample sentences than by working with the sentences plus statements of the grammatical rules (Reber, 1976); right-left confusions are less likely in spatial tasks that don't involve words than in those that do (e.g., Maki, 1979); individuals can't ignore false labeling even if they did the labeling themselves (Rozin, Millman, & Nemeroff, 1986); remembering faces and some other classes of stimuli that are difficult to put into words is impaired by naming the stimuli (Schooler & Engstler-Schooler, 1990). Perhaps it's appropriate to conclude that some things are better left unsaid.

INTRINSIC VERSUS EXTRINSIC CONSEQUENCES

Instructions have a role in a distinction between *intrinsic* and *extrinsic* reinforcers (e.g., Lepper & Greene, 1978). Some reinforcers are intrinsically effective, whereas the effectiveness of others must be established. For example, music is an intrinsic consequence of playing an instrument, but the music teacher's praise or grades are an extrinsic consequence. In one experiment (Lepper, Greene, & Nisbett, 1973), one group of children received gold stars for artwork; after the gold stars were discontinued, children in this group engaged in less artwork than those in a second group who never received gold stars. The gold stars, extrinsic

reinforcers, were said to have undermined the intrinsic reinforcers, the natural consequences of drawing.

The children were told to earn the gold stars, however, and the experiment didn't test their effectiveness as reinforcers. If they were reinforcers at all, they were reinforcers established by instructions. Thus, the results probably had nothing to do with a difference between intrinsic and extrinsic reinforcers; instead, they were probably a demonstration of the insensitivity of instructed behavior to contingencies (Schwartz, 1982, provides another example of stereotypy determined by verbal behavior but attributed to reinforcers). To produce such effects, it may be sufficient merely to get the children talking about the relevant behavior and contingencies (cf. Wilson & Lassiter, 1982).

We don't ordinarily expect behavior to occur in educational settings if it has no consequences. What would happen to performance in most college courses if instructors simply guaranteed grades of A at the start of the semester and then assumed that all students would complete all assignments and study hard for all exams? The answer is obvious, and yet such contingencies have sometimes operated in elementary and high school education, with students promoted to higher grades without regard to the completion of earlier ones.

Such consequences are remote from what happens in the classroom, so let's consider instead the child who's learning to read. What are the natural consequences of learning to name the letters of the alphabet, or even of learning to read whole words? It's only when the child can do at least that much that the natural consequences of reading can start to take hold. Only then is the child perhaps ready to read a story, so that reading can become "its own reward." Until that happens, the teacher has no choice but to arrange artificial contingencies, using consequences such as praise or other extrinsic reinforcers.

The argument, then, is that responsible teaching adds extrinsic reinforcers only when there aren't any intrinsic ones or when the intrinsic ones aren't working. Even aside from this argument, however, the evidence from the literature on the "hidden costs of reward" is simply unconvincing, and the consequences of its application are likely to be unfortunate (cf. Cameron & Pierce, 1994, which reviews that literature and shows, among other things, that problems with reward are typically small and short-lived if they occur at all, and are most likely to arise not with contingent reward but rather, as we might have predicted, with rewards that are not contingent on performance; see also Eisenberger & Cameron, 1996).

Section C   Correspondences Between Saying and Doing

Verbal communities arrange correspondences between words and events. The correspondences operate in both directions, as in equivalence classes; we name things we see and locate things we name. Another correspondence important to the verbal community is that between what we say and what we do. Here also the correspondence can operate in both directions. If we do something we can say we've done it, and if we promise to do something we can do it (e.g., Risley & Hart, 1968; Rogers-Warren & Baer, 1976; Paniagua & Baer, 1982). To the extent that the verbal community arranges contingencies for these correspondences, we can change behavior not only by instructing the behavior but also by shaping what's said about it. If both saying and correspondences between saying and doing are reinforced, doing may follow. Through such contingencies, one's own verbal behavior may become

effective as an instructional stimulus (e.g., Lovaas, 1964; Jaynes, 1976; but see also Baer, Detrich, & Weninger, 1988; Matthews, Shimoff, & Catania, 1987).

SHAPING VERBAL BEHAVIOR

In one experiment (Catania, Matthews, & Shimoff, 1982), students' presses on two buttons occasionally produced points exchangeable for money. When a blue light above the left button was lit, a random-ratio (RR) schedule operated for presses on that button; when one above the right button was lit, a random-interval (RI) schedule operated for its presses. Between alternations of the two schedules, the students filled out guess sheets that included sentences to be completed for the left and right button of the form: "The way to produce points with this button is to . . . " Their guesses were shaped with differential points worth money. In shaping guesses, the experimenter assigned points to each guess, writing point values next to each one and passing the sheet through a partition to the student.

When the guess shaped for one button was *press quickly* and that for the other was *press slowly*, response rates on the two buttons changed in corresponding directions, without regard to schedule contingencies. Thus, shaping *press slowly* for the left button and *press quickly* for the right button produced relatively low RR rates and relatively high RI rates, opposite to those usually produced by these schedule contingencies (cf. Chapter 10). What the students said about their responding was a more powerful determinant of what they did than the consequences of their responding (e.g., students who slowed down on the RR button lost points they would have earned if they'd responded more rapidly).

In a procedure in which students were told what to guess, however, correspondences between the guesses and the response rates were inconsistent; sometimes guessing *press fast* was accompanied by fast pressing and guessing *press slow* by slow pressing, but sometimes these guesses were accompanied by equal response rates on the two buttons or by rates that differed in the opposite direction.

Like shaping in other contexts, verbal shaping is a skill. It involves treating successive verbal responses as varying along semantic dimensions, but judgments of which ones are closer or farther from the behavior to be shaped can be tricky. It's easy to pick out words related to *fast* or *slow* and *time* or *num-*

ber, but a student who comes up with a guess like *four fast presses and then three slow ones* might just start varying those two numbers on all trials thereafter. Because the possibilities for varying the numbers are unlimited, the student may be caught in a sort of verbal trap, in which further attempts to shape simpler guesses will be unsuccessful. Furthermore, it makes a difference whether what's shaped is a description of behavior or a description of the contingencies operating for that behavior.

Figure 15-1 shows data from a variation on these procedures (Catania, Shimoff, &

confirmation bias.

FIGURE 15-1   Left (L) and right (R) rates over 3-min cycles of multiple random-interval (RR) random-ratio (RI) schedules of point delivery for a student's button presses. Shaded areas show point deliveries for verbal behavior (guesses) during shaping of contingency descriptions and, right of the dashed vertical line, of performance descriptions. An interruption between sessions is shown by the unconnected points. The shaping of contingency descriptions did not produce differential response rates, but the shaping of performance descriptions did. (Adapted from Catania, Shimoff, & Matthews, 1989, Figure 1)

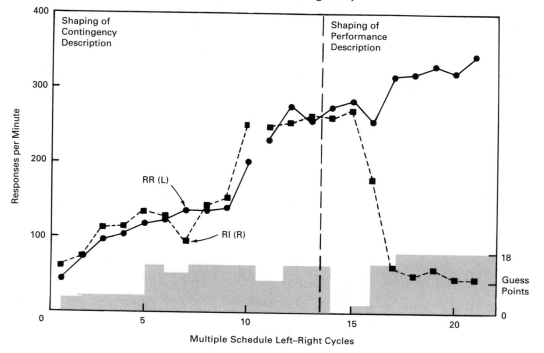

Matthews, 1989). Again, an RR schedule operated for presses on the left button (L) and an RI schedule operated for presses on the right button (R). This time the guesses that were shaped were descriptions of contingencies rather than descriptions of performances. The sentences to be completed for the left and right buttons were of the form: "The computer will let your press produce a point depending on . . . " The verbal shaping successfully produced guesses that were variations of *number of presses* for the left button contingency and variations of *time intervals* for the right button contingency (the progress of shaping is shown by the shaded areas; shaping was complete when the student's guesses were earning the maximum of 18 points per guess period). The shaped contingency descriptions were accurate, but there were no substantial differences in the RR and RI rates of button pressing.

Verbal shaping was quickly effective when it was switched to performance descriptions (right of the dashed vertical line in Figure 15-1), and produced variations on *press fast* for left RR button guesses and variations on *press slow* for right RI button guesses. The rates of pressing the buttons diverged as these performance guesses became more consistent over cycles. Unlike procedures that merely sample verbal reports during operant performance, this kind of procedure allows us to determine the direction of effect in the relation been verbal and nonverbal behavior, because we know what came first. The verbal behavior changed during shaping; then came the change in response rates. (Of course, in different circumstances the direction can go the other way, as when students whose pressing is fast or slow then accurately describe their own behavior.)

Whether descriptions of contingencies produce corresponding changes in performance depends on other verbal behavior. For example, one student, correctly identifying two schedules as RR and RI, might go on to say that point deliveries increase with higher RR rates but not with higher RI rates. Another, also correctly identifying the two schedules, might instead go on to say that because points in both are unpredictable, point deliveries are unaffected by pressing rates. We'd expect the first student but not the second to show rate differences appropriate to the schedules. In any case, descriptions of what you do in an environment differ from descriptions of how that environment works.

Correspondences between shaped verbal behavior and relevant nonverbal behavior such as those illustrated in Figure 15-1 begin early. They've been shown with children as well as adults (Catania, Lowe, & Horne, 1990; cf. Bentall & Lowe, 1987; Bentall, Lowe, & Beasty, 1985). One possibility is that they come about because of the bidirectional relations between our own behavior and the words that tact that behavior (as in naming). Procedures that affect one may then bring along the other.

The shaping of verbal behavior is a potent technique for changing human behavior, especially given that the distinction between verbally governed and contingency-governed behavior is relevant to verbal as well as nonverbal behavior (Catania, Matthews, & Shimoff, 1990). Verbal behavior that's shaped or contingency-governed is, like nonverbal shaped behavior, sensitive to its consequences, but it's also accompanied by corresponding nonverbal behavior: If what we say is shaped, we do what we say. On the other hand, verbal behavior that's instructed or verbally governed is, like nonverbal instructed behavior, relatively insensitive to its consequences, but it's less reliably accompanied by corresponding nonverbal behavior: If we're told what to say, what we do doesn't necessarily follow from what we say even if we reliably say what we were told to say.

The practical implication is that it may be easier to change human behavior by shaping what someone says than by shaping what someone does. Human nonverbal behavior is often verbally governed, but human verbal behavior is usually contingency-shaped (perhaps because we don't often talk about the variables that determine our own verbal behavior). Thus, the therapist may sometimes be effective simply by shaping a client's talk (Truax, 1966). Therapies that invoke cognitive behavior modification or cognitive efficacy are said to modify the client's behavior by changing the client's cognitions, but this is ordinarily done by changing the client's verbal behavior, either through instructions or through verbal shaping (such verbal shaping is more likely to be incidental than deliberate). Such therapies are sometimes effective, but probably for reasons other than those claimed (cf. Bandura, Adams, & Beyer, 1977; Catania, 1995; Chadwick et al., 1994).

In education, we sometimes teach by shaping what our students say through questions and discussion. More often we teach not by shaping but by instruction; in lectures, students are told what to say on exams. If the courses include no direct contact with a subject matter, the former type of teaching will probably be more likely than the latter to affect the student's interaction with the subject matter outside the classroom. Our conclusion is worth repeating: It may be easier to change human behavior by shaping what someone says than by shaping what someone does. If reinforcement sometimes appears not to work very well on human nonverbal behavior, we might be tempted to discount it as applying to human behavior at all. But if, because of the power of instruction-following as a higher-order class, the effects of reinforcement are stronger when applied to human verbal behavior than when applied to human non-

verbal behavior, it would be foolish of us to ignore it. The phenomenon can be put to good use or to bad, and the best defense against its misuse is to learn as much as we can about how it works.

Section D   The Listener's or Reader's Behavior

Given that the speaker's verbal behavior provides discriminative stimuli for the listener, the listener's behavior is what's occasioned by these verbal stimuli. The listener's responses to verbal stimuli can be as varied as the responses to any other kinds of events. Many of the possible verbal responses have already been considered, in echoic, intraverbal and other classes. Some nonverbal responses occasioned by verbal stimuli are also obvious enough that they don't require special consideration. Whether the critical stimulus is a red light, a traffic officer's outstretched hand, the word *stop* or a tree fallen across the road, the driver's stepping on the brakes illustrates stimulus control. As we move from watching an actual incident to watching the incident acted in a play or a film and then to reading the script for the actual incident and then to reading a description of the incident in a story, the common feature that holds these cases together must lie in consistencies of stimulus control over verbal and nonverbal behavior.

Listeners aren't passive, and they often behave verbally along with the speaker, saying things to themselves, planning replies and so on. Sometimes we act as our own listeners or readers, as when we carefully attend to what we're saying or think aloud or read something we've just written. We'll see in Chapter 20 that products of our own behavior can serve as discriminative stimuli and occasion our own future behavior (Skinner, 1989a).

As with nonverbal stimuli, not all responses to verbal stimuli are operant. For example, if a spoken word is paired with a stimulus that elicits autonomic responses (e.g., shock), the word may come itself to elicit these responses. This phenomenon, sometimes called *semantic conditioning* (e.g., Riess, 1946), is a verbal equivalent of the respondent conditioning of nonverbal responses. Responding generated by these procedures generalizes across semantic as well as phonological dimensions of verbal stimuli. For example, if electric shock is paired with a vehicle word, such as *truck*, the conditioned galvanic skin response is more likely to generalize to other vehicle words, such as *car* or *bus*, than to words that simply have some letters in common with the original word, such as *duck*. Semantic conditioning may contribute to instructional effects such as a child's adherence to warnings about a hot stove.

Yet if we say that a listener has under-stood something, it seems unlikely that we can provide an adequate account of the listener's response simply by appealing to relations among words (as in the giving of definitions) or of words with events (as in the teaching of tacts). The problem of meaning must reside at least in part in properties of the listener's responses to verbal stimuli. One critical property may be the correspondences between the responses occasioned by a word or utterance and the responses occasioned by the nonverbal events that the word or utterance ordinarily tacts. Many studies of verbal behavior are concerned mainly with how verbal responses occasioned by events vary together in the verbal behavior of a speaker or have common effects on a listener (cf. Chapter 16 on semantics).

Whatever else is involved in the listener's behavior, the response to a tact must share some properties with the response to what's tacted. This is demonstrated when the prop-erties of what's tacted interact with the properties of the relevant verbal behavior. For example, if words are printed in different colors, it's difficult to tact these colors rapidly if the words themselves are incompatible color-names (e.g., the word *red* printed in green; Stroop, 1935); we read words and don't ordinarily attend to physical properties such as the color in which they're printed. This relation between stimuli and the verbal responses they occasion clarifies some logical paradoxes of the language of reference. For example, consider the statement, *This statement is false*. If the statement's true, then it must be false; if it's false, then it must be true. Clearly it can't be true and false at the same time. This is a paradox of logic but not of verbal behavior. One verbal response can tact another verbal response, but it can't tact itself. In other words, *This statement is false* is not a response to itself, but "It can't be true and false at the same time" might be a response to it.

MEANINGS AS EQUIVALENCES

In dealing with the formal relations, we argued that the symmetry of stimulus and response relations favors a vocabulary in terms of words rather than one in terms of specific vocal or written modalities. Similar correspondences exist in relations between tacts and environmental events. These correspondences may be important when we speak of meaning, because the language of meaning is independent of whether words function as stimuli or as responses. This may be the most important way in which equivalence classes enter into verbal behavior. For example, consider rain as a stimulus (the sight or sound of it falling or how it feels on your skin), responses occasioned by rain (using an umbrella, putting on a raincoat, running for shelter or just enjoying it) and the word *rain*. Both rain and the word *rain*, as stimuli, may occasion either a verbal response, the word *rain*, or a nonverbal response appropriate to rain. We may look out a window, see rain and pick up an umbrella on the way out, but we might also pick up the umbrella given a verbal stimulus, as when we've just heard a weather report predicting rain. Given either the rain or the weather report, we might also phone someone who works in a windowless office and pass the news on. These relations are all summarized in Figure 15-2.

When a listener repeats what a speaker has said and we say that the listener has understood the speaker, we aren't usually satisfied in calling the relation echoic. The several relations involving *rain* as a verbal stimulus and *rain* as a verbal response in the figure are among the criteria for talking about naming, but more is involved here than naming. Presumably we judge understanding or meaning not by any single relation between stimuli and responses, but rather by the integrity of the sorts of relations illustrated in Figure 15-2. We say that someone understands something that's been said when the individual repeats what's been said not because the other person said it but for the same reasons that the other person said it (cf. Skinner, 1968, p. 139). Such behavior implies the kinds of consistent relations among verbal and nonverbal responses illustrated in Figure 15-2. Those relations are central to the concepts of meaning and understanding.

Section E   Verbal Behavior and Nonhuman Language

We've considered some of the properties of verbal behavior: instructional control, correspondences or equivalence classes, and discriminations of our own behavior in autoclitic processes, to mention just a few. In its full complexity, verbal behavior involves interactions among a variety of different processes. Just as a taxonomy of processes is required for the analysis of nonverbal behavior (Chapters 1 through 13), we need a taxonomy of verbal behavior. That taxonomy includes classes different from those in the everyday vocabulary. Textual behavior isn't equivalent to reading, although it may be its precursor. Transcription isn't equivalent to pictorial copying, but depends on the establishment of units of written verbal behavior. Tacting isn't equivalent to naming or referring, and yet as stimulus control of verbal behavior it's the point at which verbal behavior is anchored to environmental events. The effectiveness of verbal behavior depends on the coordinations of these elementary components of verbal behavior with more complex processes. By themselves they aren't even particularly verbal, but our verbal behavior is in many ways built upon them.

It's probably because verbal behavior involves so many different processes acting together that the issue of nonhuman languages

FIGURE 15-2   Relations among verbal and nonverbal responses occasioned by verbal and nonverbal stimuli (S, stimulus; R, response). Naming, meaning and other properties of verbal behavior depend on such consistencies in the relations among verbal and nonverbal events (cf. Figure 14-1).

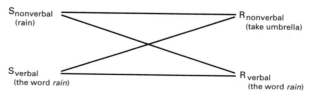

has typically engendered controversy. There certainly exist many cases in which the sounds or gestures of one nonhuman organism influence the behavior of other members of that species; some were considered in Chapter 13. Birdsong, for example, has important effects in mating and the establishment of territories. The songs of birds often depend on the social context in which they sing (West & King, 1980); those of some birds have dialects, and birds who don't hear them at an early age don't sing them as adults (Marler & Peters, 1982). The dependence of birdsong on both genetic and environmental history has some parallels in the development of human vocal behavior (as in the shaping of echoic behavior), but the functions and structures of the two kinds of behavior differ in many important ways (e.g., absolute frequency is more important in discriminating among melodies for birds than for humans; Hulse, Cynx, & Humpal, 1984). Human language involves much more than vocal releasers or stimulus control based upon vocal stimuli (for that reason, discriminations based even on very subtle events, as by the horse Clever Hans, have never counted as instances of verbal behavior; cf. Pfungst, 1911; Sebeok & Rosenthal, 1981).

The domain of animal language has often been taken to broadly encompass any case in which the behavior of one organism serves as either an eliciting or a discriminative stimulus for the behavior of another (e.g., Bright, 1985). Accounts have dealt with the full range of nonhuman communication, ranging from the flashes of fireflies and the chirps of crickets to the rivalry calls of deer and the coordinated songs of whales. Many of these cases involve stimuli or responses of special interest, but their relevance to human verbal behavior is usually limited.

As verbal classes, tacting involves stimulus control as it occurs in verbal behavior, manding involves consequences as they act in verbal behavior, and intraverbal respond-

ing involves chaining as it operates in verbal behavior. Those and other processes are important and have been studied with several species. For example, some studies have examined whether bird vocalizations can function as tacts or even as members of equivalence classes (cf. Manabe, Kawashima, & Staddon, 1995, on budgerigars; Pepperberg, 1988, on the parrot).

Other research has concentrated on structural rather than functional aspects of human languages as they might enter into nonhuman behavior (e.g., discriminations of human phonetic categories by Japanese quail; Kluender, Diehl, & Killeen, 1987). Attention, however, has more often focused on aspects of human verbal behavior that aren't obvious components of nonhuman behavior. For example, studies of the behavior of sea mammals such as dolphins and sea lions have shown them capable of sophisticated relational discriminations in both auditory and visual modes, but the sides taken on their verbal competence have depended on judgments about whether it is appropriate to regard the complex properties of their behavior as nonhuman examples of grammatical structure or of equivalence relations (cf. Herman & Forestell, 1985; Schusterman & Kastak, 1993).

In the search for nonhuman language, investigators have most often turned to the primates (e.g., chimpanzees: cf. Savage-Rumbaugh, 1986). Some of our information comes from behavior observed in natural habitats (cf. Gouzoules, Gouzoules, & Marler, 1984; Seyfarth, Cheney, & Marler, 1980; and Chapter 13). For example, the sound patternings of vocalizations may determine how well one individual can recognize kin or other individuals (cf. Rendall, Rodman, & Emond, 1996).

Early attempts to demonstrate language in chimpanzees were unsuccessful because they concentrated on language in the speech mode (Hayes & Hayes, 1951). But the chimpanzee's vocal apparatus restricts its capacity to produce differentiated vocal behavior, and the chimpanzee Viki learned to imitate only a few human utterances: *mama, papa, cup, up.* Another question was whether the chimpanzee's capacity to remember transient and arbitrary stimuli was limited.

Researchers then switched to languages based on other modalities. The chimpanzee Washoe learned the gestures of American Sign Language (Gardner & Gardner, 1969); the chimpanzee Lana learned a language based on visual displays and key presses at a computer console (Rumbaugh & Gill, 1976); and the chimpanzee Sarah learned a language based on arrangements of plastic chips of various shapes and colors on a magnetic board (Premack, 1970). In these projects, chimpanzees acquired large vocabularies and began to produce word combinations, but as each new aspect of the chimpanzees' capacities was demonstrated, questions were raised about others. For example, after the chimpanzee Nim Chimpsky was taught some of the gestural vocabulary of American Sign Language, the structure of its word combinations was compared with that of the language of a human child (Terrace et al., 1979; see also Thompson & Church, 1980). The sequential structure of Nim's word combinations was less orderly than a child's, and it was concluded that Nim's behavior couldn't be called language because it lacked adequate structure or syntax. Yet structure was deliberately avoided in the signing of Nim's teachers, so as not to impose it on Nim's signing, whereas a child's early verbal environment includes the structured speech of adults.

Other studies were concerned with the verbal implications of the chimpanzee's capacity to discriminate complex relational properties of the environment (e.g., Savage-Rumbaugh, et al., 1980; Gillan, 1981), and with the emergence of instructional control from the language of tacting (especially in

the interactions of the chimpanzees Austin and Sherman; Savage-Rumbaugh, Rumbaugh, & Boysen, 1978; cf. Epstein, Lanza, & Skinner, 1980). The syntheses of complex interactions in such studies have special value because they force all of the assumptions about what counts as verbal to be made explicit: You can't tell a pigeon or a chimpanzee what to do in an experiment; instead, you have to shape every component that will be integrated into the final performance.

The performances of nonhuman organisms will become ever more sophisticated as human investigators provide them with ever more sophisticated environments. Differences will remain, some more obvious than others (e.g., operant control of the vocal apparatus: cf. Chapter 14). For example, Kanzi, an 8-year-old bonobo monkey (*Pan paniscus*), appears capable of sentence comprehension that has so far been beyond the reach of its relative, the chimpanzee (*Pan troglodytes*) and that may be comparable to that of a 2-year-old human child (Savage-Rumbaugh et al., 1993). We've already seen how crucial verbal communities are in the shaping and maintenance of human verbal behavior, so we shouldn't be surprised that the details of verbal contingencies matter. For example, judgments of the nature of the discrimination between requests such as "Get juice from kitchen" or "Take juice to kitchen" (or their ape language equivalents) depend on such contextual features of the requests as whether juice is always present when they're made; if it is, then the discrimination is probably based on the difference between *get from* and *take to*, but if juice is present only given the request to take it to the kitchen, then the discrimination may depend only on whether juice is present when a request has *juice* in it.

Once some features of human language had been demonstrated in the behavior of a chimpanzee or a pigeon or any other nonhuman organism, that feature could no longer be regarded as uniquely human; attention then turned to the definition of language rather than to the experimental analysis of its properties. The issue of grammatical structure, which we'll consider in Chapter 16, was the focus of much controversy. Given these debates, we can't say whether chimpanzees are capable of language; the answer depends too much on how we define language. We certainly can say, however, that their behavior includes some critical components of language (e.g., Savage-Rumbaugh, 1986).

We've seen that verbal behavior includes many components: higher-order classes in naming; correspondences in formal classes; stimulus control in intraverbals and tacts; contingencies in instructional control; symbolic behavior in equivalence classes; discriminations of our own behavior in autoclitic processes. The list is incomplete. To the extent that these processes are related to those of nonverbal behavior, they hint at the origins and evolution of human language. The assumption that its primary function was to direct the behavior of others through instructional control suggests how such control might have emerged and might have been sharpened by the contingencies that operated within human social groups (cf. Jaynes, 1976; Skinner, 1986; Catania, 1991b). We'd do well to recall the constraints on selection. For example, organized complexity can evolve only if it remains advantageous at every stage of selection (cf. Chapter 3). We can then wonder about selective advantages of infant babbling, or the consistent features of those verbalizations of a mother toward an infant that we call *motherese*, or the changes that make it more difficult for adults than children to learn the different phonetic structure of a new language, and so on. Once the social selection of behavior began to operate on verbal behavior, the way was clear for the development of other functions of verbal behavior as derivatives of its primary function. That's where we should seek the foundations of human concepts such as narrative, communication, meaning and truth.

Chapter 16
Psycholinguistics: Language Structure

Three primary terms in the analysis of language have been syntax, *the study of grammatical structure;* semantics, *the study of meaning; and* pragmatics, *the study of the functions of language.* Syntax *can be traced to the Greek* taxis, *arrangement;* semantics *to the Greek* sema, *a sign or thing seen; and* pragmatics *to the Greek* prassein, *to make happen or do.* Pragmatics *is a relative of* practice. Grammar, *through the Greek* graphein, *to scratch or write, and* gramma, *a picture or a writing, is closely related to* graph, program *and* topography.

In this chapter we turn from the functions of verbal behavior to its structure. We can arrange words in sentences, and we can note how different words are similar or dissimilar in meaning. These are the topics of *syntax* and *semantics*. *Syntax* deals with how we organize words in sentences; its concern is grammatical structure. In treating syntax, we'll approach language from the point of view of psycholinguistics, noting how its vocabulary is related to the functional account of Chapters 14 and 15 when appropriate.

After syntax, we'll consider *semantics*, which deals with the problem of meaning. The introduction to verbal behavior questioned traditional concepts of meaning and reference. In this chapter we'll see what can be said about these traditional concepts. In effect, we'll ask what properties of verbal behavior lead us to say that particular words are related in meaning. Psycholinguistics deals with a speaker's vocabulary in terms of the speaker's *lexicon*, the dictionary of words available in the speaker's verbal behavior. We'll examine the structure of the lexicon. These topics, often related, pave the way for our treatment of verbal learning and memory in later chapters. (Linguistics has sometimes included a third topic, *pragmatics*, the uses of language; it corresponds most closely to the functions of language already considered in Chapters 14 and 15.)

A critical precursor of contemporary psycholinguistics was the effort to write programs for computer translation from one language to another. That history included the evolution of computers in Allied efforts to break military codes during World War II (Hodges, 1985) and later applications of mathematics to problems of language structure during post-Sputnik efforts to translate Russian technical materials into English. Early attempts simply to substitute words in one language for their equivalents in another weren't successful for a variety of reasons. For example, many words have multiple equivalents (should *bar* be translated as a noun, either a lever or a place to drink, or as a verb, to stop?), and grammatical distinctions in one language may be absent in another (given that Russian doesn't use articles, how does one decide whether an English translation of a Russian noun should be preceded by *a* or *the* or no article at all?).

One test for language translation programs is to translate a text from one language to another and then to translate the new text back to the original language: If the translation program works, you should get back the same sentence as the one you put in. One illustration of the translation problem, probably apocryphal but cited often (with variations), is the translation to Russian and then back to English of "The spirit is willing but the flesh is weak"; it comes back as "Strong vodka, rotten meat." Another is "Out of sight, out of mind"; it comes back as "Blind maniacs." And if the program generates "The lions leave by the end of summer," its source sentence, though fitting, isn't obvious ("Pride goeth before a fall").

In some respects, our treatment parallels some aspects of the evolution of computer programs in language translation. Such programs had to define explicit procedures for translation, including rules for substitution and transformation and ways to interpret ambiguous terms on the basis of context provided by earlier text. Although the programs revealed serious limitations on computer translation (e.g., Dreyfus, 1992; Winograd,

1980), they also led to more thorough descriptions of the complexities of syntax and semantics. When effects of various features of syntax and semantics were demonstrated in verbal behavior, these features were said to have *psychological reality*. We speak of the psychological reality of various structural properties of language when we can show that those properties make a difference in the behavior of speakers or listeners; we'll explore several examples.

Section A   Syntax: The Grammatical Structure of Language

How are words organized in sentences? We can count or classify and we can discriminate between grammatical and ungrammatical sentences. We can classify grammatical sentences into categories such as active voice, passive voice, past tense and so on. But how do we define the dimensions along which we make these distinctions? Any listing of grammatical sentences would be infinite if we didn't restrict sentence length, and indefinitely large even if we did. And if we produced such a list, we still wouldn't know what made a sentence grammatical. Instead of lists, we need an exhaustive description of kinds of sentences. In the language of psycholinguistics, we'd speak of writing a grammar with a finite number of rules.

We'll review two accounts of the structural regularities of grammatical sentences (Chomsky & Miller, 1963; Catania, 1972). The first describes sentence structures in terms of their *constituents* or components. The second examines the *transformations* that show how one sentence structure is related to others. For example, consider the saying "He who hesitates is lost." When we study how parts of the saying come to be named subjects and predicates or pronouns and verbs, we're dealing with constituents. When we describe its relation to such paraphrases as "He is lost who hesitates," we're dealing with grammatical transformations.

We might have tried to handle grammatical structure in terms of word sequences, as in the analysis of intraverbal behavior. The trouble is that such analyses can't handle relations between words separated by varying numbers of other words. For example, consider "The chimpanzee used sign language" and "The chimpanzee taught by the psychologist used sign language." The words *chimpanzee* and *used* are adjacent in the first sentence but separated by four other words in the second, and yet they're grammatically related in the same way in both sentences.

Another problem with sequences is that common word sequences can occur together in ungrammatical ways ("Haste makes waste not want not") whereas rare sequences may be grammatical ("Sleeping green ideas dream furiously"). The probabilities with which different words follow each other don't tell us anything about the grammaticality of sentences. Even if we resolved that problem, we'd still have the problem of ambiguous sentences. "Running experiments should be encouraged" might be read as recommending more support for research ("Encourage the running of experiments") or more research on exercise ("Encourage experiments on running"). We can't distinguish the two interpretations based on word sequences, because the same words appear in the same order in both readings (it would be more helpful to know whether the sentence was uttered in a laboratory or at a track meet; but that's a matter of function, not structure).

CONSTITUENTS AND PHRASE STRUCTURE

We determine the constituents of sentences by noting how their parts are related. Consider "A word to the wise is sufficient." We can name its constituents: *Word* is a noun, *is* a verb, *sufficient* an adjective, and so on. The relations aren't defined by how close the words are to each other. For example, *is* is more closely tied to *word* than to *wise*, even though *is* is positioned more closely to the latter. The relations among words in sentences have been represented in various ways (e.g., Wundt, 1900). Three representations, sometimes called phrase-structure diagrams, are illustrated in Figure 16-1.

The examples in Figure 16-1 provide names for the constituents. But how do we decide whether a word should be called one type of constituent or another? We can't go by the words alone. We have to look at their relations to other words in the sentence. In other words, we can't classify constituents without also identifying the structure of the sentence.

Consider "He whose laughs last laughs last." *Laughs* appears twice, first as a plural noun and then as a verb; *last* also appears twice, first as a verb and then as an adverb. So what we call *laughs* or *last* depends on the relation of each to other words in the sentence. This poses a problem. We saw earlier that we can't identify a sentence structure without classifying its constituents, but this example shows that we can't classify its constituents without identifying its structure. How then can we ever describe sentence structure? The answer is that the consistencies of sentence structure aren't in particular words or word sequences; instead, they're in various kinds of coordinations among words. We can classify words of a sentence as particular kinds of constituents because we've already learned typical structures (e.g., patterns of agreement between singular and plural nouns and verbs).

We might be tempted to look to the environment as a basis for deciding on sentence structure. But that won't work, because we can name the constituents even of some sentences partly made up of nonsense words.

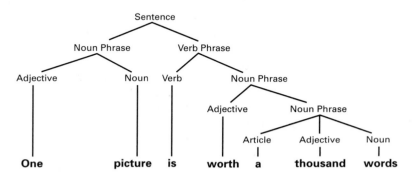

I. BOX DIAGRAM

A word	to	the wise	is sufficient
Article Noun	Preposition	Article Noun	Verb Adjective

II. TREE DIAGRAM

III. BRACKETING DIAGRAM

$$\big(\{[(A)\ (picture)][(to)\ ([the]\ [wise])]\}\{[is][redundant]\}\big)$$

FIGURE 16-1 Three methods for representing constituent structures. Each shows how a sentence can be analyzed into structural units ranging from individual words to phrases. The sentences in the box diagram (I) and the bracketing diagram (III) have equivalent structures. In psycholinguistics, a tree diagram (II) has been the most common representation. Branches come together at places called nodes; e.g., *verb phrase* in the example is a node for *verb* and *noun phrase*.

For example, compare "He who guffs merts" and "She merts his guffs." Even though *guffs* and *merts* aren't standard words, we'd call both verbs in the first sentence but we'd call *merts* a verb and *guffs* a plural noun in the second.

Grammatical classifications of words don't depend on the environment events of which we speak. They depend instead on the sentence structures within which words appear. Verbs, for example, aren't defined as the class of words occasioned by activities; they're defined in terms of conjugation and other grammatical properties. Compare the activity word, *running*, in the sentences "The child is running" and "The child's running is fun to watch." Only the first is a verb. The case is even more obvious when the activity word changes form with changes in grammatical structure, as with *move* in "The chess player moved the knight" versus "The move surprised the other player."

This doesn't mean the environment never affects our judgments of structure. For example, we've already mentioned ambiguous sentences. Consider "Time flies." Typically, as when this is said at a reunion, we call *time* a noun and *flies* a verb. But if it's said in a biology laboratory as an instruction to record how long some insects take to get from one place to another, *time* is a verb and *flies* is a plural noun. (We can also resolve such ambiguities by expanding the structure; consider "Time flies like an arrow" and "Fruit flies like a peach.")

We're left with a paradox. On the one hand are sentences with structures that allow us to name their constituents without knowing the circumstances in which they were uttered ("He who guffs merts"); on the other are sentences with structures that don't allow us to name their constituents unless we know those circumstances ("Time flies"). In other words, any account of grammar that's either exclusively structural or exclusively functional is necessarily incomplete.

In any case, and perhaps more important, our response to a sentence is typically not a matter of naming its constituents or drawing a diagram of its phrase structure. If someone asks you a question, you don't have to say which words are nouns and which are verbs before you answer. Children learn to speak and to understand sentences long before they're formally taught grammar and parts of speech. We must base our analysis of grammatical structure on something more than the capacity to name constituents or diagram structures. We must demonstrate the relation between sentence properties and the speaker's or the listener's behavior. Experiments that seek to demonstrate such relations are said to be concerned with the *psychological reality* of these dimensions of language (Fodor & Bever, 1965).

Figure 16-2 provides an example (Johnson, M., 1965). People were asked to memorize sentences with different phrase structures. When they later recalled the sentences, the probability of errors was greatest at the major breaks in phrase structure. For example, errors were highly likely at the break between

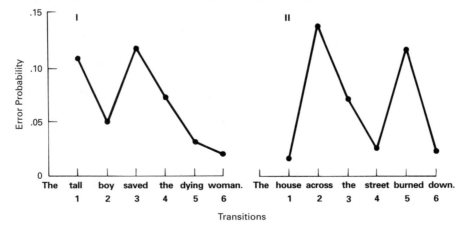

FIGURE 16-2   Probability of an error in sentence recall as a function of word transitions in two sentence types. Sentences of type I are illustrated by *(The1 tall2 boy)3 (saved4 the5 dying6 woman)*, for which error probability was highest at the break between noun phrase and verb phrase (transition **3**). Sentences of type II are illustrated by *((The1 house)2 (across3 the4 street))5 (burned6 down)*, for which error probability was highest at the break within the noun phrase (transition **2**), and next highest at the break between noun phrase and verb phrase (transition **5**). (Adapted from Johnson, 1965, Table 2)

noun phrase and verb phrase in both types of sentences, even though this break occurred at transition 3 in sentences of type I and at transition 5 in sentences of type II. Sentences with different structures were matched for number of words and other properties, so position and other nongrammatical features weren't the basis for the pattern of errors.

In another demonstration of the psychological reality of phrase structure (Fodor & Bever, 1965), listeners wearing earphones heard a sentence in one ear and a click in the other and were asked to locate where in the sentence the click occurred. The same tape recording produced all but the opening words in pairs of sentences such as *(In her hope of marrying)^X (Anna^Y was surely impractical)* and *(Your hope of marrying^X Anna)^Y (was surely impractical)*. The major sentence boundaries were in acoustically identical parts of the recording, so this ruled out effects of inflections or pauses in the reading of the sentence (Garrett, Bever, & Fodor, 1966). Instead of reliably reporting the click in the middle of *Anna*, listeners often reported it displaced in the direction of major sentence boundaries: toward X rather than toward Y in the first sentence and toward Y rather than toward X in the second. Whether we interpret the results as displacements in heard locations of clicks or systematic errors in reports of the locations, they demonstrate effects of sentence structure on behavior. That's the sense in which we're justified in saying that the structures have psychological reality.

TRANSFORMATIONS

Some sentences say different things while others say the same thing in different ways. In making such judgments, we discriminate among relations between sentences. For example, consider "He who hesitates laughs last," "He laughs last who hesitates" and "He who laughs last hesitates." The first two

sentences have something in common that neither has in common with the third. We say that the first two mean the same thing. They differ in word order, but the structural relations among their constituents are the same (e.g., *who* is similarly related to *hesitates* in both sentences). We therefore call the second sentence (but not the third) a transformation of the first.

Transformations describe changes in sentence structure that preserve certain relations among the constituents. When we transform a sentence from active to passive voice (e.g., "The rat pressed the lever" to "The lever was pressed by the rat"), we preserve the subject–object relation among the nouns and the verb. When we speak of the transformations that relate one sentence to another, we're discriminating some structural features the sentences share.

We can distinguish among structures by how they can be transformed. For example, consider "He is hard to understand" and "He is last to understand." They differ only in the adjectives *hard* and *last*. They seem structurally similar, but we can transform the first to "To understand him is hard" but not to "He understands hard"; conversely, we can change the second to "He understands last" but not to "To understand him is last." In the language of psycholinguistics, the sentences are called similar in *surface structure* (the particular order of constituents) but different in *deep structure* (the underlying structural features that distinguish them).

Figure 16-3 illustrates relations among various transformations and their combinations. The base sentence on which the transformations operate is "Haste makes waste." It provides the core material for the transformations and is called the *kernel* (in a stricter interpretation, even this present tense, active voice, positive and declarative sentence is a transformation from the raw material that makes it up: subject noun *haste*, infinitive

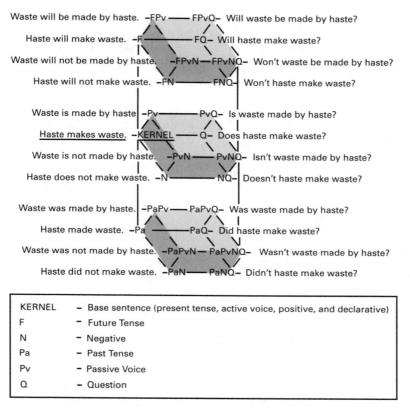

Waste will be made by haste. —FPv ——— FPvQ— Will waste be made by haste?

Haste will make waste. —F ——— FQ— Will haste make waste?

Waste will not be made by haste. —FPvN—FPvNQ— Won't waste be made by haste?

Haste will not make waste. —FN ——— FNQ— Won't haste make waste?

Waste is made by haste —Pv ——— PvQ— Is waste made by haste?

Haste makes waste. —KERNEL —— Q— Does haste make waste?

Waste is not made by haste. —PvN ——— PvNQ— Isn't waste made by haste?

Haste does not make waste. —N ——— NQ— Doesn't haste make waste?

Waste was made by haste. —PaPv ——— PaPvQ— Was waste made by haste?

Haste made waste. —Pa ——— PaQ— Did haste make waste?

Waste was not made by haste. —PaPvN— PaPvNQ— Wasn't waste made by haste?

Haste did not make waste. —PaN ——— PaNQ— Didn't haste make waste?

KERNEL	– Base sentence (present tense, active voice, positive, and declarative)
F	– Future Tense
N	– Negative
Pa	– Past Tense
Pv	– Passive Voice
Q	– Question

FIGURE 16-3 Some transformations of the kernel sentence "Haste makes waste." The middle block shows transformations from declarative to interrogative (statement to question, left-right), from active to passive voice (front-back), and from positive to negative (top-bottom). For each type, the transformation to future tense is shown in the upper block and to past in the lower block. The closeness of the relation between two sentence types depends on how many transformations separate them (e.g., the future "Haste will make waste" is closer to the kernel "Haste makes waste" than to the past passive question "Was waste made by haste?").

verb *to make,* and object noun *waste*). Possible transformations include present to past or future tense, active to passive voice, declarative to interrogative (question), positive (affirmative) to negative, or any combination. These transformations generate 24 unique sentences, and those aren't exhaustive (e.g., consider changes from singular to plural, as in "The cat pauses" and "The cats pause," or in person, as in "I am bored," "He or she is bored" and "They are bored").

What advantage does speaking in terms of transformations have over just labeling sentences according to tense and so on? With transformations, as with constituent structure, we again face the problem of behavioral significance or psychological reality. One interpretation is that the transformations correspond to something listeners or readers actually do when responding to spoken or written sentences. If so, transforming a sentence from one form to another is a kind of behavior. Even though it can't be observed directly, it may be possible to record its duration or its effects on other behavior.

In one demonstration of the psychological

reality of transformations, readers were given two sentence lists (Miller, 1962). Each sentence in list 1 was related by some transformation to one in list 2, and the reader matched list-1 sentences to corresponding list-2 sentences. For example, pairs such as "John warned the small boy" and "The small boy was warned by John" made up two lists differing by kernel to passive transformations. Time per transformation was estimated from the average time per correct match across different pairs of lists. This time was consistently shorter when lists differed by one transformation (kernel to negative, kernel to passive and passive to passive negative) than when they differed by two (kernel to passive negative and negative to passive; the transformation from kernel to passive negative breaks down into kernel to passive or to negative and then to passive negative, but that from negative to passive is indirect, by way of negative to kernel and then kernel to passive). These findings argue for recognizing transformations as properties of verbal behavior, but they don't explain verbal behavior. Describing the structural properties of sentences is the point of grammar, but describing a sentence doesn't say how it was produced or understood nor does its production or understanding require a judgment about its grammaticality.

Hierarchical Organization

Transformations change not just the form of sentences but also how the sentences or their parts can combine with one another. For example, "The canary sang" and "The cat ate the canary" can combine in "The canary that the cat ate sang" or "The cat ate the canary that sang." These structures are called *recursive*, because the addition of segments can recur again and again. With the addition of "The cat grinned," the sentence could become "The canary that the cat that grinned ate sang" or "The cat that ate the canary that sang grinned." Strictly speaking, these sentences are grammatical, even if some of them don't seem quite right. We can expand sentences by adding phrases at their beginning or end, when their structures are called left-recursive or right-recursive, or by adding parts within or around them, when their structures are called self-embedding or self-enveloping. For example, "The canary that the cat ate sang" is embedded in "The music that the canary that the cat ate sang was off key," where it's enveloped by "The music was off key" (whether we regard this structure as self-embedding or self-enveloping depends in large part on whether the conversation started with "I'm glad that the music stopped" or "I'm glad that the cat ate").

The analysis of hierarchical structure is a general problem; we considered it in our discussion of higher-order classes (Chapter 9). Different units enter into different levels of analysis in verbal behavior. Letters and phonemes combine in morphemes and words, which in turn form phrases and sentences, which in turn make up paragraphs and texts, and so on. Individual letters and phonemes can enter into a variety of different narratives, and a given narrative can be told in a variety of different words and sentences. We've been concerned here mainly with the structure of sentences, but we could extend such accounts from sentences to smaller units, such as the phonemes of speech (e.g., Liberman, 1982), or to larger units, such as story plots and other types of extended discourse (e.g., Bower, Black, & Turner, 1979). The properties of sentences have behavioral significance; to the extent that transformations describe what we do when speaking or listening or reading or writing, they correspond to some of the autoclitic processes discussed in Chapter 14. Experiments concerned with the psychological reality of constituent and transformational structure illustrate how the behavioral effects of these dimensions of syntax can be studied.

Section B   **Semantics: The Meaning of Verbal Units**

To study semantics is to grapple with the problem of meaning. Our treatment of verbal behavior made the point that traditional vocabularies of meaning and reference can mislead. Part of the problem is that the production of verbal behavior by a speaker or writer must be distinguished from its comprehension by a listener or reader (meaning what you say is different from understanding what you mean when you say it). The ordinary course of language development creates correspondences between language production and language comprehension, but we mustn't take them for granted. For example, comprehension was independent of production in the behavior of an 8-year-old boy who understood spoken English but couldn't speak because of a congenital organic defect (Lenneberg, 1962).

Our treatment of semantics will stress comprehension: What happens when someone is said to understand a word or a sentence? Let's begin with an experiment in which listeners heard a passage of text (e.g., an account of Galileo and the invention of the telescope), and were then asked whether a new sentence was one that had been in the passage (Sachs, 1967). The new sentence was either the same as the one in the passage (base sentence) or it differed in one of three ways: a change in word order that didn't affect grammatical structure (formal change); a change in grammatical voice (active to passive change); or a change in meaning (semantic change). The new sentence was presented either right after the original one in the passage or after 80 or 160 syllables of

additional text. The passages and base sentences varied across different presentations and listeners. Examples of sentences used with the passage about Galileo are the following:

Base sentence:	He sent a letter about it to Galileo, the great Italian scientist.
Formal change:	He sent Galileo, the great Italian scientist, a letter about it.
Active to passive:	A letter about it was sent to Galileo, the great Italian scientist.
Semantic change:	Galileo, the great Italian scientist, sent him a letter about it.

When the new sentence immediately followed the original one, listeners identified it as either identical or changed with better than 80% accuracy. When it was presented after 80 or 160 syllables of intervening text, accuracy decreased for all sentence types, but it stayed greater than 75% for semantically changed sentences whereas it dropped toward chance levels for the other types. In other words, listeners were likely to recognize a sentence as different only if its meaning had changed; as long as the meaning remained the same, they didn't notice formal or active to passive changes. Thus, the listeners weren't remembering words or word orders. They were remembering something more fundamental: the *gist* of the sentence, or whatever it is that sentences have in common when we say they mean the same thing.

The finding that listeners are more likely to remember semantic structure than specific words or sentences is robust (Bartlett, 1932; Fillenbaum, 1966). One study gave listeners related sentences such as "The ants were in the kitchen" and "The ants ate the sweet jelly" (Bransford & Franks, 1971). Later the listeners heard a mix of the original and new sentences and for each were asked to rate their confidence that they'd heard it before. Some new ones combined original sentences, as in "The ants in the kitchen ate the sweet jelly." The listeners were usually more confident that they'd already heard the new combined sentences than that they'd heard the simpler ones that had actually been presented. They'd learned something more abstract than particular words or sentences.

These findings should remind us of the intimate relation between semantics and syntax. When we examined transformations, we spoke of the concept of deep structure; it's the name for those properties of a sentence that remain constant over various transformations. What we hold constant when we change the syntactic structure of a sentence is its semantic structure.

THE MEASUREMENT OF MEANING

So far we've mainly considered sentences, but in semantics more attention has usually been given to individual words. What determines what a word means? Word associations were the basis for some attempts to measure meaning (Galton, 1879; cf. Chapter 14). If listeners produced longer and more varied lists of words in response to one word than another, the first word was said to be more meaningful than the second. In addition, it was assumed that words closely related in meaning would occasion overlapping lists of associates. For example, common associations to both *infant* and *baby* might include *crib* and *bottle* but probably none of these would be responses to *guitar*. The different degrees of overlap among the associates are consistent with what we already know: *Infant* and *baby* are closer in meaning than either is to *guitar*.

In word associations, concrete nouns like *leg* or *book* or *road* are likely to occasion more

responses than prepositions like *of* or *to* or *at*. Given that responses may be occasioned even by nonsense words, associations can be used to assess the meaningfulness of such words relative to each other and to standard vocabulary words (e.g., Glaze, 1928).

Word associations can be ambiguous. For example, if *night* occasions *day*, *morning*, *sun* and *moon*, are the later words responses to preceding ones or to the stimulus word itself? In this instance, we might guess that *sun* was occasioned more by *day* and *morning* than by *night*, but it's unclear whether *moon* was occasioned more by *night* or by *sun* or by *morning* (which shares three letters with it). Probably all contributed. We might want to see what each word occasions when it serves separately as a stimulus word.

The *semantic differential* was one attempt to measure meaning without such ambiguities (Osgood, Suci, & Tannenbaum, 1957). Words were rated along dimensions like *happy–sad*, *hard–soft* and *slow–fast*. Similarities among ratings were then determined by a statistical procedure, factor analysis, which created a space within which words could be placed. Words close together in this space were said to be more alike in meaning than ones far apart. Words like *good*, *beautiful*, *clean* and *pleasant* clustered together, distant from other clusters such as *bad*, *foul*, *dirty* and *ugly*. The semantic differential was intended to deal with any word in the lexicon. More recent rating methods concentrate on words in specific categories, such as emotions or probabilities (e.g., Reyna, 1981). Each method describes semantic relations among words, so meaning could be defined as just the relations measured by these methods, whatever their basis.

But such definitions leave us with little to say about the behavioral significance of meanings. Meanings aren't properties of words themselves; they're properties of our responses to them. For example, if you repeat a familiar word like your own name over and over, you may find that it loses its meaning; this implies that some response to it drops out after several repetitions. A red traffic light means *stop* and a green one means *go*, but when you stop on red and go on green, you're responding to red and green and not to their meanings. Written words in a language that no one understands have no meaning, and when we say a word has many meanings (as in *bat* in a belfry and *bat* at a baseball game), its meaning changes only in the sense that we respond differently to it in its different contexts.

If meaning is a feature of verbal behavior, then, as with syntactic structures, we should be able to measure some of its properties. For example, we might examine how different meanings affect the latencies of responses to them. In one experiment with this rationale (Collins & Quillian, 1969), readers judged whether sentences were true or false by pressing one of two buttons. Sentences were constructed from a hierarchy of semantic categories defined by sets of relevant properties. Figure 16-4 shows an example.

The assumption is that both distinctive properties and membership in the next higher class define class membership. For example, *canary* is defined by the properties *can sing* and *is yellow* and by membership in the class *bird*. The time taken to judge that a sentence is true should then depend on how far from the class a property is located. For example, given the class *canary* and the sentences "A canary can sing," "A canary has feathers" and "A canary breathes," judgment should be quickest for the first sentence and slowest for the last. In the first, the property *can sing* is characteristic of canaries; in the second, *has feathers* is characteristic of being a bird, which in turn is a property of canaries; in the third, *breathes* is characteristic of being an animal, which in turn is a property of being a bird, which in turn is a property of canaries. The structure allows for cases in which the property is incompatible with those defining the higher-level class; for example, *can't fly* is a property of penguins, so judging whether "Penguins can't fly" is true doesn't depend on first judging whether penguins are birds.

Judgment times in the experiment were consistent with hierarchical structures like those shown in Figure 16-4. Judging a sentence true took longer after sentences like "A canary eats" than after sentences like "A canary is yellow." But hierarchical structure isn't the only possible source of differences in judgment times, which may also be affected by other variables such as the sizes of

FIGURE 16-4 A hypothetical semantic structure. Each class is characterized by properties that define its members. Just a sample of properties is shown for each. (Adapted from Collins & Quillian, 1969, Figure 1)

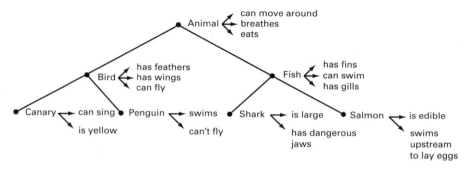

the different classes (e.g., Landauer & Meyer, 1972).

Semantics involves more than words themselves; it involves correspondences between words and classes of stimuli. When these classes don't have well-defined boundaries, they're examples of *probabilistic stimulus classes* (also called *fuzzy sets*; cf. natural concepts in Chapter 7). In such classes, each member contains some subset of features but none is common to all members; the number of features in the subset varies from one class member to another (cf. Rosch, 1973; Mervis & Rosch, 1981). Class members have family resemblances, and membership may be defined by reference to a *prototype*, a typical member of the class. A prototype is described by a weighted average of all the features of all the members of the class. For example, feathers are weighted more heavily than webbed feet among birds because more birds have feathers than have webbed feet. Thus, a robin is more prototypical than a duck because it shares more features with other birds. As these examples show, the analysis of semantic structure doesn't explain probabilistic stimulus classes; it defines some of their properties.

METAPHOR

Metaphor demonstrates another aspect of semantic structure. In Chapter 14, it illustrated the extension of verbal behavior to new events. Once particular metaphors become effective within a verbal community, they're likely to evolve and interact and spread to a variety of situations. In Chapter 14 we noted an example in the case of language itself: We speak of language in the metaphor of communicating ideas. According to this metaphor, ideas and meanings are objects placed into words and then delivered to someone else (Lakoff & Johnson, 1980;

Reddy, 1979). We *put our ideas into words*; we *have* ideas and *get them across to others*; our words *carry meaning* or are *empty*; our sentences *contain* or are *filled with* ideas; ideas can be *grasped* or *dropped* or *kicked around*; and so on. As we've seen, this metaphor is so well established that it's difficult to speak of language in other ways.

Other common systems of metaphors in our culture are those of time as money (e.g., we *spend* time or *save* it, and ask whether something is *worth* our time); of understanding as seeing (e.g., we *get the picture* or *look at things differently*, and describe arguments as *clear* or *opaque*); and of more as up and less as down (e.g., prices can *rise* or *fall*, and someone can be *under*age or *over*-charged).

Systems of metaphors may be coordinated with each other. For example, saying that a theoretical argument can be demolished by attacking its weak points combines the metaphor of discussion as war (arguments are *marshalled* or *undermined* or *shot down*, positions are *defended* or *given up*, points are *won* or *lost*) with that of theory as a building (theories are *constructed*, rest on *solid* or *shaky foundations*, can be *supported* or *buttressed*, and *stand* or *fall*). On the other hand, systems of metaphors needn't be consistent. For example, the metaphor of discussion as war may only occasionally make contact with that of discussion as exploration (issues are *gone over in depth* and *at different levels* and *from different approaches*, the *ground is covered*, the speakers *map out their territories* and make *direct* or *roundabout* arguments).

Metaphor is a pervasive property of language. Children learn it readily and adults can't ignore it (Glucksberg, Gildea, & Bookin, 1982; Winner, 1979). In semantic judgment tasks, reaction times are often shorter for metaphorical than for literal usages (Foss, 1988). The surprise of puns and other forms of verbal humor typically comes from overly literal interpretations of standard usages (for example, consider the projectionist at a slide show who, on hearing "May I have the next slide?" doesn't show it but instead pulls it out of the projector and runs up to the front of the room to hand it to the speaker). Metaphor isn't just the stuff of poetry; it's a fundamental aspect of verbal behavior.

The phenomenon of metaphor tempts us to talk about abstract properties captured by words. Yet the most important feature of metaphor is that it allows us to deal with the abstract in terms of the concrete. For example, the language of abstract dimensions like good-bad or happy-sad becomes that of a more accessible dimension, up-down (from raised spirits and the heights of cloud nine to lowered expectations and the depths of depression). Hardly any dimension can be more abstract than time, but through metaphor it becomes a concrete spatial one: Tomorrow versus yesterday becomes in-front-of versus in-back-of. We're so used to saying our past is *behind us* and our future is *before us* that it's hard to imagine taking an about-face so that the future is in back and the past lies ahead; our time line turns with us.

The ubiquity of metaphor is also evident in the etymologies that introduce each chapter. Much of our technical vocabulary evolved metaphorically from everyday sources, and much of the everyday language that applies to our own behavior also has its origins in metaphorical usages (cf. Skinner, 1989b). These etymologies demonstrate some of the very concrete origins of our fundamental concepts. The creative aspect of metaphor, in other words, is in making the abstract substantial, specific and solid or, to mix more metaphors, in bringing it down to earth.

We haven't explicitly defined *meaning* or *metaphor*. As in other cases, our failure to do so doesn't imply that the terms are meaningless. An independent specification of the stimulus isn't essential to identifying discriminative relations, and an independent specification of verbal classes isn't essential to identifying the relations between words and events that we call meanings. We speak of classes of responses in terms of operants and classes of stimuli in terms of concepts. Words can function either as responses or as stimuli, so it's reasonable that we speak of semantic classes of words in terms of meanings.

Section C   **Some Properties of Language**

Properties assumed to be characteristic of all human languages have been called *language universals*. Various grammatical relations have been proposed as such universals (e.g., Greenberg, 1966). For example, it's been argued that utterances in all human languages have subject–predicate structure, distinguish singular from plural and are limited in the transformations that can operate on embedded structures. These properties may depend as much on the conditions under which humans speak as on biological constraints on the kinds of sentences they can produce. The subject–predicate relation is one criterion for calling an utterance a sentence, so it excludes by definition utterances without subject or predicate (e.g., *Hello, Ouch!, Oh?* and *Aha!*). Differences between single objects and collections are presumably important in all human environments and to that extent determine the distinction between singular and plural; that distinction appears in all languages, but in some it's expressed by vocabulary rather than grammar (as in *one book, two book, many book*; cf. Japanese). And limits on levels of embedded phrases may have arisen as derivatives of aspects of remembering such as the limited span of immediate memory (see Chapter 19).

The inverse of the issue of language universals is that of *language relativity*. Much has been made of the many Eskimo names for snow, but the data don't compare with the claims (Pullum, 1991); anyway, skiers have many names for snow, too. It shouldn't surprise us that vocabularies are consistent with functionally important classes of events in different language communities. Language relativity gets more interesting when it seems to involve allowable grammatical relations rather than vocabulary categories. For example, languages in which nouns and verbs are exchangeable (thought versus thinking, memory versus remembering) may lead to different treatments of events and actions than those in which they're not.

Chinese grammar doesn't include convenient forms of the counterfactual conditional (*if A hadn't occurred then B would have*, or *if not A then B*) whereas English grammar does; on the other hand, English grammar doesn't include convenient forms of the exclusive and the nonexclusive *or* (*A or B but not both* versus *A or B or both*) whereas Chinese grammar does. Mastery of these two logical forms of *or* undoubtedly proceeds differently in these two language communities (cf. Braine & Rumain, 1981). Language differences are obvious when they involve formal properties, as in the artificial languages of symbolic logic, calculus and computer programming. To the extent that language is behavior, particular languages will inevitably have different functional properties. Language relativity reminds us that we must deal with each language in the context of the environment within which it was shaped.

LANGUAGE DEVELOPMENT

Children who grow up in Italy speak Italian, and those who grow up in Brazil speak Portuguese. Clearly they each learn the specific grammars and vocabularies of their native languages, and most children become fluent in them long before they begin formal education. Although there are many descriptions of language development in children, there's still much to learn about the factors critical to that development (e.g., Brown, 1973; Moerk, 1992; de Villiers & de Villiers, 1978). One question is whether general properties of human language that don't have to be learned underlie the details of particular languages. The extent to which structural properties of human language are biologically constrained has been controversial, even though the participants in the controversy typically have not been biologists (Andresen, 1990; Chomsky, 1959; Pinker, 1994; Skinner, 1957).

Between the ages of 1 and 6 years, children increase their vocabularies at an average rate of five to eight words per day; by the age of 6, a child is likely to have a productive vocabulary of thousands of words (Wagner, 1985; cf. Horne & Lowe, 1996). Many function words (e.g., *more, bye-bye, allgone*) are included along with common nouns (e.g., *mama, milk, chair*) in the early vocabulary. During the same ages, the child's syntax progresses from single-word utterances to those of two words or more, sometimes described as roughly telegraphic (e.g., *stove hot, daddy go car*), and then to constructions that more and more closely approximate the syntax of adult speech. Problems of data collection range from those of recording and sampling children's speech at different ages to those of interpreting the speech phonetically, semantically and syntactically (e.g., a young child's *more* probably has the sense of *give me* and not that of expressing a quantity; Moore & Frye, 1986).

Among the controversial issues is the extent to which consequences play a role in the child's acquisition of language, and in particular in the child's acquisition of grammatical structure. In appeals to the *poverty of the stimulus*, some have argued that the child's verbal environment isn't rich enough to support language acquisition, and therefore that some structural features of language are "prewired," in the sense that they'll emerge even in the absence of relevant contingencies (Culicover, 1992). Others have examined exchanges between parents and children, and have argued instead that contingencies play an indispensable role (Moerk, 1980, 1983; Whitehurst & Valdez-Menchaca, 1988).

Some distinctions are crucial in evaluating the different sides of these arguments. Those concerned with the poverty of the stimulus in the development of grammatical structure focus on the child's comprehension and production of grammatical forms. That verbal behavior is contingency-shaped, and must not be confused with the verbally governed behavior of someone who later learns to discriminate grammatical from ungrammatical constructions, to name sentence types and their components, and so on. Furthermore, the issue is the kind of verbal behavior available in the child's environment and not its quantity.

The case for the poverty of the stimulus argues that verbal environments don't include the negative or ungrammatical instances that should be there in support of claims that a child's grammatical behavior is shaped through natural contingencies (in the sense that such instances don't occur in the speech that children hear, or in the sense that such instances are not corrected when the child makes them, or in both senses). For example, if the muppet who is laughing is a frog, the child may hear questions in the form "Is the muppet who is laughing a frog?" but will not hear them in the form "Is the muppet who laughing is a frog?" (Crain, 1991). When the child then asks questions, they are in the former and grammatical form

and rarely if ever in the latter and ungrammatical one. What keeps the child from making the latter kind of error? One reply is that negative instances are not necessary for all kinds of learning (e.g., consider the combination of behavior classes in adduction); for example, our account of the echoic shaping of phonetic structure did not demand an environment that included nonnative as well as native speech sounds. Another reply is that a sample of a child's replies in a laboratory study does not exhibit the verbal history that led to the competencies that are revealed by that study.

The evidence on the poverty of the stimulus goes both ways (e.g., Moerk, 1992), but suppose for the sake of argument that the case had been made for grammatical universals by demonstrations that children can't learn certain types of sentence structures, or at least that they learn some types much more easily than others (cf. Pinker, 1984). Those universals would still involve structural rather than functional limitations, and it might even be appropriate to regard them as spandrels (Gould & Lewontin, 1979; cf. Chapter 3). Human language has many of the properties of other evolved systems (Pinker & Bloom, 1990), but it's not clear that it's been around long enough for the selection of those kinds of grammatical constraints.

Just as anatomical features of birds and bats determine the different ways they fly, special characteristics of our species may determine the structure of human language and how it develops. If we show that human language is limited in its structural properties or in how the structure develops, functional questions still remain about the circumstances in which verbal behavior occurs. The anatomical analogy remains valid: An account of the different properties of flight in birds and bats doesn't bear on where or when they take off or land; so too an account of language structure doesn't bear on when we speak or what we talk about.

Another part of the issue is the appropriate level of analysis for verbal classes. The child must learn not only individual phonemes and words and sentences but also larger units such as phonetic and semantic and syntactic structures. Furthermore, the consequences of verbal behavior are often subtle and probably aren't ones that need to be explicitly arranged. Contrived reinforcers such as praise or candies may be less likely to be effective than such natural consequences of verbal behavior as hearing yourself say something similar to what you've heard others say, or getting something you've asked for, or hearing someone else say something relevant to something you've just said, and so on (but the contrived reinforcers are better than none at all). With regard to the question of whether language is innate or learned, the reasonable conclusion is that both phylogeny and ontogeny contribute.

If the significant consequences of verbal behavior range from such direct outcomes as getting something you've asked for to such indirect ones as hearing a remark relevant to something you've just said, these all contribute to the shaping of verbal behavior. If among these consequences we include the correspondences between sounds one has heard and sounds one has produced oneself, as in the ontogenic shaping of echoic behavior (Chapter 14), it's not too great a leap to extend such correspondences from phonemic to semantic and syntactic properties of verbal behavior. It's presumably important to discover that the relations among words and between words and things in our own behavior correspond to those relations in the behavior of others. In this view, by engaging in verbal behavior the verbal community provides the models

the correspondence with which shapes and maintains the consistency of the child's verbal behavior.

Even if it were proved that children don't have to learn all the details of grammar because some are built in, that wouldn't mean that there aren't lots of other things about verbal behavior that they'll still have to learn. In fact, there's plenty of evidence that rich verbal environments in which parents spend lots of time interacting verbally with their children can make vast and lasting differences in their verbal competence (Hart & Risley, 1980, 1995; Moerk, 1992). Contingencies matter. The effects, described as meaningful differences in the everyday experience of young American children, appear in vocabulary growth rate, school performance and IQ scores. What else that has emerged from the analysis of behavior could have greater relevance?

Deixis

One significant feature of the development of a child's language is the evolution of a *deictic* vocabulary; deictic terms are occasioned not by intrinsic properties of events or objects but rather by their relation to the speaker and listener (de Villiers & de Villiers, 1974; Wales, 1986). Examples are *here* versus *there*, *this* versus *that* and *in front of* versus *behind*. In each case, the appropriate term depends on where one is located; for example, when you're cooking, the kitchen is *this* room and the dining room is *that* one; but when you're eating, the terms are reversed.

The acquisition of deixis follows closely upon that of other relational vocabularies (e.g., *big* and *little*, which involve relative rather than absolute size; the child is big relative to a pet frog but little relative to an adult). In combination with pronouns, the functions of deictic terms in language are analogous to those of variables in algebra; we can speak of things even if we can't name them (*what's this?*, *who was there?*, *is that it?*; cf. Clark & Sengul, 1979).

A special case of the deictic vocabulary is the personal pronouns (e.g., Charney, 1980; Huxley, 1970). Children generally learn *it* before *me* and *you*, and the distinction between first and second person (*me, you*) emerges before distinctions within those classes (*I, me, my, mine* and *you, your, yours*). But *I* and *me* aren't learned like one's name; one is called *you* rather than *I* or *me* when spoken to. How then do children come to say *I* and *me* appropriately when they become speakers instead of listeners?

It's hard to observe the conditions under which this feature of language develops. Personal pronouns are mastered by almost all children (Chiat, 1982). We can describe how the mastery evolves, but we don't know enough of its details to say what aspects of the child's verbal environment are crucial to that evolution. Given the great variability in the ways parents interact with their children, the properties that lead to deixis are probably common to human environments in general.

Personal pronouns and the deictic vocabulary involve discriminations among events as they are related to oneself, and so they're presumably related closely to the discriminations of one's own behavior that we discussed in the context of autoclitic processes and the concept of self-awareness (Damon & Hart, 1982; see also Chapters 13 and 14). Such discriminations are often expressed in mental language, as in the various ways of describing the difference between having forgotten something and never having known it (cf. Skinner, 1945). We can describe how and when this language develops (e.g., Wellman, 1990), but we still have little to say about how it can be effectively taught. These features of language development suggest,

however, that human language and human self-awareness are inextricably related.

Productivity

Another important feature of language is its novelty; when we write a sentence, it's likely to differ from any other we've written before. This feature of language is called *productivity* (language shares this property with nonverbal behavior). We can deal with novelty in terms of features that the new sentence shares with earlier ones; novel productions involve new combinations of already established syntactic and semantic classes (cf. adduction in Chapter 9 and Esper, 1973).

An illustration is provided by Berko (1958; cf. Catania & Cerutti, 1986). Children of ages from 4 to 7 years read illustrated sequences of sentences that introduced a nonsense word; the last sentence was incomplete and prompted a different grammatical form of the nonsense word. For example, a sequence that prompted a plural was: "This is a wug. Now there is another one. There are two of them. There are two _____." The regular plural in spoken English is formed by -z (as in *dogs*), by -s (as in *cats*) or by -es (as in *houses*), depending on the sound with which the spoken singular ends (e.g., -z after voiced endings such as *b, d, v*; and -s after voiceless endings such as *p, t, f*). The children usually produced standard plurals with -z and -s (e.g., most children responded *wugz* to the sample sequence above). But only about a third gave the -es plural to novel words like *tass* and *gutch* and *nizz* even though almost all of them gave *glasses* as the plural of *glass*. Thus, aspects of the standard English plural develop successively. Children first learn specific words and word sequences, but then begin to master larger units such as classes of plurals.

Other evidence that language acquisition is a progression from particular words to simple word groupings and then to syntactic and semantic structures of increasing complexity is in the usage of irregular verbs, such as *go, come* and *break* (Kuczaj, 1977). Among young children, regular but nonstandard past-tense forms are common: *goed, comed, breaked*. Children don't always start with the regular forms, however. Often, the child first learns the standard but irregular forms as individual words: *went, came, broke*. After the child learns some standard regular past-tense forms, the irregular forms are displaced by the regular but nonstandard ones, even though the irregular forms had been part of the child's vocabulary for some time. Months or years later, the standard irregular forms reappear and become permanent components of the child's verbal behavior. The progression from standard irregular to nonstandard regular and back to standard irregular past-tense forms is consistent with a progression from the mastery of individual words through a stereotyped syntactic form to the varied structure of fluent language.

These examples have mainly involved syntactic structure, but the same points apply to the development of semantic structure. Events in a novel context can occasion novel grammatical utterances (as when a child gives the standard plural of a nonsense word), but utterances can also be semantically new (as when *drinkfruit* is coined as a name for a watermelon). We speak of such cases in terms of metaphor or analogy (Esper, 1973; Jaynes, 1976). Metaphor is effective only to the extent that relations among events in the world correspond to the relations discussed here as examples of semantic structure. If grammar is a description of relations among syntactic structures, then metaphor is the grammar of semantics.

Chapter 17
Verbal Learning and Transfer

A. Verbal Learning Procedures
Serial Learning
Paired-Associates Learning
Free Recall
Verbal Discrimination
Verbal Recognition: A Special Case of Verbal
Discrimination
Summary

B. Transfer
Positive and Negative Transfer
Proaction and Retroaction
Extensions to Nonverbal Procedures
Summary

Verbal learning procedures include serial and paired-associates learning, free recall and the special case of verbal discrimination called verbal recognition. Verbal transfer involves ways in which different verbal learning tasks affect each other. Most of these terms have been related to words considered elsewhere: associates *to* consequence; *recall* to *class;* recognition *to* cognition; *and* transfer *to* differentiation. Serial, *through the Latin* serere, *to arrange or attach, is related to* series, sort *and, perhaps as an arrangement of words,* sermon.

The area traditionally called verbal learning is concerned with what happens as we learn word sequences, word combinations and word contexts. Its literature is extensive. In this chapter, we'll examine four major classes of verbal-learning procedures: serial learning, paired-associates learning, free recall and verbal discrimination (including verbal recognition as a special case). We'll illustrate each class of procedures with a sample of some characteristic findings and some experimental and theoretical issues generated by it. After this survey, we'll examine some problems of the transfer of learning: How does learning one set of verbal materials affect the learning of other materials? In positive transfer, the learning of the first set enhances that of the second; in negative transfer, the learning of the first set retards that of the second.

Section A   Verbal Learning Procedures

In a typical verbal learning procedure, we present verbal stimuli to the learner and then record verbal responses. We take a lot for granted in such arrangements. If we described them simply in terms of verbal discriminative stimuli and differentiated verbal responses, we'd omit significant features. For example, the learner's performance is only rarely generated by differential consequences; instead, it's usually generated by giving instructions. Furthermore, the consequences may be hard to specify. The experimenter designates responses as correct and incorrect or right and wrong. When the learner responds, the experimenter may say "right" or "wrong" or the learner may simply be shown the item designated as correct. These procedures are sometimes said to provide the learner with *feedback* or with *knowledge of results*. It's tempting to assume that telling or showing a learner that a response was correct is a reinforcing consequence, but such feedback might function only as an instruction (i.e., telling the learner that a response was correct is like saying, "Respond the same way next time"). Thus, it may be misleading to speak of the reinforcing properties of being correct and the punishing properties of being incorrect.

Other circumstances may affect the learner's behavior. For example, if an experiment ends as soon as a list is learned, the consequences of finishing early will differ for a learner satisfying a course requirement than for one whose pay depends on time spent learning the list. These and other experimental details that determine what the learner does are sometimes called *demand characteristics* (Orne, 1962). In this chapter we'll mainly deal with verbal stimuli and verbal responses; we won't have much to say about the consequences of verbal learning. But even if we can't specify consequences, we can usually assume that they're fairly uniform throughout an experiment.

Verbal learning materials have ranged from simple items such as numbers and letters through nonsense syllables and words to more complex materials such as sentences and extended texts. These materials are discussed in the context of specific experiments. Here we'll only distinguish between *nominal stimuli* and *functional stimuli* (cf. the nominal or descriptive and the functional classes in Chapter 7). Nominal stimuli are the verbal items as defined by the experimenter; func-tional stimuli are the features that occasion the learner's response (cf. attention in Chapter 8). For example, if the stimulus items in a learning task are the three-letter sequences OED, EAB and PBK but the learner attends only to the first letter of each, then the three-letter sequences are nominal stimuli and the first letters of each are functional stimuli.

Verbal learning experiments use verbal stimuli in both written and vocal modes, but written stimuli predominated in the early days of verbal learning research. The advantages of written stimuli are that they're uniform, easily described and can be presented at well-defined rates and durations.

An early device for presenting verbal stimuli was the memory drum, illustrated in Figure 17-1. Words were typed or printed on a paper loop and the roller advanced each item to the window at a controlled rate. In contemporary research, computer displays have displaced the memory drum. In early research, vocal verbal stimuli were less favored because it was harder to control their

FIGURE 17-1 A memory drum. Words on a paper tape are shown in the window for specified durations. For example, the items of a serial list might be presented repeatedly for 3 s each. The learner might be instructed to anticipate each item before it appears or to recite the entire list at the end of each complete presentation.

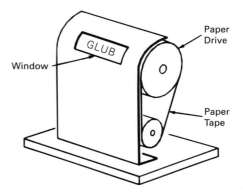

uniformity and rate of presentation. For example, an experimenter who read a list to different learners might change the inflection or loudness of words over successive readings. Tape recording eliminated this problem, and contemporary research uses either written or vocal verbal stimuli, depending on the suitability of one or the other to a particular experiment. Similarly, the choice of written or vocal responses varies with experimental requirements. Learners can usually respond more quickly vocally than in writing, but the vocal response must be recorded whereas the written response is its own record.

Table 17-1 summarizes the major classes of verbal learning procedures. As its name implies, *serial learning* is the learning of a sequence of verbal items, as when a child learns to count or to recite the days of the

week. A sequence can be learned through *serial recall* or *serial anticipation*. For example, suppose we try to teach someone the first 10 presidents of the United States through serial recall. We show each name briefly and the learner tries to recite the entire list in proper order only after all 10 have appeared; we repeat the list until the learner gives one or more correct repetitions. Alternatively, in serial anticipation, as each name appears the learner tries to say which will appear next (e.g., on seeing *Jefferson*, saying "Madison," and then on seeing *Madison*, saying "Monroe," and so on); we also repeat this list until the learner gives some number of correct repetitions. Once the list is learned, we might ask the learner questions about the positions of names in the list, such as "Who was the ninth president?" (Harrison), "Which president was Tyler?" (tenth) or "Which presi-

TABLE 17-1   Classes of Verbal Learning Procedures

NAME	DESCRIPTION	EXAMPLES
Serial learning	The items of a verbal sequence are learned in order.	Learning to recite the alphabet or the months of the year; learning a poem
Paired-associates learning	Each of several verbal stimuli occasions a different verbal response; the order of items may vary.	Given a country, naming its capital; given words in one language, providing equivalent words in another
Free recall	The items in a list are named without regard to order.	Naming the teams in a baseball or football league; naming the players on a given team
Verbal discrimination	Responses are occasioned by the classes within which verbal stimuli fall; in other words, a discrimination in which the stimulus dimension is verbal.	Identifying the nouns in a paragraph of text; given names on cards, sorting the cards into one stack of female names and another of male names
Verbal recognition	A special case of verbal discrimination. The property defining the discriminated class is whether the verbal item appeared in a specified earlier list or context.	Given a list, picking out the names of people you know; distinguishing between old and new technical terms while reading a text

dent came before Van Buren?" (Jackson). A well-learned serial list, the alphabet, illustrates the roles of context and position. We can all recite the alphabet and can probably quickly say which letter precedes or follows any other, but without counting how easy is it to give the eleventh letter or the numerical position of *S*?

Paired-associates learning generates correspondences between items on two lists, as in learning the dates of historical events or the equivalents in one language of words in another language. Each verbal stimulus sets the occasion for a verbal response. For example, if the pairs to be learned are titles and authors, the sequence might be as follows:

> *Don Quixote*
> *Don Quixote*—Cervantes
> *Candide*
> *Candide*—Voltaire
> *Moby-Dick*
> *Moby-Dick*—Melville
> *Faust*
> *Faust*—Goethe

Each title appears alone for a few seconds. Whatever the learner's response, it's then accompanied by its author. The full set is repeated, perhaps with the order changed, until the learner correctly names each author before the name appears. Questions can then be asked about effects of changing items or reversing stimuli and responses. Paired-associates experiments, however, don't typically use familiar items and pairings; they're more likely to use nonsense syllables or arbitrary combinations.

In *free recall*, the learner is asked to name, in any order, items presented earlier, as when you're asked to say what was on a misplaced shopping list or what questions were on a test. In verbal learning studies, the list consists of verbal items, but the procedure is like recall of nonverbal stimuli, as when a witness names those present at the scene of a crime; whether the stimuli are verbal or nonverbal, the responses in both cases are verbal.

Verbal discrimination is simply discrimination along some verbal dimension of stimuli, as when a child learns to distinguish vowels from consonants or nouns from verbs or grammatical sentences from ungrammatical sentences. Pairs of items are presented, and the learner chooses one item of each pair by naming it, pointing to it or perhaps pressing a left or a right button. After each pair, the learner is informed which is correct. Two examples follow, with italics indicating correct items:

JEG-*VOB*	*J*XF-MCF
ZID-*FEP*	QMH-*DXJ*
BEW-DAX	FPW-*ZJC*
SEF-*PIB*	DHJ-ZGX
BUV-HIF	*J*FM-GZB

In the left sequence, the designation of correct items is arbitrary; in the right, the correct item of each pair is the one with the letter *J*. An alternative procedure is to present items one at a time, with the learner indicating whether each item is in the designated class (e.g., by "yes" or "no"). As with other procedures, presentations continue until the learner meets some criterion.

One type of verbal discrimination is that between new and old items, as when a student in a language course distinguishes words already learned from new ones. This is called *verbal recognition*. The learner is given an initial list. Later, the learner is given another list with both new items and items from the first list. The learner must identify (recognize) the items from the first list. Except that it uses verbal materials, verbal recognition is similar to familiar instances of recognition (e.g., as in recognizing friends in a group of people or in recognizing places you've visited). We now consider each type of verbal-learning procedure in more detail.

SERIAL LEARNING

Verbal-learning procedures experimentally realized the associationist principles developed by such philosophers as David Hume and James Mill. The associationists had advocated that human thought was based upon the association of ideas. Ideas were said to become connected or associated in various ways (e.g., through similarity, common elements, contrast) but especially through contiguity in space or time. Later, with the beginnings of modern chemistry, analogies were drawn between the formation of associations and the chemical combinations of atoms into molecules. Hermann Ebbinghaus, a German investigator, was in effect the founder of research on remembering, using himself as the experimental subject. He saw the possibility of measuring the formation of arbitrary associations (Ebbinghaus, 1885), and invented the nonsense syllable as an item that hadn't yet acquired verbal functions and therefore wouldn't be contaminated by existing associations (but, as learned later, nonsense syllables did vary in meaningfulness, as measured by word-association procedures; Glaze, 1928).

The typical nonsense syllable was a three-letter consonant-vowel-consonant sequence (a *CVC trigram*). Ebbinghaus constructed many such trigrams, excluding those that were already words (e.g., DOG and CAT are CVC trigrams, but in English they are not nonsense syllables). He then arbitrarily made up lists to be learned later. He learned different lists over a period of years, recording such data as the number of repetitions

until he could reproduce a list without error. For a list of up to 7 trigrams, he required only a single reading for a correct reproduction; beyond that point, the repetitions required for a correct repetition increased with list length, up to about 55 repetitions for a 36-trigram list. Later research showed that not only total learning time but also the learning time per item increased with list length. Another of Ebbinghaus's findings was that he could learn meaningful material more rapidly than nonsense syllables. In contrast to the 55 repetitions required for a 36-item list of nonsense syllables, Ebbinghaus learned 80-syllable stanzas of poetry (from Byron's *Don Juan* in English) in about 8 repetitions.

Together with other verbal-learning procedures, serial learning provided a baseline for studying factors that influence human learning. For example, the finding that spaced practice is typically more effective than massed practice (e.g., Underwood, 1961) is often cited in support of distributing study evenly throughout a semester instead of cramming it in at the end, just before exams. The finding is so familiar that it's surprising that it was once regarded as counterintuitive. It was argued that the massing of learning trials gave the learner less opportunity to forget items from one presentation to the next than if the trials were spaced in time. But this wasn't so, and the superiority of spaced over massed practice eventually contributed to accounts of verbal learning in terms of interference between items (spaced practice is also superior to massed practice in motor-skill learning; Adams, 1954).

Other effective variables include meaningfulness (lists of words rated high in meaningfulness are learned more quickly than lists of words rated low), pronounceability (lists of easy-to-pronounce items are learned more quickly than lists of hard items), redundancy (organized lists are learned more quickly than random lists), and so on (e.g., McGeoch, 1942; Underwood & Schulz, 1960). The catalogue of factors that affect verbal learning (e.g., learning as a function of diet or hours without sleep) can be expanded indefinitely, and the effects of any variable might depend critically on details of procedure.

One prominent feature of serial learning was the serial-position effect, illustrated in Figure 17-2 (Robinson & Brown, 1926). In a list, items at the beginning are usually learned most easily, followed by items at the end, and finally by items in the middle. The serial-position effect raised questions about the role of position in the list. Serial learning

was regarded as a procedure in which each item is the stimulus that occasions the next. But learners can also answer questions about position (e.g., "What was the next-to-last item?"). This finding led to attempts to define the functional stimuli in serial learning, those features that occasioned correct responding (Woodward & Murdock, 1968). It isn't obvious, however, how position can function as a stimulus.

The beginning and end of a list are usually marked by the pause that separates presentations. The pause is inevitable in serial recall, when the learner tries to reproduce the list at the end of each presentation. In serial anticipation, on the other hand, the learner tries to name each item before it appears and the list can be repeated without in-

FIGURE 17-2   Serial-position curves (percent correct as a function of position of the item) after 1, 5, 9, 13 or 17 presentations of a list. Data are averages across 11 learners, each of whom learned 8 different 10-item lists of 3-digit numbers. At all stages of learning, percent correct was lower in the middle of the list than at its beginning or end. (Adapted from Robinson & Brown, 1926, Figure IX)

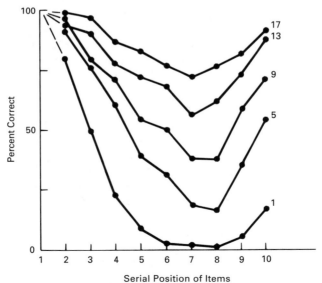

terruption. Two groups were taught a repeating 10-item list by the method of serial anticipation (e.g., *A B C D E F G H I J A B C D E* . . . , etc., where each letter represents a different item: Glanzer and Dolinsky; 1965). The first group was given standard instructions, but the second group was told that because of a procedural error the list had started with item *A* even though item *F* was actually the beginning. The serial-position effect for the first group was appropriate to a list beginning with item *A* (errors increased with items after *A* and then decreased toward the end of the list at *J*) whereas that for the second group was appropriate to a list beginning with *F* (errors increased with items after *F* and then decreased toward the end of the list at *E*). Because the lists for the two groups were identical, position as a functional stimulus can't be sought in the lists themselves; the data can be dealt with only in terms of the relation between the lists and the instructions.

Let's now return to Ebbinghaus. Other questions were raised by treating serial learning as the formation of associations among items. Could associations be formed only between successive items, or were remote associations possible (e.g., between every other or every third item)? Were associations formed both forward and backward through the list? Ebbinghaus examined these issues by relearning lists of nonsense syllables one day after original learning with item order the same as or different from that of the original list. This was called the method of *savings*: The list was ordinarily learned more quickly on the second day than the first, and effects of changing the order of items were measured by the time saved on relearning. Ebbinghaus studied savings with 16-item lists in original, scrambled and reverse orders, and with lists of every second, third, fourth or eighth item (e.g., in a list based on

every third item, the order *A B C D E F G H* becomes *A D G B E H C F*). As shown in Figure 17-3 (p. 304), the greatest savings in relearning occurred with items in the original order and the least with items in scrambled order. The reversed list produced more savings than any of the remaining ordered lists. From these data, Ebbinghaus concluded that both remote and backward associations had been formed during the original learning of each list.

If so many different kinds of associations can emerge within a serial list, serial learning might not be the way to study associations. It might be better to examine pairs of associates independently of a serial order. We could then treat serial learning as a special case of paired-associates learning. For example, consider this five-item serial list: NAJ BEF LUJ PES CED. In the presence of NAJ the learner must learn to say BEF; in the presence of BEF, LUJ; in the presence of LUJ, PES; and in the presence of PES, CED. The same relations could be created in a paired-associates list consisting of NAJ-BEF, BEF-LUJ, LUJ-PES and PES-CED. The learner who mastered the original serial list would probably quickly learn this paired-associates list, and vice versa.

PAIRED-ASSOCIATES LEARNING

Despite the relation between paired-associates and serial learning just outlined, paired-associates procedures were apparently developed independently of Ebbinghaus's work on serial learning, by Mary Calkins, an American psychologist. Her earliest experiments used colors rather than verbal items as stimuli; the response items were two-digit or three-digit numbers (Calkins, 1894). Verbal materials later became fairly standard for both stimuli and

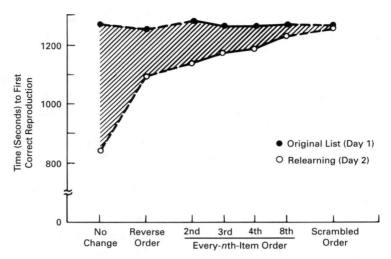

FIGURE 17-3 Original learning time (day 1) for 16-item lists of nonsense syllables and relearning time (day 2) after various reorderings of the lists: no change; reverse order; orders based on every second, third, fourth or eighth item; scrambled order. The learning times shown are averages across at least 10 different lists learned on different occasions by Ebbinghaus. The shaded area shows savings as a function of the different types of reordering. (Adapted from Ebbinghaus, 1885, Chap. IX)

responses (Calkins, 1896), and paired-associates procedures, like serial-learning procedures, examined effects of a variety of verbal properties (e.g., meaningfulness of items).

The learner's task appears simpler with a paired-associates list than with a serial list: Each item occasions a unique response and the order of items is irrelevant. But even this seeemingly simpler task can be broken down into more fundamental components. Consider paired-associates learning as an instance of discrimination learning. In contrast to procedures with a single response (as when a pigeon's pecks are reinforced during green but not red), paired-associates learning involves many stimuli and many responses. The several stimuli must be discriminated, the several responses must be differentiated and each response must be occasioned by its partic-

ular stimulus. Discrimination among the items is usually taken for granted; discriminations among various letter and word sequences are well established in human learners. But before learning associations, the learner must learn which responses are appropriate. This component of paired-associates learning has been called *response integration* or *response availability* (Underwood & Schulz, 1960).

Consider the following two paired-associates lists:

DOG — 3	DOG — 18
ANT — 1	ANT — 51
CAT — 4	CAT — 73
FLY — 2	FLY — 85
BEE — 5	BEE — 46

Each list has the same number of associations to be learned. The first list requires minimal response integration. Once the learner discovers that the responses include only the digits 1 through 5, subsequent learning involves only associations, the relations between the stimulus and response items. With the second list, however, the learner's early responses are likely to include numbers other than those on the list (e.g., 72, 86, 45). Only when the learner's responses include all the numbers in the response list and no others will response integration be complete, and the learner will make errors at least up to that time. Paired-associates learning takes longer with the second list than with the first, but the difference is one of response integration and not one of association.

Even after being separated from response integration, the learning of associations remains complicated. Presented by itself, a single stimulus–response pair can be learned very quickly. To what extent, then, is the study of association complicated merely because many pairs are learned together at one time? (The circumstances resemble those in the history of maze learning, when mazes evolved through simpler and simpler forms, culminating in T-mazes and straight-alleys; cf. Chapter 5.) It became appropriate to study the learning of single associations rather than of many associations in a single setting (e.g., Estes, 1964). The issues rekindled a long-standing dispute in the psychology of learning, the controversy over *continuity* versus *discontinuity*. The question was whether learning occurred gradually and continuously or took place discontinuously, in an all-or-none fashion. Were associations learned a little at a time or all at once?

In one experiment (Rock, 1957), a learner was given a paired-associates task involving eight pairs of CVC trigrams. Presentations were repeated until the learner responded correctly to all eight. In one group of learners, list order was changed from one presentation to the next but the pairs stayed the same. In a second group, a pair was retained in the list only if the learner had responded correctly to the stimulus item; otherwise that pair was dropped and a new pair was substituted. In other words, the only pairs retained over successive presentations of the list for the second group were those learned in just one presentation. The two groups learned their eight-pair lists at roughly equal rates; learning was as rapid with new pairs substituted as with old pairs repeated over successive presentations. Thus, trials on which a correct response hadn't yet occurred didn't seem to contribute to learning.

Unfortunately, not all pairs of CVC trigrams are equally difficult to learn. For example, a nonsense syllable pair like CEN-TER forms a common word and so is more easily learned than a similar pair like NEC-RET that doesn't form a word. The problem with Rock's experiment was that the procedure for the second group was also a method for selecting a list of those pairs that were easiest to learn; pairs that could be learned on a single presentation were kept and more difficult pairs were dropped. When the experiment was repeated with trigram pairs that had been equated for difficulty, the group with a constant list learned more rapidly than did the group for which new pairs were substituted for unlearned old pairs (Underwood, Rehula, & Keppel, 1962).

No doubt associations can at least sometimes be learned on a single trial. It may be more important to ask about the properties of the association than to ask how quickly it can be formed. For example, is it symmetrical? In other words, once the stimulus item consistently occasions the response item, will the response item occasion the stimulus item? The question isn't simple, because failures to demonstrate symmetry (cf. Chapter 9) may result from unavailability of the stimulus items as responses rather than from an irreversibility of the association. For example, the naming of written letters is a paired-associates task with written stimuli and vocal responses; if a child who can't write yet learns to say "A" when shown a written *A*, we wouldn't expect the child to write an *A* in response to the spoken letter.

Even with such factors taken into account, associations aren't necessarily symmetrical (e.g., Newman, 1972). The finding has practical implications. In learning another language, for example, when you're able to give the equivalent English word in response to a word in the other language, that doesn't guarantee you'll be able to respond in that language when the English word is the stimulus item. You'd be well-advised to learn the symmetry explicitly by studying the vocabulary in both directions (e.g., English to Russian and Russian to English). Such symmetries are among the defining characteristics of bilingual skill (e.g., Kolers, 1966).

Other practical implications follow from studies of paired-associates learning. For example, what's the most effective order in which to present pairs of items? Should easy items be presented before difficult ones? Once a stimulus item occasions a correct response, how soon and how often should it be repeated? Experiments on such questions have led to methods of sequencing items that make paired-associates learning more effective than random sequencing or even sequencing determined by the learner (Atkinson, 1972).

By definition, an association has been learned when a verbal stimulus occasions its paired verbal response (notice that this account places the association in the learning situation and not in the learner). Typically, such responding is produced by instructions rather than by differential reinforcement, but that isn't the only reason why paired-associates learning is seldom treated in the language of stimulus control. Another reason is that any human verbal learning that isn't completely arbitrary will inevitably include much more than the learning of associations.

FREE RECALL

One demonstration that a learner who's mastered a paired-associates list has learned more than associations is that the learner can usually name some response items even without any stimulus items. If the order of items is unimportant, this type of performance is called *free recall*. Recall experiments can be conducted with nonverbal stimuli. For example, we could present a collection of objects and then, after its removal, ask someone to name the items. A commonplace example is when someone asks us to name the people we met at a party or some other gathering.

In experimental settings, however, free-recall procedures typically involve lists of verbal items. These procedures usually present a list of items once, followed by an opportunity for the learner to name the items without the list. Thus, free recall resembles the first trial of a serial-learning procedure, except that the learner isn't instructed to name the items in their original order.

Given the similarity to serial-learning procedures, it's no surprise that serial-position effects also occur in free recall. Learners are most likely to recall items at the beginning and at the end of a list. These effects are often described in terms of two principles: primacy and recency. The principle of *primacy* states that the first items of a list are more likely to be recalled than later ones; the principle of *recency* states that the most recent items (i.e., those at the end of the list) are more likely to be recalled than earlier ones. It follows that items in the middle of the list are least likely to be recalled. But these principles don't explain serial-position effects generation; they just summarize what learners do.

The different sources of primacy and recency effects can be demonstrated by separating the phenomena experimentally (Glanzer & Cunitz, 1966). Groups of learners recalled list items immediately after the list was presented or after 10 s or 30 s of a counting task. A primacy effect (higher likelihood of recall for early items) occurred in all three conditions; the recency effect (higher likelihood for later items) occurred with no delay but was reduced or eliminated in the delay conditions. Imposing the delay prevented the end of the list from being the most recent event at the time of recall (cf. the stimulus suffix effect; Baddeley & Hull, 1979).

Carefully read just once through the following 60-item list, starting at the left and going down each column. Immediately after finishing it, cover the page and write down as many of the words in the list as you can before reading on:

BANANA	AUTOMOBILE	MOCCASIN
DOG	GRAPE	VAN
RESERVATION	JAGUAR	NAVAJO
CLOCK	AIRPORT	PANTHER
PEAR	LIME	TAXI
CHEROKEE	FUTURE	MOHAWK
TICKET	CHEYENNE	DATE
MELON	HAND	BEAR
BUFFALO	SEMINOLE	CHERRY
CUCKOO	PRESENT	STATION
PAPOOSE	*psychology*	PAST
LOCOMOTIVE	MANGO	LEOPARD
TIME	BUS	ORANGE
PLUM	APACHE	CHIMES
COYOTE	MOTORCYCLE	TRACKS
PUEBLO	WAMPUM	CALENDAR
CAB	DIAL	HORSE
WOLF	APRICOT	WIGWAM
TRAIN	MOOSE	APPLE
LION	PLANE	CABOOSE

If you're a typical unpracticed learner then you probably recalled considerably fewer than half the items in this list, given its length. You might or might not have recalled the earliest ones (BANANA, DOG, RESERVATION), but you were more likely to recall them than the later ones. You probably recalled one or more items from the end (WIGWAM, APPLE, CABOOSE) and you probably also recalled the distinctive one in the middle (*psychology*).

The position of an item in a list is only one of several factors influencing its likelihood of recall. The greater likelihood of recall of unusual items in a list is called the von Restorff effect (von Restorff, 1933). It works with a variety of distinctive features, such as color (e.g., a word in red on a page of standard print) or size (e.g., a word in large type). Semantic novelty may also be effective (e.g., the name of a flower in the middle of a list of carpentry tools, or a common verb embedded in a list of animal names). But did you recall PRESENT, which came just before *psychology*? Sometimes a distinctive event reduces the likelihood of recall of items that came before it. This may be a small-scale version of *retrograde amnesia*, the forgetting of what happened just before a traumatic event such as an automobile accident (Tulving, 1969).

A problem with explanations in terms of distinctiveness is that it's sometimes difficult to predict which items will be distinctive. Suppose that recall probability is much greater for one item on a list than for neighboring items. We might be tempted to say that the item must been distinctive. But this doesn't explain anything; it simply demonstrates one condition in which we call an item distinctive.

The important dimensions of free recall are in the learner and not in the list. The learner isn't passive; the learner behaves with respect to the list. For example, in free recall learners typically rehearse recent items by repeating them vocally or subvocally. In one procedure (Rundus & Atkinson, 1970), words from 20-item lists were presented for 5 s each and learners were instructed to rehearse aloud so their rehearsals could be taped. Learners had more opportunities to rehearse early words than later ones (e.g., the 4th word could be rehearsed during presentations of any of the remaining 16, but the 16th could be rehearsed only during presentations of the last 4). As illustrated in Figure 17-4, more frequent rehearsal of the early words was correlated with their higher recall probability (primacy effect). The recency effect, however, wasn't correlated with rehearsal; recall probability increased for words near the end of the list even though the opportunity to rehearse them was limited. What a learner

recalls depends on what the learner does during and after the presentation of each item.

The difference between serial recall and free recall is in the instructions to the learner. In serial recall, the learner is instructed to name the items in their original order; in free recall, the learner isn't told that order is important, or perhaps is specifically instructed to ignore order. But this doesn't mean that freely recalled items are recalled in arbitrary orders. In fact, the order of recall of items often differs systematically from the original order in the list.

Consider the 60-item list presented earlier. Words in various semantic categories were distributed throughout it (e.g., Native American words: MOHAWK, APACHE, WIGWAM, MOCCASIN; animal names: DOG, HORSE, LION, MOOSE; travel words:

FIGURE 17-4 Relation between rehearsal and recall probability. Lists of 20 nouns were presented at a rate of 5 s per item. Learners were instructed to rehearse aloud and were allowed 2 min of free recall after presentation of the list. (Adapted from Rundus & Atkinson, 1970, Figure 1)

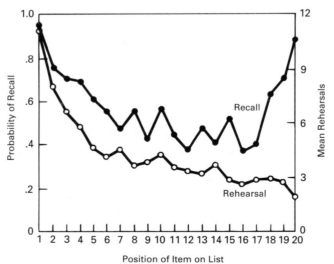

TICKET, AIRPORT, TRACKS, BUS). At recall, the items within each category are likely to be recalled in clusters. The *clustering* depends on properties of the list and the learner's verbal history. For example, the recall of RESERVATION in a cluster of Native American words might occasion some of the other travel words; a learner who closely follows Native American affairs will probably recall more items in this category than someone without such interests; and so on.

In the recall of a list like this one, learners are likely to report some items that are semantically related to words in a cluster but didn't actually appear on the list. Such *intrusions* become more likely with longer lists and with delays between list presentation and recall. For example, only some of the following were on the original list: NAVAJO, TEPEE, LOCOMOTIVE, CAR, ENGINE, PANTHER, TIGER, FOX, BISON, PEAR, PEACH, WATCH. Can you say which they are? Of the others, were any on your recall list? If so, you remembered something that never really happened. As we'll see in Chapter 18, false memories are not uncommon, and sometimes they involve events far more significant than the words presented in a recall list.

Clustering in free recall is most easily demonstrated with lists that include semantic groupings, such as the 60-item list that was our example (such clustering also provides a method for studying semantic structure; cf. Chapter 16). But it occurs with all sorts of lists and along various dimensions of verbal items (e.g., words related in spelling or pronunciation, or words that are common free associates; e.g., Bousfield, 1953). Sometimes it's hard to see consistencies of structure in the recall of just one list by a single learner, so research on clustering uses techniques for quantifying repeated recalls and recall summarized over groups of learners (e.g., Tulving, 1962). In any case, the learner isn't passive when given a verbal list. The clustering of the list items is one of several kinds of behavior the learner engages in during free recall.

VERBAL DISCRIMINATION

The distinction between simultaneous and successive discrimination (Chapter 2) is relevant with verbal as well as nonverbal procedures. Consider verbal discrimination involving a simultaneous procedure: Two verbal items are presented and the learner chooses one (by naming it, pointing or pressing one of two buttons). The learner is then told whether the choice was correct. Unlike discriminations studied in animal laboratories (e.g., a rat's lever pressing reinforced in light but not dark), the procedure usually includes many different stimulus items in both the correct and the incorrect classes. Now consider a successive procedure: Given verbal items presented one at a time, the learner is instructed to respond "yes" or "no" to each one; alternatively, the learner is instructed to sort a deck of cards with verbal items printed on them into two or more piles.

Another case of verbal discrimination is *visual search*, as when someone is instructed to find items in a list or a text (e.g., Healy, 1976). Examples are checking a word in a dictionary and proofreading a manuscript for typographical errors. Here, the words on a page are presented simultaneously, but the searcher's scanning makes it possible to interpret this as a successive task. In any case, research on visual search is usually more concerned with speed and accuracy than with the acquisition of the skill.

In simultaneous verbal discrimination, the items and their assignment by the experimenter to correct and incorrect classes are sometimes arbitrary (e.g., pairs of non-sense syllables, with the items to be correct chosen randomly). Such arbitrary discriminations may not be relevant to verbal discriminations that are already part of our everyday language (e.g., discriminations among nouns, verbs and other parts of speech, or along semantic dimensions, or along dimensions of alphabetical order or spelling). Some experiments have explored the acquisition of verbal discriminations in which some feature is always a property of the correct item. For example, a correct item might be defined as one that includes a particular letter or letter combination, or one that doesn't include a vowel, or one that falls into some semantic class. Such procedures are cases of concept formation that involve verbal stimuli (cf. Figure 14-2).

In still another type of arrangement, whether an item is correct is determined by its context. Consider the following verbal discrimination list, in which correct items are indicated by italics (assume that the order of items in each pair varies over presentations):

WOOD—*GLASS*
SPOON—STEEL
RUBBER—*KNIFE*
CEMENT—*NAPKIN*
FORK—GLASS

This list involves a conditional discrimination with respect to the item *GLASS*, which is correct in the first pair but not in the last one. The discrimination is based upon semantic classes: The correct items are all parts of a table setting and the incorrect items are common materials. Because GLASS can be a member of either class, the learner's response must be based on the class membership of the other item. In this conditional discrimination, the relevant context

isn't just the item paired with GLASS; it's also the semantic structure of all of the pairs in the list.

Verbal learning procedures usually repeat a list until the learner meets some criterion of correct responding. This is appropriate when we're interested in the relative difficulty of different types of lists. But when we're interested in teaching, we can design lists so that, through a progression of changes, they'll efficiently produce a verbal discrimination. In other words, verbal discriminations are well suited to fading procedures (cf. Chapter 8). The following progression of items is an illustration (the correct item of each pair is indicated by italics; adapted from Goldiamond, 1966):

A—*B*	DAISY MAE—*LI'L ABNER*
B—D	*ROBERT*—MELANIE
B—V	ANNA—*BOB*
O—*B*	*BOY*—GIRL
FS—*BF*	*DANNY BOY*—BETTY ANN
JB—EL	BYRON—*BETH*
EAB—*VOX*	BETSY—*WILLIAM*
ABE—JANE	DOROTHY—*GEORGE*
MARY—*BERT*	*KENNETH*—ANTONIA
BILL—CONNIE	*JOHN*—ELIZABETH

Early in the list, the discrimination is based only on the letter *B*. At the transition from letters to words, the semantic difference, male-female, is introduced, with the male item always paired with the letter *B*. Later the *B* is included in both items, and in subsequent pairs the *B* is removed so that the correct item depends only on gender. The gender discrimination in the final pair also includes a reversal of the letter discrimination that was created at the beginning of the list. The fading from pictures to written items is an effective method for teaching children early reading skills (Gleitman & Rozin, 1973).

VERBAL RECOGNITION: A SPECIAL CASE OF VERBAL DISCRIMINATION

The discrimination between items in a list may be based upon which ones appeared in some earlier list. When this is so, we speak of the discrimination as verbal recognition. For example, consider the following pairs: LION—TIGER, LEMON—MELON, WATCH—CLOCK, AUTOMOBILE—CAR, TEPEE——WIGWAM. Each pair includes one item that was on our 60-item free-recall list and another that wasn't. If you correctly identify the items from the list, we can say that you recognize them. In experiments on recognition, the response might be pointing at an item or naming it; in a less formal setting, it might be saying, "I recognize this as an item from the list." The response depends not just on the stimulus but also on the past circumstances in which the item had been presented (cf. Chapters 13 and 14 on discriminating one's own behavior).

The phenomenon of recognition isn't restricted to verbal items. Discriminations based on whether people or places or objects are familiar or unfamiliar are examples of nonverbal recognition. One study (Shepard, 1967) compared recognition of words, sentences and pictures. The procedure with words used a list equally divided between frequent words (e.g., *child, office*) and rare ones (e.g., *julep, wattled*). Immediately after inspecting a 540-word list, observers correctly identified 88% of the original words in test pairs made up of list words plus new words. Rare words were more likely to be identified correctly than frequent words. Immediately after inspecting a list of 612 sentences (e.g., "A dead dog is no use for hunting ducks"), observers correctly identified 89% of the original sentences in test pairs made up of original and new ones. The picture procedure examined recognition at different times after observers had inspected 612 pictures. After two hours, observers shown pairs made up of the original pictures and new ones correctly identified 99.7% of the original pictures, but after 120 days, accuracy decreased to 58% (50% is chance accuracy).

However, the study doesn't permit a conclusion about the superiority of recognition for nonverbal visual stimuli relative to verbal stimuli. With pairs of pictures, the observer was discriminating between pictures seen before (from the original series) and pictures probably never seen before; with words (especially frequent ones), the observer was discriminating between words both of which had been seen before in many contexts but only one of which had appeared on the original list.

Verbal recognition doesn't require discriminations between novel and familiar stimuli; instead, it's based on whether the verbal item occurred in some previous setting (i.e., a particular list). A common error in verbal recognition is recognition failure (i.e., an item from the original list isn't identified as old). False recognition (i.e., an error in which an item not from the original list is identified as old) usually occurs less often and is most likely with new items semantically related to list items (e.g., Underwood & Freund, 1968).

Recognition may also depend on how new and old items are presented. When they're presented in pairs, the observer can respond correctly by identifying either the old item as old or the new item as new. This isn't so if an old item is presented together with several new items (as in a multiple choice). In recognition studies, new items are sometimes called distractor items. Recognition accuracy decreases as the proportion of new or distractor items increases (Kintsch, 1968). The probability of identifying correctly by guessing decreases with added distractor items (e.g., the probability is 50%

when items are presented in pairs but only 25% when each old item is presented with three new ones); the adjustment for guessing, however, is too small to account for the decrease in recognition accuracy that accompanies an increase in distractor items.

It's often been assumed that recognition is involved in performances produced by other verbal learning procedures. For example, when a learner doesn't recognize a stimulus item from a paired-associates list, that item will usually not occasion the appropriate response item (e.g., Martin, 1967). It's therefore been suggested that recognition of items as stimulus items from the list is a necessary condition for paired-associates learning. The trouble is that the dependency may also go the other way. The learner may sometimes recognize a stimulus item from the list only because it has occasioned a response item.

Verbal recognition requires responding in the presence of items whereas free recall requires producing items in their absence. We can expect these two classes of behavior to have different properties. Nevertheless, many accounts of verbal learning have assumed that recognition and recall are closely related. One account (Anderson & Bower, 1972) suggests that recall occurs in two stages: First the learner generates items, and then the learner produces only those recognized as being from the list. Colloquially, we might say that the learner must think of the item first and then decide whether it was on the list.

One deduction from such accounts is that recognition accuracy should always equal or exceed recall accuracy. In many studies, recognition is superior to recall even after guessing is taken into account (in recognition with paired new and old items, guesses are correct by chance half the time, but in recall of words or CVC trigrams, guesses aren't likely to be correct by chance). However, recall accuracy can be consistently superior to recognition accuracy in some circumstances

(Tulving, 1974; Watkins & Tulving, 1975). For example, in one arrangement the learner was first given a paired-associates list (e.g., *glue-CHAIR*). Next, the learner was given free-association stimulus items likely to occasion response items from the paired-associates list (e.g., *table*, for which typical associates might be *CHAIR, CLOTH, DESK, DINNER*). Among the words produced in the free-association task, the learner was then asked to identify those that had appeared in the earlier paired-associates list (recognition). Finally, the stimulus items of the paired-associates list were presented (e.g., *glue-?*) and the learner's responses were recorded (recall). In procedures of this type, learners typically recognized fewer words from the original list than they were able to recall during the paired-associates condition.

This outcome not only makes untenable the model of recognition as a component of recall; it's also likely to surprise those who regard recognition as somehow simpler than recall. Perhaps the most important point is that recognition and recall are different classes of responses occasioned by different classes of stimuli; they are measured in different ways and therefore it may be inappropriate to compare them.

SUMMARY

We've examined the major classes of verbal-learning procedures: serial learning, paired-associates learning, free recall, verbal discrimination, and, as a special case of verbal discrimination, verbal recognition. In these procedures, performances are typically produced and maintained through instructions rather than through differential contingencies imposed on correct and incorrect responses. Although each procedure seems superficially simple, the human learner, while mastering any of these tasks, inevitably does a lot more. Thus, it's inappropriate to regard associations merely as verbal sequences; human verbal behavior has other structural properties besides the temporal ordering of events (e.g., clustering and intrusions in free recall).

We've treated verbal learning procedures in the context of their historical development. Those procedures were designed in the service of accounts of verbal learning in terms of associations. Such accounts assumed that verbal learning produced stimulus–response relations in which particular verbal stimuli came to occasion particular verbal responses. But relations produced in verbal learning weren't limited to one direction; verbal learning also produced other relations among verbal items. We'll see some implications of such treatments in Chapters 18 and 19 on remembering. By treating verbal learning as a separate topic, we've already covered some of the experimental precursors of contemporary studies of remembering. But before we turn to that topic, we must turn to transfer of learning; once one verbal task has been mastered, we may ask how the mastery of others will be affected.

Section B   **Transfer**

Does mastery of a classical language like Greek or Latin make it easier to learn economics or history or sociology? Does the discipline of mathematics make people more logical thinkers? Does the mastery of music or art create skills that are useful in studying great works of literature? Research on transfer of learning or transfer of training began with simpler questions than these (Thorndike & Woodworth, 1901). A common assumption of earlier times was that traditional educational curricula were appropriate not just because each discipline might later be important to the student, but also because they "exercised the mind" or, in other words, taught

general intellectual skills. Studies of how the learning of one task affected the learning of another were particularly relevant to this view. Yet each demonstration that transfer was specific to a particular learning task or that it was limited in some other way contradicted rather than supported the view. And the typical college curriculum gradually evolved from a fixed sequence of required courses to electives, distribution requirements and other flexible course options.

Thorndike played a critical role in this history (Jonçich, 1968). As his research interests shifted from instrumental learning in animals to human learning in educational settings, his involvement in curricular matters such as course requirements for potential teachers increased. His findings on transfer probably influenced faculty committees responsible for establishing and reviewing course requirements and curricula. The transfer of learning from one subject matter to another is difficult to analyze. Some study skills probably generalize from one course to another. But examining how the mastery of a classical language influences a student's progress in mathematics or science or philosophy requires experimental procedures that are neither practical nor acceptable in the typical educational institution (e.g., random assignment of students to course sequences; matching groups according to previous academic achievement or other criteria; controlling for different instructors and teaching methods in different classes; etc.). Perhaps inevitably, research on transfer concentrated on simpler tasks, such as transfer from one paired-associates list to another (e.g., McGeoch, 1942).

POSITIVE AND NEGATIVE TRANSFER

A complication in studies of transfer is that they necessarily compare learners. To say whether learning task X affects the later learning of Y, we must know how Y would have been learned if X hadn't been learned first. Suppose that Y is learned rapidly and with few errors after the learning of X. With just that information, we can't determine transfer from X to Y; perhaps Y was an easy task. We must compare learning Y after X with learning Y alone. When learning Y after X is essentially equal to learning just Y, transfer is zero (in *zero transfer*, learning X doesn't affect learning Y). When learning Y after X is more rapid or occurs with fewer errors than learning only Y, transfer is positive (in *positive transfer*, learning X makes Y easier to learn). When learning Y after X is slower or occurs with more errors than learning only Y, transfer is negative (in *negative transfer*, learning X makes Y harder to learn).

The history of research on transfer includes both verbal and nonverbal studies (e.g., transfer of motor skills from one hand to the other; Woodworth, 1938). Specific cases of positive or negative transfer could be catalogued, but paired-associates learning suggested an analysis from which more general principles of transfer might emerge. Studies of transfer could be based on changes in stimulus items, changes in response items or changes in their relations (Bruce, 1933). Table 17-2 illustrates several procedures in paired-associates transfer. The effect of learning one list on learning another can be examined when just stimulus items change, when just response items change, when both change or when both remain the same but their pairing changes.

Changing only stimulus items may produce positive transfer, especially if the first list includes unfamiliar response items for which no additional response integration is required (cf. paired-associates learning). Changing only response items, on the other hand, may produce negative transfer, because stimulus items continue to occasion responses from the first list during learning of the second. If relations among items are arbitrary, changing both stimulus and response items ideally should produce no transfer; in practice, the procedure assesses *generalized* or *nonspecific* transfer in the learning of successive different lists (cf. Chapter 9 on learning set). Another variation on paired-associates transfer is the re-pairing of unchanged lists of items. For example, the symmetry of associations can be studied by exchanging stimulus and response items (transfer from an A-B list to a B-A list). The roles of particular properties of items can also be studied by changing lists in various systematic ways (e.g., given A and A' as CVC

TABLE 17-2   Some Transfer Procedures With Paired-Associates Lists

	DESIGNATION*		SAMPLE ITEMS	
PROCEDURE	LIST 1	LIST 2	LIST 1	LIST 2
Stimulus change only	A-B	C-B	lan-qip	fis-qip
Response change only	A-B	A-C	req-kiv	req-zam
Stimulus and response change	A-B	C-D	xal-pom	cam-lup
Same lists, stimulus and response items re-paired	A-B	A-B$_r$	hab-lef guv-mot	hab-mot guv-lef

*The first letter in each hyphenated pair represents a stimulus-item list and the second represents a response-item list. Sample CVC items illustrate each procedure.

lists differing only in vowels, transfer from an A-B list to an A'-B list, or given B and B' as word lists in which corresponding items in each list are synonyms, transfer from an A-B list to an A-B' list).

Whether transfer from one list to another is positive or negative depends on relations among the items in the two lists, such as similarities between corresponding first-list and second-list items (Osgood, 1949). Positive transfer is maximal when stimulus and response items in the two lists are identical (A-B to A-B transfer); negative transfer is maximal when stimulus items are identical but second-list response items are incompatible with first-list response items (A-B to A-C transfer; A-B to A-B$_r$ re-pairing may also produce negative transfer). Transfer approaches zero as second-list stimulus items become more different from first-list stimulus items (A-B to C-B or A-B to C-D transfer).

The significance of this summary of transfer, however, depends largely on the definition of similarity. Consider the learner who has learned *LOUD* as the response to a stimulus item. New lists might substitute new response items related to *LOUD* by spelling (*CLOUD*), as synonyms (*NOISY*) or as antonyms (*SOFT*). How can we judge the similarity between list-1 and list-2 response items? Are words with similar spellings but different meanings more or less alike than words with different spellings but similar meanings? Are antonyms antagonistic response items, or should both antonyms and synonyms be treated as semantically similar? Do these qualify as cases of A-B to A-C transfer, or are the relations close enough to justify speaking of A-B to A-B' transfer?

In fact, transfer will probably be positive in each case. Having learned *LOUD* in response to a stimulus item in the first list, the learner would readily learn *CLOUD* in response to the same item in a new list. But that would also be true for transfer from

LOUD to *NOISY* or to *SOFT*. Transfer might even be greater with antonyms than with synonyms or spelling relations. This might lead us to say that antonyms are semantically more similar than synonyms and that similarity is better measured in semantic terms than in terms of spelling. But we'd run into problems sooner or later. For example, spelling might be more important in some verbal transfer procedures than others. Such features of transfer data are probably best regarded as part of the definition of similarity. Similarity isn't a stimulus property; rather, it's derived from behavior with respect to stimuli. It follows that doing the experiment remains the most appropriate way to judge the amount and direction of transfer from one task to another.

An understanding of transfer may be critical to the sequencing of tasks in instruction. For example, transfer may help produce some formal relations among spoken and written verbal stimuli and responses (Chapter 14). Consider the formal stimulus and response relations as a child learns the alphabet:

echoic behavior	$S_{vocal\ "a"}$ ——$R_{vocal\ "a"}$
dictation-taking	$S_{vocal\ "a"}$ ——$R_{written\ A}$
transcription	$S_{written\ A}$ ——$R_{written\ A}$
textual behavior	$S_{written\ A}$ ——$R_{vocal\ "a"}$

Ordinarily, the child acquires echoic behavior long before learning to read and write. Thus, the transition to textual behavior might be regarded as A-B to C-B transfer (stimulus change only), and to dictation-taking as A-B to A-C transfer (response change only). But the negative transfer and zero transfer predictable from the transfer relations summarized earlier probably won't be helpful. If a child hasn't learned to write letters, for example, we won't see much transfer from echoic behavior to dictation-taking. But if the child has learned transcription, we might see easy transfer to textual behavior. Thus, the order in which the classes are learned may be critical to the teaching of reading and writing; determining the most effective order is a problem of transfer. In the end, of course, we'd be more interested in equivalences across vocal and written letters than in particular stimulus–response relations.

PROACTION AND RETROACTION

We've seen how learning list 1 can affect learning list 2. This effect is called *proactive* because the direction is from an earlier to a later task. But list-2 learning can also affect later list-1 performance. For example, after transfer from an A-B to an A-C list, the learner who'd given B responses to A stimulus items may no longer be able to do so; the A stimulus items now produce C responses. This effect is called *retroactive*, because the direction is from a later to an earlier task. Most research on these effects has concentrated on cases in which learning one list interferes with rather than enhances performance on other lists (Müller and Pilzecker, 1900); such effects are called proactive and retroactive *inhibition*, or proactive and retroactive *interference*. We'll find these categories useful when we consider remembering in Chapters 18 and 19.

As with other instances of transfer, studies of proaction and retroaction compare performance on a succession of tasks with that on one task alone. The design of proaction studies is as follows:

Experimental Group	Learn Task 1	Learn Task 2	Test Task 2
Control Group	———	Learn Task 2	Test Task 2

Except that part of the task-2 performance is called a test phase, this procedure is equivalent to those discussed earlier. Task-2 learn-

ing is typically equated in some way for the two groups (e.g., number of trials or some criterion of correct responding), and some time usually separates task-2 learning and testing (on an immediate test, both groups would probably perform accurately, so there'd be no difference to observe).

The design of retroaction studies is as follows:

Experimental Group	Learn Task 1	Learn Task 2	Test Task 1
Control Group	Learn Task 1	———	Test Task 1

For the experimental group, this procedure differs from the proaction procedure only in the task tested. For a sequence of two tasks, therefore, task 1 may have a proactive effect on task 2 at the same time that task 2 has a retroactive effect on task 1. The two effects, however, would have to be assessed in two separate procedures. Proactive and retroactive effects across a variety of tasks can be studied with these procedures (e.g., task-1 serial learning and task-2 paired-associates learning, or task-1 French vocabulary and task-2 Spanish vocabulary). In a broader context, what's learned in one course may affect what's learned in a later course (proaction, as when preparation in algebra affects the mastery of calculus); conversely, what was learned in the earlier course may be affected by a later course (retroaction, as when technical vocabulary in an advanced science course affects the terminology learned in an introductory course).

EXTENSIONS TO NONVERBAL PROCEDURES

Instances of learning don't occur in isolation. Other learning preceded and is likely to follow. Every instance of learning may be affected by what came before and what follows, so proaction and retroaction are relevant to all learning. For example, a child's learning of the alphabet may be affected by earlier nonverbal discriminations among geometrical patterns (e.g., Gibson, 1965). Uppercase letters, unlike lowercase ones, don't include any up–down or left–right reversals (compare *P, B, D* and *p, b, d*), so transfer from uppercase to lowercase alphabets may depend on whether the child has already learned nonverbal up–down and left–right discriminations.

Some cases of transfer involve a shift just from one discrimination to another. For example, after reinforcing a pigeon's pecks during green but not red, we might later try reinforcing pecks during blue but not yellow or during circles but not squares. We'd probably find transfer from one color pair to another to be more rapid than transfer from a color pair to a form pair. Similarly, after reinforcing a rat's jumps toward a left but not a right stimulus, we might later try reinforcing jumps toward light but not dark, or vice versa. We might find more rapid transfer from brightness to position than from position to brightness (failures of transfer are sometimes called *fixations*).

Discrimination reversal may also be treated as a type of transfer procedure. For example, after reinforcing a rat's lever presses in the presence but not the absence of a tone, we might switch to reinforcing in the absence but not the presence of the tone. Such reversals are often more rapid if the stimuli are switched after many sessions of the original discrimination than if they are switched after only a few sessions (the overlearning reversal effect; e.g., Capaldi & Stevenson, 1957).

Related phenomena are *transposition* and *reversal* (e.g., Honig, 1962). For example, suppose the stimuli in a Lashley jumping stand are 2-cm and 4-cm squares and a rat learns to respond to the larger one. If a new pair of 4-cm and 8-cm squares is presented, the rat will probably respond to the new larger one rather than the now smaller one it responded to before. Transposition based on such relations among stimuli occurs only within certain limits; if much larger sizes are presented (e.g., 16-cm and 32-cm squares), the rat may show reversal by responding to the smaller square, closer in absolute size to the one it responded to before. (An account of transposition and reversal has been offered in terms of excitatory and inhibitory generalization gradients: Spence, 1937; cf. Chapter 8.)

Cases of transfer involving changes along the original stimulus dimension (e.g., from one color discrimination to another) are called *intradimensional shifts*. Reversals are one type of intradimensional shift. Cases involving changes from one stimulus dimension to another (e.g., from color to form discrimination) are called *extradimensional shifts*. Some effects of stimulus dimensions in transfer have been assessed by comparing intradimensional reversal shifts with extradimensional nonreversal shifts (Kendler & Kendler, 1962), as illustrated below; each task is represented by sample pairs of verbal-discrimination items in which the italicized item of each pair is designated correct:

REVERSAL SHIFT		NONREVERSAL SHIFT	
Task 1	Task 2	Task 1	Task 2
XON-map	XON-*map*	*XON*-map	*XON*-map
nij-TOY	nij-*TOY*	*nij*-TOY	nij-*TOY*

In each list, item pairs are CVC trigrams that differ along two dimensions: nonsense syllable versus common word and uppercase versus lowercase. In both task-1 cases, the correct item is the nonsense syllable, whether in uppercase or lowercase. In task 2 after the reversal shift, the correct item is now the common word instead of the nonsense syllable; whether it's uppercase or lowercase remains irrelevant. In task 2 after the nonreversal shift, however, the correct item is the uppercase one; the nonsense versus word dimension is no longer relevant.

Analogous shifts can be arranged with non-verbal items (e.g., stimuli differing in form and size). With adult humans, transfer usually occurs more rapidly with reversal than with nonreversal shifts, but the opposite is often the case with rats, monkeys and very young children. These performances have been interpreted in terms of changes in attention to individual stimuli and to stimulus dimensions (cf. Chapter 8).

SUMMARY

We assess transfer by comparing the learning of a single task with the learning of two or more tasks in succession. The learning of one task may enhance or interfere with the learning of others (positive and negative transfer), and it may affect the performance on tasks learned earlier or later (retroaction and proaction). Whether transfer is positive or negative depends on detailed relations among the stimuli and responses in the two tasks. Stimulus similarity and response similarity have been used to classify transfer effects, but the nature of similarity limits the conclusions that can be drawn from such classifications. Similarity isn't a physical property of stimuli; it's derived from behavior with respect to stimuli. Our examples of transfer were mostly from human verbal learning. But transfer is a general issue in learning, so we also considered some nonverbal examples. We can sometimes make informed guesses about both verbal and nonverbal transfer, but the best way to be sure about the direction and magnitude of transfer from one task to another is to do the experiment.

Chapter 18
The Functions of Remembering

The central metaphor of remembering involves storage, retention and retrieval, and what is stored, retained and retrieved is sometimes called a representation. Representation *combines the Latin roots* re-, prae- *and* esse, *which together have the sense of existing in front of again. Via the verb* esse, *to be, it is related to* is, yes, entity *and* interest.

By way of the Latin instaurare, *to set upright,* storage *comes from the Indo-European root* sta-, *to stand; it has a broad range of relatives, including* circumstance, exist, history *and* system. *Retention combines the Latin* re-, *back or again, and* tenere, *to hold; it is related to* maintain, continue, tenure *and* attention. Retrieval, *from the Old French* retrover, *which combines* re- *with* trover, *to find, is related to* troubador, controversy *and* tropism, *which in turn have connections with the Latin* tropus, *song, and the Greek* tropos, *a turn*

or figure of speech. Those early forms had a sense of composition or invention, which is fitting in the context of contemporary accounts of remembering as reconstruction rather than reproduction.

The term *memory* is the popular name for the topics we'll treat here, but the title of this chapter uses *remembering*. Woodworth has outlined the rationale for preferring one usage over the other:

> Instead of "memory," we should say "remembering"; instead of "thought" we should say "thinking," instead of "sensation" we should say "seeing, hearing," etc. But, like other learned branches, psychology is prone to transform its verbs into nouns. Then what happens? We forget that our nouns are merely substitutes for verbs, and go hunting for the *things* denoted by the nouns; but there are no such things, there are only the activities that we started with, seeing, remembering, and so on. . . . It is a safe rule, then, on encountering any menacing psychological noun, to strip off its linguistic mask and see what manner of activity lies behind. (Woodworth, 1921, pp. 5–6)

This chapter will emphasize functions of remembering and the next will emphasize its structure, though in both chapters we'll see that these topics often overlap. The study of remembering is concerned with how an organism's present behavior can be occasioned by past events, as when a delay is imposed between a stimulus and an opportunity to respond. Accounts of remembering often speak of what the organism does when the stimulus is presented as *memory storage*, of the intervening time as the period of *retention*, and of what the organism does when the response later occurs as *retrieval from memory*. Systematic relations between stimuli to be remembered and the responding occasioned by these stimuli are often discussed as *encoding*; for example, the learner who recites words aloud as they're presented visually is said to be encoding the visually presented words in a vocal mode.

A witness to an accident later describes what happened. How do we deal with verbal responses that depend on stimuli no longer present? What are the functions of this behavior and what structure does it have? It would be helpful to know how describing events while they occur differs from describing them later (recall how the presence of the stimulus at the time of or very shortly before a tact was a constraint on its definition: Chapter 14).

Let's start by again using the pigeon as an example. Our rudimentary example of tacting used a chamber in which a pigeon's pecks on a left or middle or right key were respectively reinforced during red or blue or green light in a window beside the keys. In that example, the pecks occurred while the colors were present and we mentioned lighting the window but not the keys. Let's assume that the keys can be lit white and that the pigeon has already learned that the keys only work when they're lit. Now we briefly present a color in the window while the keys are dark and we light the keys only after the color is gone.

If red appears for just a moment and then the pigeon immediately pecks the left key, we can still say that its peck was occasioned by the brief red stimulus even though that stimulus was gone by the time the peck oc-

curred. Now let's impose a 2-s delay between the brief presentation of red and the pigeon's opportunity to peck. If the pigeon still pecks the left key, we can still say that the peck is occasioned by the red stimulus. So far we've no reason to assume that the behavior is different in kind from that when pecks occur in the presence of the color. Imposing a delay between a stimulus and an opportunity for the response it occasions doesn't necessarily alter the control of the response by that stimulus.

In fact, control of the pigeon's pecks by color diminishes even with delays of 1 or 2 s; responding will probably be near chance levels with delays of 5 s (Blough, 1959). But maybe we can teach the pigeon to remember. We could shape different performances after red and blue and green and then chain each one to pecking on an appropriate key (e.g., first we get the pigeon to peck the left chamber wall after red, and then we get it to peck the left key if it's still pecking the left chamber wall when the keys light up; cf. *mediating behavior* in the Glossary). If each color occasions pecking in a different location, the duration over which the pigeon remembers a color will depend only on how long it can maintain its pecking in that location during the imposed delay. Under such conditions, control by the colors might extend over delays of many seconds and perhaps even minutes. We could then study how the pigeon's remembering depended on the mediating behavior by interrupting that behavior during the delay (e.g., Jans & Catania, 1980).

It's tempting to say that we really shouldn't call the pigeon's performance remembering if the temporal gap between stimulus and response is bridged by uninterrupted mediating behavior. Somehow it seems more appropriate to say that the pigeon's pecks are occasioned by its previous behavior rather than by the now-absent colors as stimuli. Yet we modify our remembering by keeping calendars and appointment books. Consider looking up a number in a phone book and then reciting it over and over to yourself until you have a chance to dial it. After you dialed successfully, you'd probably say that you had remembered the number even though your dialing depended more on your vocal repetitions than on the number as it appeared in print in the phone book. Your vocal repetition illustrates behavior sometimes called *rehearsal*; it justifies the view that what's remembered isn't so much stimuli as it is our own behavior toward those stimuli ("what is reproduced on all occasions after the first is not the original but one's own reproduction of it"; Zangwill, 1972, p. 130).

This example shows that questions about what memory is can often be translated into questions about what it is that we remember. No doubt ongoing research in the neurosciences is revealing important details of the physiology of remembering, as neuroimaging techniques such as positron emission tomography (PET scans) identify brain regions active during different sorts of remembering (e.g., Squire, 1992). For example, these techniques may be useful in the analysis of memory tasks, as when different areas are active during different tasks or components of tasks. But a researcher who seeks some memory copy of a remembered event will be disappointed in that quest if remembering depends on behavior with respect to the event, and thus only indirectly on the event itself.

Remembering is a complex subject matter with an extensive history. We discussed some of that history in the treatment of verbal learning (Chapter 17) and we'll consider it further in passing. We began this chapter by examining the language of remembering in the context of a hypothetical pigeon experiment. Now we shift to a contrasting ex-

ample, as we illustrate the complexity of human remembering in the context of the memory strategies called *mnemonic* systems. This will set the stage for a more extensive survey of research on human memory.

Section A   **Mnemonics**

Mnemonics are techniques for increasing the likelihood of remembering. Remembering may involve behavior that persists over time, as in rehearsal, but that's clearly just part of the story. If you remember an event that took place yesterday or last week or last year, we can't argue that somehow you've been rehearsing it without interruption ever since then. The use of mnemonic systems makes the learner less dependent on rehearsal, which is a major component of memorizing material by rote. A simple example of a mnemonic technique is the conversion of a sequence of symbols into a sentence, as when a beginning student of music remembers the notes on the lines of the treble clef, *EGBDF*, as the sentence "*Every good boy does fine.*"

One well-established mnemonic technique is the *method of loci* (places). It's attributed to the Greek poet Simonides (Yates, 1966). Simonides is said to have left a banquet hall just before the roof collapsed and killed all the occupants. Although the bodies were unrecognizable, Simonides was able to identify them for their relatives by where they'd been sitting at the table. This demonstration that an orderly spatial arrangement contributed to accurate remembering is supposed to have led Simonides to invent the method of loci. It became the basis for remembering sequences of topics in speeches and was described by the Greek orator Quintilian:

> In order to form a series of places in memory, he says, a building is to be remembered, as

spacious and varied a one as possible, the forecourt, the living room, bedrooms, and parlours, not omitting statues and other ornaments with which the rooms are decorated. The images by which the speech is to be remembered . . . are then placed in imagination on the places which have been memorised in the building. This done, as soon as the memory of the facts requires to be revived, all these places are visited in turn and the various deposits demanded of their custodians. We have to think of the ancient orator as moving in imagination through his memory building *whilst* he is making his speech, drawing from the memorised places the images he has placed on them. The method insures that the points are remembered in the right order, since the order is fixed by the sequence of places in the building. (Yates, 1966, p. 3)

For example, a student might imagine a systematic walk from one campus landmark to another: dormitories to dining hall to library to computer center to gymnasium and so on. To learn the items of some ordered series, the student then imagines each item at each successive location. To recall the series, the student takes the imaginary walk again, remembering each item in its appropriate place. To learn a new sequence later, the student repeats the imaginary walk in the same order, this time visualizing the new items in their places. The new series will be learned with relatively little interference from the first one (e.g., Bellezza, 1982), but the first series may no longer be well remembered. Thus, the method is useful mainly for series that need to be remembered only temporarily (e.g., shopping lists).

These mnemonic techniques work best with sequences of concrete items that are easily visualized or imagined. Unusual or bizarre items or combinations may have an advantage over common ones, but even more important is the spatial closeness or connection of the items and places. For example, in learning pairs of objects, learners remember the pairings more accurately if the objects stand in some relation to each other (e.g., one on top of the other) than if they're simply side by side (Wollen, Weber, & Lowry, 1972).

Various mnemonic devices were developed during Greek and Roman times. In the Middle Ages they became methods for remembering details of religious matters (e.g., stations of the cross; Yates, 1966). They gradually became the basis for ritualized forms of religious art, as when particular figures were used to represent vices and virtues. In the course of this evolution, the mnemonic origins of these art forms were gradually (and ironically) forgotten. Mnemonic techniques were given relatively little attention throughout much of the history of psychology, and interest in them is a fairly recent development (e.g., Bower, 1970).

Some techniques are designed so that abstract items can be converted into concrete ones. The *pegword* technique translates numbers into a sequence that can be visualized, as in *one is a bun, two is a shoe, three is a tree*, etc. An ordered list can then be learned by imagining each item together with the object corresponding to its numerical position in the list. These systems have an advantage over the method of loci, in that the learner can recall the item in any position without having to start from the beginning of the list (e.g., to recall the third item, the learner has only to remember what was imagined with *tree*).

A more elaborate system provides a code for translating numbers into letters. This system has been a part of popular mnemonic techniques for roughly a century (e.g., Loisette, 1899). One version is the following:

Number	Consonants	Rationale
1	*t, d*	*t* has one downstroke
2	*n*	*n* has two downstrokes
3	*m*	*m* has three downstrokes

4	*r*	*r* is the fourth letter of *four*
5	*l*	*l* is the Roman numeral 50
6	soft *g*, *j*	script *g* is an upside-down 6
7	*k*, hard *c*	*k* can be combined with 7: '*k*
8	*f*, *v*	both 8 and script *f* have two loops
9	*p*, *b*	backwards *p* or upside-down *b* is 9
0	*z*, *s*	*z* is the first letter of *zero*

With this code, any number can be converted into a word or a sequence of words in which consonant sounds correspond to successive digits. With a little practice, the learner can quickly translate numerical information, such as dates or telephone numbers, into a form that's easy to remember. The potential applications are limited only by the learner's ingenuity.

Consider an example. You're interested in the visual spectrum, but you sometimes forget which end is infrared and which is ultraviolet. So you construct a colorful scene from early in the American Civil War. A Union soldier, in his **blue** uniform and with his steel-**blue** *rifle* over his shoulder, is in a country kitchen taking leave of his sweetheart. Golden **yellow** *loaves* of fresh-baked bread are sitting on the counter as he *kisses* her on her **red** lips. *Rifle* translates to 485, roughly the wavelength of blue in millimicrons; *loaves* translates to 580, or yellow; and *kisses* to 700, or red. Infrared, then, is at the long wavelength end of the spectrum. It's also easy now to determine approximate wavelengths of other colors (e.g., 530 or so is a good guess for green, which is located between blue and yellow).

At this point, you might try an exercise. First choose a sequence of a dozen familiar locations, as in an imaginary stroll through your neighborhood. The places should be distinctive ones that you encounter in a definite order. For example, they might include a library, a playground, a school, a pharmacy, a parking lot, and so on. Next, construct an arbitrary sequence of 12 two-digit numbers (or, better, have someone else construct one for you); for example, 66, 57, 28, 40, 87, and so on. From the code, you can now convert each number into a word including two and only two consonant sounds; ignore unsounded letters. For example, you can code 66 as *judge*, because the *d* is silent. Concrete words are preferable to abstract ones (e.g., for 57, *lock* is preferable to *like*). Finally, as you derive each word, imagine it at the appropriate location (e.g., a giant *judge* sitting on the roof of the library, a pad*lock* attached to the playground swings, etc.). Later, you can use the successive locations to recall the words, and you can use the code to translate the words back to their respective numbers. On your first try, you may find it helpful to have the letter-to-number code handy, but with practice you should find that you can learn an arbitrary sequence with relatively little effort. Remembering 50 or more numbers isn't difficult for a practiced user of mnemonic techniques.

Such arbitrary feats may impress your friends, but whenever you encounter numerical information worth remembering (e.g., dates of events, combination lock settings, computer passwords), you can put mnemonics to practical use. More important, they demonstrate the flexibility and capacity of human memory. Educational systems have tended to emphasize learning through understanding and have correspondingly de-emphasized or even discouraged memorization. It's unlikely, however, that a learner will be disadvantaged by learning in more than one way, so mnemonics can be effective supplements to other methods of study. Mnemonics, a far cry from the pigeon example discussed earlier, illustrate how varied the phenomena of remembering are. They're classes of behavior that can be learned, and they show that what the learner remembers depends on what the learner does.

Section B   The Metaphor of Storage, Retention and Retrieval

An episode of remembering is defined by three components: the initial learning of an item, the passage of time, and then an opportunity for recall. In the research literature on memory, a metaphorical treatment of these three components has gradually evolved into a technical language. Initial learning is said to result in *storage* of the item, which determines how the item is retained over time; a period of *retention* is followed by the opportunity for recall; recall of the item is then called *retrieval* from storage. An item that's been stored is said to be *available*, but it's said to be *accessible* only if it can be retrieved. There are other memory metaphors (cf. Roediger, 1980). For example, some theories have appealed to the metaphor of resonance, as when we say "that rings a bell" when something reminds us of something else. The metaphor of storage and retrieval, however, has been most influential in determining the direction of memory research.

The stages of storage and retrieval are analogous to storing index cards in a file and retrieving them later (or storing information in computer memory and retrieving it later). The language of storage and retrieval is an effective analogy for what happens in remembering, but we must recognize its metaphorical status. In fact, one objective of some research on memory is to explore the limits of the metaphor. One way to describe the functional properties of remembering is

to determine the range of conditions over which the metaphor holds. This is a matter of function not so much because it shows us what remembering does (the functions of remembering someone's phone number or facts for an exam or how much money someone owes you are pretty obvious), but rather because it shows us how remembering works.

According to this metaphor, a remembered item is one that's been stored and retained and retrieved. The failure to remember an item may occur because the item wasn't stored in the first place, or because the item was stored and then lost from storage during retention, or because the item wasn't retrievable at the opportunity for recall (Watkins, 1990). As we examine how remembering can be affected by events during these three phases, we may have something to say about what it is that metaphorically gets stored and retained and retrieved.

STORAGE: ENCODING AND LEVELS OF PROCESSING

When you remember a stimulus, what you remember isn't so much the stimulus itself as your response to it. That response inevitably differs from the stimulus even when the two are in the same modality (as when you repeat a spoken verbal item aloud). Remembering, in other words, isn't just reproducing the stimulus. Even the immediate response to a stimulus can't be interpreted that way. The issue is long-standing. For example, this passage from the Greek philosopher Theophrastus dates from about 300 B.C.:

> . . . with regard to hearing, it is strange of him [Empedocles] to imagine that he has really explained how creatures hear, when he has ascribed the process to internal sounds and

assumed that the ear produces a sound within, like a bell. By means of this internal sound we might hear sounds without, but how should we hear this internal sound itself? The old problem would still confront us. (Stratton, 1917, p. 85)

A more contemporary version of this point is the following:

Suppose someone were to coat the occipital lobes of the brain with a special photographic emulsion which, when developed, yielded a reasonable copy of a current visual stimulus. In many quarters this would be regarded as a triumph in the physiology of vision. Yet nothing could be more disastrous, for we should have to start all over again and ask how the organism sees a picture in its occipital cortex. (Skinner, 1963; see also Skinner, 1976, p. 74)

As in the analysis of stimulus control, the problem of remembering isn't to be solved by trying to follow the stimulus into the organism; rather, we must discover how to characterize the organism's behavior with respect to the stimulus (cf. Craik, 1985, p. 200: "it is not sensible to inquire about the characteristics of the memory trace when remembering is not occurring").

The learner's behavior with respect to the stimulus to be remembered is called *encoding* (Melton & Martin, 1972). Consider the following experiment (Conrad, 1964). In one part, learners named spoken letters presented in background noise; in another, they saw a sequence of six letters and wrote them down in order. When learners erred in the first task, they did so along dimensions of common acoustic properties. For example, they were more likely to confuse *V* with rhyming letters such as *B* or *C* than with letters such as *N* or *X* that have straight lines in common with *V*. The second task used visually presented letters but produced the same kinds of errors as the first; learners again

erred more often along dimensions of common acoustic than visual properties. These errors must have occurred because the learners encoded the stimuli acoustically rather than visually. In some form or other, the learners were saying the letters to themselves. Whether they were doing that subvocally or in some other way is less important than that their remembering was based upon acoustic rather than visual properties of the letters.

Remembering depends on how the items to be remembered are encoded. For example, some tasks favor encoding based on semantic properties (defining technical terms); others favor encoding based on visual or phonological properties (learning spellings or pronunciations); still others favor encoding based on tonal or temporal properties (following the score of a musical work). Encoding can vary from time to time and within or across tasks, and it can be based on combinations of properties as well as on single dimensions. It can be as simple as the repetition of the item (sometimes called *maintenance rehearsal*) or as complex as an extensive mnemonic system (sometimes called *coding rehearsal*). We'll consider a few examples in the context of two major classes of encoding called *substitution* and *elaboration*.

Simple substitution is the most straightforward encoding and corresponds to familiar examples of codes (as in Morse-code learning; cf. Keller, 1958). Consider learning a sequence of the binary digits, 0 and 1 (Miller, 1956). The sequence 010001101011 101001 substantially exceeds the number of digits that can be remembered after a single presentation. Each group of three binary digits, however, can be replaced by a single octal digit, according to the following list:

000=0	001=1	010=2	011=3
100=4	101=5	110=6	111=7

The binary sequence then can be coded as the octal sequence 215351, which can be remembered after just one presentation. Reducing the number of items to be remembered by encoding groups of items is called *chunking* (note that chunks can be arbitrary; this factor distinguishes chunking from clustering in free recall; cf. Chapter 17). The acoustic encoding of written letters can also be regarded as substitution in that there's a unique correspondence between spoken and written letters.

A second type of encoding is called *elaborative* encoding, as when a CVC nonsense syllable or a sequence of consonants is transformed into a word or a phrase. For example, a learner might rehearse the nonsense syllable *BOH* as *BOTH without a T*, or the consonant sequence *QBF* as *Quick Brown Fox*. Another variety of elaborative encoding is visual imagery, already discussed in the context of mnemonics (cf. Paivio, 1971). Elaborative encoding doesn't guarantee the unique correspondences between items and the learner's responses that characterize substitution, so encoded items may be more likely to occasion inappropriate responses. For example, the learner using the method of loci who encodes the word *baggage* by imagining a tower of suitcases standing in a parking lot might instead say *luggage* at recall.

Encoding, whether by substitution or elaboration, is inevitably selective. Some stimulus properties are more likely to occasion responses than others. For example, written words are very likely to produce the kind of encoding called reading; it isn't easy to look at a word without reading it (cf. Stroop, 1935 and Chapter 15). Can you disobey the instruction "Don't read this sentence"? For written verbal stimuli, a reader's response is affected more by semantic properties of the text than by typeface or size. Such responding to verbal stimuli is called *semantic encoding* (cf. Chapter 16).

Simply naming something may qualify as encoding. Two experiments involved recognition tasks with rhesus monkeys and with humans (Cook, Wright, & Sands, 1991; Wright et al., 1990). The stimuli included kaleidoscope pictures or travel slides. Each stimulus was presented briefly on a screen; responses were the movement of a lever to the left or to the right. The monkey behavior was maintained by food reinforcers; the human behavior was maintained by a tone produced by correct responses (for convenience, we'll treat it as a reinforcer, though instructions and feedback presumably were also important variables). For both monkeys and humans, the task involved successive presentations of six pictures at the top of the screen and then a single picture at the bottom. If the final picture was different from the previous six, a lever movement to the left was reinforced; if it was the same, a movement to the right was reinforced. In other words, a correct response to the right corresponded to recognizing the final picture as one that had appeared among the six.

The six pictures were presented at interstimulus intervals of 0.08, 1 or 4 s. With either the kaleidoscope or the travel pictures, the monkeys were most accurate at the shorter intervals; the more slowly the pictures appeared, the more likely the monkeys were to forget earlier ones. The human performances were similar with the kaleidoscope pictures, but with the travel pictures the humans became more rather than less accurate as the pictures were presented more slowly. One interpretation was that slower presentations allowed verbal encoding and rehearsal of the travel pictures but weren't helpful with the kaleidoscope pictures because they had no names (cf. Intraub, 1979). Thus, the next stage of the experiment with humans was to teach them arbitrary names for each of the kaleidoscope pictures. The recognition task with the kaleidoscope pictures was then repeated, and the human performances became similar to those with the travel slides: The slower the presentation rate, the more accurate they became. The implication is that the names allowed them to encode and rehearse the kaleidoscope pictures.

The results are of interest both for the species difference they demonstrate and for their relevance to the role of naming in remembering. For the present purposes, the main point is that naming itself functions as a variety of encoding. That's probably why we're less likely to recall events from our infancy than from later times in our lives; if we did preverbally engage in encoding, that coding must have been very different from our later verbal encoding. Remembering in the very young is more easily demonstrated in the recall of the child's own actions than in other ways (cf. Bauer, 1996).

The several categories of encoding we've considered are neither exhaustive nor mutually exclusive. Mnemonic systems, for example, can combine substitution, as in the number-to-consonant code, with elaboration, as in visualizing objects according to the method of loci. We shouldn't expect an exhaustive listing, because types of encoding are as unlimited as the different ways in which we can respond to events in the world. For the same reason, we shouldn't expect any one type of encoding to be invariant across different learners or different tasks. Different learning histories and different contingencies upon remembering guarantee variability in the ways that we each encode stimuli.

Types of encoding differ not only in how likely they are to be used in different circumstances, but also in how likely it is that what's encoded will be remembered. Some kinds of encoding seem more superficial and therefore less memorable than others; this dimension of encoding has been called *level*

of processing or *depth of processing* (Cermak & Craik, 1979). Fewer words from a list are recalled after tasks requiring responses to formal properties of words (e.g., crossing out vowels, counting the number of letters) than after tasks requiring semantic responses (e.g., assigning words to categories, discriminating among plant and animal names). The implication is that the deeper the level of processing, the more likely an item is to be remembered. We're certainly more likely to remember items to which we've responded in rich and novel ways (semantic structure and visual imagery are important sources of richness and novelty). As with so many other concepts we've encountered, level of processing is descriptive and not explanatory. It describes relations between types of encoding and the likelihood of remembering; it doesn't explain the remembering. In other words, semantic encoding is called deeper processing because we're more likely to remember a semantically encoded item than a structurally encoded one. The issue of how we remember again becomes one of what's remembered, and the topic of encoding reminds us that remembering is behavior and the learner is active.

RETENTION: THE QUESTION OF MEMORY REORGANIZATION

According to the metaphor of storage and retrieval, after an item has been encoded it may be stored. But how does it get stored and what happens to it after it's been stored? At this point the metaphor of storage and retrieval doesn't help us much. Retention is implicit in the concept of storage, and yet we've already noted that we can't expect to find the to-be-remembered item inside the learner. We haven't even specified what an item is: a word? a sentence or logical proposition? an association? a semantic or syntactic structure tagged with various markers corresponding to its temporal and relational origins? It's only because the item emerges at recall that we assume that it somehow existed throughout retention. That may be a bit like assuming that a pianist at a keyboard releases Beethoven's sonatas from their storage in the piano or even, more simply, that the pianist releases sounds that have been stored in the strings; whoever searches for the sonatas or the sounds by disassembling the piano will be disappointed. We can't ask whether what's remembered changes during retention without resolving this point.

These considerations explain why contemporary accounts of remembering deal with it not in terms of *reproductive* processes, in which events are recalled directly or reproduced, but rather in terms of *reconstructive* processes, in which aspects of past events are derived or reconstructed from what had been encoded (e.g., Hasher & Griffin, 1978). For example, we may sometimes remember solutions to particular mathematical problems; more often, however, and usually more effectively, we remember only the methods of solving them. Analogously, we might indirectly recall the things we bought while shopping by first calculating the difference between the money we have left and what we started with and then working out the details. One crucial thing to remember about remembering is that it's *reconstruction*, not *reproduction*.

Accounts of remembering that assume that what's remembered changes during retention have included theories of *consolidation*, which argue that what's learned becomes fixed or consolidated in memory over some time following learning, and theories of *incubation*, which argue that remembered events and relations are spontaneously reorganized over time (perhaps especially during sleep), sometimes so that their combination constitutes the solution to a longstanding problem (e.g., as in some examples of scientific creativity; Hadamard, 1949). On the other hand, the evidence for subliminal learning or learning without awareness during sleep isn't persuasive (for that matter, the evidence during waking isn't either: e.g., Pratkanis, 1992). Maybe incubation depends on what's already been encoded and subliminal learning fails because it doesn't lead to encoding.

Studies of memory change during retention have used reproductions of remembered material over time (e.g., successive retellings of stories; Bartlett, 1932). Figure 18-1 provides an example using visual figures (Carmichael, Hogan, & Walter, 1932). The remembered figure changed over retention as a function of what it had been named. Gestalt psychology (Köhler, 1929) provided a theoretical case for these changes during retention. The gestalt laws of perception (such as the law of closure, which stated that incomplete figures tend to be seen as completed) were assumed to operate on what's remembered as well as on what's seen. But changes during retention couldn't be distinguished from those that might have occurred during encoding and storage or at retrieval. If a visual stimulus is remembered as a word rather than a form because of verbal encoding, the learner who remembers the word at recall will draw the corresponding picture. If so, there's no need to postulate a gradual reorganization of visual memory traces.

Events that occur between storage and retrieval, however, can affect remembering. For example, consider the following simulation of eyewitness testimony in a courtroom (Loftus & Palmer, 1974). Observers who'd viewed a film of an automobile accident were later asked to estimate the speed of the cars when they collided. In the wording for one group, the question was how fast the

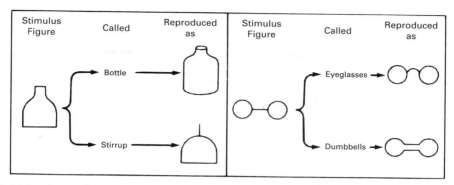

FIGURE 18-1   Examples of changes in remembered visual forms as a function of verbal labels. (Adapted from Carmichael, Hogan, & Walter, 1932, Figure 1)

cars were going when they *hit* each other; for the other, it was how fast they were going when they *smashed into* each other. The wording made a difference. Speed estimates in the first group averaged about 8 miles per hour whereas those in the second averaged more than 10. More important, when the observers were asked a week later whether there'd been broken glass at the scene of the accident, those from the second group were more likely to say, incorrectly, that there was. Whether this distortion of memory depended directly on the difference between *hit* and *smashed into* or was instead mediated by the different estimates of speed, it's clear that events during retention affect the subsequent remembering.

The effects of the wording of questions on recall raise important questions about the reliability of eyewitness testimony. For example, everything else being equal, an eyewitness asked "Did you see the broken headlight?" is more likely to say yes than one asked "Did you see a broken headlight?" (Loftus & Zanni, 1975). The observer's verbal behavior under such questioning is rehearsal of sorts, but it has the disadvantage that it's initiated long after the event. Given

that we can affect remembering by interrupting or otherwise interfering with rehearsal shortly after an event, we shouldn't be surprised that we can also do so by distorting or interfering with it later on. Some distortions of remembering may be based on the timing of the remembered event and a later recall that introduced something new; the domination of one over the other may reverse depending on their separation in time, in relations reminiscent of but in the opposite temporal direction from the reversals of preference in self-control procedures (e.g., Riccio, Rabinowitz, & Axelrod, 1994; cf. Chapter 11).

These cases are not so much concerned with retention as with successive retrievals. Perhaps that's why we usually leave out retention when we speak of the metaphor of storage and retrieval. However we look at these phenomena, they raise significant issues. For example, asking children about past events can create false memories that are more enduring than real ones (Brainerd, Reyna, & Brandse, 1995). If so, how should we interpret reports of other kinds of memories, which might range from sexual abuse in childhood to kidnapping by the alien crews of UFOs? The reality of such repressed memories has raised troublesome legal and ethical issues (Loftus, 1993). If someone claims to have just recalled an unsolved murder that occurred two decades ago, the importance of closing the case, in the absence of other kinds of evidence, must be weighed against what we know about remembering. How seriously can we take such testimony? If the sudden recall by an adult of sexual abuse in childhood is based on real events, it would be tragic to ignore it. We can't resolve these dilemmas, but at least we can consider their possible antecedents: the events that are later remembered, and verbal behavior that has been shaped by social contingencies.

An interview, whether by attorney, reporter or psychiatrist, too often lends itself to the shaping of verbal behavior by the interviewer, perhaps deliberately or perhaps inadvertently (cf. Chapter 16). With some verbal behavior to start with, such as an account of strange lights or some other unusual sighting, an interviewer, simply by reacting more enthusiastically to some parts of the descriptions than others, can shape consistent stories across individuals who've never met each other. Over time, the descriptions may come to include details of the flying saucers and their occupants. Once that's happened, there are plenty of social consequences (some monetary) to keep this verbal behavior going and to discourage reports of where it came from. If such distortions of remembering seem far-fetched, we need to be reminded that they're only more extreme cases of robust and well-documented phenomena of remembering (remembering by children may be especially susceptible to such shaping); as such they're surely not as far-fetched as UFO abduction stories. It's easy to make people think they remember words that never actually appeared on a list (e.g., intrusions in free recall: Chapter 17). Why should we be sur-

prised if we sometimes encounter more extreme cases?

RETRIEVAL: CUE-DEPENDENCY AND ACCESSIBILITY

False remembering isn't really remembering, so let's now consider remembering when it actually works. We introduce retrieval with a quotation:

> In order to understand retrieval processes, some basic principles must first be accepted. One of the most important of these was formulated by St. Augustine more than 1500 years ago; we cannot seek in our memory for anything of which we have no sort of recollection; by seeking something in our memory, "we declare, by that very act, that we have not altogether forgotten it; we still hold of it, as it were, a part, and by this part, which we hold, we seek that which we do not hold." (Tulving & Madigan, 1970, p. 460)

In other words, we aren't likely to remember an item or event in the absence of discriminative stimuli correlated with some properties of the item or event to be remembered. Sometimes these properties are specified by instructions, as when we're asked which of two items came earlier in a list, or whether we've met someone before, or where we were last year on the night of November 5. In these cases, the "parts we hold" are the items or a face or a date. At other times, circumstances define these properties, as when we can't remember the article that we were supposed to buy at the store or where we put our keys. Here, the "parts" are our presence in the store or the activity that requires the keys.

An item that's stored is said to be *available* in memory. The item, however, may or may not be remembered. When you can remember, we say it's *accessible*; when you can't, we say it's *inaccessible* (Tulving & Pearlstone,

1966). The trouble is that if you remember an item we know that it was both available and accessible, but if you can't we don't know whether it was unavailable or was available but inaccessible (cf. Watkins, 1990).

The accessibility of an item depends on the stimuli or cues present at the moment of recall. Their influence on remembering is called *cue-dependency*. For example, visualizing a place used in the method of loci reinstates one condition that existed when you encoded the item. Similarly, reciting the al-

phabet may help you to remember a forgotten name, because producing the person's initial reinstates one part of saying the name. When we use such techniques, we generate our own retrieval cues. The most critical feature of retrieval is producing conditions similar to those during encoding and storage.

Consider the recall experiment illustrated in Figure 18-2 (Tulving & Psotka, 1971). Six 24-word lists each included six semantic categories of four words each (e.g., military ranks: captain, corporal, sergeant, colonel;

FIGURE 18-2   Words recalled from six 24-word lists in original learning, cued recall and noncued recall. Each list consisted of 4-word groups in 6 semantic categories (e.g., insects, metals, tools) and was shown three times at a rate of 1 word/s; categories differed from list to list. Original learning data show recall of each list immediately after its three presentations. Noncued recall data, obtained after all 6 lists were presented, show recall as a function of the number of intervening lists (those already recalled). Cued recall data were also obtained after all 6 lists were presented, but learners were given the category names for each list. Cued recall was about equal to recall after original learning. During noncued recall the words were available but not accessible; category names in cued recall made them accessible. (Data from Tulving & Psotka, 1971, as presented in Tulving, 1974, Figure 2)

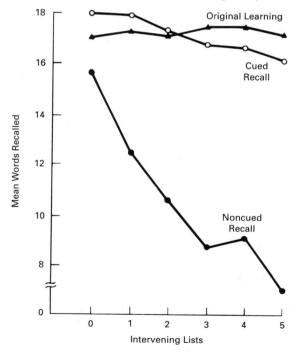

earth formations: cliff, river, hill, volcano); the categories differed from list to list. Recall was compared under three conditions. One was recall of each list immediately after its presentation (original learning); another was recall only after all six lists had been presented (noncued recall); the third was recall only after all six lists had been presented but with the category names within each list provided (cued recall). Noncued recall was poorer than recall immediately after original learning, but cued recall showed that the words hadn't been forgotten; in cued recall, when category names were provided, recall was roughly equivalent to recall immediately after original learning. In other words, according to the metaphor of storage and retrieval, the words were available but inaccessible during noncued recall; the category names in cued recall made them accessible.

Chapter 17 illustrated a similar cue-dependency in an experiment that made recall more likely than recognition. Recall is usually best when encoding and recall cues are based on common properties of the item to be remembered. Cue-dependency implies that differences between the conditions at storage and those at retrieval are an important factor in forgetting. Those conditions include not only the to-be-remembered stimuli and the learner's behavior with respect to them, but also the situation within which the learning took place. In a special case of cue-dependency called *state-dependent learning*, recall is affected by the similarity of the learner's condition at retrieval to that at storage. Conditions studied include drugs and physiological states (e.g., electroconvulsive shock) as well as experimental settings (e.g., Bower, 1981; Overton, 1964). For example, the sober learner may be less likely to remember something learned while drunk than the learner who has become drunk again.

Cue-dependencies and state-dependencies may have important practical implications. But we might not want to advise a student who's preparing for an exam to study in the room in which the exam will be held. For one thing, what's been learned will be useless after the course is over if the student can't remember it anywhere else. More important, what's learned will be best remembered if many of the conditions for remembering arise out of the subject matter itself (cf. Marholin & Steinman, 1977). A systematic subject matter is one in which each component prompts and is prompted by other components. To outline the subject matter, therefore, is to create an encoding that determines not only how well the various parts are remembered but also how the recall of one part may aid in the recall of another.

We've surveyed some memory research influenced by the metaphor of search. According to this metaphor, during retrieval the learner searches through the memory store for items having certain characteristics until the appropriate one is found. The store might be analogous to a stack of index cards or to the memory banks of a computer. But how does the metaphor deal with how rapidly and accurately humans can discriminate between knowing something and not knowing it (e.g., Kolers & Palef, 1976)? Why should search ever take longer when an appropriate item exists to be found than when such an item doesn't exist, and therefore when the search must examine every item in metaphorical storage?

Aside from the problem of how rapidly we can say we don't know something, the metaphor is also strained by the vast capacity of human memory; if nothing else, a search through memory storage at every instance of remembering seems inefficient. Cue-dependency suggests a more restricted search limited by the conditions at recall. At this point, extending the metaphor demands that we distinguish among kinds of search.

A random search through an unorganized list differs from one through an ordered list (as in finding a word in an alphabetized index); both differ from a systematic search through categories organized hierarchically (as in finding an item in a department-store catalogue with sections for different types of merchandise). As we'll see in Chapter 20, types of search may be distinguished by their quantitative properties. An undifferentiated metaphor of search isn't adequate for a general account of human memory, but differentiated versions may be relevant to special classes of memory tasks.

Section C   Metamemory

Remembering is behavior, and remembering can be learned. Not only do we learn patterns of rehearsal and mnemonic techniques, but we also learn to judge the properties of our own remembering (e.g., Flavell, Friedrichs, & Hoyt, 1970; Nelson, 1992). What we do when we remember will depend at least partly on the past consequences of our remembering. We can therefore define *metamemory* in terms of the differentiation and discrimination of our own remembering.

RUNNING OR WORKING MEMORY

Continually updating what's remembered by dropping some items and adding others is sometimes called *running memory* or *working memory*. Consider the short-order breakfast cook working on three orders of waffles, a stack of pancakes, two eggs over easy and two scrambled. As each dish is handed out to be served and each new order is called in, some items can be forgotten while others must be added to what's being remembered. Earlier breakfast orders over the course of the morning are potentially a major source of

proactive interference. Nevertheless, this task is often performed with considerable skill. It can't be done well simply through undifferentiated remembering. The number of orders that can be remembered and worked on at a given time is limited: The short-order cook must distinguish among orders that have been finished and can be forgotten, those in progress that must be watched, and those not yet started that must be remembered. The updating of what can be forgotten and what must still be remembered is crucial to doing the job successfully (e.g., Bjork, 1978). Other examples are keeping track of cards played in a card game or following the changing statistics during an athletic event (most appropriately, running memory of races run, laps completed, relative positions of competitors and other information at a track meet). In such circumstances, what can be forgotten is as important as what must be remembered.

The learning of some verbal items can be affected when the learner is instructed to forget other items (e.g., Bjork, 1970). Interference by a given item is reduced by an instruction to forget it. As might be expected, the reduction is greater when the instruction to forget precedes the presentation of the item than when it follows. But what sort of behavior occurs when the learner is instructed to forget? Are the items somehow deleted from memory, or do they remain while the learner somehow discriminates those to be remembered from those to be forgotten? One experiment (Waugh, 1972) examined free recall of a 40-item list of common one-syllable words. In one condition, some of the first 20 items of the 40-item list were repeated among the last 20. Even with the instruction to forget the first 20 items, the recall probability for these items in the last 20 was greater than that for others. Whatever the learner did when instructed to forget didn't cancel the effects of the items to be forgotten; the learner was more likely to recall those items when they appeared again in the second half of the list than to recall the items that hadn't appeared before.

DISCRIMINATED REMEMBERING

Not only can learners learn to remember and to forget differentially, as when they're more likely to remember unfinished than finished tasks (the Zeigarnik effect; Zeigarnik, 1927), but they can also discriminate among properties of their own remembering. The "tip-of-the-tongue" phenomenon (Brown & McNeill, 1966; cf. Chapter 14) is an example of a discrimination based upon the likelihood of remembering. We can sometimes say that we'll be able to recognize a word even though we're unable to recall it at the moment. The accuracy of this discrimination can be assessed on the basis of partial reports of the word to be remembered. When a word is "on the tip of your tongue," you can often report its initial letter or the number of syllables or some other property, and you're likely to recognize it when you see it.

Both at storage and retrieval, learners can estimate the likelihood of remembering; they can also usually discriminate between never having learned something and having learned and then forgotten it (Kolers & Palef,

1976). Having remembered something, we often discriminate among its sources. In recalling some incident, for example, you may be able to report that some facts are based on your own experience whereas you deduced others (e.g., Johnson & Raye, 1981). Another instance of discriminating your remembering is when you describe your confidence about something you've recalled.

Our capacity to make such judgments changes over time (cf. Lachman, Lachman, & Thronesbery, 1979, on metamemory through the adult life span; Skinner, 1983, on intellectual self-management in old age). Such judgments, closely related to the autoclitic processes of Chapter 14, aren't memory but probably are important components of it. For example, the student who can't distinguish between having learned something well and having learned it inadequately isn't likely to be able to study effectively or to ask appropriate questions (e.g., Bisanz, Vesonder, & Voss, 1978; Miyake & Norman, 1979). Remembering is a higher-order class, and many aspects of it are presumably shaped by natural contingencies. But the various dimensions of metamemory should remind us of the possibilities for differentiating it further. In other words, to propose a metaphor perhaps worth storing and occasionally retrieving, remembering is a skill that can be sharpened.

Chapter 19
The Structure of Remembering

Memory *has its source in an Indo-European root* smer- *or* mer-, *to remember, through which it is related to* remember *and* mourn. *The root does not seem to be linked to the Indo-European* men-, *to think, which is the source of* mnemonic, amnesia, memento, reminiscence, automatic, *and, perhaps most interesting,* mind *and* mental. *Forget has a source in the Indo-European root* ghend-, *to seize or take. Through the Middle English* gessen, *to try to get, it is related to* guess, *and through the Latin* prehendere, *to hold before, it is related to* apprehend *and* comprehend.

Many theories of memory have been concerned with how memory works, but a dominant theme in experiments on memory is the study of what we remember. Analyses of what's remembered, like analyses of the effects of reinforcement, tell us about the properties of behavior classes. Our example of the pigeon's remembering at the start of Chapter 18 required continued behavior that bridged the temporal gap between the stimulus and the later response. The subsequent mnemonic examples didn't include such uninterrupted intervening behavior. Clearly the cases differ. We'd similarly distinguish between remembering an appointment after seeing it on a calendar and remembering without consulting such a record. These are different varieties of remembering.

One criterion for organizing kinds of remembering is the time period over which something's remembered; another is what's remembered. We'll sample both classifications. First we'll treat the duration of remembering by examining three phenomena: (1) the relatively brief persistence of stimulus effects; (2) the maintenance of responding occasioned by a stimulus, as in rehearsal; and (3) remembering after some time elapses without rehearsal. These categories have been respectively called (1) *iconic memory*, (2) *short-term memory*, and (3) *long-term memory*. Then we'll treat categories of remembering defined by what's remembered, as in *autobiographical* or *episodic* memory and *semantic* memory; autobiographical memory involves remembering events in the learner's past, and semantic memory involves remembering properties of the learner's language, such as word meanings. The structure of what's remembered will be relevant to the distinctions among these types of remembering, but as in Chapter 18 we'll discover that structure and function often interact.

Section A   Iconic Memory: The Persisting Effects of Stimuli

The effects of a stimulus may continue even after the stimulus is gone. Persisting aftereffects of visual stimuli are called *icons*, and the topic of *iconic memory* is concerned with their time course (an afterimage is one persisting effect of a visual stimulus; on the relation between icons and visual afterimages, see Long, 1980). How do we measure that time course? If an observer reports some letters that have been briefly presented, how do we tell the difference between a report based on the sensory aftereffect and one based on the observer's continued rehearsal of the letters?

We can solve the problem by showing more items in the stimulus display than the observer can remember in a single trial and asking the observer for some sample of these items at various times after the display. We're limited in the number of items we can rehearse or remember after a single brief presentation. This limit, typically within the range of seven plus or minus two items (Miller, 1956), is called the *span of immediate memory*. For the present purposes, it serves as a tool for studying iconic memory. The range of the span of immediate memory is to some extent independent of the nature of the items. For example, you can remember roughly five to nine words almost as easily as five to nine letters, even though the words

themselves include many more than nine letters (cf. chunking in Chapter 18).

Just as an exam tests only part of the material that a student is supposed to have learned during a course and assumes that the score represents what proportion of the entire course has actually been learned, a sampling of what the observer reports at different times after the display assumes that the observer's responses represent the proportion of items that can be reported. The time course of iconic memory is measured over fractions of a second, but during this time the observer in effect can still read the items in the display even though the display is no longer there.

Figure 19-1 shows data from one experiment based on this rationale (Sperling, 1960). A 4-by-3 matrix of letters and numbers was presented to observers for 50 ms (0.05 s). An example is the following:

```
7 I V F
X L 5 3
B 4 W 7
```

Observers couldn't report this many items, so a tone of high or medium or low frequency served as an instruction to report the characters in just the top or middle or bottom line of the matrix. The tone sounded either before the display, at the moment it ended or at some time after it was gone (x-axis in Figure 19-1). The mean number of characters correctly reported from the single line was multiplied by three and taken as an estimate of the total reportable characters in the matrix (y-axis in Figure 19-1).

About 10 characters from the matrix were reportable when the instruction tone preceded the display or occurred as it ended (delays of -0.10 and 0 s); as the instruction tone followed the display with delays of 0.15 s or longer, the reportable characters decreased with increasing delay. When it was

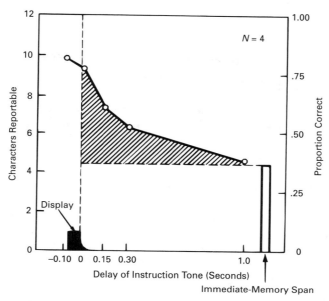

FIGURE 19-1 Characters reportable from a 3-by-4 matrix of letters and numbers when the signal for reporting occurs at various times relative to the display. The signal was a tone of high, medium or low frequency that instructed the observer to report the characters in the top, middle or bottom row of the matrix. With increasing delays of the instruction tone, accuracy approached the immediate-memory span. Data are means across four observers. (Adapted from Sperling, 1960, Figure 7)

delayed by 1 s, the reportable characters were about equal in number to the span of immediate memory in this task (this span of about 4 to 5 items, at the extreme low end of the usual 5- to 9-item range, probably depended on the relative complexity of the observer's task, which included mixed letters and numbers and the matrix format). The shaded area between the data points and the immediate-memory span is assumed to represent the persistence of the sensory effects of the display; this is the extent to which the observer can still read some of the matrix even though it's no longer there.

This experiment demonstrates that the sensory effects of a stimulus continue briefly after the stimulus has been removed. Similar effects have been demonstrated with auditory presentations of verbal stimuli, as

when different sequences of spoken letters were simultaneously presented in three auditory channels (left ear, right ear or both ears; Darwin, Turvey, & Crowder, 1972). Effects of auditory stimuli appear to decrease more slowly, perhaps over several seconds, than those of visual stimuli. The auditory case is called *echoic memory* (but shouldn't be confused with echoic verbal behavior as in Chapter 14; echoic memory involves the persisting effects of auditory stimuli, without regard to the nature of the listener's response to the stimuli, whereas echoic verbal behavior is defined by the correspondences between auditory stimuli and the listener's vocal responses).

Obviously the finding that the sensory effects of a stimulus continue for a brief time after the stimulus ends has only a little to do with remembering over longer periods. Visual stimuli must be seen and auditory stimuli must be heard to be remembered, but remembering over minutes or days can't be attributed to the persisting but brief sensory effects.

Section B   Short-Term Memory: The Role of Rehearsal

The recall of a human learner immediately after presentation of a verbal sequence, usually limited to about five to nine items, is the span of immediate memory (Jacobs, 1887; Miller, 1956). For example, you can probably correctly repeat the sequence 706294 after a single hearing, but you're not likely to manage the longer sequence 549628367999102.

The limit on the span of immediate memory provided the historical basis for studies of what's come to be called *short-term memory* (STM or, in some usages, *primary memory*, as in Waugh & Norman, 1965; cf. Daniels, 1895; Smith, W., 1895). A major question is whether the response is occasioned directly by prior stimuli or is instead occasioned indirectly by intervening behavior such as rehearsal.

One way to address the question is with a task that prevents the learner from rehearsing items between their presentation and the opportunity for recall. The tasks used to measure the span of immediate memory incidentally create such conditions. If a long sequence of items is presented, the learner can't simultaneously rehearse the early items and listen to the later ones. Some of the later items therefore interfere with or prevent the behavior on which the recall of earlier items depends.

Consider now the short-term memory experiment of Peterson and Peterson (1959; see also Brown, 1958). Vocal stimuli consisted of three consonants and then a three-digit number. The learner's instructions were to begin counting backward by threes from the number and then, when a signal light flashed, to recall the consonants. A trial might start with the spoken items, CHJ 506; the learner then counted backward, 506, 503, 500, 497, and so on until the signal light, which set the occasion for naming the consonants. The time from the consonants to the onset of the signal varied from 3 to 18 s. Under these conditions, recall accuracy decreased with delay until, at delays of 15 or 18 s, the proportion correct was less than 10%. In two other conditions, learners were allowed periods of vocal or silent rehearsal before they were given the number from which to count backward.

Figure 19-2 compares data from the original procedure (open circles) and data with 3 s of either silent rehearsal (filled triangles) or vocal rehearsal (filled circles) before the backward-counting task. The more overtly the learners could rehearse, the better was their recall. Recall is determined more by our behavior with respect to past stimuli than by the stimuli themselves.

These and related findings led to proposals for two distinct types of memory: short-term memory and long-term memory (e.g., Shiffrin & Atkinson, 1969). Items were said to be rapidly lost from short-term memory unless maintained there through rehearsal; by some means, perhaps through rehearsal itself, items in short-term memory were sometimes transferred to a more permanent long-term memory. Some accounts distinguish between two types of rehearsal (e.g., Craik & Lockhart, 1972; Rundus, 1977, 1980). In *maintenance* rehearsal, an item is simply repeated (as in reciting something to be memorized); in *coding* rehearsal, the item is

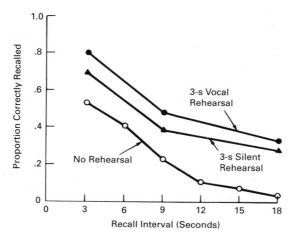

FIGURE 19-2 Proportion of three-consonant items correctly recalled as a function of delay between presentation and opportunity for recall. In one condition (open circles), rehearsal was prevented by instructing the learner to count backwards by threes from a number that immediately followed each item. In two other conditions, the learner was allowed 3 s of silent rehearsal (filled triangles) or vocal rehearsal (filled circles) before starting to count backwards. (Adapted from Peterson & Peterson, 1959, Figure 3 and Table 1)

transformed or elaborated in some way (as in mnemonic encoding). Note that both types of rehearsal depend on encoding; even naming a stimulus is a type of encoding.

Only a few items at a time can be held in short-term memory, but the capacity of long-term memory is virtually unlimited. More detailed analyses of data from short-term memory procedures complicated this view, however.

Without rehearsal (Figure 19-2, open circles), the data at first seem to represent the gradual fading or decay of items to be remembered. But several lines of evidence suggest this isn't so. Consider first the effects of varying the number of letters to be remembered, as in Figure 19-3 (Melton, 1963) (p. 340). A stimulus item containing one to five consonants and then a three-digit number was presented visually; the learner read the consonants aloud and then began counting backward by threes or fours until a visual signal set the occasion for recall. When the item consisted of just a single consonant, recall accuracy remained high even over 32 s. The proportion of items recalled decreased more rapidly over time as the number of consonants increased. But now which set of data represents the time course of short-term memory? If recall of a single consonant is nearly perfect, then adding new consonants may simply interfere to some extent with recall of the old.

The two extreme possibilities in these procedures are perfect recall and no recall at all. Perhaps the backward-counting task prevented rehearsal only partially, and intermediate outcomes occurred because learners had some opportunities for rehearsal even while engaging in that task. More rehearsal is presumably necessary for recall of more consonants, so recall accuracy at a given delay should decrease with the number of consonants. Thus, the form of the short-term

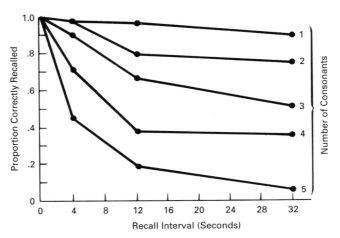

FIGURE 19-3 Proportion of consonants correctly recalled as a function of delay between presentation and recall, with number of consonants as a parameter. The consonants and a three-digit number were presented visually; the learner read the consonants aloud and then began counting backwards by threes or fours until a visual signal for recall. (From Melton, 1963, Figure 2)

memory function may depend mainly on the learner's opportunity to respond to the stimulus items (cf. Crowder, 1976, p. 196). Perhaps it's relevant that the recall probability of three consonants was greater in Melton's experiment (Figure 19-3) than in Peterson and Peterson's (Figure 19-2). Melton's learners recited the consonants aloud and were therefore guaranteed at least one rehearsal before they began the backward counting, whereas the Petersons' learners didn't do so. One experiment used visual stimuli and the other used vocal stimuli, but the opportunity for immediate responding was probably more important than the modality difference.

Once we recognize that each item can affect the recall of others, we can ask whether the numbers in the backward-counting task prevent rehearsal or interfere with recall in some other way. If each number produced by the learner during backward counting is an item, does recall vary with time or with number of items? This problem was addressed by surveying memory experiments in which delays between items and recall included various numbers and rates of intervening items (Waugh & Norman, 1965). Data from many studies indicated that the number of intervening items during the delay was more important than its duration. For example, learners were given numbers at rates of 1 or 4 per s and then were asked to name the number at a particular location in the sequence. Recall probability after 4 items in 1 s was about equal to that after 4 items in 4 s, even though the delay between the first item and recall was about 1 s in the former case and 4 s in the latter; and recall probability was greater after a delay with 2 intervening items in 2 s than after one with 8 items in 2 s. If any rehearsal occurs while items are presented, items presented slowly should permit more rehearsal than items presented rapidly. It's difficult to reconcile this outcome with an account of short-term memory in terms of the effects of restricting rehearsal.

Still another problem is that recall probability changes over the first few trials of a short-term memory procedure (e.g., Keppel & Underwood, 1962). For example, recall of a three-consonant item on the first trial of a short-term memory session is nearly perfect at a delay of either 3 or 18 s; over the next three to six trials, recall probability decreases, but the decrease is much greater when the delay is 18 s than when it's 3 s. In other words, the relation between recall probability and the delay imposed by an interpolated task, as in Figures 19-2 and 19-3, is absent at the beginning of sessions and builds up over several trials. This is an example of proactive inhibition (cf. Chapter 17): Learning the consonants on the first trial interferes with the recall of other consonants on later trials. We'll have more to say about such proactive effects later.

Changes in stimulus items can temporarily eliminate the proactive effect in short-term memory. For example, recall probability increases substantially for a trial or more after the items to be remembered are changed from letters to numbers or vice versa. Similar effects also occur with words as stimulus items (e.g., with changes in semantic categories, as from food to furniture; Wickens, 1970). These procedures may be more relevant to defining verbal classes than to analyzing short-term memory.

Short-term memory procedures are usually designed to prevent rehearsal rather than to encourage it. It's therefore curious that rehearsal has played such a substantial role in their interpretation. There's no single short-term memory function. Furthermore, interference among items, both within and across trials, makes it inappropriate to speak of short-term memory as the passive decay of items. Nevertheless, the recall of an item

after its uninterrupted rehearsal differs from its recall if there's been no rehearsal. This difference, together with the limited span of immediate memory, justifies the distinction between short-term memory and other types of memory.

Section C   **Long-Term Memory:**
              Interference and Forgetting

In studies of short-term memory, the time from item presentation to recall is usually a matter of seconds, whereas in studies of long-term memory (sometimes abbreviated LTM) it may be minutes, hours, days or even years. It's been argued on the one hand that short-term and long-term memory are separate types of remembering with different properties, and on the other that short-term and long-term memory are merely extremes on a single continuum determined by variables that affect remembering (Melton, 1963; Tulving & Madigan, 1970). The account here will mainly elaborate on a simple procedural consequence of the existence of a span of immediate memory.

When the number of items in a list exceeds the span of immediate memory, a single presentation isn't enough for the learner's recall, even if recall follows immediately after the list ends. The only way to study the remembering of such lists is to arrange repeated presentations of some or all of the items to be learned. In other words, the number of items to be remembered determines whether repeated presentations are needed; that's why they're more important in distinguishing between short-term and long-term memory than the period of time over which remembering is measured. Long-term memory includes all cases in which the items to be remembered exceed the immediate memory span. Such remembering doesn't allow uninterrupted rehearsal between presentation and recall; such remembering requires repeated presentations of the to-be-remembered items; so, inevitably, such remembering is likely to be studied over relatively longer time periods than those common to research on short-term memory.

Data from the classic study of long-term memory by Ebbinghaus (1885) are shown in Figure 19-4. The remembering of nonsense-syllable lists was assessed by the method of savings (cf. Chapter 17) at 20 min, 1 and 8.8 hr, and 1, 2, 6 and 31 days after original learning. The largest decrease in the proportion remembered (in other words, the most forgetting) occurred shortly after original learning. Even after 31 days, however, the savings on relearning exceeded 20%. Ebbinghaus entertained the alternative possibilities that memories deteriorated over time or that they remained intact but were gradually overlaid by or hidden beneath other memories. (In more contemporary vocabulary, the distinction might be expressed as one between decreasing *availability* of items with time as

items are lost from memory, and decreasing *accessibility* with unchanged availability as items remain in memory but become harder and harder to retrieve.)

These two views were the precursors of many theories of forgetting. Those based upon the passive decay of memories, sometimes called *trace* theories, usually assumed correspondences between remembering and hypothetical processes in the nervous system. Those based upon competition among different memories, sometimes called *interference* theories, were more likely to rely on stimulus and response variables. A third kind of theory, memory *consolidation*, argued that memory is impermanent immediately after learning and that time is required for it to become fixed or consolidated; during that time, various events can disrupt it (e.g., trauma). Consolidation theories were influenced by the phenomenon of *reminiscence* (Ballard, 1913; Kamin, 1957). Reminiscence, most likely to occur with incompletely learned materials, is an increase in recall probability as time passes since the end of learning, and it only occurs under certain

FIGURE 19-4 Ebbinghaus's forgetting curve. Ebbinghaus learned and relearned 13-syllable lists. With different times between original learning and relearning, he measured how much was saved from the original learning. Forgetting was substantial even soon after original learning (the first point is at 20 min), but after 31 days savings were still greater than 20%. (Adapted from Ebbinghaus, 1885, Chap. VII)

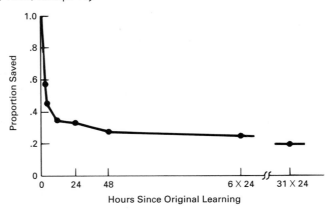

conditions. For example, it's more likely with pictures than with verbal material (Erdelyi & Kleinhard, 1978). An important implication of reminiscence is that there's no such thing as a single function that describes remembering or forgetting; there are even circumstances in which recall becomes more rather than less likely over time.

The notion of memories as traces that fade or decay over time was implicit in many early generalizations (e.g., Jost's law: If two associations are of equal strength but different ages, the older will lose strength or be forgotten more slowly than the newer; Jost, 1897). The problem with such generalizations is that what's remembered varies with how we measure it: Forgetting as measured by savings on relearning a list differs from that measured by recall or recognition of the items; an easily learned list isn't necessarily better remembered than a list learned with difficulty; two lists that differ in difficulty or in the time to meet learning criteria may be forgotten at approximately equal rates if mastery of the items on the two lists is equated (Underwood, 1964).

In one form or another, accounts in terms of interference have come to dominate analyses of long-term memory. For example, interference theories were consistent with effects of sleep. Although we've already seen that there's no convincing evidence for learning during sleep (Chapter 18), less forgetting of what's learned while awake occurs during sleep than during equal waking periods (Jenkins & Dallenbach, 1924). One interpretation is that events during waking are more likely than events during sleep to interfere with what's been learned.

Early treatments of forgetting in terms of interference assumed that events between learning and recall were the major source of interference. They were assumed to act retroactively, so that recent events affected what was learned earlier. But that assumption was wrong. The critical finding for analyses in terms of interference was that interference worked the other way around: Earlier learning had substantial proactive effects, influencing the forgetting of more recently learned material (Underwood, 1957; Underwood & Postman, 1960). Figure 19-5

FIGURE 19-5 Recall of items on a list as a function of the number of lists previously learned. Each circle represents data from a different study. Forgetting was greater as the number of previous lists increased; in other words, forgetting depended on proactive interference from the earlier lists. (Adapted from Underwood, 1957, Figure 3)

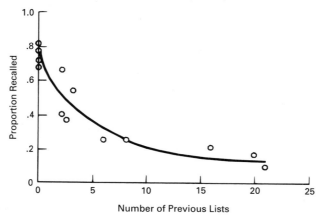

summarizes data from several experiments, and shows how the forgetting of a list varies as a function of the number of lists learned earlier (Underwood, 1957).

The demonstration of proactive interference was significant because most data on human memory over more than half a century had been obtained from practiced learners who'd served in experiments involving the learning of many lists. Ebbinghaus himself typified that circumstance, and even learners who didn't participate in experiments with many lists under many conditions were usually given practice lists before the experiment proper began. From those studies, the estimate of forgetting over 24 hours had been about 75%; Underwood's analysis showed that most of this forgetting is produced by proactive interference from the earlier lists, and that without such interference forgetting is only about 25% (zero lists, Figure 19-5). In other words, a predominant cause of forgetting is that older learning interferes with the remembering of what's been learned more recently.

The data in Figure 19-5 showed that the remembering of one list learned in the laboratory was hindered by the prior learning of other lists in the laboratory. If this much forgetting was produced by proactive interference from what was learned in the laboratory, how much of the forgetting that was left was produced by proactive interference from sources outside the laboratory (Underwood & Postman, 1960)? Even someone in an experiment on verbal learning for the first time enters with an extensive verbal history. If learning a list in the laboratory can have some effect, then learning outside it should act the same way. Transfer is also relevant: Depending on the tasks, some kinds of prior learning might have larger proactive effects than others. The implications are tantalizing: Could it be that there'd be little forgetting or none at all were it not for proactive interfer-

ence? (Probably not; there are some retroactive contributions to forgetting.)

Section D   The Structure of Memory: What Is Remembered?

We've considered various properties of memory. Many kinds of events and relations can be remembered. For example, the pigeon that pecks a key today because pecks yesterday occasionally produced food can be said to be remembering the past contingency between pecks and food. We've already questioned whether remembering of this sort is related in any simple way to remembering in human verbal learning. The vocabulary of memory may be occasioned by almost any situation in which current behavior is influenced by past events. We remember words, particular incidents, contingencies, stimuli, definitions, syntax and our own behavior, among other things. Structure exists in what's remembered in specific instances. It also exists at the higher-order level of relations among different kinds of remembering. We've already seen how the two major classes of short-term memory and long-term memory are related by the span of immediate memory and its implications for what can be mastered on a single presentation. Those two classes provide the foundation for a taxonomy of remembering that's supplemented by other classes of remembering that we'll review.

PROCEDURAL AND DECLARATIVE MEMORY

Given the variety of kinds of remembering, we might expect their properties to depend on what's remembered (cf. Roediger & Craik, 1989). Remembering how things are done is called *procedural* memory. Motor memory is an example (e.g., Baddeley, 1976). Two classes of motor memory have been distinguished: discrete skills, such as typing or changing gear in a manual-shift car; and continuous skills, such as tracking a continuously moving target or steering a car. The distinction is important mainly because discrete skills can be forgotten whereas continuous skills rarely are (one doesn't forget how to swim or to ride a bicycle). The two skills seem closely related. If a memory difference can be observed even in this comparison, we must be alert for others.

Procedural memory is usually contrasted with *declarative* memory, which is verbal remembering or the remembering of facts (e.g, Tulving, 1985; cf. the distinction between knowing how and knowing that in Chapter 1). A substantial proportion of the examples we've considered here and in Chapter 18 has involved declarative memory.

IMPLICIT AND EXPLICIT MEMORY

Procedural memory doesn't necessarily involve words. Some types of remembering can't be assessed simply by asking what someone remembers. We may not know how much we know. This is as true for the remembering of verbal material as for the remembering of ways of doing things, and it's the basis for distinguishing between *implicit* and *explicit* memory (e.g., Craik, 1983; Foss, 1988; Johnson & Hasher, 1987). These two types of remembering are usually well integrated in normal adults, but in those individuals with certain types of verbal deficits called *aphasias* they can be dissociated. For example, suppose an observer has the task of reporting tachistoscopically presented words (written words that are presented very briefly); one measure of the threshold for seeing the word is the duration at which the observer can reliably report it. This threshold can be reduced if a priming word (the same word or a semantically related word) is shown at some time before the test word. With aphasic adults, thresholds can be reduced by priming words even though these aphasics can't remember what the priming words were. In other words, verbal stimuli can have effects on later verbal behavior (they're implicitly remembered) even though they can't be reported later (they aren't explicitly remembered). Similar effects can occur in normal remembering (cf. Watkins, 1989).

AUTOBIOGRAPHICAL AND SEMANTIC MEMORY

When we speak of everyday remembering, we're usually concerned with particular incidents that occurred at certain times and places. This kind of remembering is called *autobiographical* or *episodic* memory, in that it involves the recall of episodes from our own lives. Even this class of remembering may include subclasses, such as differences between ordinary day-to-day memory and memory of emotionally charged events. One special case of autobiographical memory, sometimes called *flashbulb* memory, involves remembering the details of where we were at the time of hearing about a significant event such as a major disaster (Neisser & Harsch, 1992). Despite our intuitions about it, even this type of remembering can be modified substantially by the conditions under which we retell the story. (Flashbulb memory shouldn't be confused with *eidetic* memory, the vivid recall of visual scenes; cf. Chapter 18.)

Autobiographical memory can be contrasted with *semantic* memory (or the related lexical memory), which is our remembering of properties of language: word usages, idioms and the functional aspects of grammar

(Tulving, 1972). You can't understand a sentence if you can't remember what the words mean. But there's a difference between remembering what a word means and remembering where you saw it last. Only the former is semantic memory. In serial learning, for example, the learner's task is to recall the items that appeared on a particular list in a particular setting. That list constituted an episode in the learner's life, and therefore the learner's recall still qualifies as autobiographical memory.

Such autobiographical remembering differs from that of remembering word meanings or mathematical relations, which aren't recalled on the basis of a date or place of occurrence. The difference is implied by those cases of amnesia involving the forgetting of personal history without loss of language, but in many other respects autobiographical and semantic memory have similar functional properties (e.g., Anderson & Ross, 1980; McClosky & Santee, 1981). The difficulty is that semantic properties of words were presumably learned in the context of particular episodes, so the two kinds of learning are rarely comparable in terms of the frequencies and recencies of remembering.

In any case, the study of semantic memory usually deals with the structure of what's remembered rather than the functional properties of remembering (cf. Anderson & Bower, 1973; Shimp, 1976). Relevant research was presented in Chapter 16, in the context of psycholinguistics. For example, a learner is more likely to remember semantic than syntactic properties of a sentence in a text (Sachs, 1967). Remembering a particular sentence that appeared in a particular text is autobiographical memory. But semantic structure is defined by how we generalize across syntactic transformations of sentences; one way we determine the nature of semantic and syntactic classes is by examining what's remembered. The correspondence between what's presented and what's remembered (recalled or recognized) defines structural classes in memory in the same way that the correspondence between the behavior that's reinforced and the behavior that's generated defines the structure of operant classes (cf. Chapter 7). In other words, using remembering to study the structure of verbal behavior is likely to be more profitable than using verbal behavior to study the nature of remembering.

A variety of experiments have examined the structure of what's remembered. Analyses of how stories and texts are remembered have led to accounts of the hierarchical structure of components of story plots or texts (e.g., Mandler & Johnson, 1977). Analyses of the remembering of words and texts in different languages have shown that the structure of the semantic classes of bilingual speakers extends across language boundaries, as when the learner's remembering of meaning is independent of the language in which items are presented (e.g., Kolers, 1966; MacLeod, 1976). Analyses of the implications that learners can derive from remembered and logically related sentences have shown how items of information can be organized into integrated structures (e.g., Moeser & Tarrant, 1977). Such studies inevitably combine autobiographical and semantic components of memory, because they include the remembering of both specific dated items and general structural relations.

OTHER KINDS OF REMEMBERING

We haven't exhausted the list of kinds of remembering. For example, we haven't considered *spatial* memory (remembering paths and things located on them), though such remembering was involved in the treatment of cognitive maps and in the mnemonic method of loci. Some accounts deal with specific sensory systems (e.g., smell: Herz & Engen, 1996). Another memory distinction is that between *retrospective* and *prospective* memory, which is concerned with the difference between remembering tasks on the basis of past events or of what's to be done in the future (e.g., Urcuioli & Zentall, 1986; cf. Wixted, 1989). For example, you might arrive at a hardware store remembering what you wanted to repair or remembering the tool that you came there to buy.

Some accounts of kinds of remembering have attempted to organize them into a hierarchy of memory systems. Tulving (1985), for example, suggests that procedural memory comes first: It's shared by both verbal and nonverbal organisms. Semantic memory is then built upon procedural memory: Until a language exists, it isn't possible to talk about remembered events. Finally comes autobiographical memory. It's implicit in such a hierarchy that discriminations relevant to one's own remembering emerge last (cf. metamemory in Chapter 18).

SUMMARY

In Chapter 18, we examined the phases of an episode of remembering in terms of the metaphor of storage and retrieval; we also considered metamemory. In this chapter, we identified three memory classes: the persisting stimulus effects called iconic memory; the momentary recall, extendable through rehearsal but limited in capacity, called short-term memory; and the durable remembering called long-term memory. We also reviewed other classifications of memory based on what is remembered. In so doing, we've emphasized remembering as something the learner does. We've seen how memory can be enhanced by mnemonic encoding and distorted by verbal contingencies. We also noted that remembering becomes more likely as the circumstances of recall approach those of original learning.

It almost seems redundant to summarize these topics here in greater detail. The essential vocabulary of memory has been included in the section headings of these chapters. These headings can be listed and remembered in a variety of ways: by rote rehearsal, by mnemonic techniques, or by reviewing the relations among particular experiments and concepts. Undoubtedly the reader who learns this material merely as a sequence of words won't remember it as well as the one who's responded in other ways (we spoke of that difference as depth of processing). The reader who's explored all of the resources— the headings, the figures, the glossary, the index, and yes, even the etymologies— will remember more than the reader who has more narrowly used this book.

We haven't explained memory for words, texts, specific events, structures or our own behavior, but we've seen that what's remembered defines important units of behavior. Just as the relation between contingencies and their behavioral products defines functional response classes, the relation between what's happened and what's remembered defines the structure of memory.

Chapter 20
Cognition and Problem Solving

A. Cognitive Processes
Visual Imagery
Simulations
Processing Stages
Mental Representations

B. Problem Solving
Functional Fixity
The Construction of Solutions

The Indo-European root gno- *is the source through Old English of* know *and* knowledge *and through Germanic of* cunning *and* can, *in the sense of being able to. Its Latin derivative is* gnoscere, *to know or to get acquainted with, and this is a root of* cognition, ignorant *and* recognize. *Synonyms of* knowledge *are often related to sensory language. For example, the Indo-European* weid-, *to see, leads to* view *and* vision *through the Latin* videre, *to* idea *and* history *through the Greek* eidos, *and to* guidance *and* wisdom *through various Old English and Germanic forms. The word* see *itself implies understanding, as in the phrase* I see, *and has such relatives as the word* insight.

The Indo-European root leu-, *to loosen or divide, is the source of* loss *and the suffix* -less. *Probably in combination with* se-, *apart, it provides* solve *and* solution; *in combination with* an-, *up or again, it provides* analysis. *The origins of* synthesis *can be found in the Greek roots,* syn-, *together, plus* tithenai, *to put.*

Early in this text, before embarking on our treatment of the effects of stimuli and contin-
gencies, we distinguished between structural and functional problems in the analysis of behavior. Structural problems are those concerned with properties of response and stimuli classes; these classes are the fundamental units of behavior. We've now considered many response classes and stimulus classes, some defined by contingencies (reinforcers, operants and discriminated operants) and others defined by what's occasioned or what's remembered (semantic and syntactic classes).

We indicated, in our initial discussions of function and structure, that concern with functional problems is often correlated with a behavioral vocabulary, whereas concern with structural problems is often correlated with a cognitive vocabulary. This text began by emphasizing the experiments and vocabulary that grew out of a behavioral tradition. That treatment was extended to verbal behavior, which began the transition to topics that are a primary concern of contemporary cognitive psychology. Those topics were examined in the context of psycholinguistics, verbal learning and memory. This chapter further illustrates research methods and issues in cognitive psychology; it then proceeds to a brief treatment of problem solving, in which structural and functional analyses converge.

Section A   **Cognitive Processes**

We can't see what someone else is thinking or imagining, but imagining, like walking or talking, is something we do. Some might argue that these sorts of events shouldn't be called behavior. Yet our treatment of behavior hasn't been limited to movements; operants, for example, aren't defined by response topography. Certainly it's difficult to say just what a person does when imagining (cf. Chapter 14 on private events). Nevertheless, it's plausible to assume that such behavior shares something with the behavior of looking at things (we can discriminate imagining from seeing; when we fail to do so, we're said to be hallucinating; cf. Skinner, 1953). The difficulty is that such behavior is relatively inaccessible to anyone but the one who engages in it. We may recall the recommendation to convert psychological nouns to verbs: Instead of "cognition and thought" we should say "knowing and thinking" (Woodworth, 1921; cf. Kolers & Roediger, 1984; Malcolm, 1971).

Consider attending to something. In Chapter 8, we treated attention as the control over responding by some stimulus features but not others. We converted a word from the everyday vocabulary into a technical term, but that didn't remove it from our everyday language. Attending is something we do. Our present concern is with the kind of behavior it is: How can we identify it and how can we measure its properties?

It isn't good enough just to ask whether someone is attending. The problems of introspection (the reporting of private events) were amply demonstrated in the history of psychology. Introspection wasn't reliable. Different individuals and even the same individual at different times reported events in different ways. Attending presented particular difficulties: How do you attend to your own attending? The difficulties were inevitable. A private event is by definition available only to the person behaving, but the language of private events must be linked at some point to public events accessible to the verbal community (cf. Skinner, 1945, and Chapter 14). Thus, consistencies in the reports of private events must depend on consistencies across the public and private vocabularies. Imagining an object, for example, must share something with seeing the object.

Attending isn't necessarily movement, but we'd probably want to distinguish between sustained attention, perhaps analogous to maintenance of a posture, and switching attention from one thing to another. For visual stimuli, attention may seem superficially like looking toward or even pointing at something. This kind of extension was implicit when we gave a pigeon's key pecks functions similar to those of attending and called them observing responses (cf. Chapter 11). We can create contingencies for discrete responses such as pecks that approximate those for other responses we can't count so easily. But we can look without seeing, as when we daydream or are "lost in thought" (we then say we weren't paying attention). If we treated attending and observing as mere eye movements, we'd make the mistake of regarding looking without seeing as equivalent to looking and seeing. Attending shares something with what we do when we say we're watching for or looking for something, but we might want to distinguish among separate acts of looking at a given place if what we look for differs each time. For example, what we notice when we scan a page to find a name isn't the same as when we scan to find a definition (cf. search image in Chapter 8; in such contexts, attention has been called perceptual set or readiness).

When behavior doesn't involve movement, we may be able to record other properties, such as duration or latency (cf. Chapter 16 and Posner, 1982). Shifts in attention are particularly well suited for such measurement, as illustrated in an experiment by Sperling and Reeves (1980). Observers were instructed to look at a visual fixation point. Just to the left of this point, letters were presented in rapid sequence one at a time. Just to the right, a sequence of numerals was similarly presented. The observers could see both the letters and the numerals without moving their eyes (an infrared beam reflected off their corneas detected eye movements, so that data from trials with eye movements could be discarded). Their instructions were to attend to the letters until seeing a particular one (e.g., *B*), and then to shift attention to the numerals and report the one they saw. The observers were able to perform this task with rates of stimulus projection in excess of 20/s. The time between the critical letter and each numeral was known, so it was possible to derive the time taken to switch attention from the letters to the numerals from the numeral that was reported. The observers couldn't report the one that appeared simultaneously with the critical letter; instead, they reported one that appeared some fraction of a second later. These durations provided latencies or reaction times for shifting attention. Like the reaction times of more obvious responses, such as button presses, these reaction times depended on task difficulty and other variables.

VISUAL IMAGERY

"Think of a cube, all six surfaces of which are painted red. Divide the cube into twenty-seven equal cubes by making two horizontal cuts and two sets of two vertical cuts each. How many of the resulting cubes will have three faces painted red, how many two, how many one, and how many none?" It is possi-

ble to solve this without seeing the cubes. . . . But the solution is easier if one can actually see the twenty-seven small cubes and count those of each kind. This is easiest in the presence of actual cubes, of course, and even a sketchy drawing will provide useful support, but many people solve the problem visually without visual stimulation. (Skinner, 1953, p. 273)

Even if a shift of attention is a response, what about more complex private events such as visualizing or imagining? We considered imagery in connection with mnemonic techniques in Chapter 18. The methods for measuring imagery are necessarily indirect, but experimental techniques have been developed to study it (Paivio, 1971). Here again, temporal measures have been particularly effective.

For example, observers were shown pictures of pairs of three-dimensional figures, with instructions to report whether the figures were the same or different (e.g., by pressing a left or right button: Shepard & Metzler, 1971). When they were the same, one was rotated relative to the other, as illustrated in Figure 20-1. For such figures, the latency of the report that they were the same was linearly related to the difference in orientation, in degrees of rotation. In other words, mental rotation, or rotation of an image, has some of the same properties as the rotation of an actual object: In both cases, the time taken to do the rotation is proportional to the distance through which the object rotates. (The behavior of pigeons is different; when they're taught to discriminate same versus mirror-image rotated figures, their reaction times don't increase with the amount of rotation of one figure relative to the other; Hollard & Delius, 1982.)

By treating the image as a thing we mustn't be misled into using it to explain behavior; we shouldn't set out to find a screen somewhere in the observer's head on which the image is projected. The controversy over

A

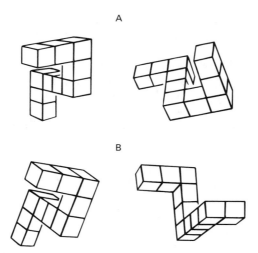

B

FIGURE 20-1   Pairs of figures from a study of mental rotation in which observers were instructed to report whether two figures were the same or different. In A, they're the same but the right figure is rotated 80° from the left one in the picture plane; in B, they're different and can't be matched by any rotation. (From Shepard & Metzler, 1971, Figure 1)

whether the image is pictorial or propositional (verbal) is less important than the recognition that the imagining of the object, like the rotation itself, is something the observer does (cf. Kolers & Smythe, 1979). The temporal properties of rotating real and imagined objects are similar because of the correspondence between what the observer does when seeing an object and what the observer does when imagining it. This correspondence has been discussed in terms of the functional equivalence of imagery and movement (e.g., Johnson, 1982). Imagining is visual behavior in the absence of the visual stimulus.

It's been suggested that John B. Watson, the founder of behaviorism, denied the existence of images because he himself was incapable of visual imagery (Skinner, 1959). His denial, unfortunately, retarded the behavioral analysis of imagery. What's at issue is the role of private events in accounts of behavior. Our primary concern must be to de-

termine their properties rather than to base accounts of other kinds of behavior upon them. A behavioral account doesn't deny the existence of such events, but it limits the conditions under which they can properly serve as explanations of behavior (cf. Paivio, 1975, p. 287).

The example of mental rotation used visual stimuli. The response of visualizing also occurs in the absence of such stimuli, as we saw in the case of visual encoding as a mnemonic technique. In such cases, there's even more temptation to speak of the image as a thing seen rather than of imagining as behavior. In the "photographic" memory of someone with eidetic imagery, for example, reports of the details of past scenes are accompanied by eye movements similar to those when scanning a current visual scene (e.g., Haber, 1969). Yet to say that the reports or the eye movements are caused by the remembered image doesn't explain anything; an account of visualizing must be derived from the behavior of seeing and not from the hypothetical stimulus properties of a private event.

Consider further research on visual imagery (Moyer & Dumais, 1978). In one experiment, observers were given pairs of words (e.g., *mouse* and *elephant*) and were instructed to choose the larger. The greater the difference in size between the two named classes, the shorter the reaction time (e.g., the response to *truck-cat* was faster than that to *book-chair*). The words themselves didn't differ systematically in size, and the relation between size difference and reaction time was similar to that with pictures rather than words as stimuli. These and related experiments (e.g., Paivio, 1975) suggest that the task involved imagery occasioned by words, presumably analogous to the visual encoding discussed in Chapter 18.

In another type of experiment, learners are given pairs of statements such as "A is taller than B" and "A is shorter than C," or "X is to the left of Y" and "Z is to the right of Y," and then are instructed to indicate whether such statements as "B is taller than C" or "Y is to the left of Z" are true or false (e.g., Huttenlocher, 1968). Latency measures in this verbal task and in analogous visual tasks suggest that performance in the verbal task is better described as the visualizing of spatial relations than as verbal responding occasioned by the statements. The private construction of a spatial array in such a task seems to parallel the behavior of moving objects into various spatial arrangements. Such experiments identify visualizing as a behavior class and then demonstrate that it enters into what the learner does.

Treating imagery as a kind of behavior as opposed to something an observer "has" or "doesn't have" raises the possibility that visualizing can be taught (cf. rehearsal of pictures; Graefe & Watkins, 1980). An artist presumably learns some of this behavior in progressing from sketching live models to sketching without a model. Shaping of visualizing might proceed by gradually dimming a scene as an observer describes or sketches it and gradually increasing the time between presentation of a scene and the observer's description or sketch. There are few systematic studies of such phenomena.

SIMULATIONS

Our imagining isn't limited to the visual mode. We not only visualize; we hold imaginary conversations, take imaginary journeys and perform imaginary actions. These are all *simulations*, imitations in the absence of relevant stimulation of some parts of the behavior that might occur in various situations. Games have been used to simulate various properties of economic, political and social situations. Just as war games played on game boards or computers or in the actual field may demonstrate potential consequences of various strategies, so also our imaginings may bring us into contact with possible consequences of our own actions. But just as military simulations may be imperfect because they fail to incorporate important variables in a combat situation, our imaginings will also often be fallible because they involve not real contingencies but only our own partial re-creations of them.

Dawkins (1976) makes the point by comparing computer simulations and human imagination. With respect to the computer simulation:

A model of some aspect of the world is set up in the computer. This does not mean that if you unscrewed the lid you would see a little miniature dummy inside with the same shape as the object simulated. In the chess-playing computer there is no "mental picture" inside the memory banks recognizable as a chess board with knights and pawns sitting on it. The chess board and its current position would be represented by lists of electronically coded numbers. . . . But it does not matter how the computer actually holds its model of the world in its head, provided that it holds it in a form in which it can operate on it, manipulate it, do experiments with it, and report back to the human operators in terms which they can understand. Through the technique of simulation, model battles can be won or lost, simulated airliners fly or crash, economic policies lead to prosperity or to ruin. (Dawkins, 1976, p. 62)

In other words, the important properties of the computer program aren't whether they generate or manipulate copies of the world but rather whether they operate in ways analogous to the workings of events in the real world (cf. Chapter 3 on blueprints versus recipes). Dawkins continues by discussing similar features of human behavior (he refers to organisms as survival machines that have been built by their genes):

> . . . when you yourself have a difficult decision to make involving unknown quantities in the future, you do go in for a form of simulation. You *imagine* what would happen if you did each of the alternatives open to you. . . . just as in the computer, the details of how your brain represents its model of the world are less important than the fact that it is able to use it to predict possible events. Survival machines which can simulate the future are one jump ahead of survival machines who can only learn on the basis of overt trial and error. The trouble with overt trial is that it takes time and energy. The trouble with overt error is that it is often fatal. Simulation is both safer and faster. (Dawkins, 1976, pp. 62–63)

Organisms that have evolved with a capacity to simulate some consequences of their own behavior have some obvious advantages over those that haven't. And once just a little bit of simulation has become possible, natural selection is likely to produce organisms that can more and more effectively simulate the environmental contingencies with which they come in contact (cf. Chapter 3 and Gallistel, 1990).

PROCESSING STAGES

As we've seen, temporal measures such as reaction times have been an important feature of the analysis of cognitive processes. Besides showing that private events take time, cognitive analyses have also demonstrated other properties of these processes. One concern is how cognitive tasks can be decomposed into their separate components or stages (cf. Posner, 1978):

> One of the oldest ideas in experimental psychology is that the time between stimulus and response is occupied by a train of processes or *stages*—some being mental operations—which are so arranged that one process does not begin until the preceding one has ended. This *stage theory* implies that the reaction-time (RT) is a *sum*, composed of the durations of the stages in the series, and suggests that if one could determine the component times that add together to make up the RT, one might then be able to answer interesting questions about mental operations to which they correspond. (Sternberg, 1969, p. 421)

Early treatments attempted to identify particular stages. For example, it was assumed that a discriminative stage could be derived by subtracting simple reaction times to a single visual stimulus from discriminated reaction times to one of two stimuli. One problem was that stage durations were highly variable, presumably because most tasks can be performed in varied ways. A second and more important problem was that stage durations were calculated by assuming that the presence or absence of one stage has no effect on the duration of others. But consider one task made up of stages

A-B-D and another made up of stages A-B-C-D. If D is longer or shorter when it follows B than when it follows C, the actual duration of C won't equal the difference between the times to complete the first and the second task.

One solution is to devise tasks in which a stage is repeated several times (e.g., A-B-C-C-C-D). Here, the immediate contexts of stages B and D are unaltered by changing the repetitions of C. Thus, the increase in latency produced by adding a repetition of C may be taken as the duration of C. This was the rationale for experiments (Sternberg, 1969) in which an observer was first given a set of digits, the positive set (e.g., 1, 3, 4, 9). Then digits from 0 through 9 were presented visually, and instructions were to press one button if the digit was from the positive set and another if it wasn't. Latencies from digit presentations to button presses were recorded with different numbers of digits in the positive set (data were discarded when responses were incorrect).

To speak of search here is again a metaphor, but what properties does such a metaphorical search have? The observer must decide whether the presented digit matches one in the positive set, so let's assume that the observer searches by in some sense comparing the presented digit with the positive-set digits. Can we tell whether the observer completes all the comparisons before dealing with a match (*exhaustive search*) or stops as soon as a match is found (*self-terminating search*). Each possibility has different quantitative implications.

Consider how reaction time is related to list length with exhaustive versus self-terminating search. In exhaustive search the observer compares the presented digit with all positive-set digits, even if it matches one of them. This means that each digit added to the positive set should add a fixed amount

to all reaction times. With self-terminating search, however, a match will be found on the average after only half the comparisons for digits in the positive set (any comparison from first to last might yield a match), whereas all comparisons must be tried for digits that have no match. Now digits in the positive set on the average add only half the time to reaction times than digits not in the positive set.

It may seem paradoxical, but the data show that search in this task is exhaustive rather than self-terminating. Having found a match, why does the observer continue with comparisons through the end of the list? One possibility is that comparing and then dealing with a match are themselves separate stages; if switching between them takes time, then exhaustive comparisons may be more efficient with relatively short lists than individual comparisons each followed by dealing with a match. The task is highly specific, so changes in detail change the outcome (cf. Baddeley, 1976; Crowder, 1976). For example, some variations produce data characteristic of self-terminating rather than exhaustive search. The metaphor of search is strengthened by the quantitative detail of the data, but its range of application is limited.

Furthermore, the metaphor is based on the assumption of *serial search*, in which the observer makes comparisons one at a time, rather than *parallel search*, in which items are compared simultaneously instead of successively. Parallel search may seem to imply that search should take a fixed time regardless of how many items are in the positive set, but it's as reasonable to assume that parallel search becomes slower as number of items increases. Thus, it's possible to develop accounts in terms of parallel search that are equivalent in outcome to those for serial search (Townsend, 1971).

This is just one example of many lines of research concerned with cognitive processing. For example, the distinction between *top-down* versus *bottom-up* processing involves whether we start with major categories and then move down to the finer details, or start with the details and then work up to the whole from the parts (e.g., Kinchla & Wolfe, 1979). *Information processing* is another common metaphor, but to the extent that it implies that the organism attends to and in some way interacts with informative stimuli, it's undercut by the literature on observing responses (cf. Watkins, 1981). As we saw in Chapter 11, such responses are maintained by the reinforcing and not by the informative properties of stimuli.

MENTAL REPRESENTATIONS

The temporal properties of attending and visualizing and searching help to define the structure of these behavior classes. Other aspects of the structure of behavior are its sequential and hierarchical organization. For example, consider the sequential and hierarchical components of completing a college major. The major consists of individual courses the order of which may be constrained by prerequisites; the courses may be decomposed into smaller units consisting of assignments and examinations; these in turn may be further reduced to reading particular passages or answering certain questions, again perhaps in specified orders; and so on. The completion of the major corresponds in structure to the contingencies established by the educational environment. The development of cognitive structure can be regarded as the development of correspondences between the structure of the environment and the structure of behavior. Analyses of concept learning or strategies in

problem solving are sometimes based on demonstrations of such correspondences (e.g., Garner, 1974; Markman, Horton, & McLanahan, 1980).

The development of cognitive structure has been a central theme in the work of Piaget (e.g., Piaget & Inhelder, 1969; see also Fischer, 1980). Only a brief and inevitably oversimplified discussion is provided here. The several phases of child development in Piaget's system (sensory-motor, preoperational, concrete operational and formal operational) correspond to a progression from relatively simple relations between motor responses and their consequences (as in reaching for and manipulating objects) to complex relations that depend on correspondences between verbal and nonverbal behavior as well as environmental and behavioral structure.

Piaget speaks of the development of such correspondences in terms of *accommodation* and *assimilation*; the child must accommodate to the constraints that environmental structures and contingencies impose upon her or his behavior, but these structures and contingencies are assimilated to the extent that they become incorporated into the child's behavior. What's assimilated, however, is sometimes said to be a structure, such as a mental representation. Cognitive development, therefore, is assumed to be the gradual enrichment of representations of the world; these representations then become the basis for behavior. (Piaget studied biology and evolution, but with orthogenesis rather than Darwinian selection as the then dominant evolutionary theory; thus, it's fitting that his treatment of development often seems more like the unfolding of a progression of competencies than their selection by contingencies: cf. Chapter 3. Unfortunately, some arguments against using contingencies in teaching have been based on an improper implication of that unfolding: if children haven't learned something yet it's only because they're not ready.)

The phenomenon called *conservation* illustrates some aspects of cognitive structure dealt with in terms of representations. If the water in a short wide beaker is poured into a tall narrow beaker, a preschool child is likely to report that there's more water in the second beaker than in the first. This report is based on the higher level at which the water stands in the tall narrow beaker. In Piaget's account of development, this type of response is characteristic of the preoperational phase; one property of this phase is that responding is based upon single properties of environmental events rather than upon relations among properties. Later, in the concrete operational phase, the child says that the amount of water is the same in one beaker as in the other. The child's reports are still restricted to specific cases, and it's only in the subsequent formal operational phase that the child begins to speak abstractly of these relations in terms of the conservation of matter. These properties of the child's verbal behavior are also consistent with what we know about the acquisition of naming and related higher-order classes (cf. Chapter 14). Conservation is assessed by verbal reports, and it would be useful to know how nonverbal responses such as choices among beakers differently filled with favorite drinks would be correlated with the verbal competencies that define the several developmental phases.

One way to deal with conservation and related phenomena is to attribute the increasing sophistication of the child's performance to successive refinements in the child's mental representations of events in the world. As the child moves from actually manipulating objects to imagining or talking about or thinking about manipulating those objects, the structure of the child's mental representations may be said to approximate more and more closely the structure of the contingencies that operate for manipulating objects in the world. But the structure of these mental representations is derived from correspondences between behavior and environmental contingencies, so it's inappropriate to use them to explain the behavior. The representations exist in the child only in a metaphorical sense; their concrete existence is in our own discriminative behavior as we observe the child or, in other words, in the consistencies and correspondences that we observe in her or his behavior.

The issue isn't different from one raised in the context of remembering, and it may be useful to extend an analogy introduced then. If you take a piano apart to find the music, you'll be disappointed. You may have just listened to a performance of Beethoven's Waldstein Sonata, but when you're done you'll have only pieces of wire and wood and felt and so on. You'll also be disappointed if you try to find behavior inside the organism. The environment plays upon organisms as the pianist plays upon the piano. Just as it may take different virtuosi to bring out what's special about pianos and what's special about violins, what an environment brings out may depend on which organism it plays upon. Or, to take the analogy further, just as some musicians may bring out some music more skillfully from some instruments than from others, different environments may bring out some sorts of behavior more effectively from some organisms than from others.

But wait, you say, what about the player piano? In that case you can find a representation of the music: a roll of paper with holes punched in it. No matter that one can substitute, in more contemporary versions, a magnetic tape or a computer chip (the choice of a piano rather than some instrument less compatible with representations, such as a violin or a trumpet, anticipated this feature of the analogy). The holes in the paper aren't music, and even though they can be translated into the action of the keyboard, we can't complete the account unless we can say how the holes got punched in the first place. If we wish to deal with representations, we must start by putting them not inside the organism but rather inside the human observer who discovered the spatial or relational properties of the environment to which the organism was responding. In other words, the issue isn't so much about the existence of representations as it is about which organism they belong in.

In any case, the development of conservation in children isn't incompatible with properties of behavior that we've already considered. Several progressions must occur in parallel, and each is part of a hierarchy in which more complex classes of behavior are based upon simpler classes. At first, the child's discriminations are based upon a single dimension of objects (in this instance, height); discriminations based upon two or three dimensions (area and volume) come later. At the same time, the child's vocabulary becomes more finely differentiated (from *big-little* to *bigger-smaller* and then to *taller-shorter*, *fuller-emptier* and so on; cf. Ward, 1980). Verbal behavior occasioned by specific instances becomes the foundation for the more general classes we call abstractions. Saying whether or not the quantity of water in one container equals that in another isn't the same as choosing the contents of one or the other container or filling two containers to equal volumes, and none of these is equivalent to a statement of the principle of conservation of matter. On the one hand, it's important to recognize how very different these classes of behavior are; on the other, it's important to recognize that equivalences across these different classes are

inevitable consequences of the way in which verbal and nonverbal behavior is related to events in the world.

The argument has been that organisms don't have to produce copies of stimuli before they can respond to them. But it's also important to note that not all representational accounts are copy theories. An organism that has responded to a stimulus is a changed organism. "Whether internal representations are copies or interpretations of images, something called 'seeing them' is still required. Notions such as 'convex edge,' 'concave edge,' and 'occluding edge' are a step in the right direction. They are the beginnings of an analysis of the stimulus rather than a replication" (Skinner, 1988, p. 337). Cognitive processing doesn't require copies. For example, no copies are involved in the simulations of complex behavior created by the variety of computer programming called parallel distributed processing (Donahoe & Palmer, 1989; cf. Chapter 3 on copy theories in phylogenic selection). "Organisms are changed by contingencies of selection, they do not store them" (Skinner, 1988, p. 472).

Section B   Problem Solving

We've examined only a few samples of research in cognition. Cognition is after all not learning; yet many issues in cognition are closely related to problems in learning. As the last experimental topic in this book, we turn to problem solving. Problem solving has sometimes been treated in the context of cognitive approaches, with emphasis on the structure of problems. An analysis of problem solving also raises functional questions, as when we're concerned with conditions that make the solution of a problem more or less likely.

Let's begin with a structural approach to problem solving in the Hobbits-and-Orcs problem (Thomas, 1974). Three hobbits and three orcs are traveling together. The orcs won't leave the hobbits behind, but they'll overpower them if ever any hobbits are outnumbered by orcs. The group reaches a river that must be crossed and finds a boat that can hold only one or two at a time. How do the hobbits organize the crossing so that no hobbits are ever outnumbered by orcs? This problem was presented to solvers to explore the effects of feedback and other variables.

The problem allows only a few possible moves, and its solution can be presented economically as in Figure 20-2. Except for an alternative first move not shown and the two cases of branching moves at the beginning and end of the sequence, the only allowable alternatives to correct moves are ones that move backward through the sequence (solvers seldom recognized this property of the problem). For our purposes, it's sufficient to note that errors were more likely at some points in the sequence (states 321 and 110) than at others. These and other features of the data indicated that the solver's performance didn't consist simply of the separate moves. Instead, the solution was based on larger units consisting of sequences of moves that led to some intermediate arrangement of hobbits and orcs on the two sides of the river. Thus, the analysis demonstrated correspondences between the structure of the problem and the structure of the solver's solution.

Problems in which the steps are as explicit as this lend themselves well to computer solution (e.g., Newell, Shaw, & Simon, 1958). The computer can perform large numbers of calculations in short periods of time, and in problems involving well-defined alternatives it can select those branches leading to a solution more rapidly than a human can.

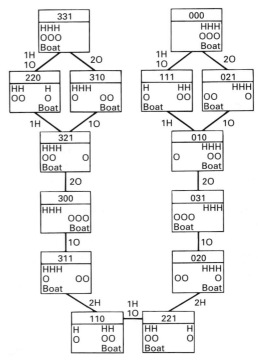

FIGURE 20-2 Successive states in solving the Hobbits-and-Orcs problem. Three hobbits and three orcs must cross a river. They have a single boat that holds only one or two creatures, and under no circumstances may orcs outnumber hobbits. Each state is coded by three digits: number of hobbits on starting side, number of orcs on starting side, and boat on starting side. In each state, positions of the hobbits (*H*), the orcs (*O*) and the boat are shown below the code, and the creatures transported by the boat are shown in the transitions between states. Except for a transition to state 320 from the first state (crossing of one orc and the boat, not shown), no other moves in which orcs don't outnumber hobbits are possible. (Adapted from Thomas, 1974, Figure 1)

Part of the field of *artificial intelligence*, or *AI*, is devoted to the design of computer programs for simulating such activities as problem solving. But computer programs are limited when those who write the programs can't provide an exhaustive list of alternatives at some steps in the solution of a problem, or can't define the terms entering into it, or can't reduce it to a manageable size even for a computer (e.g., Dreyfus, 1992; Winograd, 1980). Each of these constraints was important in limiting the application of computer programs to language translation, as discussed in Chapter 16.

Computer programs designed to play chess are a case in point (Frey, 1977). Chess-playing programs have gradually evolved to play better chess. The best programs now challenge human grandmasters. For the purposes of a computer program, chess is well-defined: All possible moves of each piece in any position are exactly specified by the rules of the game. Given 16 pieces on each side and a board of 64 squares, however, possible moves and countermoves multiply so rapidly that even the most rapid programs on the largest computers are limited in the number of moves ahead that they can calculate (the quantities exceed the number of atoms in the universe). If the computer doesn't find a forced checkmate of its opponent in, say, the next 50 moves, how does it evaluate the relative strengths of all those possible future positions so as to select its best next move? More accurately, how does a human write a program that allows the computer to do that?

Some of the most spectacular chess games are those in which a checkmate is forced through the sacrifice of several pieces. If the computer evaluates positions on the basis of the relative number of pieces lost and if the mating move itself is beyond the horizon of its calculations of future moves, it will never embark upon such a forced mate. The computer plays chess carefully; it doesn't make the mistakes of the amateur human player, such as exposing an unprotected piece to capture by the opponent. Nevertheless, chess-playing programs that now challenge human grandmasters do so in part by brute force, in the sense that they include extensive libraries of many standard chess openings and explore very many alternatives a great many moves ahead. They don't play chess like human grandmasters, who not only calculate the consequences of various moves and countermoves but also see various strengths and weaknesses to be exploited in the pattern of pieces on the board. The most successful future chess-playing programs will probably be those that most closely capture the structure of what the chess master sees in a form that can be used by the computer. The writers of such programs will presumably be expert in both chess and computer programming.

The prediction that computer programs capable of defeating any human chess grandmaster are imminent goes back some decades. No doubt the prediction will eventually come to pass as computers become ever more powerful. Meanwhile, there's a curious irony in the successes of artificial intelligence. Instead of teaching things to children, the programmers of artificial intelligence have taught things to computers. We might have hoped that what they discovered would be applicable to improvements in education, but that hasn't happened. Part of the problem may be that intelligence has not been adequately defined or has been defined for inappropriate domains. But more likely it's that teaching chess or other skills to computers doesn't have anything to do with teaching things to children.

If chess grandmasters could describe what they did when analyzing a chess position, their descriptions could be used to design chess-playing computer programs. Playing chess by following the instructions of such a program would be verbally governed rather than contingency-shaped chess playing (cf. Chapter 15). But the higher-order behavior classes of chess masters haven't been identified; grandmasters can't describe what they do in a way that can be translated into a computer program. Grandmaster chess play is called intuitive, which is another way of saying that it's contingency-shaped rather than verbally governed. This kind of expert performance isn't independent of verbal behavior, however, and it therefore suggests that there may be more than one variety of contingency-shaped behavior.

Dreyfus and Dreyfus (1986) made some observations about expert performance in the context of discussing limits on the capacity of computers to simulate human judgments. Their examples included chess, medicine and other areas. They noted that education in complex human skills often begins with verbal antecedents, or rules; they suggest that proficiency develops when intuitive judgments begin to mix with rules, and that expertise involves performance that no longer depends on the rules. Their distinctions between the functions of rules and intuitions are much like those between verbally governed and contingency-shaped behavior, but for them verbally governed behavior comes first; intuitive or contingency-shaped behavior eventually grows out of it.

Their distinction is compatible with our earlier treatment of verbally governed behavior if we expand our taxonomy to include three classes of skilled behavior: contingency-shaped behavior that's never depended on verbal antecedents, corresponding to the kinds of contingency-shaped behavior ordinarily treated in behavior analysis (as in nonhuman behavior); verbally governed behavior, in which verbal antecedents override effects of nonverbal contingencies (as treated in Chapter 15); and, finally, expert performance, in which continuing contact with the environment attenuates control by verbal antecedents and allows behavior to become

sensitive to subtle changes in contingencies (in what might be regarded as a second and different kind of contingency-shaped behavior that's yet to be explored in detail).

We can't write the rules of human expertise even in restricted domains such as chess. But that poses a problem, because we don't have ways to incorporate human expertise into computers except by writing programs that tell computers what to do. Unless and until new computer technologies such as parallel distributed processing (Donahoe & Palmer, 1989) can introduce contingencies of selection into computation, computer simulations of human expertise will inevitably be limited to simulations of verbally governed behavior.

The rules of chess are defined very explicitly. If the problems to be surmounted in writing expert computer programs are so formidable even in this limited domain, what about those domains in which the terms are less well-defined? Furthermore, once a computer program has been written to solve one problem, how can it be used to solve other problems? The question is relevant not just to computer programming but also to human problem solving, to which we now return. In the teaching of problem-solving skills within well-defined areas such as mathematics (e.g., Wertheimer, 1959), for example, analyses start with the solution of single problems and then move on to the transfer of solving strategies from one problem to another. Experiments on problem solving, therefore, have often dealt with the effects on problem solution of the solver's history of solving problems.

FUNCTIONAL FIXITY

The Luchins' water-jar problem provides an example of such an experiment (Luchins & Luchins, 1950). Given a water supply and three jars of different capacity, the problem is to produce a specified amount of water. For example, if jars A, B and C have respective capacities of 21, 127 and 3, how can you arrive at exactly 100 units of water? In this instance, the solution is to fill B and then to pour out enough to fill A once and C twice. One group was given several successive problems that could be solved this way while a second group wasn't. Later, both groups were tested on problems such as the following: How does one arrive at a quantity of 20 if jars A, B and C have respective capacities of 23, 49 and 3? The first group solved the problem in the same old way, whereas the second group solved it more efficiently, by filling A and then pouring out enough to fill C.

As an example of negative transfer or problem-solving rigidity, this is obviously a case in which the consequences of past behavior have affected current behavior. The literature on problem solving includes many variations on such situations (e.g., Saugstad & Raaheim, 1960). For example, solvers who were instructed to mount a candle on a wall were given either a box of candles and a box of matches and a box of tacks, or separate stacks of candles, matches, tacks and boxes (Duncker, 1945). The solution was to tack a box to the wall so that it provided a flat surface on which a candle could be mounted. Those who received the candles and matches and tacks in boxes, however, were much slower to solve the problem than those who received the boxes separately; they received the boxes as containers and continued to treat them that way. Instances of failure to solve a problem requiring an unusual use of common tools or materials are sometimes described as cases of *functional fixity*; the commonplace items occasion responses appropriate to their everyday functions instead of the novel responses appropriate to the problem solution (cf. Chapter 15 on insensitivity to contingencies).

Before we consider another class of examples, guess how many seven-letter words in this chapter end in *-ing*; then guess how many end in *-_n_*, where the spaces can be any letter (it might be a good idea to write your answers down). The other class of examples comes from experiments on probability judgment (cf. Estes, 1976, p. 53: "the term *probability learning* characterizes a type of problem situation rather than a type of learning"). Decision theory is concerned with the finding that our estimates of the probabilities of events often differ substantially from the probabilities calculated from actual event frequencies (e.g., Tversky & Kahneman, 1983).

Now let's discuss your guesses. There's a good chance they demonstrate the *conjunction fallacy*, which occurs when people judge the probability of several events occurring together as greater than the separate probabilities of each. If your first number was bigger than your second, your answer was mathematically impossible. At least as many words must end in *-_n_* as end in *-ing*, because those ending in *-_n_* include all those ending in *-ing*.

Consider a different kind of judgment in the context of an imaginary diagnostic situation in a psychiatric hospital. You're a staff member who's discovered a new clinical syndrome called *narapoia*. Narapoids are the opposite of paranoids; they're under the delusion that other people are plotting to do them good. You know that narapoids can't possibly make up more than 1% of your clinical population, and you've developed a test for narapoia that has only a 5% error rate. You give the test to someone who's being screened for admission to the hospital, and the person scores as a narapoid. Does the test score provide sufficient grounds for admission?

To make this question easier to answer, assume you give the test to 1000 patients in your hospital. No more than 1% are nara-poids, so they total 10 or so; with your 5% error rate most or all of them will correctly score as narapoid. But of the 990 or so others, roughly 50 will be false alarms; they're not narapoid, but because of your 5% error rate they'll score so. In other words, you'll get a total of about 60 narapoid scores, but given that only 10 or so are actually narapoid the chance that anyone with that score has been correctly diagnosed is only 1 in 6. You can't justify admission on the basis of the test alone; you need other diagnostic criteria (perhaps that's just as well, because you'll be hard-pressed to devise an effective treatment; whenever you try to help your narapoid patients, you'll only be confirming their delusions).

Narapoia is an imaginary syndrome, but the probability relations it illustrates are of practical significance. For example, even with low error rates such judgments can lead to many false alarms in cases where false alarms can be very costly (as in lie detection or medical diagnoses). These types of biases in probability estimation are likely whenever there's some error as we sample for events that occur with low frequencies in large populations. Most of our everyday probability judgments are made in the context of more symmetrical distributions of event probabilities, and our histories of such judgments, as in functional fixity, transfer too easily to extreme cases in which the familiar probability relations no longer hold. Teaching the mathematics of probability is one way to make such probability judgments more accurate; another is to provide experience with probability judgments over a range of situations that include these sorts of extremes (note that the former solution involves verbally governed behavior whereas the latter involves contingency-shaped behavior).

THE CONSTRUCTION OF SOLUTIONS

These experiments show how problem solving can be affected by antecedent events and by contingencies. But what constitutes problem solving? Consider an example from Skinner:

> You have been asked to pick up a friend's suitcase from an airport baggage claim. You have never seen the suitcase or heard it described; you have only a ticket with a number from which a match is to be found among the numbers on a collection of suitcases. To simplify the problem, let us say you find yourself alone before a large rotary display. A hundred suitcases move past you in a great ring. They are moving too fast to be inspected in order. You are committed to selecting suitcases essentially at random, checking one number at a time. How are you to find the suitcase? You may, of course, simply keep sampling. You will almost certainly check the same suitcase more than once, but eventually the matching ticket will turn up. . . . A much more effective strategy is to mark each case as it is checked—say, with a piece of chalk. No bag is then inspected twice, and the number of bags remaining to be examined is reduced as rapidly as possible. Simple as it seems, this method of solving the problem has some remarkable features. . . . It is the use of the chalk which introduces something new. Marking each suitcase as it is checked . . . is constructing a discriminative stimulus. (Skinner, 1969, pp. 136–137)

Problem solving, in other words, is behavior. The discriminative features of the situation define the problem, and the reinforcer is the solution of the problem. Often we solve problems by manipulating stimuli: looking something up, converting a verbal problem into a mathematical equation, and so on. It's important to recognize how we can alter our own behavior by modifying our environment. Consider, for example, a problem in multiplication. We might multiply 23 by 14 in the following form.

$$
\begin{array}{r}
23 \\
\times 14 \\
\hline
92 \\
23 \\
\hline
322
\end{array}
$$

In the intermediate products, 92 and 23, we create discriminative stimuli that allow us to reach the solution, 322. But what if we had to solve the problem without a pencil? Presumably the intermediate products would still enter into the solution, even we had no written record of them. If we didn't say them aloud, an observer might say we'd been doing mental arithmetic (cf. Ashcraft, 1982). But the intermediate products have the same role in both cases, even though they're more public and permanent in one than the other.

Now that we've seen how problem solutions can be affected by antecedents and contingencies, we've come nearly full circle. Let's return to the problem Köhler set for his apes, but with a different organism (Epstein, 1981; cf. Chapter 2). We start with a pigeon in a compartment with a movable box in a far corner and, hanging out of reach, a model banana (chosen, instead of a simple key, in deference to Köhler). Earlier, the pigeon's pecks at the banana had been reinforced with access to food. Also, the pigeon was taught through shaping to move the box across the floor by pecking at it. Finally, the pigeon's feathers were trimmed so that it couldn't fly, and its jumping and wing-flapping dropped to a low rate in the presence of the hanging banana. Under these circumstances, the pigeon looks from the banana to the box and back again. Soon it goes to the box and moves it under the banana. Once the box is there, the pigeon climbs it and pecks the banana, operating the feeder.

This is novel behavior. The pigeon solved the problem of getting to the banana by moving the box and then climbing it, even though it had never done so before (this spontaneous combination of two operant classes is adduction: cf Chapter 9). Presumably it was important that the competing responses of jumping and wing-flapping had already been reduced in probability. The pigeon doesn't look like a chimpanzee, but its performance is functionally just like Sultan's in Köhler's insight experiment. The main difference between this demonstration and Köhler's is that we know a lot more about the pigeon's history than we do about Sultan's. An experimenter interested in problem solving might start simply by watching the solver's behavior. Like Köhler in his study of insight in apes, the experimenter will discover what the solver already can do. That's where we began. But now we can see how much more was involved in the environments Köhler constructed for his apes.

PART V   CONCLUSION

Chapter 21
Structure and Function in Learning

A. **Two Psychologies of Learning:**
   A Capsule History

B. **Structure and Function**

C. **Learning and Evolution**

D. **Behavior Analysis and Behavior**
   Synthesis

The word psychology *comes from the Greek* psukhein, *to breathe, and* psukhe, *breath. When the psyche was said to leave the body of a mortally wounded warrior in the Homeric epics, it may be understood to mean the warrior's breath and not his soul. A curious parallel exists between this word and* spirit, *from the Latin* spirare, *another word meaning to breathe; no evidence links these Greek and Latin words etymologically. A similar relation between air and spirit exists in the Latin* anima, *originally a breath of air but later soul or spirit in such words as* animate *and* animosity, *and in the Greek* atmos, *vapor or air as it enters into the English* atmosphere *but breath or soul in the related Sanskrit* atman.

We've considered the varied phenomena of learning. We began with experimental operations. The first and simplest, apart from observation, was presenting stimuli. Stimuli produce responses, but they can also have other effects. For example, they can modulate how responses are distributed in time. As responses can follow stimuli, stimuli can follow responses. We dealt with the effects of contingencies, the consequences of responding, in treating the operations of reinforcement and punishment. Their effects led us to distinguish among positive reinforcement, positive punishment, negative reinforcement (escape and avoidance) and negative punishment (timeout and omission procedures). In exploring these procedures, we noted the importance of some consequences, less dramatic than biologically significant stimuli such as food and water, that affected an organism's orientation within its environments. In this context, we examined sensory–motor learning, visual fixation, latent learning and other phenomena not usually classified according to the effects of reinforcers and punishers.

We distinguished between reinforcement and punishment by whether response consequences raised or lowered response probability, but we also recognized that distinguishing between the positive and negative cases was sometimes arbitrary. As in reinforcement by a change in temperature, it was sometimes ambiguous whether a case should be treated in terms of presenting or removing stimuli (e.g., presenting heat or removing cold). Instead, we treated these cases in terms of relations between reinforced responses and the responses occasioned by their consequences. We noted that stimuli could have multiple effects and that a stimulus that served as a reinforcer for a response might also have eliciting effects on that or other responses. The task of an experimental analysis is to separate such different effects and to observe how elicitation and consequences can combine to create a performance.

We also turned to the signalling effects of stimuli, in stimulus control. This operation can be superimposed either on the consequential operations of reinforcement and punishment, when we speak of discrimination learning, or on stimulus-presentation operations, when we speak of respondent conditioning. Within these contexts, we explored a variety of behavioral phenomena and procedures: attention, stimulus-control gradients, reinforcement schedules, novel behavior, self-control, sensory preconditioning and conditioned suppression, to mention just a few. Along the way, we considered their various applications to significant human problems, such as parenting, education and the nurturing of the developmentally disabled.

Having examined the effects of these operations, we shifted our attention to the problem of characterizing the dimensions along which stimuli and responses vary. In discussing differentiation and discrimination, we saw that the relevant dimensions included not only relatively simple ones such as topography or intensity, but also complex ones involving the structure of stimuli and responses and their relations. The correspondences between the classes of responses with particular consequences (descriptive or nominal operants) and the classes of responses generated by those consequences (functional operants) was critical to defining behavioral classes; we distinguished between those defined by response properties, called operants, and those defined by stimulus properties, called discriminated operants.

In our examinations of natural categories, concept formation and verbal behavior, we were forced to conclude that behavioral relations were primary: We couldn't appeal to physical measures to define such classes. Responses like attending, remembering, imagining and thinking aren't easily observed directly, but we decided early that it would be inappropriate to define behavior in terms of movement. Furthermore, in our analyses of symbolic matching we discovered relations among stimuli and responses that weren't implicit in the three-term contingencies among antecedents, behavior and consequences. The relations of reflexivity, symmetry and transitivity can be demonstrated only within procedures that allow stimulus and response terms to be exchanged. They led us to define symbolic behavior in terms of equivalence classes, and those classes later entered into our treatment of language.

Much of our account classified learning phenomena according to experimental operations. But there's no guarantee that imposing a particular procedure on a given organism's behavior will be effective. A procedure in which one organism learns may be one in which another doesn't, and an organism that learns under one procedure may not do so under another. Such findings don't invalidate our behavioral taxonomy, because the classifications are merely ways of naming phenomena and relating them to each other. That wouldn't be so if we assumed that all learning was based on some one process or some small number of processes that act across all organisms and procedures.

When we moved from learning without words to learning with words, by way of social learning, we discovered that the basic operations were relevant to verbal as well as nonverbal behavior. Verbal classes such as tacting and manding were, in effect, names for the relevant processes as they entered into verbal behavior. They also provided the context within which we more fully developed the implications of higher-order classes and recognized potentials for novel behavior in adduction and other sources of emergent behavior. The taxonomy of verbal behavior then allowed us to treat issues in a range of areas, including remembering, cognition, problem solving and metaphor, among others. Speaking metaphorically, we've traveled a long way.

Section A   **Two Psychologies of Learning: A Capsule History**

The psychology of learning evolved on the basis of the different outcomes of a variety of experimental procedures. As each procedure was considered in its historical turn, it was assigned importance in proportion to its demonstrated effectiveness. At different times, the available findings led to theoretical formulations dominated by laws of association or contiguity, rules of respondent conditioning, or principles of reinforcement and punishment. Sometimes this domination was so substantial that one or another process was presumed to be the fundamental and exclusive basis of all learning. Such formulations were inevitably open to challenge, because the phenomena of learning can't be accounted for exhaustively by any single process. Thus, the history of the psychology of learning, a tale of confusions and controversies, has been more often told in terms of theorists and their systems than in terms of the phenomena of learning.

The psychology of learning has at times been regarded as a foundational component of experimental psychology, but in the psychological laboratories of the late 19th century it was overshadowed by other issues, such as those of sensation and perception. By the turn of the century, research on animal behavior had been stimulated by the work of Darwin (1859), and the fundamentals of research on human memory and verbal learning had been provided by Ebbinghaus (1885). Both historical lines found homes within university laboratories, but despite their academic proximity they remained separate.

Early in the 20th century, John B. Watson addressed what came to be called his behaviorist manifesto (Watson, 1913) to a psychology marked by substantial disagreements about its methods and its subject matter. Researchers claimed to be able to study the content of consciousness through introspection, but couldn't agree on such fundamentals as the nature of the basic mental units. In this context, Watson advocated behavior, as opposed to consciousness or mind, as the only legitimate subject matter of psychology. On methodological grounds he excluded mental events such as images as proper areas of inquiry, and his version of behaviorism came to be called *methodological* behaviorism. In other words, Watson rejected the study of private events. The study of private events would require a different kind of behaviorism, sometimes called *radical* behaviorism (perhaps because in its interest in the behavior of the scientist, it had turned its own science upon itself: cf. Catania, 1993; see also Burns & Staats, 1991, and Staats, 1986, on *paradigmatic* behaviorism).

In the study of animal behavior, much early research was devoted to invertebrates (e.g., Jennings, 1906; Loeb, 1900; Lubbock, 1882), but attention gradually shifted to vertebrates. Instrumental learning had been introduced by the mazes of Small (1899–1900) and Yerkes (1907) and by the problem boxes of Thorndike (1898). Thorndike soon moved from animal studies to analyses of human learning (e.g., Thorndike, 1921), but in so doing he was exceptional. Other students of animal learning were more likely to make the extension from animal to human behavior through theoretical statements than through experiments. Pavlov (1927; 1957, p. 285), for example, manifested an interest in human language in his theory of the second signal system, but his main impact was through his canine research. Once instrumental learning and respondent conditioning had been distinguished as phenomena in the early decades of the 20th century, the stage was set for elaborations of discrimination learning, in the progression from jumping stands to rat chambers and pigeon boxes (Lashley, 1930; Skinner, 1930, 1938). The phenomena of reinforcement schedules were to follow later (Ferster & Skinner, 1957).

Preoccupation with the scientific legitimacy of psychology disposed researchers to look to other sciences for principles of scientific method, and gradually the behaviorism of Watson (1919) converged with the operationism that was newly developing in physics (Bridgman, 1927) and with the logical positivism that was being introduced as a revolutionary change in the philosophy of science (Ayer, 1946). Behaviorism became a major orientation within psychology, and the 1930s and 1940s became a period of grand behavioral theories. Applications to human behavior and to language became an issue in the competition among the systems of Guthrie (1935), Skinner (1938) and Tolman (1948), among others, but attempts to integrate the processes of animal learning with the properties of language gradually lost influence as the fortunes of early behaviorist theories based on stimulus–response associations declined (even so, methodological behaviorism remains the basis for virtually all of contemporary experimental psychology,

in such methodological practices as the operational definition).

Meanwhile, the field of human learning and memory went its separate way. The precedence of Ebbinghaus dominated detailed studies of serial-position effects, massed versus spaced practice, meaningfulness, backward associations, interference and so on. Some controversies were long-lasting. For example, plateaus in Morse-code learning at various stages of competence, demonstrated at the turn of the century (Bryan & Harter, 1899), remained a part of psychological lore until well into the 1950s, when the phantom phenomenon was at last put to rest (Keller, 1958). Thorndike and Woodworth (1901), inspired perhaps by questions about the educational value of such classical disciplines as Greek and Latin, had begun investigations of transfer of learning. Findings from these and other studies made the practical relevance of studies of human learning seem obvious, and the effects on verbal learning of such variables as sleep and distraction and motivation became the basis for advice on study habits. The theoretical underpinnings of these areas were the same as those of animal learning, but although laws of effect, contiguity, association and generalization gave a superficial appearance of unity, the two experimental lines originated as separate entities and remained so.

By the 1940s, the pattern was firmly entrenched and was most clearly illustrated by two textbooks of the time. *Conditioning and learning* by Hilgard and Marquis (1940) was devoted primarily to animal research; *The psychology of human learning* by McGeoch (1942) was concerned mainly with human learning and remembering. Each appeared later in revised editions (Kimble, 1961; McGeoch & Irion, 1952). Beyond the common appeal to theoretical principles such as association, there was little evidence in either the original or the revised editions that the two research traditions had substantially influenced each other.

It can reasonably be claimed that these two psychologies of learning remain separate in contemporary psychology. Having examined their histories we might ask the point of treating these disparate subject matters together. Perhaps animal learning and conditioning and human learning and remembering have so little relevance to each other that they should go their separate ways. But here we've argued otherwise. Such a course would be a serious mistake for several reasons: Learning phenomena studied with animals also occur in human behavior; the nature of complex human learning is clarified by analyses in terms of more elementary processes; and perhaps most important, human behavior especially is characterized by the interplay between verbal and nonverbal responses, and we've yet to understand the origins of either.

We must identify not just the properties of our behavior unique to humans but also those we hold in common with other organisms. Given the myriad properties of human language, both elementary phenomena of animal learning and conditioning and the complexities of human learning and remembering must enter into any effective account. Our treatments of such phenomena as equivalence classes, awareness, instructional control and problem solving couldn't have proceeded without prior analyses of antecedent stimuli. To the extent that such important varieties of human behavior as autoclitics, self-control, deixis and metamemory are based on both verbal behavior and discriminations of our own behavior, any analysis of them that fails to build upon the more elementary processes of stimulus control and contingencies is bound to be deficient. We must therefore conclude that the union of these two psychologies of learning

is long overdue; we need a single psychology of learning encompassing all of the varieties of animal and human learning.

Section B   Structure and Function

Early in our account we distinguished between structural and functional analyses (cf. Titchener, 1898; Catania, 1973). A structural analysis holds relations among stimuli and responses constant while varying critical properties of one or the other. We noted the properties of formal verbal units (as in phonemes and letters), hierarchical organizations in text structure (as in relations among words, phrases and sentences) and correspondences between stimulus and response structure (as in relations between text and speech). A functional analysis holds the stimuli and responses of interest constant while changing their relations. We study interactions between behavior and environment in terms of contingency relations among discriminative stimuli, responses and consequences.

Structural and functional problems are often interrelated. For example, the design of an illustrated reader for an elementary school class should consider both its structural features, in the details of text and pictures, and its functional features, in how the pictures are related to the sentences they illustrate. A problem exists if the pictures set the occasion for verbal descriptions that correspond so closely to the accompanying text that a teacher can't tell whether a child is responding to the picture, reading the text or doing both in some combination. It can be addressed by changing the relation between the pictures and the child's responses (e.g., making the pictures reinforcing consequences of reading rather than antecedents of it). A systematic analysis might show that, as consequences, pictures maintain the picking up of books and the turning of pages, but as antecedents they compete with the text in setting the occasion for verbal responses. This analysis might lead to a rationale for sequencing the relations among words and pictures to maximize both stimulus control by the words and reinforcing effects of the pictures. At the same time, a structural analysis of text and pictures could provide the basis for organizing the textual material, deciding on appropriate levels of complexity, and perhaps even determining how quickly pictures could be faded out (e.g., Harzem, Lee, & Miles, 1976).

Structure and function are complementary, not mutually exclusive. There's no reason why structural concerns shouldn't enter into functional experiments, or vice versa. But in the evolution of psychology the distinction between structural and functional approaches became correlated with and eventually confused with another distinction, between the two languages of cognitive psychology and behaviorism. The cognitivist prefers to summarize the organization of the organism's behavior in terms of structures the organism knows, for which the language of mind is convenient. The behaviorist prefers to anchor accounts of action to the detailed functional relations among observable events, for which the language of stimuli and responses is appropriate. Yet relations between stimuli and responses must be implicit in the cognitive vocabulary, as it deals with relations between the structures of the environment and knowledge, just as structure is implicit in the behavioral vocabulary, as it deals with the properties that define operants.

Biology also distinguished between structure and function, in anatomy and physiology, but an equivalent schism didn't emerge within biology because the languages of anatomy and physiology didn't diverge. For example, the debate over mechanism versus vitalism, perhaps analogous to that between

behaviorism and mentalism, remained reasonably independent of the distinction between anatomy and physiology (e.g., Hein, 1972; Catania, 1978). In psychology, the respective correlations of cognitive and behavioral languages with structural and functional problems made it difficult to recognize that the problems were different and therefore that these research areas might be complementary rather than mutually exclusive.

There's always a certain ambiguity in the distinction between structure and function. But when the biologists of an earlier time debated the issues, their concerns weren't so much with whether structural or anatomical problems could be distinguished from functional or physiological ones as they were with whether one or the other problem should be given priority (e.g., Russell, 1916). The emergence of structure from undifferentiated beginnings has long been a fundamental problem in science. For example, debates over the development of the embryo pitted the unfolding of preexisting structure (preformationism) against the functional differentiation of unstructured systems (epigenesis), and gave rise to the widely cited but usually misleading generalization that ontogeny recapitulates phylogeny (Gould, 1977).

The arguments were based on assumptions about how, in the evolution of a species, the functions of an organ might determine its structure or how, in the development of an organism, the structure of an organ might determine its functions. With the advent of Darwin's (1859) account of evolutionary process in terms of selection, both structure and function in biology came to be seen as derivatives of selection, each reciprocally constrained by the other. For example, the properties of animal locomotion, whether on land or at sea or in air, are jointly determined by common functions (e.g., capturing prey, escaping predators) and by structural limitations that arise from differences in vertebrate and invertebrate body plans (e.g., muscle configuration, number of limbs). The problem was resolved not with the domination of one or the other position, but rather with the recognition that structure and function are mutually determined by selection.

Similar controversies over the primacy of structure or function exist in the history of the psychology of learning, although the issues are usually expressed differently. For example, consider latent learning: A hungry rat explores a maze with an empty goalbox; when later given food there, it demonstrates that it's learned the maze by negotiating it as rapidly and with as few blind-alley entries as a rat that's always found food there. The rat's running, itself not learning, occurs because of its relation to food in the goalbox; presumably it reflects what the rat learned. It was once important to distinguish between learning and performance, but the distinction was merely a basis for asserting the primacy of structure over function. What's structure here? It seems to be the particular sequence of turns. To say that the structure was learned, however, isn't to say that it caused the learning. A theorist who wanted to reinstate the primacy of function over structure might then argue that the structure was learned because of the contingencies: Certain turns at certain choicepoints led to certain new maze locations, and the rat learned these functional relations even without food in the maze. Even in negotiating the environment, the consequences of behavior matter. Then comes the argument that if contingencies define what is learned, they too can't be a cause of learning. And so it goes.

The theorist arguing for primacy of structure was probably a cognitivist, and the theorist arguing for primacy of function was probably a behaviorist, and their different languages weren't likely to help matters. Yet these structures and functions of behavior were both outcomes of learning. The problems can be resolved only by recognizing that behavioral structure and behavioral function are mutually determined by the relations between behavior and the environment. Both the structure and the function of behavior are to be understood in terms of their origins, and neither has primacy over the other. The relative provinces and provenances of structure and function remain controversial, but the controversies are perhaps amenable to the same sorts of solutions that worked for biology.

Both structure and function have limits, and as learning theories evolved, they were necessarily refined and qualified, thereby restricting the range of phenomena to which they could be applied. Recognizing the boundary conditions for learning was implicit in these restrictions. Limits on learning pose no problems when they can be easily traced to an organism's sensory or motor capacities. For example, we aren't surprised if certain stimuli are more likely to produce responses in some species than in others. We know that the visual and auditory systems of pigeons and bats make pigeons capable of visual discriminations impossible for bats and make bats capable of auditory discriminations impossible for pigeons. We also aren't troubled by different capacities for responding. Pigeons and bats fly differently at least in part because the anatomical structures of their wings are different. Although the examples are obvious, they aren't trivial. They illustrate how much we take the different sensory and motor capacities of different species for granted.

Like sensory and motor capacities, the

effectiveness of different stimuli as reinforcers or punishers varies across species. Once we recognized the relativity of reinforcement, it was no longer good enough just to identify which reinforcers or which punishers might be effective for a given species. These consequences can only be defined in relation to the responses that produce them. Within a species, a reinforcer effective for one response may not be effective for others. As demonstrated by phenomena such as food aversion and acknowledged by the concept of preparedness, we can't specify limits on learning in terms of stimuli alone or responses alone. Instead, we must express the limits in terms of the types of relations that can be created in a given species. Organisms may be predisposed to learn different relations among stimuli and responses in different situations. These predispositions are limitations on the structure of behavior.

An organism's behavior in its current environment is determined by phylogeny as well as ontogeny. The relative contributions of nature and nurture have been a long-standing issue in psychology, and though the emphasis has often shifted in one direction or the other it remains clear that neither operates to the exclusion of the other. Some aspects of behavior are highly determined by evolutionary factors (e.g., the human vocal apparatus) and others by experience (e.g., the human language one speaks). Nature and nurture are extremes on a continuum, and we must therefore recognize that learning as well as evolutionary history can impose constraints on behavior.

Like nature and nurture, behavior too is best represented not by all-or-none categories but rather by dimensions along which processes can be located. Reinforcement and punishment are extremes on a continuum of

contingencies ranging from those that increase responding through those that don't affect responding to those that decrease responding. Differentiation and discrimination are extremes on a continuum of the relative contributions of response properties and stimulus properties to the criteria for differential reinforcement. Contingency-shaped and verbally governed behavior are extremes on a continuum of the relative contributions of contingencies and verbal antecedents to the behavior of a listener. Behavioral and cognitive processes are extremes on a continuum that represents the relative accessibility or inaccessibility of things that organisms do. And so on.

One crucial part of the distinction between behavioral and cognitive psychologies is the insistence by the former that its subject matter is behavior. Our interpretation of cognitive processes such as remembering and imagining, for example, has been in terms of what organisms do. When some type of cognitive process, such as the processing of information, is expressed in terms that aren't explicitly related to behavior, its status becomes similar to that of the tacting of private events (cf. Watkins, 1981). A consistent vocabulary can be developed for a cognitive process only if at some point it makes contact with the environment, just as the consistent tacting of a private event can be developed only if some correlate of that event is publicly available to the verbal community. That may be one reason why the status of representations as copies or as transformations of stimuli has been the basis for so much controversy.

Another source of controversy has been the relation between behavior and physiology. Asserting that behavior is a subject matter in its own right doesn't deny its intimate dependence on physiology. Consider again the evolutionary analogy. Natural selection overcame challenges from orthogenesis and other alternatives and emerged as the primary account of evolution long before molecular biology worked out mechanisms of genetic transmission. Early geneticists had no biochemical evidence about genes and based their conclusions only on the data of reproduction. Molecular biologists needed the findings of genetics and mutation and natural selection to know what to look for in cells. They'd have looked differently, and undoubtedly with less success, if they'd started with orthogenetic or Lamarckian assumptions.

Similarly, those studying the neurophysiology of learning need to know what happens in learning and behavior to know what they should look for in the nervous system. The neurophysiologist who thinks of learning mainly in terms of stimulus–response associations will look for different things than the one who thinks of learning in terms of ontogenic selection. Skinner compared the relation between behavior analysis and neuroscience to that between genetics and biochemistry: "It is the function of the science of behavior at the present time to give neurologists their assignments, as it was the function of genetics prior to the discovery of DNA to give modern geneticists their assignment with respect to the gene" (Skinner, 1988, p. 60; see also p. 461).

We've made progress in our understanding of the neurophysiology of some relatively simple systems (e.g., Carew, 1992; Kandel & Schwartz, 1982), but neuroscience has given only scant attention to mechanisms for ontogenic selection (Stein, Xue, & Belluzzi, 1993). Neural mechanisms presumably underlie the environmental contingencies that create behavioral structure (cf. Hebb, 1949). Perhaps the accumulating evidence for growth and reorganization within the nervous system will turn out to be consistent with a selectionist account (e.g., Catania, K. C., & Kass, 1996; Donahoe, Burgos, & Palmer, 1993; Donahoe & Palmer, 1994; Kaas, 1991; Recanzone et al., 1992; Shull, 1995; Yates, 1986).

Section C   Learning and Evolution

In discussing types of selection, we've argued that properties of learning parallel those of evolution, because the selection or survival of patterns of behavior in an organism's lifetime has much in common with the selection or survival of individuals in the evolution of a species (e.g., Skinner, 1966, 1975; Catania, 1978). Our discussion of social learning made a similar case for the selection of cultural practices (cf. Dawkins, 1976; Harris, 1977; Petroski, 1992; Skinner, 1981); our own verbal behavior makes this variety of selection of special interest to us. Each type of selection involves some kind of variation that provides the source materials upon which it operates, and each involves some mechanism for selecting what survives. Whatever else happens at every level, behavior gets selected and the environment does the selecting.

The parallels between Darwinian natural selection and operant selection also extend to the problems of acceptance each has faced (Catania, 1987). Like Galileo's displacement of the earth from the center of the universe to an orbit around the sun and like Freud's challenge to the central status of human consciousness, these accounts overturned traditional ways of thinking about the place of our species in nature. (By the way, Freud's message at least took consciousness for granted while reducing its scope, in the sense that his unconscious processes, in the interactions of ego and superego and id, were supplements to consciousness: e.g., Freud, 1917. In a behavioral account, however, consciousness itself is derivative, because it demands discrimination of one's own behavior, which has to exist already if it's to be discriminated. In other words, the unconscious has to be there first or there'll be nothing to be conscious of.)

In any case, phylogenic and ontogenic selection have faced similar substantive challenges. For example, artificial selection was familiar in Darwin's time; what was questioned was whether selection could operate naturally. The operant parallel is provided by shaping, which is also an artificial selection procedure, as when an experimenter shapes a pigeon's figure-8 turns or as when a behavior therapist shapes the vocalizations of a nonverbal autistic child. The effectiveness of shaping is self-evident; what's questioned is whether it operates naturally to produce some of the varied patterns of behavior that we see in everyday life.

It isn't good enough to argue that in humans the effects of shaping are likely to be often masked by verbally governed behavior. It would be best to document cases in which the changes in contingencies are identified early and tracked. Typically, however, we only have outcomes, after the natural contingencies have done their work. For example, we can assume that ontogenic selection was involved in shaping the skill with which grizzly bears catch salmon in the rivers of the Pacific Northwest, but we mainly see the differences between the inefficient performances of the young novices and the well-coordinated actions of the experienced adults; we don't see the shaping itself, because it continues over too long a time.

Furthermore, shaping can be hard to see if one doesn't know what to look for; someone who's actually done shaping is more apt to notice it when it happens naturally than someone who's only read about it. Thus, the parents who always wait a while before attending to a crying child may not notice that they've gradually shaped louder and more annoying cries. The attention reinforces the crying, and annoying cries are, by definition, the ones most likely to get attention. If one watches what a parent does when a child throws tantrums, it's often easy to guess where the tantrums came from.

Time is another factor in the acceptance of both types of selection. For Darwinian natural selection, the question was once whether the earth had existed long enough for such selection to have taken place; upward revisions of the age of the earth resolved the problem. The comparable problem is easier to deal with for operant selection. Even with rapid breeders like the fruit fly, genetic experiments take days. Shaping, however, can be demonstrated within minutes. If reinforcers can do so much to behavior when contingencies are deliberately arranged over relatively short periods of time, isn't it reasonable to assume that they'll also affect behavior when natural contingencies operate over substantial periods in an organism's lifetime? Many contingencies may take hold of behavior over the course of a year in the life of a young child. Compared to how long most artificial examples of shaping last, a year is an extremely long time. Some contingencies may be subtle, especially when we recognize the very broad range of events that can serve as reinforcers. Some may produce behavior that is desirable; others may do the opposite. Given what artificial contingencies can do in a short time, natural contingencies should be able to do a lot in a long time. It's certainly more appropriate to be alert for the effects of such contingencies than to assume they don't exist.

In both natural and artificial environments, it's difficult to determine the boundaries of behavioral classes. Here again is a parallel between ontogenic and phylogenic selection. In each case, we must deal not with particular instances but rather with populations or classes of events. We speak of populations of organisms as species, and we speak of behavioral populations as response classes, such as operants, discriminated operants and respondents (and in social learning we speak of populations of socially maintained response classes as cultural practices and as classes of verbal behavior).

It might be argued that our notions of response classes are much vaguer than the classes Darwin spoke of as species in his account of evolution (Darwin, 1859). Yet even though the word *species* is in Darwin's famous title, *On the Origin of Species*, Darwin knew the term couldn't be unambiguously defined. In his book, he commented often on the problem of definition:

> I look at the term species, as one arbitrarily given for the sake of convenience to a set of individuals closely resembling each other [p. 52]; . . . the amount of difference necessary to give two forms the rank of species is quite indefinite [p. 59]; [and] . . . we shall have to treat species in the same manner as those naturalists treat genera, who admit that genera are merely artificial combinations made for convenience. This may not be a cheering prospect; but we shall at least be freed from the vain search for the undiscovered and undiscoverable essence of the term species. (Darwin, 1859, p. 485)

In Darwin's account of evolution, the relations among populations of organisms couldn't be expressed adequately in terms of similar topographies (for example, males and females within some species differ more from each other in form than some pairs of organisms within completely unrelated species; the social insects in particular provide striking instances).

For Darwin, the important basis for distinguishing among populations was descent. We define relations among populations by looking at where they came from. Darwin's achievement, in fact, was more description than explanation. His account of evolution didn't depend on any theory specifying the mechanics of evolution (his work predated genetics, and he even argued at times that acquired traits might be the source of variation on which evolution acted). He'd described the properties of evolution (Gould, 1975, p. 824). Darwin himself was skeptical about explanation: "It is so easy . . . to think that we give an explanation when we only restate a fact" (Darwin, 1859, pp. 481–482).

What does this have to do with learning? The analogies between behavior and biology suggest that some solutions appropriate to biology will be appropriate to behavior analysis. We've seen the importance of descriptions of what happens in learning and gave such descriptions priority over theories or mechanisms or models. For example, we found that *reinforcement*, a term that once served explanatory functions, now functions just as a name for a behavioral phenomenon. We no longer ask whether it explains behavior. Instead, we regard questions about the generality of reinforcement as about the range of circumstances to which the name can be applied. Similarly, the study of memory doesn't explain what's remembered; instead, what's remembered is the basis for determining behavioral structure, as in the analysis of the psychological reality of syntax and semantics. Theories and models come and go, but the descriptions of behavior remain (it's fitting that we've sometimes considered the results of experiments conducted a century ago).

Darwin's treatment rejected the concept of immutable species in favor of classes defined by their descent or evolution. The psychology of learning has sometimes moved in the opposite direction. It sought to *explain* learning by inventing sources for responses (neural traces, associations, cognitive structures). But that was getting it backwards. We should use the development of behavior to define behavioral classes. We should define behavioral classes in terms of their descent: where they come from or how they are learned. To some extent, we already do that, though seldom explicitly. We distinguish innate behavior from behavior acquired through experience. We speak of behavior produced by stimuli as elicited, and we speak of behavior occurring independently of stimuli as emitted. We say that responses elicited by stimuli are respondent behavior, and responses occasioned by stimuli that signal consequences are operant behavior. We say that responses engendered by verbal antecedents are verbally governed, and responses engendered by consequences are contingency-shaped. Such distinctions constitute our behavioral taxonomy.

In the analysis of behavior, we deal with populations of responses. These populations are sometimes not well-defined. The problem isn't different from Darwin's. Darwin clearly recognized the arbitrary nature of the concept of species, but unambiguous definitions of species were no more critical to his account than unambiguous definitions of stimulus or response classes are to a behavioral account (like natural categories, these too are probabilistic classes). When we distinguish among words by the circumstances in which they're uttered (e.g., *fire* as a mand, a tact, an echoic or a textual response), we're simply distinguishing among classes of verbal responses on the basis of their origins. Ambiguous cases will necessarily occur because, just as organisms have many ancestors, responses have many origins. But there would be no need for an analysis if that weren't so.

Section D   Behavior Analysis and Behavior Synthesis

A behavior analysis begins with complex behavior and breaks it down into its components. These are the elements of our behavioral taxonomy, and they can be combined in various ways, when it may be appropriate to speak of behavior synthesis. For example, we can synthesize some kinds of sequential performances through chaining procedures. In a more complex instance, we may combine discriminative stimuli, reinforcement schedules and delays of reinforcement so that the resulting contingencies are analogous to those when we speak of self-control. In the verbal domain, we may integrate echoic behavior, tacting and listener behavior into a higher-order class called naming. If our syntheses are successful, we may use them to clarify the properties of behavior; if they're unsuccessful, we may use them to identify components of performance that were missed or taken for granted in preceding analyses (e.g., as when we study variables affecting the likelihood of commitment responses in self-control procedures, or as when we discover, in designing an animal analogue of some human performance, that verbal behavior had a role we hadn't allowed for). Because many important human problems involve creating new behavior (e.g., teaching developmentally delayed children), the applications of our methods are often matters of behavior synthesis (cf. Catania & Brigham, 1978).

The term *learning* has receded into the background in all of this; perhaps it's outlived its usefulness. We can modify behavior hierarchies, shape new responses, construct higher-order classes, generate discriminations, form equivalence classes, solve problems and create novel behavior through adduction. Our understanding of these phenomena depends at least in part on whether we've developed a language consistent with them. We've recognized ambiguities in the present vocabulary of behavior; we can assume it will evolve as research progresses. Yet in emphasizing behavioral operations and processes, this vocabulary at least adheres closely to what is done and what is observed in research on behavior. The success of behavior analysis will be measured by its survival in the behavior of those who practice it and by the effectiveness of the behavior syntheses that follow from it.

Glossary

As the psychology of learning evolves, its terminology is progressively refined. This glossary defines some of that terminology. A set of definitions must be treated as a preliminary guide to the basic classifications and concepts in the relevant literature rather than as an inflexible set of rules. This glossary has been prepared in that spirit. A fuller and more technical glossary restricted to the experimental analysis of behavior is available in Catania (1991a); the evolution of some of the terminology can be examined by comparing current entries with those in an earlier version now out of print (Catania, 1968).

The present glossary attempts to acknowledge alternative definitions and to point out difficulties or potential ambiguities in existing usages. Nevertheless, sooner or later the reader must expect to encounter particular usages in the literature that disagree with the usages defined here.

Definitions are merely words that can substitute for other words, and the substitution is sometimes just an approximation. Because the framing or mastering of a definition is primarily verbal, it can't be counted on to produce the discriminations on which the development and evolution of that verbal behavior was based. For example, the student who has learned to define *reinforcement* may be able to offer a correct definition, but it doesn't follow that the student will then be able to discriminate reliably between actual instances of reinforcement and nonreinforcement in laboratory or real-world settings.

Glossaries are hardly ever exhaustive. This one's no exception. Over time old terms are modified or dropped and new ones are added. This glossary covers some major terminology of the psychology of learning as it appears in this volume and in closely related literature. With some exceptions, it doesn't cover aspects of vocabulary consistent with everyday usage (e.g., technical terms defined adequately in standard dictionaries), terms likely to be encountered in specialty areas or other disciplines (e.g., drug classification in psychopharmacology), or specialized technical terms that appear only in passing in the text and can be located via the index. For a review of other glossaries in behavior analysis, psychology and related disciplines, see Catania (1989); for a useful general dictionary of psychology, see Reber (1985); for a general English dictionary that includes Indo-European etymologies, see *The American Heritage Dictionary* (1992).

Time is usually expressed in seconds (abbreviated s in technical contexts); the abbreviation for minutes is min, and for milliseconds (thousandths of a second) is ms. Arbitrary quantities of time or number are indicated by *t* and *n*, which are constants unless otherwise stated. In cross-references among definitions, identified by FULL CAPITALIZATION, cf. (as opposed to *see*) usually refers to useful contrasts and critical distinctions among related terms rather than to synonymous usages. Most cross-references are given at the end of entries, but some are contained within entries. Some matters of usage pertinent to the glossary as a whole are discussed under OPERATION.

A

Abstraction: discrimination based on a single stimulus property, independent of other properties; thus, generalization among all stimuli with that property (e.g., all red stimuli as opposed to specific red objects). Cf. CONCEPT.

Accessibility: in the metaphor of memory storage, the retrievability of a stored item; an item stored but not retrievable is *inaccessible*. Cf. AVAILABILITY.

Acquisition: the addition of new behavior to an organism's repertoire. The behavior may be a discriminated operant, a topographically complex operant, a conditional reflex relation or the performance controlled by a schedule, or, in other words, changes in performance caused by any change in contingencies. Cf. LEARNING, REPERTORY.

Adaptation: a reduction, usually during the prolonged presentation of a stimulus, in the behavior produced by that stimulus (e.g., adaptation to an experimental chamber). Cf. HABITUATION, POTENTIATION.

Adduction: the production of novel behavior when new combinations of stimulus properties that separately control different classes or properties of behavior engender new combinations of those classes or properties (as when a child appropriately combines a color name and an animal name on seeing a horse of a different color for the first time); the novel coming together of different repertoires. Adduction is most obvious in verbal behavior.

Adjunctive behavior: responding that reliably accompanies some other response produced or occasioned by a stimulus, especially with stimuli presented according to temporally defined schedules. The stimulus rather than the responding it engenders is usually emphasized (e.g., in rats, food deliveries reliably produce eating followed by drinking; the adjunctive drinking is said to be *induced* by the schedule of food delivery and not by the eating).

Adjusting (adj) schedule: a schedule varying as a function of some property of performance (e.g., an adjusting FR schedule in which the ratio increases or decreases depending on the duration of postreinforcement pauses; an adjusting avoidance schedule in which schedule parameters change as a function of how often aversive stimuli occur).

Aggression: a side effect of presenting aversive stimuli or removing positive reinforcers. These events may generate responses that injure other organisms (e.g., biting) and/or make the opportunities for such responses effective as reinforcers.

Alternative (alt) schedule: a schedule in which a response is reinforced when either of two (or more) requirements is satisfied (e.g., in alternative FR 10 FI 60-s, the 10th response or the first response after 60 s is reinforced, whichever comes first; both schedule requirements then start over).

Analysis of behavior: see BEHAVIOR ANALYSIS.

Antecedent: a stimulus or event that precedes some other event or a contingency; a discriminative stimulus in a three-term contingency is one kind of antecedent.

Anticipation: see SERIAL LEARNING.

Anxiety: see EMOTIONAL BEHAVIOR, PREAVERSIVE STIMULUS.

Appetitive stimulus: usually, a positive reinforcer, especially one the effectiveness of which is modifiable by deprivation.

Arbitrary matching: see MATCHING-TO-SAMPLE.

Arousal: a state of readiness for behaving, metaphorically extended from arousal in the colloquial sense of awakening.

Artificial reinforcer: see CONTRIVED REINFORCER, EXTRINSIC REINFORCER.

Artificial selection: in the Darwinian account of evolution, the variety of selection practiced by humans, in selective breeding in horticulture, animal husbandry, etc. The distinction between artificial and NATURAL SELECTION is also relevant in ontogenic selection.

Association: see CONTIGUITY.

Attention (attending): discriminative responding based on some stimulus or stimulus property.

An organism is said to *attend to* a stimulus or property when variations in that stimulus or property change behavior (e.g., a pigeon discriminating blue light from its absence is said to attend to color rather than brightness if variations in wavelength but not intensity change its performance). Cf. DISCRIMINATION, FUNCTIONAL STIMULUS.

Audience: the discriminative stimuli that set the occasions on which verbal behavior has consequences. Different audiences set the occasion for different verbal classes. Audience stimuli are typically social (as when a speaker is influenced by cues provided by an attentive listener) but they're not exclusively so (as when someone interacts verbally with a computer terminal).

Augmenting stimulus: see INCENTIVE.

Autobiographical memory: episodic memory. See REMEMBERING.

Autoclitic: a unit of verbal behavior that depends on other verbal behavior for its occurrence and that modifies the effects of that other verbal behavior on the listener. *Descriptive autoclitics* involve discriminations of one's own behavior, as when the word *not* depends on a mismatch between what one's inclined to say and the appropriateness of saying it; including *not* in the statement cancels some of its effects on the listener. *Relational autoclitics* involve verbal units coordinated with other units in such a way that they can't stand alone, as when plurals depend on quantitative features of events or grammatical tenses depend on temporal features; novel verbal behavior is sometimes the product of novel combinations of such units: see ADDUCTION.

Autology: the scientific study of the self. "It is because our behavior is important to others that it eventually becomes important to us" (Skinner, 1957, p. 314). Cf. PRIVATE EVENTS.

Automaintenance: the maintenance of autoshaped responding by continuing the AUTOSHAPING procedure. In *negative automaintenance*, reinforcers are omitted on trials with and presented on trials without responses.

Automatic reinforcer: a reinforcer related to a response in such a way that it's usually produced automatically by the response (as in the relation between sexual activity and orgasm). Cf. CONTRIVED REINFORCER, INTRINSIC REINFORCER, PRIMARY REINFORCER.

Autoshaping: a respondent procedure that generates skeletal responses. In the commonest ex-ample, a pigeon's key pecks are engendered by presentations of a fixed duration of keylight followed by food, which isn't presented at other times. In some procedures, pecks on the key, once they occur, produce food immediately rather than at keylight offset. Cf. AUTOMAINTENANCE.

Availability: in the metaphor of memory storage, the status of a stored item; if it's stored, it's said to be available whether or not it can be retrieved. A retrievable item is both available and accessible; an unretrievable one might be either unavailable or available but inaccessible. Cf. ACCESSIBILITY.

Aversive control: see specific cases: ESCAPE, AVOIDANCE, PUNISHMENT, PREAVERSIVE STIMULUS.

Aversive stimulus: a stimulus effective as a *negative reinforcer* or as a *punisher*, or that suppresses positively reinforced operant behavior during another stimulus that precedes it (cf. PREAVERSIVE STIMULUS). A stimulus with any one of these effects is likely also to have the others, but it's not guaranteed to do so. Cf. NOXIOUS STIMULUS, PUNISHMENT, REINFORCEMENT.

Avoidance: the prevention of an aversive stimulus by a response. In *deletion* procedures, the response cancels presentations of the aversive stimulus; in *postponement* procedures, the response only delays them. In *discriminated, discrete-trials* or *signaled avoidance*, an exteroceptive stimulus (sometimes called a *warning stimulus*) precedes the aversive stimulus; a response during this stimulus prevents the aversive stimulus on that trial. If no response occurs and the aversive stimulus is presented, escape from it typically depends on the same response that's effective for avoidance. In *continuous, free-operant* or *Sidman avoidance*, no exteroceptive stimulus is arranged and, typically, there's no provision for escape. Each response postpones the aversive stimulus (usually, brief shock) for a fixed period called the *response–shock (RS) interval*; in the absence of responses, shocks are delivered regularly according to a *shock–shock (SS) interval*. Cf. NEGATIVE REINFORCEMENT.

B

Backward conditioning: respondent conditioning in which the CS follows rather than precedes the US. This procedure can work with aversive stimuli but is otherwise usually ineffective.

Bait-shyness: see TASTE AVERSION.

Bar: lever. See OPERANDUM.

Baseline: a stable and usually recoverable performance on which effects of experimental variables are superimposed (e.g., a drug effect may be expressed as the change produced in baseline response rate by a dosage of the drug). The term is also used occasionally to refer to the horizontal starting position (zero responses) of a cumulative recorder pen. Sometimes what the baseline should be is ambiguous; for example, if pecks occur at higher rates when they produce shock than when they don't because shocks are correlated with reinforcers, should the baseline be a no-shock condition with reinforcers or a shock condition without them? Cf. STEADY STATE.

Behavior: anything an organism does. The definition is too inclusive as it stands but can't easily be restricted further. For example, shifts of attention needn't involve eye movement but qualify as behavior. The word is often used as a substitute for *responses* (*a behavior, several behaviors*), but this text adheres to colloquial usage, in which *behavior* is a collective term (*kinds of behavior*). See specific cases: COVERT, EMOTIONAL, SPECIES-SPECIFIC, OPERANT, OVERT and RESPONDENT BEHAVIOR.

Behavioral contrast: see CONTRAST.

Behavior analysis: breaking complex behavior down into its functional parts. A successful analysis should allow the behavior to be synthesized by putting the parts back together.

Bias: a systematic error in measurement (e.g., if a device can't record all responses when they follow each other rapidly, data recorded with the device will be biased toward low response rates). For other usages, see MATCHING LAW, PREFERENCE, SIGNAL DETECTION ANALYSIS.

Biofeedback: FEEDBACK based on physiological measures (e.g., blood pressure, heart rate, muscle tension).

Blackout: a timeout arranged by turning off all lights in the chamber.

Blocking: an attenuation of respondent conditioning with one stimulus because of prior conditioning with another (e.g., if tone and bell together precede food but bell is already a CS, tone may remain ineffective as a CS even though it and bell have the same contingent relation to food). Cf. OVERSHADOWING.

Break: an abrupt transition from responding to no responding (cf. RATIO STRAIN).

Burst: high-rate responding bounded by lower-rate responding.

C

Categories: see specific cases: ABSTRACTION, CONCEPT, EQUIVALENCE CLASS, NATURAL CONCEPT, POLYMORPHOUS STIMULUS CLASS, PROBABILISTIC STIMULUS CLASS, PROTOTYPE.

CER: conditioned emotional response. See PREAVERSIVE STIMULUS.

Chain: a sequence of discriminated operants such that responses during one stimulus are followed by other stimuli that reinforce those responses and set the occasion for the next ones (see CHAINED SCHEDULE, CONDITIONED REINFORCER). Not all temporally integrated sequences are maintained through chaining; those that are should be distinguished from those that aren't. Parts of a chain are called *components, links* or *members*. Procedures for creating chains often start at the end closest to the reinforcer and then work back (*backward chaining*); starting from the other end (*forward chaining*) is more difficult, because early responses may extinguish while later ones are being shaped. Chains with topographically similar responses are *homogeneous* (e.g., pecks maintained by a chained schedule); those with topographically dissimilar responses are *heterogeneous* (e.g., alley running and then lever pressing).

Chained (chain) schedule: a compound schedule in which reinforcers are produced by successive completions of two or more component schedules, each operating during a different stimulus. Equivalent arrangements with the same stimulus during each component are *tandem* schedules.

Chamber: a space designed to minimize interference from stimuli irrelevant to experimental conditions (e.g., laboratory noises) and including devices for recording behavior (see OPERANDUM) and presenting stimuli. Typical chambers may contain mechanisms for delivering reinforcers (e.g., food dispensers), discriminative stimulus sources (e.g., speakers for auditory stimuli, lamps or projectors for visual stimuli), aversive stimulus sources (e.g., see SHOCK), a houselight for general illumination, feedback devices that produce stimuli such as clicks after each response, and auditory sources that mask outside noise (often, a fan that provides masking noise along with ventilation).

Changeover: the switch from one response to another, as when a pigeon in a two-key chamber moves from left-key pecking to right-key pecking. Cf. CONCURRENT OPERANTS.

Changeover delay (COD): a feature sometimes used with concurrent schedules to prevent sequences in which a reinforcer produced by one response closely follows the other response. As usually arranged, the COD provides that no response can be reinforced within t s after a changeover (but CODs may be timed from other events, such as the last response before the changeover).

Changeover ratio (COR): a changeover contingency that provides that no response can be reinforced until at least n responses after the last changeover. Cf. CHANGEOVER DELAY.

Chaos: a branch of mathematics dealing with nonlinear systems, which are drastically affected even by very small changes in initial values (e.g., the path of a storm system may be influenced by the flaps of a butterfly's wings weeks before). Like the weather, behavior is a nonlinear system. For measurement at any level of precision, the mathematics of chaos demonstrates that we can predict kinds of things that will happen but we can't predict specific details (e.g., we can predict that a pigeon will peck a key but not precisely when). This makes interpretation far more important. In many behavioral applications it's all that's feasible.

Choice: the emission of one of two or more alternative and, usually, incompatible responses. Cf. CONCURRENT OPERANTS, PREFERENCE.

Chunking: the arbitrary creation of larger verbal units, as when a mnemonic system is used to convert a number sequence to a single word.

Classical conditioning: see RESPONDENT CONDITIONING.

Closed economy: in operant contexts, the availability of appetitive stimuli only within the session, as reinforcers, with none provided independently of behavior on a supplementary basis outside of the session. Cf. OPEN ECONOMY.

Clustering: In free recall, the reorganization of items by the learner so that related ones are recalled together rather than in the order in which they appeared on the list.

cm: centimeters (abbreviation). One cm is about 0.4 inches.

COD: see CHANGEOVER DELAY.

Coding, coding response: an inferred variety of mediating behavior, as when humans remember visually presented letters on the basis of sound rather than geometric properties, perhaps as a result of saying or subvocally rehearsing them. Errors based on acoustic rather than visual similarity support the inference. Tacting is one kind of coding. Cf. DECODING, ENCODING.

Cognition, cognitive processes: knowing and the ways in which it takes place. Processes said to be cognitive are often varieties of BEHAVIOR that aren't manifested as movements and so must be measured indirectly (e.g., doing mental arithmetic, shifting attention, imagining). Cf. COVERT BEHAVIOR.

Cognitive map: a spatial schema or representation. In learning a coordinated set of spatial relations, an organism is sometimes said to develop a cognitive map. The term is most likely to be invoked when an organism orients toward locations it can't see or otherwise directly respond to.

Collateral behavior: responding that, like MEDIATING BEHAVIOR, appears in a consistent sequential relation to reinforced behavior while not itself instrumental in producing reinforcers. It doesn't carry the implication that the responding mediates the reinforced behavior.

Comparison stimulus: see MATCHING-TO-SAMPLE.

Component: one of the schedules, or the stimulus associated with it, in a compound schedule. The term is usually restricted to cases in which the schedules making up the compound operate successively and not simultaneously.

Compound schedule: a schedule that combines two or more component schedules. The components may operate successively, in alternation (MULTIPLE and MIXED) or as a sequence (CHAINED and TANDEM), or simultaneously (CONCURRENT and CONJOINT); they may also interact (ALTERNATIVE, CONJUNCTIVE, INTERLOCKING). See these and other specific cases: ADJUSTING, CONCURRENT-CHAIN, HIGHER-ORDER, PERCENTILE-REINFORCEMENT, PROGRESSIVE.

Concept: a class of stimuli such that an organism generalizes among all stimuli within the class but discriminates them from those in other classes. Concepts are to analyses of discriminative stimuli as operants are to analyses of response classes (Keller & Schoenfeld, 1950). Cf. ABSTRACTION, DISCRIMINATION, GENERALIZATION, STIMULUS.

Concurrent-chain schedules: concurrent schedules in which the reinforcers are themselves schedules that operate separately and in the presence of different stimuli, as when equal and independent concurrent VI VI schedules operate for a pigeon's pecks on two white keys and, according to the VI schedules, left pecks produce an FI schedule on a blue key and right pecks produce an FR schedule on a yellow key. The concurrent VI VI schedules are *initial links* and the separate schedules they produce are *terminal links*. The initial links can be thought of as doors that admit the pigeon to separate rooms containing the terminal links. PREFERENCE for terminal links is given by relative response rates in initial links.

Concurrent operants: two or more classes of alternative responses. Concurrent operants may be compatible (as when a rat simultaneously presses one lever with its left paw and another with its right) or incompatible (as when the pigeon, having only one beak, pecks only one of two keys at a time) as long as the organism can emit either or change over from one to the other at any time (responding and not responding are sometimes treated as concurrent operants). Discriminated operants can be concurrent if the organism has an opportunity to produce the stimuli that occasion them at any time. For example, in a *changeover-key procedure*, a pigeon changes the stimuli and their associated schedules on one key (the *main* key) by pecking a second key (the *changeover* key). In this case, two CONCURRENT SCHEDULES operate on one key, and the CHANGEOVER is an explicit response on a second key. See also PREFERENCE.

Concurrent (conc) schedules: two or more schedules operating simultaneously and independently, each for a different response, as when separate VI schedules are arranged for a pigeon's pecks on each of two keys. Cf. CONJOINT SCHEDULES.

Conditional: an often-preferred alternative to *conditioned*.

Conditional discrimination: a discrimination in which reinforcement of responding during a stimulus depends on (is conditional on) other stimuli (e.g., matching-to-sample involves a conditional discrimination in the sense that the comparison response that'll be reinforced depends on the sample). Conditional discrimination procedures involve four-term contingencies: They arrange stimuli during which different three-term contingencies operate.

Conditional probability: the PROBABILITY of one event given another event (e.g., if A and B occur equally often but A is followed by A 75% of the time and by B 25% of the time, the simple probability of A is .5 but its conditional probability given a prior A is .75). See INTERRESPONSE TIME for another example.

Conditioned: see CONDITIONAL.

Conditioned aversive stimulus: a stimulus that acquired its aversive properties by reliably accompanying another aversive stimulus (e.g., in discriminated avoidance, the warning stimulus may become a conditioned aversive stimulus). Cf. PREAVERSIVE STIMULUS.

Conditioned emotional response (CER): see PREAVERSIVE STIMULUS.

Conditioned reflex or **conditional reflex:** a reflex produced by a contingent relation between stimuli (see CONTINGENCY). One stimulus, originally neutral, sets the occasion for a second stimulus, the *unconditioned stimulus* (*US*). A conditioned reflex is created when the neutral stimulus becomes a *conditioned stimulus* (*CS*), eliciting a response by virtue of its contingent relation to the US. This response, a *conditioned response* (*CR*), is often related to but isn't necessarily the same as the *unconditioned response* (*UR*) elicited by the US. Responses elicited by the CS before conditioning (e.g., orienting responses) tend to disappear as conditioning progresses (cf. HABITUATION).

The most typical respondent procedure, in which a CS is followed within no more than 5 s by the US, is called *simultaneous conditioning* (brief delays were incorporated into most so-called simultaneous procedures because the CR can't be measured independently of the UR if the CS and US are simultaneous, and strict simultaneity is less effective in conditioning than a brief delay between CS and US). Effective USs in respondent conditioning are often effective positive or negative reinforcers in operant selection, and an older usage of *reinforcement* referring to US presentations still survives in some parts of the learning literature. See BACKWARD, DELAY, HIGHER-ORDER, TEMPORAL and TRACE CONDITIONING; cf. UNCONDITIONED REFLEX, RESPONDENT.

Conditioned reinforcer or **conditional reinforcer:** a stimulus that functions as a reinforcer because of its contingent relation to another reinforcer. Such stimuli have also been called *secondary* reinforcers, but this designation is best reserved for cases in which the modifier specifies how many stimuli separate the conditioned from the primary reinforcer (e.g., secondary related directly to primary, tertiary to secondary, etc.). Convenience often dictates the assigned order (e.g., feeder operations are usually called primary reinforcers even though the auditory and/or visual stimuli that accompany them are actually conditioned reinforcers that precede eating).

Conditioned response or **conditional response (CR)** and **conditioned stimulus** or **conditional stimulus (CS)**: see CONDITIONED REFLEX.

Conditioned suppression: see PREAVERSIVE STIMULUS.

Conditioning: see RESPONDENT CONDITIONING. The term appears occasionally in conjunction with *operant*, but *operant conditioning* is becoming a rarer usage.

Conflict: a situation in which a single response produces both reinforcers and punishers (*approach–avoidance* conflict), or two or more incompatible responses produce different reinforcers (*approach–approach* conflict), or two or more incompatible responses each avoid only one of two or more aversive stimuli (*avoidance–avoidance* conflict). Approach–avoidance conflicts often produce vacillating behavior (as in love–hate relationships).

Conjoint (conjt) schedules: two or more component schedules, usually involving different reinforcers, operating for a single response (e.g., lever presses simultaneously are reinforced according to an FR schedule and postpone shock according to an avoidance schedule). Cf. CONCURRENT SCHEDULES.

Conjugate reinforcement: reinforcement in which some property of a reinforcer varies systematically with some response property (as when the sharpness of focus of a visual reinforcer increases with the momentary rate of responding).

Conjunctive (conj) schedule: a schedule that reinforces a response when each of two (or more) schedule requirements is satisfied (e.g., in conj FI 60-s FR 10, a response is reinforced only after at least 60 s have elapsed and at least nine other responses have been emitted since the last reinforcer).

Consequence: an event produced by some other event; especially, in operant contexts, an event produced by a response (e.g., stimulus presentation or removal, a change in contingencies or any other environmental change). The term is particularly useful for referring to events with an unknown status as reinforcers or punishers (presenting such events contingent on responding has sometimes been called *consequation*).

Consolidation of memory: a theoretical process based on the assumption that remembering is relatively impermanent immediately after learning and takes some time to become fixed or consolidated.

Constituent grammars: phrase-structure grammars. See GRAMMARS.

Constructive memory: see RECONSTRUCTION.

Consummatory response: the behavior occasioned by a reinforcer. The term originated with reinforcers that were consumed (food, water) but has been extended to other kinds (e.g., if opportunities to run in a wheel are reinforcers, wheel running is the consummatory response).

Context: the constant features of an situation (e.g., the chamber in which an operant session occurs). Experimental contexts acquire behavioral function because they're imbedded in the still larger contexts that include the experimental session.

Contiguity: the juxtaposition of two or more events when they occur simultaneously or very closely together (e.g., the succession of a response and a reinforcer in a superstition procedure or of a CS and a US in a respondent procedure). Cf. CONTINGENCY.

Contingency: in the operant case, the conditions under which a response produces a consequence (e.g., in an FI, the reinforcer is *contingent on* a response of a given force, topography, etc., as well as on the passage of time). An organism is said to *come into contact with a contingency* when its behavior produces some consequences of the contingency.

Studies of reinforcement schedules analyze contingencies and their effects (as in comparing contingencies of reinforcement for various IRTs in VI and VR schedules). In this most general usage, contingencies describe any relation, whether completely specified in a procedure or an incidental and perhaps fortuitous consequence of them. In a more specific sense, contingencies are the conditional probabilities relating some events (e.g., responses) to others (e.g., stimuli). When responses produce reinforcers, the contingent relation is defined by two conditional probabilities: probability of the reinforcer (1) given a response and (2) given no response. Without both probabilities specified, the contingent relations can't be distinguished from the incidental temporal *contiguities* of responses and reinforcers that occur independently over time. Response–reinforcer relations involve two terms, but when correlated with discriminative stimuli they produce a *three-term contingency*. Conditional discriminations add a fourth term, and so on for other contingency relations of various orders of complexity.

When applied to respondent cases, *contingency* refers to the conditions under which some stimuli are followed by others. By analogy to the operant case, *stimulus–stimulus contingencies* expressed as conditional probabilities specify conditions more completely than descriptions in terms of temporal *contiguities*, and distinguish cases in which two stimuli always occur together from those in which they're frequently paired but also occur independently. Stimuli correlated with stimulus–stimulus contingencies (sometimes called *occasion setters*) may enter into three-term or higher-order relations.

Contingency-governed behavior or **contingency-shaped behavior:** operant behavior. The terminology is ordinarily used to contrast responding that isn't occasioned by verbal behavior with *verbally governed behavior*, behavior controlled by verbal antecedents (e.g., instructions).

Contingency space: any coordinate system within which contingencies expressed as conditional probabilities are plotted.

Contingent associations: associations that involve all possible combinations, so that their learning is contingent on the entire configuration of each item, as when a verbal discrimination task uses two lists of three-letter words arranged so that every possible letter combination appears in both lists. For example, with list-1 items FIT FAN PIN PAT and list-2 items FIN FAT PIT PAN, every possible letter and pair of letters appears as often in list 1 as in list 2 (e.g., F--, -I-,--T; PA-, P-N, -AN). Only whole items can consistently occasion correct responses; no part will work. Lists constructed this way can be exceedingly difficult to learn (Wickelgren, 1969). Contingent associations may account for the difficulty of learning some artificial languages that include very little redundancy (e.g., Loglan).

Contingent stimulus: a stimulus the presentation of which depends on a response-stimulus contingency.

Continuous avoidance: see AVOIDANCE.

Continuous reinforcement (CRF): reinforcement of every response within the limits of an operant class.

Continuous repertoire or **continuous repertory:** behavior that tracks continuous changes in some environmental property, as when a driver steers a car to keep it in its lane.

Continuum: see STIMULUS CONTINUUM.

Contrast or **behavioral contrast:** a change in the rate of one response that occurs when either the rate of a second response or the reinforcement rate produced by that response changes in the opposite direction, where the reinforcement rate main-

taining the first response remains constant. For example, the rate of reinforced responding in one multiple-schedule component typically increases if reinforcement is reduced or discontinued in the other. The effect is most appropriately measured relative to a baseline in which responses in both components are maintained by the same reinforcement rate but has also been measured relative to rates in prior nonbaseline conditions. The term usually applies to effects during successive stimuli, as in multiple schedules, but similar phenomena occur in concurrent schedules.

Contrived reinforcer: an artificial reinforcer. Cf. CONDITIONED REINFORCER, EXTRINSIC REINFORCER.

Control: the systematic modification or maintenance of behavior by changes in relevant conditions. The manipulation of conditions distinguishes control from *prediction* and *interpretation*. If control isn't possible because relevant conditions aren't manipulable, adequate information about relevant variables may allow prediction (as in the history of astronomy before space flight). Interpretation usually occurs after the fact. Given an outcome, a plausible account of the relevant variables can be offered, but it may be difficult to determine its adequacy. Nevertheless, such analyses are often expected or demanded of students of behavior (as when a psychologist is asked to explain in a court of law why a defendant acted in some way). In its commonest behavior analytic usage, the term appears in conjunction with some variable that has a demonstrable effect on behavior (e.g., *schedule control*, *stimulus control*). Cf. CHAOS.

Coordinate: the value of a point plotted on a graph. In a two-dimensional system, the one plotted along the x-axis is called the *abscissa* and the one plotted along the y-axis is called the *ordinate*; the terms don't refer to the axes themselves.

COR: see CHANGEOVER RATIO.

Correction procedure: the repetition or continuation of conditions and/or stimuli after certain responses or their absence (especially after errors in simultaneous discrimination trials). For example, stimuli may be repeated in a new trial if an error occurred in the last one or, with trials of limited duration, if no response occurred; or a multiple VI extinction schedule may be arranged so that each response during the extinction component delays the onset of the VI component. The term can refer to any procedure that arranges continued or repeated opportunities for responses in alternative classes until a given response does (or doesn't) occur. Its colloquial origins imply procedures that eventually force an organism to emit a correct response (cf. ERROR), but the usage doesn't exclude procedures in which the alternative response classes can't easily be categorized as correct responses and errors.

Correlated stimuli or **correlated reinforcers:** see CONJUGATE REINFORCEMENT.

Correlation: see STATISTICS. The term is often applied to stimulus control procedures (as when a schedule operating during the presence but not the absence of a stimulus is said to be *correlated with* the stimulus) and to *molar* analyses (as in studies of the correlation between overall response rates and overall reinforcement rates).

Correspondence (between saying and doing): see VERBALLY GOVERNED BEHAVIOR.

Cost: see RESPONSE COST.

Covert behavior: behavior that isn't observed or observable and so is only inferred. Alternatively, behavior inside an organism, but of such a sort or on such a small scale that it's not recordable or is recordable only with special equipment (e.g., thinking or counting to oneself, perhaps inferred from a verbal report, or muscle contractions too small to produce obvious movement).

CR: conditioned response. See CONDITIONED REFLEX.

CRF: see CONTINUOUS REINFORCEMENT.

Critical feature: a feature, perhaps one of several, on which discrimination among stimuli depends (e.g., letters of the alphabet include straight versus curved, open versus closed, etc., as critical features). Cf. FUNCTIONAL STIMULUS.

Critical period: the time during which a stimulus can become imprinted (cf. IMPRINTED STIMULUS). More generally, any time period to which the operation of some behavioral process is limited.

CS: conditioned stimulus. See CONDITIONED REFLEX.

Cue-dependent learning: see STATE-DEPENDENT LEARNING.

Cultural selection: the selection of behavior as it's passed on from one organism to another (examples include imitated behavior and verbal behavior). Cf. OPERANT SELECTION.

Cumulative record: a record that shows total responses plotted as a function of time, usually made by a marker or pen that moves a fixed distance with each response across a paper advancing at a constant speed. Thus, the faster the responding, the steeper the slope. Moment-to-moment changes in slope show the details of changing response rates over time. Cumulative recorders typically include additional features; for example, the pen can be reset to its starting position (sometimes called the *baseline*) after a full excursion across the paper or after some event; it can be briefly displaced downward or to one side, producing a pip, to indicate a reinforcer or other brief event; it can be held in its downward position, producing a displaced line, to indicate stimuli or other extended conditions; and an event pen at the bottom of the record can be used to indicate other events. Cf. RATE OF RESPONDING.

CVC trigram: a verbal item made up of a consonant, a vowel and a consonant, in that order (often a nonsense syllable).

D

Data; datum: recorded information, usually in numerical form. *Data* is plural; *datum* is singular.

Declarative memory: see REMEMBERING.

Decoding: the learner's behavior with respect to an item to be remembered at the time it's recalled. Cf. ENCODING.

Deep structure: the common structural features of sentences related to each other by grammatical transformations. Cf. SURFACE STRUCTURE.

Defensive conditioning: respondent conditioning with an aversive or noxious stimulus as US.

Deictic verbal behavior, deixis: verbal behavior in which terms have functions that vary relative to the speaker (e.g., personal pronouns, *here* versus *there*, *this* versus *that*). Deixis depends on discriminations of the speaker's own behavior and so shares some properties with autoclitic behavior.

Delay conditioning: respondent conditioning in which the CS is presented for some fixed extended time before the US (in most usages, no less than 5 s).

Delay of reinforcement: the time from a response to a reinforcer. Reinforcers lose their effectiveness with increasing delays, but procedural complications stand in the way of measuring delay-of-reinforcement effects. When delay procedures interpose a stimulus between a response and its delayed reinforcer (*signaled delay of reinforcement*), the stimulus probably functions as an immediate conditioned reinforcer. When procedures interpose no stimulus, either additional responses reset the delay, thereby limiting response rate because a reinforcer is delivered only after a pause equal to the delay, or they don't reset the delay, thereby allowing the actual delay to be reduced to the now shorter time between those additional responses and the reinforcer.

Delayed matching-to-sample: see MATCHING-TO-SAMPLE, DELAYED RESPONSE.

Delayed response: a response that occurs some time after a discriminative stimulus is removed, as when the sample in a matching-to-sample procedure is turned off several seconds before the comparison stimuli are presented (see MEDIATING BEHAVIOR for an example). Cf. REMEMBERING.

Deletion: see AVOIDANCE.

Density: a synonym for rate (as in *reinforcement density* or *shock density*). Cf. RATE OF REINFORCEMENT.

Dependency: roughly, a contingency completely specified by the experimenter or with a conditional probability very close to 1.0. Cf. CONTINGENCY.

Deprivation: a reduction in the availability of a reinforcer. With food reinforcers, percentage of free feeding weight and the time since free feeding have been used as criteria for deprivation levels. Deprivation may be a condition for making any positive reinforcer effective (e.g., a rat's opportunity to run in a running wheel). Cf. ESTABLISHING OPERATION.

Descriptive autoclitic: see AUTOCLITIC.

Development of language: see LANGUAGE DEVELOPMENT.

Dictation-taking: a formal verbal class in which a vocal verbal stimulus occasions a corresponding written response. The correspondence is defined by the one-to-one relation of verbal units (e.g., letters or words). Cf. ECHOIC BEHAVIOR, TEXTUAL BEHAVIOR, TRANSCRIPTION.

Differential conditioning: usually, producing a discrimination in respondent conditioning. See RESPONDENT DISCRIMINATION.

Differential reinforcement: reinforcement of some responses but not others, depending on intensive, temporal, topographical or other properties of the responses (including the stimuli during which they're emitted; cf. DISCRIMINATED OPERANT); differential reinforcement defines operant classes. When the proportion of responses within the limits of the operant class increases as a result of differential reinforcement, responding is said to be *differentiated*.

Differential-reinforcement schedules: schedules of differential reinforcement, especially when reinforcers depend on the temporal spacing of responses. Contingencies can be based on interresponse times (IRTs), response rates or periods of no responding. They're usually arranged for free-operant responding but also can be arranged within discrete trials.

In *differential-reinforcement-of-long-interresponse-times, differential-reinforcement-of-low-rate* (*DRL*) or *IRT>t* schedules, a response is reinforced only if at least t s has passed since the last response. An alternative and less common method is based on rates rather than IRTs; it reinforces a response only if fewer than n responses were emitted during the last t s.

In *differential-reinforcement-of-high-rate* (*DRH*) or *IRT<t* schedules, a response is reinforced if n responses were emitted during the last t s. The alternative based on IRTs rather than rates is less common because reinforcing single short IRTs tends to produce short IRTs separated by pauses rather than sustained high response rates.

A *paced-response* or *differential-reinforcement-of-pacing* (*DRP*) schedule arranges upper and lower limits on reinforced IRTs (e.g., an IRT between 2 and 4 s) or on reinforced response rates (e.g., between 10 and 15 responses during the last 5 s). When the schedule is based on IRTs rather than rates, it's sometimes called *DRL with limited hold.*

Another type delivers a reinforcer after a response is followed by t s of no responding (cf. DELAY OF REINFORCEMENT). Still another reinforces not responding by delivering a reinforcer after t s without a response; this schedule's called *differential reinforcement of zero behavior* or *other behavior* (*DRO*). See also INTERRESPONSE TIME, RATE OF RESPONDING.

Differentiation: see DIFFERENTIAL REINFORCEMENT.

Discrete trials: see TRIAL.

Discriminated operant: an operant defined in terms of the stimuli during which it occurs as well as its environmental effect. This operant depends on the relations among three events (the *three-term contingency*): a *stimulus* in the presence of which a *response* may have *consequences*. In one sense, the stimulus sets the occasion on which the response may be reinforced; in another, it defines a property of the operant and so sets the occasion for the response. The joint dependence of the response on both stimulus and reinforcer distinguishes the relation from that of a reflex. See also OPERANT.

Discrimination: any difference in responding in the presence of different stimuli; in a more restricted usage, a difference resulting from differential consequences of responding in the presence of different stimuli. See also DISCRIMINATED OPERANT, GENERALIZATION, RESPONDENT DISCRIMINATION, SIMULTANEOUS DISCRIMINATION, STIMULUS, SUCCESSIVE DISCRIMINATION, VERBAL DISCRIMINATION. Usually the organism is said to discriminate among relevant stimuli. In some cases, however, it's useful to speak of responses as discriminating (e.g., if response rate varies with color whereas response location varies with form, rate discriminates color while location discriminates form). Further, when discriminated responding is produced by differential contingencies in the presence of different stimuli, it's appropriate to say that the stimuli are discriminated but not that the contingencies are discriminated.

Discriminative stimulus: any stimulus with a discriminative function; according to an older usage, a stimulus correlated with reinforcement when another is correlated with extinction. The latter usage has become less common because it isn't applicable to stimuli correlated with different schedules (e.g., multiple FI FR); it was the source of S^D ("S-dee": discriminative stimulus) and S^Δ ("S-delta": absence of discriminative stimulus) as abbreviations for stimuli correlated with reinforcement and with extinction. The abbreviations have lost ground to S+ (positive stimulus) and S- (negative stimulus). Strictly, S^0 ("S-zero") is more appropriate for the absence of reinforcement but S- is typographically more convenient.

Displacement activity: an ethological term referring to a response occurring not in the presence of the RELEASER that usually produces it but rather in the presence of one that usually produces some other response. Displacement activity and VACUUM ACTIVITY depend on deprivation of opportunities to complete a FIXED ACTION PATTERN, but displacement activity is likely to occur at lower levels of deprivation than vacuum activity.

Distributed practice: spacing periods of activity on a task. Cf. MASSED PRACTICE.

Distribution: a classification of events by location along a continuum. For example, an IRT distribution classifies IRTs into several temporal categories (e.g., less than 1 s, 1 but less than 2 s, 2 but less than 3 s, and 3 or more s). *Frequency distributions* show the number of events per category; *relative frequency distributions* show the events per category as a proportion of the total. Each category is called a *class interval*, and class intervals are ordinarily of equal size. Distributions often include a category for all events falling beyond some point on the continuum (e.g., in the above example, 3 or more s) so that a category exists for any event no matter how extreme. Cf. INTERRESPONSE TIME, STATISTICS.

DMTS: delayed matching-to-sample. See DELAYED RESPONSE, MATCHING-TO-SAMPLE.

DRH: differential reinforcement of high rate. See DIFFERENTIAL-REINFORCEMENT SCHEDULES.

Drive operation: see ESTABLISHING OPERATION.

DRL: differential reinforcement of long interresponse times or low rate. See DIFFERENTIAL-REINFORCEMENT SCHEDULES.

DRO: differential reinforcement of zero behavior or other behavior. See DIFFERENTIAL-REINFORCEMENT SCHEDULES.

DRP: differential reinforcement of paced responding or pacing. See DIFFERENTIAL-REINFORCEMENT SCHEDULES.

Duration of response: the time from the beginning to the end of a response (sometimes called *holding time*). Analyses of this property of responding depend heavily on procedural details. For example, if a reinforcer is delivered when a lever is pressed, response duration is short because the reinforcer occasions quick release, but if it's delivered on lever release, then each member of the chain (press, hold, release) may be differently affected by the contingencies.

Duration of stimulus: see TEMPORAL DISCRIMINATION.

E

Echoic behavior: a formal verbal class in which a vocal verbal stimulus occasions a corresponding vocal verbal response. The correspondence is defined by the one-to-one relation of verbal units (e.g., phonemes or words) and not by acoustic similarity. Cf. DICTATION-TAKING, TEXTUAL BEHAVIOR, TRANSCRIPTION.

Echoic memory: see REMEMBERING.

Effect, Law of: see LAW OF EFFECT.

Eidetic memory: sometimes called photographic memory, a rare type of remembering, usually in children, in which visual stimuli are described in detail as if seen long after they were presented.

Elaborative rehearsal: see REHEARSAL.

Elicitation: the reliable production of a response by a stimulus in unconditioned or conditioned reflexes. Cf. RESPONDENT BEHAVIOR.

Emergent relation: a new behavioral relation (especially conditional stimulus control) emerging as a byproduct of other relations rather than through differential reinforcement. For example, if arbitrary matching has been trained only for AB and BC (where the first letter of each corresponds to the sample and the second to the matching comparison) and transitivity testing demonstrates matching with the new pair AC, this new matching relation is said to be emergent. Cf. ADDUCTION.

Emission: the occurrence of OPERANT BEHAVIOR. A response that occurs without an eliciting stimulus is said to be *emitted*. The term applies to responding occasioned by discriminative stimuli as well as to undiscriminated responding.

Emotional behavior: correlated changes in a range of response classes (e.g., if a preaversive stimulus simultaneously alters heart rate, respiration, blood pressure, defecation and operant behavior maintained by reinforcement, it's said to produce emotional behavior). This and related terms evolved from an imprecise colloquial vocabulary, so types of emotional behavior can't be defined unambiguously in terms of response classes. The operations that produce them allow them to be more consistently defined (e.g., *fear, anxiety* or, with another organism present, *anger*, produced by primary or conditioned aversive stimuli; *relief*, produced by the termination of aversive stimuli; *joy* or *hope*, produced by primary or conditioned reinforcers; and *sorrow*, produced by the termination of reinforcers), but they still don't function as technical terms. Cf. AGGRESSION, FRUSTRATION, PREAVERSIVE STIMULUS.

Encoding: the learner's behavior with respect to the item to be remembered at the time it's presented. Cf. DECODING, REHEARSAL.

Episodic memory: autobiographical memory. See REMEMBERING.

Equivalence class: a stimulus class (usually produced through conditional discrimination in matching-to-sample) that includes all possible EMERGENT RELATIONS among its members. The properties of an equivalence class are derived from the logical relations of reflexivity, symmetry and transitivity. *Reflexivity* refers to the matching of a sample to itself, sometimes called identity matching (AA, BB, CC; in these examples, each letter pair represents a sample and its matching comparison). *Symmetry* refers to the reversibility of a relation (if AB, then BA). *Transitivity* refers to the transfer of the relation to new combinations through shared membership (if AB and BC, then AC). If these properties are characteristics of matching-to-sample, then training AB and BC may produce AC, BA, CA and CB as emergent relations (reflexivity provides the three other possible relations, AA, BB and CC). Given AB and BC, for example, the combination of symmetry and transitivity implies the CA relation. The emergence of all possible stimulus relations after only some are trained through contingencies is one criterion for calling the three stimuli members of an equivalence class. The class can be extended by training new stimulus relations (e.g., if CD is learned, then AD, DA, BD, DB and DC may be created as emergent relations). Stimuli that are members of an equivalence class are likely also to be *functionally equivalent*. It remains to be seen whether the logical properties of these classes are fully consistent with their behavioral ones. Cf. EQUIVALENCE RELATION.

Equivalence relation: a term with various usages, including functional equivalence (the relation between stimuli that have become members of a *functional class*) as well as the mathematical relations that define an *equivalence class* (especially the CA relation). The terminology of equivalence relations has often been interchanged with that of equivalence classes, but functionally equivalent stimuli needn't be members of an equivalence class. Cf. EQUIVALENCE CLASS.

Error: in simultaneous discriminations, a response to a stimulus not correlated with reinforcement; in successive discriminations, a response during a stimulus correlated with extinction. Because of its colloquial origins, the term often assumes evaluative as well as descriptive functions. Cf. CORRECTION PROCEDURE.

Escape: the termination of an aversive stimulus by a response. A reduction in the magnitude of an aversive stimulus by a response is sometimes called partial or fractional escape. Cf. REINFORCEMENT.

Establishing operation: any operation that changes the status of a stimulus as a reinforcer or punisher: deprivation, satiation, procedures that establish formerly neutral stimuli as conditioned reinforcers or as conditioned aversive stimuli, and stimulus presentations that change the reinforcing or punishing status of other stimuli (as when an already available screwdriver becomes a reinforcer in the presence of a screw that needs tightening).

Estes-Skinner procedure: see PREAVERSIVE STIMULUS.

Ethology: an area of biology concerned with the analysis of behavior patterns that evolve in natural habitats, either in species or in individual organisms, with particular emphasis on those patterns that don't depend on or aren't known to depend on prior operant selection or respondent conditioning. Cf. FIXED ACTION PATTERN, SPECIES-SPECIFIC BEHAVIOR, RELEASER.

Event recorder: a device that records events as displacements of markers or pens along timelines generated at a constant rate (as in Figure 12-2).

Evocation: the production of a response, usually by an establishing operation (as when food deprivation is said to *evoke* behavior that has led to food in the past). Sometimes responding is said to be evoked if it's unclear whether it was emitted or elicited.

Evolution: changes in populations over time. Evolution can operate at phylogenic, ontogenic and cultural levels. Evolution happens; NATURAL SELECTION is a theory of how it works. Cf. CULTURAL SELECTION, ONTOGENIC SELECTION.

Excitation: roughly, the production of behavior or the variables that produce it, used especially in contrast with *inhibition*.

Exercise, Law of: see LAW OF EXERCISE.

Expectancy: a colloquial term referring to behavior that precedes predictable events. Expectancy depends on a history with respect to the events (it can't depend on events that haven't yet occurred).

EXT: extinction. See EXTINCTION.

Exteroceptive stimulus: any stimulus presented at or outside of the organism's skin. Cf. INTEROCEPTIVE STIMULUS.

Extinction: in operant behavior, discontinuing the reinforcement of responding (or the reduction in responding that it produces). In negative reinforcement (escape and avoidance), extinction has often referred to the discontinuation of aversive stimuli, although the term applies more appropriately to discontinuing the consequences of responding, so that aversive stimuli occur but responses no longer prevent them. The discontinuation of punishment (see RECOVERY) is

rarely referred to as a variety of extinction. In respondent conditioning, extinction is presenting the CS without, or no longer in a contingent relation to, the US (or the diminution in conditioned responding that follows this operation).

Extinction gradient: following differential extinction, a gradient obtained along a continuum that contains the extinction stimulus. In one type, responding is first reinforced during several stimuli along the continuum and is then extinguished during only one of them. In another, reinforcement is correlated with one stimulus and extinction with another, but only the second is represented on the continuum along which the gradient is determined (e.g., the first stimulus is a form and second is a color, and the gradient is determined for color). Cf. INHIBITORY GRADIENT.

Extrinsic reinforcer: a reinforcer that has an arbitrary relation to the responses that produce it (as when a musician plays for money rather than because the playing produces music). The term has also been applied to stimuli presumed to function as reinforcers because their function has been instructed (as when children are told that it's important to earn good grades); despite their label, such stimuli are often ineffective reinforcers. Cf. INTRINSIC REINFORCER, CONDITIONED REINFORCER.

F

Facilitation: an occasional synonym for *potentiation*.

Fading: a procedure for transferring control of responding from one stimulus or set of stimuli to another by gradually removing one while the other is gradually introduced. Stimuli may be faded in or out (e.g., once a pigeon discriminates key colors, the discrimination may be transferred to line orientation by maintaining differential reinforcement while gradually fading out color intensity and fading in line intensity). Cf. SHAPING.

Feature-positive stimulus: in successive discrimination between reinforcement and extinction stimuli, a stimulus property present only during reinforcement components (as when, in discrete trials with pigeons, a star appears on green during reinforcement trials but green appears alone during extinction trials). Stimulus control is more easily produced when such stimuli are correlated with reinforcement (*feature positive*) than when they're correlated with extinction (*feature negative*). Cf. SIGN-TRACKING.

Feedback: roughly, a stimulus or stimulus property correlated with or produced by the organism's own behavior. The stimulus may in turn change the behavior, which again changes the stimulus, and so on. Mathematical relations between the behavior and the stimulus are called *feedback functions.*

FI: fixed interval. See INTERVAL SCHEDULE.

Fixed action pattern: an ethological term for a sequence of responses, usually but not necessarily produced by a RELEASER, the consistent patterning of which can't be attributed to an operant chain. When the stimuli that elicit or set the occasion for a fixed action pattern are absent, their presentation, and thereby an opportunity to engage in the fixed action pattern, may serve as a reinforcer. Cf. DISPLACEMENT ACTIVITY, VACUUM ACTIVITY.

Fixed consecutive number (FCN): a two-operandum procedure with trials initiated by responses on one operandum and terminated by a changeover to the other. The changeover is reinforced if at least *n* responses preceded it (e.g., reinforcing a pigeon's left peck only if at least 10 right pecks preceded the changeover to the left).

Fixed-interval schedule: see INTERVAL SCHEDULE.

Fixed-ratio schedule: see RATIO SCHEDULE.

Fixed-time schedule: see TIME SCHEDULE.

Fixity, functional: see FUNCTIONAL FIXITY.

Flashbulb memory: the detailed remembering of the context of a surprising and significant event in one's life (e.g., where one was on hearing the news of the Challenger disaster).

Fluency: accurate performance that occurs at high rates and/or with short latencies, and that's well retained after long periods without practice. Skills that become fluent, such as mastery of mathematical skills, may also be more likely to combine with other behavior in novel ways. Cf. ADDUCTION.

Foraging: searching for food. Foraging in natural habitats has been treated as a chain that includes search, prey identification, prey capture and handling and/or consumption of prey, with concurrent or concurrent-chain performances treated as analogous to parts of this chain (e.g., the foraging patterns according to which organisms switch from partially depleted patches of food to fresh ones can be characterized in terms of strategies examined within concurrent performances, such as *matching, momentary maximizing* and *optimizing*).

Forced choice: see FREE CHOICE.

Formal verbal classes: see DICTATION-TAKING, ECHOIC BEHAVIOR, TEXTUAL BEHAVIOR, TRANSCRIPTION.

FR: fixed ratio. See RATIO SCHEDULE.

Fractional escape: see ESCAPE.

Free choice: the availability of two or more concurrent operants even if one is consistently chosen over the other. With only one operant available, choice is said to be *forced* (as when one of the two arms in a T-maze is blocked).

Free feeding weight: the stable weight maintained by a mature organism with unlimited access to food and water. A percentage of this weight (e.g., 80%) may serve as a criterion for a level of deprivation; 80% of free feeding exceeds the weight at which many wild animals maintain themselves.

Free operant: see OPERANT.

Free recall: a verbal learning procedure in which the learner recalls the items of a list, usually after a single presentation, without regard to the original order of items.

Frequency of reinforcement: total reinforcers over a fixed time (occasionally, over a session of variable duration, over a fixed number of responses or, in a trial procedure, over a fixed number of trials). Cf. FREQUENCY OF RESPONDING, RATE OF REINFORCEMENT.

Frequency of responding: total responses over a fixed time, over a session of variable duration or, in a trial procedure, over a fixed number of trials. Cf. FREQUENCY OF REINFORCEMENT, RATE OF RESPONDING.

Frustration: any operation that reduces an organism's opportunities for highly probable responses (or the consequences of such operations, especially emotional behavior, aggression or escape from correlated stimuli). The term is most commonly applied to extinction after food reinforcement, which eliminates the opportunity to eat; in this usage it's a label for some side effects of extinction.

FT: fixed time. See TIME SCHEDULE.

Functional analysis: an analysis in terms of behavioral functions (effects of responses); alternatively, an analysis in terms of functional relations (e.g., the production of pupillary constriction by light might be discussed as a pupillary reflex, but a functional analysis deals with it as a transition from one point to another on a continuous mathematical function relating pupillary diameter to light intensity).

Functional class: a class in which members have common behavioral functions, either produced by similar histories or acquired through emergent relations. If two stimuli are members of a functional class, then the behavior occasioned by one will also be occasioned by the other; such stimuli are *functionally equivalent*. Cf. EQUIVALENCE CLASS; see also EQUIVALENCE RELATION, OPERANT, STIMULUS.

Functional fixity: problem-solving behavior in which the usual function of a tool, object or material makes it less likely that the solver will use it effectively in a novel way.

Functional relation: a mathematical function appealed to by a FUNCTIONAL ANALYSIS.

Functional stimulus: the properties of a stimulus that control behavior, as opposed to the properties of the *nominal stimulus* (e.g., for a pigeon attending to the color but not the form of a green circle, the functional stimulus is just green even though the nominal stimulus is a green circle).

Fuzzy set: see PROBABILISTIC STIMULUS CLASS.

G

g: gram (abbreviation).

Generalization: the spread of the effects of reinforcement (or other operations such as extinction or punishment) during one stimulus to other stimuli differing from the original along one or more dimensions. To the extent that responding is similar during two different stimuli, the organism is said to *generalize* between them (the stimuli are said to be *generalized*). If responding is identical during different stimuli, generalization between them is said to be complete (this outcome may also be described as the absence of DISCRIMINATION). Cf. ATTENTION, INDUCTION, STIMULUS.

Generalization gradient: a gradient obtained after reinforcement correlated with a single stimulus (occasionally two or more stimuli, in studies of the summation of gradients), when no discrimination has been trained between this and other stimuli along the continuum of the gradient.

Generalized imitation: see HIGHER-ORDER CLASS OF BEHAVIOR.

Generalized reinforcer: a conditioned reinforcer based on several primary reinforcers. It's more

likely to remain effective across different establishing operations than a conditioned reinforcer based on just one primary reinforcer. Money is often offered as an example of a generalized reinforcer of human behavior.

Goal gradient: systematic changes in responding with changes in an organism's spatial or temporal separation from a reinforcer (e.g., changes in running speed as a rat approaches the goalbox of a maze).

Go–no go discrimination: usually, a successive discrimination using trials with reinforcement in the presence of one stimulus (*go*) and extinction in presence of the other (*no go*).

Gradient: a measure of responding during different stimuli as a function of their location along a continuum (cf. STIMULUS). Gradients are usually determined by presenting stimuli successively but in irregular order in extinction. The slope or steepness of a gradient is determined by how much responding changes from one point on the continuum to another; the larger the change, the steeper the gradient. The case in which responding doesn't change is usually called a *flat* gradient, although it may also be called the absence of a gradient. See specific cases: EXTINCTION GRADIENT, GENERALIZATION GRADIENT, INHIBITORY GRADIENT, POSTDISCRIMINATION GRADIENT.

Grain: a reinforcer effective with food-deprived pigeons; also a characteristic of cumulative records (see RATE OF RESPONDING).

Grammars: descriptions of the structural or syntactic properties of verbal behavior. *Phrase-structure* grammars describe structures in terms of relations among sentence *constituents* (e.g., noun and verb phrases); *transformational* grammars describe them in terms of relations among different sentences (e.g., active and passive voice). The two are complementary.

H

Habit: recurrent behavior or behavior that's highly resistant to change. The term is mainly colloquial; it often occurs in conjunction with evaluations of the behavior (good habits versus bad habits) but without specifying the contingencies that maintain it.

Habituation: a reduction, over repeated presentations, in the respondent behavior elicited by a stimulus. Cf. ADAPTATION, POTENTIATION.

Helplessness, learned: see LEARNED HELP-LESSNESS.

Hierarchical organization: the nesting of some classes of behavior within others. Cf. HIGHER-ORDER CLASS OF BEHAVIOR.

Hierarchy, of behavior or responses: a ranking of response classes based on their relative probabilities. A more probable class is said to be higher in the response hierarchy.

Higher-order class of behavior: an operant class that includes within it other classes that can themselves function as operants, as when generalized imitation includes all the component imitations that could be separately reinforced. Higher-order classes may be a source of novel behavior (as in the imitation of behavior that the imitator hadn't seen before). Contingencies operate differently on the higher-order class than on the classes that are its components. For example, if all instances of imitation are reinforced except those within one component class (e.g., jumping whenever the model jumps), that class may change with the higher-order class rather than with the contingencies arranged for it (i.e., imitations of jumping won't extinguish, even though no longer reinforced). Control by the contingencies arranged for the higher-order class defines membership in the class; the component classes are sometimes said to be *insensitive* to the lower-order contingencies arranged for them. A higher-order class may be called a *generalized* class, in that contingencies arranged for some of its components generalize to all the others. Generalized matching and verbally governed behavior are examples of higher-order classes.

Higher-order conditioning: respondent conditioning in which the stimulus that functions as the US in producing one conditioned reflex is itself the CS of another.

Higher-order schedule: a schedule that reinforces a higher operant consisting of completion of a schedule requirement (e.g., with FR 10 reinforced according to an FI 50-s schedule, every 10th response that occurs at least 50 s after the last reinforcer is reinforced; the FR is the first-order schedule and the FI the second-order schedule). Such schedules often include a stimulus presented on each completion of the first-order schedule (e.g., in the example, flashing a light after every 10th response). The notation for such schedules includes the first-order schedule and the stimulus it produces in parentheses: FI 50-s (FR 10: stimulus). A *percentage-reinforcement*

schedule is a higher-order schedule in which the second-order schedule is an RR schedule.

Hill-climbing: changes in behavior that come about because the organism moves gradually from one performance to another that produces a somewhat higher reinforcement rate. The metaphorical paths made possible by different contingencies determine whether the organism approaches *optimizing* or gets trapped in a dead end. Cf. MAXIMIZING, SHAPING.

History: conditions that an organism has been exposed to and its performances under them; often an abbreviation for *experimental history*, simply because experimental organisms are rarely observed continuously throughout their lives. History is particularly important when its effects are irreversible or only slowly reversible.

Houselight: see CHAMBER.

I

Iconic memory: see REMEMBERING.

Identity matching: see MATCHING-TO-SAMPLE.

Imitation: behavior that duplicates some properties of the behavior of a model. Imitation needn't involve a matching of stimulus features (e.g., when one child imitates the raised hand of another, the felt position of the child's own limb has different stimulus dimensions than the seen position of the other child's). Cf. HIGHER-ORDER CLASS OF BEHAVIOR.

Immediate memory: usually, short-term memory. See REMEMBERING.

Implicit learning: in human learning, contingency-shaped learning (as in learning to speak grammatically even though one can't state the grammatical rules).

Implicit memory: remembering demonstrated by the effect of an item on other behavior rather than by its recall (as when a priming stimulus enhances a learner's later recognition of a semantically related word even though the learner can't report what the priming stimulus was).

Imprinted stimulus: a stimulus that, by virtue of the conditions of its presentation, has become effective as a reinforcer. Imprinting is noted primarily in some bird species (e.g., ducks) and usually occurs within a few days of hatching. Conditions that affect imprinting include movement of the stimulus and time spent in its presence. Imprinting doesn't occur as easily with older ducklings because they avoid novel stimuli and therefore don't spend enough time in their presence.

Impulsiveness or **impulsivity:** see SELF-CONTROL.

Incentive: discriminative effects of reinforcing stimuli (as when the smell of food makes responses reinforced by food more likely); occasionally, a stimulus that changes the reinforcing or punishing status of other stimuli. A verbal response that has such effects is sometimes called an *augmenting* stimulus. Cf. ESTABLISHING OPERATION.

Incidental chaining or **incidental reinforcement:** see SUPERSTITION.

Incidental learning: human learning that occurs in the absence of instructions or consequences, usually contrasted with *intentional learning*.

Induction: the spread of the effects of reinforcement to responses outside the limits of an operant class (sometimes called *response generalization*). This phenomenon is essential to shaping because without it new responses more closely approximating some final form might never be emitted (e.g., reinforcement of a 10-N key peck may be followed by the first instance of a 15-N peck; cf. SHAPING). With discriminated operants, induction occasionally refers to the spread of the effects of reinforcement to stimuli other than those defining the operant class (as when, after extinction during green and red, reinstating reinforcement during green produces both responding during green and a transient increase in responding during red; cf. GENERALIZATION).

Information: strictly, the reduction in uncertainty provided by a stimulus, as quantified in *bits*, the number of binary decisions needed to specify the stimulus. One bit specifies 2 alternatives, two bits 4, three bits 8, and so on in increasing powers of 2. The term more often appears in its nontechnical sense, as when applied to *information processing*; the value of such usages is undermined by the finding that reinforcers rather than information maintain observing behavior.

Informative stimulus: a predictive stimulus; a discriminative stimulus though not necessarily a conditioned reinforcer (e.g., a stimulus correlated with differential punishment that's superimposed on ongoing reinforced behavior is informative, but its onset doesn't ordinarily maintain observing responses).

Inhibition: a process inferred from a response decrement. The term, extended to behavior by analogy to physiological usage, is appropriate only when it's been shown that the decrement is produced by an increment in something else (e.g., if reinforcing one response reduces the rate of another, the reinforcement may be said to inhibit the second response). The term is sometimes extended to accounts of the extinction process, in part because extinction may be accompanied by increments in other responses (e.g., behavior characterized as emotional). Such accounts are often unsupported by demonstrations that the increments produce the decrement rather than simply accompany it. When they don't distinguish between conditions that reduce responding and those that fail to maintain it they may be misleading. See also PROACTION, RETROACTION.

Inhibitory gradient: an extinction gradient in which responding increases along the continuum as the distance from a stimulus previously correlated with extinction increases. This is taken to indicate that the extinction stimulus reduces response rate rather than just failing to maintain it. Cf. EXTINCTION GRADIENT, INHIBITION.

Inhomogeneous data: data derived from more than one type of performance and that misrepresent the performances from which they were derived when summarized statistically (as when an avoidance schedule produces both moderate response rates and bursts of high-rate responding after shock, so that the average rate doesn't represent either contribution to overall rate).

Initial links: see CONCURRENT-CHAIN SCHEDULES.

Innate behavior: see SPECIES-SPECIFIC BEHAVIOR.

Insensitivity to contingencies: see HIGHER-ORDER CLASS OF BEHAVIOR.

Insight: the sudden solution of a problem, especially in contrast to gradual "trial-and-error" learning. This now nontechnical term is mainly of historical interest.

Instinctive behavior: see SPECIES-SPECIFIC BEHAVIOR.

Instructional stimulus, instruction: in nonverbal settings, a conditional discriminative stimulus (occasionally a simple discriminative stimulus is also said to have instructional functions); in verbal settings, a verbal antecedent of either verbal or nonverbal behavior. Cf. VERBALLY GOVERNED BEHAVIOR.

Instrumental behavior: see OPERANT BEHAVIOR.

Intentional learning: the opposite of *incidental learning.*

Interdependent schedules: schedules in which the operation of one depends on some property of the other (e.g., in one version of interdependent concurrent VI VI schedules, each VI arranges setups only during runs of responding on the other).

Interdimensional: between or across dimensions.

Interference: see PROACTION, RETROACTION; cf. INHIBITION.

Interim behavior: varying responding that occurs, usually early or midway rather than late within interstimulus intervals, in superstition procedures or temporal conditioning. Cf. SUPERSTITION, TERMINAL BEHAVIOR.

Interlocking schedule: a schedule in which time, number and/or IRT requirements vary together according to some function (as with interlocking intervals and ratios scheduled so that the number of responses that will produce a reinforcer decreases linearly as time passes since the last one).

Intermittent reinforcement: reinforcement of some but not all responses. See specific schedules.

Interoceptive stimulus: a stimulus inside the organism. The stimulus may be presented from outside, as when an experimenter passes electric current through a brain area, or it may be produced by the organism itself, as when responses produce proprioceptive stimulation on the basis of which the organism discriminates among different movements. With self-produced stimulation, the stimuli and their discriminative functions are usually inferred rather than demonstrated.

Interpretation: see CONTROL.

Interresponse time (IRT): the time between two responses (or, more strictly, if response duration is appreciable, from response onset to onset, or from response offset to offset). The time from a reinforcer to the next response is a latency and not an IRT, even if the reinforcer is response-produced. Reinforcing the response that ends an IRT is said to reinforce that IRT. An *IRT distribution* summarizes the temporal spacing of the responses making up a response rate (it doesn't show sequential patterning). In assessing probabilities of different IRT classes, calculating proportions of IRTs falling into a class may be misleading because short IRTs reduce the organism's opportunity to produce longer ones. For this reason, conditional probabilities, *IRTs per op-*

portunity (*IRTs/Op*), are often calculated: the probability of IRTs in a class interval, given enough time elapsed since the last response to permit an IRT to end in that class interval. For example, if 80 of 100 IRTs were less than 1 s, 10 were 1 but less than 2 s, and the remaining 10 were 2 or more s, then the organism had only 20 opportunities to complete the 10 IRTs of 1 but less than 2 s and the conditional probability for this IRT class was .5 (10/20). Cf. CONDITIONAL PROBABILITY, RATE OF RESPONDING, DIFFERENTIAL-REINFORCEMENT SCHEDULES.

Intertrial interval (ITI): see TRIAL.

Interval schedule: a schedule in which some minimum time must elapse before a response is reinforced; early responses have no effect. The time is measured from some event, usually a stimulus onset or the last reinforcer (an alternate method times each interval from the end of the last one, without regard to the time from the end of the last interval to the reinforced response). In *fixed-interval* (*FI*) schedules, the time is constant from one interval to the next, and performance is characterized by a pause after the reinforcer followed by a gradual or an abrupt transition to a moderate response rate. In *variable-interval* (*VI*) schedules, the time varies from one reinforcer to the next; compared with FI schedules, the response rate is relatively constant between reinforcers. Interval schedules are usually identified by average interval (e.g., FI 50-s arranges one reinforcer per 50 s).

Historically, VI schedules used intervals selected in irregular order from a set of intervals, often described by a mathematical progression (e.g., arithmetic or geometric). Current practice favors schedules with a constant reinforcement probability over time within the interval (with probability measured by *reinforcers per opportunity* or *Rf/Op*: probability that a response will be reinforced at a given time in an interval, given that the organism has reached that time). Such conditions are met by a type of VI schedule called *random interval* (*RI*), which arranges a setup (makes the next response eligible to produce a reinforcer) with a fixed probability every *t* s. In RI schedules, the average interval equals *t* divided by the probability (e.g., arranging a setup once per second with a probability of .02 produces RI 50-s). In one version, the schedule stops operating after a setup until the scheduled reinforcer is produced, so that low response rates make the obtained reinforcement rate lower than what had been scheduled; in another, the schedule continues and successive setups accumulate, so that obtained and scheduled reinforcement rates remain about equal even with low response rates.

Intradimensional: within a dimension.

Intraverbal: a verbal response occasioned by a verbal stimulus, where the relation between stimulus and response is an arbitrary one established by the verbal community. Intraverbal behavior is chaining as it occurs in verbal behavior; an example is reciting the alphabet. Either the speaker or someone else may provide the verbal stimulus (intraverbals aren't autoclitic because they don't require discrimination of one's own behavior).

Intrinsic reinforcer: a reinforcer that's naturally related to the responses that produce it (as when a musician plays not for money but because the playing produces music). Cf. EXTRINSIC REINFORCER.

IRT: see INTERRESPONSE TIME.

ITI: intertrial interval. See TRIAL.

J

Jumping stand: an apparatus used to study discrimination, especially with rats. The rat is forced to jump from a platform to one of two doors on which stimuli are displayed. One door is unlocked and by jumping to it the rat gains access to a reinforcer behind it; if the rat jumps to the other door, which is locked, it falls into a net below the doors.

K

Key: see OPERANDUM.

Kinesis (plural: kineses): undirected movement that depends on stimulus magnitude (as when the random movements of an insect larva increase with light and stop when it reaches the dark).

Kinesthetic stimulus: see PROPRIOCEPTIVE STIMULUS.

Knowledge of results (KOR): A kind of feedback, usually verbal, given during human performance in various tasks (e.g., verbal learning, motor skills).

KOR: see KNOWLEDGE OF RESULTS.

L

Language: the practices shared by the members of a verbal community, including consistencies of vocabulary and grammar. Cf. LINGUISTICS.

Language development: the emergence of language in the individual. Much of the controversy about language development revolves around assumptions about the respective phylogenic and ontogenic contributions to it.

Language relativity: the dependence of the behavior within a verbal community, both verbal and nonverbal, on the verbal discriminations incorporated within its language.

Language universals: the structural features common to all human languages, especially if they have phylogenic sources. If there are such features, what they are is controversial; furthermore, some may be spandrels.

Lashley jumping stand: see JUMPING STAND.

Latency: the time from an event, usually a stimulus onset, to a response.

Latent learning: see LEARNING.

Law of effect: Thorndike's classic statement of the principle of reinforcement and, in one version, punishment. Reinforcers and punishers were called satisfying and annoying states of affairs that an organism tended respectively to maintain or renew and to put an end to or avoid. The *strong* law included both cases; the *weak* law deleted the effects of annoyers or punishers.

Law of exercise: the statement, in early accounts of learning, that repetition of a response contributes to its strength. The law has also been expressed in terms of effects of use and disuse. A more contemporary version states that the elicitation of a response may increase the likelihood of its emission.

Learned helplessness: a retardation in the acquisition of escape or avoidance responding produced by a history in which responding during aversive stimuli has had no consequences.

Learning: roughly, acquisition, or the process by which behavior is added to an organism's repertory; a relatively permanent change in behavior. The term has been used in so many different ways in both technical and colloquial vocabularies that it's of limited usefulness. Decisions about whether learning has occurred and what's been learned sometimes depend on what the experimenter looks at. Latent learning provides an example. A rat explores a maze and the results of its exploration are assessed later when food reinforcers are available for the first time at the end of its run through the maze. Latent learning is said to have occurred if the rat negotiates the maze more rapidly and/or accurately than if it hadn't explored. The difficulty is that exploring the maze involves other contingencies (e.g., which turns lead where); these contingencies act on behavior but their effects are harder to get at than those involving food reinforcers. Cf. ACQUISITION, PERFORMANCE.

Learning set or **learning-to-learn:** a case of transfer in which, on the basis of similar relations among stimuli in a sequence of discrimination problems, accuracy in later ones improves more rapidly over trials than in the earlier problems (perhaps to a point at which correct responses occur on the first trials of a new problem). Cf. HIGHER-ORDER CLASS OF BEHAVIOR, TRANSFER.

Level of processing: the abstractness or richness of coding (e.g., encoding the number 2001 as a year or as the title of a film involves deeper levels of processing than encoding it as an arbitrary sequence of four digits).

Lever: see OPERANDUM.

LH: see LIMITED HOLD.

Limited hold (LH): termination of reinforcer availability if the response to be reinforced doesn't occur soon enough (e.g., in FI 100-s with a 10-s limited hold, the first response between 100 and 110 s after the start of the interval is reinforced; if there's no response during that time, the interval ends without a reinforcer).

Linguistics: the study of language, usually divided into the topics of *syntax* or grammatical structure, *semantics* or meaning, and *pragmatics* or the functions of language. *Psycholinguistics* is a branch of psychology concerned with demonstrating the psychological reality of linguistic categories and concepts. Cf. PSYCHOLOGICAL REALITY.

Link: a response in a chain or a component in a chained schedule.

Local rate: see RATE OF RESPONDING.

Long-term memory (LTM): see REMEMBERING.

LTM: long-term memory. See REMEMBERING.

M

Maintenance: continuation of the conditions that generated a performance. As a subject matter, maintained performance differs from but is compatible with acquisition (e.g., research concerned with effects of schedule parameters on performance doesn't really begin until acquisition is completed). Cf. STEADY STATE.

Maintenance rehearsal: see REHEARSAL.

Mand: a verbal response that specifies its reinforcer. In human verbal behavior, manding is usually a higher-order class, in the sense that a newly acquired tact can be incorporated into a novel mand (as when a child asks for a toy on learning its name).

Manipulandum: see OPERANDUM.

Massed practice: uninterrupted activity on a task (as in cramming for an exam). Massed practice is usually less effective than distributed practice.

Matching: in performances involving concurrent operants, distributing responses so that the relative response rate of each roughly matches its relative reinforcement rate. See MATCHING LAW; cf. MAXIMIZING, MELIORATION, OPTIMIZING.

Matching law: a quantitative formulation stating that the relative rates of different responses tend to equal the relative reinforcement rates they produce. The *generalized matching law* summarizes this relation in an equation in which relative response rate equals a constant multiplied by the relative reinforcement rate raised to a power. The constant takes into account units of measurement and includes *bias* (e.g., one response might call for a larger constant than another that's more effortful); the performance is described as *undermatching* when the exponent (the power to which the function is raised) is less than 1 and *overmatching* when it's greater than 1.

Matching-to-sample: a simultaneous conditional discrimination procedure, or the performance maintained by it. As it's typically arranged for pigeons, a *sample* stimulus is presented on the middle key of three keys. A peck on the sample turns on *comparison* stimuli on two side keys. A peck on the matching side key is reinforced (perhaps according to a schedule); a peck on the other side key may produce timeout or invoke a *correction procedure*. When the criterion for a match is physical correspondence (as when a pigeon must peck a green comparison given a green sample and a red comparison given a red one), the procedure is sometimes called *identity matching*, though accurate matches may be based on features other than the identity relation, such as stimulus configurations. When matches are based on arbitrary relations (as when a pigeon must peck a circle given a green sample and a triangle given a red one), the procedure is called *arbitrary matching* (*symbolic matching*, an alternative terminology, has the disadvantage of suggesting that the samples and comparisons have other functions besides those in the matching-to-sample procedure). Cf. CONDITIONAL DISCRIMINATION, ODDITY PROCEDURE.

Maximizing: given two or more responses, emitting the one with the higher probability of reinforcement. If reinforcement probabilities change from moment to moment and responding follows the one currently highest, the maximizing is said to be *momentary maximizing*. Note that matching requires a population of responses whereas maximizing can occur with a single response. Cf. HILL-CLIMBING, MATCHING, OPTIMIZING.

Maze: an apparatus through which an organism locomotes, usually from a startbox to a goalbox containing some reinforcer such as food, and often including alternative paths that divide at *choicepoints* and some of which end in a *blind alley* or *cul-de-sac*. Mazes come in a variety of configurations, including T-mazes or Y-mazes with a single choicepoint, mazes with a single sequence of choices between blind alleys and a continuing path, and radial mazes with paths arranged like the spokes of a wheel.

Meaning: in verbal behavior, a response to verbal stimuli; or the defining properties of classes, usually including verbal components, in which the members can serve as either stimuli or responses.

Mediating behavior: behavior that occurs in a consistent relation to reinforced behavior and that, though reinforcers aren't explicitly arranged for it, is maintained because it makes reinforcers more likely. For example, a stereotyped pattern of drinking is said to mediate spaced responding if, when the pattern is maintained, the next response is more likely to be late enough after the last response that it will be reinforced; or, two different postures held after one or another sample stimulus are said to mediate delayed matching-to-sample if a correct match is more likely when the organism has held the posture since the sample was presented (e.g., it leans to the right after a red but not a green sample and later is more likely to respond to red rather than green if still leaning to the right). Cf. COLLATERAL BEHAVIOR, SUPERSTITION.

Mediation: the contribution of intervening behavior to the relation between other events (as when coding mediates between the presentation of an item and its recall). Consider a mediational account of a pigeon experiment in which (i) response-independent food is delivered during green but not red; then (ii) pecking is shaped and maintained with food reinforcers with the key white; finally (iii) green and red alternate during extinction and for a while the pigeon pecks more during green, formerly correlated with food, than during red, even though pecking had never been reinforced during either (Morse & Skinner, 1958). In (i) food presumably generated incidental responding occasioned by both green and food (Reid, 1958); in (ii), peck-produced food generates the same behavior, which is followed by pecks that in turn produce food. With green and red reinstated in (iii), more pecks occur during green because green but not red occasions responding that had often been followed by reinforced key pecks in (ii). Cf. MEDIATING BEHAVIOR.

Melioration: allocating time to two or more response classes so all local reinforcement rates are equal. For example, assume a pigeon whose pecks in a changeover-key procedure are maintained by concurrent VI 20-s VI 60-s schedules. In an hour, the former provides about 180 reinforcers and the latter about 60, but if the pigeon allocates 45 min to the VI 20-s schedule and 15 min to the VI 60-s schedule both local reinforcement rates will equal about 4 per min (180 in 45 min and 60 in 15 min). Cf. MATCHING, MAXIMIZING, OPTIMIZING.

Memory: see REMEMBERING.

Memory search: see SEARCH.

Memory span: the number of items that can be remembered after a single presentation, given that they aren't coded or rehearsed.

Metacognition: differentiation and discrimination of one's own cognitive processes (as in shifting attention among tasks or distinguishing between seeing something and just imagining it).

Metamemory: differentiation and discrimination of one's own remembering (as when keeping track of a constantly changing list of items in *running* or *working* memory, or judging whether some material just studied will be remembered).

Metaphor: the extension of concrete terms to complex and/or abstract events or relations for which relevant verbal responses are otherwise unavailable (as when pain is described not by how it feels but rather by the properties of objects that can produce it: e.g., pains as sharp or stinging or dull).

Metastability: see STABILITY.

Metathetic stimuli: see STIMULUS CONTINUUM.

Microanalysis: see MOLAR AND MOLECULAR ANALYSES.

min: minute (abbreviation).

Misbehavior: a nontechnical term sometimes used to refer to the intrusion of behavior with phylogenic origins into ongoing operant behavior. For example, raccoons ordinarily rub and wash food before eating it; if food is used to reinforce their deposit into a container of objects they've picked up, they may begin to rub the objects together instead of releasing them into the container. The procedure raises the probability of rubbing, so the effect illustrates the relativity of reinforcers. Intrusions in the opposite direction (as when food-reinforced behavior intrudes into a fixed action pattern) are rarely referred to as misbehavior.

Mixed (mix) schedule: a compound schedule with two or more component schedules operating in alternation, all during the same stimulus. Occasionally, a VI or VR schedule with a limited number of schedule values is called a mixed schedule (e.g., a VR schedule that randomly alternates between FR 10 and FR 20 may be called mixed FR 10 FR 20). Cf. MULTIPLE SCHEDULE.

Mnemonics: techniques for enhancing remembering.

Modeling: providing behavior to be imitated. Cf. IMITATION.

Molar and molecular analyses: analyses distinguished by the level of detail in the data they consider. Molar analyses consider overall measures such as average response rates over sessions, whereas molecular analyses break such measures down into components such as the distribution of the IRTs that make up a response rate. Many levels of analysis are possible, so molar or molecular are sometimes defined relative to each other. Both rely on data sampled over some time and should be distinguished from *microanalysis*, which proceeds at the level of individual stimuli and responses.

Momentary maximizing: see MAXIMIZING.

Motivation: see ESTABLISHING OPERATION.

Motor programs: coordinations that don't depend on response feedback (e.g., in producing phonemes, movements of lungs, vocal chords, tongue and lips must be initiated at different times; thus, their coordination must be organized before the sound begins). Such coordinations can't be based on chaining.

Movement: cf. BEHAVIOR.

ms: a millisecond or thousandth of a second (abbreviation).

Multiple causation of behavior: the determination of behavior by two or more variables acting at the same time. Behavior is always determined by multiple variables; some may be more important than others. The aim of *behavior analysis* is to examine the multiple factors controlling behavior one at a time.

Multiple (mult) schedule: a compound schedule in which two or more component schedules alternate, each during a different stimulus. Alternation of the components is usually arranged after reinforcers or after fixed or variable time periods. The equivalent arrangement with the same stimulus during each component is a *mixed* schedule.

N

n: usually, number.

N: Newtons, a unit of force.

Naming: a higher-order class that involves arbitrary stimulus classes (things or events with particular names) and corresponding arbitrary verbal topographies (the words that serve as their names) in a bidirectional relationship. Prerequisites for naming include at least three components: (i) listener behavior, in looking for things and pointing based on what's been said; (ii) echoic behavior, in repeating names when they're spoken; and (iii) tacting, in saying the names given the objects. Naming is generated from the ordinary interactions between children and their caregivers. Once available as a higher-order class, naming allows expansions of vocabulary in which the introduction of new words in particular functional relations (such as tacting) involves those words in a range of other emergent functions.

Natural concept: a discriminative class produced through presentations of complex natural stimuli (as when a pigeon discriminates between pictures with and pictures without trees in them). Cf. PROBABILISTIC STIMULUS CLASS.

Natural reinforcer: sometimes used in place of *primary reinforcer* or *intrinsic reinforcer*. The relativity of reinforcers limits the usefulness of the term: cf. REINFORCEMENT.

Natural selection: at the phylogenic level, the Darwinian account of EVOLUTION as the selection of members of a population over generations. Different features survive in a population as a result of interactions between the available range of genetic variations in the population and the properties of evolutionary environments. Natural selection can also occur at the ontogenic level; cf. ARTIFICIAL SELECTION.

Negative automaintenance: see AUTOMAINTENANCE.

Negative reinforcement: see REINFORCEMENT.

Negative stimulus: see DISCRIMINATIVE STIMULUS.

Negative transfer: see TRANSFER.

Neophobia: avoidance of novel stimuli, especially of new foods.

Nominal operant or **nominal stimulus:** see FUNCTIONAL STIMULUS, OPERANT.

Nonsense syllable: an arbitrary sequence of letters, usually a *CVC trigram*, that isn't a word. Nevertheless, nonsense syllables vary in meaningfulness (e.g., the resemblance of LUQ to LUCK makes it more meaningful than QUL).

Novel behavior: see ADDUCTION, HIGHER-ORDER CLASS OF BEHAVIOR, SHAPING.

Noxious stimulus: often used as a synonym for aversive stimulus, but more strictly defined as a stimulus that affects pain receptors or produces tissue damage. In this strict sense, the term is useful for referring to an extensive class of stimuli without specifying behavioral consequences.

O

Observational learning: learning based on observing the responding of another organism (and/or its consequences). Observational learning does not imply imitation (e.g., organisms may come to avoid aversive stimuli on seeing what happens when other organisms produce them).

Observing response: a response that produces or clarifies a discriminative stimulus and that may be maintained by the effectiveness of the stimulus as a conditioned reinforcer. Some observing responses are only inferred (as when a pigeon's head movements are assumed to bring a visual stimulus into view or better focus), but conditions may be arranged to control them (e.g., in matching-to-sample the pigeon may be more likely to observe the sample if a peck on the sample key is required; in a more explicit arrangement, pigeon's pecks on one key may produce stimuli correlated with components of a multiple schedule on a second key).

Occasion: an opportunity for a response or some other event, or the circumstances under which a contingency operates, as when discriminative stimuli *set the occasion* on which responses have some consequence. When a stimulus is said to *occasion* a response, the term serves as a verb and distinguishes responses emitted in the presence of discriminative stimuli from those elicited by stimuli in a reflex relation.

Occasion setter: see CONTINGENCY.

Oddity procedure: a conditional discrimination procedure in which one of three or more stimuli differs from the others in some property (e.g., color) and responses to the odd one are reinforced. Versions of matching-to-sample in which responses to the comparison that doesn't match the sample are reinforced (mismatching) also qualify as oddity procedures. Cf. MATCHING-TO-SAMPLE.

Omission training: a version of differential reinforcement of zero behavior (see DIFFERENTIAL-REINFORCEMENT SCHEDULES): a reinforcer is delivered only if no response has occurred in a trial or within a given time. It's formally analogous to avoidance, with reinforcers substituted for aversive stimuli.

Ontogenic selection: the selection of populations of responses within the lifetime of the individual organism. See DIFFERENTIAL REINFORCEMENT, OPERANT SELECTION, SHAPING. Cf. CULTURAL SELECTION, NATURAL SELECTION, ARTIFICIAL SELECTION.

Ontogeny: the development or life history of an individual organism. Cf. PHYLOGENY.

Open economy: in operant contexts, the availability of appetitive stimuli not only as reinforcers within the session but also, independently of behavior, on a supplementary basis outside the session (as when food is provided after a session of food-reinforced responding to maintain the organism at a standard percentage of free feeding weight). Cf. CLOSED ECONOMY.

Operandum: any device operable by an organism that defines an operant class in terms of an environmental effect (*descriptive* or *nominal operant*; see OPERANT). Many operanda (plural) consist of switches (as in rats' lever presses and pigeons' key pecks, or as when a rat operates a switch by stepping off a platform). In the broadest sense, an operandum is any apparatus by means of which behavior is recorded. The term replaces an earlier one, *manipulandum*, which suggested a device that's handled. For other examples, see JUMPING STAND, WHEEL RUNNING.

Operant: a class of responses. Responses are assigned to classes because no two can be exactly the same. Special cases include the *free operant*, in which the completion of one response leaves the organism in a position to emit the next, and the discrete or constrained operant (see TRIAL). Classes defined descriptively (*descriptive* or *nominal operant*) are usually distinguished from those defined functionally (*functional operant*).

In the descriptive usage, usually for the purpose of recording responses, the class is defined in terms of its environmental effect (e.g., a lever press defined by operation of a switch; see OPERANDUM). To count as a member of an operant, a response must have a certain force, topography and so on; another defining property may be the stimuli in the presence of which it occurs (see DISCRIMINATED OPERANT). The effect that defines an operant in this usage may be different from scheduled consequences of responses (e.g., in a schedule, every response in the class doesn't necessarily produce a reinforcer).

In the functional usage, an operant is a class modifiable by the consequences of responses in it. It's defined by the relation between consequences and subsequent responding. According to this definition, a response class isn't an operant until its modifiability has been demonstrated. In most cases, operants defined descriptively and those defined functionally include roughly the same responses. If they don't, it may be appropriate either to change recording methods or to search for the variables that are limiting the modifiability of the class. See also OPERANT BEHAVIOR.

Operant behavior: behavior that can be modified by its consequences. It's also been called *instrumental* and often corresponds closely to behavior colloquially called purposive. Because of its relation to consequences, it's said to be *emitted* rather than elicited. Few responses, however, are either exclusively emitted or exclusively elicited. Many emitted responses (e.g., a pigeon's pecks) can be made more probable by certain stimuli (e.g., spots on the pigeon's key); many elicited responses can occur in the absence of typical eliciting stimuli (e.g., spontaneous salivation). Operant and respondent classes are best regarded as extremes on a continuum along which the probability varies that a stimulus will produce a response. See also OPERANT.

Operant level: the baseline level of an operant; the rate at which responses occur before they've been reinforced.

Operant selection: the selection of behavior during the lifetime of an individual organism; the modification of operant behavior by its consequences (see DIFFERENTIAL REINFORCEMENT, SHAPING). This type of selection was once called *operant* or *instrumental conditioning*. Those who work in this research area are sometimes called *behavior analysts*.

Operation: any experimental procedure or condition (e.g., presenting a stimulus, reinforcing a response, arranging a schedule). The behavioral vocabulary often fails to provide separate terms for operations and their behavioral outcomes, processes. For example, *a response was reinforced* may mean that the response produced a reinforcer or that it increased in rate because it produced a reinforcer; the correct reading is usually given by context. This dual usage is common to several fundamental terms (e.g., conditioning, extinction, punishment). In this glossary, the process definitions of such terms are usually indicated parenthetically. Ambiguity can be avoided by restricting such terms to operations and describing outcomes directly in terms of changes in responding (e.g., *A response was reinforced and as a result its rate increased*).

Optimizing: responding that produces the maximum possible reinforcers over some extended time rather than from moment to moment, especially in concurrent schedules. Contingencies can be designed under which optimizing requires a performance different from *matching, melioration* or *momentary maximizing*.

Orienting response: in operant behavior, a response that puts an organism in a position to emit other responses or allows it to attend to a discriminative stimulus (cf. OBSERVING RESPONSE). In respondent behavior, a response elicited by initial presentations of a stimulus (e.g., the first few times a bell sounds or its sound is paired with food, a dog may prick up its ears and/or turn its head toward the bell; cf. CONDITIONED REFLEX).

Overall rate: see RATE OF RESPONDING.

Overmatching: see MATCHING LAW.

Overshadowing: an attenuation of respondent conditioning with one stimulus because of the presence of another stimulus (e.g., if soft tone and loud bell together precede food, tone may remain ineffective as a CS even though it and the bell have the same contingent relation to food). Cf. BLOCKING.

Overt behavior: behavior that's observed or observable, or that affects the organism's environment. Cf. COVERT BEHAVIOR.

P

Paced response; pacing: see DIFFERENTIAL-REINFORCEMENT SCHEDULES.

Paired-associates learning: a verbal learning procedure in which each of several stimuli (usually verbal) sets the occasion for a different verbal response. The stimulus items are presented repeatedly in varied order until the learner meets some learning criterion.

Pairing: see CONTIGUITY and cf. CONTINGENCY.

Paradigm: a symbolic representation of relations. For example, a three-term contingency in which a response (R) produces a reinforcer (Rf) in the presence of a discriminative stimulus (S^D) might be written as: S^D:R→Rf. Paradigm is often used incorrectly as a synonym for *procedure*.

Parameter: a variable that's held constant while some other variable changes. When different values of a parameter are examined, the parameter distinguishes different functions within a family of functions (e.g., a graph of avoidance behavior can show avoidance response rate as a function of either RS interval with SS interval as a parameter or SS interval with RS interval as a parameter).

Passive avoidance: a misnomer for punishment. To avoid passively is to not respond when responding's been punished. For example, a rat's on a platform above an electrified grid. Its failure to step down onto the grid is called passive avoidance, in the sense that in doing so it's not shocked. But defining contingencies in terms of the absence of responses may be misleading. It's more appropriate to say that stepping down is punished by shock.

Pause: a period of no responding, not necessarily bounded by responses. Cf. INTERRESPONSE TIME, LATENCY, RATE OF RESPONDING.

Pavlovian conditioning: see RESPONDENT CONDITIONING.

Peak procedure: omitting some proportion of the reinforcers arranged by an FI schedule and thereby allowing responding to continue for some time after the usual end of the interval. Response rate typically passes through a maximum (the peak) and then decreases over time (the increasing and then decreasing rates are sometimes treated as the two sides of a temporal generalization gradient).

Peak shift: see POSTDISCRIMINATION GRADIENT.

Percentage reinforcement: the omission of a fixed proportion of scheduled reinforcers. For example, in an FR 100 schedule with 50% reinforcement, only half of the completed ratios end with a reinforcer. A stimulus (e.g., a brief tone) is often substituted for the omitted reinforcer; without such a stimulus, the above schedule is the same as a VR 200 schedule in which the constituent ratios are all multiples of 100 responses.

Percentile-reinforcement schedule: a schedule in which the eligibility of a response to produce a reinforcer depends on its location within a distribution (e.g., a schedule for long IRTs might reinforce any IRT in the top 25% of an IRT distribution taken over the last 100 responses). The schedule must specify both the percentile criterion for reinforcement and the reference response distribution. Its criteria for differential reinforcement are relative rather than absolute, so it operates consistently over a range of changes in performance and makes automated shaping possible.

Performance: behavior, usually over extended time periods. A subject matter in itself, performance has often been treated instead as an index of something else (e.g., learning, motivational states).

Phenomenon (plural **phenomena**): an event; something that happens.

Phrase structure grammar: see GRAMMARS.

Phylogenic constraints: limitations on learning or differential capacities for learning that depend on phylogenic selection, including properties of the behavior classes that can be produced and limits on the contingencies that can modify behavior (e.g., it may be impossible to shape alternating as opposed to synchronized wing flapping in newly hatched birds). The terminology is rarely invoked when the limitations involve obvious anatomical features. See TASTE AVERSION for an example; cf. PREPAREDNESS.

Phylogenic selection: see NATURAL SELECTION; cf. ONTOGENIC SELECTION.

Phylogeny: the development or evolutionary history of a species. Cf. ONTOGENY.

Place learning versus response learning: the historical issue of whether organisms learned stimuli or movements (e.g., whether a rat in a maze learns a sequence oriented to stimuli outside the maze or just a particular sequence of turns; the outcome can go one way or the other depending on stimuli outside the maze).

Pliance: instruction-following based on social contingencies rather than the correspondence between verbal behavior and environmental events. Cf. TRACKING, VERBALLY GOVERNED BEHAVIOR.

Polydipsia: the schedule-induced enhancement of water intake. See ADJUNCTIVE BEHAVIOR.

Polymorphous stimulus class: a probabilistic stimulus class in which each member includes exactly *n* of *m* distinguishing features (as when a stimulus is a member of a class by virtue of containing exactly 2 of 3 critical features). In such cases, any feature may also appear in stimuli outside the class.

Positive reinforcement: see REINFORCEMENT.

Positive stimulus: see DISCRIMINATIVE STIMULUS.

Positive transfer: see TRANSFER.

Postdiscrimination gradient: a gradient obtained after a discrimination between one stimulus correlated with reinforcement and another correlated with extinction (occasionally, between two stimuli correlated with different reinforcement schedules), usually with both stimuli represented on the continuum along which the gradient is determined. It often includes a *peak shift*, a displacement of the point of maximum responding to one side of the reinforcement stimulus in a direction away from the extinction stimulus.

Postponement: see AVOIDANCE.

Postreinforcement pause: the period of no responding following a reinforcer, especially in an FR or an FI. In an FR, the pause is sometimes measured as the time to some response other than the first (e.g., the fifth response in FR 100), because pauses may separate the first few responses before the roughly constant rate of the FR run begins. It might more appropriately be called a preresponse pause (e.g., in multiple FR FR, the duration of the pause is influenced by the stimulus of the current rather than the prior component).

Potentiation: an increase, over repeated presentations, in the respondent behavior elicited by a stimulus (especially, an aversive stimulus). Cf. HABITUATION.

Pragmatics: see LINGUISTICS.

Preaversive stimulus: a stimulus that reliably precedes an aversive stimulus and thus may be a conditioned aversive stimulus. Such stimuli may

reduce the responding maintained by positive reinforcers, an effect variously called *anxiety, conditioned emotional response (CER)* or *conditioned suppression*. In some contexts, the stimulus increases responding, as when presented during avoidance responding or during positively reinforced responding after a history of avoidance; this has been called *conditioned acceleration* or *conditioned facilitation*.

Prediction: see CONTROL.

Predictive stimulus: a discriminative stimulus. A stimulus predicts an event if the probability of the event given the stimulus differs from that given no stimulus. Cf. INFORMATIVE STIMULUS.

Preference: the probability of one of two or more alternative responses, derived from the relative frequencies of the responses over an extended sequence of choices. The term doesn't apply when the different probabilities of each response are engendered by the different schedules according to which each is reinforced (e.g., higher VR than DRL rates don't imply that VR is preferred). Preferences quantify the relative effectiveness of different consequences as reinforcers (cf. REINFORCEMENT); when each response produces a different consequence, the organism is said to prefer the consequence produced by the response that's most probable. If different probabilities of two or more responses can't be accounted for, as when they occur despite identical consequences and schedules for each response, the preference may be called a *bias*. Cf. CHOICE, CONCURRENT-CHAIN SCHEDULES, CONCURRENT OPERANTS.

Premack principle: the relativity of reinforcers and punishers. See REINFORCEMENT.

Preparedness: a capacity, presumably of phylogenic origin, to learn some response–stimulus or stimulus–stimulus contingencies more readily than others (e.g., organisms may learn relations between tastes and gastrointestinal consequences more easily than those between lights or sounds and such consequences). See TASTE AVERSION.

Primacy: see SERIAL-POSITION EFFECT.

Primary memory: an earlier term for short-term memory. See REMEMBERING.

Primary reinforcer: a reinforcer the effectiveness of which doesn't depend on its contingent relation to another reinforcer. Cf. CONDITIONED REINFORCER.

Priming: presenting a stimulus that affects behavior after the stimulus is removed (as when the brief presentation of one word lowers the recognition threshold of a semantically related word presented later).

Private events: in verbal behavior, events accessible only to the speaker (usually, events inside the skin). Private events have the same physical status as public events, but it's more difficult for the verbal community to shape tacts of private events.

Proaction: effects of learning at one time on other learning later. When the later learning is impaired, the effect is a variety of negative TRANSFER called *proactive interference* or *proactive inhibition*. Cf. RETROACTION.

Probabilistic stimulus class: a class in which each member contains some subset of features but none is common to all members. The number of features in the subset may vary from one class member to another (cf. POLYMORPHOUS STIMULUS CLASS). Such classes, sometimes called *fuzzy sets*, don't have well-defined boundaries, though class members may have family resemblances. Examples include *natural concepts* and classes defined by reference to a *prototype*.

Probability: a proportion or relative frequency, either scheduled or derived from data. The probability of an event is given by how often it occurs divided by how often it's possible. For example, if a response occurs on 40 of 50 occasions during which it's sampled, its probability is .8 (40/50). Response probability can be based on response frequencies in the presence of a stimulus, within successive short time periods or relative to other responses. Cf. CONDITIONAL PROBABILITY.

Probe: a condition or stimulus introduced into a performance to clarify the variables controlling it (e.g., the interruption of FR responding by an occasional brief stimulus correlated with reinforcement of another response can be used to probe how strongly the FR responses are chained together).

Problem solving: constructing discriminative stimuli, either overtly or covertly, in situations involving novel contingencies; these stimuli may set the occasion for effective behavior (as when a verbal problem is converted into a familiar mathematical formula or a listing of options clarifies complex contingencies). Cf. SIMULATION.

Procedural memory: see REMEMBERING.

Procedure: An experimental arrangement or operation. Cf. PARADIGM.

Process: the changes in behavior produced by an experimental operation. See OPERATION.

Processing: whatever goes on within an organism between the presentation of a stimulus and subsequent responding. Cf. COGNITIVE PROCESSES.

Processing, level of: see LEVEL OF PROCESSING.

Productivity: the generation of novel behavior through the recombination and reorganization of existing classes of behavior.

Programming: arranging experimental conditions such as reinforcement schedules. In some usages, *programming* is restricted to arranging systematic changes in conditions (as in shaping or the transfer of stimulus control through fading) and so is distinguished from *scheduling*, arranging maintained conditions.

Progressive schedule: a schedule in which requirements change progressively with each reinforcer (e.g., in one progressive ratio schedule, the ratio increases by 5 responses after each reinforcer). The schedule sometimes allows the requirement to be reset to its initial value (e.g., by a second response and according to some schedule).

Proprioceptive stimulus: an interoceptive stimulus produced by the effects of movements and postures on receptors in muscles, tendons or joints.

Prospective memory: see REMEMBERING.

Prothetic stimuli: see STIMULUS CONTINUUM.

Prototype: a typical member of a probabilistic class, described by a weighted average of all features of all members of the class (e.g., feathers are weighted more heavily than webbed feet among birds because more birds have feathers than have webbed feet; thus, a robin is a more prototypical bird than a duck because it shares more features with other birds than does a duck). Cf. PROBABILISTIC STIMULUS CLASS.

Pseudoconditioning: the elicitation of responding by one stimulus as a result of its presentation in the same context as another, even though neither had been presented in a contingent relation to the other. See SENSITIZATION for an example.

Pseudotrial: a time period corresponding to that of a trial but within which no trial stimuli occur. Pseudotrials are used to assess response probability in the absence of the trial stimuli over time periods that correspond to those of trials.

Psycholinguistics: see LINGUISTICS.

Psychological reality: the role various classes of events play in behavior, especially in psycholinguistics (as when grammatical transformations are demonstrated as something that speakers do with sentences).

Psychophysics: an area of psychology that evolved out of the philosophical concern with the relation between mind and body. Psychophysics relates behavioral properties of stimuli to properties defined in physical terms. Studies of detection or discrimination examine *absolute thresholds* or minimum effective stimulus intensities, and *difference thresholds* or minimum effective differences between stimuli along some continuum (see also SIGNAL DETECTION ANALYSIS). Studies of scaling relate the effects of changes in the properties of one stimulus to those of changes in the properties of another (e.g., if responding depends on auditory or visual stimulus intensity, determining how much one must increase to equal the effect of doubling the other).

Punisher: see PUNISHMENT.

Punishment: the response-produced presentation of positive punishers or the termination of negative punishers (or the response decrement or suppression that results). The terminology closely parallels that of reinforcement. *Punishers* are stimuli, *punishment* is an operation (or process), and responses rather than organisms are said to be punished. A stimulus is a *positive punisher* if its presentation reduces the likelihood of responses that produce it, or a *negative punisher* if its removal reduces the likelihood of responses that terminate it. Like reinforcers, punishers are relative and may be defined independently of their behavioral consequences (e.g., the probabilities of two responses can be assessed by forcing the organism to choose between engaging in one or the other, and if the more probable response then forces the organism to engage in the less probable one, the forced responding will punish the more probable response). These definitions parallel the definitions of reinforcers; punishers are equivalent except for the difference in sign. Cf. AVERSIVE STIMULUS, REINFORCEMENT.

R

R, r: usually, response.

Random control: a procedure for presenting two stimuli randomly in time, as a baseline against which to compare effects of stimulus–stimulus contingencies. The random presentations are usually arranged in the context of a sequence of pseudotrials and therefore typically include incidental stimulus–stimulus contiguities as well as presentations of each stimulus alone.

Random-interval schedule: see INTERVAL SCHEDULE.

Randomness: variability generated by a process that produces events that are completely independent of one another, in the sense that none can be predicted from any of the others. It's a property of a distribution of events (or the process that generates the distribution); no single event can be random.

Random-ratio schedule: see RATIO SCHEDULE.

Rate dependency: changes in the effects of a variable that depend on baseline response rate, especially in reference to drug effects (as when a drug dosage increases low response rates but decreases high ones).

Rate of reinforcement: reinforcers per unit time; often used in preference to reinforcement frequency because frequency sometimes refers not to reinforcers per unit time but to reinforcers per response, per session or per trial.

Rate of responding: responses per unit time. Several types have been distinguished: *overall* or *average rate*, determined over a substantial time such as an experimental session; *local, momentary* or *moment-to-moment rate*, determined over a short time, particularly when rate is relatively constant throughout that time; *running rate*, roughly equivalent to local rate, but usually with the provision that it's determined over a time bounded by pauses; and *terminal rate*, determined over a short time just before a reinforcer, especially in an FI. Criteria for distinguishing rates, such as how a running rate is determined, may be informal (e.g., visual inspection) or explicitly defined (as when a period of no responding qualifies as a pause only if it's more than 5 s long).

Other terms distinguish changes in rate: *acceleration* or *positive acceleration* is increasing rate, appearing as concave upward curvature in a cumulative record; *deceleration* or *negative acceleration* is decreasing rate, appearing as concave downward curvature; cyclic changes are repeated increases and decreases, each completed over a roughly constant time; and compensation is a low rate immediately after an unusually high one, or a high one immediately after an unusually low one. The acceleration typically produced by an FI schedule is often called a *scallop*, especially in reference to what it looks like in a cumulative record. When extended to other schedules, the term is mostly restricted to accelerations bounded by some event, such as a reinforcer. The curvature in an FI has been measured in terms of *quarterlife* (time to complete one quarter of the responses within an interval) and *index of curvature* (a statistic based on the number of responses in successive fractions of an interval). Moment-to-moment changes in rate are often described as *grain* (e.g., the fine grain of a roughly constant rate, the coarse or steplike grain of a rate that fluctuates), again especially in reference to what they look like in a cumulative record. Cf. CUMULATIVE RECORD, INTERRESPONSE TIME.

Ratio schedule: a schedule in which the last of a specified number of responses is reinforced. In a *fixed-ratio (FR) schedule*, the number is constant from one reinforcer to the next; performance is characterized by pauses after the reinforcer followed by a relatively high and constant response rate. In a *variable-ratio (VR) schedule*, the number of responses varies from reinforcer to reinforcer; relative to FR schedules, the postreinforcement pause is reduced or eliminated. A VR schedule is usually identified in terms of the average responses per reinforcer. In the variety of VR schedule called *random ratio (RR)*, the ratio specifies the probability with which responses are reinforced. For example, in RR 20 that probability is .05 (1/20) and is independent of the number of responses emitted since the last reinforcer. In some VR schedules, successive ratios are selected in irregular order from a set of ratios described by a mathematical progression, analogous to those used in VI schedules (see INTERVAL SCHEDULE).

Ratio strain: the appearance of pauses in VR responding, or in FR responding at times other than after a reinforcer (cf. POSTREINFORCEMENT PAUSE); a result of large ratio size and/or low reinforcement frequency.

Reaction time: usually equivalent to latency.

Reality, psychological: see PSYCHOLOGICAL REALITY.

Recall, verbal: see FREE RECALL.

Recency: see SERIAL-POSITION EFFECT.

Recognition, verbal: see VERBAL DISCRIMINATION.

Reconstruction: memory interpreted as a way of reconstructing rather than replicating what is remembered. Remembering interpreted in this way is more like following a recipe than like reading a blueprint.

Recovery: return to an earlier level of responding after it's been reduced by an operation such as extinction or punishment. The vocabulary doesn't distinguish between recovery during maintained conditions and recovery after the conditions are discontinued (e.g., *recovery during punishment* refers to a return of responding toward prepunishment levels while punishment continues, and *recovery after punishment* refers to a return toward those levels after punishment is discontinued).

Reflex: see UNCONDITIONED REFLEX, CONDITIONED REFLEX.

Reflexive relation or **reflexivity:** the identity relation. See EQUIVALENCE CLASS.

Regression: the reappearance of previously extinguished behavior during the extinction of more recently reinforced behavior.

Regular reinforcement: see CONTINUOUS REINFORCEMENT.

Rehearsal: behavior that occurs between storage and retrieval. In most usages, rehearsal includes encoding; occasionally it refers only to behavior that follows encoding. Some usages also distinguish among kinds of rehearsal: *maintenance rehearsal* involves repetitions of encoded items and *elaborative rehearsal* involves further encoding and/or processing. See also REMEMBERING; cf. MEDIATING BEHAVIOR.

Reinforcement: the response-produced presentation of positive reinforcers or termination of negative reinforcers (or the increase or maintenance of responding resulting from this operation). *Reinforcers* are stimuli (e.g., food); *reinforcement* is an operation (e.g., presentation of food given a response) or a process. The operation reinforces responses, not organisms; organisms are sometimes said to be *rewarded*, but this term often implies effects of stimuli other than reinforcing effects. Earlier in its history, reinforcement was also applied to presentations of the US in respondent conditioning, but that usage is now unusual.

A stimulus is a *positive reinforcer* if its presentation increases responding that produces it, or a *negative reinforcer* if its removal increases responding that terminates or postpones it. The distinction matters mainly when responses produced by the reinforcer can compete with the reinforced response (e.g., reinforcement by heat of a rat's lever presses in cold is more likely to be called negative reinforcement by removal of cold than positive reinforcement by presentation of heat because cold produces huddling and shivering that may compete with lever pressing).

Reinforcers can also be defined independently of their behavioral consequences. The effectiveness of a reinforcer depends on the relative probabilities of the responses it occasions and the responses to be reinforced; these can be altered by limiting the organism's opportunities to engage in one or the other response (*response deprivation*: cf. ESTABLISHING OPERATION). If a less probable response produces a stimulus that occasions a more probable response, then the stimulus will reinforce the less probable response. This definition takes into account the *relativity of reinforcers*; the reinforcement relation is reversible (e.g., if water deprivation makes drinking more probable than wheel running, the opportunity to drink will reinforce running, but if limited access to the wheel makes running more probable than drinking, the opportunity to run will reinforce drinking). Cf. OPERANT, PUNISHMENT.

Reinforcer: see REINFORCEMENT.

Relational autoclitic: see AUTOCLITIC.

Relational discrimination or **relational learning:** discrimination based on relational rather than absolute properties of stimuli (e.g., to the left of or to the right of; same or different; greater than or less than; see also MATCHING-TO-SAMPLE).

Relational frame: a description of the relations characterizing a higher-order class, especially in cases of complex stimulus control (e.g., if relations AB and AC both satisfy the frame *opposite of*, then the relation BC is one of sameness). Cf. EQUIVALENCE CLASS.

Relative rate: the rate of one event (especially a response or a reinforcer) as a proportion of the summed rates of that and other events (e.g., given rates *a* and *b*, the relative rate of *a* is *a* divided by the sum of *a* plus *b*).

Relativity (of language): see LANGUAGE RELATIVITY.

Relativity (of reinforcers): see REINFORCEMENT.

Releaser: an ethological term for a stimulus that elicits a stereotyped pattern of behavior (cf. FIXED ACTION PATTERN). Releasers are often USs provided by the behavior or physical features of another organism. In some usages, releasers have some properties of discriminative stimuli that occasion operant behavior. The comparison is complicated because the functions of releasers are usually analyzed differently from those of CSs, USs and discriminative stimuli. For example, releasers are usually presented for extended time periods and may vary during those times (particularly when they depend on another organism's behavior), whereas CSs and USs are more often presented briefly, in discrete trials. An artificial releaser that's

more likely to produce a fixed action pattern than its natural counterpart is called a *supernormal* stimulus. Cf. DISPLACEMENT ACTIVITY, RESPONDENT BEHAVIOR, VACUUM ACTIVITY.

Remembering: a response occasioned by a stimulus no longer present, perhaps directly or perhaps through the mediation of other behavior with respect to that stimulus. Remembering is often discussed in terms of a metaphor of storage and retrieval, where *storage* occurs when the stimulus is presented and *retrieval* when it's recalled. The time between storage and retrieval is sometimes called the *retention* interval. See REHEARSAL, RETRIEVAL, STORAGE.

Types of remembering are sometimes distinguished by their time courses. *Iconic memory* and *echoic memory* refer respectively to the brief persistence of effects of visual and auditory stimuli. *Short-term memory* (*STM*) is remembering based on a single presentation of items and without coding and/or rehearsal; it's of short duration (e.g., 10 to 20 s) and limited to roughly 5 to 9 items (historically, the span of immediate memory). *Long-term memory* (*LTM*) occurs after coding or rehearsal and/or multiple presentations of items, and is therefore of unlimited duration and capacity.

Remembering is also classified in terms of what is remembered. Examples include: *procedural memory* (remembering operations or ways of doing things), often contrasted with *declarative memory* (remembering facts); *autobiographical* or *episodic memory* (remembering specific events in one's life); *semantic memory* (remembering aspects of one's language); *spatial memory* (remembering paths and things located on them); and *retrospective memory* (remembering past events), often contrasted with *prospective memory* (remembering things one has to do in the future). See also METAMEMORY.

Reminiscence: an increase in recall as time passes since learning. Reminiscence is an occasional phenomenon and usually appears, if at all, shortly after learning.

Repeated acquisition: a procedure that examines acquisition as steady-state performance. For example, assume a monkey must emit a sequence of presses on four levers to produce a reinforcer and the required sequence changes each session. After many sessions, the monkey has had enough contact with correction procedures and other experimental details that all it has to learn within a session is the new sequence of presses. The repeated acquisition of new sequences may then be used as a baseline for studying how acquisition is affected by different variables (e.g., drugs). The consistent way in which the monkey masters each new sequence in steady-state performance may be called a *strategy*. Cf. HIGHER-ORDER CLASS OF BEHAVIOR, LEARNING SET.

Repertoire or **repertory:** the behavior an organism can emit, in the sense that the behavior exists at a nonzero level, has been shaped or, if extinguished, may be rapidly reinstated. The organism need not engage in behavior for it to be in its repertoire (e.g., a rat that's learned a maze has maze running in its repertory even when not in the maze). To the extent that some responses in it are more likely than others, a repertoire consists of a hierarchy; operant procedures modify the relative positions of responses in the hierarchy.

Replicative memory: see REPRODUCTION.

Representation: a transformation of stimuli occurring either when an organism responds to them or later (e.g., in remembering). In some accounts they're copies; in other accounts representations have arbitrary relations to stimuli, as when a visually presented letter is represented by its sound. The latter are more like recipes than like copies and have behavioral dimensions. Cf. CODING, REMEMBERING.

Reproduction: memory interpreted as the production of copies of what's remembered. Current accounts of remembering instead favor RECONSTRUCTION.

Resistance to change: see STRENGTH.

Resistance to extinction: the responses emitted, time elapsed or number of trials until performance meets some extinction criterion (e.g., number of responses emitted before 10 min pass with no response). The measure must be specified, because one contingency or schedule may produce more resistance to extinction than another according to one measure but less according to a different one.

Respondent: a class of responses defined in terms of stimuli that reliably produce them (e.g., salivation elicited by food or acid in the mouth is a member of one respondent class and salivation elicited by a CS is a member of another; spontaneous salivation, in the absence of identifiable stimuli, isn't strictly a member of a respondent class, although it's sometimes loosely referred to as such). Cf. OPERANT.

Respondent behavior: behavior elicited by stimuli (cf. RESPONDENT, UNCONDITIONED REFLEX, CONDITIONED REFLEX). Respondent behavior was once considered primarily autonomic (e.g., responses of glands and smooth muscles), but the reflex relation defines respondent behavior regardless of the character of the response. Thus, skeletal responses may have respondent characteristics (see AUTOSHAPING; cf. OPERANT BEHAVIOR).

Respondent conditioning: the modification of respondent behavior by stimulus–stimulus contingencies, also referred to as *classical conditioning* or *Pavlovian conditioning*. Cf. CONDITIONED REFLEX.

Respondent discrimination: differential conditioning, a type of respondent conditioning in which one stimulus is followed by the US but a second isn't (e.g., food in the mouth follows bell but not tone). Discrimination has occurred when the CR is elicited by the first stimulus but not the second. The term doesn't refer to respondent conditioning in general, even though such conditioning entails discrimination between the presence and absence of stimuli.

Response: a unit of behavior; a discrete and usually recurring segment of behavior. Cf. OPERANT, RESPONDENT, STRENGTH; see also specific properties: DURATION OF RESPONSE, RATE OF RESPONDING, TOPOGRAPHY OF RESPONSE.

Response competition: the reduction of one response by the time and/or effort involved in concurrent responding. Such reductions should be distinguished from those caused by the reinforcers produced by concurrent responding. Cf. INHIBITION.

Response cost: any property or consequence of responding that may reduce or punish it. Examples include increases in response effort or force and response-contingent loss or reduction of reinforcers (especially, with humans, point loss superimposed on responding maintained by points; in such cases, however, the effectiveness of points as reinforcers is often assumed rather than confirmed experimentally).

Response deprivation: see ESTABLISHING OPERATION, REINFORCEMENT.

Response generalization: an alternative term for *induction*.

Response-independent reinforcer: the delivery of a reinforcer without reference to the organism's behavior. See TIME SCHEDULE.

Response induction: see INDUCTION.

Response rate: see RATE OF RESPONDING.

Response strength: see STRENGTH.

Resurgence: see REGRESSION.

Retention: the time between storage and retrieval in the storage-retrieval metaphor of memory.

Retrieval: in the memory metaphor of storage and retrieval, what the learner does at the time something is remembered. Retrieval is typically occasioned by a discriminative stimulus that sets the occasion for it (e.g., a question or an instruction). Cf. DECODING, REMEMBERING.

Retroaction: effects of learning at one time on other learning that occurred earlier. When the earlier learning is impaired, the effect is a variety of negative TRANSFER called *retroactive interference* or *retroactive inhibition*. Cf. PROACTION.

Retrospective memory: see REMEMBERING.

Reversible effects: changes in performance that are eliminated, either immediately or over some time, when the operations that produced them are discontinued (e.g., if responding returns to earlier levels after punishment, the effects of punishment are reversible). Effects that aren't completely eliminated are sometimes said to be partially reversible.

Reward: see REINFORCEMENT.

Rf: reinforcement or reinforcer. See REINFORCEMENT.

RI: random interval. See INTERVAL SCHEDULE.

RR: random ratio. See RATIO SCHEDULE.

RS interval: response-shock interval. See AVOIDANCE.

Rule-governed behavior: verbally governed behavior. Because of varied definitions of *rule* both inside and outside the discipline, this is one of the more problematic expressions in behavior analytic terminology. In many cognitive usages, for example, rules are regarded not as instances of verbal behavior but rather as the internal codification of central processes or concepts, so they have no verbal status. With rules defined as verbal antecents, any verbal antecedent qualifies as a rule in some usages (as when one is told to do or say something); in others, rules are only those verbal antecedents that specify contingencies (as when one is told what will happen if one does or says something). See VERBALLY GOVERNED BEHAVIOR and cf. CONTINGENCY-SHAPED BEHAVIOR, SPECIFICATION.

Run: a sequence of responses bounded by pauses or some event (e.g., an FR run is the response sequence within a single ratio).

Running memory: see METAMEMORY.

Running rate: see RATE OF RESPONDING.

S

s: seconds.

S: stimulus.

S+, S^D ("S-dee"): positive stimulus. See DISCRIMINATIVE STIMULUS.

S–, S^Δ ("S-delta"): negative stimulus. See DISCRIMINATIVE STIMULUS.

Sample-specific behavior: in matching-to-sample, differential responding to each sample, usually introduced to ensure stimulus control by the sample. For example, pigeon matching-to-sample may be arranged with a fixed-duration sample after which a peck on the sample turns on the comparisons only if some differential criterion is met (e.g., more than five pecks given green samples or fewer than four given red); the trial ends without comparisons if sample responding doesn't meet the criterion. Sample-specific responding may guarantee attention to samples but doesn't necessarily do so for the sample–comparison relation.

Sample stimulus: see MATCHING-TO-SAMPLE.

Satiation: an establishing operation, continued presentation or availability of a reinforcer, that reduces its effectiveness (or, as a process, the reduction in effectiveness it produces). Satiation may occur as responses are reinforced or it may be arranged independently of responses. A criterion for satiation with food reinforcers is prefeeding (presenting food for some fixed time or in some fixed amount before a session). Cf. DEPRIVATION.

Scallop: see RATE OF RESPONDING.

Schedule: a specification of the criteria by which responses become eligible to produce reinforcers. The term has been extended to other operations (e.g., schedules of escape, avoidance or punishment). See specific cases: COMPOUND SCHEDULES, DIFFERENTIAL-REINFORCEMENT SCHEDULES, HIGHER-ORDER SCHEDULES, INTERVAL SCHEDULES, LIMITED HOLD, RATIO SCHEDULES, TIME SCHEDULES.

Schedule-induced behavior: see ADJUNCTIVE BEHAVIOR.

Schema: in cognition, an organized representation of events, especially in complex contexts (e.g., spatial schemas relating lengths, areas and volumes, or social ones arranged in scripts, scenarios and narratives). Cf. COGNITIVE MAP, REPRESENTATION.

Search: in the storage and retrieval metaphor of memory, search for a match to some target item. The search may be *exhaustive* (all items are checked) or *self-terminating* (the search ends when a match is found).

Secondary reinforcer: see CONDITIONED RE-INFORCER.

Second-order: see HIGHER-ORDER CLASS OF BEHAVIOR, HIGHER-ORDER CONDITION-ING, HIGHER-ORDER SCHEDULE.

Selection by consequences: operant selection or the ontogenic analogue of phylogenic or Darwinian selection, expressed as an abbreviated form of *the selection of behavior by its consequences*. In a more general sense, all varieties of selection involve consequences (e.g., the evolution of the eye depends on the consequences of more finely differentiated seeing). See ARTIFICIAL SELEC-TION, CULTURAL SELECTION, ONTOGENIC SELECTION, PHYLOGENIC SELECTION, NAT-URAL SELECTION.

Self-control: a term derived from the colloquial vocabulary that applies to cases in which a relatively immediate small reinforcer is deferred in favor of a later large reinforcer or in favor of avoiding a later large aversive event, or in which a relatively immediate small aversive event is accepted when the acceptance leads to a later large reinforcer or avoids a later large aversive event. Examples include deferring a small purchase to save for a large one, refusing a drink to avoid a hangover, exercising to perform well in a later athletic event, and undergoing preventive dental procedures. The opposite of self-control is called *impulsiveness* or *impulsivity*.

Self-reinforcement: a misnomer for the delivery of a reinforcer to oneself based on one's own behavior. In so-called self-reinforcement, the contingencies and establishing operations that affect the behavior that's purportedly reinforced are confounded with those that affect the delivery of the reinforcer to oneself. The organism that appears to self-reinforce must be able to discriminate behavior that qualifies for the reinforcer from behavior that doesn't; this behavior is more appropriately described as an example of the discrimination of properties of one's own behavior.

Semantic memory: see REMEMBERING.

Semantics: see LINGUISTICS.

Sensitivity: the organism's capacity to respond differentially to different stimuli or conditions. In most behavioral usages, sensitivity is measured in terms of *thresholds*. Cf. PSYCHOPHYSICS.

Sensitivity to contingencies: see HIGHER-ORDER CLASS OF BEHAVIOR.

Sensitization: the lowering of a threshold, as when prior delivery of an aversive stimulus lowers the intensity at which a noise elicits a startle response.

Sensory preconditioning: in respondent conditioning, a type of higher-order conditioning in which a contingent relation between two stimuli precedes making one of them a CS. Sensory preconditioning is said to have occurred if the other stimulus elicits the CR solely by virtue of its relation to the first one. Preconditioning procedures have been extended to operant cases (e.g., correlating response-independent reinforcers with one stimulus that later signals reinforcement but not with a second one that later signals extinction sometimes facilitates acquisition of an operant discrimination between the stimuli; see MEDIA-TION).

Sequential dependencies: conditional probabilities of successive events (e.g., given concurrent responses A and B, the probabilities of A followed by A, A followed by B, B followed by A, and B followed by B).

Sequential grammar: see GRAMMARS.

Serial anticipation: see SERIAL LEARNING.

Serial learning: learning an ordered list of items. In *serial recall*, the learner has an opportunity for recall after the entire list is presented. In *serial anticipation*, items are presented one at a time and the learner has an opportunity to say which comes next. In both cases, list presentations continue until the learner meets some learning criterion.

Serial-position effect: differential recall of an item depending on its position in a list, especially in free recall. Early items are more likely to be recalled than later ones (*primacy*), and the most recent items are more likely to be recalled than earlier ones (*recency*). Thus, items at the beginning or end are more likely to be recalled than ones in the middle. Primacy effects are usually stronger than recency effects.

Serial recall: see SERIAL LEARNING.

Set: loosely, a disposition to respond. The term may refer to stereotyped patterns of operant behavior (especially under stimulus control) or to effects of the conditional stimuli of a conditional discrimination. A common usage is provided by instructions at the start of an experiment, often said to produce in humans a *set* to attend to particular features of the situation. Cf. ATTENTION.

Setup: in reinforcement schedules (especially interval schedules), an arrangement that makes a response eligible to produce a reinforcer.

Shaping: gradually modifying some property of responding (often but not necessarily topography) by differentially reinforcing successive approximations to a target operant class. Shaping is used to produce responses that, because of low operant levels and/or complexity, might not otherwise be emitted or might be emitted only after a considerable time. The variability of the responding that follows reinforcement usually provides opportunities for reinforcing further responses that still more closely approximate the criteria that define the target operant class. Shaping is a variety of operant selection.

Shock: a stimulus sometimes used as an aversive stimulus. Shock is usually delivered through a grid floor on which the organism stands. The parallel bars of the grid are far enough apart that feces or urine can't short-circuit them. A complication is that the organism's behavior may alter shock level (as when rats contact the shock source through either a furred or unfurred body area).

Short-term memory (STM): see REMEMBERING.

SIB: self-injurious behavior (abbreviation).

Side effect: any effect that accompanies the main effect with which an experimenter is concerned. The distinction is often arbitrary, because no stimulus has a single effect (e.g., a researcher interested in aggression induced by extinction may regard the decrease in previously reinforced responding during extinction as a side effect, whereas another researcher interested in operant extinction may regard the aggression as the side effect). Cf. MULTIPLE CAUSATION OF BEHAVIOR.

Sidman avoidance: see AVOIDANCE.

Signal: roughly, a discriminative stimulus or an occasion-setting stimulus; a stimulus that sets the occasion on which some contingency operates or on which another stimulus may be presented. Cf. INFORMATIVE and PREDICTIVE STIMULUS.

Signal detection analysis: an analysis of stimulus detectability in terms of conditional probabilities of a response given a signal in noise or noise alone. A response given a signal in noise is a *correct detection* or *hit* and one to noise alone is a *false alarm*; no response given a signal in noise is a *miss* and given noise alone is a *correct rejection*. A mea-

sure of *sensitivity* to the signal derived from these measures is called d' (d-prime); another measure based on whether false alarms or misses are favored is called *bias*.

Sign-tracking: responding directed toward some feature of a stimulus correlated with reinforcement. Cf. FEATURE-POSITIVE STIMULUS.

Simulation: imagining; especially, covert problem solving. Simulation that takes actual contingencies into account may mediate effective behavior in actual environments. Cf. THINKING.

Simultaneous discrimination: a discrimination in which two or more stimuli are presented at the same time rather than successively (e.g., see JUMPING STAND) and which therefore involves two or more alternative responses. The locations of the stimuli are ordinarily at or close to those of the alternative responses (e.g., stimuli on each of two pigeon keys) and the organism is said to respond to one or the other stimulus. Cf. SUCCESSIVE DISCRIMINATION.

Skinner box: a term not in current usage. See CHAMBER.

Span, memory: see MEMORY SPAN.

Spandrel: an incidental byproduct of selection.

Species-specific behavior: behavior observed in all or most members of a species (of only one or of both sexes, and perhaps only over limited times in each organism's life). Different usages may include: emitted behavior before its selection by consequences; unconditioned respondent behavior; and, in fairly consistent environments, stereotyped operant behavior maintained by species-specific primary reinforcers or conditioned reflexes that depend on species-specific unconditioned reflexes. See also specific examples: DISPLACEMENT ACTIVITY, FIXED ACTION PATTERN, RELEASER, VACUUM ACTIVITY.

Species-specific defense reaction (SSDR): avoidance or escape responding that has a phylogenic origin. Such behavior presumably evolved because natural environments don't allow organisms to learn certain types of avoidance or escape responses (e.g., a mouse that fails to avoid a predatory cat on its first encounter will probably never have another opportunity to do so).

Specification: the correspondence between a verbal response and what it tacts, when the verbal response occurs outside of the tact relation (as when a mand is said to specify its reinforcer even though the reinforcer may be absent). The term is often used in an informal rather than a technical sense, especially in reference to effects on a listener (as when a response to a word is said to share properties with responses to what the word ordinarily tacts).

Spontaneous recovery: in operant or respondent extinction, an increment in responding at the start of one session of extinction, relative to the level of responding at the end of the preceding one. Cf. WARMUP.

SS interval: shock–shock interval. See AVOIDANCE.

Stability: session-to-session variability in performance (the lower the variability, the more stable the performance). A performance that can shift from one to another of two or more steady-state baselines maintained by the same conditions is said to be *metastable*. Cf. STEADY STATE.

State-dependent learning: learning that's most likely to be demonstrated when the learner is in the same context as during the original learning. The term is often reserved for learning under specific physiological conditions such as drug states (e.g., the learner who learned an item while drunk is more likely to remember it when drunk again than when sober).

Statistics: quantitative methods for summarizing data (descriptive statistics) or evaluating data (statistical inference). Descriptive statistics include measures of *central tendency* or average value (e.g., mean, median, mode); measures of *variability* or dispersion, or the spread of successive measures around an average value (e.g., range, standard deviation, variance); measures of *regression* or the relation between two variables (e.g., the function best describing how two response measures vary together); and measures of *correlation* or how well one variable predicts the value of another (e.g., correlation coefficients, which are positive when two variables vary directly and negative when they vary inversely, and which range from 1.0 when one of the variables is perfectly predicted by the other to zero when one is completely independent of the other). See also DISTRIBUTION, PROBABILITY.

Statistical inference estimates whether an experimental outcome is likely to have been produced by experimental operations or is better regarded as having occurred by chance. It compares an experimental outcome with a theoretical distribution of possible outcomes (e.g., normal, chi-square, or, in analyses of variance, F) based on the assumption that the outcome depended on chance. If the outcome was highly unlikely on

this basis (e.g., probability less than .05), the outcome is said to be *statistically significant*. Statistical and substantive significance are unrelated.

Steady state: performance maintained by a set of conditions after systematic session-to-session changes have become negligible (e.g., when the rate and pattern of responding within an FI doesn't vary systematically over sessions, FI performance is said to have reached a steady state). Steady-state performance is a preferred baseline for analyzing effects of variables (if a baseline is unstable, it might be impossible to assess where it would've been if the variable hadn't been introduced). The decision as to when performance has reached a steady state depends on the criteria for saying that systematic changes have become negligible; such criteria range from informal observation to stringent quantitative assessments.

Stereotyped response: a response with properties (especially topography) that are relatively invariant over successive occurrences.

Stimulus (plural: stimuli): any physical event, combination of events or relation among events. The stimulus vocabulary classifies aspects of the environment in much the same way that the response vocabulary classifies aspects of behavior. Like responses, stimuli may be described in terms of physical or behavioral properties and, again like responses, they may be defined in terms of descriptive (nominal) or functional classes (cf. OPERANT). The term may refer to any of the following: specific instances of physical events (e.g., the sound of a bell); combinations of events, sometimes also referred to as *compound stimuli* or *stimulus complexes* (e.g., feeder operation, with accompanying auditory and visual components); the absence of events (e.g., a dark chamber as a stimulus); a relation among events (e.g., matches in a matching-to-sample problem); specific physical properties of events (e.g., green referred to as a stimulus even though it's only one of many properties of a light); classes defined by physical properties (e.g., a stimulus class consisting of all lights within certain limits of intensity and wavelength); and classes defined in terms of behavioral functions (e.g., classes of effective discriminative stimuli or of stimuli effective as reinforcers or punishers).

When *stimulus* is used descriptively, the *continua* or dimensions along which stimuli vary (e.g., intensity, wavelength or frequency, spatial extent, duration) may be discussed in at least two distinct ways: A change in some stimulus property is said to produce a change in the stimulus, or it's said to change one stimulus to another. The usage is typically determined by convenience of exposition rather than convention (e.g., *the light was changed from green to blue* is equivalent to *the green light was replaced by blue*). When *stimulus* is used functionally, an event isn't a stimulus unless it exerts control over behavior. Functional classes can often be characterized verbally even though their limits can't be specified adequately in physical terms (e.g., red stimuli don't necessarily include wavelengths in the red region of the spectrum). See also ABSTRACTION, CONCEPT, DISCRIMINATION, GENERALIZATION.

Stimulus continuum (plural: continua): a stimulus dimension. Stimulus continua that vary along intensive dimensions (e.g., brightness, loudness) are called *prothetic*; those that vary along nonintensive dimensions (e.g., color, pitch) are called *metathetic*. See also STIMULUS.

Stimulus control: the discriminative control of behavior (including control in a respondent discrimination). See CONTROL, DISCRIMINATION, GENERALIZATION, STIMULUS.

Stimulus generalization: see GENERALIZATION.

Stimulus substitution: an account of respondent conditioning, no longer widely accepted, in which the CS becomes a substitute for the US. But a CR isn't just a UR now elicited by a new stimulus; one of several problems is that CRs typically differ from URs in many ways (e.g., chemical composition may distinguish CS-elicited from US-elicited salivation).

STM: short-term memory. See REMEMBERING.

Storage: in the memory metaphor of storage and retrieval, what the learner does when something to be remembered is presented. Some of the behavior relevant to the stimulus that occurs at or after storage has been called *rehearsal*. Cf. ENCODING, REHEARSAL, REMEMBERING.

Strain: see RATIO STRAIN.

Strategy: a higher-order discriminated operant characterized by relations among different stimuli, responses and/or consequences occurring across trials and/or conditions rather than by specific stimulus or response properties within trials and/or conditions. Different strategies may be appropriate to different settings. For example, if the availability of reinforcers is more likely to alternate between two levers than to remain with one lever, a *win-shift lose-stay* strategy (change

levers after each reinforcer) will be more effective than a *win-stay lose-shift* strategy (stick with the lever that produced the last reinforcer).

Strength: as a property of behavior, the resistance of behavior to change (e.g., resistance to extinction, to disruption by added stimuli and/or to effects of reinforcing alternative responses). The term has also been used, in place of specific measures, to describe the general state of a response or reflex, on the assumption that different measures vary together and reflect an underlying disposition to respond (e.g., if response latency decreases while magnitude, duration and resistance to extinction increase, response strength is said to have increased). With operants, measures such as rate, latency, force and duration have been used as indices of strength, but each is independently modifiable by differential reinforcement. For brevity without sacrificing generality, processes that might otherwise be described in terms of each of several measures (especially rate, latency and probability of response) are often described just as increments or decrements in responding.

Stroop effect: a demonstration of competition between verbal and nonverbal responses to a visual verbal stimulus. It's difficult to name rapidly the different colors in which color words are printed if the colors and the color words don't correspond (e.g., blue printed in red).

Substitution: see STIMULUS SUBSTITUTION.

Successive discrimination: a discrimination in which two or more stimuli are presented one at a time rather than simultaneously and which therefore usually involves only a single response (as in a multiple schedule). In the most accurate usage, the organism responds *in the presence of* each stimulus, but this is often abbreviated to responding *in, during* or *to* each. Cf. SIMULTANEOUS DISCRIMINATION.

Summation: the accumulated effect of a repeated stimulus. A stimulus that doesn't elicit responding if presented only once may do so if presented repeatedly at a high enough rate.

Supernormal stimulus: see RELEASER.

Superstition: the modification or maintenance of behavior by *accidental* (also *adventitious, incidental* or *spurious*) relations between responses and reinforcers, as opposed to those either explicitly or implicitly arranged (cf. CONTINGENCY). Classes of superstitions include: simple superstitions, in which responses are maintained, usually unstably, by reinforcers delivered independently of behavior; concurrent superstitions, in which one response is maintained by reinforcers produced by a different response; sensory superstitions, in which identical contingencies maintain different performances during different stimuli; and topographical superstitions, in which reinforcers produce and maintain a response topography that varies over a much narrower range than that specified by the limits of the operant class. Interpretations in terms of superstitious behavior must be drawn with caution, because (i) it's inevitably variable either within or across organisms, and because (ii) performances that superficially appear to be superstitious can sometimes be shown to depend instead on subtle contingencies. Many human superstitions depend on verbally governed behavior rather than, or in addition to, accidental contingencies (e.g., to be superstitious about breaking mirrors, one needn't first have seven years of bad luck after doing so).

Suppression: a reduction in responding produced directly or indirectly by an aversive stimulus (e.g., by punishment or by a preaversive stimulus). The term is sometimes extended to any reduction of responding by a stimulus (e.g., an extinction stimulus), but such usages aren't always accompanied by a demonstration that the stimulus reduced responding as opposed to having failed to maintain responding. Cf. INHIBITION.

Surface structure: the arrangement of constituents in a particular sentence. Cf. DEEP STRUCTURE.

Symbolic behavior: in some usages, verbal behavior; in a fairly specialized usage, behavior the function of which has transferred from one stimulus to another by virtue of the membership of both in an *equivalence class*.

Symbolic matching: see MATCHING-TO-SAMPLE.

Symmetrical relation or **symmetry:** see EQUIVALENCE CLASS.

Syntax: see LINGUISTICS.

Synthesis: putting the parts obtained through analysis back together again. Cf. BEHAVIOR ANALYSIS.

T

T, t: usually time, or an arbitrary number of seconds.

Tact: a verbal discriminative response (as when the verbal response *apple* in the presence of an apple is said to *tact* the apple). The tact captures stimulus control as it enters into verbal behavior. The tact relation includes only responses in the presence of or shortly after a stimulus, so it isn't equivalent to naming or reference.

Tandem (tand) schedule: a compound schedule in which a reinforcer is produced by the successive completion of two or more component schedules, all of which operate during a single stimulus. Cf. CHAINED SCHEDULE.

Taste aversion: rejection of substances with a given taste after their ingestion has been followed later by gastrointestinal distress or nausea (e.g., as produced by x-irradiation). It might be interpreted as operant behavior (punishment of ingestion of substances with this taste) or as respondent conditioning (where gastrointestinal distress is the US and taste becomes a CS). In either case, its special characteristic is the long delay (sometimes hours) between the taste and its aftermath. The procedure is ineffective over such delays if stimuli such as sounds or lights are substituted for taste. For this reason, taste aversion is often cited as an example of *preparedness*.

Taxis (plural: taxes): phylogenically determined movement or orientation toward or away from a stimulus (e.g., negative phototaxis is movement away from light). Cf. KINESIS.

Temporal conditioning: respondent conditioning in which a US is presented at regular intervals (e.g., every 10 min). Conditioning is said to have occurred when the CR tends to occur shortly before each US.

Temporal discrimination: discrimination based on temporal properties of stimuli (i.e., duration), often appealed to in accounts of spaced responding. For example, if a response is more likely to be emitted at 10 s than at 5 s since the last one, the two durations may be said to be discriminated. When changes in contingencies alter response rate, the temporal spacing of responses necessarily changes too. Thus, it's preferable to study temporal discrimination directly, as by reinforcing one response after one stimulus duration and a second after another. Duration as a discriminable property of stimuli has some unique features: It's not determined until time has passed, so a discriminative response can't occur in its presence; and durations can't change discontinuously, unlike other stimulus properties such as intensity.

Temporal integration: control of behavior by the distribution of events in time. Behavior can be affected by events extended over some time, and recent events may weigh more heavily than those further in the past. The way in which the events combine to affect current behavior is called temporal integration. When events are so far removed in time that they no longer contribute, they're said to be beyond the organism's *time horizon*.

Terminal behavior: stereotyped behavior that reliably occurs late in interstimulus intervals in superstition procedures or temporal conditioning, and usually related topographically to the behavior produced by the reinforcer or the CS (e.g., with pigeons, pecking given food presentations). Cf. INTERIM BEHAVIOR.

Terminal link: see CONCURRENT-CHAIN SCHEDULES.

Terminal rate: see RATE OF RESPONDING.

Textual behavior: A formal verbal class in which a written stimulus occasions a corresponding vocal verbal response. The correspondence is defined by the one-to-one relation of verbal units (e.g., letters or words). Textual behavior isn't equivalent to reading, because it doesn't include the additional behavior called understanding or reading for meaning. Cf. DICTATION-TAKING, ECHOIC BEHAVIOR, TRANSCRIPTION.

Thinking: behavior, especially covert and/or verbal behavior. Thinking isn't some other sort of thing that produces behavior. "It is not some mysterious process responsible for behavior but the very behavior itself in all the complexity of its controlling relations" (Skinner, 1957, p. 449). Productive thinking occurs when verbal responses are reinforced by specific consequences (as in solving a mathematical problem).

Three-term contingency: see CONTINGENCY.

Threshold: see PSYCHOPHYSICS.

Timeout (TO): a period of nonreinforcement arranged either by extinction during a stimulus or by removal of an opportunity to respond (e.g., with pigeons, which only rarely peck keys in darkness, by turning off all lights in the chamber). The term is occasionally extended to other cases (e.g., *timeout from avoidance*, during which no shocks are delivered) and so is more precisely specified as *timeout from positive reinforcement*. Timeout as used with children was derived from the procedure, but the practices following from such extensions deviate from technical specifications in various ways.

Time schedule: a schedule of response-independent reinforcer deliveries. Aside from the absence of a required response, time schedules are classified like interval schedules. In *fixed-time* (*FT*) schedules, the time between reinforcers is constant (cf. TEMPORAL CONDITIONING); in *variable-time* (*VT*) schedules, it varies from one delivery to the next. A *random-time* (*RT*) schedule arranges a constant probability of reinforcer delivery at the end of constant recycling time periods. Cf. INTERVAL SCHEDULE.

Timing behavior: see MEDIATING BEHAVIOR, TEMPORAL DISCRIMINATION.

Titration schedule: a schedule in which one response changes a variable in one direction and either a second response or nonoccurrence of the first changes it in the other (e.g., one response raises stimulus intensity while another lowers it, or each response produces an increment while each 5-s period of no responding produces a decrement).

TO: see TIMEOUT.

Token reinforcer: a conditioned reinforcer (e.g., a coin) that the organism may accumulate and later exchange for other reinforcers.

Topographical drift: gradual changes over time in the topography of responses maintained by a superstition procedure.

Topographical tagging: the identification of different functional properties of responding by correlating each with a different topography, especially a different spatial location. For example, shock avoidance in rats often consists of moderate rates of lever pressing interrupted by occasional high-rate bursts after shock. If an escape lever is added, so that presses on the original lever continue to avoid shock but the rat can terminate shock once it's delivered only by pressing the escape lever, the high-rate bursts move to that lever. Thus, the moderate rates on the original lever are tagged by their location as depending on the avoidance contingency, whereas the high-rate bursts are tagged as depending on shock deliveries and the escape contingency (Boren, 1961).

Topography of response: spatial configuration or form (e.g., how an organism operates an operandum or moves from one place to another), sometimes also specifying location (e.g., the place on a key the pigeon's beak strikes). Topographies can be complex and are more often described verbally than quantitatively (e.g., specifying the limb with which a rat presses a lever).

Trace conditioning: respondent conditioning in which a brief CS presentation is followed by the US after some fixed, extended time period (according to general usage not less than 5 s, but usually considerably longer). Cf. TEMPORAL CONDITIONING.

Tracking: instruction-following based on a history of correspondences between verbal behavior and environmental events. Cf. PLIANCE, VERBALLY GOVERNED BEHAVIOR.

Transcription: A formal verbal class in which a written stimulus occasions a corresponding written response (some usages have also included dictation-taking as transcription; Skinner 1957). Correspondence is defined by the one-to-one relation of verbal units (e.g., letters, words). It's not equivalent to visual copying because the units are not defined by form (e.g., it may involve print to script, lowercase to uppercase). Cf. DICTATION-TAKING, ECHOIC BEHAVIOR, TEXTUAL BEHAVIOR.

Transfer: substituting one set of discriminative stimuli for another (or, as a process, the stimulus control maintained after such a substitution). Transfer may be based on common properties of two sets of stimuli or on similar correlations of the two sets of stimuli with differential contingencies. In verbal learning, transfer from one task to another is usually assessed with reference to a control group that didn't learn the first task; it's positive if the first task enhances performance on the second and negative if it does the opposite. Cf. GENERALIZATION, LEARNING SET, PROACTION, RETROACTION, TRANSPOSITION.

Transformational grammar: see GRAMMARS.

Transitive relation or **transitivity:** see EQUIVALENCE CLASS.

Transposition: in transfer experiments, a reversal of stimulus function depending on control by relations among stimuli on a continuum rather than by absolute values (e.g., a rat learns to choose the larger of two circles and the smaller one is then replaced by a new one larger than either of the others; transposition with respect to size is shown if the rat chooses the new larger circle rather than the circle, now smaller, it had previously chosen).

Trial: a discrete period, usually stimulus-correlated, during which an organism has an opportunity to respond. Trials are separated by intertrial intervals that may consist of any of the following: a stimulus condition (e.g., a dark chamber); removal of the operandum (or operanda); or removal of the organism from the chamber (especially when the organism, after emitting a response such as running an alley, is no longer in a

position to respond again). Trials distinguish discrete-operant procedures from free-operant procedures. Cf. OPERANT, PSEUDOTRIAL.

Two-factor theory: in general, any behavioral theory involving the interaction of operant and respondent processes; more specifically, an avoidance theory stating that avoidance responses are operants reinforced by termination of conditioned aversive stimuli established through a respondent process.

U

Unconditioned reflex or **unconditional reflex:** a relation between a stimulus and a response that doesn't depend on prior conditioning. A reflex is the reliable production of a response by a stimulus. The stimulus is an *unconditioned stimulus* (*US*) and the response is an *unconditioned response* (*UR*). The stimulus is said to elicit the response. Examples of unconditioned reflexes are the salivary reflex (salivation elicited by food or acid in the mouth) and the patellar reflex (a knee jerk elicited by a blow on the patellar tendon). In each case, the elicitation of the response by the stimulus, not the response alone or the stimulus alone, defines the reflex. Cf. RESPONDENT.

Unconditioned or **unconditional response (UR)** or **stimulus (US):** see UNCONDITIONED REFLEX.

Undermatching: see MATCHING LAW.

Universals of language: see LANGUAGE UNIVERSALS.

UR: unconditioned response. See UNCONDITIONED REFLEX.

US: unconditioned stimulus. See UNCONDITIONED REFLEX.

V

Vacuum activity: an ethological term referring to responding (see FIXED ACTION PATTERN) in the absence of the stimulus (see RELEASER) that ordinarily produces it. Cf. DISPLACEMENT ACTIVITY.

Variability: see STATISTICS. Variability is the raw material on which selection operates. It's also a property for which contingencies can be arranged, but no single response can have variability because variability can only be a property of a population of responses.

Variable-interval schedule: see INTERVAL SCHEDULE.

Variable-ratio schedule: see RATIO SCHEDULE.

Variable-time schedule: see TIME SCHEDULE.

Variation: see VARIABILITY; cf. SELECTION BY CONSEQUENCES.

Verbal behavior: any behavior involving words, without regard to modality (e.g., spoken, written, gestural). Verbal behavior involves both listener behavior shaped by its effects on speaker behavior and speaker behavior shaped by its effects on listener behavior. The field of verbal behavior is concerned with the behavior of individuals, and the functional units of their verbal behavior are determined by the practices of a verbal community. Cf. LANGUAGE, VOCAL BEHAVIOR.

Verbal discrimination: any discrimination among verbal stimuli, as in discriminating among nouns and verbs in a sentence. Discrimination among items on the basis of whether they appeared in a given context, *verbal recognition*, is a special case of verbal discrimination.

Verbal learning: see FREE RECALL, PAIRED-ASSOCIATES LEARNING, SERIAL LEARNING, VERBAL DISCRIMINATION, VERBAL RECOGNITION.

Verbally governed behavior: behavior, either verbal or nonverbal, under the control of verbal antecedents. Verbally governed behavior has also been called RULE-GOVERNED BEHAVIOR and *instruction-following*. Contingencies operate for the following of instructions, so instruction-following is a higher-order class. Verbal antecedents may alter the functions of other stimuli (as when something neutral becomes a reinforcer after one is told that it's worth having). They may also produce instruction-following; they don't qualify as discriminative stimuli if they do so even when they're no longer present. The verbal behavior of one individual may provide verbal antecedents for another, but verbal antecedents may also be shaped or self-generated. Once verbal contingencies have created correspondences between saying and doing so that saying is often accompanied by doing, other behavior may be modified by such shaped or self-generated verbal behavior. Cf. CONTINGENCY-SHAPED BEHAVIOR, HIGHER-ORDER CLASS OF BEHAVIOR.

Verbal recognition: see VERBAL DISCRIMINATION.

VI: variable interval. See INTERVAL SCHEDULE.

Vicarious learning: see OBSERVATIONAL LEARNING.

Vocal behavior: Behavior of lips, tongue, etc., that modulates air flow and produces sound. Vocal behavior isn't necessarily verbal. Cf. VERBAL BEHAVIOR.

Von Restorff effect: the enhanced likelihood of recall of a distinctive item in a list.

VR: variable ratio. See RATIO SCHEDULE.

VT: variable time. See TIME SCHEDULE.

W

Warmup: a low or zero response rate at the start of a session followed by an increase to the rate maintained later, especially in avoidance performances.

Warning stimulus: a stimulus that precedes an avoidable aversive stimulus. See AVOIDANCE.

Wheel running: sometimes taken as an index of level of activity, especially in rats. The rat runs inside the wheel, which usually turns in only one direction to simplify recording of revolutions or distance run. Wheel running has a high baseline level and is relatively continuous compared to such discrete responses as lever presses.

Win-shift lose-stay or **win-stay lose-shift:** see STRATEGY.

Working memory: see METAMEMORY.

Y

Yoking: connecting chambers so that the performance of an organism in one determines the stimuli and/or schedules for an organism in the other (e.g., equating VR and VI reinforcement rates by letting the times between reinforcers in one organism's VR performance determine the intervals of another's VI schedule). In within-organism yoking, an experimental condition is yoked to some property of the organism's own performance in an earlier condition.

Conclusions from yoking must be cautiously drawn. For example, assume two types of rats equally distributed among groups in a yoking experiment on the role of avoidance in shock-induced ulcers. Sensitive types are prone to ulcers when shocked; they also respond rapidly at low shock levels receiving few shocks but sporadically at higher levels receiving many shocks. Insensitive types are resistant to ulcers when shocked; they also respond slowly at low shock levels receiving many shocks but rapidly at higher levels receiving few shocks. For each shock received by an avoidance rat, an unavoidable shock is delivered to its yoked partner. At low shock levels, only yoked rats develop ulcers (only insensitive avoidance rats respond slowly and receive frequent shocks; they don't develop ulcers, but all their yoked partners also receive frequent shocks and half of those are sensitive). At higher levels, more avoidance rats develop ulcers than do their yoked partners (sensitive avoidance rats respond sporadically, thereby receiving frequent shocks and developing ulcers; all their yoked partners also receive frequent shocks but only half of those are sensitive and develop ulcers).

Thus, a yoking experiment done at one shock level would yield a different conclusion about avoidance and shock-induced ulcers than one done at another level.

Z

Zeigarnik effect: the greater likelihood of remembering an unfinished than a finished task, as when you can't figure out how to end a ;-)

Acknowledgments

Thanks go to the sources below and the authors for granting permission to use material from copyrighted works. Full citations appear in the references.

Fig. 2-1, from Tinbergen & Perdeck (1950) with permission of E. J. Brill Publishers. Fig. 2-3, from Lashley (1930) by permission of the Journal Press.

Fig. 5-12, from Tolman & Honzik (1930), published by the Regents of the University of California; by permission of the University of California Press. Fig. 5-13, from Held & Hein (1963), copyright by the American Psychological Association; reprinted by permission. Fig. 6-3, from Camp, Raymond, & Church (1967), copyright by the American Psychological Association; adapted by permission. Fig. 6-4, from Holz & Azrin (1961), copyright by the Society for the Experimental Analysis of Behavior; published with permission of the Society. Fig. 6-5, from Fowler & Trapold (1962), copyright by the American Psychological Association; adapted by permission. Fig. 8-2, from Reynolds (1961b), copyright by the Society for the Experimental Analysis of Behavior; adapted with permission of the Society. Fig. 8-5, from Honig, Boneau, Burstein, & Pennypacker (1963), copyright by the American Psychological Association; reprinted by permission. Fig. 10-2 from Catania &

Reynolds (1968), copyright by the Society for the Experimental Analysis of Behavior, Inc.; adapted with permission of the Society. Fig. 10-5, from Catania, Matthews, Silverman, & Yohalem (1977), copyright by the Society for the Experimental Analysis of Behavior; published with permission of the Society. Fig. 10-7, from Dews (1962), copyright by the Society for the Experimental Analysis of Behavior; published with permission of the Society. Fig. 11-9, from Reynolds (1961b), copyright by the Society for the Experimental Analysis of Behavior; adapted with permission of the Society. Fig. 12-8, from Geller (1960), copyright by the Society for the Experimental Analysis of Behavior; published with permission of the Society. Fig. 12-9, from Blackman (1968), copyright by the Society for the Experimental Analysis of Behavior; adapted with permission of the Society. Fig. 12-10, from Rescorla (1968), copyright by the American Psychological Association; adapted by permission. Fig. 12-11, from Revusky & Garcia (1970), with permission of Academic Press.

Fig. 16-2, from N. F. Johnson (1965), adapted with permission of Academic Press. Fig. 16-4, from Collins & Quillian (1969), adapted with permission of Academic Press. Fig. 17-4, from Rundus & Atkinson (1970), adapted with permission of Academic Press. Fig. 18-2, from Tulving (1974), published with permission of American Scientist. Fig. 18-3, from Sperling (1960), copyright by the American Psychological Association; adapted by permission. Fig. 19-5, from Melton (1963), with permission of Academic Press. Fig. 20-1, from Shepard & Metzler (1971), copyright by the American Association for the Advancement of Science. Fig. 20-2, from Thomas (1974), adapted with permission of Academic Press.

References

[Bracketed numbers indicate the pages on which each reference is cited.]

Adams, J. A. (1954). Psychomotor performance as a function of intertrial rest interval. *Journal of Experimental Psychology, 48,* 131–133. [301]

Ader, R., & Cohen, N. (1985). CNS-immune system interactions: Conditioning phenomena. *Behavioral and Brain Sciences, 8,* 379–394. [201]

The American Heritage Dictionary of the English Language (1992, 3rd edition). Boston: Houghton Mifflin. [377]

Anderson, J. R., & Bower, G. H. (1972). Recognition and retrieval processes in free recall. *Psychological Review, 79,* 97–123. [312]

Anderson, J. R., & Bower, G. H. (1973). *Human associative memory.* Washington, DC: Winston. [346]

Anderson, J. R., & Ross, B. H. (1980). Evidence against a semantic-episodic distinction. *Journal of Experimental Psychology: Human Learning and Memory, 6,* 441–466. [346]

Andresen, J. T. (1990). Skinner and Chomsky thirty years later. *Historiographia Linguistica, 17,* 145–166. [292]

Andronis, P. T. (1983). *Symbolic aggression by pigeons: Contingency coadduction.* Ph.D. dissertation, University of Chicago. [161]

Anger, D. (1956). The dependence of interresponse times upon the relative reinforcement of different interresponse times. *Journal of Experimental Psychology, 52,* 145–161. [171]

Anger, D. (1963). The role of temporal discriminations in the reinforcement of Sidman avoidance behavior. *Journal of Experimental Psychology, 6,* 477–506. [105]

Antonitis, J. J. (1951). Response variability in the white rat during conditioning, extinction, and reconditioning. *Journal of Experimental Psychology, 42,* 273–281. [115]

Ashcraft, M. H. (1982). The development of mental arithmetic: A chronometric approach. *Developmental Review, 2,* 213–236. [363]

Atkinson, R. C. (1972). Optimizing the learning of a second-language vocabulary. *Journal of Experimental Psychology, 96,* 124–129. [306]

Austin, J. L. (1962). *How to do things with words.* Cambridge, MA: Harvard University Press. [258]

Ayer, A. J. (1946). *Language, truth and logic* (2nd ed.). New York: Dover. [367]

Ayllon, T., & Azrin, N. H. (1968). *The token economy.* New York: Appleton-Century-Crofts. [186]

Azrin, N. H. (1956). Some effects of two intermittent schedules of immediate and nonimmediate punishment. *Journal of Psychology, 42,* 3–21. [92, 179]

Azrin, N. H., & Hake, D. F. (1969). Positive conditioned suppression: Conditioned suppression using positive reinforcers as the unconditioned stimuli. *Journal of the Experimental Analysis of Behavior, 12,* 167–173. [216]

Azrin, N. H., & Holz, W. C. (1966). Punishment. In W. K. Honig (Ed.), *Operant behavior: Areas of research and application* (pp. 380–447). New York: Appleton-Century-Crofts. [92, 94]

Azrin, N. H., Hutchinson, R. R., & Hake, D. F. (1966). Extinction-induced aggression. *Journal of the Experimental Analysis of Behavior, 9,* 191–204. [75]

Azrin, N. H., Hutchinson, R. R., & Hake, D. F. (1967). Attack, avoidance, and escape reactions to aversive shock. *Journal of the Experimental Analysis of Behavior*, **10**, 131–148. [104]

Azrin, N. H., Hutchinson, R. R., & McLaughlin, R. (1965). The opportunity for aggression as an operant reinforcer during aversive stimulation. *Journal of the Experimental Analysis of Behavior*, **8**, 171–180. [75]

Baddeley, A. D. (1976). *The psychology of memory*. New York: Basic Books. [345, 354]

Baddeley, A., & Hull, A. (1979). Prefix and suffix effects: Do they have a common basis? *Journal of Verbal Learning and Verbal Behavior*, **18**, 129–140. [307]

Badia, P., Suter, S., & Lewis, P. (1966). Rat vocalization to shock with and without a CS. *Psychonomic Science*, **4**, 117–118. [50]

Baer, D. M., Peterson, R. F., & Sherman, J. A. (1967). The development of imitation by reinforcing behavioral similarity to a model. *Journal of the Experimental Analysis of Behavior*, **10**, 405–416. [229]

Baer, R. A., Detrich, R., & Weninger, J. M. (1988). On the functional role of the verbalization in correspondence training procedures. *Journal of Applied Behavior Analysis*, **21**, 345–356. [270]

Balda, R. P., Kamil, A. C., & Grim, K. (1986). Revisits to empty cache sites by nutcrackers. *Animal Behaviour*, **34**, 1289–1298. [144]

Ballard, P. B. (1913). Obliviscence and reminiscence. *British Journal of Psychology Monograph Supplements*, **1** (No. 2). [342]

Bandura, A. (1986). *Social foundations of thought and action*. Englewood Cliffs, NJ: Prentice-Hall. [227, 228]

Bandura, A., Adams, N. E., & Beyer, J. (1977). Cognitive processes mediating behavioral change. *Journal of Personality and Social Psychology*, **35**, 125–139. [273]

Baron, A., & Leinenweber, A. (1995). Effects of a variable-ratio conditioning history on sensitivity to fixed-interval contingencies in rats. *Journal of the Experimental Analysis of Behavior*, **63**, 97–110. [267]

Barrett, J. E., & Stanley, J. A. (1980). Maintenance of responding by squirrel monkeys under a concurrent shock-postponement, fixed-interval shock-presentation schedule. *Journal of the Experimental Analysis of Behavior*, **34**, 117–129. [95]

Bartlett, F. C. (1932). *Remembering*. Cambridge: Cambridge University Press. [287, 328]

Bauer, D. W., & Miller, J. (1982). Stimulus-response compatibility and the motor system. *Quarterly Journal of Experimental Psychology*, **34A**, 367–380. [221]

Bauer, P. J. (1996). What do infants recall of their lives? Memory for specific events by one- to two-year-olds. *American Psychologist*, **51**, 29–41. [327]

Baum, W. M. (1973). The correlation-based law of effect. *Journal of the Experimental Analysis of Behavior*, **20**, 137–153. [77]

Bechterev, V. M. (1933). *General principles of human reflexology* (tr. E. Murphy & W. Murphy). London: Jarrolds. [201, 210]

Bellezza, F. S. (1982). Updating memory using mnemonic devices. *Cognitive Psychology*, **14**, 301–327. [322]

Bem, D. J. (1967). Self perception: An alternative interpretation of cognitive dissonance phenomena. *Psychological Review*, **74**, 183–200. [227, 231, 254]

Bentall, R. P., & Lowe, C. F. (1987). The role of verbal behavior in human learning: III. Instructional effects in children. *Journal of the Experimental Analysis of Behavior*, **47**, 177–190. [272]

Bentall, R. P., Lowe, C. F., & Beasty, A. (1985). The role of verbal behavior in human learning: II. Developmental differences. *Journal of the Experimental Analysis of Behavior*, **43**, 165–181. [272]

Berko, J. (1958). The child's learning of English morphology. *Word*, **14**, 150–177. [295]

Bernstein. D. J., & Ebbesen, E. B. (1978). Reinforcement and substitution in humans: A multiple-response analysis. *Journal of the Experimental Analysis of Behavior*, **30**, 243–253. [81]

Bisanz, G. L., Vesonder, G. T., & Voss, J. F. (1978). Knowledge of one's own responding and the relation of such knowledge to learning. *Journal of Experimental Psychology*, **25**, 116–128. [334]

Bjork, R. A. (1970). Positive forgetting: The non-interference of items intentionally forgotten. *Journal of Verbal Learning and Verbal Behavior*, **9**, 225–268. [333]

Bjork, R. A. (1978). The updating of human memory. In G. H. Bower (Ed.), *The psychology of learning and motivation. Volume 12* (pp. 235–259). New York: Academic Press. [333]

Blackman, D. E. (1968). Conditioned suppression or facilitation as a function of the behavioral baseline. *Journal of the Experimental Analysis of Behavior.* **11**, 53–61. [216, 217]

Blackman, D. E. (1977). Conditioned suppression and the effects of classical conditioning on operant behavior. In W. K. Honig & J. E. R. Staddon (Eds.), *Handbook of operant behavior* (pp. 340–363). Englewood Cliffs, NJ: Prentice-Hall. [214, 216]

Blakemore, C., & Cooper, G. F. (1970). Development of the brain depends on the visual environment. *Nature,* **228**, 477–478. [87]

Blough, D. S. (1958). New test for tranquillizers. *Science,* **127**, 586–587. [114]

Blough, D. S. (1959). Delayed matching in the pigeon. *Journal of the Experimental Analysis of Behavior.* **2**, 151–160. [320]

Blough, D. M. (1989). Odd-item search in pigeons: Display size and transfer effects. *Journal of Experimental Psychology: Animal Behavior Processes,* **15**, 14–22. [143]

Blough, D. S. (1992). Effects of stimulus frequency and reinforcement variables on reaction time. *Journal of the Experimental Analysis of Behavior,* **57**, 47–50. [259]

Boakes, R. A. (1973). Response decrements produced by extinction and by response-independent reinforcement. *Journal of the Experimental Analysis of Behavior,* **19**, 293–302. [76]

Bolinger, D. (1973). Truth is a linguistic question. *Language,* **49**, 539–550. [255]

Bolles, R. C. (1970). Species-specific defense reactions and avoidance learning. *Psychological Review,* **77**, 32–48. [103, 104]

Bolles, R. C. (1975). *Theory of motivation* (2nd edition). New York: Harper & Row. [58, 78]

Boren, J. J. (1961). Isolation of post-shock responding in a free operant avoidance procedure. *Psychological Reports,* **9**, 265–266. [414]

Boren, J. J., & Devine, D. D. (1968). The repeated acquisition of behavioral chains. *Journal of the Experimental Analysis of Behavior,* **11**, 651–660. [125, 157]

Boren, M. C. P., & Gollub, L. R. (1972). Accuracy of performance on a matching-to-sample procedure under interval schedules. *Journal of the Experimental Analysis of Behavior,* **18**, 65–77. [187]

Bousfield, W. A. (1953). The occurrence of clustering in the recall of randomly arranged associates. *Journal of General Psychology,* **49**, 229–240. [309]

Bower, G. H. (1970). Analysis of a mnemonic device. *American Scientist,* **58**, 496–510. [322]

Bower, G. H. (1981). Mood and memory. *American Psychologist,* **36**, 129–148. [332]

Bower, G. H., Black, J. B., & Turner, T. J. (1979). Scripts in memory for text. *Cognitive Psychology,* **11**, 177–220. [286]

Bowler, P. J. (1983). *The eclipse of Darwinism.* Baltimore: The Johns Hopkins University Press. [30]

Braine, M. D. S., & Rumain, B. (1981). Development of comprehension of "or": Evidence for a sequence of competencies. *Journal of Experimental Child Psychology,* **31**, 46–70. [292]

Brainerd, C. J., Reyna, V. F., & Brandse, E. (1995). Are children's false memories more persistent than their true memories? *Psychological Science,* **6**, 359–364. [329]

Brandauer, C. (1958). *The effects of uniform probabilities of reinforcement on the response rate of the pigeon.* Unpublished doctoral dissertation, Columbia University. [167]

Bransford, J. D., & Franks, J. J. (1971). The abstraction of linguistic ideas. *Cognitive Psychology,* **2**, 331–350. [287]

Breland, K., & Breland, M. (1961). The misbehavior of organisms. *American Psychologist,* **16**, 681–684. [220]

Bridgman, P. W. (1927). *The logic of modern physics.* New York: Macmillan. [367]

Bright, M. (1985). *Animal language.* Ithaca, NY: Cornell. [276]

Brogden, W. J. (1939). Sensory preconditioning. *Journal of Experimental Psychology,* **25**, 323–332. [208]

Brown, J. (1958). Some tests of the decay theory of immediate memory. *Quarterly Journal of Experimental Psychology,* **10**, 12–21. [338]

Brown, P. L., & Jenkins, H. M. (1968). Autoshaping of the pigeon's key-peck. *Journal of the Experimental Analysis of Behavior,* **11**, 1–8. [212]

Brown, R. (1973). *A first language.* Cambridge, MA: Harvard University Press. [292]

Brown, R., & McNeill, D. (1966). The "tip of the tongue" phenomenon. *Journal of Verbal Learning and Verbal Behavior,* **5**, 325–337. [251, 334]

Bruce, R. W. (1933). Conditions of transfer of training. *Journal of Experimental Psychology,* **16,** 343–361. [314]

Bryan, W. L., & Harter, N. (1899). Studies on the telegraphic language: The acquisition of a hierarchy of habits. *Psychological Review,* **6,** 345–375. [367]

Burns, G. L., & Staats, A. W. (1991). Rule-governed behavior: Unifying radical and paradigmatic behaviorism. *Analysis of Verbal Behavior,* **9,** 127–143. [366]

Butler, R. A. (1957). The effect of deprivation of visual incentives on visual exploration motivation in monkeys. *Journal of Comparative and Physiological Psychology,* **50,** 177–179. [84]

Bykov, K. M. (1957). *The cerebral cortex and the internal organs* (tr. W. H. Gantt). New York: Chemical Publishing. [201]

Calkins, M. W. (1894). Association. *Psychological Review,* **1,** 476–483. [303]

Calkins, M. W. (1896). Association. II. *Psychological Review,* **3,** 32–49. [304]

Cameron, J., & Pierce, W. D. (1994). Reinforcement, reward, and intrinsic motivation: A meta-analysis. *Review of Educational Research,* **64,** 363–423. [270]

Camp, D. S., Raymond, G. A., & Church, R. M. (1967). Temporal relationship between response and punishment. *Journal of Experimental Psychologyy,* **74,** 114–123. [94, 95]

Capaldi, E. D., & Davidson, T. L. (1979). Control of instrumental behavior by deprivation stimuli. *Journal of Experimental Psychology: Animal Behavior Processes,* **5,** 355–367. [231]

Capaldi, E. J., & Stevenson, H. W. (1957). Response reversal following different amounts of training. *Journal of Comparative and Physiological Psychology,* **50,** 195–198. [317]

Caramazza, A., & Brones, I. (1980). Semantic classification by bilinguals. *Canadian Journal of Psychology,* **34,** 77–81. [246]

Carew, T. J. (1992). Aplysia: Development of processes underlying learning. In L. R. Squire (Ed.), *The encyclopedia of learning and memory* (pp. 51–56). New York: Macmillan. [372]

Carmichael, L. C., Hogan, H. P., & Walter, A. A. (1932). An experimental study of the effect of language on the reproduction of visually perceived form. *Journal of Experimental Psychology,* **15,** 73–86. [328]

Carr, E. G., Newsom, C. D., & Binkoff, J. A. (1980). Escape as a factor in the aggressive behavior of two retarded children. *Journal of Applied Behavior Analysis,* **13,** 101–117. [98]

Carrigan, P. F., Jr., & Sidman, M. (1992). Conditional discrimination and equivalence relations: A theoretical analysis of control by negative stimuli. *Journal of the Experimental Analysis of Behavior,* **58,** 183–204. [153]

Carter, D. E., & Werner, T. J. (1978). Complex learning and information processing by pigeons: A critical analysis. *Journal of the Experimental Analysis of Behavior,* **29,** 565–601. [153]

Catania, A. C. (1963a). Concurrent performances: A baseline for the study of reinforcement magnitude. *Journal of the Experimental Analysis of Behavior,* **6,** 299–300. [190]

Catania, A. C. (1963b). Concurrent performances: Reinforcement interaction and response independence. *Journal of the Experimental Analysis of Behavior,* **6,** 253–263. [190]

Catania, A. C. (1968). Glossary. In A. C. Catania (Ed.), *Contemporary research in operant behavior* (pp. 327–349). Glenview, IL: Scott, Foresman. [377]

Catania, A. C. (1969). Concurrent performances: Inhibition of one response by reinforcement of another. *Journal of the Experimental Analysis of Behavior,* **12,** 731–744. [189]

Catania, A. C. (1970). Reinforcement schedules and psychophysical judgments: A study of some temporal properties of behavior. In W. N. Schoenfeld (Ed.), *The theory of reinforcement schedules* (pp. 1–42). New York: Appleton-Century-Crofts. [121]

Catania, A. C. (1971). Reinforcement schedules: The role of responses preceding the one that produces the reinforcer. *Journal of the Experimental Analysis of Behavior,* **15,** 271–287. [76, 177]

Catania, A. C. (1972). Chomsky's formal analysis of natural languages: A behavioral translation. *Behaviorism,* **1,** 1–15. [280]

Catania, A. C. (1973). The psychologies of structure, function, and development. *American Psychologist,* **28,** 434–443. [240, 368]

Catania, A. C. (1975). The myth of self-reinforcement. *Behaviorism,* **3,** 192–199. [232]

Catania, A. C. (1978). The psychology of learning: Some lessons from the Darwinian revolution.

Annals of the New York Academy of Sciences, **309**, 18–28. [38, 369, 372]

Catania, A. C. (1981). The flight from experimental analysis. In C. M. Bradshaw, E. Szabadi, & C. F. Lowe (Eds.), *Quantification of steady-state operant behaviour* (pp. 49–64). Amsterdam: Elsevier/North-Holland. [188]

Catania, A. C. (1987). Some Darwinian lessons for behavior analysis. A review of Peter J. Bowler's *The eclipse of Darwinism. Journal of the Experimental Analysis of Behavior*, **47**, 249–257. [30, 372]

Catania, A. C. (1989). Speaking of behavior. *Journal of the Experimental Analysis of Behavior*, **52**, 193–196. [377]

Catania, A. C. (1991a). Glossary. In I. H. Iversen & K. A. Lattal (Eds.), *Experimental analysis of behavior. Part 2.* (pp. G1–G44). Amsterdam: Elsevier/North-Holland. [377]

Catania, A. C. (1991b). The phylogeny and ontogeny of verbal behavior. In N. A. Krasnegor, D. M. Rumbaugh, R. L. Schiefelbusch, & M. Studdert-Kennedy (Eds.), *Biological and behavioral determinants of language development* (pp. 263–285). Hillsdale, NJ: Erlbaum. [278]

Catania, A. C. (1993). The unconventional philosophy of science of behavior analysis. *Journal of the Experimental Analysis of Behavior*, **60**, 449–452. [366]

Catania, A. C. (1994). The natural and artificial selection of verbal behavior. In S. C. Hayes, L. J. Hayes, M. Sato, & K. Ono (Eds.), *Behavior analysis of language and cognition* (pp. 31–49). Reno, NV: Context Press. [230]

Catania, A. C. (1995). Higher-order behavior classes: Contingencies, beliefs, and verbal behavior. *Journal of Behavior Therapy and Experimental Psychiatry*, **26**, 191–200. [228, 232, 273]

Catania, A. C., & Brigham, T. A. (Eds.) (1978). *Handbook of applied behavior analysis: Social and instructional processes.* New York: Irvington. [376]

Catania, A. C., & Cerutti, D. (1986). Some nonverbal properties of verbal behavior. In T. Thompson & M. D. Zeiler (Eds.), *Analysis and integration of behavioral units* (pp. 185–211). Hillsdale, NJ: Erlbaum. [162, 295]

Catania, A. C., & Gill, C. A. (1964). Inhibition and behavioral contrast. *Psychonomic Science*, **1**, 257–258. [183]

Catania, A. C., & Harnad, S. (Eds.). (1988). *The selection of behavior: The operant behaviorism of B. F. Skinner.* New York: Cambridge University Press. [113]

Catania, A. C., Horne, P., & Lowe, C. F. (1989). Transfer of function across members of an equivalence class. *Analysis of Verbal Behavior*, **7**, 99–110. [154]

Catania, A. C., & Keller, K. J. (1981). Contingency, contiguity, correlation, and the concept of causation. In P. Harzem & M. D. Zeiler (Eds.), *Predictability, correlation, and contiguity* (pp. 125–167). New York: Wiley. [76, 173, 177]

Catania, A. C., Lowe, C. F., & Horne, P. (1990). Nonverbal behavior correlated with the shaped verbal behavior of children. *Analysis of Verbal Behavior*, **8**, 43–55. [272]

Catania, A. C., Matthews, B. A., & Shimoff, E. (1982). Instructed versus shaped human verbal behavior: Interactions with nonverbal responding. *Journal of the Experimental Analysis of Behavior*, **38**, 233–248. [270]

Catania, A. C., Matthews, B. A., & Shimoff, E. H. (1990). Properties of rule-governed behaviour and their implications. In D. E. Blackman & H. Lejeune (Eds.), *Behaviour analysis in theory and practice* (pp. 215–230). Hillsdale, NJ: Erlbaum. [272]

Catania, A. C., Matthews, T. J., Silverman, P. J., & Yohalem, R. (1977). Yoked variable-ratio and variable-interval responding in pigeons. *Journal of the Experimental Analysis of Behavior*, **28**, 155–161. [170]

Catania, A. C., & Reynolds, G. S. (1968). A quantitative analysis of the responding maintained by interval schedules of reinforcement. *Journal of the Experimental Analysis of Behavior*, **11**, 327–383. [168, 173]

Catania, A. C., & Sagvolden, T. (1980). Preference for free choice over forced choice in pigeons. *Journal of the Experimental Analysis of Behavior*, **34**, 77–86. [192]

Catania, A. C., Sagvolden, T., & Keller, K. J. (1988). Reinforcement schedules: Retroactive and proactive effects of reinforcers inserted into fixed-interval performances. *Journal of the Experimental Analysis of Behavior*, **49**, 49–73. [189]

Catania, A. C., Shimoff, E., & Matthews, B. A. (1989). An experimental analysis of rule-governed behavior. In S. C. Hayes (Ed.), *Rule-*

governed behavior: Cognition, contingencies, and instructional control (pp. 119–150). New York: Plenum. [271, 272]

Catania, A. C., Yohalem, R., & Silverman, P. J. (1980). Contingency and stimulus change in chained schedules of reinforcement. *Journal of the Experimental Analysis of Behavior*, **33**, 213–219. [186]

Catania, K. C., & Kaas, J. H. (1996). The unusual nose and brain of the star-nosed mole. *BioScience*, **46**, 578–586. [372]

Cermak, L. S., & Craik, F. I. M. (Eds.). (1979). *Levels of processing in human memory*. Hillsdale, NJ: Erlbaum. [327]

Chadwick, P. D. J., Lowe, C. F., Horne, P. J., & Higson, P. J. (1994) Modifying delusions: The role of empirical testing. *Behavior Therapy*, **25**, 35–49. [273]

Charney, R. (1980). Speech roles and the development of personal pronouns. *Journal of Child Language*, **7**, 509–528. [295]

Chase, S. (1938). *The tyranny of words*. New York: Harcourt, Brace & World. [267]

Chiat, S. (1982). If I were you and you were me: The analysis of pronouns in a pronoun-reversing child. *Journal of Child Language*, **9**, 359–379. [295]

Chomsky, N. (1959). Review of B. F. Skinner's *Verbal behavior*. *Language*, **35**, 26–58. [240, 292]

Chomsky, N., & Miller, G. A. (1963). Introduction to the formal analysis of natural languages. In R. D. Luce, R. R. Bush, & E. Galanter (Eds.), *Handbook of mathematical psychology. Volume II* (pp. 269–321). New York: Wiley. [280]

Chung, S.-H. (1965). Effects of effort on response rate. *Journal of the Experimental Analysis of Behavior*, **8**, 1–7. [190]

Church, R. M. (1963). The varied effects of punishment on behavior. *Psychological Review*, **70**, 369–402. [92]

Church, R. M. (1969). Response suppression. In B. A. Campbell & R. M. Church (Eds.), *Punishment and aversive behavior* (pp. 111–156). New York: Appleton-Century-Crofts. [94]

Clark, H. H., & Sengul, C. J. (1979). In search of referents for nouns and pronouns. *Memory and Cognition*, **7**, 35–41. [295]

Collier, G. H., & Rovee-Collier, C. K. (1981). A comparative analysis of optimal foraging behavior: Laboratory simulations. In A. C. Kamil & T. D. Sargent (Eds.), *Foraging behavior* (pp. 39–76). New York: Garland. [135]

Collins, A. M., & Quillian, M. R. (1969). Retrieval time from semantic memory. *Journal of Verbal Learning and Verbal Behavior*, **8**, 240–247. [289]

Conrad, R. (1964). Acoustic confusions in immediate memory. *British Journal of Psychology*, **55**, 75–84. [325]

Cook, R. G., Wright, A. A., & Sands, S. F. (1991). Interstimulus interval and viewing time effects in monkey list memory. *Animal Learning and Behavior*, **19**, 153–163 [326]

Cott, A., Pavlovski, R. P., & Black, A. H. (1981). Operant conditioning and discrimination of alpha: Some methodological limitations inherent in response-discrimination experiments. *Journal of Experimental Psychology: General*, **110**, 398–414. [232]

Craik, F. I. M. (1983). On the transfer of information from temporary to permanent memory. *Philosophical Transactions of the Royal Society of London B*, **302**, 341–359. [345]

Craik, F. I. M. (1985). Paradigms in human memory research. In L. Nilsson & T. Archer (Eds.), *Perspectives on learning and memory* (pp. 197–221). Hillsdale, NJ: Erlbaum. [325]

Craik, F. I. M., & Lockhart, R. S. (1972). Levels of processing: A framework for memory research. *Journal of Verbal Learning and Verbal Behavior*, **11**, 671–684. [338]

Crain, S. (1991). Language acquisition in the absence of experience. *Behavioral and Brain Sciences*, **14**, 597–650. [293]

Critchfield, T. S. (1993). Signal-detection properties of verbal self-reports. *Journal of the Experimental Analysis of behavior*, **60**, 495–514. [232]

Crowder, R. G. (1976). *Principles of learning and memory*. Hillsdale, NJ: Erlbaum. [340, 354]

Culicover, P. W. (1992). Language learning: Humans. In L. R. Squire (Ed.), *The encyclopedia of learning and memory* (pp. 327–331). New York: Macmillan. [293]

D'Amato, M. R., Salmon, D. P., Loukas, E., & Tomie, A. (1985). Symmetry and transitivity of conditional relations in monkeys (Cebus apella) and pigeons (Columba livia). *Journal of the Experimental Analysis of Behavior*, **44**, 35–47. [153]

Damon, W., & Hart, D. (1982). The development of self-understanding from infancy through adolescence. *Child Development*, **53**, 841–864. [295]

Daniels, A. H. (1895). The memory after-image and attention. *American Journal of Psychology*, **6**, 558–564. [338]

Darwin, C. (1859). *On the origin of species*. London: John Murray (reprinted Cambridge, MA: Harvard University Press, 1966). [30, 35, 366, 369, 374]

Darwin, C. J., Turvey, M. T., & Crowder, R. G. (1972). An auditory analogue of the Sperling partial report procedure: Evidence for brief auditory storage. *Cognitive Psychology*, **3**, 255–267. [337]

Davis, H., & Pérusse, R. (1988). Numerical competence in animals: Definitional issues, current evidence, and a new research agenda. *Behavioral and Brain Sciences*, **11**, 561–615. [143]

Davison, M., & McCarthy, D. (1988). *The matching law: A research review*. Hillsdale, NJ: Erlbaum. [188]

Dawkins, R. (1976). *The selfish gene*. New York: Oxford University Press. [30, 226, 255, 352, 353, 372]

Dawkins, R. (1982). *The extended phenotype*. San Francisco: Freeman. [32, 34, 35, 226]

Dawkins, R. (1986). *The blind watchmaker*. New York: Norton. [30, 31, 32, 35]

Dawkins, R., & Krebs, J. R. (1978). Animal signals: Information or manipulation? In J. R. Krebs & N. B. Davies (Eds.), *Behavioral ecology* (pp. 282–309). Sunderland, MA: Sinauer. [226]

Day, W. F. (1969). On certain similarities between the philosophical investigations of Ludwig Wittgenstein and the operationism of B. F. Skinner. *Journal of the Experimental Analysis of Behavior*, **12**, 489–506. [255]

DeCasper, A. J., & Fifer, W. P. (1980). Of human bonding: Newborns prefer their mothers' voices. *Science*, **208**, 1174–1176. [242]

Delgado, L. E., & Lutzger, J. R. (1988). Training young parents to identify and report their children's illnesses. *Journal of Applied Behavior Analysis*, **21**, 311–319. [142]

Delius, J. D., & Nowak, B. (1982). Visual symmetry recognition by pigeons. *Psychological Research*, **44**, 199–212. [143]

Deluty, M. Z. (1978). Self-control and impulsiveness involving aversive events. *Journal of Experimental Psychology: Animal Behavior Processes*, **4**, 250–266. [195]

Dennett, D. C. (1987). *The intentional stance*. Cambridge, MA: MIT Press. [226]

de Rose, J. C., McIlvane, W. J., Dube, W. V., Galpin, V. C., & Stoddard, L. T. (1988). Emergent simple discrimination established by indirect relation to differential consequences. *Journal of the Experimental Analysis of Behavior*, **50**, 1–20. [154]

Derrickson, J. G., Neef, N. A., & Cataldo, M. F. (1993). Effects of signalling invasive procedures on a hospitalized infant's affective behavior. *Journal of Applied Behavior Analysis*, **26**, 133–134. [215]

Deutsch, R. (1974). Conditioned hypoglycemia: A mechanism for saccharin-induced sensitivity to insulin in the rat. *Journal of Comparative and Physiological Psychology*, **86**, 350–358. [201]

De Villiers, J. G., & De Villiers, P. A. (1978). *Language acquisition*. Cambridge, MA: Harvard University Press. [292]

De Villiers, P. A., & De Villiers, J. G. (1974). On this, that, and the other: Nonegocentrism in very young children. *Journal of Experimental Child Psychology*, **18**, 438–447. [294]

de Waal, F. (1989). *Peacemaking among primates*. Cambridge, MA: Harvard University Press. [227]

Dews, P. B. (1960). Free-operant behavior under conditions of delayed reinforcement: I. CRF-type schedules. *Journal of the Experimental Analysis of Behavior*, **3**, 221–234. [172]

Dews, P. B. (1962). The effect of multiple S^Δ periods on responding on a fixed-interval schedule. *Journal of the Experimental Analysis of Behavior*, **5**, 369–374. [176, 177]

Dews, P. B. (1970). Drugs in psychology. A commentary on T. Thompson & C. R. Schuster's *Behavioral Pharmacology*. *Journal of the Experimental Analysis of Behavior*, **13**, 395–406. [181]

Dill, L. M. (1974). The escape response of the zebra danio (*Brachydanio rerio*) II. The effect of experience. *Animal Behavior*, **22**, 723–730. [54]

Dinsmoor, J. A. (1983). Observing and conditioned reinforcement. *Behavioral and Brain Sciences*, **6**, 693–728. [182]

Dinsmoor, J. A. (1995). Stimulus control. *The Behavior Analyst*, **18**, 51–68 and 253–269. [140]

Donahoe, J. W., Burgos, J. E., & Palmer, D. C. (1993). A selectionist approach to reinforcement. *Journal of the Experimental Analysis of Behavior*, **60**, 17–40. [112, 372]

Donahoe, J. W., & Palmer, D. C. (1989). The interpretation of complex human behavior: Some reactions to *Parallel Distributed Processing*. *Journal of the Experimental Analysis of Behavior*, **51**, 399–416. [357, 360]

Donahoe, J. W., & Palmer, D. C. (1994). *Learning and complex behavior*. Boston: Allyn and Bacon. [129, 372]

Dorsey, M. F., Iwata, B. A., Ong, P., & McSween, T. E. (1980). Treatment of self-injurious behavior using a water mist: Initial response suppression and generalization. *Journal of Applied Behavior Analysis*, **13**, 343–353. [93]

Dreyfus, H. L. (1992). *What computers still can't do*. Cambridge, MA: MIT Press. [280, 359]

Dreyfus, H. L., & Dreyfus, S. E. (1986). *Mind over machine*. New York: Macmillan. [360]

Dube, W. V., McIlvane, W. J., Callahan, T. D., & Stoddard, L. T. (1993). The search for stimulus equivalence in nonverbal organisms. *Psychological Record*, **43**, 761–778. [154]

Duncker, K. (1945). On problem solving. *Psychological Monographs*, **58**, (5), Whole No. 270. [361]

Dunham, P. J. (1977). The nature of reinforcing stimuli. In W. K. Honig & J. E. R. Staddon (Eds.), *Handbook of operant behavior* (pp. 98–124). Englewood Cliffs, NJ: Prentice-Hall. [81]

Dworkin, B. R., & Miller, N. (1986). Failure to replicate visceral learning in the acute curarized rat preparation. *Behavioral Neuroscience*, **100**, 299–314. [115]

Ebbinghaus, H. (1885). *Über das Gedächtnis*. Leipzig: Duncker & Humblot (*Memory*, tr. H. A. Ruger & C. E. Bussenius, New York: Teachers College, 1913; reprinted by Dover, 1964). [248, 301, 304, 342, 366]

Eckerman, D. A., Hienz, R. D., Stern, S., & Kowlowitz, V. (1980). Shaping the location of a pigeon's peck: Effect of rate and size of shaping steps. *Journal of the Experimental Analysis of Behavior*, **33**, 299–310. [112]

Eimas, P. D., Siqueland, E. R. Jusczyk, P., & Vigorito, J. (1971). Speech perception in early infancy. *Science*, **171**, 303–306. [242]

Eisenberger, R., & Cameron, J. (1996). Detrimental effects of reward: Reality or myth? *American Psychologist*, **51**, 1153–1166. [270]

Eisenberger, R., Karpman, M., & Trattner, T. (1967). What is the necessary and sufficient condition for reinforcement in the contingency situation? *Journal of Experimental Psychology*, **74**, 342–350. [81]

Epstein, R. (1981). On pigeons and people: A preliminary look at the Columban Simulation Project. *Behavior Analyst*, **4**, 43–55. [363]

Epstein, R., Lanza, R. P., & Skinner, B. F. (1980). Symbolic communication between two pigeons (*Columba livia domestica*). *Science*, **207**, 543–545. [277]

Epstein, R., Lanza, R. P., & Skinner, B. F. (1981). "Self-awareness" in the pigeon. *Science*, **212**, 695–696. [229]

Epstein, R., & Skinner, B. F. (1980). Resurgence of responding after the cessation of response-independent reinforcement. *Proceedings of the National Academy of Sciences*, **77**, 6251–6253. [73]

Erdelyi, M. H., & Kleinbard, J. (1978). Has Ebbinghaus decayed with time?: The growth of recall (hypermnesia) over days. *Journal of Experimental Psychology: Human Learning and Memory*, **4**, 275–289. [343]

Esper, E. A. (1973). *Analogy and association in linguistics and psychology*. Athens, GA: University of Georgia Press. [161, 253, 295, 296]

Estes, W. K. (1944). An experimental study of punishment. *Psychological Monographs*, **57**, No. 263. [91]

Estes, W. K. (1964). All-or-none processes in learning and retention. *American Psychologist*, **19**, 16–25. [305]

Estes, W. K. (1971). Reward in human learning: Theoretical issues and strategic choice points (pp. 16–36). In R. Glaser (Ed.), *The nature of reinforcement*. New York: Academic Press. [158]

Estes, W. K. (1976). The cognitive side of probability learning. *Psychological Review*, **83**, 37–64. [361]

Estes, W. K., & Skinner, B. F. (1941). Some quantitative properties of anxiety. *Journal of Experimental Psychology*, **29**, 390–400. [214]

Falk, J. L. (1977). The origin and functions of adjunctive behavior. *Animal Learning and Behavior*, **5**, 325–335. [52]

Fantino, E., & Abarca, N. (1985). Choice, optimal foraging, and the delay-reduction hypothesis. *Behavioral and Brain Sciences*, **8**, 315–330. [191]

Favell, J. E., McGimsey, J. F., & Jones, M. L. (1978). The use of physical restraint in the treatment of self-injury and as positive reinforcement. *Journal of Applied Behavior Analysis*, **11**, 225–241. [79]

Fearing, F. (1930). *Reflex action*. Baltimore, MD: Williams and Wilkins. [42]

Felton, M., & Lyon, D. O. (1966). The post-reinforcement pause. *Journal of the Experimental Analysis of Behavior*, **9**, 131–134. [174]

Ferrari, M. & Harris, S. L. (1981). The limits and motivating potential of sensory stimuli as reinforcers for autistic children. *Journal of Applied Behavior Analysis*, **14**, 339–343. [77]

Ferster, C. B. (1958). Control of behavior in chimpanzees and pigeons by time out from positive reinforcement. *Psychological Monographs*, **72**, (8, Whole No. 461). [108]

Ferster, C. B. (1960). Intermittent reinforcement of matching to sample in the pigeon. *Journal of the Experimental Analysis of Behavior*, **3**, 259–272. [149]

Ferster, C. B., & Skinner, B. F. (1957). *Schedules of reinforcement*. New York: Appleton-Century-Crofts. [40, 70, 121, 164, 169, 195, 367]

Fetterman, J. G. (1996). Dimensions of stimulus complexity. *Journal of Experimental Psychology: Animal Behavior Processes*, **22**, 3–18. [160]

Field, T. M., Woodson, R., Greenberg, R., & Cohen, D. (1982). Discrimination and imitation of facial expressions by neonates. *Science*, **218**, 179–181. [226]

Fillenbaum, S. (1966). Memory for gist: Some relevant variables. *Language and Speech*, **9**, 217–227. [287]

Findley, J. D. (1962). An experimental outline for building and exploring multioperant behavior repertoires. *Journal of the Experimental Analysis of Behavior*, **5**, 113–166. [174]

Findley, J. D., & Brady, J. V. (1965). Facilitation of large ratio performance by use of conditioned reinforcement. *Journal of the Experimental Analysis of Behavior*, **8**, 125–129. [187]

Fischer, K. W. (1980). A theory of cognitive development: The control and construction of hierarchies of skills. *Psychological Review*, **87**, 477–531. [355]

Fisher, W., Piazza, C. C., Bowman, L. G., Hagopian, L. P., Owens, J. C., & Slevin, I. (1992). A comparison of two approaches for identifying reinforcers for persons with severe and profound disabilities. *Journal of Applied Behavior Analysis*, **25**, 491–498. [78]

Flavell, J. H., Friedrichs, A. G., & Hoyt, J. D. (1970). Developmental changes in memorization processes. *Cognitive Psychology*, **1**, 324–340. [333]

Fodor, J. A., & Bever, T. G. (1965). The psychological reality of linguistic segments. *Journal of Verbal Learning and Verbal Behavior*, **4**, 414–420. [283, 284]

Foss, D. J. (1988). Experimental psycholinguistics. *Annual Review of Psychology*, **39**, 301–348. [290, 345]

Fowler, C. A., Wolford, G., Slade, R., & Tassinary, L. (1981). Lexical access with and without awareness. *Journal of Experimental Psychology: General*, **110**, 341–362. [245]

Fowler, H., & Trapold, M. A. (1962). Escape performance as a function of delay of reinforcement. *Journal of Experimental Psychology*, **63**, 464–467. [99]

Fraenkel, G. S., & Gunn, D. L. (1961). *The orientation of animals*. New York: Dover. [36]

Freeman, R. D., Mitchell, D. E., & Millidot, M. A. (1972). Neural effect of partial visual deprivation in humans. *Science*, **175**, 1384–1386. [87]

Freud, S. (1917). *Wit and its relation to the unconscious* (trans. A. A. Brill). London: Allen & Unwin. [373]

Frey, P. W. (Ed.). (1977). *Chess skill in man and machine*. New York: Springer-Verlag. [359]

Fromkin, V. A. (1971). The non-anomalous nature of anomalous utterances. *Language*, **47**, 27–52. [243]

Fujita, K. (1983). Formation of the sameness-difference concept by Japanese monkeys from a small number of color stimuli. *Journal of the Experimental Analysis of Behavior*, **40**, 289–300. [151]

Galbicka, G., Kautz, M. A., & Jagers, T. (1993). Response acquisition under targeted percentile schedules: A continuing quandary for molar models of operant behavior. *Journal of the Experimental Analysis of Behavior*, **60**, 171–184. [179]

Galef, B. G., Jr., & Stein, M. (1985). Demonstrator influence on observer diet preference: Analysis of critical social interactions and olfactory signals. *Animal Learning and Behavior*, **13**, 31–38. [227]

Gallistel, C. R. (1980). *The organization of action*. Hillsdale, NJ: Erlbaum. [40, 43, 219]

Gallistel, C. R. (1990). *The organization of learning.* Cambridge, MA: MIT Press. [85, 144, 353]

Gallup, G. G., Jr. (1979). Self-awareness in primates. *American Scientist, 67,* 417–419. [229]

Galton, F. (1879). Psychometric experiments. *Brain, 2,* 149–162. [247, 288]

Garcia, E., Baer, D. M., & Firestone, I. (1971). The development of generalized imitation within topographically determined boundaries. *Journal of Applied Behavior Analysis, 4,* 101–112. [229]

Garcia, J., & Koelling, R. A. (1966). Relation of cue to consequence in avoidance learning. *Psychonomic Science, 4,* 123–124. [221, 222]

Gardner, R. A., & Gardner, B. T. (1969). Teaching sign language to a chimpanzee. *Science, 165,* 664–672. [277]

Garner, W. R. (1974). *The processing of information and structure.* Hillsdale, NJ: Erlbaum. [355]

Garrett, M., Bever, T. G., & Fodor, J. (1966). The active use of grammar in speech perception. *Perception and Psychophysics, 1,* 30–32. [284]

Geller, I. (1960). The acquisition and extinction of conditioned suppression as a function of the base-line reinforcer. *Journal of the Experimental Analysis of Behavior, 3,* 235–240. [214]

Gibbon, J., Farrell, L., Locurto, C. M., Duncan, H. J., & Terrace, H. S. (1980). Partial reinforcement in autoshaping with pigeons. *Animal Learning and Behavior, 8,* 45–59. [202]

Gibson, E. J. (1965). Learning to read. *Science, 148,* 1066–1072. [142, 244, 317]

Gibson, J. J. (1979). *The ecological approach to visual perception.* Boston: Houghton Mifflin. [9, 129]

Gillan, D. J. (1981). Reasoning in the chimpanzee: II. Transitive inference. *Journal of Experimental Psychology: Animal Behavior Processes, 7,* 150–164. [277]

Glanzer, M., & Cunitz, A. R. (1966). Two storage mechanisms in free recall. *Journal of Verbal Learning and Verbal Behavior, 5,* 351–360. [307]

Glanzer, M., & Dolinsky, R. (1965). The anchor for the serial position curve. *Journal of Verbal Learning and Verbal Behavior, 4,* 267–273. [303]

Glaze, J. A. (1928). The association value of nonsense syllables. *Journal of Genetic Psychology, 35,* 255–267. [288, 303]

Gleick, J. (1987). *Chaos.* New York: Viking. [32]

Gleitman, L. R., & Rozin, P. (1973). Teaching reading by use of a syllabary. *Reading Research Quarterly, 8,* 447–483. [244, 310]

Glencross, D. J. (1977). Control of skilled movements. *Psychological Bulletin, 84,* 14–29. [221]

Glucksberg, S., Gildea, P., & Bookin, H. B. (1982). On understanding nonliteral speech: Can people ignore metaphors? *Journal of Verbal Learning and Verbal Behavior, 21,* 85–98. [290]

Goldiamond, I. (1966). Perception, language, and conceptualization rules. In B. Kleinmuntz (Ed.), *Problem solving* (pp. 183–224). New York: Wiley. [310]

Gollub, L. R. (1977). Conditioned reinforcement: Schedule effects. In W. K. Honig & J. E. R. Staddon (Eds.), *Handbook of operant behavior* (pp. 288–312). Englewood Cliffs, NJ: Prentice-Hall. [186, 187]

Gormezano, I. (1972). Investigations of defense and reward conditioning in the rabbit. In A. H. Black & W. F. Prokasy (Eds.), *Classical conditioning II* (pp. 151–181). New York: Appleton-Century-Crofts. [201]

Gould, S. J. (1975). Darwin's "Big Book." *Science, 188,* 824–827. [374]

Gould, S. J. (1977). *Ontogeny and phylogeny.* Cambridge, MA: Harvard University Press. [31, 369]

Gould, S. J. (1989). *Wonderful life.* New York: Norton. [29]

Gould, S. J. (1996). *Full house.* New York: Harmony Books. [33]

Gould, S. J., & Lewontin, R. C. (1979). The spandrels of San Marco and the Panglossian paradigm: A critique of the adaptationist programme. *Proceedings of the Royal Society of London B, 205,* 581–598. [35, 36, 293]

Gouzoules, S., Gouzoules, H., & Marler, P. (1984). Rhesus monkey (*Macaca mulatta*) screams: Representational signalling in the recruitment of agonistic aid. *Animal Behaviour, 32,* 182–193. [227, 276]

Graefe, T. M., & Watkins, M. J. (1980). Picture rehearsal: An effect of selectively attending to pictures no longer in view. *Journal of Experimental Psychology: Human Learning and Memory, 6,* 156–162. [352]

Gray, J. (1953). *How animals move.* London: Cambridge University Press. [219]

Green, C. W., Reid, D. H., White, L. K., Halford, R. C., Brittain, D. P., & Gardner, S. M. (1988). Identifying reinforcers for persons with profound handicaps: Staff opinion versus systematic assessment of preferences. *Journal of Applied Behavior Analysis, 21,* 31–43. [78]

Green, D. M., & Swets, J. A. (1966). *Signal detection theory and psychophysics.* New York: Wiley. [268]

Greenberg, J. H. (Ed.) (1966). *Universals of language.* Cambridge, MA: MIT Press. [291]

Greenspoon, J. (1955). The reinforcing effect of two spoken sounds on the frequency of two responses. *American Journal of Psychology, 68,* 409–416. [262, 263]

Grosch, J., & Neuringer, A. (1981). Self-control in pigeons under the Mischel paradigm. *Journal of the Experimental Analysis of Behavior, 35,* 3–21. [195]

Groves, P. M., & Thompson, R. F. (1970). Habituation: A dual-process theory. *Psychological Review, 77,* 419–450. [50]

Guthrie, E. R. (1935). *The psychology of learning.* New York: Harper. [204, 367]

Guthrie, E. R., & Horton, G. P. (1946). *Cats in a puzzle box.* New York: Rinehart. [76]

Guttman, N. (1959). Generalization gradients around stimuli associated with different reinforcement schedules. *Journal of Experimental Psychology, 58,* 335–340. [138]

Guttman, N., & Kalish, H. I. (1956). Discriminability and stimulus generalization. *Journal of Experimental Psychology, 51,* 79–88. [138]

Haber, R. N. (1969). Eidetic images. *Scientific American, 220,* 36–44. [351]

Hadamard, J. (1949). *The psychology of invention in the mathematical field.* Princeton, NJ: Princeton University Press. [328]

Hailman, J. P. (1969). How an instinct is learned. *Scientific American, 221* (6), 98–106. [18]

Hall, R. V., Lund, D., & Jackson, D. (1968). Effects of teacher attention on study behavior. *Journal of Applied Behavior Analysis, 1,* 1–12. [78]

Hall, W. G., & Oppenheim, R. W. (1987). Developmental psychobiology: Prenatal, perinatal, and early postnatal aspects of behavioral development. *Annual Review of Psychology, 38,* 91–128. [40, 54]

Hanson, H. M. (1959). Effects of discrimination training on stimulus generalization. *Journal of Experimental Psychology, 58,* 321–334. [137, 138]

Harlow, H. F. (1949). The formation of learning sets. *Psychological Review, 56,* 51–65. [155]

Harlow, H. F., & Harlow, M. K. (1966). Learning to love. *American Scientist, 54,* 244–272. [223]

Harris, A. H., & Turkkan, J. S. (1981). Generalization of conditioned blood pressure elevations: Schedule and stimulus control effects. *Physiology and Behavior, 26,* 935–940. [115]

Harris, C. S. (1965). Perceptual adaptation to inverted, reversed, and displaced vision. *Psychological Review, 72,* 419–444. [86]

Harris, M. (1977). *Cannibals and kings.* New York: Random House. [225, 372]

Hart, B. L. (1973). Reflexive behavior. In G. Bermant (Ed.), *Perspectives on animal behavior* (pp. 171–193). Glenview, IL: Scott, Foresman. [37]

Hart, B. M., Reynolds, N. J., Baer, D. M., Brawley, E. R., & Harris, F. R. (1968). Effect of contingent and non-contingent social reinforcement on the cooperative play of a preschool child. *Journal of Applied Behavior Analysis, 1,* 73–76. [75]

Hart, B., & Risley, T. R. (1980). In vivo language intervention: Unanticipated general effects. *Journal of Applied Behavior Analysis, 13,* 407–432. [294]

Hart, B., & Risley, T. R. (1995). *Meaningful differences in the everyday experience of young American children.* Baltimore: Paul H. Brookes. [294]

Hartman, A. M. (1975). Analysis of conditions leading to the regulation of water flow by a beaver. *Psychological Record, 25,* 427–431. [104]

Harzem, P., Lee, I., & Miles, T. R. (1976). The effects of pictures on learning to read. *British Journal of Educational Psychology, 46,* 318–322. [369]

Hasher, L., & Griffin, M. (1978). Reconstructive and reproductive processes in memory. *Journal of Experimental Psychology, 4,* 318–330. [328]

Hayes, K., & Hayes, C. (1951). The intellectual development of a home-raised chimpanzee. *Proceedings of the American Philosophical Society, 95,* 105–109. [243, 276]

Hayes, S. C. (1994). Relational frame theory: A functional approach to verbal events. In S. C. Hayes, L. J. Hayes, M. Sato, & K. Ono (Eds.), *Behavior analysis of language and cognition* (pp. 9–30). Reno, NV: Context Press. [151, 158]

Hayes, S. C., Zettle, R. D., & Rosenfarb, I. (1989). Rule-following. In S. C. Hayes (Ed.), *Rule-*

governed behavior: Cognition, contingencies, and instructional control (pp. 191–220). New York: Plenum. [266]

Healy, A. F. (1976). Detection errors on the word *the*: Evidence for reading units larger than letters. *Journal of Experimental Psychology: Human Perception and Performance, 2,* 235–242. [309]

Hearst, E. (1958). The behavioral effects of some temporally defined schedules of reinforcement. *Journal of the Experimental Analysis of Behavior, 1,* 45–55. [171]

Hearst, E., Besley, S., & Farthing, G. W. (1970). Inhibition and the stimulus control of operant behavior. *Journal of the Experimental Analysis of Behavior, 14,* 373–409. [138]

Hearst, E., & Jenkins, H. M. (1974). *Sign-tracking: The stimulus-reinforcer relation and directed action.* Austin, TX: Psychonomic Society. [213]

Hearst, E., Koresko, M. B., & Poppen, R. (1964). Stimulus generalization and the response-reinforcement contingency. *Journal of the Experimental Analysis of Behavior, 7,* 369–379. [137]

Hebb, D. O. (1949). *The organization of behavior.* New York: Wiley. [372]

Hebb, D. O. (1956). The distinction between "classical" and "instrumental." *Canadian Journal of Psychology, 10,* 165–166. [210]

Hefferline, R. F. (1958). The role of proprioception in the control of behavior. *Transactions of the New York Academy of Sciences, 20,* 739–764. [232]

Hein, A., Vital-Durand, F., Salinger, W., & Diamond, R. (1979). Eye movements initiate visual-motor development in the cat. *Science, 22,* 1321–1322. [86]

Hein, H. (1972). The endurance of the mechanism-vitalism controversy. *Journal of the History of Biology, 5,* 159–188. [369]

Held, R., & Hein, A. (1963). Movement-produced stimulation in the development of visually guided behavior. *Journal of Comparative and Physiological Psychology, 56,* 872–876. [85]

Hemmes, N. S. (1973). Behavioral contrast in pigeons depends upon the operant. *Journal of Comparative and Physiological Psychology, 85,* 171–178. [183]

Henton, W. W., & Iversen, I. H. (1978). *Classical conditioning and operant conditioning.* New York: Springer-Verlag. [190]

Herman, L. M., & Forestell, P. H. (1985). Reporting presence or absence of named objects by a language-trained dolphin. *Neuroscience and Biobehavioral Reviews, 9,* 667–681. [276]

Herrick, R. M., Myers, J. L., & Korotkin, A. L. (1959). Changes in S^D and in S^Δ rates during the development of an operant discrimination. *Journal of Comparative and Physiological Psychology, 52,* 359–364. [129]

Herrnstein, R. J. (1961). Relative and absolute strength of response as a function of frequency of reinforcement. *Journal of the Experimental Analysis of Behavior, 4,* 267–272. [188]

Herrnstein, R. J. (1964a). Aperiodicity as a factor in choice. *Journal of the Experimental Analysis of Behavior, 7,* 179–182. [190]

Herrnstein, R. J. (1964b). Secondary reinforcement and rate of primary reinforcement. *Journal of the Experimental Analysis of Behavior, 7,* 27–36. [190]

Herrnstein, R. J. (1966). Superstition: A corollary of the principles of operant conditioning. In W. K. Honig (Ed.), *Operant behavior: Areas of research and application.* (pp. 33–51). New York: Appleton-Century-Crofts. [76, 171]

Herrnstein, R. J. (1970). On the law of effect. *Journal of the Experimental Analysis of Behavior, 13,* 243–266. [188]

Herrnstein, R. J., & Hineline, P. N. (1966). Negative reinforcement as shock-frequency reduction. *Journal of the Experimental Analysis of Behavior, 9,* 421–430. [105]

Herrnstein, R. J., & Loveland, D. H. (1975). Maximizing and matching on concurrent ratio schedules. *Journal of the Experimental Analysis of Behavior, 24,* 107–116. [146]

Herrnstein, R. J., Loveland, D. H., & Cable, C. (1976). Natural concepts in pigeons. *Journal of Experimental Psychology: Animal Behavior Processes, 2,* 285–311. [146]

Herrnstein, R. J., & Morse, W. H. (1957). Some effects of response-independent positive reinforcement on maintained operant behavior. *Journal of Comparative and Psychological Psychology, 50,* 461–467. [216]

Herrnstein, R. J., & Sidman, M. (1958). Avoidance conditioning as a factor in the effects of unavoidable shocks on food-reinforced behavior. *Journal of Comparative and Physiological Psychology, 51,* 380–385. [216]

Herz, R. S., & Engen, T. (1996). Odor memory: Review and analysis. *Psychonomic Bulletin and Review, 3,* 300–313. [347]

Hilgard, E. R. (1951). Method and procedures in the study of learning. In S. S. Stevens (Ed.), *Handbook of experimental psychology* (pp. 517–567). New York: Wiley. [60]

Hilgard, E. R., & Marquis, D. G. (1940). *Conditioning and learning*. New York: Appleton-Century-Crofts. [367]

Hineline, P. N. (1970). Negative reinforcement without shock reduction. *Journal of the Experimental Analysis of Behavior, 14*, 259–268. [105]

Hineline, P. N. (1977). Negative reinforcement and avoidance. In W. K. Honig & J. E. R. Staddon (Eds.), *Handbook of operant behavior* (pp. 364–414). Englewood Cliffs, NJ: Prentice-Hall. [105, 107]

Hineline, P. N. (1981). The several roles of stimuli in negative reinforcement. In P. Harzem & M. D. Zeiler (Eds.), *Predictability, correlation, and contiguity* (pp. 203–246). New York: Wiley. [105, 106]

Hinson, J. M., & Staddon, J. E. R. (1981). Maximizing on interval schedules. In C. M. Bradshaw, E. Szabadi, & C. F. Lowe (Eds), *Quantification of steady-state operant behavior* (pp. 35–47). Amsterdam: Elsevier/North-Holland. [188]

Hodges, A. (1985). *Alan Turing: The enigma of intelligence*. London: Unwin. [280]

Hoffman, H. S. (1996). *Amorous turkeys and addicted ducklings: A search for the causes of social attachment*. Boston: Authors Cooperative. [47, 57]

Hoffman, H. S., & Fleshler, M. (1959). Aversive control with the pigeon. *Journal of the Experimental Analysis of Behavior, 2*, 213–218. [99]

Hoffman, H. S., & Fleshler, M. (1962). The course of emotionality in the development of avoidance. *Journal of Experimental Psychology, 64*, 288–294. [217]

Hoffman, M. L. (1975). Developmental synthesis of affect and cognition and its implications for altruistic motivation. *Developmental Psychology, 11*, 607–622. [227]

Hogan, J. A. (1971). The development of a hunger system in young chicks. *Behavior, 39*, 128–201. [55]

Holland, J. G. (1958). Human vigilance. *Science, 128*, 61–67. [173]

Holland, P. C., & Ross, R. T. (1981). Within compound associations in serial compound conditioning. *Journal of Experimental Psychology: Animal Behavior Processes, 7*, 228–241. [209]

Hollard, V. D., & Delius, J. D. (1982). Rotational invariance in visual pattern recognition by pigeons and humans. *Science, 218*, 804–806. [350]

Holt, G. L., & Shafer, J. N. (1973). Function of intertrial interval in matching-to-sample. *Journal of the Experimental Analysis of Behavior, 19*, 181–186. [150]

Holz, W. C., & Azrin, N. H. (1961). Discriminative properties of punishment. *Journal of the Experimental Analysis of Behavior, 4*, 225–232. [96, 97]

Honig, W. K. (1962). Prediction of preference, transposition, and transposition-reversal from the generalization gradient. *Journal of Experimental Psychology, 64*, 239–248. [317]

Honig, W. K., Boneau, C. A., Burstein, K. R., & Pennypacker, H. S. (1963). Positive and negative generalization gradients obtained after equivalent training conditions. *Journal of Comparative and Physiological Psychology, 56*, 111–116. [139]

Horne, P. J., & Lowe, C. F. (1996). On the origins of naming and other symbolic behavior. *Journal of the Experimental Analysis of Behavior, 65*, 185–241. [154, 256, 292]

Hull, C. L. (1920). Quantitative aspects of the evolution of concepts: An experimental study. *Psychological Monographs, 28*, No. 123. [250]

Hull, C. L. (1934). Learning: II. The factor of the conditioned reflex. In C. Murchison (Ed.), *Handbook of general experimental psychology* (pp. 382–455). Worchester, MA: Clark University Press. [201]

Hull, C. L. (1943). *Principles of behavior*. New York: Appleton-Century-Crofts. [11, 101, 204]

Hulse, S. H., Cynx, J., & Humpal, J. (1984). Cognitive processing of pitch and rhythm structures by birds. In H. L. Roitblat, T. G. Bever, & H. S. Terrace (Eds.), *Animal cognition* (pp. 183–198). Hillsdale, NJ: Erlbaum. [276]

Hunter, W. S. (1928). The behavior of raccoons in a double-alternation temporal maze. *Journal of Genetic Psychology, 35*, 374–388. [123]

Hursh, S. R. (1980). Economic concepts for the analysis of behavior. *Journal of the Experimental Analysis of Behavior, 34*, 219–238. [167]

Huttenlocher, J. (1968). Constructing spatial images: A strategy in reasoning. *Psychological Review, 75*, 550–560. [352]

Huxley, R. (1970). The development of the correct use of subject personal pronouns in two children. In G. B. F. d'Arcais & W. J. M. Levelt (Eds.), *Advances in psycholinguistics* (pp. 141–165). Amsterdam: Elsevier/North-Holland. [295]

Intraub, H. (1979). The role of implicit naming in pictorial encoding. *Journal of Experimental Psychology: Human Learning and Memory, 5*, 78–87. [326]

Ison, J. R., & Hoffman, H. S. (1983). Reflex modification in the domain of startle: II. The anomalous history of a robust and ubiquitous phenomenon. *Psychological Bulletin, 94*, 3–17. [50, 204]

Iwata, B. A., Pace, G. M., Cowdery, G. E., & Miltenberger, R. G. (1994). What makes extinction work: An analysis of procedural form and function. *Journal of Applied Behavior Analysis, 27*, 131–144. [119]

Iwata, B. A., Pace, G. M., Kalsher, M. J., Cowdery, G. E., & Cataldo, M. F. (1990). Experimental analysis and extinction of self-injurious escape behavior. *Journal of Applied Behavior Analysis, 23*, 11–27. [119]

Jacobs, J. (1887). Experiments on "prehension." *Mind, 12*, 75–79. [338]

James, W. (1890). *The principles of psychology. Volume 1.* New York: Holt. [159]

Jans, J. E., & Catania, A. C. (1980). Short-term remembering of discriminative stimuli in pigeons. *Journal of the Experimental Analysis of Behavior, 34*, 177–183. [320]

Jaynes, J. (1976). *The origin of consciousness in the breakdown of the bicameral mind.* Boston, MA: Houghton Mifflin. [230, 253, 270, 278, 296]

Jenkins, H. M., & Harrison, R. H. (1960). Effect of discrimination training on auditory generalization. *Journal of Experimental Psychology, 59*, 246–253. [136]

Jenkins, H. M., & Moore, B. R. (1973). The form of the auto-shaped response with food or water reinforcers. *Journal of the Experimental Analysis of Behavior, 20*, 163–181. [213]

Jenkins, H. M., & Sainsbury, R. S. (1970). Discrimination learning with the distinctive feature on positive or negative trials. In D. I. Mostofsky (Ed.), *Attention: Contemporary theory and analysis* (pp. 239–273). New York: Appleton-Century-Crofts. [140, 182]

Jenkins, J. G., & Dallenbach, K. M. (1924). Obliviscence during sleep and waking. *American Journal of Psychology, 35*, 605–612. [343]

Jennings, H. S. (1906). *Behavior of the lower organisms.* New York: Macmillan. [366]

Johanson, I. B., & Hall, W. G. (1979). Appetitive learning in 1-day-old rat pups. *Science, 205*, 419–421. [40]

Johnson, D. F., & Cumming, W. W. (1968). Some determiners of attention. *Journal of the Experimental Analysis of Behavior, 11*, 157–166. [134]

Johnson, K. R., & Layng, T. V. J. (1992). Breaking the structuralist barrier: Literacy and numeracy with fluency. *American Psychologist, 47*, 1475–1490. [72, 161, 162]

Johnson, M. K., & Hasher, L. (1987). Human learning and memory. *Annual Review of Psychology, 38*, 631–668. [345]

Johnson, M. K., & Raye, C. L. (1981). Reality monitoring. *Psychological Review, 88*, 67–85. [334]

Johnson, N. F. (1965). The psychological reality of phrase-structure rules. *Journal of Verbal Learning and Verbal Behavior, 4*, 469–475. [283]

Johnson, P. (1982). The functional equivalence of imagery and movement. *Quarterly Journal of Experimental Psychology, 34A*, 349–365. [351]

Jonçich, G. (1968). *The sane positivist. A biography of Edward L. Thorndike.* Middletown, CT: Wesleyan University Press. [313]

Jost, A. (1897). Die Associationsfestigkeit in ihrer Abhängigkeit von der Verteilung der Wiederholungen. *Zeitschrift für Psychologie, 14*, 436–472. [343]

Kaas, J. H. (1991). Plasticity of sensory and motor maps in adult mammals. *Annual Review of Neuroscience, 14*, 137–167. [372]

Kamil, A. C., Yoerg, S. I., & Clements, K. C. (1988). Rules to leave by: Patch departure in foraging blue jays. *Animal Behaviour, 36*, 843–853. [191]

Kamin, L. J. (1956). The effects of termination of the CS and avoidance of the US on avoidance learning. *Journal of Comparative and Physiological Psychology, 49*, 420–424. [105]

Kamin, L. J. (1957). The retention of an incompletely learned avoidance response. *Journal of Comparative and Physiological Psychology. 50*, 457–460. [342]

Kamin, L. J. (1969). Predictability, surprise, attention and conditioning. In B. A. Campbell & R. M. Church (Eds.), *Punishment and aversive behavior* (pp. 279–296). New York: Appleton-Century-Crofts. [206]

Kandel, E. R., & Schwartz, J. H. (1982). Molecular biology of learning: Modulation of transmitter release. *Science, 218,* 433–443. [372]

Kawamura, S. (1959). The process of sub-culture propagation among Japanese macaques. *Primates, 2,* 43–60. [225]

Kazdin, A. E. (1977). The influence of behavior preceding a reinforced response on behavior change in the classroom. *Journal of Applied Behavior Analysis, 10,* 299–310. [76]

Kelleher, R. T., & Gollub, L. R. (1962). A review of positive conditioned reinforcement. *Journal of the Experimental Analysis of Behavior, 5,* 543–597. [183, 185]

Kelleher, R. T., Riddle, W. C., & Cook, L. (1962). Observing responses in pigeons. *Journal of the Experimental Analysis of Behavior, 5,* 3–13. [181]

Keller, F. S. (1941). Light aversion in the white rat. *Psychological Record, 4,* 235–250. [99, 100]

Keller, F. S. (1958). The phantom plateau. *Journal of the Experimental Analysis of Behavior, 1,* 1–13. [325, 367]

Keller, F. S., & Schoenfeld, W. N. (1950). *Principles of psychology.* New York: Appleton-Century-Crofts. [73, 145, 381]

Keller, K. (1974). The role of elicited responding in behavioral contrast. *Journal of the Experimental Analysis of Behavior, 21,* 249–257. [183, 213]

Kendall, S. B. (1965). Spontaneous recovery after extinction with periodic time-outs. *Psychonomic Science, 2,* 117–118. [73]

Kendler, H. H., & Kendler, T. S. (1962). Vertical and horizontal processes in problem solving. *Psychological Review, 69,* 1–16. [317]

Keppel, G., & Underwood, B. J. (1962). Proactive inhibition in short-term retention of single items. *Journal of Verbal Learning and Verbal Behavior, 1,* 153–156. [341]

Kiesler, C. A., Nisbett, R. E., & Zanna, M. P. (1969). On inferring one's beliefs from one's behavior. *Journal of Personality and Social Psychology, 11,* 321–327. [254]

Killeen, P. (1972). A yoked-chamber comparison of concurrent and multiple schedules. *Journal of the Experimental Analysis of Behavior, 18,* 13–22. [190]

Killeen, P. R. (1994). Mathematical principles of reinforcement. *Behavioral and Brain Sciences, 17,* 105–172. [177]

Killeen, P. R., & Amsel, A. (1987). The kinematics of locomotion toward a goal. *Journal of Experimental Psychology: Animal Behavior Processes, 13,* 92–101. [63]

Kimble, D. P., & Ray, R. S. (1965). Reflex habituation and potentiation in *Rana pipiens. Animal Behavior, 13,* 530–533. [50]

Kimble, G. A. (1947). Conditioning as a function of the time between conditioned and unconditioned stimuli. *Journal of Experimental Psychology, 37,* 1–15. [202]

Kimble, G. A. (1961). *Hilgard & Marquis' Conditioning and learning* (2nd edition). New York: Appleton-Century-Crofts. [1, 73, 367]

Kimble, G. A. (1993). A modest proposal for a minor revolution in the language of psychology. *Psychological Science, 4,* 253–255. [98]

Kimmel, H. D. (1976). Notes from "Pavlov's Wednesdays": Pavlov's law of effect. *American Journal of Psychology, 89,* 553–556. [210]

Kinchla, R. A., & Wolfe, J. M. (1979). The order of visual processing: "Top-down," "bottom-up," or "middle-out." *Perception and Psychophysics, 25,* 225–231. [355]

King, A. P., & West, M. J. (1985). Social metrics of song learning. *Learning and Motivation, 15,* 441–458. [113]

Kintsch, W. (1968). An experimental analysis of single stimulus tests and multiple-choice tests of recognition memory. *Journal of Experimental Psychology, 76,* 1–6. [311]

Kish, G. B. (1966). Studies of sensory reinforcement. In W. K. Honig (Ed.), *Operant Behavior: Areas of research and application* (pp. 109–159). New York: Appleton-Century-Crofts. [84]

Kluender, K. R., Diehl, R. L., & Killeen, P. R. (1987). Japanese quail can learn phonetic categories. *Science, 237,* 1195–1197. [276]

Köhler, W. (1927). *The mentality of apes* (tr. E. Winter; 2nd revised edition). London: Routledge & Kegan Paul. [15]

Köhler, W. (1929). *Gestalt psychology.* New York: Liveright. [328]

Kolers, P. A. (1966). Reading and talking bilingually. *American Journal of Psychology, 79,* 357–376. [246, 306, 346]

Kolers, P. A. (1985). Skill in reading and memory. *Canadian Journal of Psychology, 39,* 232–239. [245]

Kolers, P. A., & Palef, R. (1976). Knowing not. *Memory and Cognition, 4,* 553–558. [332, 334]

Kolers, P. A., & Roediger, H. L., III (1984). Procedures of mind. *Journal of Verbal Learning and Verbal Behavior, 23,* 425–449. [349]

Kolers, P. A., & Smythe, W. E. (1979). Images, symbols, and skills. *Canadian Journal of Psychology, 33,* 158–184. [351]

Konorski, J. (1948). *Conditioned reflexes and neuron organization.* New York: Cambridge University Press. [205]

Koriat, A. (1995). Dissociating knowing and the feeling of knowing: Further evidence for the accessibility model. *Journal of Experimental Psychology: General, 124,* 311–333. [231]

Krechevsky, I. (1932). Hypotheses' in rats. *Psychological Review, 39,* 516–532. [123, 124]

Kroodsma, D. E., & Miller, E. H. (Eds.) (1982). *Acoustic communication in birds. Volume 2.* New York: Academic Press. [227]

Kuczaj, S. A., III. (1977). The acquisition of regular and irregular past tense forms. *Journal of Verbal Learning and Verbal Behavior, 16,* 589–600. [296]

Lachman, J. L., Lachman, R., & Thronesbery, C. (1979). Metamemory through the adult life span. *Developmental Psychology, 15,* 543–551. [334]

Lakoff, G. (1987). *Women, fire, and dangerous things.* Chicago: University of Chicago. [160]

Lakoff, G., & Johnson, M. (1980). *Metaphors we live by.* Chicago: University of Chicago Press. [290]

Lalli, J. S., Mace, F. C., Wohn, T., & Livezey, K. (1995). Identification and modification of a response-class hierarchy. *Journal of Applied Behavior Analysis, 28,* 551–559. [120]

Lamb, M. R., & Riley, D. A. (1981). Effects of element arrangement on the processing of compound stimuli in pigeons (Columba livia). *Journal of Experimental Psychology: Animal Behavior Processes, 7,* 45–58. [151]

Landauer, T. K., & Meyer, D. E. (1972). Category size and semantic-memory retrieval. *Journal of Verbal Learning and Verbal Behavior, 11,* 539–549. [290]

Lane, H. (1960). Control of vocal responding in chickens. *Science, 1960, 132,* 37–38. [243]

Lane, H. (1965). The motor theory of speech perception: A critical review. *Psychological Review, 72,* 275–309. [241]

Lashley, K. S. (1930). The mechanism of vision. I. A method for rapid analysis of pattern vision in the rat. *Journal of Genetic Psychology, 37,* 453–460. [24, 367]

Lashley, K. S. (1951). The problem of serial order in behavior. In L. A. Jeffress (Ed.), *Cerebral mechanisms in behavior* (pp. 112–146). New York: Wiley. [125, 126]

Lattal, K. A. (1974). Combinations of response reinforcer dependence and independence. *Journal of the Experimental Analysis of Behavior, 22,* 357–362. [171]

Lawrence, D. H. (1949). Acquired distinctiveness of cues: Transfer between discriminations on the basis of familiarity with the stimulus. I. *Journal of Experimental Psychology, 39,* 770–784. [134]

Lea, S. E. G. (1979). Foraging and reinforcement schedules in the pigeon: Optimal and non-optimal aspects of choice. *Animal Behavior, 27,* 875–886. [135]

Lea, S. E. G., & Harrison, S. N. (1978). Discrimination of polymorphous stimulus sets by pigeons. *Quarterly Journal of Experimental Psychology, 30,* 521–537. [146]

Leitenberg, H. (1966). Conditioned acceleration and conditioned suppression in pigeons. *Journal of the Experimental Analysis of Behavior, 9,* 205–212. [216]

Lenneberg, E. H. (1962). Understanding language without ability to speak: A case report. *Journal of Abnormal and Social Psychology, 65,* 419–425. [287]

Lepper, M. R., & Greene, D. (Eds.). (1978). *The hidden costs of reward.* Hillsdale, NJ: Erlbaum. [269]

Lepper, M. R., Greene, D., & Nisbett, R. E. (1973). Undermining children's intrinsic interest with extrinsic reward: A test of the "overjustification" hypothesis. *Journal of Personality and Social Psychology, 28,* 129–137. [269]

Levitsky, D., & Collier, G. (1968). Schedule-induced wheel running. *Physiology and Behavior, 3,* 571–573. [53]

Ley, R. (1990). *A whisper of espionage.* Garden City Park, NY: Avery. [15]

Liberman, A. M. (1982). On finding that speech is special. *American Psychologist, 37,* 148–167. [241, 286]

Loeb, J. (1900). *Comparative physiology of the brain and comparative psychology.* New York: Putnam. [366]

Loftus, E. F. (1993). The reality of repressed memories. *American Psychologist, 48*, 518–537. [330]

Loftus, E. F., & Palmer, J. C. (1974). Reconstruction of automobile destruction: An example of the interaction between language and memory. *Journal of Verbal Learning and Verbal Behavior, 13*, 585–589. [328]

Loftus, E. F., & Zanni, G. (1975). Eyewitness testimony: The influence of the wording of a question. *Bulletin of the Psychonomic Society, 5*, 86–88. [329]

Logan, F. A. (1960). *Incentive.* New Haven, CT: Yale University Press. [78]

Loisette, A. (1899). *Assimilative memory, or, How to attend and never forget.* New York: Funk & Wagnalls. [322]

Long, G. M. (1980). Iconic memory: A review and critique of the study of short-term visual storage. *Psychological Bulletin, 88*, 785–820. [336]

Lorenz, K. (1937). The companion in the bird's world. *Auk, 54*, 245–273. [56]

Lovaas, O. I. (1964). Cue properties of words: The control of operant responding by rate and content of verbal operants. *Child Development, 35*, 245–256. [270]

Lovaas, O. I., & Simmons, J. Q. (1969). Manipulation of self-destruction in three retarded children. *Journal of Applied Behavior Analysis, 2*, 143–157. [119]

Lowe, C. F. (1980). Determinants of human operant behavior. In P. Harzem & M. D. Zeiler (Eds.), *Advances in the analysis of behavior. Volume 1.* New York: Wiley. [267]

Lubbock, J. (1882). *Ants, bees, and wasps.* New York: D. Appleton. [366]

Lubinski, D., & Thompson, T. (1987). An animal model of the interpersonal communication of interoceptive (private) states. *Journal of the Experimental Analysis of Behavior, 48*, 1–15. [232]

Luchins, A. S., & Luchins, E. H. (1950). New experimental attempts at preventing mechanization in problem solving. *Journal of General Psychology, 42*, 279–297. [360]

MacLeod, C. M. (1976). Bilingual episodic memory: Acquisition and forgetting. *Journal of Verbal Learning and Verbal Behavior, 15*, 347–364. [346]

MacPhail, E. M. (1968). Avoidance responding in pigeons. *Journal of the Experimental Analysis of Behavior, 11*, 629–632. [103]

Mahoney, M. J., & Bandura, A. (1972). Self-reinforcement in pigeons. *Learning and Motivation, 3*, 293–303. [232]

Maier, S. F., Albin, R. W., & Testa, T. J. (1973). Failure to learn to escape in rats previously exposed to inescapable shock depends on nature of escape response. *Journal of Comparative and Physiological Psychology, 85*, 581–592. [157]

Maier, S. F., Seligman, M. E. P., & Solomon, R. L. (1969). Pavlovian fear conditioning and learned helplessness: Effects on escape and avoidance behavior of (a) the CS-US contingency and (b) the independence of the US and voluntary responding. In B. A. Campbell & R. M. Church (Eds.), *Punishment and aversive behavior* (pp. 299–342). New York: Appleton-Century-Crofts. [157]

Maki, R. H. (1979). Right-left and up-down are equally discriminable in the absence of directional words. *Bulletin of the Psychonomic Society, 14*, 181–184. [269]

Malcolm, N. (1971). The myth of cognitive processes and structures. In T. Mischel (Ed.), *Cognitive development and epistemology* (pp. 385–392). New York: Academic Press. [349]

Malone, J. C. (1990). *Theories of learning.* Belmont, CA: Wadsworth. [120, 187]

Malott, R. W., & Cumming, W. W. (1964). Schedules of interresponse time reinforcement. *Psychological Record, 14*, 221–252. [121]

Manabe, K., Kawashima, T., & Staddon, J. E. R. (1995). Differential vocalization in budgerigars: Towards an experimental analysis of naming. *Journal of the Experimental Analysis of Behavior, 63*, 111–126. [276]

Mandler, J. M., & Johnson, N. S. (1977). Remembrance of things parsed: Story structure and recall. *Cognitive Psychology, 9*, 111–151. [346]

Marholin, D, II, & Steinman, W. M. (1977). Stimulus control in the classroom as a function of the behavior reinforced. *Journal of Applied Behavior Analysis, 10*, 465–478. [332]

Markman, E. M., Horton, M. S., & McLanahan, A. G. (1980). Classes and collections: Principles of organization in the learning of hierarchical relations. *Cognition, 8*, 227–241. [355]

Marler, P., & Peters, S. (1982). Long-term storage of learned birdsongs prior to production. *Animal Behaviour, 30*, 479–482. [276]

Martin, E. (1967). Relation between stimulus recognition and paired-associate learning. *Journal of Experimental Psychology*, **74**, 500–505. [312]

Matthews, B. A., Shimoff, E. H., & Catania, A. C. (1987). Saying and doing: A contingency-space analysis. *Journal of Applied Behavior Analysis*, **20**, 69–74. [270]

Matthews, B. A., Shimoff, E., Catania, A. C., & Sagvolden, T. (1977). Uninstructed human responding: Sensitivity to ratio and interval contingencies. *Journal of the Experimental Analysis of Behavior*, **27**, 453–467. [267]

Max, L. W. (1934). An experimental study of the motor theory of consciousness. I. History and critique. *Journal of General Psychology*, **11**, 112–125. [245]

Mayr, E. (1982). *The growth of biological thought.* Cambridge, MA: Harvard University Press. [32]

Mazur, J. E. (1986). *Learning and behavior.* Englewood Cliffs, NJ: Prentice-Hall. [221]

Mazur, J. E. (1991). Choice. In I. H. Iversen & K. A. Lattal (Eds.), *Experimental analysis of behavior. Part 1* (pp. 219–250). Amsterdam: Elsevier/North-Holland. [189]

Mazur, J. E. (1996). Procrastination by pigeons: Preference for larger, more delayed work requirements. *Journal of the Experimental Analysis of Behavior*, **65**, 159–171. [195]

McCloskey, M., & Santee, J. (1981). Are semantic memory and episodic memory distinct systems? *Journal of Experimental Psychology: Human Learning and Memory*, **7**, 66–71. [346]

McGeoch, J. A. (1942). *The psychology of human learning.* New York: Longmans, Green. [302, 313, 367]

McGeoch, J. A., & Irion, A. L. (1952). *The psychology of human learning* (2nd edition). New York: Longmans, Green. [367]

McGraw, M. B. (1945). *The neuromuscular maturation of the human infant.* New York: Columbia University Press. [55]

Meehl, P. E. (1950). On the circularity of the Law of Effect. *Psychological Bulletin*, **47**, 52–75. [70]

Mehler, J., Jusczyk, P., Lambert, G., Halsted, N., Bertoncini, J., & Amiel-Tison, C. (1988). A precursor of language acquisition in young infants. *Cognition*, **29**, 143–178. [242]

Meisch, R. A., & Thompson, T. (1971). Ethanol intake in the absence of concurrent food reinforcement. *Psychopharmacologia*, **22**, 72–79. [53]

Melton, A. W. (1963). Implications of short-term memory for a general theory of memory. *Journal of Verbal Learning and Verbal Behavior*, **2**, 1–21. [339, 340, 341]

Melton, A. W., & Martin, E. (Eds.), (1972). *Coding processes in human memory.* Washington, DC: Winston. [325]

Mervis, C. B., & Rosch, E. (1981). Categorization of natural objects. *Annual Review of Psychology*, **32**, 89–115. [290]

Michael, J. (1975). Positive and negative reinforcement, a distinction that is no longer necessary; or a better way to talk about bad things. *Behaviorism*, **3**, 33–44. [98]

Michael, J. (1982). Distinguishing between discriminative and motivational functions of stimuli. *Journal of the Experimental Analysis of Behavior*, **37**, 149–155. [26, 78]

Milgram, S. (1963). Behavioral study of obedience. *Journal of Abnormal and Social Psychology*, **67**, 371–378. [267]

Miller, G. A. (1956). The magical number seven plus or minus two: Some limits on our capacity for processing information. *Psychological Review*, **63**, 81–97. [325, 336, 338]

Miller, G. A. (1962). Some psychological studies of grammar. *American Psychologist*, **17**, 748–762. [286]

Miller, G. A., & Selfridge, J. A. (1950). Verbal context and the recall of meaningful material. *American Journal of Psychology*, **63**, 176–185. [248]

Miller, J. D., & Bowe, C. A. (1982). Roles of the qualities and locations of stimuli and responses in simple associative learning. *Pavlovian Journal of Biological Science*, **17**, 129–139. [221]

Miller, N. E., & Carmona, A. (1967). Modification of a visceral response, salivation in thirsty dogs, by instrumental training with water reward. *Journal of Comparative and Physiological Psychology*, **63**, 1–6. [115, 211]

Mineka, S., Davidson, M., Cook, M., & Keir, R. (1984). Observational learning of snake fear in Rhesus monkeys. *Journal of Abnormal Psychology*, **93**, 355–372. [227]

Mitchell, D., Scott, D. W., & Williams, K. D. (1973). Container neophobia and the rat's preference for earned food. *Behaviorial Biology, 9,* 613–624. [220]

Miyake, N., & Norman, D. A. (1979). To ask a question, one must know enough to know what is not known. *Journal of Verbal Learning and Verbal Behavior, 18,* 357–364. [334]

Moerk, E. L. (1980). Relationships between parental input frequencies and children's language acquisition: A reanalysis of Brown's data. *Journal of Child Language, 7,* 1–14. [293]

Moerk, E. L. (1983). A behavioral analysis of controversial topics in first language acquisition: Reinforcements, corrections, modeling, input frequencies, and the three-term contingency pattern. *Journal of Psycholinguistic Research, 12,* 129–155. [293]

Moerk, E. L. (1992). *First language: Taught and learned.* Baltimore: Paul H. Brookes. [292, 293, 294]

Moeser, S. D., & Tarrant, B. L. (1977). Learning a network of comparisons. *Journal of Experimental Psychology: Human Learning and Memory, 3,* 643–659. [346]

Montee, B. B., Miltenberger, R. G., & Wittrock, D. (1995). An experimental analysis of facilitated communication. *Journal of Applied Behavior Analysis, 28,* 189–200. [22]

Moore, B. R., & Stuttard, S. (1979). Dr. Guthrie and *Felis domesticus* or: Tripping over the cat. *Science, 205,* 1031–1033. [76]

Moore, C., & Frye, D. (1986). Context, conservation and the meanings of *more. British Journal of Developmental Psychology, 4,* 169–178. [292]

Morgan, C. L. (1920). *Animal behaviour.* London: Edward Arnold. [15]

Morgan, M. J., Fitch, M. D., Holman, J. G., & Lea, S. E. G. (1976). Pigeons learn the concept of an "A." *Perception, 5,* 57–66. [146]

Morse, W. H., & Kelleher, R. T. (1977). Determinants of reinforcement and punishment. In W. K. Honig & J. E. R. Staddon (Eds.), *Handbook of operant behavior* (pp. 174–200). Englewood Cliffs, NJ: Prentice-Hall. [95, 187]

Morse, W. H., & Skinner, B. F. (1958). Some factors involved in the stimulus control of operant behavior. *Journal of the Experimental Analysis of Behavior, 1,* 103–107. [397]

Mowrer, O. H. (1960). *Learning theory and behavior.* New York: Wiley. [205]

Mowrer, O. H., & Jones, H. M. (1943). Extinction and behavior variability as a function of effortfulness of task. *Journal of Experimental Psychology, 33,* 369–385. [75]

Moyer, R. S., & Dumais, S. T. (1978). Mental comparison. In G. H. Bower (Ed.), *The psychology of learning and motivation. Volume 12* (pp. 117–155). New York: Academic Press. [352]

Müller, G. E., & Pilzecker, A. (1900). Experimentelle Beiträge zür Lehre vom Gedächtnis. *Zeitschrift für Psychologie,* Ergänzungsband 1. [316]

Neisser, U., & Harsch, N. (1992). Phantom flashbulbs: False recollections of hearing the news about *Challenger.* In E. Winograd & U. Neisser (Eds.), *Affect and accuracy in recall: Studies of "flashbulb memories"* (pp. 9–31). New York: Cambridge University Press. [345]

Neiworth, J. J., & Rilling, M. E. (1987). A method for studying imagery in animals. *Journal of Experimental Psychology: Animal Behavior Processes, 13,* 203–214. [143]

Nelson, T. O. (1992). Metamemory. In L. R. Squire (Ed.), *The encyclopedia of learning and memory* (pp. 412–415). New York: Macmillan. [333]

Neuringer, A. (1986). Can people behave randomly?: The role of feedback. *Journal of Experimental Psychology: General, 115,* 62–75. [126, 161]

Neuringer, A., & Neuringer, M. (1974). Learning by following a food source. *Science, 184,* 1005–1008. [228]

Neuringer, A., & Schneider, B. A. (1968). Separating the effects of interreinforcement time and number of interreinforcement responses. *Journal of the Experimental Analysis of Behavior, 11,* 661–667. [190]

Nevin, J. A. (1969). Signal detection theory and operant behavior: A review of David M. Green & John A. Swets's *Signal detection theory and psychophysics. Journal of the Experimental Analysis of Behavior, 12,* 475–480. [268]

Nevin, J. A. (1992). An integrative model for the study of behavioral momentum. *Journal of the Experimental Analysis of Behavior, 57,* 301–316. [71, 122]

Newell, A., Shaw, J. C., & Simon, H. A. (1958). Elements of a theory of human problem solving. *Psychological Review, 65,* 151–166. [358]

Newman, S. E. (1972). In search of associative symmetry. In C. P. Duncan, L. Sechrest, & A. W.

Melton (Eds.), *Human memory* (pp. 133–153). New York: Appleton-Century-Crofts. [306]

Nisbett, R. E., & Wilson, T. D. (1977). Telling more than we can know: Verbal reports on mental processes. *Psychological Review, 84,* 231–259. [231]

Olton, D. S. (1979). Mazes, maps, and memory. *American Psychologist, 34,* 583–596. [134, 145]

Olton, D. S., & Samuelson, R. J. (1976). Remembrance of places passed: Spatial memory in rats. *Journal of Experimental Psychology: Animal Behavior Processes, 2,* 97–116. [135]

Orne, M. T. (1962). On the social psychology of the psychological experiment: With particular reference to demand characteristics and their implications. *American Psychologist, 17,* 776–783. [298]

Ortony, A., & Turner, J. (1990). What's basic about basic emotions? *Psychological Review, 97,* 315–331. [215]

Osgood, C. E. (1949). The similarity paradox in human learning: A resolution. *Psychological Review, 56,* 132–143. [315]

Osgood, C. E., Suci, G. J., & Tannenbaum, P. H. (1957). *The measurement of meaning.* Urbana, IL: University of Illinois. [288]

Overton, D. A. (1964). State-dependent or "dissociated" learning produced with phenobarbital. *Journal of Comparative and Physiological Psychology, 57,* 3–12. [332]

Page, S., & Neuringer, A. (1985). Variability is an operant. *Journal of Experimental Psychology: Animal Behavior Processes, 11,* 429–452. [126, 161]

Paivio, A. (1971). *Imagery and verbal processes.* New York: Holt, Rinehart & Winston. [326, 350]

Paivio, A. (1975). Neomentalism. *Canadian Journal of Psychology, 29,* 263–291. [351, 352]

Paniagua, F. A., & Baer, D. M. (1982). The analysis of correspondence training as a chain reinforceable at any point. *Child Development, 53,* 786–798. [270]

Parsons, H. M. (1974). What happened at Hawthorne? *Science, 183,* 922–932. [84]

Pavlov, I. P. (1927). *Conditioned reflexes* (tr. G. V. Anrep). London: Oxford University Press. [20, 21, 42, 199, 367]

Pavlov, I. P. (1957). *Experimental psychology and other essays.* New York: Philosophical Library. [367]

Peele, D. B., & Ferster, C. B. (1982). Autoshaped key pecking maintained by access to a social space. *Journal of the Experimental Analysis of Behavior, 38,* 181–189. [213]

Pennypacker, H. S., & Iwata, M. M. (1990). MammaCare: A case history in behavioural medicine. In D. E. Blackman & H. Lejeune (Eds.), *Behaviour analysis in theory and practice* (pp. 259–288). Hillsdale, NJ: Erlbaum. [142]

Pepperberg, I. M. (1988). The importance of social interaction and observation in the acquisition of communicative competence: Possible parallels between avian and human learning. In T. R. Zentall & B. G. Galef, Jr. (Eds.), *Social learning* (pp. 279–299). Hillsdale, NJ: Erlbaum. [276]

Peterson, L. R., & Peterson, M. J. (1959). Short-term retention of individual verbal items. *Journal of Experimental Psychology, 58,* 193–198. [339]

Peterson, N. (1960). Control of behavior by presentation of an imprinted stimulus. *Science, 132,* 1395–1396. [57]

Peterson, N. (1962). Effect of monochromatic rearing on the control of responding by wavelength. *Science, 136,* 774–775. [139]

Peterson, R. F. (1968). Some experiments on the organization of a class of imitative behaviors. *Journal of Applied Behavior Analysis, 1,* 225–235. [229]

Petroski, H. (1992). *The evolution of useful things.* New York: Knopf. [372]

Pfungst, O. (1911). *Clever Hans (the horse of Mr. Von Osten): A contribution to experimental animal and human psychology* (tr. C. L. Rahn). New York: Holt. [21, 22, 276]

Piaget, J., & Inhelder, B. (1969). *The psychology of the child* (tr. H. Weaver). New York: Basic Books. [355]

Pinker, S. (1984). *Language learnability and language development.* Cambridge, MA: Harvard University Press. [293]

Pinker, S. (1994). *The language instinct.* New York: Morrow. [292]

Pinker, S., & Bloom, P. (1990). Natural language and natural selection. *Behavioral and Brain Sciences, 13,* 707–784. [293]

Pitts, R. C., & Malagodi, E. F. (1991). Preference for less frequent shock under fixed-interval schedules of electric-shock presentation. *Journal of the Experimental Analysis of Behavior, 56,* 21–32. [96]

Platt, J. R. (1973). Percentile reinforcement: Paradigms for experimental analysis of response shaping. In G. H. Bower (Ed.), *The psychology of learning and motivation. Volume 7* (pp. 271–296). New York: Academic Press. [112]

Pliskoff, S. S., & Goldiamond, I. (1966). Some discriminative properties of fixed ratio performance in the pigeon. *Journal of the Experimental Analysis of Behavior, 9,* 1–9. [231]

Posner, M. I. (1978). *Chronometric explorations of mind.* Hillsdale, NJ: Erlbaum. [353]

Posner, M. I. (1982). Cumulative development of attentional theory. *American Psychologist, 37,* 168–179. [350]

Poulson, C. L. (1984). Operant theory and methodology in infant vocal conditioning. *Journal of Experimental Child Psychology, 38,* 103–113. [70, 242]

Poulson, C. L., Kymissis, E., Reeve, K. F., Andreatos, M., & Reeve, L. (1991). Generalized vocal imitation in infants. *Journal of Experimental Child Psychology, 51,* 267–279. [228, 241]

Powers, R. B., & Osborne, J. G. (1976). *Fundamentals of behavior.* St. Paul, MN: West Publishing. [20]

Pratkanis, A. R. (1992). The cargo-cult science of subliminal persuasion. *Skeptical Inquirer, 16,* 260–272. [328]

Premack, D. (1959). Toward empirical behavior laws: I. Positive reinforcement. *Psychological Review, 66,* 219–233. [79]

Premack, D. (1962). Reversibility of the reinforcement relation. *Science, 136,* 255–257. [79]

Premack, D. (1970). A functional analysis of language. *Journal of the Experimental Analysis of Behavior, 14,* 107–125. [277]

Premack, D. (1971). Catching up with common sense or two sides of a generalization: Reinforcement and punishment. In R. Glaser (Ed.), *The nature of reinforcement* (pp. 121–150). New York: Academic Press. [79, 93]

Provine, R. R. (1976). Development of function in nerve nets. In J. Fentress (Ed.), *Simpler networks and behavior* (pp. 203–220). Sunderland, MA: Sinauer. [55]

Provine, R. R. (1981). Development of wing-flapping and flight in normal and flap-deprived domestic chicks. *Developmental Psychobiology, 14,* 279–291. [219]

Provine, R. R. (1984). Wing-flapping during development and evolution. *American Scientist, 72,* 448–455. [34]

Provine, R. R. (1989a). Contagious yawning and infant imitation. *Bulletin of the Psychonomic Society, 27,* 125–126. [226]

Provine, R. R. (1989b). Faces as releasers of contagious yawning: An approach to face detection using normal human subjects. *Bulletin of the Psychonomic Society, 27,* 211–214. [219]

Provine, R. R. (1996). Laughter. *American Scientist, 84,* 38–45. [226]

Provine, R. R., & Fischer, K. R. (1989). Laughing, smiling, and talking: Relation to sleeping and social context in humans. *Ethology, 83,* 295–305. [219]

Pryor, K. (1985). *Don't shoot the dog!* New York: Bantam. [126, 161]

Pryor, K. W., Haag, R., & O'Reilly, J. (1969). The creative porpoise: Training for novel behavior. *Journal of the Experimental Analysis of Behavior, 12,* 653–661. [126, 161]

Pullum, G. K. (1991). *The great Eskimo vocabulary hoax and other irreverent essays on the study of language.* Chicago: University of Chicago. [292]

Rachlin, H. (1967). The effect of shock intensity on concurrent and single-key responding in concurrent-chain schedules. *Journal of the Experimental Analysis of Behavior, 10,* 87–93. [94]

Rachlin, H. (1971). On the tautology of the matching law. *Journal of the Experimental Analysis of Behavior, 15,* 249–251. [188]

Rachlin, H. (1974). Self-control. *Behaviorism, 2,* 94–107. [195]

Rachlin, H., & Baum, W. M. (1972). Effect of alternative reinforcement: Does the source matter? *Journal of the Experimental Analysis of Behavior, 18,* 231–241. [189]

Rachlin, H., & Burkhard, B. (1978). The temporal triangle: Response substitution in instrumental conditioning. *Psychological Review, 85,* 22–47. [81]

Rachlin, H., & Green, L. (1972). Commitment, choice and self-control. *Journal of the Experimental Analysis of Behavior, 17,* 15–22. [192, 193, 194]

Ratner, S. C. (1970). Habituation: Research and theory. In J. H. Reynierse (Ed.), *Current issues in animal learning* (pp. 55–84). Lincoln, NE: University of Nebraska Press. [50]

Reber, A. S. (1976). Implicit learning of synthetic languages: The role of instructional set. *Journal of Experimental Psychology: Human Learning and Memory*, **2**, 88–94. [269]

Reber, A. S. (1985). *The Penguin dictionary of psychology*. New York: Viking Penguin. [377]

Recanzone, G. H., Merzenich, M. M., Jenkins, W. M., Garjski, K. A., & Dinse, H. R. (1992). Topographic reorganization of the hand representation in cortical area 3b of owl monkeys trained in a frequency-discrimination task. *Journal of Neurophysiology*, **67**, 1031–1056. [372]

Reddy, M. J. (1979). The conduit metaphor—a case of frame conflict in our language about language. In A. Ortony (Ed.), *Metaphor and thought* (pp. 284–324). New York: Cambridge University Press. [290]

Reid, A. K., & Staddon, J. E. R. (1982). Schedule-induced drinking: Elicitation, anticipation, or behavior interaction? *Journal of the Experimental Analysis of Behavior*, **38**, 1–18. [53]

Reid, R. L. (1958). The role of the reinforcer as a stimulus. *British Journal of Psychology*, **49**, 202–209. [73, 397]

Rendall, D., Rodman, P. S., & Emond, R. E. (1996). Vocal recognition of individuals and kin in free-ranging rhesus monkeys. *Animal Behaviour*, **51**, 1007–1015. [276]

Repp, A. C., & Deitz, S. M. (1974). Reducing aggressive and self-injurious behavior of institutionalized retarded children through reinforcement of other behaviors. *Journal of Applied Behavior Analysis*, **7**, 313–325. [77]

Rescorla, R. A. (1967). Pavlovian conditioning and its proper control procedures. *Psychological Review*, **74**, 71–80. [205, 206]

Rescorla, R. A. (1968). Probability of shock in the presence and absence of CS in fear conditioning. *Journal of Comparative and Physiological Psychology*, **66**, 1–5. [217, 218]

Rescorla, R. A. (1980). *Pavlovian second-order conditioning*. Hillside, NJ: Erlbaum. [206, 208]

Rescorla, R. A. (1988). Pavlovian conditioning: It's not what you think it is. *American Psychologist*, **43**, 151–160. [206]

Rescorla, R. A., & Solomon, R. L. (1967). Two process learning theory: Relationships between Pavlovian conditioning and instrumental learning. *Psychological Review*, **74**, 151–182. [214]

Rescorla, R. A., & Wagner, A. R. (1972). A theory of Pavlovian conditioning: Variations in the effectiveness of reinforcement and nonreinforcement. In A. H. Black & W. F. Prokasy (Eds.), *Classical conditioning II* (pp. 64–99). New York: Appleton-Century-Crofts. [206]

Restle, F. (1957). Discrimination of cues in mazes: A resolution of the "place versus response" question. *Psychological Review*, **64**, 217–228. [134]

Revusky, S. H., & Garcia, J. (1970). Learned associations over long delays. In G. H. Bower (Ed.), *The psychology of learning and motivation. Volume 4* (pp. 1–44). New York: Academic Press. [221, 222]

Reyna, V. F. (1981). The language of possibility and probability: Effects of negation on meaning. *Memory and Cognition*, **9**, 642–650. [288]

Reynolds, G. S. (1961a). Attention in the pigeon. *Journal of the Experimental Analysis of Behavior*, **4**, 203–208. [133]

Reynolds, G. S. (1961b). Behavioral contrast. *Journal of the Experimental Analysis of Behavior*, **4**, 57–71. [183, 184]

Reynolds, G. S. (1966). Discrimination and emission of temporal intervals by pigeons. *Journal of the Experimental Analysis of Behavior*, **9**, 65–68. [231]

Riccio, D. C., Rabinowitz, V. C., & Axelrod, S. (1994). Memory: When less is more. *American Psychologist*, **49**, 917–926. [329]

Richards, R. W. (1988). The question of bidirectional associations in pigeons' learning of conditional discrimination tasks. *Bulletin of the Psychonomic Society*, **26**, 577–579. [153]

Richter, C. P. (1927). Animal behavior and internal drives. *Quarterly Review of Biology*, **2**, 307–343. [77]

Riess, B. F. (1946). Genetic changes in semantic conditioning. *Journal of Experimental Psychology*, **36**, 143–152. [274]

Risley, T. R. (1977). The development and maintenance of language: An operant model. In B. C. Etzel, J. M. LeBlanc, & D. M. Baer (Eds.), *New developments in behavioral research* (pp. 81–101). Hillsdale, NJ: Erlbaum. [242]

Risley, T. R., & Hart, B. (1968). Developing correspondence between the non-verbal and verbal behavior of preschool children. *Journal of Applied Behavior Analysis*, **1**, 267–281. [270]

Rizley, R. C., & Rescorla, R. A. (1972). Associations in second-order conditioning and sensory preconditioning. *Journal of Comparative and Physiological Psychology*, **81**, 1–11. [209]

Robinson, E. S., & Brown, M. A. (1926). Effect of serial position upon memorization. *American Journal of Psychology*, **37**, 538–552. [302]

Rock, I. (1957). The role of repetition in association learning. *American Journal of Psychology*, **70**, 186–193. [305]

Roediger, H. L., III. (1980). Memory metaphors in cognitive psychology. *Memory and Cognition*, **8**, 231–246. [324]

Roediger, H. L., III, & Craik, F. I. M. (Eds.). (1989). *Varieties of memory and consciousness.* Hillsdale, NJ: Erlbaum. [344]

Rogers-Warren, A. R., & Baer, D. M. (1976). Correspondence between saying and doing: Teaching children to share and praise. *Journal of Applied Behavior Analysis*, **9**, 335–354. [270]

Rosch, E. H. (1973). Natural categories. *Cognitive Psychology*, **4**, 328–350. [146, 290]

Rosenfarb, I. S., Newland, M. C., Brannon, S. E., & Howey, D. S. (1992). Effects of self-generated rules on the development of schedule-controlled behavior. *Journal of the Experimental Analysis of Behavior*, **58**, 107–121. [268]

Rosenfeld, H. M., & Baer, D. M. (1970). Unbiased and unnoticed verbal conditioning: The double agent robot procedure. *Journal of the Experimental Analysis of Behavior*, **14**, 99–105. [262, 263]

Rozin, P., & Kalat, J. W. (1971). Specific hungers and poison avoidance as adaptive specializations of learning. *Psychological Review*, **78**, 459–486. [221]

Rozin, P., Millman, L., & Nemeroff, C. (1986). Operation of the laws of sympathetic magic in disgust and other domains. *Journal of Personality and Social Psychology*, **50**, 703–712. [269]

Rudolph, R. L., Honig, W. K., & Gerry, J. E. (1969). Effects of monochromatic rearing on the acquisition of stimulus control. *Journal of Comparative and Physiological Psychology*, **67**, 50–57. [139]

Rudy, J. W., Vogt, M. B., & Hyson, R. L. (1984). A developmental analysis of the rat's learned reactions to gustatory and auditory stimulation. In R. Kail & N. E. Spear (Eds.), *Comparative perspectives on the development of memory* (pp. 181–208). Hillsdale, NJ: Erlbaum. [40]

Rumbaugh, D. M., & Gill, T. V. (1976). The mastery of language-type skills by the chimpanzee (*Pan*). *Annals of the New York Academy of Sciences*, **280**, 562–578. [277]

Rundus, D. (1977). Maintenance rehearsal and single-level processing. *Journal of Verbal Learning and Verbal Behavior*, **16**, 665–681. [338]

Rundus, D. (1980). Maintenance rehearsal and long-term recency. *Memory and Cognition*, **8**, 226–230. [338]

Rundus, D., & Atkinson, R. C. (1970). Rehearsal processes in free recall: A procedure for direct observation. *Journal of Verbal Learning and Verbal Behavior*, **9**, 99–105. [308]

Russell, E. S. (1916). *Form and function.* London: John Murray. [369]

Ryle, G. (1949). *The concept of mind.* New York: Barnes & Noble. [2]

Sachs, J. S. (1967). Recognition memory for syntactic and semantic aspects of connected discourse. *Perception and Psychophysics*, **2**, 437–442. [287, 346]

Salapatek, P., & Kessen, W. (1966). Visual scanning of triangles by the human newborn. *Journal of Experimental Child Psychology*, **3**, 155–167. [86]

Saugstad, P., & Raaheim, K. (1960). Problem solving, past experience and availability of functions. *British Journal of Psychology*, **51**, 97–104. [361]

Saunders, R. R., & Green, G. (1992). The nonequivalence of behavioral and mathematical equivalence. *Journal of the Experimental Analysis of Behavior*, **57**, 227–241. [154]

Savage-Rumbaugh, E. S. (1986). *Ape language.* New York: Columbia University Press. [276, 278]

Savage-Rumbaugh, E. S., Murphy, J., Sevcik, R. A., Brakke, K. E., Williams, S. L., & Rumbaugh, D. M. (1993). Language comprehension in ape and child. *Monographs of the Society for Research in Child Development*, **58** (3–4, Serial No. 233). [277]

Savage-Rumbaugh, E. S., Rumbaugh, D. M., & Boysen, S. (1978). Symbolic communication between two chimpanzees (*Pan troglodytes*). *Science*, **201**, 641–644. [277]

Savage-Rumbaugh, E. S., Rumbaugh, D. M., Smith, S. T., & Lawson, J. (1980). Reference: The linguistic essential. *Science*, **210**, 922–925. [277]

Sawisch, L. P., & Denny, M. R. (1973). Reversing the reinforcement contingencies of eating and keypecking behaviors. *Animal Learning and Behavior*, 1, 189–192. [80]

Schlinger, H., & Blakely, E. (1987). Function-altering effects of contingency-specifying stimuli. *The Behavior Analyst*, 10, 41–45. [265]

Schlosberg, H. (1937). The relationship between success and the laws of conditioning. *Psychological Review*, 44, 379–394. [205, 210]

Schoenfeld, W. N. (1950). An experimental approach to anxiety, escape and avoidance behavior. In P. H. Hoch (Ed.), *Anxiety* (pp. 70–99). New York: Grune & Stratton. [105]

Schoenfeld, W. N. (1966). Some old work for modern conditioning theory. *Conditional Reflex*, 1, 219–223. [54]

Schoenfeld, W. N. (1969). "Avoidance" in behavior theory. *Journal of the Experimental Analysis of Behavior*, 12, 669–674. [105]

Schoenfeld, W. N., & Cole, B. K. (1972). *Stimulus schedules: The t-τ systems*. New York: Harper & Row. [164, 179]

Schooler, J. W., & Engstler-Schooler, T. Y. (1990). Verbal overshadowing of visual memories: Some things are better left unsaid. *Cognitive Psychology*, 22, 36–71. [269]

Schroeder, S. R., & Holland, J. G. (1968). Operant control of eye movements. *Journal of Applied Behavior Analysis*, 1, 161–166. [86]

Schuster, C. R., & Balster, R. L. (1977) The discriminative stimulus properties of drugs. In T. Thompson & P. Dews (Eds.), *Advances in behavioral pharmacology* (Vol. 1, pp. 85–138). New York: Academic Press. [142]

Schusterman, R. J., & Kastak, D. (1993). A California sea lion (*Zalophus californianus*) is capable of forming equivalence relations. *Psychological Record*, 43, 823–839. [154, 276]

Schwartz, B. (1974). On going back to nature: A review of Seligman & Hager's *Biological boundaries of learning*. *Journal of the Experimental Analysis of Behavior*, 21, 183–198. [221]

Schwartz, B. (1982). Reinforcement-induced stereotypy: How not to teach people to discover rules. *Journal of Experimental Psychology: General*, 111, 23–59. [269]

Schwartz, B., Hamilton, B., & Silberberg, A. (1975). Behavioral contrast in the pigeon: A study of the duration of key pecking maintained on multiple schedules of reinforcement. *Journal of the Experimental Analysis of Behavior*, 24, 199–206. [183]

Schwartz, B., & Williams, D. R. (1972). Two different kinds of key peck in the pigeon: Some properties of responses maintained by negative and positive response-reinforcer contingencies. *Journal of the Experimental Analysis of Behavior*, 18, 201–216. [213]

Sebeok, T. A., & Rosenthal, R. (Eds.). (1981). *The Clever Hans phenomenon: Communication with horses, whales, apes, and people*. New York: New York Academy of Sciences. [276]

Secan, K. E., Egel, A. L., & Tilley, C. S. (1989). Acquisition, generalization, and maintenance of question-answering skills in autistic children. *Journal of Applied Behavior Analysis*, 22, 181–196. [229]

Sechenov, I. M. (1863). *Reflexes of the brain* (tr. S. Belsky). (reprinted Cambridge, MA: MIT Press, 1965). [44, 54, 55]

Seligman, M. E. P. (1970). On the generality of the laws of learning. *Psychological Review*, 77, 406–418. [103, 221]

Seyfarth, R. M., Cheney, D. L., & Marler, P. (1980). Monkey responses to three different alarm calls: Evidence for predator classification and semantic communication. *Science*, 210, 801–803. [227, 276]

Shahn, B. B. (1972). *Ben Shahn*. New York: Abrams. [244]

Sheffield, F. D. (1965). Relation between classical conditioning and instrumental learning. In W. F. Prokasy (Ed.), *Classical conditioning* (pp. 302–322). New York: Appleton-Century-Crofts. [108, 211]

Shepard, R. N. (1967). Recognition memory for words, sentences, and pictures. *Journal of Verbal Learning and Verbal Behavior*, 6, 156–163. [311]

Shepard, R. N. & Metzler, J. (1971). Mental rotation of three-dimensional objects. *Science*, 171, 701–703. [350, 351]

Sherman, T. M., & Cormier, W. H. (1974). An investigation of the influence of student behavior on teacher behavior. *Journal of Applied Behavior Analysis*, 7, 11–21. [78]

Sherrington, C. (1906). *The integrative action of the nervous system*. New York: Scribner's. [42]

Shettleworth, S. J. (1978). Reinforcement and the organization of behavior in golden hamsters: Punishment of three action patterns. *Learning and Motivation*, 9, 99–123. [95]

Shiffrin, R. M., & Atkinson, R. C. (1969). Storage and retrieval processes in long-term memory. *Psychological Review*, **76**, 179–193. [338]

Shimoff, E., Catania, A. C., & Matthews, B. A. (1981). Uninstructed human responding: Sensitivity of low-rate performance to schedule contingencies. *Journal of the Experimental Analysis of Behavior*, **36**, 207–220. [267]

Shimp, C. P. (1966). Probabilistically reinforced choice behavior in pigeons. *Journal of the Experimental Analysis of Behavior*, **9**, 443–455. [188]

Shimp, C. P. (1976). Organization in memory and behavior. *Journal of the Experimental Analysis of Behavior*, **26**, 113–130. [346]

Shimp, C. P., Sabulsky, S. L., & Childers, L. J. (1989). Preference for starting and finishing behavior patterns. *Journal of the Experimental Analysis of Behavior*, **52**, 341–352. [143, 231]

Shull, R. L. (1995). Interpreting cognitive phenomena: Review of Donahoe and Palmer's *Learning and Complex Behavior*. *Journal of the Experimental Analysis of Behavior*, **63**, 347–358. [372]

Sidman, M. (1952). A note on functional relations obtained from group data. *Psychological Bulletin*, **49**, 263–269. [63]

Sidman, M. (1953). Two temporal parameters in the maintenance of avoidance behavior by the white rat. *Journal of Comparative and Physiological Psychology*, **46**, 253–261. [102]

Sidman, M. (1960). *Tactics of scientific research.* New York: Basic Books. [82]

Sidman, M. (1971). The behavioral analysis of aphasia. *Journal of Psychiatric Research*, **8**, 413–422. [246]

Sidman, M. (1994). *Equivalence relations and behavior: A research story.* Boston, MA: Authors Cooperative. [152]

Sidman, M., Cresson, O., Jr., & Willson-Morris, M. (1974). Acquisition of matching to sample via mediated transfer. *Journal of the Experimental Analysis of Behavior*, **22**, 261–273. [153]

Sidman, M., Herrnstein, R. J., & Conrad, D. G. (1957). Maintenance of avoidance behavior by unavoidable shocks. *Journal of Comparative and Physiological Psychology*, **50**, 553–557. [215]

Sidman, M., & Stoddard, L. T. (1967). The effectiveness of fading in programming a simultaneous form discrimination for retarded children. *Journal of the Experimental Analysis of Behavior*, **10**, 3–15. [141]

Sidman, M., Wynne, C. K., Maguire, R. W., & Barnes, T. (1989). Functional classes and equivalence relations. *Journal of the Experimental Analysis of Behavior*, **52**, 261–274. [154]

Siegel, S. (1977). Morphine tolerance acquisition as an associative process. *Journal of Experimental Psychology: Animal Behavior Processes*, **3**, 1–13. [201]

Siegel, S., Hinson, R. E., Krank, M. D., & McCully, J. (1982). Heroin "overdose" death: The contribution of drug-associated environmental cues. *Science*, **216**, 436–437. [202]

Silverman, P. J. (1971). Chained and tandem fixed-interval schedules of punishment. *Journal of the Experimental Analysis of Behavior*, **16**, 1–13. [186]

Simpson, G. G. (1951). *Horses.* New York: Oxford University Press. [33]

Sizemore, O. J., & Lattal, K. A. (1977). Dependency, temporal contiguity, and response-independent reinforcement. *Journal of the Experimental Analysis of Behavior*, **27**, 119–125. [172, 173]

Skiba, E. A., Pettigrew, L. E., & Alden, S. E. (1971). A behavioral approach to the control of thumbsucking in the classroom. *Journal of Applied Behavior Analysis*, **4**, 121–125. [77]

Skinner, B. F. (1930). On the conditions for elicitation of certain eating reflexes. *Proceedings of the National Academy of Sciences*, **16**, 433–438. [63, 367]

Skinner, B. F. (1931). The concept of the reflex in the description of behavior. *Journal of General Psychology*, **5**, 427–458. [8, 43]

Skinner, B. F. (1933). The rate of establishment of a discrimination. *Journal of General Psychology*, **9**, 302–350. [22]

Skinner, B. F. (1934). The extinction of chained reflexes. *Proceedings of the National Academy of Sciences*, **20**, 234–237. [124]

Skinner, B. F. (1935a). The generic nature of the concepts of stimulus and response. *Journal of General Psychology*, **12**, 40–65. [114]

Skinner, B. F. (1935b). Two types of conditioned reflex and a pseudotype. *Journal of General Psychology*, **12**, 66–77. [205, 210]

Skinner, B. F. (1938). *The behavior of organisms.* New York: Appleton-Century-Crofts. [23, 43, 63, 72, 367]

Skinner, B. F. (1945). The operational analysis of psychological terms. *Psychological Review*, **52**, 270–277. [254, 295, 349]

Skinner, B. F. (1948). "Superstition" in the pigeon. *Journal of Experimental Psychology*, **38**, 168–172. [75, 76]

Skinner, B. F. (1950). Are theories of learning necessary? *Psychological Review*, **57**, 193–216. [63, 149]

Skinner, B. F. (1953). *Science and human behavior*. New York: Macmillan. [25, 110, 195, 349, 350]

Skinner, B. F. (1956). A case history in scientific method. *American Psychologist*, **11**, 221–233. [63, 195]

Skinner, B. F. (1957). *Verbal behavior*. New York: Appleton-Century-Crofts. [240, 241, 242, 247, 248, 262, 292, 379, 415]

Skinner, B. F. (1959). John Broadus Watson, behaviorist. *Science*, **129**, 197–198. [351]

Skinner, B. F. (1963). Behaviorism at fifty. *Science*, **140**, 951–958. [254, 325]

Skinner, B. F. (1966). The phylogeny and ontogeny of behavior. *Science*, **153**, 1204–1213. [39, 372]

Skinner, B. F. (1968). *The technology of teaching*. New York: Macmillan. [275]

Skinner, B. F. (1969). An operant analysis of problem solving. In B. F. Skinner, *Contingencies of reinforcement* (pp. 133–157). New York: Appleton-Century-Crofts. [265, 362]

Skinner, B. F. (1972). A lecture on "having" a poem. In B. F. Skinner, *Cumulative record* (3rd ed.) (pp. 345–355). New York: Appleton-Century-Crofts. [243]

Skinner, B. F. (1975). The shaping of phylogenic behavior. *Journal of the Experimental Analysis of Behavior*, **24**, 117–120. [145, 372]

Skinner, B. F. (1976). *Particulars of my life*. New York: Alfred A. Knopf. [325]

Skinner, B. F. (1977). Herrnstein and the evolution of behaviorism. *American Psychologist*, **32**, 1006–1012. [220]

Skinner, B. F. (1981). Selection by consequences. *Science*, **213**, 501–504. [38, 225, 372]

Skinner, B. F. (1983). Intellectual self-management in old age. *American Psychologist*, **38**, 239–244. [334]

Skinner, B. F. (1984). The evolution of behavior. *Journal of the Experimental Analysis of Behavior*, **41**, 217–221. [36]

Skinner, B. F. (1986). The evolution of verbal behavior. *Journal of the Experimental Analysis of Behavior*, **45**, 115–122. [243, 278]

Skinner, B. F. (1988). Replies to commentators. In A. C. Catania & S. Harnad (Eds.), *The selection of behavior*. New York: Cambridge University Press. [34, 357, 372]

Skinner, B. F. (1989a). The listener. In B. F. Skinner, *Recent issues in the analysis of behavior* (pp. 35–47). Columbus, OH: Merrill. [273]

Skinner, B. F. (1989b). The origins of cognitive thought. *American Psychologist*, **44**, 13–18. [253, 291]

Small, W. S. (1899–1900). Experimental studies of the mental processes of the rat. *American Journal of Psychology*, **11**, 1–89. [62, 366]

Smith, B. H. (1968). *Poetic closure*. Chicago, IL: Chicago University Press. [243]

Smith, J. B. (1974). Effects of response rate, reinforcement frequency, and the duration of a stimulus preceding response-independent food. *Journal of the Experimental Analysis of Behavior*, **21**, 215–221. [217]

Smith, J. D., Schull, J., Strote, J., McGee, K., Egnor, R., & Erb, L. (1995). The uncertain response in the bottlenosed dolphin (*Tursiops truncatus*). *Journal of Experimental Psychology: General*, **124**, 391–408. [259]

Smith, K. (1954). Conditioning as an artifact. *Psychological Review*, **61**, 217–225. [205]

Smith, T. L. (1986). Biology as allegory: A review of Elliott Sober's *The nature of selection*. *Journal of the Experimental Analysis of Behavior*, **46**, 105–112. [38]

Smith, W. G. (1895). The relation of attention to memory. *Mind*, **4**, 47–73. [338]

Snapper, A. G., Kadden, R. M., & Inglis, G. B. (1982). State notation of behavioral procedures. *Behavior Research Methods and Instrumentation*, **14**, 329–342. [179]

Solnick, J. V., Rincover, A., & Peterson, C. R. (1977). Some determinants of the reinforcing and punishing effects of timeout. *Journal of Applied Behavior Analysis*, **10**, 415–424. [108]

Solomon, R. L., & Corbit, J. D. (1974). An opponent-process theory of motivation: I. Temporal dynamics of affect. *Psychological Review*, **81**, 119–145. [50, 58]

Solomon, R. L., & Turner, L. H. (1962). Discriminative classical conditioning in dogs paralyzed by curare can later control discriminative avoidance responses in the normal state. *Psychological Review*, **69**, 202–219. [211]

Spalding, D. (1873/1954). Instinct with original observations on young animals. *Macmillan's Magazine*, **27**, 282–293. Reprinted in *British Journal of Animal Behaviour*, **2**, 2–11. [39]

Spence, K. W. (1937). The differential response in animals to stimuli varying within a single dimension. *Psychological Review*, **44**, 430–444. [138, 317]

Spence, K. W., & Ross, L. E. (1959). A methodological study of the form and latency of eyelid responses in conditioning. *Journal of Experimental Psychology*, **58**, 376–381. [46]

Sperling, G. (1960). The information available in brief visual presentations. *Psychological Monographs*, **74**, (11, Whole No. 498). [336, 337]

Sperling, G., & Reeves, A. (1980). Measuring the reaction time of a shift of visual attention. In R. S. Nickerson (Ed.), *Attention and performance VIII* (pp. 347–360). Hillsdale, NJ: Erlbaum. [350]

Spetch, M. L., Wilkie, D. M., & Pinel, J. P. J. (1981). Backward conditioning: A reevaluation of the empirical evidence. *Psychological Bulletin*, **89**, 163–175. [204]

Squier, L. H. (1993). The science and art of training: A review of Pryor's *Lads before the wind*. *Journal of the Experimental Analysis of Behavior*, **59**, 423–431. [112]

Squire, L. R. (1992). (Ed.) *The encyclopedia of learning and memory*. New York: Macmillan. [321]

Staats, A. W. (1986). Behaviorism with a personality: The paradigmatic behavioral assessment approach. In R. O. Nelson & S. C. Hayes (Eds.), *Conceptual foundations of behavioral assessment* (pp. 242–296). New York: Guilford. [366]

Staddon, J. E. R., & Simmelhag, V. L. (1971). The "Superstition" experiment: A reexamination of its implications for the principle of adaptive behavior. *Psychological Review*, **78**, 3–43. [53, 76]

Stein, L., Xue, B. G., & Belluzzi, J. D. (1993). A cellular analogue of operant conditioning. *Journal of the Experimental Analysis of Behavior*, **60**, 41–53. [372]

Sternberg, S. (1969). Memory-scanning: Mental processes revealed by reaction time experiments. *American Scientist*, **57**, 421–457. [353, 354]

Stewart, G. R. (1975). *Names on the land*. New York: Oxford University Press. [253]

Stokes, P. D., & Balsam, P. D. (1991). Effects of reinforcing preselected approximations on the topography of the rat's bar press. *Journal of the Experimental Analysis of Behavior*, **55**, 213–231. [76]

Stratton, G. M. (1897). Vision without inversion of the retinal image. *Psychological Review*, **4**, 341–360; 463–481. [86]

Stratton, G. M. (1917). *Theophrastus and the Greek physiological psychology before Aristotle.* New York: Macmillan. [325]

Straub, R. O., Seidenberg, M. S., Bever, T. G., & Terrace, H.S. (1979). Serial learning in the pigeon. *Journal of the Experimental Analysis of Behavior*, **32**, 137–148. [124]

Stroop, J. R. (1935). Studies of interference in serial verbal reactions. *Journal of Experimental Psychology*, **18**, 643–662. [274, 326]

Sturgis, E. T., Tollison, C. D., & Adams, H. E. (1978). Modification of combined migraine-muscle contraction headaches using BVP and EMG feedback. *Journal of Applied Behavior Analysis*, **11**, 215–223. [232]

Svartdal, F. (1992). Sensitivity to nonverbal operant contingencies: Do limited processing resources affect operant conditioning in humans? *Learning and Motivation*, **23**, 383–405. [267]

Terrace, H. S. (1963a). Discrimination learning with and without "errors." *Journal of the Experimental Analysis of Behavior*, **6**, 1–27. [141]

Terrace, H. S. (1963b). Errorless transfer of a discrimination across two continua. *Journal of the Experimental Analysis of Behavior*, **6**, 223–232. [141]

Terrace, H. S. (1966). Stimulus control. In W. K. Honig (Ed.), *Operant behavior: Areas of research and application.* (pp. 271–344). New York: Appleton-Century-Crofts. [184]

Terrace, H. S. (1975). Evidence of the innate basis of the hue dimension in the duckling. *Journal of the Experimental Analysis of Behavior*, **24**, 79–87. [139]

Terrace, H. S., & Chen, S. (1991). Chunking during serial learning by a pigeon: III. what are the necessary conditions for establishing a chunk. *Journal of Experimental Psychology: Animal Behavior Processes*, **17**, 107–118. [143]

Terrace, H. S., Petitto, L. A., Sanders, R. J., & Bever, T. G. (1979). Can an ape create a sentence? *Science*, **206**, 891–902. [277]

Thelen, E., & Fisher, D. M. (1983). From spontaneous to instrumental behavior: Kinematic analysis of movement changes during very early learning. *Child Development*, **54**, 429–440. [219]

Thelen, E., Fisher, D. M., Ridley-Johnson, R., & Griffin, N. J. (1982). Effects of body build and arousal on newborn infant stepping. *Developmental Psychobiology*, **15**, 447–453. [56]

Thistlethwaite, D. (1951). A critical review of latent learning and related experiments. *Psychological Bulletin*, **48**, 97–129. [82]

Thomas, J. C., Jr. (1974). An analysis of behavior in the hobbits-orcs problem. *Cognitive Psychology*, **6**, 257–269. [358]

Thomas, J. R. (1979). Matching-to-sample accuracy on fixed-ratio schedules. *Journal of the Experimental Analysis of Behavior*, **32**, 183–189. [187]

Thompson, C. R., & Church, R. M. (1980). An explanation of the language of a chimpanzee. *Science*, **208**, 313–314. [277]

Thorndike, E. L. (1898). Animal intelligence: An experimental study of the associative processes in animals. *Psychological Review Monograph Supplements*, **2** (No. 4). [19, 61, 367]

Thorndike, E. L. (1921). *Educational psychology. Volume II. The psychology of learning*. New York: Teachers College. [54, 367]

Thorndike, E. L., & Woodworth, R. S. (1901). The influence of improvement in one mental function upon the efficiency of other functions. *Psychological Review*, **8**, 247–261. [313, 367]

Timberlake, W. (1980). A molar equilibrium theory of learned performance. In G. H. Bower (Ed.), *The psychology of learning and motivation. Volume 14* (pp. 1–58). New York: Academic Press. [81]

Tinbergen, N. (1960). *The Herring Gull's world* (revised edition). New York: Basic Books. [16]

Tinbergen, N. (1972). *The animal in its world. Volume 1. Field studies*. Cambridge, MA: Harvard University Press. [37, 145]

Tinbergen, N., & Perdeck, A. C. (1950). On the stimulus situation releasing the begging response in the newly hatched Herring Gull chick (*Larus a. argentatus Pontopp*). *Behavior*, **3**, 1–38. [17]

Titchener, E. B. (1898). The postulates of a structural psychology. *Philosophical Review*, **7**, 449–465. [368]

Tolman, E. C. (1948). Cognitive maps in rats and men. *Psychological Review*, **55**, 189–208. [82, 145, 367]

Tolman, E. C., & Honzik, C. H. (1930). Introduction and removal of reward, and maze performance in rats. *University of California Publications in Psychology*, **4**, 257–275. [82, 83]

Touchette, P. E. (1969). Tilted lines as complex stimuli. *Journal of the Experimental Analysis of Behavior*, **12**, 211–214. [140]

Townsend, J. T. (1971). A note on the identifiability of parallel and serial processes. *Perception and Psychophysics*, **10**, 161–163. [354]

Truax, C. B. (1966). Reinforcement and nonreinforcement in Rogerian therapy. *Journal of Abnormal Psychology*, **71**, 1–9. [273]

Tulving, E. (1962). Subjective organization in free recall of "unrelated" words. *Psychological Review*, **69**, 344–354. [309]

Tulving, E. (1969). Retrograde amnesia in free recall. *Science*, **164**, 88–90. [307]

Tulving, E. (1972). Episodic and semantic memory. In E. Tulving & W. Donaldson (Eds.), *Organization of memory* (pp. 381–403). New York: Academic Press. [346]

Tulving, E. (1974). Cue-dependent forgetting. *American Scientist*, **62**, 74–82. [312, 331]

Tulving, E. (1985). How many memory systems are there? *American Psychologist*, **40**, 385–398. [345, 347]

Tulving, E., & Madigan, S. A. (1970). Memory and verbal learning. *Annual Review of Psychology*, **21**, 437–484. [330, 341]

Tulving, E., & Pearlstone, Z. (1966). Availability versus accessibility of information in memory for words. *Journal of Verbal Learning and Verbal Behavior*, **5**, 381–391. [331]

Tulving, E., & Psotka, J. (1971). Retroactive inhibition in free recall: Inaccessibility of information available in the memory store. *Journal of Experimental Psychology*, **87**, 1–8. [331]

Tversky, A., & Kahneman, D. (1983). Extensional versus intuitive reasoning: The conjunction fallacy in probability judgment. *Psychological Review*, **90**, 293–315. [361]

Twitmyer, E. B. (1974). A study of the knee jerk (1902). *Journal of Experimental Psychology*, **103**, 1047–1066. [201]

Underwood, B. J. (1957). Interference and forgetting. *Psychological Review*, **64**, 49–60. [343, 344]

Underwood, B. J. (1961). Ten years of massed practice on distributed practice. *Psychological Review*, **68**, 229–247. [301]

Underwood, B. J. (1964). Degree of learning and measurement of forgetting. *Journal of Verbal Learning and Verbal Behavior*, **3**, 112–129. [343]

Underwood, B. J., & Freund, J. S. (1968). Errors in recognition learning and retention. *Journal of Experimental Psychology*, **78**, 55–63. [311]

Underwood, B. J., & Postman, L. (1960). Extra-experimental sources of interference in forgetting. *Psychological Review*, **67**, 73–95. [343, 344]

Underwood, B. J., Rehula, R., & Keppel, G. (1962). Item-selection in paired-associate learning. *American Journal of Psychology*, **75**, 353–371. [305]

Underwood, B. J., & Schulz, R. W. (1960). *Meaningfulness and verbal learning.* Philadelphia, PA: Lippincott. [302, 304]

Urcuioli, P. J. (1985). On the role of differential sample behaviors in matching-to-sample. *Journal of Experimental Psychology: Animal Behavior Processes*, **11**, 502–519. [150]

Urcuioli, P. J., & Zentall, T. R. (1986). Retrospective coding in pigeons' delayed matching-to-sample. *Journal of Experimental Psychology: Animal Behavior Processes*, **12**, 69–77. [347]

Vaughan, W., Jr. (1988). Formation of equivalence sets in pigeons. *Journal of Experimental Psychology: Animal Behavior Processes*, **14**, 36–42. [159]

Verhave, T. (1967). Contributions to the history of psychology: IV. Joseph Buchanan (1785–1829) and the "law of exercise" (1812). *Psychological Reports*, **20**, 127–133. [54]

Vesonder, G. T., & Voss, J. F. (1985). On the ability to predict one's own responses while learning. *Journal of Memory and Language*, **24**, 363–376. [231]

Vollmer, T. R., & Iwata, B. A. (1991). Establishing operations and reinforcement effects. *Journal of Applied Behavior Analysis*, **24**, 279–291. [78]

Von Holst, E. (1973). *The behavioural physiology of animals and man. Selected papers.* Coral Gables, FL: University of Miami Press. [40]

Von Restorff, H. (1933). Über die Wirkung von Bereichsbildungen im Spurenfeld. *Psychologische Forschung*, **18**, 299–342. [307]

Wagner, A. R., Thomas, E., & Norton, T. (1967). Conditioning with electrical stimulation of motor cortex: Evidence of a possible source of motivation. *Journal of Comparative and Physiological Psychology*, **64**, 191–199. [210]

Wagner, K. R. (1985). How much do children say in a day? *Journal of Child Language*, **12**, 475–487. [292]

Wahler, R. G. (1975). Some structural aspects of deviant child behavior. *Journal of Applied Behavior Analysis*, **8**, 27–42. [119]

Walcott, C., Gould, J. L., & Kirschvink, J. L. (1979). Pigeons have magnets. *Science*, **205**, 1027–1029. [145]

Wales, R. (1986). Deixis. In Fletcher, P., & Garman, M. (Eds.), *Language acquisition* (2nd ed.) (pp. 401–428). New York: Cambridge University Press. [294]

Walters, G. C., & Glazer, R. D. (1971). Punishment of instinctive behavior in the Mongolian gerbil. *Journal of Comparative and Physiological Psychology*, **75**, 331–340. [94]

Wanchison, B. A., Tatham, T. A., & Hineline, P. N. (1988). Pigeons' choices in situations of diminishing returns: Fixed- versus progressive-ratio schedules. *Journal of the Experimental Analysis of Behavior*, **50**, 375–394. [191]

Ward, T. B. (1980). Separable and integral responding by children and adults to the dimensions of length and density. *Child Development*, **51**, 676–684. [357]

Washburn, D. A., Hopkins, W. D., & Rumbaugh, D. M. (1991). Perceived control in rhesus monkeys (*macaca mulatta*): Enhanced video-task performance. *Journal of Experimental Psychology: Animal Behavior Processes*, **17**, 123–129. [143]

Wasik, B. H. (1970). The application of Premack's generalization on reinforcement to the management of classroom behavior. *Journal of Experimental Child Psychology*, **10**, 33–43. [80]

Wason, P. C., & Johnson-Laird, P. N. (1970) A conflict between selecting and evaluating information in an inferential task. *British Journal of Psychology*, **61**, 509–515. [182]

Wasserman, E., Franklin, S., & Hearst, E. (1974). Pavlovian appetitive contingencies and approach vs. withdrawal to conditioned stimuli in pigeons. *Journal of Comparative and Physiological Psychology*, **86**, 616–627. [212]

Wasserman, E. A., Kiedinger, R. E., & Bhatt, R. S. (1988). Conceptual behavior in pigeons: Categories, subcategories, and pseudocategories. *Journal of Experimental Psychology: Animal Behavior Processes*, **14**, 235–246. [151]

Watkins, M. J. (1981). Human memory and the information-processing metaphor. *Cognition,* 10, 331–336. [355, 371]

Watkins, M. J. (1989). Willful and nonwillful determinants of memory. In H. L. Roediger, III, & F. I. M. Craik (Eds.), *Varieties of memory and consciousness* (pp. 59–71). Hillsdale, NJ: Erlbaum. [345]

Watkins, M. J. (1990). Mediationism and the obfuscation of memory. *American Psychologist,* 45, 328–335. [324, 331]

Watkins, M. J., & Tulving, E. (1975). Episodic memory: When recognition fails. *Journal of Experimental Psychology: General,* 104, 5–29. [312]

Watson, J. B. (1913). Psychology as the behaviorist views it. *Psychological Review,* 20, 158–177. [366]

Watson, J. B. (1919). *Psychology from the standpoint of a behaviorist.* Philadelphia, PA: Lippincott. [42, 367]

Watson, J. B., & Rayner, R. (1920). Conditioned emotional reactions. *Journal of Experimental Psychology,* 3, 1–14. [209, 210]

Waugh, N. C. (1972). Retention as an active process. *Journal of Verbal Learning and Verbal Behavior,* 11, 129–140. [333]

Waugh, N. C., & Norman, D. A. (1965). Primary memory. *Psychological Review,* 72, 89–104. [338, 340]

Weiner, J. (1994). *The beak of the finch.* New York: Knopf. [30]

Weiss, B., & Laties, V. G. (1961). Behavioral thermoregulation. *Science,* 133, 1338–1344. [101]

Weiss, B., & Laties, V. G. (1969). Behavioral pharmacology and toxicology. *Annual Review of Pharmacology,* 9, 297–326. [181]

Wellman, H. M. (1990). *The child's theory of mind.* Cambridge, MA: MIT Press. [295]

Werker, J. F. (1989). Becoming a native listener. *American Scientist,* 77, 54–59. [242]

Wertheimer, M. (1959). *Productive thinking.* New York: Harper and Row. [360]

West, M. J., & King, A. P. (1980). Enriching cowbird song by social deprivation. *Journal of Comparative and Physiological Psychology,* 94, 263–270. [276]

Wetherington, C. L. (1982). Is adjunctive behavior a third class of behavior? *Neuroscience and Biobehavioral Reviews,* 6, 329–350. [52]

Whitehurst, G. J., & Valdez-Menchaca, M. C. (1988). What is the role of reinforcement in early language acquisition? *Child Development,* 59, 430–440. [293]

Wickelgren, W. A. (1969). Context-sensitive coding, associative memory, and serial order in (speech) behavior. *Psychological Review,* 76, 1–15. [384]

Wickens, D. D. (1970). Encoding categories of words: An empirical approach to meaning. *Psychological Review,* 77, 1–15. [341]

Wildemann, D. G., & Holland, J. G. (1972). Control of a continuous response dimension by a continuous stimulus dimension. *Journal of the Experimental Analysis of Behavior,* 18, 419–434. [229]

Williams, D. R., & Williams, H. (1969). Automaintenance in the pigeon: Sustained pecking despite contingent non-reinforcement. *Journal of the Experimental Analysis of Behavior,* 12, 511–520. [212]

Wilson, D. M. (1959). Long term facilitation in a swimming sea anemone. *Journal of Experimental Biology,* 36, 526–531. [50]

Wilson, T. D., & Lassiter, G. D. (1982). Increasing intrinsic interest with superfluous extrinsic constraints. *Journal of Personality and Social Psychology,* 42, 811–819. [269]

Winett, R. A., & Winkler, R. C. (1972). Current behavior modification in the classroom: Be still, be quiet, be docile. *Journal of Applied Behavior Analysis,* 5, 499–504. [108]

Winner, E. (1979). New names for old things: The emergence of metaphoric language. *Journal of Child Language,* 6, 469–491. [290]

Winograd, T. (1980). What does it mean to understand language? *Cognitive Science,* 4, 209–241. [280, 359]

Wixted, J. T. (1989). The vocabulary of remembering. A review of Kendrick, Rilling, and Denny's *Theories of animal memory. Journal of the Experimental Analysis of Behavior,* 52, 441–450. [347]

Wolf, M. M., Risley, T. R., & Mees, H. (1964). Application of operant conditioning procedures to the behavior problems of an autistic child. *Behavior Research and Therapy,* 1, 306–312. [108]

Wollen, K. A., Weber, A., & Lowry, D. (1972). Bizarreness versus interaction of mental images as determinants of learning. *Cognitive Psychology,* 3, 518–523. [322]

Wolpe, J. (1958). *Psychotherapy by reciprocal inhibition.* Stanford, CA: Stanford University Press. [209]

Wolpe, J. (1990). *The practice of behavior therapy.* (4th ed.). New York: Pergamon. [209]

Woodward, A., Jr., & Murdock, B. B., Jr. (1968). Positional and sequential probes in serial learning. *Canadian Journal of Psychology, 22,* 131–138. [302]

Woodworth, R. S. (1921). *Psychology* (revised edition). New York: Holt. [319, 349]

Woodworth, R. S. (1938). *Experimental Psychology.* New York: Holt. [314]

Wright, A. A., Cook, R. G., Rivera, J. J., Shyan, M. R., Neiworth, J. J., & Jitsumori, M. (1990). Naming, rehearsal, and interstimulus interval effects in memory processing. *Journal of Experimental Psychology: Learning, Memory, and Cognition, 16,* 1043–1059. [326]

Wundt, W. (1900). *Die Sprache.* Leipzig: Engelmann. [281]

Yates, F. A. (1966). *The art of memory.* Chicago, IL: University of Chicago Press. [321, 322]

Yates, F. E. (1986). *Self-organizing systems.* New York: Plenum. [372]

Yerkes, R. M. (1907). *The dancing mouse.* New York: Macmillan. [366]

Yerkes, R. M., & Watson, J. B. (1911). Methods of studying vision in animals. *Behavior Monographs, 1* (no. 2). [23]

Young, F. A. (1958). Studies of pupillary conditioning. *Journal of Experimental Psychology, 55,* 97–110. [201]

Zangwill, O. L. (1972). *Remembering* revisited. *Quarterly Journal of Experimental Psychology, 24,* 123–138. [321]

Zeigarnik, B. (1927). Das Behalten erledigter und unerledigter Handlungen. *Psychologische Forschung, 9,* 1–85. [334]

Zelazo, P. R. Zelazo, N. A., & Kolb, S. (1972). "Walking" in the newborn. *Science, 176,* 314–315. [55, 56]

Zener, K., & McCurdy, H. G. (1939). Analysis of motivation factors in conditioned behavior. I. Differential effect of change in hunger upon conditioned, unconditioned and spontaneous salivary secretion. *Journal of Psychology, 8,* 321–350. [55, 115]

Zentall, T. R., & Galef, B. G., Jr. (1988). *Social learning.* Hillsdale, NJ: Erlbaum. [227]

Zentall, T. R., & Levine, J. M. (1972). Observational learning and social facilitation in the rat. *Science, 178,* 1220–1221. [227]

Zentall, T. R., & Urcuioli, P. J. (1993). Emergent relations in the formation of stimulus classes by pigeons. *Psychological Record, 43,* 795–810. [151, 154]

Zettle, R. D., & Hayes, S. C. (1982). Rule-governed behavior: A potential theoretical framework for cognitive-behavioral therapy. In P. C. Kendall (Ed.), *Advances in cognitive-behavioral research and therapy, Volume I* (pp. 73–118). NY: Academic Press. [266]

Zimmerman, J., Hanford, P. H., & Brown, W. (1967). Effects of conditioned reinforcement frequency in an intermittent free-feeding situation. *Journal of the Experimental Analysis of Behavior, 10,* 331–340. [186]

Index